INTERNATIONAL ECONOMICS
AND DEVELOPMENT

Raúl Prebisch

INTERNATIONAL ECONOMICS AND DEVELOPMENT

Essays in Honor of RAÚL PREBISCH

Edited by LUIS EUGENIO DI MARCO

Universidad Nacional de Córdoba
Córdoba, Argentina

and

Universidad Nacional de Rosario
Rosario, Argentina

1972

ACADEMIC PRESS New York and London

ACADEMIC PRESS, INC.
111 Fifth Avenue, New York, New York 10003

United Kingdom Edition published by
ACADEMIC PRESS, INC. (LONDON) LTD.
24/28 Oval Road, London NW1

LIBRARY OF CONGRESS CATALOG CARD NUMBER: 72-87230

PRINTED IN THE UNITED STATES OF AMERICA

My Dear Friend,

I am delighted with your undertaking which has succeeded so brilliantly.

I am also deeply grateful for your friendly gesture in which one can discern that spirit of solidarity so characteristic of the work of economists in this area.

At the same time I wish to express my appreciation to all the economists who collaborated in this enterprise.

With warmest regards,

Raúl Prebisch

ECONOMIC THEORY AND MATHEMATICAL ECONOMICS

Consulting Editor: Karl Shell

UNIVERSITY OF PENNSYLVANIA
PHILADELPHIA, PENNSYLVANIA

Franklin M. Fisher and Karl Shell. **The Economic Theory of Price Indices:** ***Two Essays on the Effects of Taste, Quality, and Technological Change.***

Luis Eugenio Di Marco (Ed.). **International Economics and Development:** ***Essays in Honor of Raúl Presbisch.***

In preparation

Erwin Klein. **Mathematical Methods in Theoretical Economics:** ***Topological and Vector Space Foundations of Equilibrium Analysis.***

CONTENTS

LIST OF CONTRIBUTORS

Numbers in parentheses indicate the pages on which the authors' contributions begin.

AKIHIRO AMANO (47), Kobe University, Kobe, Japan

SAMUEL ARANCIBIA (369), Banco Central de Chile, Santiago, Chile

BELA BALASSA (159), Johns Hopkins University, Baltimore, Maryland and International Bank for Reconstruction and Development, Washington, D.C.

JAGDISH BHAGWATI (181), Massachusetts Institute of Technology, Cambridge, Massachusetts

JOHN CHEH (181), Massachusetts Institute of Technology, Cambridge, Massachusetts

JOHN S. CHIPMAN (209), University of Minnesota, Minneapolis, Minnesota

W. M. CORDEN (191), Nuffield College, Oxford, England

BENJAMIN CORNEJO (465), Universidad Nacional de Córdoba, Córdoba, Argentina

ALDO ANTONIO DADONE (15), Universidad Nacional de Córdoba, Córdoba, Argentina

CAMILO DAGUM (245), The University of Ottawa, Ottawa, Canada

G. DESTANNE DE BERNIS (267), Institut de Recherche Economique et de Planification, Université des Sciences Sociales de Grenoble, Grenoble, France

Luis Eugenio Di Marco (3, 15), Universidad Nacional de Córdoba, Córdoba, Argentina and Universidad Nacional de Rosario, Rosario, Argentina

Victor Jorge Elias (301), Universidad Nacional de Tucumán, Tucumán, Argentina

Ricardo M. Ffrench-Davis (369), Universidad Catolica de Chile, Santiago, Chile

Albert Fishlow (311), University of California, Berkeley, California

Harry G. Johnson (447), London School of Economics and Political Science, London, England and University of Chicago, Chicago, Illinois

Murray C. Kemp (61), University of New South Wales, Kensington, New South Wales, Australia

Charles P. Kindleberger (387), Massachusetts Institute of Technology, Cambridge, Massachusetts

Jan Kňákal (97), Economic Commission for Latin America, Santiago, Chile

John M. Letiche (405), University of California, Berkeley, California

W. Arthur Lewis (75), Princeton University, Princeton, New Jersey

Gunnar Myrdal (37), University of Stockholm, Stockholm, Sweden

Anibal Pinto (97), Economic Commission for Latin America, Santiago, Chile

John P. Powelson (429), University of Colorado, Boulder, Colorado

John Tinbergen (129), Nederlandse Economische Hogeschool, Rotterdam, The Netherlands

Paul Zarembka (135), University of California, Berkeley, California

PREFACE

The study and comprehension of the field of international economics, particularly as it relates to the problems of the underdeveloped countries, has never been more crucial to the world than it is today. With this in view, the primary purpose of this book is to bring together the main lines of development in this vast field of thought and to suggest something of the interrelationships which link them together. A second purpose of the book, and one in which I take particular pleasure, is to honor the many contributions of Professor Raúl Prebisch to international economics. His work and ideas have, over the years, profoundly affected generations of economists in general, and more concretely, are reflected in many of the papers which appear in the volume. Although the gist of Prebisch's ideas has been summarized in three of the papers, the reader can doubtless find many reflections of his ideas in the theories and hypotheses of these papers, many of which make special reference to his work.

A brief biography of Prebisch's career is included in the book, but it seems appropriate here to draw special attention to his well-known work at the Economic Commission for Latin America, his crucial and influential role at the United Nations Conference on Trade and Development, and the many other facets of this "economist turned executive and author of so many decisive ideas in the world of today." Most of the contributions in the volume draw directly on Professor Prebisch's work. This is especially true of the papers by Letiche ("he has had a greater influence on Latin American international development policy than any other economist"), Powelson, who deals with the proposals emanating from the ECLA, and Johnson, who draws our attention to "the success of Dr. Prebisch and of UNCTAD in putting trade policy on the agenda of development assistance." It is the

Editor's hope that papers such as these, as well as the essay which recapitulates the broad features of Prebisch's economic thought, will help the reader to better evaluate the contributions of this Argentinian economist, of whom his country and continent are so rightfully proud.

During the compilation of the essays in this volume, the Editor approached a number of economists, asking them to contribute articles covering their most recent work, with emphasis wherever possible on the connections with Prebisch's own work over the years. Rather than stressing the "classical" treatment, it was decided to follow a topical analysis of the broad themes of discussion and controversy in the field of economic development, those which arouse the interest of economists, politicians, and the public alike. Among the topics covered are such issues as the relationship between the Center and the Periphery, industrial policies for development, problems of economic integration in less-developed countries, the contribution of trade to the national income, aspects of international income distribution, and an analysis of the influence of foreign capital movements on economic development.

Following this general scheme, the sections of the book have been divided into eight more or less homogenous categories, and it should be stressed that the actual arrangement of material is more the product of the need to divide the topics conceptually than the reflection of a purely academic classification. There is no doubt that many of the papers deal with subjects which could well be placed under different topic headings, or for that matter, under several. Each section of the book is introduced briefly with a sketch of its contents and an abstract of each of the included articles.

The preparation of such a volume is, obviously, impossible without the cooperation and collaboration of a number of people, and special thanks are due to the various authors for their spontaneous and decisive support and encouragement for this undertaking. A number of other prominent international economists also lent their support to the project, though unable to make personal contributions, and they, too, have our thanks for their assistance. The Editor would be remiss if he did not also express his gratitude for the helpful suggestions and valuable stimulus received from Dr. Francisco Giner de los Rios, the work by Mrs. Lelia B. V. de Ortiz, who did her best to improve my English syntax, Miss M. B. Bederian, who prepared the bibliography related to Dr. Prebisch, Miss S. V. Burgos, who typed the manuscript, and Misses O. V. Mammana and A. M. Vitale for their cheerful secretarial work. And finally, of course, I want to express my thanks to my wife who, as co-author of my university work, helped bring this dream to its realization.

BIOGRAPHICAL NOTES ON DR. PREBISCH

These biographical notes outline the most outstanding features of the life of this distinguished economist of the Argentine Republic. We limit ouselves here to a brief summary of the positions Dr. Prebisch has held and the work he has done, since at the end of the volume we include—as an Appendix—a fairly complete list of the published work of Dr. Raúl Prebisch.

In January, 1963, Dr. Prebisch was appointed Secretary-General of the United Nations Conference on Trade and Development (Geneva, March–June, 1964) by Secretary-General U Thant. Dr. Prebisch is Director-General of the Latin American Institute for Economic and Social Planning (United Nations) and former Executive Secretary of the United Nations Economic Commission for Latin America (ECLA).

Born on April 17, 1901, in Tucumán, Argentina, Dr. Prebisch graduated with a degree in economics from the University of Buenos Aires in 1923. He was Professor of Political Economy at the School of Economics in the University of Buenos Aires from 1925 to 1948.

In addition to his academic work, Dr. Prebisch held various other positions. From 1925 to 1927 he was Deputy Director of the Department of Statistics (Argentina), and from 1927 to 1930, Director of Economic Research for the National Bank of Argentina. He was Under-Secretary of Finance (1930–1932) and served as Adviser to the Ministries of Finance and Agriculture from 1933 to 1935.

He was one of the founders and the first Director-General of the Argentine Central Bank (1935–1943). Upon his retirement from the Argentine Central Bank, Dr. Prebisch devoted his time to research and university tasks (1943–1948).

After a short time with the Mexican Central Bank, he joined the Secretariat of the United Nations Economic Commission for Latin America and was appointed its Executive Secretary in 1950. He resigned this position in 1963.

At the end of 1955, Dr. Prebisch was appointed to his former chair of Political Economy at the University of Buenos Aires, on an honorary basis. He was also made an honorary member of the Faculty of Economics of the University of Chile in Santiago, and the Universities of San Andrés, La Paz (Bolivia), and San Marcos, Lima (Perú). He has been awarded honorary doctorates by Columbia University, New York, Universidad de los Andes, Colombia, and the University of Punjab, India.

In May, 1962, Dr. Prebisch was appointed Director-General of the Latin American Institute for Economic and Social Planning, established in Santiago (Chile) by the United Nations Economic Commission for Latin America, with financial assistance from the United Nations Special Fund and the Inter-American Development Bank.

In July, 1962, Dr. Prebisch attended the Cairo Conference on the Problems of Economic Development, as an observer for the United Nations.

After his appointment as Secretary-General of the United Nations Conference on Trade and Development, Dr. Prebisch visited a number of geographic areas for regional discussions of trade problems and conferred with a number of individual governments on questions relating to the Conference, which was held from March 23 to June 15, 1964, in Geneva. He submitted a report outlining issues before the Conference and suggested a program of action as a basis for discussion.

On December 30, 1964, the nineteenth session of the General Assembly approved the creation of the United Nations Conference on Trade and Development as a permanent organ of the General Assembly and decided, as well, on the establishment of a 55-member Trade and Development Board that was to have the same functions as the Conference when the latter is not in session. The Secretary-General of the United Nations was requested to proceed immediately with the organization of the permanent secretariat that was to serve the needs of the Conference, the Board, and its subsidiary bodies. On February 10, 1965, the General Assembly unanimously confirmed the appointment of Dr. Raúl Prebisch as Secretary-General of the United Nations Conference on Trade and Development.

The first session of the Trade and Development Board was held from April 5 to 30, 1965, in New York. It decided, among other things, to establish a 55-member Committee on Commodities and two 45-member Committees on Manufactures and Invisibles, as well as a 45-member Committee on Maritime Shipping.

At the same time, it also determined the terms of reference for these Committees, approved the program of work for 1965, including preparations for the Conference that was held in 1968 (New Delhi). It also recommended that the headquarters of the Secretariat of the Conference be located in Europe, preferably Geneva, although a liaison office would be maintained in New York to coordinate certain activities with other substantive departments of the United Nations Secretariat and with international institutions that function in the United States, whose work is related to the Conference field of operations.

When his term of activities with the Conference was over (on March 1, 1969), Dr. Prebisch reassumed once again, on a full-time basis, his functions as Director-General of the Latin American Institute for Economic and Social Planning. In that capacity he has simultaneously agreed to act as a Special Adviser in Washington to the President of the Inter-American Development Bank and to the President of the Inter-American Committee of the Alliance for Progress. In addition, at the request of Secretary-General U Thant, Dr. Prebisch has also agreed to act as advisor to the United Nations Secretary-General and to the Under-Secretary-General of the Department of Economic and Social Affairs on activities pertaining to the Second Development Decade.

I. INTRODUCTION

In requesting the contributions for this volume, we suggested that Dr. Prebisch's "international image" should be primarily emphasized; his work as economist at the Economic Commission for Latin America (ECLA); his performance at the United Nations Conference on Trade and Development; as well as "many other features of the Economist turned into an Executive, author of so many decisive ideas in the world of today." Our request was taken into good account, to the extent that a great many of the contributions refer to Dr. Prebisch's work, particularly those of Letiche ("He has had a greater influence on Latin American international development policy than any other economist"), Powelson (who deals with the "theories emanating from the ECLA"), and Johnson (who points out "the success of Dr. Prebisch and of UNCTAD in putting trade policy on the agenda of development assistance"). It has been found convenient, however, to embody Dr. Prebisch's main economic ideas into a single paper. This is one of the reasons for these introductory contributions.

The main purpose of the first essay is to offer the reader an orderly summary of Prebisch's economic thought, which should allow him better to evaluate those contributions which make specific reference to the topics dealt with by the Argentine economist. Briefly, *Di Marco*'s paper constitutes a review of Prebisch's theories from that famous plan of industrialization through import substitution, to his recent concept of how to attain economic development through a shift in the commercial policy of more advanced countries.

The second essay, written by *Dadone* and *Di Marco* about the impact of Prebisch's ideas on modern economic analysis, intends to make an outline, necessarily incomplete, of what has been said and done, as well as the reactions which at the time arose from the economic concepts of the Argentine thinker, in their relation to both economic theory and policy. In its first section, the essay offers a brief statement about the Latin American school of economics and its effects upon the existing economic analysis. The subject is focused by means of the thorough study of the great problems facing underdeveloped countries, carried out by the above school. The second chapter aims to sketch the consequences of Prebisch's propositions about economic policy of less-developed countries. This analysis comprises three well-defined aspects: what the various national positions in relation to a series of economic policy alternatives have been; how the attitude of underdeveloped countries has been cast in international conferences; and a specified analysis of the problem, referring to economic integration as a response to problems of growth. The third section of this paper intends to give a brief outline of the reactions of economists and governments of developed areas to the ideas and policies emerging from Prebisch's work. In terms of certain aspects which were the inspiration of ECLA's theories, the writers try to visualize what the orthodox economists' replies and critiques have been. The final part of this section aims to be a thorough examination of the individual and joint position of developed countries in terms of the reports and claims of the underdeveloped world.

Dadone and Di Marco conclude their work by pointing out that Prebisch's work has played a dominant role in the analysis of international economic relationships. With regard to theory, it should be stated that Prebisch has questioned the postulates of traditional analysis of growth by emphasizing the necessity of considering the different frameworks within which theory is supposed to play. Regarding policy, Prebisch's vision is particularly remarkable upon the need of considering more concise factors in the formulation of a policy for development.

THE EVOLUTION OF PREBISCH'S ECONOMIC THOUGHT

LUIS EUGENIO DI MARCO

Universidad Nacional de Córdoba, Córdoba, Argentina
and Universidad Nacional de Rosario, Rosario, Argentina

> *We talk of freedom, but today political freedom does not take us very far, unless there is economic freedom. In fact, there is no such thing for a man who is starving or for a country which is poor. The poor, whether they are countries or individuals have little place in the world.*
>
> Jawaharlal Nehru

I

It is the purpose of this short essay to give a rapid insight into the evolution of Raúl Prebisch's economic ideas. Since we are especially interested in the task of emphasizing his international achievements, we will only deal with the evolution of his thought during the time he worked with the United Nations, through its technical organizations (that is, from around 1948).

As is known, Prebisch entered ECLA's Secretariat in 1949, after a long period of intense public and academic activities in Argentina. It is most evident that all his experience—and writings and ideas as expressed in a number of documents—constituted the preparation for this task, which occupied his energies for about two decades of fruitful work [4].

The fundamental core of Prebisch's body of thought is concerned with *the industrialization process* which less-developed countries should undergo in order to attain a level of income that makes possible an adequate increase in the standards of living of these countries. Prebisch is particularly concerned with Latin America, for which, according to some writers, he himself has constructed a quite complete theory of development.

Before going into the details of Prebisch's ideas, we think it appropriate to put special stress on what might be considered the very essence of his original thought. We refer to the well-known theory of the evolution of the terms of trade. As Buchanan and Ellis [1, Vol. 2, pp. 36 ff.] have pointed out, Prebisch thinks that the relationship between primary goods prices and industrial prices has been deteriorating since the 1870s, which means that wages and profits in industrial countries have increased in comparison to productivity; otherwise, prices would have *declined* as productivity increased. In other words, the rate of increase of incomes in "peripheral" countries has been lower than the rate of productivity gain.

Consequently, benefits derived from technical progress have been channeled in obvious disproportion to the "central" countries. This trend will surely continue until less-developed regions can, in turn, reach successful levels of industrialization. As will be seen later, the essential point which may serve to explain the uneven evolution of income, is the negotiating power of worker-unions in more advanced countries. The point is that during an economic "boom," or cyclical peak, monetary wages rise parallel to prices, whereas in periods of depression they resist downward pressure. This resistance—as the argument runs—maintains additional incomes in industrialized countries, at the expense of the "peripheral" ones, in which workers are not usually unionized.

In brief, the deterioration in the terms of trade[1] is the result—in addition to technological and institutional factors already mentioned—of a low income-elasticity of demand for primary products, so that the only way to overcome the existing conditions would be through a higher level of efficiency of the economic system (raising productivity levels), which can only be attained by industrialization.

II

In the following notes we will make a rather comprehensive analysis of the topics dealt with by Raúl Prebisch. One idea that constantly emerges in discussions about economic development is that referring to the need for properly allocating human and physical resources. In other words, economic development and planning are complements: the planning of development seems to be a *sine qua non* required to achieve development. Prebisch's ideas should be analyzed within this framework.[2]

[1] Prebisch's analysis uses price indexes published by the British "Board of Trade" for the period 1876–1947.

[2] Prebisch's voluminous production at the ECLA—particularly, his "economic surveys" —shows him as one of the most prominent planners of our time. It is not surprising then to find him again as a member of a body—the Latin American Institute for Economic and Social Planning—devoted to the training of planners for development and the preparation of experts in that field.

III

In his "Wealth of Nations," Adam Smith set forth his well-known theory about "the international division of labor." Prebisch has stressed the invalidity of such a theory. His position is contained in two essays [7, 8] simply known as "Prebisch's thesis."

We must first characterize the institutional framework in which the theory is supposed to play. Thus, Prebisch's thesis starts by postulating a disparity between national economic development in advanced countries (the *center* in the author's terminology) and that in the still developing countries (the *periphery*, according to Prebisch). Economies in the former are self-sustained through technological progress, whereas the peripheral ones play the role of raw material suppliers for industrial centers.

The problem resides in the fact that communities of the periphery have not shared in the profits of technological progress in the same manner as the countries from the center. It is also argued that increases in productivity actually achieved in economies of the Periphery have benefited the Center.[3]

On the other hand, the poor communities remain trapped inside a vicious circle of low productivity and low savings, followed by more of the same.

The validity of the Smithian scheme of the international division of labor implicitly depends on the assumption that the participating economies are strictly complementary: there are specific differences in structures and functions among countries that participate in international trade. In fact, Prebisch's thesis is derived from his view that too much emphasis has been given to such differences, which are differences rather of degree than of essence. The fact is that we find that commercial interchange between peripheral and central countries based on exports of primary and industrial goods, respectively, is of a sort which does not facilitate economic development in the Periphery. Let us examine these facts in a more detailed fashion.

Poor countries must face a twofold problem: how to achieve a higher rate of growth in technical progress (widely diffused among all economic sectors) than has been achieved up to now; and how to retain the benefits from increased productivity in order to promote balanced economic growth. Since the forties, the Periphery has been engaged in its own unique industrial revolution, whose "takeoff" is characterized by a radical change in production methods, and whose final outcome will (hopefully) be the raising of the standards of living of the great national majorities.

In other words, in the course of the 19th century, a "schema," consisting of a certain type of international division of labor between the Center and the

[3] We must not forget that industries achieving productivity increases are usually foreign, and they constitute appendages of advanced economies. This is approximately the argument.

Periphery was established. The former should produce manufactured goods—which implied a whole battery of complex processes based on capitalist techniques—and the latter should supply raw materials and foodstuffs, to which purpose the peripheral economies should adapt their productive structures, by having a relatively developed export sector.[4] However, in the present century, as a consequence of two world wars and economic changes at the international level as a result of the Great Depression, these peripheral countries—the Latin American ones in particular—are anxious to break down the Smithian scheme. Industrialization has been fostered and countries are not so willing as before to accept what they see as colonial status, a subservient role as simple suppliers of materials and foodstuffs.

IV

Prebisch—through the ECLA—stated in 1950 that the solution was to industrialize. In one of his famous papers he pointed out the following [8, p. 251]:

> ...Although it is not an end in itself, [industrialization is] the principal means at the disposal of those countries for obtaining a share of the benefits of technical progress and of progressively raising the standard of living of the masses.... Historically, the spread of technical progress has been uneven, and it has contributed to the division of the world economy into an industrial center and countries engaged in primary production, with differences in income growth.

The industrializing power of peripheral countries has on occasion been questioned. Yet, Prebisch discounts the argument that states that Latin American nations will worsen their position through industrialization, despite the fact that their industrial production might be less efficient than that of the nations of the Center. The growth of domestic industry is not incompatible with a sustained expansion of primary production. Hence, the standard of living could be raised through the process of industrialization without any decline in the volume or efficiency of primary production.

V

In fact, the real problem in Latin America is how to foment industrialization on a large scale. Prebisch has contended[5] that the Periphery is in a disadvantageous position to promote development. Generally, Latin American in-

[4] The difference in negotiating power led to a distortion of relative prices: fluctuations in the terms of trade always favored rich countries. This is another of Prebisch's arguments which embodies the well-known encouragement of industrial import substitution that, in parallel to changes in relative prices, may also lead to national economic development.

[5] Although these statements were made in the fifties, we can still say that, on the average, conditions have not changed in a fundamental way.

comes are low, and there is a distinctly limited capacity to save and invest. On the other hand, peripheral countries strongly depend upon foreign trade, and in this respect two circumstances should be noted: (a) the prices that Latin America receives for its primary products are not keeping pace with the price increases in the manufactured goods it has to buy, while its industrialization depends on the capacity to import generated by its exports; (b) the demand for the primary goods sold by Latin American countries has been declining, and this fact, added to what was stated in (a), has resulted in serious balance of payments problems.

This decreasing growth in demand for Latin American products, means that export receipts are insufficient to create the capacity to import necessary to provide the region with capital goods needed for rapid economic development. Consequently, there exists an "undeclared war" between industrial centers and peripheral communities, despite the vaunted interdependence between the two in the world economy.

It would be convenient to put some emphasis on the prominent features of the two types of systems. Thus, some of the characteristics of central areas are: their ability to benefit from or internalize their own increases in productivity and to distribute the gains among all their members (in the way of higher salaries and profits); their ability to save about 15 per cent of their national income, this saving being used to generate new capital goods; their ability to reduce the weekly working hours of their working class (i.e., to increase paid leisure hours); and their ability to support greater public expenditure for the benefit of the community. The peripheral regions, on the contrary, are typified by domestic consumption which sometimes exceeds the level of national production. As they have low savings capacity (about 5 per cent), they are subject to the impact of any fluctuations arising from the more or less competitive working of the international capital market. It should also be noted that benefits from the low productivity gains generally fall into the hands of a few privileged ones who, in most cases, either do not reinvest them productively or hoard their wealth abroad.

Some other comparative features are to be noted. Technical progress varies according to the environment. Inventions and new production methods diffuse very slowly and in an irregular way from the Center to the Periphery, and even within the latter, the spread of new methods and the application of more complex techniques are subject to the form (and to the prices) in which different sectors operate in order to export their primary goods.

With regard to prices, we can say that they are relatively inflexible downwards in advanced areas: the successful operation of large firms and the bargaining power of unions prevent prices and salaries from falling, even in times of crisis. On the other hand, prices in the Periphery are affected by the smallest fluctuations in world markets, and unions owe their existence to the willingness of industry or the government, and, therefore, lack effective bargaining power.

VI

For purposes of the present essay (and as Prebisch has pointed out for such a situation), the Center is practically taken as synonymous with the United States. Within this context, we will consider the following relation: The U.S. import coefficient[6] has always been low, whereas that of Latin America remains very high. Taking this into account, and considering that the United States is the main economic power in the world, every time there is a cyclical contraction in the industrial center, the import coefficient declines, thus creating a large disequilibrium in the Periphery. The situation is still worse, since the shortfall or reduction in imports from the Periphery represents for this area a major reduction in its foreign exchange receipts, and their low reserves tend to disappear. Partly in reaction against this, and as a way to counterbalance situations as the one just described, the countries concerned began to adopt measures such as import quotas, exchange controls, higher tariffs, and devaluation of their currencies, among others [10, pp. 5–9]. Prebisch himself wrote [7, p. 11]:

> ...Exchange control was not the result of a theory, but was imposed by the circumstances. None who experienced firsthand the complications of every kind that it involved, would have adopted such a measure had there been other alternatives or had it been within the power of the Latin American countries to eliminate the fundamental causes of the evil.

The picture is obviously quite different when there is full employment in the Center, which is a situation that generates a sort of economic welfare in the Periphery.[7]

VII

The low rate of savings—which according to Prebisch is the root of poverty in the Periphery—seems to be the genesis of a vicious circle in the economies of the communities located there. Our writer explains it as follows [7, p. 37]:

> ...Productivity in these countries is very low, owing to lack of capital; and the lack of capital is due to the narrow margin of savings resulting from this low productivity:

[6] Defined as the ratio of the import value of a country's imports to its national income.

[7] The reading of the text shows us clearly the case of economic dependence of poor countries (say, economies which are primary exporters, usually having a single type of farming).

Throughout most of Latin America, the characteristic lack of savings is the result, not only of this narrow margin, but in many cases, of its improper use. Savings means refraining from consumption and is thus incompatible with certain types of consumption peculiar to relatively high income groups.

Thence the need for foreign capital in order to break the vicious "low productivity–low savings" circle. The problem, however, originates not only in the complex and unbalanced situation between the Center and the Periphery. Prebisch himself has pointed out that it would not be surprising to find a large part of foreign exchange reserves of poor countries spent on products not essential for their economic development.[8]

The search for a solution to the problem of economic development in Latin America has shifted from an emphasis on the need to adopt policies to overcome perverse labor supply curves (backward bending) in peripheral communities, to a call for greater foreign assistance in order to achieve the necessary "push" which would help the Latin American economies break out of the so-called "vicious circle of poverty." As Nurkse has stated [6, p. 13], this means "a circular constellation of forces tending to act and react upon one another in such a way as to keep a poor country poor."

Prebisch's prescription was the achievement of an increase in industrialization in Latin America, with the purpose of eliminating this growing evil. This was the only way to counteract efficiently the prevailing forces of disequilibrium. The "Prebisch thesis" took shape and in the present, two decades later, has been accepted by most Latin American economists.

As already stated, the foundation of Prebisch's scheme was laid after a careful economic evaluation of the double need: to increase productivity in the Periphery and to retain the fruits of that productivity.

In this connection, foreign investment could[9] be the key factor, since the level of economic activity would improve if foreign capital were able to increase productivity. If this is not the case, no net increase in savings will be realized toward reaching the rate of an adequate net capital formation, which is the only way to break the "vicious circle" of poverty. Prebisch's recommendation for industrialization is through import substitution, this being essential for the progressive growth of peripheral countries. Beyond the industrializing process itself, Prebisch foresees that such a process could be used to increase labor productivity as a whole, and to allow a transfer to highly

[8] We can state that the governments (of the peripheral regions) have not usually dared to encourage investment in their countries with the increased income coming from inflation regulating, for instance, a progressive taxation of profits. As a matter of fact, Latin American inflation has tended towards decapitalization rather than to net capital formation.

[9] "Could" in the sense that depends on *how* investment is allocated, *what* the fruits (gains) of the investments are, and *how* the Latin American entrepreneur may have access to the new technology that might be involved in the foreign investment.

productive employment of those engaged in low-yield occupations. Industrialization would also be a means to maintain a high and increasing wage level.

VIII

Prebisch's thesis,[10] has had its share of critics, however. Thus, when Prebisch points out that [3, p. 195] many of the modern techniques applied to agriculture will set laborers free who will be able to work in areas offering better prospects in terms of wages, Viner [9, p. 73 ff,] criticizes this statement by arguing that Prebisch's study stubbornly identifies agriculture with poverty, adding that this is not true if we consider cases such as those of Australia, New Zealand, and Denmark. It is also evident that industrialization is not synonymous with prosperity if we observe the cases of Italy and Spain. Viner tends to the conclusion that the problem in poor countries is not to be found in agriculture as such, or in the lack of manufactures as such, but in underdevelopment owing to poverty and backwardness, to *poor* agriculture and *poor* industry.

To all those disturbed by the overemphasis given to industrialization, Prebisch has clearly stressed that Latin American industrialization is not incompatible with an efficient development of primary production. On the contrary, Prebisch declares, the availability of better capital equipment and the prompt adoption of new techniques are essential, if industrial development is to fulfill the social objective of raising the standard of living. And all of this holds true with regard to mechanization (and industrialization) of farm production.

Another critical approach to Prebisch's analysis runs in the following terms: Suppose that foreign aid is obtained in the form of capital goods, which are to be used to rationalize the production of some agricultural good, hitherto almost entirely labor intensive. Because of the new capital intensive technique, less labor input is needed, and total employment of the industry drops (and thus, productivity rises). But what will happen to workers who have lost their jobs? As it is assumed that they are relatively unskilled, the possibilities of new job opportunities are scanty. All this implies that in order to get new jobs, they will have to accept lower salaries, or even worse, bid existing wages down so as to get a secure job. The real implication of this is that industrial wages will fall, hence causing a further transfer of real income from the Periphery to the Center in the form of lower prices.

[10] More than his ideas, it has been his theoretical formulation and his recommendations on economic policy which have been the object of controversy, and many outstanding international economists have participated in the debate.

To solve the problem of job shortage, Prebisch suggests that emphasis be put on a certain kind of industrialization, in addition to the rationalization of primary production, so as to provide the increased number of productive jobs necessary to absorb the unemployed workers released from the exporting sector, after a program of retraining. In this way, the surplus labor would be readily employed in jobs which were at least as productive as those that were left behind. There would be no unemployment (other than frictional) and no bidding down of wages. On the contrary, wages could rise due to the higher level of productivity, and through these higher incomes an increased level of savings will result, so as to provide the greater amount of capital needed to accelerate economic development.

Despite all the critiques, Prebisch's thesis "subsists as the most practical, cohesive, and feasible solution for an immediate and progressive development of Latin America" [4, p. 31]. The two decades since Prebisch's theory on industrialization have made it possible to consolidate many of its features. The arguments in favor of or against it have served to show the advantages of a position Prebisch strongly supported both from his workdesk and in his discussions with officials and scholars of every latitude.

IX

Before concluding this review of Prebisch's economic ideas, it might be appropriate to emphasize the policy tools which the great Argentine economist, with his realistic orientation, has suggested over the years. Putting it briefly, let us say that in the fifties, Prebisch felt that the industrialization process should be promoted through import substitution, so that at the same time the terms of trade[11] were improved, an increased capacity to import would develop, a capacity necessary to confront the large capital needs of development. This process obviously had an important period of application.

By the end of the fifties ECLA's idea that development problems should be considered a joint task took shape: the efforts of twenty stagnant compartments were not satisfactory. It was then that the idea of creating a structure like the Latin American Common Market came into prominence. At the present time, this idea has advanced a few steps, although no massive concretion has been achieved.

Finally, Prebisch experimented with a new technique. Industrialization might continue using the substitution policy; it might be necessary to go on stressing the economic integration of the Latin American countries, with the

[11] In Di Marco [2] an empirical analysis is made of the terms of trade at a national level between two Argentine regions, in which the author tries to isolate their behavioral causes.

whole series of measures which would put such policies into effect. However, at the beginning of the sixties, a new ingredient is incorporated into the problem of development: the patterns of commercial policy of the advanced countries must be changed so as to make it possible for those in the process of development to export nontraditional products.[12] This meant a great shift: international cooperation schemes should not depend on grants and aid but must rather be the result of reasonable trade policies under which all may share the fruits of progress. And it is here that Prebisch showed himself as the skilled and able executive,[13] as the intelligent man willing to materialize what, in his opinion, opened a new path to international understanding.

X

We have thus sketched the economic and political ideas of Raúl Prebisch.[14] His theories—despite the critiques—show him as an individual in dialogue with his world, a scholar who has mastered the problems of his time. In brief, we can say that Prebisch has achieved the final goal of every creative economist. He has suggested patterns which may unite nations in common effort, promoting respect and freedom for the members of the international community.

REFERENCES

[1] Buchanan, N. S., and Ellis, H. S., "Approaches to Economic Development." 20th Century Fund, New York, 1955.

[2] Di Marco, L. E., Los Términos del Intercambio: Construcción de Modelos y Un Caso de Estudio. Doctoral thesis, School of Economics, Univ. of Córdoba, 1969.

[3] Frankenhoff, Ch., The Prebisch Thesis: A Theory of Industrialism for Latin America, *J. Int. Stud.* **IV-2**, 1962.

[4] Freyman, C., Dr. Raúl Prebisch, A Most Distinguished Latin American Economist, paper, St. Mary's Univ., San Antonio, Texas, 1970.

[5] Kafka, A., Algunas Reflexiones Sobre la Interpretación Teórica del Desarrollo Económico de América Latina, "El Desarrollo Económico y América Latina" (H. S. Ellis ed.). Fondo de Cultura Económico, México, 1960.

[12] Naturally, this implies a whole set of measures, among which we can mention the elimination of artificial policy barriers of rich countries, and the creation of preferential tariffs for poor countries.

[13] We refer to his brilliant performance in the organization and execution of the U.N. Conference on Trade and Development (UNCTAD).

[14] Aspects related to the "social question" in Prebisch's doctrine are dealt with in Cornejo's paper included in Part VIII of this volume.

[6] Nurkse, R., "Problems of Capital Formation on Underdeveloped Countries." Blackwell, Oxford, 1955.
[7] Prebisch, R., "The Economic Development of Latin America and its Principal Problems," Dept. of Econ. Affairs, N. Unidas, 1950.
[8] Prebisch, R., Commercial Policy in Underdeveloped Countries, *Amer. Econ. Rev.*, **XLIV**, 1959.
[9] Viner, J., "International Trade and Economic Development." Free Press, Glencoe, Illinois, 1966.
[10] Whipple, R. D., "Prebisch Revisited." St. Mary's Univ., San Antonio, Texas, 1967.

THE IMPACT OF PREBISCH'S IDEAS ON MODERN ECONOMIC ANALYSIS

ALDO ANTONIO DADONE

Universidad Nacional de Córdoba, Córdoba, Argentina

LUIS EUGENIO DI MARCO

Universidad Nacional de Córdoba, Córdoba, Argentina
and Universidad Nacional de Rosario, Rosario, Argentina

I. Introduction

It would be an almost insurmountable task to attempt a synthesis of the consequences which the ideas emerging with Prebisch have had, either in economic theory or economic policy. This paper will attempt to offer a view, a necessarily incomplete one, of what has often been said and done on the subject, and the responses which have been elicited by the economic concepts of the Argentine thinker.

Let us mention, in brief, that this essay includes as its first part an abridged description of the Latin American school and its effects upon existing economic analysis. The question is dealt with through an examination of the great problems affecting underdeveloped countries, as carried out by the abovementioned school. A second section aims to outline the consequences of Prebisch's propositions about economic policy in less-developed countries. This analysis consists of three quite different topics: what the different national positions have been in their relation to a set of alternative economic policies; how the attitude of underdeveloped countries has been presented in international conferences; and a specific study of the problem of economic integration as a response to problems of growth. A third section of this paper gives a brief sketch of the reactions of economists and governments in developed areas to the ideas and policies emanating from the Prebisch circle.

In terms of certain policy aspects which were incorporated in ECLA'S theories, we have tried to elucidate the objections and critiques of orthodox economists. The final part of this section is a careful study of the individual and joint positions of the developed countries in terms of the proposals and claims of the underdeveloped world.

In short, we can state that Prebisch's work has played a prominent role in the analysis of international economic relations among countries of different degrees of development. With respect to theory, we can say that his work has questioned the claims of traditional analysis of development, by emphasizing the necessity of taking different structures into account, and showing where theory is supposed to play its part. With regard to policy, Prebisch's viewpoint draws our attention to the need for considering more tangible factors in the formulation of a policy for development.

II. The Latin American Economic School

A.

In this part of the paper we will examine, in brief, the main characteristics of the so-called Latin American School, which recognizes Prebisch as one of its principal mentors. The problems we will analyze are those specifically dealt with by the members of this school, with emphasis on economic development and the distribution of income between industrial countries and the less-developed ones.

Productive structures in Latin American countries had conformed to the international division of labor from political independence to the great breakdown in the international trade system during the 1930s. Up to that time there was no reason whatsoever for people with an economic background in Latin America to suspect that the economic theory devised mainly in England, France, Germany, and the United States was not the most adequate to solve the problems posed in that area of the world. Ten years later, after the breakdown of the free trade system and international division of labor, most of the influential Latin American economists continued to hold on to theories originating in the developed countries. This delay is easily explained, since these economists had to undergo a long process to be certain that the problems posed were different from those of the more-developed countries and that the elements of the analysis received from more advanced countries possibly rested on some implied assumptions not met in the case of Latin American economies.

This new school of economic thought appeared at the beginning of the

1950s with Raúl Prebisch, the Argentine economist, as its first exponent [13, p. 294]. The center from which the new ideas radiated was the Economic Commission for Latin America (ECLA), where a group of economists made a thorough study of the main lines of Prebisch's thought, which are outlined as follows:

One of the outstanding aspects of this new school was its critical stance against the classical and neoclassical doctrines. In addition, the main points of interest for the economists belonging to this group centered on the analysis of the external sector with special reference to problems of inflation, development, and the government attitude facing economic difficulties. This approach was surely conditioned by international economic relations, partly because of ECLA's nature and its interests; hence the emphasis given to the external sector, which is perhaps the point where the problems of each nation become most evident (for instance, the inflationary effect of the exchange rate, the slow growth of the export sector, problems inherent in the balance of payments, etc.). Thus, the second characteristic of this school is confirmed—its approach to national problems with special reference to the external sector.

B.

In recent decades, people of many countries have become more and more conscious of the necessity of rapid growth so as to be able to reach the position which is today occupied by the advanced countries. They have met many difficulties, however, on the way to that goal. Some economists have emphatically pointed out the unfavorable prospects for economic development in the institutions, attitudes, and conditions of underdeveloped countries. Yet, no school has placed so much emphasis on the analysis of the external sector in its relation to development as the group of economists from ECLA has done. They feel they have detected in that sector an obstinate tendency to create difficulties for developing economies, among others, the increasing problems in obtaining the necessary imports: in underdeveloped countries there are trade aberrations—fluctuating in one or the other direction—that make it hard to get the required amount of foreign exchange for the usual imports [8, p. 28]. Subsequently, they enter into a stage of import substitution. This substitution, in its turn, becomes more and more problematic for various reasons.

In the beginning, imported goods are substituted by domestic products whose manufacture is technically simple; then substitution takes place for goods which are more complex and is consequently harder to attain. Besides, greater amounts of imported capital inputs as well as strategic raw materials are required. All this leads to the impossibility of reducing imports beyond some given amount, since it would bring domestic industry to a full stop. The strategy of import substitution, paradoxically, makes national economies depend on the external sector even more than before, since, prior to the substitution process, the reduction in imported goods left a rather superfluous part of the population's desires unsatisfied. But after substitution, any import reduction implies the paralysis of a vast sector of the economy needing raw materials, semimanufactured products, or capital goods which are obtained from abroad. In addition, the common inefficiency of the import substitution sector often causes commodity prices to rise, at the expense of exports themselves. To this aspect of things great attention has been given to the experience of the Latin American countries, since it is expected that the same path and identical problems will be faced by other less-developed countries in the future [8, pp. 27, 73]. Finally, it has been pointed out that trends in the relative development of countries lead us to think that the now existing gap between industrial countries and the rest of the world will actually increase in the years to come. Doubtless, this is a real paradox that reality seems to impose on less-developed countries despite their desires and ambitions. They had hoped that this gap would diminish in the coming years.

C.

In the economic analysis of problems dealt with by Prebisch and his followers, the thesis of the secular deterioration of the terms of trade has played a fundamental role. This is one of the most elaborate points of the analysis and is based upon statistical data which show how export earnings have been declining. The argument rests upon some fundamental observations, the most important one being technological progress, as it is upon this that the remaining elements pivot to a greater or lesser extent.

Technical advance is brought about in different sectors of the economy, though in more advanced countries it shows a bias towards substitution against often imported raw materials. Raw materials from underdeveloped countries are thus replaced by synthetics or in any case, the amount of foreign input is reduced in the final product. At the same time, the sectors producing substitutes for imports which come from less-developed countries become more and more efficient, particularly in the obtention of agricultural products [16, p. 13]. Technical progress in both sectors (agriculture and industry) causes income to increase. However, this increase brings about a higher demand for manufactured products than for primary ones, according to the explanation contained in Engel's law [16, p. 167].

If we consider that less-developed countries are, in general, exporters of raw materials and importers of manufactured products, this would imply a lesser increase in demand for exports from those countries (raw materials) than in their import demands (manufactures). This fact tends to produce unfavorable changes in the terms of trade of underdeveloped countries.[1] But there are two elements to add to the complexity of the problem: one, related to protective restrictions imposed by more advanced countries against the inflow of primary products from other regions, and another, which relates to market structure. As regards the former, there is no significant treatment at a theoretical level within the framework of the school of ECLA's economists. It is the second element that plays a relevant role. We refer to the existence of monopolistic sectors in advanced countries and competitive ones in underdeveloped countries [16, pp. 166–167]. All this is closely linked to the fundamental argument of technological process. Let us examine this point in detail.

Productivity increases in every economic sector, and the increase in industrial centers is equivalent to the one observed in underdeveloped countries. Yet, this increase manifests itself differently in prices: in developing countries, these increases are reflected in lower prices, particularly because exporting sectors work competitively. But in exporting sectors of industrial countries there are monopolistic forces, such as those represented by the unions, that prevent cost decreases from being transferred to prices but preempt such decreases by means of negotiation [11, p. 58]. This would virtually mean the closing of the analysis, since it would start a secular trend downwards for prices of primary products (as a result of the competition under which exporters from underdeveloped countries operate) and an upward movement or maintenance of manufactured goods prices (since monopolistic sectors of advanced countries prevent technical progress from being translated into lower prices). For the sake of completeness, we can say that the worsening of the terms-of-trade will occur even in the absence of a clearly-defined trend and with just cyclical fluctuations, if during the depressive stage manufactured goods' prices decrease less than primary goods' prices. This is likely to happen owing to the monopolistic characteristics under which industrial goods production operates. This disparity of forces prevents international trade gains from being equally distributed among participants; rather, the greater part of such gains falls into the hands of wealthier countries, making distribution regressive at the world level.

[1] To a certain extent, as Meier and Baldwin recognize, the main argument of the idea of agricultural inferiority in relation to industry as an economic activity, shows certain similarity to the position of M. Manoilesco in favor of tariffs to protect industry.

III. Consequences of Prebisch's Propositions for Economic Policy in Underdeveloped Countries

The present section aims at examining the national position of different countries in light of the ideas emerging from Prebisch's line of thinking. We shall briefly analyze examples of national policies which have been followed (tariffs, commercial or industrial policies, economic planning, etc.) and study the attitude of less-developed countries at the international conferences which have been held; finally, we shall look at a definite idea that prevails in Prebisch's thinking as well as that of ECLA, that of economic integration as the most coherent response to the problem of underdevelopment.

A.

It is beyond the limits of this paper to offer a detailed analysis of every economic policy followed by countries in the process of development and compare them to propositions which either directly or indirectly relate to Prebisch. It should suffice to illustrate some of the most typical recent cases.

Powelson [13] has placed the problem of the policy implications of ECLA's economic theories within a consistent historical perspective. In short, although the prevailing attitude during the 1950s was invoking LDC "weaknesses" (leading to claims among other measures, for the unilateral trade privileges from advanced countries), in the 1960s there was a shift towards a "strong" policy (which was made apparent in a series of measures taken independently by underdeveloped countries). This is particularly valid for Latin American countries.

The first type of attitude—that of "weakness"—had as its starting stage, the idea of waiting passively to see what the "strong" would do in favor of those adopting this stance. The promising opportunities to express such a position were to be found at the international conferences. There was an enormous turnout of officials from every level to attend such meetings which, at the beginning, seemed to be quite promising. On the other hand, it was possible to arouse great popular expectations about their results, which were hoped to be substantial real benefits for great majorities in the rather proximate future. Not to cite the ascendant number of hemispheric meetings—one of which was attended by nearly all the presidents of countries of the American continent—it will suffice to refer only to the so-called "Pan American Operation," whose historical extension has been known as the "Alliance for Progress." Readers interested in this point may refer to the many reports which have critically studied the operation of these programs. Their evaluation will surely be negative.

Examples of the new policy of "strength" can be found—among others—by the recent firm attitudes of countries on the South American continent. Thus, they have asserted national sovereignty, with all its consequences, over coastal waters out to 200 miles by collecting duties from those carrying on fishing activities in these territorial waters (e.g., Ecuador's decisive action regarding tuna boats). We could also make reference to the attitude of the Peruvian government in nationalizing the International Petroleum Company and that of the Chilean government in completely nationalizing the copper sector and in partially nationalizing many other industries (such as textiles, automobiles, etc.), as well as the increasing state administration of Chilean banking.

We might also mention the different positions which underdeveloped countries represented in the international arena. Generally speaking, we can say that up to the end of World War II, their argument was for "aid, not trade." The truth is that such an "aid policy" has developed much more vigorously than trade measures, at least insofar as grants to underdeveloped countries are concerned [16, Chap. 4]. But, as soon as World War II ended, their position changed: "trade, not aid" became the slogan of less-developed countries. Their increasing need for development dictated this change in posture: it was, they felt, necessary to export industrial products in order to acquire the foreign exchange which would facilitate sustained domestic growth. In fact, the success of this new commercial policy depended, to a great extent, on the willingness of the advanced countries to sweep aside the obstacles which prevented the proposed traffic.[2] At any rate, we all recognize that the formula "trade, not aid" has profound political connotations (that is, the elimination of economic dependence, which is implied in the aid programs).

Leaving aside all these considerations, which are rather political in nature, we shall examine from another angle those taking greater account of economic relations in a stricter sense. Thus, it is possible to judge the attitude of some countries in terms of Prebisch's original idea about import substitution policy as a means for the industrialization of less-developed economies.

On this point, there are two kinds of strategies to distinguish: the "inward-looking" strategy of development (the import substitution of manufactured goods through high protective barriers), and the "outward-looking" strategy

[2] Among the impediments erected by developed countries, we can mention: tariff barriers, quantitative restrictions, administrative procedures, discriminatory practices of private firms. (On the other hand, one must also point out the protectionist practices employed by less-developed countries in their mutual trade of industrial goods.) Johnson [8] states that many policies of developed countries have been adopted for reasons of domestic economic policy but not to prevent other countries' growth, and quite often, such policies are due to problems of world commercial competition with other developed countries (but not with the underdeveloped world).

(a policy oriented towards exports, usually involving changes in the system of incentives in order to favor export activity). In the light of this scheme, B. Balassa [1] has considered the industrial policies followed by Korea and Taiwan, where special emphasis has been placed upon an elaborate "system of incentives" in order to foster exports. The decline of the substitution policy, after the "easy" period, has prompted some less-developed countries to choose the other alternative. As a consequence of the application of the "outward-looking" strategy, many countries have been able to partially eliminate undue protection for their manufacturing production (with corresponding administrative economies). Primary activities, in turn, have gained with more realistic exchange rates in force (with a subsequent improvement of the balance of payments). In the case of overpopulated countries, the export of goods which are labor intensive has meant not only progress for the external sector, but has also made it possible to accelerate the growth rate of the economy as a whole.

Finally, the experience of a semi-industrialized country like Argentina is worth mentioning in order to observe how its economic policy has been changing through time. The substitution scheme of the 1950s was applied to sectors of light industry, particularly those which were labor intensive, with a little application to the basic sectors. Due to the restrictive net effect of import substitution, ECLA has proposed that the solution to the Argentine economic problem was to be found in the use of international public capital This ECLA "mechanism," although suggesting autarchy as the final outcome, was hard to achieve. By the end of the 1950s, there appeared a new "desarrollista," scheme, postulating a semiautarchic model, with strong participation by foreign private capital (the ways to implement it were indicated at the time, and, according to some economists, it constituted the most consistent strategy). In terms of the progress attained in the 1960s—introduction of foreign economic policy tools, restraint of the national market, emphasis upon capital-intensive projects, and the decline of substitution policy—it was said that "the basic problem of our economy consists in the changing of an economic structure, the agricultural and above all an industrial structure operating at the lowest level of efficiency, into an efficient and more industrial one." [3] The new strategy proposed for Argentine economic development—it is thus said—will make a nationalistic economic policy possible (the use of minimal capital requirements, and an effective encouragement of industrial exports, to make the financing of the process possible with resources at hand), with a proper consideration for the spatial structure of the Argentine economy.

[3] The interested reader should refer to Di Tella [4] to see other elements apart from those defined by Di Tella as a strategy of "indirect development."

B.

It is now necessary—within the proposed outline—to point out the attitudes of underdeveloped countries (as a group) in their relations with the industrialized group, as shown at international meetings and in world organizations. The agenda concerning less-developed countries constitutes an extraordinary set of problems. However, according to priorities set at the IInd United Nations Conference on Trade and Development (UNCTAD) by the countries themselves, the most important questions could be summarized under four main headings: (a) trade preferences for manufactured goods; (b) agreements on raw materials and foodstuffs; (c) compensatory finance; and (d) cost of sea transportation.

Point (a) refers to unilateral preferences in international trade in favor of underdeveloped countries. Point (b) refers to a system of compensatory finance owing to fluctuations in primary goods' prices (which destabilize earnings proceeds from primary exports). All this could be attained by increasing the capital inflow supplied by international lending agencies. Point (c) refers to the necessity of striking effective international agreements or some other form of agreement which will improve the terms of trade (which, according to the evaluation made by underdeveloped countries mentioned above, generally turn against them). Point (d) refers to the high cost that developing countries must bear in matters of sea transportation, tourism, and insurance: amounts paid to industrial countries for such services reach huge figures.[4]

The great problems affecting the underdeveloped countries of the world, outlined in this way through their controversy with the more advanced ones, are illuminated in a significant fact which attracts our attention: at the world meetings (such as the one held in Geneva in 1964 and New Delhi, 1968; Argel, 1967), as well as in the regional conferences (CECLA), underdeveloped countries presented their case as a united front (neglecting problems which might divide them), while the advanced countries (western as well as socialist) showed great fissures in their facades. In order to portray in greater detail the collective attitude of underdeveloped countries in supranational events, we will refer to the two well-known meetings of UNCTAD held in 1964 (Geneva) and in 1968 (New Delhi). The creation of UNCTAD was, fundamentally, the result of Prebisch's personal efforts, and he traveled throughout the world in the months prior to March, 1964, in an effort to assemble the opinions and viewpoints of underdeveloped countries.

[4] Thus, Latin America spends annually 500 million dollars to pay for maritime services from developed countries, as well as for air services and insurance. See *Comercio Exterior*, México, April 1968, "El Balance de la Segunda UNCTAD."

In recent years UNCTAD has operated as a complementary body to GATT (General Agreement on Trade and Tariffs), whose main concern has been (due to its origin and date of creation) questions relating to industrialized countries in matters of commercial policy and the like. Although some of the problems presently discussed explicitly and treated with priority at UNCTAD were also discussed by GATT, this has only happened sporadically. In short, we can say that UNCTAD was created to discuss the international economic relations linking industrialized and less-developed countries.

UNCTAD represented, in fact, an extraordinary effort.[5] Over 2000 delegates representing 120 countries attended the meeting in Geneva. The work sessions were divided into 5 commissions, dealing with different topics: (a) international problems related to goods; (b) trade in semimanufactured and manufactured goods; (c) development financing; (d) continuation of institutional arrangements; (e) expansion of international trade and its significance for economic development. Obviously, at the conference the underdeveloped countries (75 in number) formed a "majority front." Inspired by Prebisch, this front succeeded in maintaining the principle of jointly submitting agreed-upon propositions, even in the case of questions where the interests of members of the front were at variance (for instance, regarding surplus food disposal and nondiscriminatory preferences in advanced countries' markets). In short, it was necessary to find the way to reconcile the form and content of the statements about the issues discussed at the Conference.

To this point, we have outlined the organizational and mechanical aspects of the task of putting UNCTAD into motion. There is still a point left to be examined, which is the underlying philosophy of the discussions. We can say, in brief, that the goal of the LDCs was to obtain a new commercial policy for development. President Kennedy had promulgated the idea that the 1960s ought to be a "development decade." Underdeveloped areas felt that it was imperative to look for a new international forum to replace the negative policy they sensed GATT represented, in the sense of removing restrictions on trade only within a framework of reciprocity and nondiscrimination. The essential goal of the "new international deal" consisted of a political decision by developed countries to aid less-developed ones more effectively.

Historically, it is possible to distinguish three phases in the development of international economic relations. At the time when the United Kingdom was considered the world's economic center, trade was characterized by the well-known "double flow": the Periphery imported manufactures and exported primary goods. When, in the 1930s, the United States became the "Center," the previous scheme was broken down because of the large resource endow-

[5] References to this meeting are based on Johnson [8, Chap. 1].

ment of the North American country and its strong protective policy. After the outbreak of World War II and during the postwar period, less-developed countries undertook great projects aimed at industrialization (particularly those belonging to the "inward-looking" type, that is, an import-substitution policy); Europe reconstruction was also undertaken and led to consequent modernization. As a result of this new order in the international economy, commercial policy also had to be changed: underdeveloped countries needed markets to absorb their exports (especially those coming from the economically dynamic sector, that is, industrial exports).

The behavior of less-developed countries has been absolutely consistent. Their demands for better export performance serve a main object, which is to relieve the pressure of a chronic deficit in the external sector. This situation appears to be inherent in the present process of development. Consequently, the prevailing tendency towards lack of external equilibrium should be offset by means of a policy of industrialization and this in turn should be made compatible with an intelligent commercial policy [15]. Therefore, it is necessary to close the "trade gap" existing between foreign-exchange requirements and the possibilities to obtain such exchange. The needs for more foreign exchange are underscored by increasing imports and the external debt-services requirements, if the goal of the "development decade" is to be fulfilled. One is pessimistic about the chances to raise foreign exchange proceeds due to the low increase of earnings coming from exports.[6]

Needless to say, many of UNCTAD's decisions have only meant an expression of good but unfulfilled wishes. However, we should summarize the proposals made by underdeveloped countries at the 1964 Meeting. Besides the universal desire for increased exports (industrial ones, in particular) as a means to attain a substantial improvement in the international balance of payments, less-developed countries demanded international agreements on certain goods (favoring a parity-price system), a system of compensatory finance (payments made in order to compensate for losses incurred), and a "real" trade reciprocity[7] (that is, a reduction of tariffs by the advanced countries in favor of the underdeveloped ones, so that the latter could increase their capacity to import from developed areas, thus expanding world trade). Another of the issues dealt with was that of external aid, which would offset, among other things, the effects of unfavorable terms of trade, fund the existing

[6] The commercial gap just mentioned, has been estimated at 20 billion dollars by the UN Secretariat and 12 billion dollars by Balassa. (See Johnson [8, Chap. 1].) The objective of the development decade was to reach a growth rate of 5 per cent per annum.

[7] "Real" reciprocity in Prebisch's terminology is distinguished from "conventional" reciprocity, which means a simple interchange of connections, which make underdeveloped countries more and more dependent upon their primary goods exports (with low rates of growth in gross product and a decrease in international trade).

debt, help obtain an extension of the corresponding payment schedules, and meet expenses for overseas shipment and contingency freights.[8]

We will now cast a rapid glance at the outcome of UNCTAD II (New Delhi, 1968). Since the main goals of less-developed countries have not changed much in comparison with those already dealt with in some detail in connection with UNCTAD I, we will only review the most outstanding characteristics of the meeting held in New Delhi. On the basis of four main problem areas proposed by underdeveloped countries, the issues discussed were: preferences for manufactures, agreements on raw materials, compensatory finance, and the high cost of overseas transportation. UNCTAD II, which ". . . submitted to world opinion, in a rather dramatic fashion, a complete outline of the demands of about eighty underdeveloped countries from Latin America, Africa, and Asia . . . also advanced some of the solutions in the field of international economic relations. . . ."[9] With regard to their proposals, it should be pointed out that the one relating to preferential access to markets of more advanced countries for manufactures and semimanufactured goods coming from underdeveloped areas was unanimously approved. What was not mentioned, however, was the date on which such a policy would be put into force, nor the kind of goods covered. The most positive result on this front was the creation of a Special Committee on Preferences (within UNCTAD), in charge of seeing to the execution of the decision taken.

Regarding basic products, the results obtained were limited, despite the conciliatory attitude of the group of 77 (among which we should emphasize the participation of Argentina, Brazil, Mexico, and Venezuela). The ground covered included practically every issue in the framework of the exchange of raw materials, from their production to their marketing at the international level. It was also anticipated that a series of world conferences about different products would be called, that stabilizing reserve would be created, measures would be taken to ameliorate competition in byproducts, and that there would be limitations on some competitive products in industrial countries. Obviously, this set of measures was only partially accepted by the developed world. In the other aspects, such as marine transportation, tourism, and insurance, it was possible to break through the "hostile front" of advanced countries. We have continually emphasized the financial significance of such items in the international balance of payments of less-developed countries.

In short, as was affirmed by the president of UNCTAD II, the meeting was discouraging in many aspects, although to some extent, successful. The

[8] Other aspects of the attitudes of less-developed countries can be found in Powelson's paper, included in the present volume. The writer explains what, in his opinion, a "Latin American strategy" should be and outlines the elements for a "strong policy."

[9] See *Comercio Exterior*, April 1968. The analysis in the text is based on information from the February, March, and April, 1968, issues.

new session of UNCTAD reemphasized the cohesion of the underdeveloped countries (and, in turn, the lack of common aims among developed countries), a situation relatively favorable to the former in the attainment of their goals. Raúl Prebisch interpreted the most important achievements to be the declaration on preferences and the decisions related to compensatory financing; with regard to the overall success of the Conference, he pointed out its impact on what may happen in the future.

C.

In the present section, there is still an issue left to be analyzed, that is, the joint response of less-developed countries to the proposals made in ECLA by Prebisch, relating to economic integration. We shall particularly refer to the case of Latin America, making a brief analysis of the causes leading to their efforts at integration and examining the achievements of some of the experiences (Latin American Free Trade Association, Central American Common Market, Andean Pact, Plata Basin).

Evidently, the main objective of economic integration is to accelerate economic development. Let us make a rapid review of the reasoning employed by ECLA [5, Chap. 5] in this context. The starting point is given by the painful slowness of Latin American economic growth in recent years. Thus, in the period 1945–1965, Latin American income per capita increased only by 50 per cent (from 280 to 430 dollars). With this trend in mind, and in view of the high rate of demographic growth, future prospects were not very promising that Latin America might participate in a major economic expansion of one of the great geographic areas of the world. The causes of the failure of different development policies have been analyzed by ECLA, and the results can be summarized by stating that their failure has been the outcome of a series of independent efforts carried out in isolated compartments (3). Countries on the road to development have few resources available or technical capacity even to compete with the relatively more-developed ones in the same underdeveloped regions, much less with the developed areas. Consequently, it is necessary to establish a gradual process of economic integration between Latin American countries. It has been pointed out that this is the only way to solve the problem of bottlenecks in the countries' foreign trade as a whole. There are also a variety of other ideas in ECLA's theories related to the long-run deficiencies of an import-substitution policy and questions of the external debt, as well as some considerations about the overall deficit in Latin American foreign trade. In short, regional economic integration should serve as a decisive instrument of national development, by helping to settle the balance of payments deficit, overcoming difficulties arising from the size of national markets, raising productivity and the efficient use of regional resources, and also by serving as a strong stimulus for the incorporation of technical progress and many other objectives in international policy, which would make too long a list to detail in this space.

Let us now briefly examine what has happened by way of implementation of these designs for integration.[10] At the beginning of the 1960s treaties were signed at Montevideo and Managua, creating the Latin American Free Trade Association (LAFTA) and Central American Common Market (CACM), respectively. Within the framework of LAFTA a significant event was that of increasing intrazonal trade in the following years. However, the integration process in LAFTA has evolved neither in a continuous nor in an increasing manner. Another important aspect to be noted is that the bulk of commercial flows has consisted of traditional products, so that intrazonal trade has enjoyed but a very small influx of new products.

A plausible explanation for the lack of dynamism in commercial relations within Latin America lies in the inherent deficiency of the very structural conformation of the regional economy. In fact, although economic integration requires adequate market size in order to carry out the development process, it also requires adequate purchasing power (on the part of the population), capable of creating high effective demand. In Latin America, the changing structure of income distribution serves as a limiting factor in the process of economic integration. Thus, in the work done by OECEI it has been suggested that where scale economies play a relevant part, the scale of effective demand be regarded as most significant from the moment the industries are set in motion. Consequently, in order to consolidate the dynamic role of basic industries, one must pay attention to the decisive question of market dimensions, that is, the number of inhabitants and income level.[11]

In discussing LAFTA's achievements, it is pertinent to turn to a consideration of some of the specific purposes of the Montevideo Treaty. We must not forget that it constituted the basic instrument for only trade liberalization, not for economic integration, which was foreseen as a later stage. In other words, the characteristics of the document signed at Montevideo in 1960 were such that it eliminated or, at least, limited the scope of the program's capacity to

[10] The interested reader should consult the different issues of *Comercio Exterior*—among other specialized publications—and also OECEI (Oficinas de Estudios para la Colaboración Económica, [12]).

[11] Another feature—among the great number which might be considered—is that of differences of degree in relative development attained by Latin America countries. The various degrees of economic potential is another of the limiting factors in the process of integration. Other points to be consider for instance, are the integrating capacity of physical infrastructure, investment feasibility of projects in the region as a whole, and the agricultural as well as the industrial bases, apart from legal-institutional questions.

support economic integration. Nevertheless, the future of the efforts to create a Common Market in Latin America appears very promising. In 1967, presidents of member countries signed the "Charter of Punta del Este," whose *Program of Action* contains two basic points. The first—and most important in our opinion—refers to the commitment assumed by the heads of governments to "create the Latin American Common Market in a progressive way, starting in 1970, so as to be in full operation in no more than 15 years." Besides the signatory countries of the treaties of Montevideo and Managua, those belonging to LAFTA and CACM, the Common Market should also incorporate the remaining countries of Latin America. The second basic point deals with the necessity of sponsoring a sustained multinational effort to strengthen and expand the physical infrastructure of the region to meet future requirements.

As a final evaluation, we might add that the declaration of Punta del Este is considered the joint political decision of highest importance that Latin American countries have adopted on the subject of economic integration. Another question to be considered is the term foreseen (fifteen years) for putting the Common Market into effect. In fact, the 1970s promise to pose problems quite similar to those of the early 1960s for countries undertaking the integration task in Latin America. In short, the attainment of those goals depends in the final analysis on the political decision of every country as an entity and upon the body of Latin American countries as a whole.

IV. The Response of the Economists and Governments in Advanced Areas

The theories emerging in the group of economists who recognize Prebisch as the creator of their principal lines of argument, as well as the policies and attitudes adopted by underdeveloped countries (as a whole or independently) have not been exempted from critical analysis by the economists from more developed areas. Those who have shown the greatest interest in these doctrines have been the English-speaking economists. There has been a small but outstanding group which has accepted, modified and enlarged Prebisch's concepts. The rest have severely criticized the whole approach, uncovering a set of both theoretical and empirical deficiencies in the analysis. If, as Joan Robinson has stated, there is no doctrine without ideology, this is a good example to show how the national interest of the country can exert a remarkable influence upon the formulation of the theory. In particular, the bulk of economists from developed areas have questioned the Prebisch approach, whereas those coming from less-developed ones have supported it.

A.

Before going into detail, it should be emphasized that in every case the critics have been sympathetic to the great importance attributed to the external sector in problems of development. The first and still principal of their attacks has been aimed at the empirical support of Prebisch's ideas. His analysis of the terms of trade was thoroughly reviewed and a number of deficiencies were unearthed which, in most cases, obscure the conclusions of the Prebisch analysis. The major critiques in this respect were directed to several points, but fundamentally they take aim at inadequacies in the indices used to measure fluctuations in the terms of trade. In the first place, it is argued that the quality of tradable goods is not taken into account. This fact produces a bias, since manufactured goods have shown substantial improvements in quality which are not balanced by equivalent changes in primary products. Nor have new products, which have been incorporated in international trade, been taken into account, although they have supplanted ones from previous periods under examination and embody extraordinary technical advances. Such has been the case with new cars, which can now replace carriages and even older vehicles.

In the second place, in the analysis of British imports and exports, it is argued that no change in transportation costs through time has been taken into consideration. These costs have been gradually declining, and by taking the CIF figures for British imports and FOB figures for exports, the Prebisch school introduced a bias, in the sense that there only *appeared* to be a decrease in import prices—including freight—in relation to export prices, which excluded shipping. Finally, the question of the adequacy of the sample has been discussed: even if Prebisch is correct, the conclusions obtained from the analysis of the English case cannot be necessarily extended to other countries. This last critique gave rise to some subtleties. On the one hand, attempts were made to distinguish between what might happen in the terms of trade of manufactured goods versus primary goods, and on the other hand, what might happen to the terms of trade for goods sold by underdeveloped countries versus those sold by more advanced ones. These trends should not necessarily be equal, since many developed countries export primary products, and sometimes they even regulate their prices. Besides, it would be unlikely that the prices of oil, cacao, wheat, rubber, meat, etc., would all change in the same direction. Some empirical studies show us movements in either direction but with different intensities in the case of some primary goods; the same result is obtained for manufactured goods.

These are the main critiques at the empirical level of the statistical foundation for Prebisch's theories. But, as the conclusions reached on the basis of available data are rather eclectic, orthodox economists have been forced to make a critical analysis of the theoretical foundations of the ideas we have just developed here. Those who have been most successful in dealing with this point [11, p. 59] are Harberler [7, pp. 275–297] and Flanders [6, pp. 305–326].

Harberler presents some arguments which it will be worthwhile to analyze briefly here. In the first place, he deals with the empirical aspects mentioned above (quality, transportation costs and other services, significance of British terms of trade). Another of these aspects, which is more theoretical in character, refers to the explanations given for the assumed trend on the grounds of (a) the existence of monopolistic factors in industrial countries, and (b) the operation of Engel's law. Regarding point (a), in a very obscure paragraph, Harberler tries hard to contradict the postulate, without, in our opinion, being successful at it. In his argument, he alludes to the monopoly structure in industrial areas, but disregards the conditions in the underdeveloped world. He recognizes that in most advanced countries, monetary as well as fiscal policies have been such that have led to increasing monetary wages and stable prices. Harberler concludes his paper by saying that there is no evidence to prove that this wage–price behavior will injure raw materials producers, but rather those who receive fixed incomes in developed countries. As for point (b) it is said that Engel's law refers to foodstuffs, so it cannot be equally applicable to *every* export from underdeveloped countries.

Flanders, in his paper, deals with the same subject from the standpoint of its relation to economic cycles. We believe that, although the analysis in his paper is quite detailed, it does not lessen the possibility that different structures in the labor market of the Center and Periphery may encourage the fruits of technical progress to move from underdeveloped countries to more advanced ones.

In this way, we have given an answer to the proposals supported by Prebisch and his followers from a different point of view: even in the case of a real deterioration in the terms of trade, what loss would this imply for general welfare? How could this loss be compared with the gains obtained by underdeveloped countries from foreign trade and technical progress? Taking the most unfavorable hypothesis as a starting point (that is, assuming that on balance foreign trade meant an absolute loss for the countries of the periphery), this would still not be of much importance compared to the loss in national income due to the lack of capital, the use of inefficient agricultural techniques, land tenure system, unstable political situation, inflation, inadequate tax system, etc. [2, p. 262].

Finally, it has been argued that the Prebisch position places undue emphasis on the commodity terms of trade [11, p. 259], whereas what is perhaps more relevant would be an analysis of trade at the national welfare level, that is, the income terms of trade (referring to the income level) or the single factoral terms of trade (explaining the changes in productivity). Meier, for instance, writes:

> It is clearly possible, as already noted, that a country's income terms and single-factoral terms might improve at the same time as its commodity terms deteriorate. Since the exports from poor countries have grown so considerably, and productivity in export production has increased, the income terms and single-factoral terms have undoubtedly improved for poor countries.... Although their double factoral terms of trade may have deteriorated this did not affect the welfare of poor countries.... Their capacity to import and their imports per unit of productive resources exported have increased-regardless of any changes in the relative prices for their products.

B.

Having now reviewed the opinions of a group of economists from developed areas, we may now examine the behavior of the advanced countries, individually and collectively, in relation to the position taken by the underdeveloped world, particularly in light of political recommendations growing out of Prebisch's ideas. Following the lines of argument developed in Sect. III, we will deal with the position of the developed countries represented at the major recent international gathering (GATT, and the UNCTAD I and II conferences), and try to glance, as well, at their attitudes as expressed on other occasions.

It was pointed out above that industrial countries (western and socialist), did not forge a united front at the meetings held at Geneva and New Delhi. In general, the communist countries had little to offer of real significance to underdeveloped countries, and regarding the countries of the western part of the world, their attitudes were quite varied [8, Chap. 1]. The United States reaction was absolutely negative towards the new policies proposed by the underdeveloped countries. Following GATT lines, the United States opposed the idea of giving preferences to underdeveloped countries in the markets of the industrial ones. They were willing to help in terms of regional cooperation to increase trade between underdeveloped countries and collaborate in the solution of financial problems (to increase the availability of compensatory financing, reduce the debt service burden, and increase public and private capital supply for development). The United States identified itself with the so-called "soft options."[12] France, and in general, the members of the European Common Market, proposed a complex scheme to "organize"

[12] It must not be forgotten, however, that the United States is the most important donor for development in the whole world, and that many of the restrictive measures in her commercial relations have much to do with the increasing difficulties in her balance of payments.

markets for primary goods and the importation of manufactures (and semi-manufactures) in order to secure high prices, according to the degree of economic development of the countries participating in international trade. The United Kingdom and other countries belonging to the European Free Trade Association, besides being sympathetic to financial problems, were willing to accept the extension of Commonwealth Preferences to *every* underdeveloped country. Yet, in other aspects, her position was rather ambiguous. With regard to the stance adopted by the advanced countries at UNCTAD II, the most important issue was the French proposal that developed countries should annually devote to external aid one per cent of their GNP. As has often been pointed out, this "decision" lacks substance, since developed countries refuse to implement it, arguing that they, too, have serious problems in their balance of payments and other great difficulties in the international monetary system. France proposed that such a quantitative measure should be put in force by 1972; other countries advocated 1975. The United States stated vaguely that the measure would be put in force "when her economic situation would allow it."

In general, we can say that the developed countries have offered many explanations but very few positive proposals in matters of underdevelopment. The United States (and to a certain extent, the United Kingdom) pointed out that they could not increase their aid flows to underdeveloped countries because of difficulties in their balance of payments and responsibilities at the international level. France considered that the possibility for a series of agreements on primary goods was quite encouraging, although the political situation was not too promising for rapid progress in that direction. West Germany promised to increase her aid, but "took advantage of this opportunity to preach to poor countries that they should help themselves through an adequate policy of economic and social changes."[13] Nor has the position of the socialist countries changed much since UNCTAD I.

By way of conclusion, we can say that the two UNCTAD meetings have on balance been positive occasions, and have thus helped to overcome the *impasse* resulting from the GATT conferences. Developed countries—partly because of a slow change in their position and partly because of strong third-world pressure—have dropped serious hints of greater flexibility, so that a new dialogue has been broached in international economic relationships. Less-developed countries operated together in a very wise way, and have tried hard to reach their goals through specific policies. At the same time, they received encouraging support from the highest ranks in international

[13] *Comercio Exterior*, March 1968. For a complete view of the other proposals in the framework of commercial relationships at the international level, see, for instance, Lary [9, in particular, pp. 127–138].

organisms. It is perhaps at this point, that we can say that Prebisch's work has found its highest expression in favor of greater equality and justice in the modern world.

REFERENCES

[1] Balassa, B., Industrial Policies in Taiwan and Korea, this volume.

[2] Buchanan, N. S., and Ellis, H. S., "Approaches to Economic Development." 20th Century Fund, New York, 1955.

[3] ECLA, El Mercado Común Latinoamericano, E/CN. 12/531, UN Sales 59, II, G.4 (July 1959).

[4] Di Tella, G., Por una Nueva Estrategia del Desarrollo, *Criterio*, Buenos Aires (December 1970).

[5] "El Pensamiento de la CEPAL." Editorial Univ., Santiago, Chile, 1966.

[6] Flanders, M. J., Prebisch on Protectionism: An Evaluation, *Econ. J.* (1964).

[7] Harberler, G., Terms of Trade and Economic Development, "Economic Development and Latin America" (H. S. Ellis, ed.). St. Martin's Press, New York, 1961.

[8] Johnson, H. G., "Economic Policies Toward Less Developed Countries." The Brookings Inst., Washington, D. C., 1967.

[9] Lary, H. B., "Imports of Manufactures from Less Developed Countries." Columbia Univ. Press, New York, 1968.

[10] Meier, G. M., and Baldwin, R. E., "Economic Development: Theory, History, Policy." Wiley, New York, 1959.

[11] Meier, G. M., "The International Economics of Development." Harper and Row, New York, 1968.

[12] OECEI, Mercado ALALC, "Fundamentos Macroeconómicos para su Evaluación," Buenos Aires, 1971.

[13] Powelson, J. P., "Latin America: Today's Economic and Social Revolution." McGraw-Hill, New York, 1964.

[14] Powelson, J. P., The International Politics of Latin American Economics, this volume.

[15] Prebisch, R., Hacia una Nueva Política Comercial en Pro del Desarrollo, E/conf. 46/3, UN Sales 64, II, B.4 (1964).

[16] Singer, H. W., "International Development: Growth and Change." McGraw-Hill, New York, 1964.

II. ON INSTITUTIONS AND IDEAS

In this section, we have included a very interesting work written by Gunnar *Myrdal*, in relation to ambiguities implicit in certain terminologies, which in turn tend to support biased theories. By way of summary, we can say that Myrdal poses the question: Has the wrong name been given to what might be called the international entity par excellence, the United Nations? There are a number of reasons to support his point of view.

The second part of the essay is devoted to a problem which has always been of real concern to the U.N. since the creation of the organization, namely, the economic and social development of underdeveloped countries. The writer points out the necessity of distinguishing between static concepts ("backward regions") and dynamic ones ("underdeveloped countries"). The distinction is not only important because of the economic implications which derive from it, but also because an error in terminology may lead to serious biases in the scientific approach to development questions in less developed countries.

Finally, Myrdal draws attention to the theoretical and empirical advantages of changing the existing situation and adopting a new terminology, in scientific as well as public documents, and in general the adequate use of words to overcome biases in intellectual work.

TWISTED TERMINOLOGY AND BIASED THEORIES

GUNNAR MYRDAL

University of Stockholm, Stockholm, Sweden

There is a tendency for all knowledge, like all ignorance, to deviate from truth in an opportunistic direction [1, pp. 977 ff., 2, 3, p. 3]. This becomes reflected in twisted terminology. I shall illustrate this in regard to some of the major world problems, to which my highly esteemed friend and former colleague Raúl Prebisch has devoted so many years of his working life, and whom we are honoring by this collective volume.

The very name of the system of intergovernmental organizations, which we both have served, the "United Nations," is logically fallacious. Indeed, the very first words of its charter, where the active subjects enacting it are said to be "We the peoples of the United Nations," is a pious falsehood. The members of the United Nations and of all the composite organizations within that system are not peoples, or nations, but governments of states.

The assembly or plenary meeting of an organization is thus in no real sense equal to the legislative assembly of a country. The delegates are not elected by constituencies of voters as in a democratic state. As there is no suprastate world government, it is still less equal to that resemblance to a legislative assembly that is often created by authoritarian governments, with members appointed or chosen in some way other than elected under universal suffrage by free and secret voting. The delegates represent nations only indirectly, if at all.

It should be added that the large and rapid increase of member states since the enacting of the charter has very much increased the proportion of such governments upon whose policies the broad masses of people in their nations, and very often even the majority of their educated and alert upper strata, have little or no influence. Their legitimation for membership is not that they can truly be said to represent nations but that they control a territory recognized to be a state.

Even if for practical reasons no more adequate term can now be substituted for the "United Nations," this qualification should constantly be borne in mind. Indeed, the adjective "international" in the name of some of the intergovernmental organizations in the system and generally used to characterize relations or problems stretching over the boundary of the states, is mostly a misnomer. In any case, the term "international organizations" should in correct language be substituted by the term "intergovernmental organizations."

Terminology, and the meaning given to terms, does matter. It represents opportunities for logical gliding of our thoughts in unrealistic directions, if not critically watched most carefully. There is likewise an opportunistic tendency with all of us to want to believe that the United Nations, and all the intergovernmental organizations within its system, is a suprastate, or at least the beginning of it: having goals and promising, establishing, and implementing collectively decided policies like the government of an individual state.

The hierarchical structure of the organizations within the system contributes to giving a semblance of realism to this analogy with a state. So does the largely fictitious "purposes and principles" expressed in the charter and founding constitutional documents of all the composite organizations, which are afforded not only "functions" but also "powers." And that terminology works on our mind in the same opportunistic direction. The vague idea of this system of intergovernmental organizations constituting a suprastate entity in its own right lingers on in all popular, political, and often even scientific discussion. It is this otherworldly conception of what the United Nations is that inspires both the pessimists and the optimists.

In reality, an intergovernmental organization in our time, and as far ahead as we can think, is ordinarily no more, and no less, than an agreed matrix for the multilateral pursuit of the policies of the participant governments: indeed a created instrumentality for the diplomacy of a number of disparate individual states. In this context, I shall not pursue the analysis further, except by pointing out that this does not necessarily imply that the intergovernmental organizations cannot be important. Everything depends on the will of governments, working under internal and external influences and pressures of all sorts, to reach agreement on substantive issues.

One world problem that hardly was clearly perceived at the time when the U.N. Charter was framed, but that has gradually taken on increasing weight in the deliberations taking place and the agreements sought and sometimes reached in the intergovernmental organizations, concerns the development of the underdeveloped countries. To this, Raúl Prebisch has, as we all know, made major contributions.

In colonial times and right up to World War II, there was little interest devoted to this problem. If anybody at that time sought a common term for the nonindustrialized and very poor parts of the world, the term used was usually the *static* one: "backward regions." Most of them were not then countries.

To this terminology corresponded what I have called the colonial theory [1, pp. 977 ff., 3, pp. 4 ff.]. Both in its popular and more sophisticated versions this theory, as is now apparent in retrospect, was plainly apologetic, aimed at protecting and relieving the colonial powers and the developed, rich countries generally from moral and political responsibility for the poverty and lack of development of the peoples living there. Nothing very much could be done about it. In any case, the idea that a request could be made to all the developed states to alter their commercial policies in favor of these territories and assist their development by financial aid was simply absent.

After the war, because of the avalanche of decolonization that swept over the globe, and certain other changes in the world's political climate, the term coming into use was the *dynamic* one: "underdeveloped countries." The term does not merely recognize their poverty and state of underdevelopment. As it was used, it also implied the value premises that their governments should initiate and pursue planned policies for their development and that the governments of the developed countries should assist them.

But then diplomacy—of the lower order—entered the field. The term did not seem polite enough and also, more importantly, tended to imply too much of commitments on behalf of the underdeveloped as well as the developed countries' governments. A number of euphemisms, all playing down the dynamic and value-loaded aspect of the earlier used term, entered the field. The main one was "developing countries," which even tended to play down their state of underdevelopment.

This term has now acquired a sort of official status by being used almost exclusively in all documents produced in the United Nations organizations and by all governments when presenting a view or a position. It has also been widely accepted not only in popular but also scientific writings, occasionally substituted by some other euphemism of the same character.

The term "developing country" is defective already because it does not state the thought that is pressing for expression: that a country is underdeveloped and should develop. It is also plainly illogical since it begs the question of whether a country is developing or not, or whether it is foreseeable that it will develop.

Such a terminological politesse may seem to be unimportant *per se*. But semantics *is* important. The twisted term indicates deeper biases in the scientific approach to the problems of the development of underdeveloped countries.

Elsewhere I have attempted to demonstrate in some detail that the larger part of the huge postwar economic literature was from the beginning heavily biased in a *diplomatic* and *overoptimistic* direction [1, Prologue, 3]. Much of elaborated and "elegant" learnedness serves the need of providing an escape from having to deal with awkward facts which are part of their underdevelopment and which raise inhibitions and obstacles to development. I shall not in this context enter upon the sources for the biases. Neither shall I again critically analyze the faulty approaches and methods used. I shall restrict myself to point to the *interests* that are served and only do it in the broadest terms.

Were these diplomatic and overoptimistic views that dominate even the most technical economic literature on the development problems of underdeveloped countries correct, it would be much cheaper for the developed countries to aid them in an effective way. The existence and strength of this interest to keep down the requests for aid is revealed by the fact that the statistics on aid and financial assistance is grossly juggled and falsified, giving the appearance that aid and assistance from the developed to the underdeveloped countries is much bigger than it really is.

In practically all underdeveloped countries, political power is exerted by shifting alliances within the tiny upper strata. This is mostly true both in the countries where there are general elections to a parliament and in countries under more authoritarian government. These ruling oligarchies have an interest in the biased views such that, if they were correct, they could expect to see their countries develop without having to carry out the radical egalitarian reforms which are necessary for rapid and steady development.

I am then thinking of land and tenancy reforms, which mostly have remained a sham; reforms of the distribution of taxation and of tax collection; of educational reforms that lay a stress on the content and direction of education on all levels, on decreasing the dropping out and wastage, particularly on the primary level, and on adult education; on the spread of birth control among the masses; on the stamping out of corruption, which is mostly on the increase in almost all underdeveloped countries; and generally on enforcing more social discipline.

The overcoming of the biases and a rectification of the situation in both theoretical speculation and empirical research are needed for three reasons: They are needed because knowledge as presented in our literature should be true and relevant, which is a general demand on our scientific endeavors. They are also needed if we hope to succeed in impressing upon people in the developed countries the necessity of undertaking sacrifices in order to assist underdeveloped countries to develop. They are needed, finally, to give the support which true knowledge can give to the liberal forces in underdeveloped countries who, against heavy odds, are struggling for domestic reforms.

REFERENCES

[1] Myrdal, G., "Asian Drama." Pantheon Books, New York, 1968.
[2] Myrdal, G., "Objectivity in Social Research." Pantheon Books, New York, 1969.
[3] Myrdal, G., "The Challenge of World Poverty." Pantheon Books, New York, 1970.

III. THEORETICAL APPROACHES

Despite the apparent thematic diversity, it has been found desirable to gather under this heading all those contributions whose essence has been the theoretical approach. The main object of these notes is to provide a brief summary of the papers included in this part of the book. This will allow the reader a synthetic or panoramic view of the topics dealt with by each writer.

The expression "apparent" thematic diversity makes sense if one bears in mind that, except for the papers written by Amano and Kemp—which are nonrelated topics—all the rest have a common frame of reference: the problem of economic development of the countries newly involved in the process of growth. Besides, the essays written by Lewis and Zarembka have more than one point of contact, since both deal with the same topic, although from different points of view: the underlying theory which best interprets the problems of economies of lesser relative development on the world scene.

Although the Pinto and Kñákal paper contains a great number of historical features, it also constitutes an analysis which attempts to explain the relationships between the underdeveloped and socialist economic areas in the world.

Regarding the essay contributed by Tinbergen, we can say that this strikes at the essence of the underdevelopment issue, although its approach—as might be expected—is that of aspects of economic policymaking. Let us proceed to a brief synthesis of the essays included in this part of the book.

The paper written by *Amano* on the stability conditions in the real and monetary models of international trade, considers such conditions as a whole, in contrast to the traditional approach, where different assumptions are established, depending on whether the author refers to problems of pure theory or monetary theory of international trade. Given the basic assumptions of the analysis, the paper develops an original model and later compares the stability conditions in the real and monetary models under a system of flexible exchange rates. The second section is an exercise in comparative statics, and considers the effect of the expansion of output on the terms of trade. The analysis that follows demonstrates the comparative operation of the real and monetary models under a system of fixed exchange rates (showing that devaluation improves the balance-of-trade if and only if the elasticity criterion is satisfied with stability in the original system). Finally, Amano's excellent mathematical work shows us that the assumption of full employment is crucial to establish a parallel between real and monetary models (i.e., the models in which the reasoning is based on classical and not on Keynesian postulates).

Kemp's contribution consists of a reformulation of the short-run theory of foreign exchange and constitutes a mathematical effort to surmount the existing imprecision in the conventional analysis. The theory, as it stands, lacks a foundation by which it might be incorporated into the micro-economic scheme, is not elegant, and lacks generality. Kemp proposes a theory in which all the market participants should have essentially the same goals and be able to manage speculative operations as well as those of arbitrage. The analytical construction permits pure activities (speculation and arbitrage) as extreme cases; and, within a reasonable time horizon, the analysis permits today's arbitrageur to emerge as tomorrow's speculator. The expository part covers, successively, the model's assumptions and symbols, the simplest example of planning (one-day), and a study of a two-day horizon. Finally, the author considers what should be the "next steps" in model building, when more realistic assumptions are made in relation to the speculator–arbitrageur, the unity of decision of the outlined system, and what happens when the time horizon is extended (i.e., when a generalization of the analysis is obtained).

Lewis' reflections on unlimited labor supply constitutes an effort to put into an orderly way his own ideas in this field, in the light of recent writings drawing on his seminal contribution. His paper begins by pointing out some conceptual errors, and the author once again defines certain concepts. Lewis indicates what the opinions of a number of other writers have been and adduces a series of historical examples to support his thesis. He also includes an analysis of the so-called "turning points," which is done within the framework of three versions considered by his model: (a) a closed economy without international trade; (b) a closed economy in which the capitalist sector depends on the traditional one (food and raw material supply); and (c) an open economy whose capitalist sector trades with the surplus resources of labor or with the world at large. In this study, Lewis draws attention to the behavior of the key economic variables (prices, profits, terms of trade, salaries, etc.) as the economic expansion proceeds.

Pinto and *Kñákal* contribute to this volume a brief but yet complete analysis of the changes registered in the Center–Periphery system in the decades from 1950–1970, with particular emphasis on the 1960s. The paper contains four main chapters. In the first, the writers try to explain clearly the concept of the system: ECLA's 1949 *Economic Survey*—which bears the indelible seal of Raúl Prebisch—serves as a starting point. Once the key terms of the analysis are explained—Center, Periphery, socialist world—the writers devote the second chapter to an investigation of the recent main changes in the international economic system, the rapid rate of expansion in the world economy, how that development has been polarized, the "internal" differentiation within the capitalist Center, and the implications of the rise of a socialist system. These problems are dealt with successively. In the third chapter—about other facets of the structure and operation of the Center–Periphery system, Pinto and Kñákal consider some of the following points: the problems of marginalization and "dependent integration" in the Periphery, Center–Periphery relationships from some specific viewpoints (Europe–Africa, U.S.A.–Latin America, Japan–Asia, and Soviet Union–Socialist Europe), and changes in the internal structure and relationships of the Periphery. The essay concludes with three connected reflections on the new scheme of relations between Center and Periphery, which suggest an implied contradiction between what the writers call "marginalization" and "dependent integration," and with some thoughts on the possibilities or alternatives open to the Periphery.

Tinbergen's contribution to this volume is a study of the consequences of the existence of "immobile" or "national" industries, characterized by primary production and the production of nontradables.

The writer makes a clear statement of the concept of what should be understood by these productive patterns and their quantitative importance to the national income. In subsequent sections of his work, Tinbergen turns to the basic issues at hand, the analysis of the consequences emanating from the existence of these "national" industries—within this framework, the author gives special attention to the developing countries—and considers the following: (a) balance-of-payments problems, (b) macroplanning for development, and (c) the selection of the sectors to develop. Tinbergen concludes by reemphasizing the necessity of taking into account the existence of "national" sectors inside the economy, owing to the difficulties that they can create in planning for development.

Zarembka's paper on a long-run economic growth model for developing countries, is an analytical and empirical contribution to the theory of economic development of depressed geographical areas. To this purpose, the writer has built an econometric model of economic growth around the basic principle of profit maximization. His theoretical approach employs a general equilibrium model with special emphasis on commodity supply. In the first part of the essay, he develops the basic characteristics of the model (production functions, factor markets, wage–rate determination, domestic prices, and the international market). The second part offers parameter estimates for Columbia and prewar Japan for those equations relating directly to the foreign sector with a very interesting contrast between the structuralist and monetarist hypotheses of inflation in less-developed areas. Finally, Zarembka outlines a comparison of his own model with two well-known approaches (those of Lewis and Fei-Ranis and of Jorgenson) and concludes by pointing out some lines for future investigation with regard to the methodological aspects of goods allocations.

STABILITY CONDITIONS IN THE REAL AND MONETARY MODELS OF INTERNATIONAL TRADE *

AKIHIRO AMANO

Kobe University, Kobe, Japan

I. Introduction

Traditionally international trade theorists have developed two sets of instruments: one to analyze the real aspects of international trade flows, and the other to resolve the problems of international monetary systems. In the comparative statics analyses of the former aspects, the stability condition that the sum of the elasticities of offer curves be greater than one is usually called for, while in the devaluation analysis a somewhat different set of "stability conditions" is presented without sufficient explanation of its relation to the stability conditions of the real or barter system.

The purpose of this paper is to consider the relationship between stability conditions of real and monetary models of international trade under the following basic assumptions:

(i) There are only two commodities, two countries, and two currencies;
(ii) Full employment is maintained by the price flexibility;
(iii) Perfect competition prevails, and there are no trade impediments;
(iv) The trade balance is zero initially; and
(v) Goods and money are separable in the consumer's utility function.

* The author wishes to acknowledge his indebtedness to Professors K. Inada, R. Komiya, T. Shizuki, and H. Uzawa for valuable comments.

The last assumption has been shown by Negishi [13] as a sufficient condition for the classical dichotomy to be valid in the comparative statics analyses of international trade theory. This paper will attempt to demonstrate that this conclusion carries over to the stability conditions as well under the variable exchange rate system with fairly natural assumptions concerning the dynamic adjustment behavior. A similar comparison between the real and the monetary models will also be made for the system of fixed exchange rates.

In Sect. II the basic model will be presented. In Sect. III the stability conditions of real and monetary models under the variable exchange-rate system will be compared. As an example of comparative statics analysis, the effect of output expansion upon the terms of trade under the variable exchange-rate system will be considered in Sect. IV. Section V then deals with the comparison of real and monetary models under the fixed exchange-rate system. In particular, attention will be focused on the condition for the devaluation to be effective. In Sect. VI the same comparative statics problem as in Sect. IV will be considered under the fixed exchange-rate system. Finally, in Sect. VII the assumption of full employment is noted as an Achilles' tendon for the parallelism between real and monetary models.

II. The Basic Model

Let the two goods be good i ($i = 1, 2$), and the two countries be the home and the foreign countries. The variables pertaining to the foreign country will be designated by attaching an asterisk. We define the variables as follows:

D_i demand for good i,
X_i supply (or output) of good i,
M demand for imports,
A_i demand for money by residents, deflated by the price of good i,
E_i total expenditure, deflated by the price of good i,
Y_i national income, deflated by the price of good i,
P_i the price of good i in terms of home currency,
$\bar{A}$ the initial supply of money (assumed as given),
B the balance of trade of the home country in terms of good 1,
R the price of foreign currency in terms of home currency, and
α a parameter presenting conditions of production.

Under assumption (v) we may express the demand for each good as a function of commodity prices and total expenditure alone. If we further assume, as is usually done, that the demand functions are homogeneous of degrees zero in prices and total expenditure, we can write[1]

$$D_i = D_i(P_2/P_1, E_1), \qquad D_i^* = D_i^*(P_2/P_1, E_2^*), \tag{2.1}$$

where

$$E_1 = \sum_i P_i D_i/P_1, \qquad E_2^* = \sum_i P_i D_i^*/P_2. \tag{2.2}$$

As for the demand for money, we shall assume that a national currency is held only by its residents. It is a function of commodity prices, national income, and the initial amount of money. Again, it is assumed that the function is homogeneous of degree one in its arguments:

$$A_1 = A_1(P_2/P_1, Y_1, \bar{A}/P_1), \qquad A_2^* = A_2^*(P_2/P_1, Y_2^*, R\bar{A}^*/P_2). \tag{2.3}$$

Under assumptions (ii) and (iii), output of each industry depends only on the commodity price ratio,

$$X_i = X_i(P_2/P_1, \alpha), \qquad X_i^* = X_i^*(P_2/P_1), \tag{2.4}$$

where the parameter α in the home supply functions can be disregarded until Sect. IV.

We shall assume that the home country exports good 1, and foreign country exports good 2. Thus, the demand for imports is given by

$$M = D_2 - X_2, \qquad M^* = D_1^* - X_1^*. \tag{2.5}$$

Since national income is either spent or hoarded, we have

$$Y_1 = E_1 + A_1 - \bar{A}/P_1, \qquad Y_2^* = E_2^* + A_2^* - R\bar{A}^*/P_2, \tag{2.6}$$

where, by definition,

$$Y_1 = \sum_i P_i X_i/P_1, \qquad Y_2^* = \sum_i P_i X_i^*/P_2.$$

[1] See, for example, Pearce [15, Chap. 2] and also [14]. Here we assume that the consumer's utility function is represented by

$$U = U(D_1, D_2, \phi(P_1, P_2, A, \bar{A})),$$

where A is the nominal amount of desired money balances and ϕ is assumed to be homogeneous of degree zero in its arguments. Commodity and money demand functions are derived by maximizing utility subject to the restraint Eqs. (2.2) and (2.6). Aggregation problems are assumed away as in most other models of international trade.

The initial amount of money, $\bar{A}$, is included in the ϕ-function to account for the fact that a consumer's preference may be affected by the amount of real balances which he is initially endowed. Without this term, the marginal propensity to hoard out of real income and that out of real cash balances would become identical. For the analyses based on this identity, see Lloyd [9] and Komiya [6].

Equation (2.7) defines the trade balance of the home country,

$$B = M^* - (P_2/P_1)M. \tag{2.7}$$

Equilibrium conditions for goods markets,

$$X_i + X_i^* = D_i + D_i^*,$$

may be written in a more familiar form as

$$Y_1 = E_1 + B, \qquad Y_2^* = E_2^* - (P_1/P_2)B. \tag{2.8}$$

That is, in the absence of nontraded goods, the absorption condition represents the equilibrium condition for the exportables of the country under consideration. Equilibrium conditions for money markets require different treatment according to whether the system is under variable or fixed exchange rates. Under the variable exchange rate system, money markets are in equilibrium when

$$A_1 - \bar{A}/P_1 = 0, \qquad A_1^* - R\bar{A}^*/P_2 = 0, \tag{2.9a}$$

and the foreign exchange market is in equilibrium when

$$B = 0. \tag{2.10a}$$

Under the fixed exchange-rate system, on the other hand, the monetary authority buys and sells foreign exchanges in an indefinite amount at a fixed exchange rate in exchange for domestic currency. The foreign exchange market is always in equilibrium, in that any excess demand on the part of the private sector is always matched by the compensatory supply of the monetary authority. Equilibrium conditions for the money markets, therefore, become

$$A_1 - \bar{A}/P_1 - B = 0, \qquad A_2^* - R\bar{A}^*/P_2 + (P_1/P_2)B = 0. \tag{2.9b}$$

It may immediately be noticed that under the variable exchange-rate system any one of Eqs. (2.6), (2.8), or (2.9a) is not independent for each country. We have therefore 20 independent equations in 20 unknowns. Similarly, under the fixed exchange-rate system, any one of Eqs. (2.6), (2.8), or (2.9b) is not independent for each country. Now, 19 equations determine 19 unknowns for any given R.

By eliminating variables other than P_1, P_2, R, and B, we have the following reduced form equations for each exchange-rate system:

$$\begin{aligned} &A_1(P_2/P_1, \tilde{Y}_1(P_2/P_1, \alpha), \bar{A}/P_1) - \bar{A}/P_1 = 0, \\ &A_2^*(P_2/P_1, \tilde{Y}_2^*(P_2/P_1), R\bar{A}^*/P_2) - R\bar{A}^*/P_2 = 0, \\ &\tilde{M}^*(P_2/P_1, A_2^*(\cdot) - R\bar{A}^*/P_2) - (P_2/P_1)\tilde{M}(P_2/P_1, A_1(\cdot) - \bar{A}/P_1) = 0, \end{aligned} \tag{2.11a}$$

for the variable exchange rate system, and

$$A_1(\cdot) - \bar{A}/P_1 = 0,$$
$$(2.11b) \qquad A_2{}^*(\cdot) - R\bar{A}^*/P_2 + (P_1/P_2)B = 0,$$
$$B = \tilde{M}^*(\cdot) - (P_2/P_1)\tilde{M}(\cdot),$$

for the fixed exchange-rate system. In these expressions, we write

$$Y_1 = \sum_i P_i X_i(P_2/P_1, \alpha)/P_1 \equiv \tilde{Y}_1(P_2/P_1, \alpha),$$
$$Y_2{}^* = \sum_i P_i X_i{}^*(P_2/P_1)/P_2 \equiv \tilde{Y}_2{}^*(P_2/P_1),$$

and

$$M = D_2(P_2/P_1, E_1) - X_2(P_2/P_1, \alpha) \equiv \tilde{M}(P_2/P_1, A_1(\cdot) - \bar{A}/P_1, \alpha),$$
$$M^* = D_1{}^*(P_2/P_1, E_2{}^*) - X_2{}^*(P_2/P_1) \equiv \tilde{M}^*(P_2/P_1, A_2{}^*(\cdot) - R\bar{A}^*/P_2),$$

since

$$E_1 = \tilde{Y}_1(P_2/P_1, \alpha) - A_1(P_2/P_1, \tilde{Y}_1(P_2/P_1, \alpha), \bar{A}/P_1) + \bar{A}/P_1,$$
$$E_2{}^* = \tilde{Y}_2{}^*(P_2/P_1) - A_2{}^*(P_2/P_1, \tilde{Y}_2{}^*(P_2/P_1), R\bar{A}^*/P_2) + R\bar{A}^*/P_2.$$

Equations (2.11a) and (2.11b) form our starting point for the following discussions. In what follows, we shall assume for convenience that P_1, P_2, and R are set equal to unity at the initial equilibrium position.

III. Stability Conditions under the Variable Exchange-Rate System

In the real model of international trade between two countries, it is well known that the stability of trading equilibrium requires the sum of the elasticities of offer curves to be greater than unity [1, 4, 5]. In view of the importance of this condition in the comparative statics analyses, it may be quite natural to ask whether the same condition can be extended to a monetary world.

To study the dynamic stability of the system, it is necessary to postulate some kind of market adjustments in disequilibrium situations. We shall simply assume that the price of a commodity or of foreign exchanges tends to rise (or fall) when there exists a positive (or negative) excess demand for it. Let

$$Z_1 = A_1(\cdot) - \bar{A}/P_1,$$
$$(3.1) \qquad Z_2 = A_2{}^*(\cdot) - R\bar{A}^*/P_2,$$
$$Z_3 = \tilde{M}^*(\cdot) - (P_2/P_1)\tilde{M}(\cdot).$$

In view of Eqs. (2.6) and (2.8), it can be seen that the net excess supply of good 1 is $Z_1 - Z_3$ and that of good 2 is $Z_2 + Z_3$, where Z_3 represents the net excess supply of foreign exchanges. Therefore, the dynamic behavior of the present system in the neighborhood of equilibrium can be expressed as

$$(3.2) \qquad \dot{P}_1 = \varepsilon_1(Z_1 - Z_3), \qquad \dot{P}_2 = \varepsilon_2(Z_2 + Z_3), \qquad \dot{R} = \varepsilon_3 Z_3,$$

where ε_i (<0) represents a speed of adjustment. As is well known, a necessary condition for the local stability is that the Jacobian determinant of the right-hand sides of Eqs. (3.2) be negative. Denoting

$$Z_i = \tilde{Z}_i(P_1, P_2, R), \qquad i = 1, 2, 3,$$

we can express the above condition equivalently as

$$(3.3) \qquad |\tilde{Z}_{ij}| > 0,$$

where $\tilde{Z}_{ij}$ stands for the partial derivative of Z_i with respect to the jth argument. Let

$$a = \partial A_1/\partial(P_2/P_1) + (\partial A_1/\partial Y_1)(\partial \tilde{Y}_1/\partial(P_2/P_1)),$$
$$a^* = -\partial A_2{}^*/\partial(P_2/P_1) - (\partial A_2{}^*/\partial Y_2{}^*)(\partial \tilde{Y}_2{}^*/\partial(P_2/P_1)),$$

be the effects of a change in the commodity price ratio upon the demand for money;

$$h = \partial A_1/\partial(\bar{A}/P_1), \qquad h^* = \partial A_2{}^*/\partial(R\bar{A}^*/P_2),$$

be the marginal propensity to hoard out of real cash balances;

$$m = \partial M/\partial E_1, \qquad m^* = \partial M^*/\partial E_2{}^*,$$

be the marginal propensity to import; and

$$\eta = -\frac{P_2/P_1}{M}\frac{\partial \tilde{M}}{\partial(P_2/P_1)}, \qquad \eta^* = \frac{P_2/P_1}{M^*}\frac{\partial \tilde{M}^*}{\partial(P_2/P_1)},$$

be the (relative) price elasticity of imports. Then we have

$$\tilde{Z}_{11} = -a + (1-h)\bar{A}, \qquad \tilde{Z}_{12} = a,$$
$$\tilde{Z}_{21} = a^*, \qquad \tilde{Z}_{22} = -a^* + (1-h^*)\bar{A}^*,$$
$$\tilde{Z}_{31} = -M(\eta+\eta^*-1) + m\tilde{Z}_{11} - m^*\tilde{Z}_{21}, \qquad \tilde{Z}_{32} = M(\eta+\eta^*-1) + m\tilde{Z}_{12} - m^*\tilde{Z}_{22},$$
$$\tilde{Z}_{13} = 0,$$
$$\tilde{Z}_{23} = -(1-h^*)\bar{A}^*,$$
$$\tilde{Z}_{33} = -m^*\tilde{Z}_{23}.$$

Hence

$$|\tilde{Z}_{ij}| = \begin{vmatrix} -a+(1-h)\bar{A} & a & 0 \\ a^* & -a^*+(1-h^*)\bar{A}^* & -(1-h^*)\bar{A}^* \\ -M(\eta+\eta^*-1) & M(\eta+\eta^*-1) & 0 \end{vmatrix}$$

$$= M(\eta+\eta^*-1)(1-h)\bar{A}(1-h^*)\bar{A}^*.$$

Thus, the elasticity criterion in the real model, $\eta+\eta^*-1>0$, is also a necessary condition for stability in the monetary model under the variable exchange-rate system, provided that the marginal propensity to hoard is less than unity. It may be interesting to note that the above conclusion is obtained without making any restriction on the effects of changes in relative commodity prices upon the demand for money.

IV. Output Expansion and the Terms of Trade under the Variable Exchange-Rate System

As an example of the comparative statics analysis, we shall now compare the effects of output expansion on the commodity terms of trade in real and monetary models under the variable exchange rate system. A change in parameter α in the home supply functions [see Eqs. (2.4)] now represents any change in the production conditions which affects the level of output at constant relative commodity prices, say, a change in factor endowments, a change in technology, and so forth. From Eqs. (2.11a), we obtain

$$\begin{aligned} a\,d(P_2/P_1) + (1-h)\bar{A}\,dP_1 + h'(\partial\tilde{Y}_1/\partial\alpha)\,d\alpha &= 0, \\ a^*\,d(P_2/P_1) + (1-h^*)\bar{A}^*\,d(R/P_2) &= 0, \\ (M\eta^*+a^*m^*)\,d(P_2/P_1) + m^*(1-h^*)\bar{A}^*\,d(R/P_2) + (M\eta+am)\,d(P_2/P_1)& \\ + m(1-h)\bar{A}\,dP_1 - [(1-h')m-\iota](\partial\tilde{Y}_1/\partial\alpha)\,d\alpha - M\,d(P_2/P_1) &= 0, \end{aligned} \tag{4.1}$$

where $h' = \partial A_1/\partial Y_1$ is the marginal propensity to hoard out of national income, and $\iota = (\partial X_2/\partial\alpha)/(\partial\tilde{Y}_1/\partial\alpha)$ represents the relative contribution of the import-competing sector in the expansion of national product at constant relative commodity prices. Solving Eq. (4.1) for $d(P_2/P_1)$, we have

$$d(P_2/P_1) = \frac{m-\iota}{M(\eta+\eta^*-1)}\frac{\partial\tilde{Y}_1}{\partial\alpha}\,d\alpha. \tag{4.2}$$

The denominator of the right-hand side is positive if equilibrium is stable. When $(\partial\tilde{Y}_1/\partial\alpha)\,d\alpha>0$, therefore, the commodity terms of trade will turn in favor of, or against the expanding country as $m \lesseqgtr \iota$. This conclusion is exactly the same as the one obtained in the real model [3, Chap. 3].

V. Stability Conditions and the Effect of Devaluation under the Fixed Exchange-Rate System

In a truly barter model of international trade under full employment, where no private hoarding can exist in equilibrium, the balance of payments (or trade) must necessarily be zero in equilibrium [2]. It is, therefore, a little difficult to find a real trade model corresponding to the fixed exchange-rate system in which imbalances of international payments can take place. The following arrangements, though somewhat artificial, may nevertheless provide a useful reference model that will help us understand the correspondence between the real and monetary trade models.

We shall suppose that the international commodity terms of trade, the only factor now relevant to the international payments problem, are fixed by some international agreement, and that to maintain the fixed terms of trade the authorities of each country assume the responsibility of adjusting the market disequilibrium of its own exportables by appropriate changes in their buffer stocks of that same commodity. We shall also suppose that the authorities always maintain a fixed amount of buffer stocks by collecting taxes when the stock is depleting or by granting subsidies when the stock is accumulating.[2]

In the absence of money, Eqs. (2.6) should now read

$$Y_1 - T_1 = E_1, \qquad Y_2^* - T_2^* = E_2^*, \tag{5.1}$$

where T_i represents the amount of net tax revenue to the government expressed in terms of good i, which is equal to the net reduction in the buffer stock. Equations, other than Eqs. (2.3) and (2.9b), that constitute the fixed exchange-rate system remain unchanged. The reduced form of the real, fixed exchange-rate system then becomes

$$\begin{aligned} T_1 - B &= 0, \\ T_2^* + (P_1/P_2)\,B &= 0, \\ B &= \tilde{M}^*(P_2/P_1, T_2^*) - (P_2/P_1)\,\tilde{M}(P_2/P_1, T_1, \alpha), \end{aligned} \tag{5.2}$$

which determines T_1, T_2^*, and B for given P_2/P_1. If we assume that the authorities attempt to reduce the excess demand for exportables by depleting

[2] This model is essentially the same as that of Meade [10, Chap. VII]. For another approach see Jones [4], and a comment by Negishi [12].

the buffer stock, and vice versa, the dynamic behavior of the present model can be represented by

$$(5.3)\qquad \begin{aligned} \dot{T}_1 &= \varepsilon_1[\tilde{M}^*(\cdot) - (P_2/P_1)\tilde{M}(\cdot) - T_1], \\ \dot{T}_2^* &= \varepsilon_2[\tilde{M}(\cdot) - (P_1/P_2)\tilde{M}^*(\cdot) - T_2^*], \end{aligned}$$

where $\varepsilon_i > 0$. A necessary condition for stability is, therefore,

$$(5.4)\qquad m + m^* - 1 < 0.$$

Next let us consider the effect upon the trade balance of "devaluation," that is, a once and for all change in the fixed commodity terms of trade against the home country. Differentiating Eqs. (5.2) totally and solving for dB, we obtain

$$(5.5)\qquad dB = \frac{M(\eta+\eta^*-1)}{1-m-m^*}\,d(P_2/P_1).$$

Thus the devaluation improves the trade balance if and only if the elasticity criterion be satisfied, provided that the original system is stable [i.e., condition (5.4) holds].

Now, a monetary model of fixed exchange-rate system which corresponds to the above real model has been given by Eqs. (2.11b), or equivalently by

$$(5.6)\qquad Z_1 - B = 0, \qquad Z_2 + (P_1/P_2)B = 0, \qquad Z_3 - B = 0,$$

where Z_i are as defined in Eq. (3.1). Since the exchange rate is now fixed, the adjustment Eqs. (3.2) reduce to

$$(5.7)\qquad \dot{P}_1 = \varepsilon_1(Z_1 - Z_3), \qquad \dot{P}_2 = \varepsilon_2(Z_2 + Z_3),$$

where $\varepsilon_i < 0$. A necessary condition for stability is given by

$$(5.8)\qquad \begin{vmatrix} \tilde{Z}_{11} - \tilde{Z}_{31} & \tilde{Z}_{12} - \tilde{Z}_{32} \\ \tilde{Z}_{21} + \tilde{Z}_{31} & \tilde{Z}_{22} + \tilde{Z}_{32} \end{vmatrix} > 0.$$

Finally, differentiating Eq. (5.6) totally, we obtain

$$(5.9)\qquad \begin{bmatrix} \tilde{Z}_{11} & \tilde{Z}_{12} & -1 \\ \tilde{Z}_{21} & \tilde{Z}_{22} & 1 \\ \tilde{Z}_{31} & \tilde{Z}_{32} & -1 \end{bmatrix} \begin{bmatrix} dP_1 \\ dP_2 \\ dB \end{bmatrix} = - \begin{bmatrix} \tilde{Z}_{13} \\ \tilde{Z}_{23} \\ \tilde{Z}_{33} \end{bmatrix} dR,$$

Hence

$$(5.10)\qquad dB = -\frac{|\tilde{Z}_{ij}|}{\Delta}\,dR$$

where Δ is the determinant of the coefficient matrix in Eq. (5.9). Since Δ and the determinant in Eq. (5.8) are equal in absolute value with opposite signs, we conclude that the devaluation improves the trade balance if and only if $|\tilde{Z}_{ij}| > 0$, provided that the original system is stable. The condition is equivalent to the elasticity condition when the marginal propensity to hoard is less than unity [see Eq. (3.4)].

VI. Output Expansion, the Trade Balance, and the Terms of Trade under the Fixed Exchange-Rate System

We shall here re-examine the same question we posed in Sect. IV under the fixed exchange-rate system, that is, the effects of output expansion upon international trade.

First, let us consider the effect of a change in production conditions in the real model Eqs. (5.2). Differentiating Eqs. (5.2) totally and solving the resulting equations for dB, we obtain

$$dB = \frac{m - \imath}{m + m^* - 1} \frac{\partial \tilde{Y}_1}{\partial \alpha} \, d\alpha. \tag{6.1}$$

The denominator on the right-hand side of this expression is negative if the real system is stable [see Eq. (5.4)]. Therefore, the output expansion $[(\partial \tilde{Y}_1/\partial \alpha)\, d\alpha > 0]$ will worsen or improve the trade balance for the expanding country according as $m \gtrless \imath$, that is, according to whether the income effect is greater or less than the capacity effect.

A corresponding result for the monetary model may similarly be obtained by differentiating Eqs. (5.6) totally:

$$\begin{bmatrix} \tilde{Z}_{11} & \tilde{Z}_{12} & -1 \\ \tilde{Z}_{21} & \tilde{Z}_{22} & 1 \\ \tilde{Z}_{31} & \tilde{Z}_{32} & -1 \end{bmatrix} \begin{bmatrix} dP_1 \\ dP_2 \\ dB \end{bmatrix} = \begin{bmatrix} -h' \\ 0 \\ (1-h')m - \imath \end{bmatrix} \frac{\partial \tilde{Y}_1}{\partial \alpha} \, d\alpha. \tag{6.2}$$

Solving Eqs. (6.2) for dB, we obtain[3]

$$dB = \frac{(1-h)\bar{A}(1-h^*)\bar{A}^*}{\Delta} \left[(m-\imath) - \frac{M(\eta + \eta^* - 1)h'}{(1-h)\bar{A}} \right] \frac{\partial \tilde{Y}_1}{\partial \alpha} \, d\alpha. \tag{6.3}$$

If we assume that $0 < h, h^* < 1$, and that the monetary system is stable (i.e., $\Delta < 0$), then we have similar income and capacity effects as in the real model. In the present case, however, we have an additional effect [the last term in the square brackets in Eq. (6.3)], which may be called the asset effect.

[3] For simplicity's sake we assume here that $a = a^* = 0$.

The asset effect will improve the trade balance of the expanding country as has been emphasized by Mundell [11] and Komiya [7], provided that the elasticity condition is satisfied. The final outcome thus depends on the relative magnitudes of the above three effects. Expression (6.3) may be viewed as a synthesis of the traditional (or real) and the monetary approaches.

From Eqs. (6.2), we can also express the changes in the terms of trade as

$$(6.4)\quad dP_1 - dP_2 = \frac{(1-h)\bar{A} + (1-h^*)\bar{A}^*}{\Delta} \times \left[(m-\imath) + \frac{(1-h^*)\bar{A}^*(1-m-m^*)h'}{(1-h)\bar{A} + (1-h^*)\bar{A}^*}\right]\frac{\partial \tilde{Y}_1}{\partial \alpha}\,d\alpha.$$

Thus the income effect of an output expansion tends to worsen the terms of trade, whereas the capacity effect tends to improve them. The asset effect will worsen or improve the terms of trade depending on whether the sum of the marginal propensities to import in the two countries is less than or greater than unity.

VII. A Stability Condition of Underemployment Equilibrium

So far we have assumed that full employment is maintained by price flexibility. It is important to note that the parallelism between the real and monetary models is essentially of the classical nature. In this section we shall briefly consider the stability conditions in a monetary model under the Keynesian assumptions. We shall only be concerned with the variable exchange-rate system, as the other case can be handled in a similar fashion.

In order to simplify the argument, we assume that each country is completely specialized to the production of exportables whose money price is fixed in terms of domestic currency. Letting the export price in terms of export country's currency be unity by an appropriate choice of units, we may write the variable exchange-rate system as

$$(7.1)\quad D_i = D_i(R, E_1), \qquad D_i^* = D_i^*(R, E_2^*),$$

$$(7.2)\quad E_1 = D_1 + RD_2, \qquad E_2^* = (1/R)\,D_1^* + D_2^*,$$

$$(7.3)\quad A_1 = A_1(R, Y_1, \bar{A}), \qquad A_2^* = A_2^*(R, Y_2^*, \bar{A}^*),$$

$$(7.4)\quad Y_1 = E_1 + A_1 - \bar{A}, \qquad Y_2^* = E_2^* + A_2^* - \bar{A}^*,$$

$$(7.5)\quad B = M^* - RM, \qquad M = D_2, \qquad M^* = D_1^*,$$

$$(7.6)\quad Y_1 = E_1 + B, \qquad Y_2^* = E_2^* - (1/R)\,B,$$

$$(7.7)\quad A_1 - \bar{A} = 0, \qquad A_2^* - \bar{A}^* = 0,$$

$$(7.8)\quad B = 0.$$

As before, the above system can be reduced to

$$
\begin{aligned}
& Z_1 = A_1(R, Y_1, \bar{A}) - \bar{A} = 0, \\
(7.9)\quad & Z_2 = A_2{}^*(R, Y_2{}^*, \bar{A}^*) - \bar{A}^* = 0, \\
& Z_3 = \tilde{M}^*(R, Y_2{}^* - A_2{}^*(\cdot) + \bar{A}^*) - R\tilde{M}(R, Y_1 - A_1(\cdot) + \bar{A}) = 0,
\end{aligned}
$$

which determine Y_1, $Y_2{}^*$, and R.

In the present model, adjustments in commodity markets must be carried out in terms of output levels rather than prices. Assuming that the level of output responds positively to the excess demand, we have

$$
\begin{aligned}
\dot{Y}_1 &= \varepsilon_1[\tilde{Z}_1(Y_1, Y_2{}^*, R) - \tilde{Z}_3(Y_1, Y_2{}^*, R)], \\
\dot{Y}_2{}^* &= \varepsilon_2[\tilde{Z}_2(Y_1, Y_2{}^*, R) + \tilde{Z}_3(Y_1, Y_2{}^*, R)], \qquad (7.10) \\
\dot{R} &= \varepsilon_3 \tilde{Z}_3(Y_1, Y_2{}^*, R),
\end{aligned}
$$

where $\varepsilon_i < 0$. A necessary condition for stability now becomes

$$
(7.11)\quad 0 < |\tilde{Z}_{ij}| = \begin{vmatrix} h' & 0 & a \\ 0 & h^{*\prime} & -a^* \\ -m(1-h') & m^*(1-h'^*) & M(\eta+\eta^*-1) + ma + m^*a^* \end{vmatrix}
$$

$$
= h'h^{*\prime}\left[M(\eta+\eta^*-1) + \frac{ma}{h'} + \frac{m^*a^*}{h^{*\prime}}\right],
$$

where $a = \partial A_1/\partial R$ and $a^* = -\partial A_2{}^*/\partial R$.[4] Other symbols are similarly defined as in Sects. III and IV. Thus, even if we assume separability in the consumer's utility function, it is no longer true that the stability requires the classical elasticity criterion unless the private hoarding is unaffected by changes in relative commodity prices.

REFERENCES

[1] Amano, A., Stability Conditions in the Pure Theory of International Trade: A Rehabilitation of the Marshallian Approach, *Quart. J. Econ.* **LXXXII**, No. 2, 326–339 (1968).

[2] Harberger, A. C., Currency Depreciation, Income, and the Balance of Trade, *J. Political Econ.* **LVIII**, No. 1, 47–60 (1950); reprinted in R. E. Caves and H. G. Johnson (eds.), "Readings in International Economics," pp. 341–358. Irwin, Homewood, Illinois, 1968.

[4] This is the condition obtained by Laursen and Metzler [8]. It also becomes the condition for effective devaluation under the fixed exchange-rate system if the system is stable.

[3] Johnson, H. G., "International Trade and Economic Growth." Allen and Unwin, London, 1958.
[4] Jones, R. W., Stability Conditions in International Trade: A General Equilibrium Analysis, *Int. Econ. Rev.* **2**, No. 2, 199–209 (1961).
[5] Kemp, M. C., "The Pure Theory of International Trade and Investment." Prentice-Hall, Englewood Cliffs, New Jersey, 1969.
[6] Komiya, R., Monetary Assumptions, Currency Depreciation and the Balance of Trade, *Econ. Stud. Quart.* **17**, No. 2, 9–23 (1966).
[7] Komiya, R., Economic Growth and the Balance of Payments: A Monetary Approach, *J. Political Econ.* **LXXVII**, No. 1, 35–48 (1969).
[8] Laursen, S., and Metzler, L. A., Flexible Exchange Rates and the Theory of Employment, *Rev. Econ. Statist.* **32**, No. 4, 281–299 (1950).
[9] Lloyd, C., The Real Balance Effect and the Slutzky Equation, *J. Political Econ.* **LXXII**, No. 3, 295–299 (1964).
[10] Meade, J. E., "A Geometry of International Trade." Allen and Unwin, London, 1952.
[11] Mundell, R. A., "International Economics," Chap. 9. Macmillan, New York, 1968.
[12] Negishi, T., Approaches to the Analysis of Devaluation, *Int. Econ. Rev.*, **9**, No. 2, 218–228 (1968).
[13] Negishi, T., The Dichotomy of Real and Monetary Analyses in the International Trade Theory, Mimeographed (1967).
[14] Pearce, I. F., The Problem of the Balance of Payments, *Int. Econ. Rev.* **2**, No. 1, 1–28 (1961).
[15] Pearce, I. F., "A Contribution to Demand Analysis." Oxford Univ. Press (Clarendon), New York and London, 1964.

TOWARDS A REFORMULATION OF THE SHORT-RUN THEORY OF FOREIGN EXCHANGE*

MURRAY C. KEMP

University of New South Wales, Kensington, New South Wales, Australia

I. Introduction

In recent years there has been a growing interest in the theory of the short-run functioning of the foreign exchanges and, in particular, in the lines of interdependence between the spot market and the several forward markets.[1] As yet, however, the theory lacks a clear and convincing microfoundation.

In most expositions of the theory, key roles are played by the "speculator" and the "arbitrageur," with exchange rates emerging from their interaction in the market.[2] The speculator is depicted as a pure gambler who bets on uncertain events (spot rates of exchange at future points of time). The arbitrageur, on the other hand, is defined as a short-term investor whose objective it is to place his capital to greatest advantage at home or abroad but without undertaking exchange risks.

Since completely disparate objectives have been assigned to the two market

* This paper was written during the summer of 1968, when the author was a guest of the Institute of International Economic Studies, University of Stockholm.

[1] See, for example, Spraos [14, 15], Tsiang [16], Einzig [4], Sohmen [13], Grubel [6], Kenen [7], Black [3], and Frevert [5]. Serious academic study of forward exchange is comparatively new, extending back only to Keynes' *Tract* [8]. See also Kindleberger [9, Chap. 12] and, especially, Kindleberger [10].

[2] The other key roles are played by the representatives of government and by the exporter–importer, none of whom we shall be concerned with here.

participants, it has been found necessary to develop separate models of the behavior of the speculator and of the arbitrageur. The theory is, therefore, inelegant. Much more important, it lacks generality, for no provision is made for the participant who wishes to mix speculation with arbitrage, possibly in proportions which depend on market circumstances. As an implication, any elements of interdependence between speculation and arbitrage are blocked from view.[3]

To see this more clearly, consider the position of an initially pure arbitrageur. At the beginning of any particular market day he has a portfolio comprising, in part, foreign bills with various future maturity dates (and the appropriate covering contracts in forward exchange). In general, he will want to consider whether and by how much to run down his holdings of one or more maturities. If he should choose to run down a particular holding, however, it must be because he finds it advantageous to repatriate the proceeds or to invest them in foreign bills with different maturity dates. In either case he is left with a forward exchange contract which no longer covers anything. He can let it lie, or he can "undo" it, but at a price which may differ from the price of the original contract. In either case, therefore, he will make a profit or loss on the original forward sale; that is, he will be a speculator. To impose from the outset the requirement that an arbitrageur will not speculate is to rule out the possibility of his ever undoing a foreign investment.

To the current "dualistic" microtheory we may oppose a theory in which all market participants are endowed with essentially the same objectives and are free to engage in both speculation and arbitrage. In a theory constructed along these lines a place can be found for pure speculation and for pure arbitrage, but only as extreme cases. Moreover, given a sufficient change in his data, today's arbitrageur may emerge as tomorrow's speculator.

Such a theory, worked out in all detail, is bound to be ferociously complicated. This chapter is only an attempt to sketch its general outlines and set out the detail of some simple cases.

II. Assumptions and Notation

Time is viewed as a sequence of "days." At the momentary beginning of each day, spot and forward exchange contracts may be entered into and riskless short-term government securities ("bills") may be bought and sold; but for the rest of the day contracts can be neither made nor revised. The planning horizons of market participants, as well as the terms of contracts and bills, are assumed to be integral numbers of days.

[3] See Sohmen [13, p. 2, n. 2] for a contrary view.

The speculator–arbitrageur is endowed with a von Neumann–Morgenstern utility function u of his net wealth A and is supposed to maximize the value of the function expected at the end of the last day of his planning horizon. The utility function is supposed to be uniformly strictly concave ($u'' \equiv d^2u/dA^2 < 0$); in that sense, the speculator–arbitrageur is assumed to be averse to risk. However, the second derivative u'' is not invariant under the permitted positive linear transformations of u; it is, therefore, an unsatisfactory measure of risk aversion. Accordingly, we introduce the Arrow–Pratt measure of absolute risk aversion [1, 2, 11]:

(1a) $$\zeta(A) \equiv -u''(A)/u'(A).$$

Following Arrow [2, p. 35] it is assumed that ζ is a decreasing function:

(1b) $$\zeta'(A) \equiv d\zeta/dA < 0.$$

No further restrictions are placed on the utility function.

It is assumed that there are just two countries, the home country and the foreign.

Both government bills and forward exchange contracts have a term of just one day. The issue price of all bills is, in each country, one unit of the local currency.

The following symbols will be employed throughout. For the simplest case, considered in Sect. III, they are unnecessarily elaborate; but there has seemed to be virtue in maintaining a uniform notation:

- A_t the net resources of the speculator–arbitrageur at the beginning of day t or at the end of day $t-1$;
- r_t the redemption value of home bills issued on day t. Thus $r_t - 1$ is the rate of return per day;
- R_t the spot price of foreign exchange on day t;
- $R_{t,f}$ the price of foreign exchange on day t for delivery on day $t+1$;
- π_t $(R_{t,f} - R_t)/R_t$, the premium on foreign currency for delivery one day forward;
- β_t $R_{t+1} - R_{t,f}$, the difference between the spot price of foreign currency which is expected on day t to prevail one day later and the price of foreign currency on day t for delivery one day forward (this difference is sometimes called "backwardation");
- x_t the number of home bills bought on day t;
- y_t the number of units of foreign currency bought forward on day t.

If the symbol relates to the foreign country it will bear an asterisk. Thus r_t^* is the redemption value, in foreign currency, of a foreign bill issued on day t; and x_t^* is the number of foreign bills bought on day t. Finally, we introduce the following "mixed" notation:

ρ_t $(R_{t+1}/R_t)r_t^* - 1$, the expected rate of return, per day, on an uncovered investment in a foreign bill;

$\bar{\rho}_t$ $(R_{t,f}/R_t)r_t^* - 1$, the expected rate of return, per day, on a covered investment in a foreign bill.

III. The Simplest Case: A One-Day Planning Horizon

Suppose that the speculator–arbitrageur seeks to maximize the expected utility of his wealth just one day forward.[4] The supposition is bizarre, but it is implicit in most recent theoretical discussion. It is under this assumption, therefore, that any novelties or peculiarities in this approach will be most in evidence.

At the beginning of day t, the resources of the speculator–arbitrageur have a value A_t. He invests x_t in the bills of the home government and, therefore, $A_t - x_t$ in foreign bills. Moreover, he contracts to buy forward y_t units of foreign exchange. His wealth at the end of the day will be, therefore,

$$A_{t+1} = x_t r_t + (R_{t+1}/R_t)(A_t - x_t)r_t^* + y_t(R_{t+1} - R_{t,f}), \tag{2}$$

and he must calculate

$$\max_{x_t, x_t^*, y_t} E\{u(A_{t+1})\}, \tag{3a}$$

where A_{t+1} is defined by Eq. (2), and E is the instruction to take the expected value. His bill holdings are, of course, nonnegative, but he may be long $(y_t > 0)$ or short $(y_t < 0)$ of forward exchange.

It is clear at the outset that, if the return on home bills exceeds the covered return on foreign bills, the maximizing speculator–arbitrageur will hold his entire wealth in home bills, so that $x_t = A_t$ and $x_t^* = 0$; and that, if the covered return on foreign bills exceeds the return on home bills, his entire wealth will be held in foreign bills, so that $x_t = 0$ and $x_t^* = A_t/R_t$. Thus there is no question of his seeking a "balanced portfolio." To remove a small element of indeterminacy we adopt the lexicographic convention that, when home and covered foreign investment are equally attractive, the speculator–arbitrageur places everything in home bills. Thus we have two cases to consider, according as $r_t - 1$ is not less than or less than $\bar{\rho}_t$, that is, as, respectively, π_t is not greater than or greater than $(r_t - r_t^*)/r_t^*$.

[4] It may be thought that this assumption is redundant—that if all instruments are one-day instruments it makes no difference to the decisions of the speculator–arbitrageur whether his horizon is of one day or several days, that in any case it will be optimal for him to plan myopically, one day at a time. We defer discussion of this objection to Sect. IV.

If $r_t - 1 \geqslant \bar{\rho}_t$, the speculator–arbitrageur must compute

$$\max_{y_t} E\{u(A_{t+1})\}, \tag{3}$$

where

$$A_{t+1} = A_t r_t + y_t(R_{t+1} - R_{t,f}). \tag{2a}$$

The first-order condition of a maximum is

$$E\{u'(A_{t+1})(R_{t+1} - R_{t,f})\} = 0, \tag{4}$$

where $u'(A_{t+1}) \equiv du(A_{t+1})/dA_{t+1}$. Since $u''(A_{t+1}) < 0$, the second-order condition

$$E\{u''(A_{t+1})(R_{t+1} - R_{t,f})^2\} < 0 \tag{5}$$

is automatically satisfied. If, on the other hand, $r_t - 1 < \bar{\rho}_t$, the speculator–arbitrageur must compute (3) with[5]

$$A_{t+1} = (R_{t,f}/R_t)\, A_t r_t^* + y_t(R_{t+1} - R_{t,f}). \tag{2b}$$

The first- and second-order conditions are given by Eqs. (4) and (5), respectively, with A_{t+1} defined by Eq. (2b).

The comparative statical responses of investment (in home and foreign bills) to changes in the determining variables are too obvious to merit spelling out. The interesting questions concern the response of the net forward purchase of foreign exchange, y_t, to changes in interest rates, changes in the forward rate of exchange, and changes in the spot rate expected to prevail tomorrow.

Consider first the implications of a change in one or other of the two rates of interest, $r_t - 1$ and $r_t^* - 1$. It is easy to see that $dy_t/dr_t = 0$ when $r_t - 1 < \bar{\rho}_t$, and that $(dy_t/dr_t)_{r_t \geqslant \bar{\rho}_t}$ and $(dy_t/dr_t^*)_{r_t < \bar{\rho}_t}$ differ only by a positive constant $R_{t,f}/R_t \equiv \pi_t + 1$. It, therefore, suffices to calculate dy_t/dr_t on the assumption that $r_t - 1 \geqslant \bar{\rho}_t$. From Eqs. (4) and (2a), we find that

$$\frac{dy_t}{dr_t} = -A_t \frac{E\{u''(A_{t+1})(R_{t+1} - R_{t,f})\}}{E\{u''(A_{t+1})(R_{t+1} - R_{t,f})^2\}} \qquad \text{if} \quad r_t - 1 \geqslant \bar{\rho}_t. \tag{6}$$

Since $u''(A_{t+1}) < 0$, the denominator is negative, as we have noted; and, since absolute risk aversion is a decreasing function of wealth, the numerator

[5] Given that the speculator–arbitrageur's resources are invested wholly in foreign bills, it is a matter of taste only whether we think of him as covering or as not covering his investments. If he is considered to cover, by "nonspeculative" forward sales of foreign currency, then his "speculative" forward purchases of foreign currency will be that much greater, leaving the net expected value of A_{t+1} unchanged.

has the sign of y_t.[6] It follows that (6) also has the sign of y_t. Hence, if absolute risk aversion is decreasing and if the optimum y_t is nonzero, then

(7a) $$\frac{1}{y_t} \cdot \frac{dy_t}{dr_t} > 0 \qquad \text{if} \quad r_t - 1 \geqslant \bar{\rho}_t,$$

and

(7b) $$\frac{1}{y_t} \cdot \frac{dy_t}{dr_t^*} > 0 \qquad \text{if} \quad r_t - 1 < \bar{\rho}_t.$$

It is worth emphasizing that the conclusions summarized by Eqs. (7) could not be inferred from a model of pure speculation, for the expected profitability of speculation has not changed. Nor could they be inferred from a model of pure covered interest arbitrage; for, if $r_t - 1 > \bar{\rho}_t$, a small increase in the home

[6] From the assumption of decreasing absolute risk aversion, we may infer that

$$\begin{aligned} \zeta(A_{t+1}) &= \zeta(A_t r_t + y_t(R_{t+1} - R_{t,f})) \\ &\leqslant \zeta(A_t r_t) \qquad \text{if} \quad y_t(R_{t+1} - R_{t,f}) \geqslant 0, \end{aligned}$$

that is, that

(i) $$-\frac{u''(A_{t+1})}{u'(A_{t+1})} \leqslant \zeta(A_t r_t), \qquad \text{if} \quad y_t(R_{t+1} - R_{t,f}) \geqslant 0.$$

Since $u' > 0$, we have also

(ii) $$-y_t(R_{t+1} - R_{t,f})\, u'(A_{t+1}) \leqslant 0 \qquad \text{if} \quad y_t(R_{t+1} - R_{t,f}) \geqslant 0.$$

From (i) and (ii),

(iii) $$\begin{aligned} &y_t(R_{t+1} - R_{t,f})\, u''(A_{t+1}) \\ &\qquad \geqslant -\zeta(A_t r_t)\, y_t(R_{t+1} - R_{t,f})\, u'(A_{t+1}) \qquad \text{if} \quad y_t(R_{t+1} - R_{t,f}) \geqslant 0. \end{aligned}$$

By a similar argument,

(iv) $$\begin{aligned} &y_t(R_{t+1} - R_{t,f})\, u''(A_{t+1}) \\ &\qquad \geqslant -\zeta(A_t r_t)\, y_t(R_{t+1} - R_{t,f})\, u'(A_{t+1}) \qquad \text{if} \quad y_t(R_{t+1} - R_{t,f}) < 0. \end{aligned}$$

From (iii) and (iv),

(v) $$y_t(R_{t+1} - R_{t,f})\, u''(A_{t+1}) \geqslant -\zeta(A_t r_t)\, y_t(R_{t+1} - R_{t,f})\, u'(A_{t+1}).$$

Hence [from Eq. (4)],

(vi) $$\begin{aligned} y_t E\{(R_{t+1} - R_{t,f})\, u''(A_{t+1})\} &\geqslant -\zeta(A_t r_t)\, y_t E\{(R_{t+1} - R_{t,f})\, u'(A_{t+1})\} \\ &= 0. \end{aligned}$$

It follows from Eq. (vi) that

(vii) $$\operatorname{sign} E\{(R_{t+1} - R_{t,f})\, u''(A_{t+1})\} = \operatorname{sign} y_t.$$

In developing the above argument I have been guided by the method of proof employed by Arrow in establishing a similar proposition. See Sandmo [12, p. 121].

rate of interest leaves the demand for cover unchanged at zero. Missing from such models is the dependence of the purely speculative demand for forward exchange on the interest rate-induced change in wealth.

Suppose alternatively that the speculator–arbitrageur enjoys an increase in his initial wealth A_t. That his demand for forward exchange will respond in essentially the same way to this stimulus as it responds to changes in the rate of interest is obvious from Eqs. (2a) and (2b). Specifically, if $r_t - 1 < \bar{\rho}_t$ then

$$\frac{dy_t}{dA_t} = \frac{r_t}{A_t}\frac{dy_t}{dr_t},$$

and if $r_t - 1 \geqslant \bar{\rho}_t$ then

$$\frac{dy_t}{dA_t} = \frac{r_t^*}{A_t}\frac{dy_t}{dr_t^*}.$$

Thus if y_t is nonzero,

$$\frac{1}{y_t} \cdot \frac{dy_t}{dA_t} > 0. \tag{8}$$

It has not been found necessary to suppose that probability distributions can be summarized by just a few parameters, e.g., the mean and variance. It is nevertheless of interest to examine the implications for the demand for forward exchange of simple shifts in the distribution of tomorrow's expected rate of exchange, R_{t+1}. To this end, we define

$$R_{t+1}^{\alpha\beta} = E\{R_{t+1}\} + \beta(R_{t+1} + \alpha - E\{R_{t+1}\}), \qquad \alpha = 0, \quad \beta = 1. \tag{9}$$

An increase in α can be interpreted in terms of a rightward shift of the distribution of R_{t+1}, with variance and other central moments unchanged; and an increase in β can be interpreted in terms of an increase in the variance of the distribution, with mean unchanged. If the new variable $R_{t+1}^{\alpha\beta}$ is substituted for R_{t+1} in Eqs. (2a), (2b), and (4), we may calculate that

$$\frac{dy_t}{d\alpha} = -\frac{E\{u'(A_{t+1})\} + y_t E\{u''(A_{t+1})(R_{t+1} - R_{t,f})\}}{E\{u''(A_{t+1})(R_{t+1} - R_{t,f})^2\}}, \tag{10}$$

and that

$$\frac{dy_t}{d\beta} \tag{11}$$

$$= -\frac{E\{u'(A_{t+1})(R_{t+1} - E\{R_{t+1}\})\} + y_t E\{u''(A_{t+1})(R_{t+1} - R_{t,f})(R_{t+1} - E\{R_{t+1}\})\}}{E\{u''(A_{t+1})(R_{t+1} - R_{t,f})^2\}}.$$

Since u' is positive and since $E\{u''(A_{t+1})(R_{t+1}-R_{t,f})\}$ has the sign of y_t if absolute risk aversion is decreasing, we may infer from Eq. (10) that

$$dy_t/d\alpha < 0, \tag{12}$$

that is, the net demand for forward exchange is a strictly increasing function of the expected profitability of forward purchases. To attach a sign to Eq. (11) is more difficult. The first term of the numerator may be rewritten [from Eq. (4)] as

$$\begin{aligned}(13)\quad & E\{u'(A_{t+1})(R_{t+1}-E\{R_{t+1}\})\} \\ &= E\{u'(A_{t+1})(R_{t+1}-R_{t,f})\} + (R_{t,f}-E\{R_{t+1}\})\,E\{u'(A_{t+1})\} \\ &= (R_{t,f}-E\{R_{t+1}\})\,E\{u'(A_{t+1})\}.\end{aligned}$$

The second term may be rewritten as

$$\begin{aligned}(14)\quad & y_t\,E\{u''(A_{t+1})(R_{t+1}-R_{t,f})(R_{t+1}-E\{R_{t+1}\})\} \\ &= y_t\,E\{u''(A_{t+1})(R_{t+1}-R_{t,f})^2\} \\ &\quad + y_t(R_{t,f}-E\{R_{t+1}\})\,E\{u''(A_{t+1})(R_{t+1}-R_{t,f})\}.\end{aligned}$$

Since $u(A_{t+1})$ is a concave function, positive y_t implies that $R_{t,f} < E\{R_{t+1}\}$. If y_t is positive, therefore, (13) must be negative. Moreover, if y_t is positive and if absolute risk aversion is decreasing, Eq. (14) is negative also. It follows that

$$\frac{dy_t}{d\beta} < 0 \qquad \text{if} \quad y_t \text{ is positive.} \tag{15}$$

That is, if the net demand for foreign exchange is positive, an increase in the variance of the expected future spot rate will curb the demand.

It remains to consider the implications of an increase in the forward rate of exchange. Suppose that $r_t - 1 \geqslant \bar{\rho}_t$, so that the wealth of the speculator–arbitrageur is held entirely in home bills. From Eqs. (4) and (2a),

$$\frac{dy_t}{dR_{t,f}} = \frac{E\{u'(A_{t+1})\} + y_t\,E\{u''(A_{t+1})(R_{t+1}-R_{t,f})\}}{E\{u''(A_{t+1})(R_{t+1}-R_{t,f})^2\}}, \tag{16a}$$

which is negative, as was to be expected. If, alternatively, $r_t - 1 < \bar{\rho}_t$, so that the speculator–arbitrageur invests his wealth in foreign bills only, we obtain, from Eqs. (4) and (2b),

$$\frac{dy_t}{dR_{t,f}} = \frac{E\{u'(A_{t+1})\} + [y_t-(A_t/R_t)\,r_t{}^*]\,E\{u''(A_{t+1})(R_{t+1}-R_{t,f})\}}{E\{u''(A_{t+1})(R_{t+1}-R_{t,f})^2\}}. \tag{16b}$$

Expression (16b) differs from (16a) by virtue of the additional income generated by the change. The increased price of forward exchange implies a corresponding improvement in the profitability of foreign investment and a certain increase in final wealth. In view of Eq. (8), we should therefore expect, for positive y_t, a tendency for the net demand for foreign exchange to increase. If the initial level of foreign investment is sufficiently high, this factor may outweigh the changed profitability of speculation.

IV. A Two-Day Planning Horizon

The analysis of Sect. III was based on assumptions as familiar as they are special. In this first tentative exposition only one short step will be taken towards a less restricted analysis. The really heavy work of generalization is left for others.

The introduction of bills and forward contracts with maturities in excess of one day is easy if the assumption of a one-day planning horizon is retained. But then the analysis and conclusions change only in uninteresting detail. For this reason we choose in the present section to explore the implications of a longer planning horizon.

Suppose that the decisions taken by the speculator–arbitrageur at the beginning of day t are aimed at maximizing the expected utility of his wealth two days hence. His decisions will of course be influenced by his expectation of the decisions he will take on the intermediate day $t+1$. The speculator–arbitrageur cannot on day t know what those decisions will be, for part of the data with which he will be confronted on day $t+1$ will be generated by a random process. However, he must be assumed to believe that he knows how he will behave in the face of each possible random outcome. The speculator–arbitrageur, therefore, may be viewed as seeking

$$\max_{\substack{x_t, x_{t+1} \\ y_t, y_{t+1}}} E\{u(A_{t+2})\}, \tag{17}$$

where

(18)

$$A_{t+2} = x_{t+1} r_{t+1} + (R_{t+2}/R_{t+1})(A_{t+1} - x_{t+1}) r_{t+1}^* + y_{t+1}(R_{t+2} - R_{t+1,f})$$

and A_{t+1} is defined by Eq. (2). Here, however, we focus on exchange rate uncertainty by assuming that both future rates of interest are expected with certainty. It follows from this assumption that the speculator–arbitrageur will direct his initial wealth entirely to home or entirely to foreign bills, and will adopt a similar all-or-none tactic with respect to tomorrow's wealth A_{t+1}. There are, therefore, four possible patterns of investment: (a) home bills on both days, (b) home bills today, foreign bills tomorrow, (c) foreign bills today, home bills tomorrow, and (d) foreign bills on both days. Here we consider

(a) only. In this case, $x_t = A_t$, $x_{t+1} = A_{t+1}$, and $x_t^* = 0 = x_{t+1}^*$, so that Eqs. (2) and (18) take the specialized forms (2a) and

$$A_{t+1} = A_{t+1} r_{t+1} + y_{t+1}(R_{t+2} - R_{t+1,f}), \tag{18a}$$

respectively, and (17) reduces to

$$\max_{y_t, y_{t+1}} E\{u(A_{t+2})\}. \tag{17a}$$

From Eqs. (17a), (18a), and (2a) we obtain, as first-order conditions,

$$E\{u'(A_{t+2})(R_{t+1} - R_{t,f})\} = 0 = E\{u'(A_{t+2})(R_{t+2} - R_{t+1,f})\}, \tag{19}$$

and, as second-order conditions,

$$\begin{gathered} E\{u''(A_{t+2})(R_{t+1} - R_{t,f})^2\} < 0, \\ E\{u''(A_{t+2})(R_{t+2} - R_{t+1,f})^2\} < 0, \\ J \equiv \begin{vmatrix} E\{u''(A_{t+2})(R_{t+1} - R_{t,f})^2\} & E\{u''(A_{t+2})(R_{t+1} - R_{t,f})(R_{t+2} - R_{t+1,f})\} \\ E\{u''(A_{t+2})(R_{t+1} - R_{t,f})(R_{t+2} - R_{t+1,f})\} & E\{u''(A_{t+2})(R_{t+2} - R_{t+1,f})^2\} \end{vmatrix} > 0. \end{gathered} \tag{20}$$

Of the several comparative statical calculations which might be carried out with the aid of Eqs. (19) and (20), two are of special interest, namely, the calculation of dy_t/dr_t and dy_t/dA_t. For these two responses may be directly compared with their one-day-horizon counterparts to clear up the doubts expressed in footnote 4.

From Eq. (19), bearing in mind Eqs. (2a) and (18a),

$$\begin{aligned} \frac{dy_t}{dr_t} &= \frac{A_t}{r_t} \cdot \frac{dy_t}{dA_t} \\ &= -\frac{r_{t+1} A_t}{J} [E\{u''(A_{t+2})(R_{t+1} - R_{t,f})\} E\{u''(A_{t+2})(R_{t+2} - R_{t+1,f})^2\} \\ &\quad - E\{u''(A_{t+2})(R_{t+2} - R_{t+1,f})\} E\{u''(A_{t+2})(R_{t+1} - R_{t,f})(R_{t+2} - R_{t+1,f})\}]. \end{aligned} \tag{21}$$

From the second-order conditions (20), J is positive. The sign of (21) is therefore opposite to the sign of the square-bracketed expression. The latter, however, cannot be pinned down without stronger assumptions.[7] Thus

[7] An argument similar to that of footnote 6 does, however, yield a generalization of Eq. (vii) [footnote 6] which is of some interest. From Eqs. (2a) and (18a),

$$A_{t+2} = r_{t+1}[A_t r_t + y_t(R_{t+1} - R_{t,f})] + y_{t+1}(R_{t+2} - R_{t+1,f}). \tag{viii}$$

From Eq. (viii) and the assumption of diminishing absolute risk aversion,

the response of the demand for forward exchange may be of either sign. This conclusion contrasts sharply with the unambiguous conclusion expressed in Eq. (7a). Thus the length of the planning horizon does matter (cf. footnote 4). An increase in initial wealth will change the willingness to speculate but, knowing nothing about the degree of statistical association between R_{t+1} and R_{t+2}, we cannot in the two-day case say anything about the response of speculation on any particular day. The same indeterminacy emerges in cases (b)–(d).

With the aid of stronger assumptions, however, it is possible to pin down dy_t/dr_t and dy_t/dA_t. For example, we might (as suggested to me by Dr. Agnar Sandmo) postulate a simple proportionality relationship between the expected backwardations, β_t and β_{t+1}:

$$\beta_t = \lambda\beta_{t+1},$$

where λ is a positive constant which might be greater or less than one. The

---

$$\zeta(A_{t+2}) \leqslant \zeta(r_t r_{t+1} A_t) \qquad \text{if} \quad z \geqslant 0,$$

where

(ix) $$z \equiv r_{t+1} y_t (R_{t+1} - R_{t,f}) + y_{t+1}(R_{t+2} - R_{t+1,f}).$$

That is,

(x) $$-\frac{u''(A_{t+2})}{u'(A_{t+2})} \leqslant \zeta(r_t r_{t+1} A_t) \qquad \text{if} \quad z \geqslant 0.$$

Since $u' > 0$, we have also

(xi) $$-zu'(A_{t+2}) \leqslant 0 \qquad \text{if} \quad z \geqslant 0.$$

From Eqs. (x) and (xi),

(xii) $$zu''(A_{t+2}) \geqslant -\zeta(r_t r_{t+1} A_t)\, zu'(A_{t+2}) \qquad \text{if} \quad z \geqslant 0.$$

By a similar argument,

(xiii) $$zu''(A_{t+2}) \geqslant -\zeta(r_t r_{t+1} A_t)\, zu'(A_{t+2}) \qquad \text{if} \quad z < 0.$$

From Eqs. (xii) and (xiii),

(xiv) $$zu''(A_{t+2}) \geqslant -\zeta(r_t r_{t+1} A_t)\, zu'(A_{t+2}).$$

Taking expectations, and bearing in mind Eqs. (ix) and (19),

(xv) $$\begin{aligned} r_{t+1} y_t E\{(R_{t+1} - R_{t,f}) u''(A_{t+2})\} &+ y_{t+1} E\{(R_{t+2} - R_{t+1,f}) u''(A_{t+2})\} \\ &\geqslant -\zeta(r_t r_{t+1} A_t)[r_{t+1} y_t E\{(R_{t+1} - R_{t,f}) u'(A_{t+2})\} \\ &\quad + y_{t+1} E\{(R_{t+2} - R_{t+1,f}) u'(A_{t+2})\}] \\ &= 0. \end{aligned}$$

It follows that at least one of

$$y_t E\{(R_{t+1} - R_{t,f}) u''(A_{t+2})\} \qquad \text{and} \qquad y_{t+1} E\{(R_{t+2} - R_{t+1,f}) u''(A_{t+2})\}$$

is nonnegative and that, if one is negative, the other is positive.

assumption is a strong one; but is not, perhaps, wholly without interest. For, given the assumption, the expression in square brackets in the preceding equation reduces to:

$$E\{u''(A_{t+2})\lambda\beta_{t+1}\}E\{u''(A_{t+2})\beta_{t+1}^2\} - E\{u''(A_{t+2})\beta_{t+1}\}E\{u''(A_{t+2})\lambda\beta_{t+1}^2\}.$$

Since λ is not a random variable and can be factored out, this expression vanishes. Thus investment in forward exchange is independent of the rate of interest.

V. Next Steps

I have poured cold water on a theory in which pure speculators and pure arbitrageurs are assigned major roles. But it is open to any reader to ask why he should be interested in a speculator–arbitrageur who does not consume, does not borrow, does not hold money, and forms absolutely certain expectations concerning future rates of interest.

REFERENCES

[1] Arrow, K. J., Comment, *Rev. Econ. Statist.* **XLV**, No. 1, 24–27 (1963).

[2] Arrow, K. J., "Aspects of the Theory of Risk-Bearing." Yrjö Jahnssonin Säätiö, Helsinki, 1965.

[3] Black, S. W., Theory and Policy Analysis of Short-term Movements in the Balance of Payments, *Yale Econ. Essays* **8**, No. 1, 5–78 (1968).

[4] Einzig, P., "A Dynamic Theory of Forward Exchange." Macmillan, London, 1961.

[5] Frevert, P., A Theoretical Model of the Forward Exchange, *Int. Econ. Rev.* **8**, Nos. 2 and 3, 153–167, 307–326 (1967).

[6] Grubel, H. G., "Forward Exchange, Speculation, and the International Flow of Capital." Stanford Univ. Press, Stanford, California, 1966.

[7] Kenen, P. B., Trade, Speculation, and the Forward Exchange Rate, *in* "Trade, Growth, and the Balance of Payments Essays in Honor of Gottfried Haberler on the Occasion of his 65th Birthday" (R. E. Baldwin *et al.*, eds.), pp. 143–169. North-Holland Publ., Amsterdam, 1965.

[8] Keynes, J. M., "A Tract on Monetary Reform." Macmillan, London, 1923.

[9] Kindleberger, C. P., "International Short Term Capital Movements." Columbia Univ. Press, New York, 1937.

[10] Kindleberger, C. P., Speculation and Forward Exchange, *J. Political Econ.* **XLVII**, No. 2, 163–181 (1939).

[11] Pratt, J. W., Risk Aversion in the Small and in the Large, *Econometrica*, **32**, No. 1, 122–136 (1964).

[12] Sandmo, A., Portfolio Choice in a Theory of Saving, *Sweidsh J. Econ.* **LXX**, No. 2, 106–122 (1968).

[13] Sohmen, E., "The Theory of Forward Exchange," Princeton Studies in International Finance No. 17. Princeton Univ. Press, Princeton, New Jersey, 1966.
[14] Spraos, J., The Theory of Forward Exchange and Recent Practice, *Manchester School Econ. Social Stud.* **21**, No. 2, 87–117 (1953).
[15] Spraos, J., Speculation, Arbitrage and Sterling, *Econ. J.* **LXIX**, No. 1, 1–21 (1959).
[16] Tsiang, S. C., The Theory of Forward Exchange and Effects of Government Intervention on the Forward Exchange Market, *Int. Monetary Fund Staff Papers* **7**, No. 1, 75–106 (1959).

REFLECTIONS ON UNLIMITED LABOR

W. ARTHUR LEWIS

Princeton University, Princeton, New Jersey

This paper seeks to clarify and expand two articles which I published on this subject ten and fourteen years ago, respectively [25, 26]. Clarification seems necessary since the large literature to which they have given rise is somewhat confusing.

I. Some Misconceptions

The purpose of the model was to provide a mechanism explaining the rapid growth of the proportion of domestic savings in the national income in the early stages of an economy whose growth is due to the expansion of capitalist forms of production. The chief historical example on which the model was based was that of Great Britain where, as we may deduce from the later figures of Deane and Cole, net saving seems to have risen from about 5 per cent before 1780 to 7 per cent in the early 1800s, to 12 per cent around 1870, at which level it stabilized [8, pp. 265–267]. A similar rise is shown for the United States by Gallman [13, p. 11], starting around the 1840s with gross domestic saving at 14 per cent, and continuing up to 28 per cent in the 1890s, where the figure stabilizes. Similar changes can be found since the second world war for many less-developed countries such as India or Jamaica.

The explanation of capitalist sector growth provided by the model turned on the higher than average propensity to save from profit income, and on the rise of the share of profits in the national income in the initial spurt of economic development. Some such model was needed at the time of writing, since the dynamic models then in use usually assumed constant savings and profits ratios. Even today our economic journals still publish many articles on savings functions which do not distinguish between profits and other incomes; a notable exception, specially valuable for bringing in less-developed countries, is the article by Houthakker [18].

Given the purpose of the model, the division of the economy into two sectors had to turn on profits. The two sectors are a capitalist and a noncapitalist sector, where "capitalist" is defined in the classical sense as a man who hires labor and resells its output for a profit. So a domestic servant is in the capitalist sector when working in a hotel but not when working in a private home.

This distinction was vital for my purpose. Other writers, with different purposes, have made different divisions. A now popular division is between industry and agriculture, but capitalist production cannot be identified with manufacturing, as anyone familiar with a plantation economy must know. The model is intended to work equally well whether the capitalists are agriculturists or industrialists or anything else, and indeed in its first version (as we shall see in a moment) the model presupposes that the capitalist sector is self-sufficient and contains every kind of economic activity.

This explanation may serve to refute the charge that the model identifies economic growth with industrialization. A further misconception is that it necessarily identifies economic growth with capitalist production. The anti-socialist aspect of this attack is easily beaten off. Since a capitalist is one who hires labor for profit, it makes no difference to the model whether the capitalists are private or public; the model gives a pretty good explanation of the sharp rise in the share of savings in the U.S.S.R. between, say, 1929 and 1939. The accusation that the model disparages peasant production is on a different plane. The model does not deny that peasants can grow rich by producing more, or more valuable output; it does not argue that capitalist production is more valuable; it is not normative. This author is delighted that there are economies where the productivity of peasants increases steadily and that some portion of that increase goes into capital formation. This does not render it useless or dangerous to study models of economies where, in the initial stages, the dynamism of growth is located in capitalist expansion.

In the model, the noncapitalist sector serves for a time as a reservoir from which the capitalist sector draws labor. The original paper makes clear that this labor does not all come from agriculture—a fact which has escaped the attention of many subsequent writers. The paper mentions *inter alia* domestic service and the self-employed (especially in handicrafts and petty retailing). It also points out that the labor force itself expands through the increased participation of women, as well as by natural increase and by immigration. The last of these sources, immigration, played a substantial role in economic development during the nineteenth century (e.g., U.S.A., Brazil, Malaya, Australia) and, according to Kindleberger [23], is an important explanation of why some European economies have grown faster than others since the second world war.

The existence of such a reservoir is important to the model, since it explains why the capitalist labor force can for a time grow faster than the 3 per cent per annum limit which natural increase would now impose on the less-developed countries, or the 1.5 per cent population limit on Western Europe in the nineteenth century. This is important in explaining why profits can grow much faster than national income. But it receives added significance in these days, since we have observed that in one part of the capitalist sector, namely manufacturing industry, the rate of growth of productivity per head is a positive function of the rate of growth of employment. For this means that productivity can grow faster if there is a labor reservoir than if there is not.

In the model, the capitalist sector is said to have unlimited access to a labor supply, thanks to the existence of this reservoir. The use of the word "unlimited" has caused confusion. It means that if capitalists offer additional employment at the existing wage, there will be far more candidates than they require: the supply curve of labor is infinitely elastic at the ruling wage. One condition for this is that the ruling wage in the capitalist sector exceeds the earnings in the noncapitalist sector of those who are willing to transfer themselves. The other condition is that any tendency which the transfer may set in motion for earnings per head to rise in the noncapitalist sector must initially be offset by the effect of increases in the labor force (natural increase, immigration, or greater female participation). This is discussed more fully later in this paper. The model does not attempt to derive the conventional wage: as in the classical system, this depends not only on productivity but also on social attitudes. The model simply postulates as facts that in the initial stage the supply of labor at the given wage exceeds the demand, and that this condition will continue for some time despite the expansion of the capitalist sector. This postulate is inconsistent neither with history nor with reason.

Since all that the model needs is the fact that supply exceeds demand at the current wage it was not necessary to say anything about the productivity of marginal units of labor in the reservoir, beyond noting that it must be less than the wage offered by capitalists. As the original article said: "Whether marginal productivity is zero or negligible is not however of fundamental importance to our analysis" (p. 142). It was probably a mistake to mention marginal productivity at all, since this has merely led to an irrelevant and intemperate controversy.

This debate has been further confused by the fact that I did not mean by "marginal product is zero" what most of the subsequent writers have meant.

I meant (and said so explicitly) the marginal product of a man, whereas they mean the marginal product of a manhour. For example, in many countries the market stalls (or the handicraft industries) are crowded with people who are not as fully occupied as they would wish to be. If ten per cent of these people were removed, the amount traded would be the same, since those who remained would do more trade. This is the sense in which the marginal product of men in that industry is zero. It is a significant sense, and its significance is not diminished by pointing out that the fact that others have to do more work to keep the total product constant proves that the marginal product of manhours is positive. That an intelligent man like Professor Wellisz [34] believes that my model stands or falls by whether marginal productivity per manhour is zero testifies only to the obscurity of my writing.

Why did I bring in zero marginal productivity (per person)? For two reasons, neither of which is fundamental to the model. Since all the model requires is that the supply of labor exceed the demand, zero marginal productivity was not a necessary condition. My first reason for introducing it was that I was concerned with the relative rates of growth of output in the capitalist and noncapitalist sectors, since this affected the share of profits and thus of savings in national income. Relative rates of growth would depend partly on how the output of the noncapitalist sector would be affected by the loss of labor, so I mentioned zero marginal product as a limiting case. This is clearly a peripheral reference.

The second reason is not even a part of the model. I was concerned, as many others have been, with the possibility that underemployed labor might be put to productive capital formation. This again raises the question by how much the output of the noncapitalist sector would thereby be reduced, and zero is again the limiting case. But it makes no difference whether the loss of noncapitalist output is zero or positive, so long as it is less than the value added by the labor in the sector to which it is transferred.

Egypt is an excellent case, because it illustrates both the kind of labor market which the model fits, and also the misconceptions even of some distinguished writers on this subject. Here is a passage from Hansen and Marzouk [15, p. 16–17] which specifically rejects the model, while actually describing a situation which exactly fits it! After noting the "remarkable" stability of prices in the 1950s, the authors continue:

> A basic condition for the price stability is to be found in the labour market. Although the supply of labour is certainly not infinitely elastic in the Arthur Lewis sense (absolute surplus labour in agriculture probably never did exist in Egypt), there is no doubt that the supply has increased so rapidly during the postwar years that the increasing demand has never led to a real shortage, at least in the major categories of labour. Construction is probably the only sector where labour shortage and wage drift has been a real problem. And Government money wage rates have, if anything, been falling for the post-war period as a whole.

Elsewhere they state specifically, referring to agricultural labor, that "during the fifties the wage rate remained unchanged" (p. 78).

The authors' confusion, in using an infinitely elastic labor supply to explain why the price level and money wages remained constant, while at the same time denying that the labor supply was infinitely elastic, derives from their erroneous identification of infinite elasticity with a zero manhour marginal product of labor in agriculture. Elsewhere in their analysis they supply adequate explanations for the elastic labor supply:

(a) Population was growing by about 3 per cent per annum (p. 23);

(b) In spite of this, the agricultural labor force remained constant. There was terrific migration to other occupations, whose potential labor force must thus have been growing by about 6 or 7 per cent per annum (p. 61);

(c) There was considerable underemployment in the service industries, such that between 1952 and 1962 the numbers in commerce increased only by 49 per cent, whereas the volume of goods handled increased by 65 per cent (p. 320). The government service was notoriously overstaffed;

(d) The proportion of women in the labor force was only 10 per cent (p. 37).

These are typical phenomena of an infinitely elastic supply situation.

Though zero marginal productivity (whether per person or per manhour) makes no difference to my model, there is so much confused writing about marginal productivity in the agriculture of overpopulated countries that I will complete this section with a few remarks on this subject.

First as to manhour productivity, it is quite certain that if farmers were willing to work longer hours they would produce more. Agricultural extension officers show the farmers many ways of increasing output per acre (e.g., transplanting instead of broadcasting seed, or weeding their plots more frequently) which the farmers often reject because they involve more work. Moreover most of these require work not at the peak season (usually but not always the harvesting), but in earlier slack seasons when the farmers are undoubtedly underemployed. They do not work because the extra work would not in their view be adequately compensated by the extra output. So here is an example of a situation where the marginal product of persons is zero (in my sense that output would be the same with fewer people) while the marginal product of manhours is positive in the sense that more work would raise output.

So far I am assuming that the time of the farmers is not fully occupied. The proposition that, if one member of the family migrates, the others will do his work has also been attacked (e.g. [2]). The argument runs as follows: The departure of, say, the fifth working member of a family gives each of the others in effect one fourth more land to cultivate. Assuming constant returns to scale, if each works one fourth more hours on one fourth more land he will get one fourth more product, leaving total output the same as it was before the fifth member left. But the marginal value of output is diminishing in terms of leisure, so if a person was originally in equilibrium he will not work one fourth longer to get only one fourth more output.

One can reply to this in two ways. One can accept the approach through the valuation of leisure, but reject the valuation given to leisure. In particular there is no basis for the assumption that the supply curve of work is upward sloping (in terms of output) throughout the relevant range. A person is trained by his parents or his society that he should work for at least so many hours per day, and until this point is reached he may give no thought to leisure. Indeed, if he can get, say, only 6 hours at his regular job, he may gladly work an extra three hours at half price in some other situation, partly for the money, and partly for self-respect. If in addition he has a fixed idea of what his time is worth, the best representation of his supply curve of work is a horizontal straight line which turns upward sharply when he passes what he considers to be the right number of hours per day.

Figure 1 expresses this situation. Curve I shows the marginal yield of work to the individual worker when the family has five working members on its two acres. Agricultural extension agents want the worker to go beyond the point where this curve cuts the labor supply curve, but he refuses to do so, even though he has much idle time. Curve II shows the situation when the family is reduced to four working members. The farmer now works one fourth more time on one fourth more land with the same marginal product. Without empirical data one cannot assert that the supply curve of labor is horizontal in these circumstances, but this assumption is as reasonable and more likely than the assumption that the supply curve is rising throughout the day.

The other answer is to reject this type of analysis for people in these situations. A farm family with 2 acres wishes to cultivate the farm in accordance with the standards of its community. It will do what needs to be done whether there are 4 or 5 working members of the family. The mistress of the house likes it to be clean. If the opening of a nearby factory reduces the number of her servants from 5 to 4, she will still keep up the standards of her class, even if this means that she and her children must now do a little more for them-

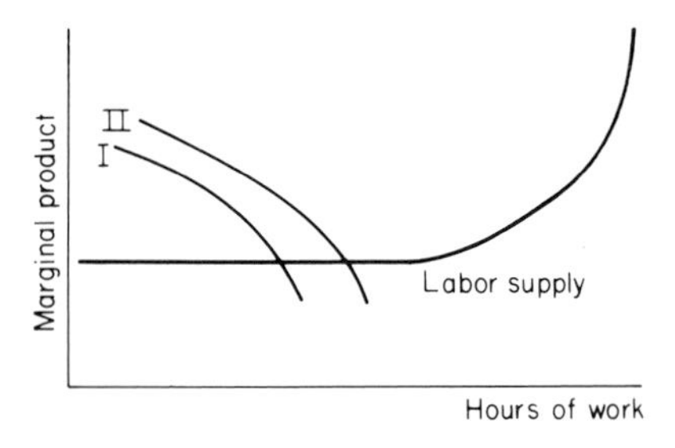

Fig. 1.

selves. Marginal analysis applies to the means by which individuals attain their goals. It is not correct to assume that the goals will be altered just because they become marginally more costly or more easy to attain. Keeping the farm cultivated is amenable to marginal analysis if it is a means, but not if it is a goal.

Let us however move away from these cases, in which the existence of leisure is implicitly accepted, and pass to the attack on underemployment itself. Nobody denies that in the overpopulated countries handicraft workers, petty traders, dock workers, domestic servants, and casual workers have a lot of spare time on their hands, and that most of them (except the domestic servants) would be glad to exchange extra work for extra income at the current rate. Neither does anybody deny that there is much seasonal unemployment in agriculture. The dispute is confined to the situation on small family farms at the peak of the agricultural season, in some parts of Asia and the Middle East.

The argument turns mostly on the labor situation at the time of harvesting, which for most crops (but not, e.g., for manioc) makes the peak demand for labor. The reason for this peak is usually that once the harvest is ready it must be reaped as quickly as possible if it is not to spoil by remaining on the stalk, or to be spoiled by a change in the weather. For this reason, no practicable number of people is too large at this time, since the more hands, the faster the harvesting is completed. It may nevertheless be possible to take off the same harvest with fewer hands if each person works more hours per day, or if the harvesting is spread over a few more days: there is no fixed ratio of number of persons to tons of crop. Harvests vary enormously from one year to another, but somehow or other even the largest harvest gets reaped—although not always the complete 100 per cent. Hansen and Marzouk [15] note that the labor force in Egyptian agriculture was the same in 1960 as in 1950, but was reaping a 25 per cent larger harvest at the later date without any significant increase in machinery. But they fail to deduce the corollary that the farmers could probably have taken off the 1950 harvest with a labor force smaller by (say) 10 per cent. In spite of all they say about labor shortage, one may surmise that if the harvest is 10 per cent larger five years from now, the present labor force will manage to take it off somehow or other.

Even if there were a fixed ratio of men to tons in harvesting, one cannot justify keeping men idle for eleven months so that they may harvest for the twelfth. In the days before harvesting machinery, the standard European solution was for these men to work at nonagricultural occupations during eleven months of the year, and go into the fields for the twelfth. Where this practice is followed, a peak demand for labor at harvest time is quite consistent with transferring men from agriculture into other occupations during the rest of the year.

I do not believe that the productivity of a manhour is zero in agriculture, domestic service, petty retailing, handicrafts, or any other part of the noncapitalist reservoir. Nevertheless, I have seen nothing in the now vast literature of underemployment to alter my belief that in India or Egypt one could mobilize a group equal to, say, ten per cent of the unskilled noncapitalist labor force without significantly reducing the output of the noncapitalist sectors from which they were withdrawn. (One might not be able to use this group effectively without drawing skilled labor, supervisors, food, raw materials, or capital equipment from the other sectors, but that is a different story.) Professor Schultz's doubtful statistics [32] about India's influenza epidemic in 1918–1919 do not meet the conditions specified, because the labor must come *only* from the small family farms and other underemployed pockets; besides at the time of which he speaks India's population was smaller by 200 million than it is today. Professor Paglin [1, 30] confuses total input with labor input. His figures actually show (though he did not spot this) that the marginal productivity of labor on small farms is zero or negative, but only because bullocks, which are also underemployed on small farms, are treated as a continuously variable input. Most of the other articles relate to the marginal productivity of manhours, or embrace the naive idea that there is a fixed ratio of men to tons harvested, and are therefore not germane.

What our colleagues want to emphasize is that even in very overpopulated countries like India or Java, agricultural output could be increased by additional inputs of labor, if the farmers could be persuaded to spend more time on transplanting, weeding, fertilizing, etc. I agree with this completely, and have always favored heavy expenditure on agricultural extension, But this position is not inconsistent with recognizing that, as things now stand in such countries, labor squads could be recruited for useful works off the farms without significantly reducing agricultural output, since those who were left behind would manage to do what needs to be done.

However, this is all an irrelevant digression, since the model in no way depends on the marginal product in agriculture, whether per person or per manhour. All we need is a situation where the supply of labor exceeds the demand, in the capitalist sector—a situation which may exist either because the capitalist wage significantly exceeds noncapitalist earnings, or because the labor force is increasing (natural increase, immigration, or female participation). We do not even need to know why supply exceeds demand; it is enough for our purposes that it does.

II. The Model's Turning Points

It is important to realize that this model comes in three different versions.

In the first version we have (i) a closed economy and (ii) no trade between the two sectors. The capitalist sector is completely self-contained, except that it imports labor. The first turning point then comes only when the labor supply ceases to be infinitely elastic and the wage starts rising through pressure from the noncapitalist sector. One can vary this model slightly to take in whole countries developed by immigration, such as Malaya or the U.S.A.; or to consider the effects of immigration on growth in Western Europe during the 1950s.

In the second version (i) we have a closed economy, but (ii) the capitalist sector depends on trade with the noncapitalist sector, e.g., for food or raw materials. Now we have an additional turning point, since the capitalist sector may be choked by adverse terms of trade, even if the labor reservoir is still teeming with people.

The third model is a variant of the second. Here we have (i) an open economy whose capitalist sector (ii) trades either with the labor reservoir or with the outside world. Here the capitalist sector can escape the stagnation of the noncapitalist sector by importing from the ouside world, but the resulting import surplus may slow growth or produce structural inflation.

A. Model One

It is useful to begin with a model in which the capitalist sector is self-contained, since this enables us to focus attention upon the labor supply, without considering the terms of trade. Besides there are many economies where the capitalist sector gets labor from the noncapitalist, but neither food nor raw materials.

In this version the supply of labor exceeds the demand at the current wage. One would expect this wage to hold constant for some time as the capitalist sector expands. There are two turning points. The first occurs when the check to the growth of the noncapitalist sector raises average earnings there to the point that the capitalist wage is forced upwards. The second turning point comes when the marginal product is the same in the capitalist and noncapitalist sectors, so that we have reached the neoclassical one-sector economy.[1]

The first turning point comes when the changes in the noncapitalist sector begin to react on the wage. We must distinguish between exogenous and endogenous changes. The supply price of labor may rise because something happens to make people richer in the noncapitalist sector, e.g., the farmers may begin to grow a profitable crop for export; or may learn to use fertilizers. Favorable exogenous changes may be expected to raise wages; we must look out for them in any attempts at historical verification, but we cannot take

[1] The second turning point is exactly the same as in Fei and Ranis [10, pp. 201–5]. The definition of the first turning point is also the same, but the mechanism for reaching it is different, since Fei and Ranis are working with Model II, in which the capitalist sector depends on the noncapitalist for agricultural products.

them into the model. (In the same way, as we shall see in a moment, the wage rate may rise exogenously for reasons which have nothing to do with the noncapitalist sector; e.g., because the government enacts minimum wage legislation.) The model incorporates only those endogenous changes in wages which result directly from the transfer of labor from the noncapitalist sector.

This transfer automatically causes consumption per head to be higher than it would otherwise be in the noncapitalist sector. If the people transferred are farmers, farm output will fall by less than their consumption, since land is assumed to be scarce (their consumption equaled average product, which exceeded marginal product). If the people transferred were in petty retailing or handicrafts, those who remain will get more trade.

Several writers (e.g., [7, 14]) have assumed that this increase in noncapitalist consumption per head must immediately force up the capitalist wage, but there are two reasons why this is not so. The first of these is that in my model, as distinct from those used by these and other writers, there is a substantial gap between the capitalist wage and noncapitalist consumption per head, and this gap is not fixed rigidly. If one transfers 5 per cent of the labor force from the noncapitalist sector one is increasing very substantially (perhaps doubling) the capitalist labor force, but the difference this makes to consumption per head in the noncapitalist sector is small and need not be enough to force up the capitalist wage. That wage is determined conventionally, and we know that conventional money wages hold stable even when prices move a few points in one direction or the other.

This is one factor which distinguishes my model from those of some other writers who, desiring to find some reasonable basis for the conventional wage, tie it rigidly to agricultural productivity. This tie seems especially appropriate if one further assumes, as they tend to do, that the reservoir consists exclusively of agriculturists, which of course is not the case. Their rigid assumptions yield precise numbers for wages and earnings, and one can calculate precisely how these numbers alter as labor transfers from one sector to the other. But what is gained in precision is lost in realism.

The second reason why the conventional wage does not necessarily rise as labor is transferred is that in my model the labor force in the noncapitalist sector is still growing in the first stage (though not proportionately as fast as in the capitalist sector). At this stage, therefore, the transfer does not raise consumption per head in the noncapitalist sector in the absolute sense; it merely prevents consumption from falling by as much as it otherwise would. The increase in the labor force may be due to population increase, to greater participation of women, or to migration.[2] We should also remember Marx's

[2] Clapham [6, pp. 168–169] remarks that as French peasants migrated to the towns at the end of the nineteenth century, Belgians, Spaniards, Poles, and Italians immigrated into French farming in their place.

point that capitalism creates its own labor force; competition from factories may put the handicraft workers out of business; increasing use of domestic appliances may throw the domestic servants onto the labor market.[3] In sum, there are forces at work tending to reduce consumption per head in the noncapitalist sector. These would not necessarily have reduced the capitalist wage, since, as we have just said, the gap between the capitalist wage and noncapitalist consumption is flexible, and the conventional wage may hold constant despite a few percentage points of rise or fall in noncapitalist consumption per head.

Thus, bearing all these factors in mind and, in particular, the population factor, there is no reason to expect the capitalist wage to rise endogenously as soon as the capitalist sector begins to grow. It may rise immediately, or an increase may be long delayed: this is a matter for historical research in each case.

Ultimately the capitalist wage must rise, since a successful transformation implies that the capitalist sector has grown rapidly enough to overtake population growth and reach the second turning point.

Critics of the model make enormous play with the question of how long it takes to reach the first turning point, i.e., the question whether there really is a period during which the wage is constant. But this question is of no consequence. The decisive turning point is not the first but the second, for it is here that we pass the boundary into the neoclassical system. The model would have achieved all that it set out to do even if it could be shown (and it cannot) that historically there never has been a case where the real wage did not begin to grow as soon as the capitalist sector began to expand.

The point becomes even clearer when we investigate what is meant by "the real wage." Everyone recognizes that we are talking about unskilled labor, so this is not the problem; skilled wages will certainly rise as skills increase. We are also talking about capitalist wages and not the wages of domestic servants —this is part of our definition. The problem is not in defining the wage, but in defining "real."

"Real" wage has many meanings. The most common is the money wage rate w divided by the cost of living c:

(1) w/c denotes cost of living wage.

However, since we are also interested in the relationship between the income of the capitalist worker and the income of the noncapitalist worker a, by which it is ultimately affected, we must also consider the relationship

(2) w/a denotes factoral wage.

[3] There is much less resistance today than there was in 1954 to the idea of an unlimited supply of labor being available to the capitalist sector, since swelling urban unemployment has emerged as the biggest problem of the seventies, *as a result of the modernization process itself.*

Ultimately, however, what interests us is profit, which depends *inter alia* on the ratio of wages to prices. A crude index of this is given by dividing the wage index by an index of the price p received by capitalists:

(3) w/p denotes wage/price ratio.

This is not a good index of profits, because profits also depend on productivity, i.e., on real output Q divided by the quantity of labor L. Also the price of the product includes the cost of raw materials, which should be deducted to get the value added price of the product v. Profit then depends on the ratio of wages to value added:

(4) wL/vQ denotes product-wage.

If the system does not import raw materials, as in this first version of the model, the product-wage becomes

$$wL/pQ.$$

Given this wide variety of types of real wage, what do we mean when we talk about the real wage being constant, for the purpose of this model? The answer derives from what we are seeking. Our interest is in the share of profits in the national income, which is determined by two factors: the share of the capitalist sector as a whole in the national income, and the share of profits in the capitalist sector (which is unity minus the product wage) The share of the capitalist sector in national income will grow so long as the product-wage is favorable to growth. We can therefore concentrate our attention in the first instance on the product-wage.

We can now formulate more precisely what we are after. The model postulates that the product-wage will fall (the profit ratio rise) during an initial period because capitalists will not have to share with their workers the fruit of technological advance (Q/L). During this initial period the wage-price ratio (w/p) is assumed to be constant, but sooner or later the rise in noncapitalist consumption per head (a) forces up w. This is the first turning point. From here on both w/p and Q/L are rising. Sooner or later w/p will be rising faster than Q/L, which means that the profit ratio will have begun to fall. We enter the neoclassical system at the second turning point, where the marginal product of labor is the same throughout the system. We also believe that at this point the product-wage wL/pQ stabilizes, although we have no theoretical explanation why this should happen. It is sufficient for our purposes that sooner or later we expect the product-wage to start rising, as we move from the first turning point towards the second.

Thus to test the historical validity of the model, the questions to ask for any particular country are (i) was w/p initially constant, and (ii) did wL/pQ ultimately rise?

As to the first question, the data are not easy to find, since even in those cases where we can put together some kind of money wage index it is very hard to make an index of the price of domestic capitalist output (which has, in an open economy, to be not p but v). In a closed economy with a self-contained capitalist sector, if we can assume that the prices of capital goods and consumer goods all move together, we can write

$$p = v = c,$$

and ask ourselves the simpler question—whether the real cost of living wage remained constant initially. This is also difficult to answer, but it is easier to find data for w/c than for w/v. However, even if we get an answer for w/c we have to remember that in the real world p, v, and c are not equal to each other, and that therefore the answer we get for the cost-of-living wage is not conclusive for w/p.

When the first article was being written, the historical wages data uppermost in my mind were those for the cost of living wage in Great Britain in the first half of the nineteenth century, and the U.S.S.R. in the 1930s. Historians still dispute what happened to the real wage rate in the first half of the nineteenth century [16, 17], but it seems a good bet that the rate of increase was slight. Deane and Cole's version [8] of Wood's data on money wage rates shows a rise in Great Britain from 70 in 1790 to 100 in 1840. Phelps Brown and Hopkins's index [4] of the price of consumables rises in that period from 68 to 100, indicating a slight *decline* in the real wage rate over those 50 years. Indeed the Phelps Brown–Hopkins index of the real wage rate of building craftsmen shows it only 4 per cent higher in 1840–1844 than it had been ninety years earlier in 1750–1754. One can get different results with different figures, but it is safest to conclude that the cost-of-living wage did not rise substantially in Great Britain during the first fifty years of the industrial revolution. (This is not inconsistent with the standard of living rising through a fall in underemployment or movement from worse into better paid jobs; wages per head can rise even if wage rates are constant.)

The British case is not necessarily typical. The wage–price ratio (w/p) will remain constant only if noncapitalist earnings a are not rising, or if the capitalists are not sharing productivity gains with their workers. Both conditions may have been met in Britain 150 years ago, but there are plenty of other cases. Thus, in the U.S.A. productivity on family farms was rising sharply in the middle of the nineteenth century, through the adoption of machinery, so industrial wages could not have been held constant. Similarly, in Japan farm productivity was rising at the end of the century. Okhawa's cost of living data [29] starting only in 1893, show real wages rising by 17 per cent in the 18 years from 1893/95 to 1911/13. They did not rise as fast as industrial productivity; he puts the productivity increase in secondary industry at 38 per cent, which is rather low for our purpose, since it includes handicrafts. Thus the capitalists conceded part of the increase in productivity to the workers, but they did not concede it proportionately. According to Okhawa the terms of trade between primary and secondary sectors altered little in this period, so profits in the industrial sector must have risen relatively to wages.

Study of the Japanese materials brings out another important phenomenon, which is also found elsewhere, namely, a widening gap between industrial and agricultural wages. The data given in Minami [28] show the real agricultural wage constant in the two decades before the first world war, when the industrial wage was rising, and agricultural productivity rising even faster. How do agricultural wages remain constant while farmers' incomes are rising? The answer is already in our model. The agricultural wage initially exceeds the marginal product of labor. It is established conventionally for the landless (or insufficiently landed) class. Farmers employ laborers for tasks whose productivity exceeds the wage; less productive tasks they do at other times with their own family labor. The agricultural wage of landless laborers is not tied to the farmers' incomes, and may stay constant or rise very slowly for a long time, even though farm income is rising.

In sum, we are now talking about three different kinds of earnings:

(1) the wages of landless laborers,
(2) the earnings of small farmers,
(3) the earnings of unskilled industrial workers.

The crucial test of whether labor is in surplus supply in the countryside will be what happens to the wages of landless agricultural laborers. If, as in Japan, or allegedly in Egypt, these remain constant while the other two are rising, we can be quite sure that a labor surplus exists. What interests our model, however, is the wage that the capitalists have to pay, and there is no doubt that this may rise even in the face of a labor surplus in the countryside.

When we turn to the less-developed countries of our own times and ask what is happening to the industrial wage, the answer, from a very large number, if not from all, is that the cost of living wage w/c is rising, even in situations where there is open mass urban unemployment, not to speak of underemployment. Why is this happening?

In some countries rising a is clearly a contributing factor. The small farmers' output of food per head is more or less constant, but their output of coffee, cocoa, peanuts, rubber, cotton, etc., has been rising swiftly, and in some countries, especially in Africa, the increase in output per head has been greater than the decline in the price received by the farmers. In those countries one would expect the capitalist wage to be forced up.

However, the evidence, even from such favorably placed countries, is that in most places the gap between w and a has widened; wages have risen much faster than farmers' incomes. This means that the capitalists are sharing productivity gains with the workers to a greater extent than one would expect if the abundance of the labor supply were the only element to be considered. Why they are doing this is not clear,[4] though explanations have been offered [12, 27, 31].

It seems therefore that what we should expect in overpopulated countries is that the real agricultural wage will remain constant, if the laborers are landless. What happens to the urban wage will depend partly on what is happening to a (the farmers' income) and partly on the extent to which the capitalists share technological gains with their workers. The industrial wage may well be rising faster than industrial prices, but this will not cut into profit unless it is also rising faster than industrial productivity. If we assume that the capitalists share technological gains equally, the product-wage will remain constant. It makes little difference to the model whether one assumes w/p constant or wL/pQ constant. The system expands faster on the first assumption than on the second, but it is still capable of rapid expansion until wages start rising faster than productivity.

Whether the product-wage stays constant or falls somewhat in the initial stages of development, it must ultimately rise when the combination of rising a and diminution of the labor reservoir combine to push up w/p faster than labor productivity. We cannot document this historically, since we do not have profit–wage data for the first three quarters of the nineteenth century for the countries which are now developed, but contemporary cross-country data throw light on the situation.

The United Nations' "The Growth of World Industry 1953–1965" [33] summarizes data from censuses of manufactures taken between 1961 and 1963 (with the exception of Venezuela, which are from 1953). Comparable data for the percentage share of wages and salaries in value added can be computed for several countries, e.g.,

Denmark	59	Venezuela	38	Ghana	26
Sweden	57	Japan	37	Brazil	26
U.K.	53	Jamaica	33	Nigeria	25
Norway	51	Colombia	32	Philippines	24
U.S.A.	49	Peru	29	Ivory Coast	24
Israel	46			Iran	22

The difference between the highly industrialized and the least industrialized countries is striking. Some part of the difference is due to heavier depreciation

[4] That they will pay a w higher than a to get higher productivity through higher consumption of food, etc., is clear enough. But this does not explain why the gap between w and a should *widen* continually for unskilled labor.

cost in the least industrialized countries (imported capital costs relatively more, and the life of equipment is relatively shorter), but removing this element would still leave net profits much lower relative to wages in the most-developed countries.

The cross-country data do not, like the historical data, support the notion that the real wage or even the product-wage is constant initially (most of the countries shown here are not overpopulated). They show very high initial profits, and, since the capitalist sector is growing very rapidly (the modal rate of growth of large scale manufacturing in Asian and African countries is about 10 per cent per year), they are consistent with a rapid increase in the share of profits in the national income as a whole, in the countries at the bottom of the list. The generalization which the cross-country data would support for our own times (as distinct from the 19th century) is that the share of profits in national income grows rapidly at the start because both the profit margin and the rate of growth of the capitalist sector (relative to the whole) are high, and that the share of profits declines and eventually stabilizes at a lower level, because both the profit margin and the relative growth rate of the capitalist sector are reduced. For evidence that initially the profit margin increases before beginning to decline and ultimately stabilizing (second turning point), we have to look at historical data from countries known to have had large labor reservoirs (England and Japan).

The cross-country data support the proposition that the profit margin ultimately stabilizes. More appropriate evidence can be derived from the U.S. Censuses of Manufactures. From these one can calculate the following ratios of wages and salaries to value added:

1899	48.6%
1909	50.3%
1929	46.7%
1963	48.6%

Recognizing that 1909 was a relatively depressed and 1929 a relatively prosperous year, one may surmise that changes in the later stages of development are very small in comparison with those which occur in the middle years.

Let us return for a moment to the widening of the gap between w and a which results from capitalists sharing the gains of technology in spite of the abundance of labor. Whatever their reason for doing this, the consequences for unemployment and underemployment are serious. The ratio of w to a is one of the factors determining how many people flock into the capitalist sector looking for work. Apart from full-time jobs this sector offers much casual employment (at the docks, in building, etc.), so everybody who looks for work stands some statistical chance of getting casual employment—

whether for 5, 10, or 20 days per month. Others can become self-employed, in retailing or handicrafts, doing some business, though not much. The higher the wage, the greater the inflow, and the less work for each person, though presumably to each level of w/a there corresponds some degree of underemployment which would be enough to stop further migration. As the ratio of w to a has risen since 1950, there has been a massive exit from the countryside into unemployment and underemployment in the towns. This is now one of the major problems of underdeveloped countries.

Here we tie into another problem, namely, what is the appropriate capital intensity for economies where the wage rate in the capitalist sector exceeds the marginal product outside that sector. This has been investigated by a long line of writers, summarized by Chenery [5], and the debate continues [9, 11, 24]. But the issue is largely political, and our model throws no light on it.

In sum, the model seems to survive the tests of its relevance if one sticks to what is crucial in it, namely, first, the abundance of labor at the current wage, which facilitates the rapid growth of capitalist output and profits; and second, the notion that in due course wages will rise faster than profits until some upper leveling-off is reached. If the model is not destroyed by showing that the marginal product of manhours in agriculture is not zero, neither is it rendered useless by showing that the real (cost of living) wage is not necessarily constant.

B. Model Two

In this version our two sectors produce different commodities and therefore trade with each other. Thus the capitalist sector faces the additional hazard that it may be checked by adverse terms of trade, arising out of the pressure of its own demands, long before any shortage of labor begins to be felt.

This is the version which has been worked out in great detail by Fei and Ranis working with models in which each of the variables is or can be precisely determined. Jorgensen and others also prefer to work with this model. It is a good model for studying the economic history of countries before about 1870, when railways, steamships, and the Suez Canal began the great explosion of world trade. Until then transport costs were so high that countries had virtually to be self-sufficient in basic necessities. But since then the terms of trade are determined by international rather than national forces. If the capitalists were hindered by failure of the noncapitalist sector to produce what was wanted, the capitalists would simply import from other countries whatever they might need (including food for their workers and raw materials for their machines).

This is true for the great majority of countries now underdeveloped, and mainly dependent on foreign trade. It is still not true, however, of huge economies like those of the U.S.S.R. or India, which have been developing with their price levels largely isolated from those of the world market. It is still possible for such economies to grind to a standstill through overemphasis on industry and underemphasis on agriculture, showing up in shortages of food, raw materials, and foreign exchange—contemporary Indian experience illustrates only too vividly the continued relevance of this model. Let us, therefore, pursue it.

For the moment (until we reach model three), we assume a closed economy without international trade. We simplify by assuming that just two commodities are produced, and our interest is in the terms of trade between them. Thus our specifications are altered. The division between the two sectors now turns on commodities rather than on capitalists; it makes no difference to us whether there are capitalists in the slow-growing sector, provided we specify that their profits are not reinvested in the fast-growing sector. What we still need is a substantial initial difference between real wages in the two sectors, so that labor supply is not initially a problem to the fast-growing sector. Following the conventions, we will now divide the economy into an industrial and an agricultural sector, with industry paying significantly higher wages than agriculture.

Thus stated, the problem is an exercise in the study of unbalanced growth in a closed economy. It is normally approached by specifying the conditions under which balance (which here means constant terms of trade) would be maintained. But this balance carries no normative implications. The industrial sector may grow quite rapidly for some time, even if the terms of trade are moving against it. And since industry has no intrinsic merit over agriculture, economic policy does not require that the terms of trade be moved in favor of industry. The only economists who wish to impoverish the peasants are those who have set the creation of a modern industrial state as their target for its own sake.

Since what we are studying is the behavior of the terms of trade between two sectors, ready answers are already available in the corpus of international trade theory; such an answer was given by Johnson [19]. We define the variables as follows:

e price elasticity of demand,
z income elasticity of demand,
r rate of growth of output,
p price of agricultural products relatively to manufactures,
a subscript denoting the agricultural sector,
m subscript denoting the industrial sector.

Then, after various manipulations detailed by Johnson (p. 141), we get the annual change in the terms of trade:

$$\frac{dp}{dt} \times \frac{1}{p} = \frac{z_a r_m - z_m r_a}{e_a + e_m - 1} .$$

From this, it follows that the terms of trade will be constant if

$$z_a r_m = z_m r_a ,$$

i.e., if

$$z_m / z_a = r_m / r_a .$$

This equality means that the terms of trade will be constant if the relative growth rates of industry and agriculture are the same as the relative income elasticities. For example, if the income elasticity of demand for manufactures is twice that for agricultural products, then the output of manufactures must grow twice as fast as the output of agricultural products if the terms of trade are to remain constant.

This neat answer reminds us that the terms of trade may move in either direction. If agricultural productivity is rising very fast, the terms of trade will move in favor of industry, which can then pay a lower product-wage and expand faster. (Since labor is available, expansion does not depend on consumption; more capital can be used to hire proportionately more workers [25].) But if agricultural productivity rises too slowly, rapid growth of manufacturing will be checked by a constantly rising product-wage. Several writers (e.g., [3]) have explored the case of "immiserizing growth," which is an extreme form of this proposition.

It should be noted that nothing in the analysis requires the terms of trade to be constant; movement checks or helps the rate of expansion of the industrial sector, by checking or spurring the rate of growth of profits, but since industry and industrial workers are not more valuable than agriculture or farmers, the analysis has no emotional content. Also, even if the terms of trade are rising, industrial expansion will not necessarily cease. Productivity is rising in the industrial sector, so if real wages (w/c) are constant, the profit margin will not fall unless the terms of trade rise faster than industrial productivity. Real wages cannot be constant if agricultural productivity is rising significantly, since this would be moving the factoral terms of trade against industry. So what will happen to profits in any particular case will depend on a race between agricultural productivity, industrial productivity, real wages (which may rise on their own for exogenous reasons), and the commodity terms of trade. If one makes precise assumptions about these magnitudes one can get precise answers, as Fei and Ranis have done. We will not dwell on this model, since it has nothing to add to their work.

C. Model Three

As mentioned, in most of the world since 1870 the terms of trade are determined increasingly, not by the relative growths of the two sectors of the same economy, but by the world market in which it is possible to buy and sell.

In model three, a rapidly growing industrial sector faced by a too slow agricultural sector is forced to import and to pay for its imports by exporting.

However, in order to export more it may have to lower its prices, thus squeezing its profits. Its real wages, in terms of agricultural products, are fixed by definition. If we take as given the propensity to import and the inflexibility of the agricultural sector, we can see that the possible rate of growth of such an economy is determined by its propensity to export.

Alternatively the country may devalue its currency. This raises (in domestic currency) the price of food and raw materials, and therefore by definition raises money wages. This is the well-known case of "structural inflation," in which a spiral of rising wages and prices is set off.

The open economy may run into trouble even if the agricultural sector is not stagnant. As the economy develops, the product-wage rises. This change in the distribution of income will alter the propensity to import—favorably if the economy specializes in consumer goods, but unfavorably if it specializes in producing capital goods.

This gives us a different aspect of "balanced growth." A country must plan its development in such a way as to be sure that its exports will keep pace with needed imports. If it fails to do this, the rate of growth of output will be constrained by the rate of growth of export earnings. All this is now familiar ground [27, pp. 38–55].

Finally, the behavior of capitalists as profit margins diminish relatively to wages cannot be predicted. The original article drew attention to the temptation to export capital, but Kindleberger [23] has pointed out that dynamic capitalists may react rather by speeding up labor-saving innovations. We are still in the dark as to why entrepreneurs act more creatively in some countries than in others, or at one period rather than another in the history of the same country.

REFERENCES

[1] Bennett, R. L., Surplus Agricultural Labour and Development: Comment, *Amer. Econ. Rev.* (March 1967).

[2] Berry, R. A., and Soligo, R., Rural-Urban Migration, Agricultural Output, and the Supply Price of Labour in a Labour-Surplus Economy, *Oxford Econ. Papers* (July 1968).

[3] Bhagwati, J., International Trade and Economic Expansion, *Amer. Econ. Rev.* (December 1958).
[4] Brown, E. H. Phelps, and Hopkins, S. V., Seven Centuries of the Prices of Consumables, Compared with Builders' Wage Rates, *Economica* (November 1956).
[5] Chenery, H. B., Comparative Advantage and Development Policy, *Amer. Econ. Rev.* (March 1961).
[6] Clapham, J. H., "The Economic Development of France and Germany 1815–1914." Cambridge Univ. Press, London and New York, 1951.
[7] Cumper, G. E., Lewis's Two-Sector Model of Development and the Theory of Wages, *Social Econ. Stud.* (March 1963).
[8] Deane, P., and Cole, W. A., "British Economic Growth 1688–1959." Cambridge Univ. Press, London and New York, 1964.
[9] Dixit, A. K., Optimal Development in the Labour Surplus Economy, *Rev. Econ. Stud.* (January 1968).
[10] Fei, J. C., and Ranis, G., "The Development of the Labour Surplus Economy." Irwin, Homewood, Illinois, 1964.
[11] Fei, J. C., and Ranis, G., Innovation, Capital Accumulation and Economic Development, *Amer. Econ. Rev.* (June 1963).
[12] Frank, C. R., Jr., Urban Unemployment and Economic Growth in Africa, *Oxford Econ. Papers* (July 1968).
[13] Gallman, R. E., Gross National Product in the United States 1834–1909, *in* "Studies in Income and Wealth," Vol. 30, New York, 1966.
[14] Hagen, E. E., "The Economics of Development." Irwin, Homewood, Illinois, 1968.
[15] Hansen, B., and Marzouk, G. A., "Development and Economic Policy in the U.A.R." London, 1965.
[16] Hartwell, R. M., The Rising Standard of Living in England, 1800–1850, *Econ. Hist. Rev.* (April 1961). Also rejoinder to Hobsbawm in *Econ. Hist. Rev.* (August 1963).
[17] Hobsbawm, E. J., The Standard of Living During the Industrial Revolution, *Econ. Hist. Rev.* (August 1963).
[18] Houthakker, H. S., On Some Determinants of Saving in Developed and Underdeveloped Countries, *in* "Problems in Economic Development" (E. A. G. Robinson, ed.). London, 1965.
[19] Johnson, H. G., "International Trade and Economic Growth." London, 1958.
[20] Jorgenson, D. W., The Development of a Dual Economy, *Econ. J.* (June 1961).
[21] Jorgenson, D. W., Testing Alternative Theories of the Development of a Dual Economy, *in* "The Theory and Design of Economic Development" (I. Adelman and E. Thorbecke, eds.) Johns Hopkins Press, Baltimore, 1966.
[22] Jorgenson, D. W., Surplus Agricultural Labour and a Dual Economy, *Oxford Econ. Papers* (November 1967).
[23] Kindleberger, C. P., "Europe's Postwar Growth." Cambridge, Massachusetts, 1967.
[24] Lefeber, L., Planning in a Surplus Labor Economy, *Amer. Econ. Rev.* (June 1968).
[25] Lewis, W. A., Economic Development with Unlimited Supplies of Labor, *Manchester School* (May 1954).
[26] Lewis, W. A., Unlimited Labor: Further Notes, *Manchester School* (January 1958).
[27] Lewis, W. A., "Development Planning." Harper, London and New York, 1966.
[28] Minami, R., The Turning Point in the Japanese Economy, *Quart. J. Econ.* (August 1968).
[29] Okhawa, K., "The Growth Rate of the Japanese Economy since 1878." Tokyo, 1957.
[30] Paglin, M., Surplus Agricultural Labour and Development, *Amer. Econ. Rev.* (September 1965).

[31] Reynolds, L. G., Wages and Employment in a Labour Surplus Economy, *Amer. Econ. Rev.* (January 1965).
[32] Schultz, T. W., "Transforming Traditional Agriculture." New Haven, Connecticut, 1964.
[33] United Nations, "The Growth of World Industry 1953–1965." New York, 1967.
[34] Wellisz, S., Dual Economies, Disguised Unemployment and the Unlimited Supply of Labor, *Economica* (February 1968).

THE CENTER–PERIPHERY SYSTEM 20 YEARS LATER

ANIBAL PINTO and JAN KÑÁKAL

*Economic Commission for Latin America, Santiago, Chile**

I. Introduction: An Idea of the System

From the outset, and particularly in the 1949 Economic Survey [3]—inspired and written by Dr. Raúl Prebisch—the Economic Commission for Latin America (ECLA) paid special attention to the relations between Latin America and the industrialized economies, with particular regard to circumstances prevailing in the 1930s and 1940s.

It is not necessary here to focus on the different aspects of the problem [4], but one is prompted to recall the analytical category that had been coined in examining such relationships, that is, the "Center–Periphery."

The creator of this term remarked some time ago that it was derived from the preoccupation with economic cycles during the immediate postwar periods. From that standpoint, the distinction between Center and Periphery was principally inspired by the unequal role played by the two segments of the world economy in the system's periodic fluctuations: the first playing an active role; the second, a passive or reflexive role.

The approach also stemmed from the difference in the functions assigned to primary exporters and industrial exporters by the international division of labor, whose end result was an unequal distribution of technical progress.

The main hypotheses about the relationships and terms of trade between the Periphery and the Center were established on this basis. They deal with the implications of the substitution of the United States for the United

* The ideas expressed in this paper are those of the authors and do not necessarily reflect the opinions of ECLA.

Kingdom as the system's principal center. We may outline these implications without a formal review of the 1949 Economic Survey as follows:

(i) Latin America's capacity to import from the Center declined continuously in the first postwar period owing to a decrease in exports and more particularly, to worsening in the terms of trade.[1]

Period	Quantum Index of Exports	Price Indices		Terms of Trade	Index of Capacity to Import	
		Export	Import		Total	Per Capita
1930–1934	−8.8	−44.3	−26.7	−24.3	−31.3	−36.6
1935–1939	−2.4	−30.5	−22.1	−10.8	−12.9	−26.3
1940–1944	−7.9	−11.4	11.1	−20.3	−26.7	−44.9
1945–1949	16.6	56.7	49.0	4.4	22.1	−15.6

(ii) The Center's imports depend basically on the rate of its domestic economic development, not on its terms of trade with the Periphery.[2]

(iii) "If because of a decrease in national income or any other restriction, imports into the United States and Great Britain are reduced, the consequent relative fall of import prices does not seem to cause imports to rise again. Rather, this fall of prices is simply a mean of enabling the centres to acquire their imports with a smaller proportion of their money income." (See ECLA [3, p. 34].)

(iv) The relatively high independence of the new U.S. center from external activities[3] has serious implications for the operation of the world economy in general, and particularly for the Center–Periphery relationship.

[1] "The capacity to import depends fundamentally upon the volume of a country's exports and the price relationship between its exports and imports. Of course, foreign capital investments affect import capacity, but the ability to make the interest and amortization payments on these investments also depends on the total volume of exports and their relative prices. We will not consider this question at this stage, however." The percentages of variation of the respective indices (as compared with the 1925–1929 yearly average) were (see ECLA [3, p. 15, and Table 2B]):

[2] "The fluctuation of real income in the United States has been the dominant factor in the rise and fall of imports from Latin America. This correlation is not absolute since in the 1930s imports fluctuated more sharply than income, and over the whole period they revealed minor fluctuations which did not follow the movement of income. There is, however, a definite connexion between these factors which seems to indicate that the fluctuations of income outweigh those of other factors in their influence upon the volume of imports." (See ECLA [3, p. 22].)

[3] The average import coefficient for the period 1945–1949 was only 3% for U.S.A., while the corresponding relation for the United Kingdom reached almost 30% before the Great Depression and 18% in 1945–1949 (see ECLA [3, p. 33]).

Since domestic investment constitutes the dynamic factor determining the course of U.S. economic activity, the responsiveness of its economy to external stimuli—in order to increase exports—as well as its capacity to send them back to the other countries, through greater U.S. imports, seems to be much smaller than those of the previous British center.[4]

(v) The lower external openness of the U.S. economy led to certain changes in the working of the gold standard in the world monetary system. Immediately after World War II, in 1949, the United States held about half of the world's gold and foreign exchange reserves, and almost three-fourths of the gold.[5]

With the magnitude of the gold accumulation in the U.S.A., the world monetary system appeared threatened because of an increasing shortage of dollars.[6]

[4] "Thus, should the cyclical upswing be initiated elsewhere than in Great Britain, or develop there more intensely than in Great Britain, the increased income in the other centre and the extension of this phenomenon to other countries would react favourably on British exports. This increase in British exports would, in turn, quickly stimulate domestic activity and hence produce an increase in the total income of Great Britain, owing to the effect of the increase on consumption as well as on capital investment, first in the export industries and thereafter in other industries. On the other hand, since in the United States exports comprise a much smaller proportion of the national income, as a dynamic element they are not comparable to capital investment, which, as all well know, is of decisive influence in economic activity. Consequently, if capital investments in the United States were scarce, there is little likelihood that increased exports would be able to act as a dynamic factor affecting domestic activity, at least with sufficient vigour to make up for the deficiency of investments. The British centre was not only more sensitive to external impetus than the United States, but also its capacity to return an external impetus was much greater, a fact chiefly due to the difference in magnitude of the respective import coefficients." (See ECLA [3, p. 36].)

[5] See Table III on p. 110.

[6] "The new cyclical centre does not now possess the same power to expel gold. It is less sensitive to an external stimulus than was the British centre and far slower in transmitting it to the rest of the world by means of increased imports; hence the international monetary system works on lines very different from those followed before the First World War. For this and other reasons analysed elsewhere, gold tends to become concentrated in the United States. This leads to the dollar shortage. It should be pointed out, nevertheless, that the problem is partly due to European reconstruction requirements, as well as to inflation. These transitory factors must therefore be recognized together with the persistent tendency of gold to accumulate in the United States. Owing to the weakness of the expelling mechanism, gold tends to be retained in that country, thereby hampering the reconstruction of the monetary reserves of the rest of the world. Little wonder, then, that new regulatory and differential measures are adopted to curb the effects of this phenomenon.

Rather than being the mere effect of a particular monetary policy, these facts have far deeper roots. However favourable to the United States the credit balance of its external accounts may be, the magnitude of this balance is rather small in relation to the national income. The increase in income, accruing from the favourable balance of payments would,

It is evident from the foregoing summary, that the Center–Periphery *perspective* in the original hypotheses of ECLA arose from the standpoint of commercial transactions, that is, from specialization (primary and manufactured goods) either imposed by or deriving from the unequal spread of economic and technical progress. Thus, the characteristics and implications of financial links established by foreign credit and investment were not introduced into the initial analysis. These factors were included shortly afterwards, but the main stress still remained on the importance of this matter for the balance of payments and the saving–investment process [9, Chap. 4].

This clear restriction—which was to be more than offset by discussions which started in the second half of the 1950s—has an obvious explanation in the fact that in the thirties and the forties foreign credit and investment was small in amount and significance. As we shall see later, there are no difficulties in considering financial ties within the analytical approach of the Center–Periphery system. Likewise (although this is not the time to discuss the topic) no difficulties would arise by including in that context the elements considered in other approaches, such as those emphasized in discussions about imperialism, "dependence," or distinction between developed and underdeveloped countries.[7]

It seems to be true, however, that the concepts of "Center" and "Periphery" are subject to some ambiguity, especially if we do not confine ourselves to working with only one dominant pole, and if we separate these concepts from their original link with cyclical movements. Of course, they are not to be identified with the concept of "developed" or "developing" countries. All central nations are obviously developed (because of their income levels and economic structure), but not every developed country is a central one.[8] In today's world, we must also consider groupings of countries (like the European Economic Community) and not only the great national units.

Tentatively we may say that a central economy—in addition to its income level and development structure, and the basically endogenous nature of the dynamism of its growth—is further defined by the essential fact that it is capable of having a *perceptible* influence upon the course of events in peripheral economies—but not vice versa, except for some very special cases and structures and/or in a marginal or incidental way.

Several points pertinent to this matter are worth mentioning. First, the Center's evident capacity to influence the Periphery and/or its various parts

in the light of the foregoing, require considerable time before bringing about an increase in imports and in other items on the debit side of the balance of payments, sufficient, ultimately, to achieve a true balance." (See ECLA [3, p. 42].)

[7] On this point see, among other analyses, Cardozo and Faletto [2].

[8] We may cite, as an illustration, the relationship between Canada's economy and that of the U.S.A.

may or may not be exercised in different degrees by the central units, but it is they who decide whether to do so, as well as when and the means of so doing. Secondly, in general, central area members undoubtedly influence each other, that is, they are also "dependent" to a greater or smaller extent according to their economic capacity and on the internal ties or integration they have within the Center.

In contrast to some periods of the past, e.g., in centuries of unquestionable British hegemony, the Center is now not identified with one single country, but comprises several units (nations or associated countries). Under these circumstances we may speak of the "central area," of the "principal center," and of "subcenters." Nevertheless, for the sake of simplicity, we shall indiscriminately refer to the "Center" (as a dominant group), the principal center, and the rest of the "centers," although these should really be referred to as subcenters.

Finally we must consider a completely new ingredient in the study of the postwar Center–Periphery system: the socialist world. This compels us to discuss its own internal relationships as well as those established with the capitalist Center and the Periphery.[9]

From a methodological viewpoint, the international statistical classification of the world's large areas—usually applied in United Nations surveys—as "developed" and "developing" countries with market economies, and countries with "centrally planned economies" is equivalent to the concepts of Center, Periphery, and socialist countries. Despite the difference between our criteria for "Centers" and developed countries as discussed above, the use of the United Nations classification is justified by the fact that countries and/or groups integrating the Center (U.S.A., EEC, EFTA, and Japan) constitute—as we shall see later—about 90 per cent of the aggregate economic activity of developed areas with market economies.

As previously stated, the analysis of the Center–Periphery system that was started in the 1949 Economic Survey was necessarily based upon the evolution of the two previous decades, and on the characteristics of the world economic framework in the late 1940s. This was the objective basis utilized in analyzing its main aspects and hypotheses.

Having this essential aspect in mind, we now wish to make a brief outline of the most important changes which have occurred in the Center–Periphery system in the last two decades, and particularly those of the 1960s. Our purpose is to examine closely the transformations experienced by the world economy with regard to the Center structure and the ties between the Center and the Periphery. We want, in particular to emphasize the relationship between Latin America and the U.S.A., which continues to be the "principal cyclical

[9] The external economic (not political) impact of the U.S.S.R., the first socialist state, was very small until World War II.

center" in the words of the 1949 Economic Survey.

As a consequence of this preliminary analysis some hypotheses emerge regarding the changes recorded and their effects upon the Center–Periphery system.

As will be seen in Sect. III of this paper, some aspects differ distinctly from the outlook and the prospect as viewed in 1949 while in other essential points the premises formerly elaborated still remain valid.

II. Principal Changes in the World Economic System

From the standpoint of the Center–Periphery system, the complex development of the world economy in the postwar period points to four principal characteristics, namely: (a) a general expansion of the world economy; (b) a polarization of that growth; (c) an internal differentiation of the capitalist center; and (d) the establishment of a socialist center.

In this chapter we shall examine these four characteristics within the framework of some important aspects of domestic economy (gross domestic product, industrial output), and of external economy (exports, foreign investment, exchange reserves), making a distinction between the poles of the system, Center and Periphery, as well as the new socialist center.

A. General Expansion of the World Economy

The postwar period is marked by a high rate of general economic expansion for almost the entire world, which contrasts with the postwar situation in the 1920s.

During the twenty years under consideration, 1950–1970, the world aggregate gross product increased 2.7 times, industrial output 2.8 times, and exports 3.8 times. The higher rate of growth in trade and industrial output with respect to total output shows that the industrialization process has gone on with its development; so, to an even greater extent, has the international division of labor. Furthermore, capital exports, and particularly foreign direct investment by the principal center, also expanded (see Table I).

If we compare world export development during both postwar periods (1921–1938 and 1950–1967), we observe that in the first period, the total increase was only 15 per cent, whereas in the second it reached 250 per cent. Figure 1 shows that world trade developed in a cyclical fashion and with

TABLE I

GENERAL EXPANSION OF THE WORLD ECONOMY BETWEEN 1950 AND 1970[a,b]

	Gross Domestic Product	Industrial Output	Exports	Direct Foreign Investment
World	270	280	385	...
North America	210	250	295	540[c]
South America	250	300	195	...
Europe	260	310	470	...
U.S.S.R.	435	700	740	...
Africa	...	...	305	...
Asia	325	820	440	...

[a] Aggregate volume indices for year 1970: 1950 = 100.
[b] Source: "Statistical Yearbook" [13] Preliminary Evaluation.
[c] The U.S.A. only for the 1950–1968 period in current prices. See ECLA [5].

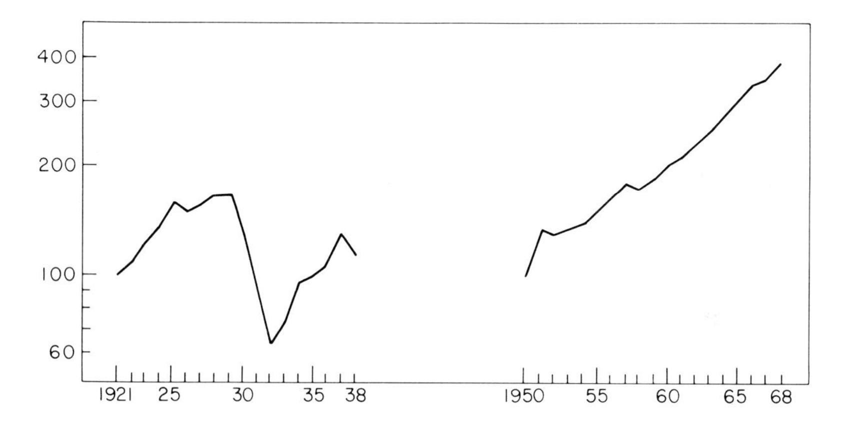

Fig. 1. Growth of world exports in postwar periods. Indices of current values in FOB dollars (semilog scaling).

sharp fluctuations in the first period: in 1929 an increase of 67 per cent is recorded, and in 1932 a decline of 35 per cent in relation to 1921. After World War II the great trade expansion was essentially smooth, with only small declines in 1952 and 1958, and trade always recovered in the following year.

As a matter of fact, the sense of "malaise" in the third quarter of this century allows no simple or dogmatic economic explanations. It requires more complex interpretations, and has been the subject of multiple essays and discussions that we will not consider here.[10] Indeed, the experience of the last decades forces us to be cautious with "catastrophic" forecasts (as those of the early postwar years) as well as with "optimistic" ones. Both have confronted the paradoxical fact of an economic expansion without parallel coexisting with sharp social conflicts and internal and external struggles.

Examining the postwar economic expansion again—and turning back to Table I—we observe it to have been unequal in various parts of the world. This situation, along with its structural qualitative repercussions in the Center–Periphery system, will be discussed later. What we want to point out now is that this inequality *occurs in the relative rates of development in both poles* without contradicting the fact of a general expansion in absolute terms. Thus, North America in the twenty years under consideration had a lower growth rate in gross product and in its industrial output than other large world regions. Notwithstanding, it increased total output and industrial production 2.1 and 2.5 times, respectively, that is, an expansion without precedent over previous periods.[11] The same may be said for Latin America, whose lower relative export increase still led to its doubling in the period analyzed (see again Table I).

Having now observed the prime characteristic of postwar development—the general expansion of the world economy—we shall now look in more detail at some of its aspects.

B. Center–Periphery: Polarized Expansion

First, we must observe that this global phenomenon is distinguished by the fact that economic progress—always in relative terms—has been concentrated in one part of the system, the Center, thus leading to an increasing gap between the Center and the Periphery. Such a polarization is present in the three main dimensions we are to observe here, namely: (i) in the relative economic capacity of the respective pole either domestically or externally, and particularly in "per capita" terms; (ii) in the zonal and sectoral flows of trade; (iii) in the distribution of foreign investment; and (iv) in the accumulation of international reserves.

[10] Marcuse, Galbraith, Garaudy, the Yugoslavian and Italian "neomarxists," Mandel, Silberman, etc., are just a few names involved in the "great debate."

[11] We have to take into account that the United States economic growth starts from a much greater base than, say, the USSR's which, in turn, achieved a much higher rate than that of the United States. On the other hand, we may observe that in the most dynamic period of the U.S.A. economy (1870/1–1913) the rise in the real product per capita was 2.2 per cent yearly, while in the first part of the sixties (1960–1966) that rate was 3.1 per cent (see Fores [10]).

1. Relative Economic Capacity

In light of the changes that occurred in the postwar period in the relative economic capacity of both poles, we may visualize some of the main circumstances.

The Periphery's total gross domestic product for the period 1950–1968 experienced an average annual growth rate of 4.8 per cent, that is, a little higher than that of the Center, which attained 4.4 per cent (see Table II). However, this small difference disappears if we consider the associated demographic increases. From this standpoint, as should be clear, the Periphery has a much smaller per capita rate than that of the Center, 2.5 and 3.3 per cent, respectively. Moreover, in the sixties, the decade of international effort "for the development of the underdeveloped " the gap between "rich" and "poor" countries became larger, since the Center's economic expansion almost doubled that of the Periphery in per capita terms (see again Table II). Therefore the Periphery's share in the system's global product, which had been only 17 per cent in 1963, was reduced even further toward the end of the sixties, though almost three quarters of world population was living there (excluding socialist countries).

The Latin American situation does not differ substantially from that of the rest of the peripheral areas. Its aggregate growth is slightly higher but, on the other hand, it falls with greater intensity in "per capita" terms owing to higher rates of demographic growth.

2. International Trade

The degree of polarization of the system is even more significant if we consider international trade. Between 1948–1968, in global terms, the average annual rate of increase of the Center's exports is much higher than that of the Periphery, 7.9 and 4.8 per cent, repectively (and only 3.2 per cent for Latin America). The role of the Periphery in the system's overall trade having reached its peak in the first postwar period (32 per cent in 1948) it was thereafter reduced to only 21 per cent, that is, less than in the prewar period, when it accounted for 28 per cent. The Latin American position turns out to be still weaker: it declined from 12 per cent in 1948 to 6 per cent in 1968 (see indicators 2(a) and 2(b) in Table II).

The increasing polarization is closely related to the development of integration and the sectoral composition of trade in each of the two universes.

Intrazonal trade in goods, that is, the commodity interchange among economies constituting each pole, experienced a great increase in the central area

TABLE II

POLARIZED EXPANSION OF THE CENTER–PERIPHERY SYSTEM[a]

Indicator	Period/ Year	Center[b]	Periphery[c]	Latin America	Total System
1. Gross Domestic Product					
(a) Weight in per cent	1963	83	17	6	100
(b) Annual average rate:					
Total	1950–1968	4.4	4.8	5.2	4.5
	1960–1968	5.0	4.8	5.0	5.0
Per capita	1950–1968	3.3	2.5	2.4	2.5
	1960–1968	4.0	2.3	2.0	2.8
2. Exports					
(a) Total export growth, average annual rate	1948–1968	7.9	4.8	3.2	7.1
	1958–1968	9.0	5.9	4.0	8.3
(b) Percentage share of pole in system's total exports	1938	72	28	8	100
	1948	68	32	12	100
	1958	74	26	8	100
	1968	79	21	6	100
(c) Intrazonal trade in per cent of the pole's total export	1948	64	29	9	—
	1968	76	20	11	—
(d) Manufactures[d] as percentage of pole's total exports	1955	64	13	9	49
	1968	74	22	17	63
3. U.S.A. Direct Investment					
(a) Total distribution between poles	1950	48	49	38	100
	1969	67	28	16	100
(b) Manufacturing activities as percentage of total investment	1950	52	15	17	32
	1969	51	26	31	42
4. International Gold and Foreign Exchange Reserves					
Total distribution between poles	1949	85	15	5	100
	1969	79	21	6	100

[a] Sources: "U.N. Statistical Yearbook," 1965, 1969; *U.N. Monthly Bulletin of Statistics*, March 1961, 1962, and 1970 and U.S. Department of Commerce: *Survey of Current Business*, several issues; International Monetary Fund: *International Financial Statistics*, 1954 and 1970.

[b] Developed countries according to U.N. classification.

[c] Developing countries according to U.N. classification.

[d] Chemical products, machinery and transport equipment and other manufactured products (groups 5–8 in "SITC" classification).

whereas that conducted among peripheral countries declined perceptibly. If we consider the total Center exports, we determine that the share of intrazonal exports rose from 64 to 76% between 1948 and 1968 (see Table II, indicator 2(c)). On the other hand, the lower level of economic relationships among peripheral economies led to a fall from 29 to 20% in percentages representing internal interchange between the years mentioned. In this respect Latin American development was slightly different, since there was some progress in regional integration. Whereas in 1948 only 9 per cent of total exports were directed to other countries of the area, in 1968 this figure was 11 per cent.

The Center's progressively closer trade relationship is also related to its concentration in the interchange of manufactured products. In other words, the increased share of central economies in world trade was basically due to the commerce in manufactured products among industrial countries. Regarding the Periphery, the opposite conclusion may be drawn: its smaller share in world interchange was principally due to its continued specialization in the sale of primary goods, though there have been some significant changes in this field.

The above may be verified from the information displayed in Table II, where we observe (see indicator 2(d)) that manufactured exports from central countries rose from 64 per cent in 1955 to 74 per cent in 1968 as a proportion of total volume. In fact, between these years the interchange of industrial goods increased at a rate of 9.6 per cent per annum.

In the Periphery, there was also a perceptible rise in the export value of manufactured products, which climbed from 13 per cent in 1955 to 22 per cent in 1968 (the respective figures for Latin America are 9 per cent and 17 per cent). At any rate, this essential difference between a 22 per cent and 74 per cent share of manufactures in exports at the end of the sixties makes clear the respective situation of the division of labor between the respective poles. It is necessary to realize that the share of manufactured products in the exports of each area corresponds almost exactly to that existing in their intrazonal trade, which in 1968 was 20 per cent and 76 per cent for the Periphery and the Center, respectively (see indicators 2(c) and 2(d) in Table II). Incidentally, it should be added that there seems to be a reciprocal and dynamic relationship between industrialization and integration, as experience indicates—especially in European associations and those of socialist countries: greater integration has contributed to the deepening and acceleration of industrialization, and vice versa: the latter having been decisive in the fostering of the integration processes.

3. Foreign Investment and International Reserves

The polarization of growth seen in international trade and its sectoral composition is also present in a third dimension: the distribution of foreign investment, which is mostly attached to developed countries and to the industrial activity. To illustrate, we can refer to the regional and sectoral distribution of U.S.A. direct investment abroad.[12]

With regard to the first point, it is possible to verify from Table II that the central economies' share in the gross U.S.A. investment increased from 48 to 67 per cent between 1950 and 1969, with a consequent decrease in the share corresponding to underdeveloped areas, particularly Latin America, where a decline from 38 to 16 per cent was registered during those years.

On the other hand, considering the sectoral allocation of capital it is observed that manufacturing activities, which absorbed 32 per cent of total investments in 1950, have increased their share to 42 per cent in 1969 (see indicators 3(a) and 3(b) in Table II).

Finally, we should mention the evolution and changes that occurred in the volume and allocation of international reserves (that is, gold and foreign exchanges).

If the 1949 and 1969 situations are compared, we observe an increase in the world total of such reserves from 50.6 to 70.2 billion dollars, that is, a 39 per cent increase. As far as the Periphery is concerned, its absolute holdings of reserves rose from 7.7 to 14.6 billion dollars, which means an increase of 88 per cent. Thus, the share of peripheral countries in total reserves has risen from 15 per cent in 1949 to 21 per cent in 1969 (see again Table II, indicator 4).

This is the only indicator which evolves to show a more positive balance for the Periphery at the end of the period. Of course, this does not compensate for the points stressed above. On the other hand, there exists a highly significant counterpart to this reverse shift, namely, the substantial rise of indebtedness in the peripheral economies. In this respect and as far as Latin America is concerned, it may be recalled that the imputed total external debt has increased more than seven times between 1950 and 1968: from 2.2 to 16.4 billion dollars in those years [6].

In short, the polarized expansion of the Center–Periphery system, i.e., the world economy's expansion, has taken the place of a wide variety of interrelated levels: the growth of output per person, the share in world trade, the share in manufactured exports, and the distribution of private capital investments. These changes have widened the gap between Center and Periphery with a relative marginalization of the latter. However, the Periphery seems to have become much more dependent on the Center in many basic aspects, which we shall examine later.

[12] The scanty data on direct investment of other central economies forces us to restrict the discussion to the U.S.A. investment. We will return to the topic in connection with the considerable absolute and relative increase of capital investment by certain European countries—especially West Germany—and Japan.

C. Internal Differentiation of the Center

The third principal characteristic of postwar economic expansion consists in the internal differentiation of the central group.

Despite the fact that the U.S.A.'s dominant postion in the capitalist world—derived from the displacement of Great Britain as a result of the Second World War—is still in force, it is no less true than the fact that in the last twenty years we can perceive—especially in the sixties—a clear tendency toward the relative decline of U.S.A. economic hegemony. This is due to a more dynamic expansion of other centers or subcenters, namely, Western Europe—principally the European Economic Community—and Japan. Extending the definition of the world economic system, this differentiation is also evident in the development of a new socialist center (or system), which we shall discuss later.

The above outlined transformations may be verified using the same criteria applied to the analysis of the previous section.

The extent to which the principal center still holds its absolute predominance is evident if we consider such indicators as aggregate output and direct investment, in which the U.S.A. still represents more than half of the total for developed countries, although, a dynamic approach also reveals the changes we have pointed out above. The relative decline reveals itself in nearly all foreign trade figures, in total private capital flows, and in the distribution of world gold and foreign exchange reserves (see Table III.) In the following paragraphs we shall examine each of these aspects.

1. Production and Trade

If we look at the evolution of growth of gross domestic product and industrial output, it is evident that the European Economic Community and Japan have surpassed the U.S.A. The average annual rates of expansion of GNP in the period 1950–1968 were 5.3, 9.9, and 3.7 per cent[13], respectively; and 6.5, 13.6, and 4.1 per cent[13] for industrial output. The EEC relative advantage was achieved primarily in the fifties, whereas between 1960 and 1968 the differences decreased. (See indicators 1 and 2 in Table III.) The EFTA showed an even smaller growth rate than that of the U.S.A. especially because of the United Kingdom's serious postwar economic problems. At any rate. in the later sixties, however, the U.S.A. remained the main center, in spite of its lesser relative growth.

The differentiation of the Center was much more considerable insofar as postwar trade is concerned. Between 1948 and 1968 the growth rate of exports

[13] For the U.S.A. 1953–1968.

TABLE III INTERNAL DIFFERENTIATION OF THE CAPITALIST CENTER[a]

Indicator	Period/ Year	U.S.A.	EEC	EFTA	Japan	Developed Countries Total
1. Gross Domestic Product						
(a) Weight	1963	52	22	12	6	100
(b) Average annual rate	1950–1968	3.7[b]	5.3	3.2	9.9[b]	4.4
	1960–1968	4.7	4.9	3.4	10.8	5.0
2. Industrial Output						
(a) Weight	1963	52[c]	24	12	6	100
(b) Average annual rate	1950–1968	4.1[b]	6.5	3.8	13.6[b]	5.1
	1960–1968	5.4	5.7	3.8	13.3	5.8
3. Exports						
(a) Total exports average annual rate	1948–1968	5.1	12.0	6.1	21.6	7.9
	1958–1968	6.8	10.6	6.9	16.3	9.0
(b) Center share in per cent of total exports of developed countries	1938	20	(29)	(27)	7	100
	1948	34	18	26	1	100
	1958	25	33	23	4	100
	1968	20	38	19	8	100
(c) Intrazonal trade in per cent of center's total exports	1948	22[d]	28	17	—	64
	1968	35[d]	45	24	—	76
4. Direct Foreign Investment						
(a) Accumulated investment in per cent	1966	57	15	22	1	100[e]
(b) Average annual net flows (outflows −, inflows +) in billions of dollars	1960–1962	−2.5	+0.3[f]	−0.2[g]	—	—
	1963–1965	−3.8	+0.7[f]	−0.3[g]	—	—
	1966–1968	−4.5	+0.5[f]	−0.3[g]	−0.1	—
5. Total Private Capital Average annual net flows (outflows −, inflows +) in billions of dollars (EEC, EFTA and Japan combined)	1960–1962	−3.5		+1.1		—
	1963–1965	−4.8		+1.7		—
	1966–1968	−3.3		−1.7		—
6. Gold and Foreign Exchange (distribution in %)						
(a) Gold and foreign exchange	1938	53	23[h]	10[g]	1	100[i]
	1949	48	11[h]	3[g]	—	100[i]
	1969	21	37[h]	4[g]	4	100[i]
(b) Gold	1938	56	23[h]	11[g]	1	100[i]
	1949	71	10[h]	4[g]	—	100[i]
	1969	30	45[h]	4[g]	1	100[i]

[a] Sources: GDP, Industrial Output and Exports: see Table II; accumulated direct investment, based on S. H. Robock and K. Simonds computation in *Columbia Journal of World Business*, May–June 1970; direct investment and total private capital flows: "U.N. Statistical Yearbook," 1962, 1966, 1968, 1969. Gold and foreign exchange: International Monetary Fund, *International Financial Statistics*, September 1954 and May 1970.

[b] 1953–1968. [c] North America. [d] U.S.A. and Canada.

[e] Includes the U.S.A., Canada, EEC and EFTA countries, and Japan.

[f] Germany, France, Netherlands, and Italy. [g] United Kingdom.

[h] Continental Europe (Austria, Belgium, Denmark, France, Germany, Italy, Netherlands, Norway, Sweden, and Switzerland). [i] World reserves (excluding socialist countries).

more than doubled in the EEC and was four times greater in Japan than in the U.S.A. Therefore, the U.S.A. share in total exports of developed countries decreased from 34 to 20 per cent between 1948 and 1968. At the same time that corresponding to the EEC and Japan together rose from 19 per cent in 1948 to 46 per cent in 1968, that is, a share more than double that of the U.S.A.

Although postwar changes in the trade position of the various centers are substantial, it must be recalled that to some extent, they involve a reestablishment of the pre-World War II situation. Indeed, the relationship of the two trade positions, with the U.S.A., on one side, and Western Europe[14] and Japan, on the other, was 20 and 63 per cent in 1938, and 20 and 65 per cent in 1968. In short, after two decades of rapid changes, a structure similar to the prewar one was established.

2. Foreign Investment and International Reserves

With regard to direct foreign investment, it has already been noted that the U.S.A. center maintained its hegemonic position. Furthermore, U.S.A. direct investment outflows had experienced a perceptible growth. For instance, from an annual average of 2.5 billion dollars in 1960–1962 they rose to 4.5 billion dollars in 1966–1968. The main EEC countries (Germany, France, Netherlands, and Italy) showed a net inflow in direct investment in the sixties especially from U.S.A. sources (see again Table III, indicator 4(b)). The United Kingdom's net direct investment outflows—and even more those of Japan—were insignificant in relation to those of the U.S.A.

As we know, the expansion of the U.S.A.'s foreign direct investments—significantly enlarged by local capital attraction in recipient countries—is related to the increase in the activities of international corporations which, in a number of cases bring the conglomerate company to the international level and represent, by their sales volume a sort of "third world power."[15]

If we employ another perspective and examine overall international financial transactions and their effects on the U.S.A. domestic economy itself, we once more recognize a tendency toward the Center's differentiation and the relative weakening of its position.

With regard to total private capital flows, that is, including portfolio investment and other types of financial capital, it is useful to compare the relationship among the five major European countries[16] and Japan, on one side, and the U.S.A., on the other. From this standpoint, we may verify that in the years 1963–1965 net private capital flows from abroad were still positive,

[14] Countries presently integrating EEC and EFTA.

[15] See the well-known book of J. J. Servan-Schreiber, "The American Challenge" [11]. See also the recent ECLA Survey [7].

[16] Germany, France, Netherlands, Italy, and the United Kingdom.

e.g., there was a net capital inflow (of 1.7 billion dollars), for the first group of countries, and negative (that is, net capital outflow) for the United States (of 4.8 billion dollars). The situation changed radically in the second half of the sixties when, in the 1966–1968 period the (average) totals were −1.7 and −3.3 billion dollars (see indicator 5 in Table III). This means that European centers and Japan became net exporters of private capital, competing with the United States.

These recent developments can be seen even more clearly if we contrast some rates of expansion of capital flows to developing countries. In a recent survey we read that "United States' direct and portfolio investments [reinvestment included] in developing countries has grown at an average annual rate of 15.4 per cent between 1964 and 1968. Japan's in the same period has expanded by 32 per cent, and Western Germany's at 50 per cent yearly" [7].

One of the illustrative aspects of the growing influence of European centers in the world's capital market is the importance of the "Eurodollar" market, which has achieved relative autonomy from the main center. The "Eurodollar market" serves the U.S.A. capital market as an important financial source of its foreign investments.

The growth of investment from other centers in the U.S.A. also deserves our attention. The total foreign investment in this country was only about 8 billion dollars in 1950 but rose to 32 billion dollars in 1967, thus representing almost 40 per cent of the corresponding U.S.A. foreign investment in the rest of the capitalist world countries [12].

The relative decrease in the U.S.A. center's hegemonic weight may also be noted in the redistribution of reserves in the world monetary system. Back in 1949, the U.S.A. held approximately three quarters of world gold and nearly half of total monetary reserves. In the last twenty years, the continuous gold outflow from the U.S.A. has diminished its gold reserves to approximately half the earlier level, that is, to 30 per cent of the world's gold. Its share of total gold and foreign exchange reserves has declined even more, to just 21 per cent. It is obvious that the rest of the centers were the beneficiaries. The share of continental Europe in world gold and foreign exchange rose from 11 per cent in 1949 to 37 per cent in 1969, that is, it nearly doubled the U.S.A. share (see indicator 6 in Table III).

The redistribution of gold and foreign exchange within the Center was derived principally from the larger external openness of the main power, the U.S.A. Although the U.S.A. import coefficient held at about 5 per cent in the sixties,[17] the international corporate expansion became decisive, as we have

[17] We should not forget that the coefficient's numerical stability veils an extraordinary and sustained increase of imports in this period, which might be considered as an "absolute openness."

already discussed, and particularly the U.S.A.'s political, military, and economic involvements. Thus, the U.S.A. net unilateral transfers—namely, military gifts, commodities, services, and others—represented about 4 billion dollars annually throughout the postwar period, exceeding the positive balances on commercial account. In conclusion, we observe a continuous balance of payments deficit and a persistent gold outflow from the United States.

D. Changes in the World Economic System: The Socialist Countries

The postwar changes in the Center must also be appraised from the broad standpoint of world economic system, since the constitution of a new social system stands out in the early postwar period. We are referring to the socialist countries.[18] This is no doubt a transcendental change insofar as it opens up another dimension in a previously bipolar order of an industrialized capitalist world and an underdeveloped one.[19]

It is evident from Table IV that the socialist countries' share appears to be much greater in world output than in world trade.[20] The socialist share in world output was 26 per cent in 1963, whereas the capitalist Center and the Periphery shared a 61 and 13 per cent share, respectively. During the postwar period, the socialist area has shown a more dynamic rate of growth than that of the rest of the world, doubling that corresponding to the capitalist Center. However, a certain retardation in the expansion of the socialist economies is apparent throughout the sixties, during which the domestic growth rates of these three areas approach one another more closely (see indicators 1 and 2 in Table IV).

During the sixties the share of all socialist countries in world trade was nearly three times smaller than that in world output. Although this share increased from 6 to 11 per cent between 1948 and 1958, it stabilizes at the same relative level at the end of the last decade. We may further state that this percentage is equivalent to that corresponding to the same geographical area (the present socialist countries) in the prewar period.

[18] Owing to the nature of this essay, we will not go into detail here on the well-known political and social aspects of the origin and development of this new world system. We refer only to its economic relationships.

[19] It has already been made clear that the U.S.S.R.'s external economic weight was very small in the prewar period.

[20] Of course, given the known differences of statistical concepts in the capitalist and socialist worlds, the comparisons made here have a very relative and approximate character. The scanty availability of data concerning Asian socialist countries should be noted. This latter fact actually forces us to limit the concept of "socialist countries" principally to those of Eastern Europe—including, of course, the U.S.S.R.

TABLE IV

CHANGES IN THE WORLD ECONOMIC SYSTEM: THE SOCIALIST COUNTRIES[a]

Indicator	Period/ Year	Center[b]	Periphery[c]	Socialist Countries	World
1. Gross Domestic Product					
(a) Weight in per cent	1963	61	13	26[d]	100[e]
(b) Average annual rate	1950–1968	4.4	4.8	8.0[d]	5.4[e]
	1960–1968	5.0	4.8	6.7[d]	5.4[e]
2. Industrial Output					
(a) Weight in per cent	1963	63	8	29[d]	100[e]
(b) Average annual rate	1950–1968	5.1	6.9	10.3[d]	6.4[e]
	1960–1968	5.8	6.7	8.7[d]	6.8[e]
3. Exports					
(a) Average annual rate	1948–1968	7.9	4.8	10.5	7.4
	1958–1968	9.0	5.9	8.4	8.3
(b) Regional share as percentage of world exports	1938	65	25	(10)	100
	1948	64	30	6	100
	1958	66	23	11	100
	1968	71	18	11	100
(c) Intrazonal trade as percentage of total regional exports	1948	64	29	44	—
	1968	76	20	62	—
(d) Manufactures as percentage of total regional exports	1955	64	13	49	49
	1968	74	22	62	63

[a] Source: See Table II.
[b] Developed countries under U.N. classification.
[c] Developing countries.
[d] Eastern Europe.
[e] Excluding China, North Korea, Mongolia, and North Vietnam.

These relationships are much different from those prevailing in the other two parts of the Center–Periphery system. Thus the socialist complex appears to be much less "integrated" in the world economy than the developed capitalist Center and Periphery, whose trade shares are in both cases larger than their world output shares (see again Table IV, indicators 1(a) and 3(b)).

As we can see, the relatively "closed" character of postwar socialist development derives from its high degree of internal integration. The intrazonal trade of socialist countries increased its share in the *total* exports of the area from 44 per cent in 1948 to 62 per cent in 1968, thus approaching the degree of internal coherence of the much more extensive and varied capitalist Center and substantially surpassing the respective levels of both European communities.[21]

On the other hand, the high level of trade integration within the socialist center became in general an important stimulus to industrialization and particularly of "trade industrialization." The manufacturing share in the socialist countries' total exports rose from 49 per cent in 1955 to 62 per cent in 1968, generating a substantial change in their international division of labor (see indicators 3(c) and (d) in Table IV).

We shall later consider other aspects of the new socialist Center's relationships with the Periphery.

E. Some General Conclusions about the Expansion, Polarization, and Differentiation of the System

What has been stated thus far enables us to draw some conclusions about the changes that occurred in certain particular aspects, and to visualize some important differences in the situations which formed the basis of ECLA's original hypotheses about the Center–Periphery system.[22]

The most relevant points are the following:

(i) The world economy was characterized in the 1950s and 1960s—and contrary to the situation after World War I—by a considerable, continuous, and general expansion in every principal area.

(ii) At the same time the polarization of the Center–Periphery system was stressed. The distance between both poles of the system increased along the "domestic" as well as along the external lines of the relationship.

(iii) The developed capitalist Center experienced a considerable internal differentiation. Although the principal economy (U.S.A.) kept its hegemonic position, mainly in aggregate output and direct foreign investment, its role in world trade and finance declined sharply, and that of European Centers and Japan increased concurrently.

(iv) In the broader sense of the "world economic system," differentiation of the Center is extended with the entrance of the socialist world, which has a high degree of internal integration and a relatively larger share in world output than in world trade.

If these rough summary elements are compared with the 1949 ECLA hypotheses, we can notice the coincidence of ECLA's diagnosis with the

[21] The percentage of intrazonal trade was 45 per cent for EEC and 24 per cent for EFTA in 1968 (see Table III).

[22] See Sect. I.

concentration of technical progress and its fruits in the Center and in the Periphery's relative backwardness (which we shall examine in the next section).

On the other hand, the first hypotheses were certainly somewhat pessimistic insofar as the dynamism and regularity of the later expansion were concerned. Finally, it seems to be clear that the tendency toward the Center's internal differentiation and especially the decrease of the U.S.A.'s hegemonic weight were not anticipated by the forecasts (and not only those of ECLA).

In a more extensive paper we shall examine and assemble some outstanding hypotheses about the capitalist Center's behavior in the last 25 years, when it became so different from the past with regard to the points discussed. Nevertheless, it would be useful to draw attention to the following instances:

(a) The "Cold War" and the peaceful competition–coexistence between the capitalist Center and the socialist world;

(b) Technological innovations renewing or establishing alternative "advanced" sectors in the centers, especially in the U.S.A., which are closely related to military requirements;

(c) The adoption of well-known Keynesian-type policies (full employment, government countercyclical monetary and fiscal policies, etc.) which, among other things, have caused the emergence or enlargement of a "mass market";

(d) The increasing capitalist Center integration, wherein international corporations play a decisive role, accounting both for domestic output as well as international trade and, particularly, intrazonal trade.

It seems necessary to recall that colonial or neocolonial "exactions" constitute a subordinate aspect of the Center's dynamization in that period, although they might have been significant for certain peripheral countries. The best evidence for this, which contradicts known arguments,[23] may be found in the extraordinary development of those Center areas lacking colonial bases, e.g., Japan, Italy, France, and Netherlands.

This evidence confirms the obvious fact that the Center's expansion and working depend fundamentally on endogenous elements. In Marxist terms, it depends on the transformations in production forms.

Obviously, changes recorded in the world economy affected the Center–Periphery system operation and relationships. In the next chapter we shall discuss some views of the subject and confront them with the pertinent hypotheses of the 1949 Economic Survey.

We shall start with a general assessment of some of the mutations in the Center–Periphery relationship, then later discuss briefly the subject from

[23] For instance, in a recent study, it is asserted that the capitalist system "exists and develops thanks to an international structural relationship which *generates development in certain countries* and, simultaneously, the underdevelopment of others. This is the reason for its permanence" Caputo and Pizarro [1]. (The italics added.)

certain more particular angles, and, finally, conclude with a reference to the "intraperipheral" structure and relationships.[24]

III. Principal Changes in the Working of the Center–Periphery System

A. Marginalization and "Dependent Integration" of the Periphery

The Center–Periphery system in its "classical" stage operated on the basis of neat and congruent relationships. These may be conceived of as a circular process binding two flows. On one side, the Center-oriented primary goods flow; on the other, the Periphery-oriented industrial goods flow. Capital flows move along this connection mainly increasing the Periphery's export and import capacity. These capital flows were compensated for with a part of export incomes. Insofar as the main center (Great Britain) expanded its basic imports and capital transfers, it provided resources so that the Periphery, deferring its manufactured purchases, could pay the metropolis for its investment.

Transformations taking place in the last two decades have affected the Center–Periphery relationship to a very substantial degree. They seem to derive from two parallel and contradicting processes that might be called relative marginalization and "dependent integration."

With regard to the first, it seems evident that the link between both poles of the capitalist system has lost importance on the whole, despite the absolute increase in all the variables discussed, which are the effects of a considerable global expansion of the system.

In this context, it is possible to state that an approximately similar world concentration and marginalization process has taken place. It was already implicit in the ECLA's pioneer approach (especially, as far as the Periphery marginalization is concerned) and anticipated the national situations that occurred in many developing countries [9]. In other words: the Periphery, for the reasons advanced by ECLA (low income-elasticity of demand for primary products, technological substitution, etc.) [4], has gradually become less "necessary" to the Center as a supplier and as a market, both for goods and services and for capital.

It must be noted that marginalization within what Prebisch called the "old scheme" of interchange implied the continuation of the deterioration of price relationships (terms of trade)—the most obvious and perhaps the main "exaction mechanism" working on incomes in the Periphery (see Table V).

[24] The analysis of these topics has a very preliminary character and should be considered as an introduction to a more detailed study, being presently worked out by the authors.

TABLE V

TERMS OF TRADE[a,b]

		Center	Periphery
Terms of Trade Relationship	1960–1969	111	90
Export Quantum	1960–1969	132	156
Export Purchasing power	1960–1969	147	136

[a] Source: *U.N. Monthly Bulletin of Statistics*, November 1967, 1969, and 1970
[b] Average annual indices: 1955–1959 = 100.

The above situation must be considered together with another force working in the opposite direction: parts of the Periphery and of Latin America (generally the more developed or dynamic) have gradually been integrated into the central system by means of capital movements and, especially, by direct investment oriented to satisfy its domestic markets.

This process, which to some extent counteracts that of marginalization, might be called "dependent integration."[25] This term is justified mainly by the substantial differences found in comparing this phenomenon with that stemming from the Center's own advancing cohesion. The dependent condition arises from several considerations which demonstrate the inequality involved in the relationship between the Periphery and the Center. We may observe the following:

(a) The mere fact of structural specialization in primary products reduces—for many well-known reasons—the relative bargaining power of the Periphery in world trade and in its relationships with the Center;

(b) The new modes and orientation in foreign private investment represent (apart from the resource transfers, to which we shall refer later) an obvious diminution in the national decision-making power vital for development;

(c) Even the system of financing, insofar as it derives from or increases external indebtedness in the Periphery, has negative effects on the autonomy of national policy;

(d) Enlargement and diversification in the field of foreign ownership and management sharpens the problem of technological subordination, which is no longer confined to the export sector, as in the past;

(e) The above realities are translated into other means of subjection at the political, military, etc. levels.

A remarkable dissociation and a clear difference from the old scheme have gradually emerged from both processes we have described. Thus, the Periphery (or important areas of it) has lost its traditional role as primary supplier

[25] These observations in no way attempt to cover the many general considerations on dependence. In this respect, see the work of Cardozo and Faletto [2].

for the Center although, at the same time, it has an increasing significance as an outlet for capital investment (yet this may be not relevant *vis à vis* the nexus between centers).

As we can see, this imbalance nurtures an important contradiction between the servicing and/or repayment of that capital (mostly generated by benefits created within the countries instead of net transferences *from* the Centers) and the actual possibilities of achieving it. Contrary to the old model, primary exports do not grow *pari-passu* with the increasing foreign claims and other import needs. In this context, all we need to consider is the relationship between capital inflows and remittances of profits, which showed a negative balance for Latin America of about 10 billion dollars in the 1960–1968 period. Total net payments in profits and interest reached 18 billion dollars between 1960 and 1969. The relationship between these transfers and export incomes went from 12.4 to 15.3 per cent between the decades of the fifties and the sixties. From a broader perspective, in the late sixties, total capital services represented percentages which are closer to or even greater than 35 per cent. For some countries, like Mexico and Chile, they exceeded 50 per cent.[26]

In this context, the discernible options are clear: if certain conditions in the balance of payments do not so permit "nonrealizable" services will tend to be transformed into new asset purchases of the central country. If the transfer is feasible (as in countries of easy convertibility, e.g., Mexico or Venezuela) the "current" leakage will increase in relation to the relatively less dynamic export incomes.

Some "realizable" possibilities could likewise be created through "nontraditional" exports, either oriented toward economies with remittance facilities, or (this being mostly difficult) toward the Center. In this context, we have to analyze the important and rising share of international corporations in the region's "nontraditional" exports.

Although we are not here in a position to describe and/or systematize the present framework's implications,[27] it seems evident that this development does not fit within "traditional" treatments. In short, new contradictory relationships characterize the Center–Periphery system's *general* model, although it is clear that we have just given emphasis to those emanating in the last decades from developed capitalist centers (particularly the U.S.A.) and Latin America.

[26] See ECLA [4, 6]. To some extent, payments recorded might be considered as the other great "exaction mechanism" (along with the terms of trade). This has been noticed in some papers, but they obviously should not be taken as a whole because of their different natures, e.g. we would err in estimating as such, for instance, the interest paid on development loans granted by the World Bank or the IDB. And thus there are a number of different situations we should distinguish and evaluate.

[27] Some of them have been discussed in "Diagnóstico, estructura y esquemas de desarrollo en América Latina," Third Part, FLACSO, 1970, mimeo.

B. Center–Periphery Relationships from More Particular Standpoints

The Center–Periphery relationship must also be analyzed from the viewpoint of relations between various centers and areas of the Periphery.

With this in mind, some "vertical" associations that have taken shape in the postwar period can be observed; they correspond to previous prevailing situations (e.g., colonial relations). Among them we may point out those existing between Europe and Africa, the U.S.A. and Latin America, Japan and Asia, and the Soviet Union and countries of the European socialist sphere.

1. Relationships with the Capitalist Center

With regard to the first, we know the special connections existing between several Western European countries (or their regional associations) and different African economies, which in many cases were their former colonies. Although with different and enlightened patterns, these relationships are still generally established to expand the traditional interchange between primary products and manufactures, aided with preferential treatment in European markets and with capital transfers.

This scheme repeats itself as far as the U.S.A.–Latin America relationship is concerned, albeit with some noteworthy differences. One of them is that, in general, there has been no preferential treatment as in the European case, partly because of U.S.A.'s opposition, but to a larger extent because of Latin American distrust of establishing ties which would enlarge its dependence on the regional superpower. As we know, the Latin American position on this matter has been that of obtaining special treatment for the *whole* Periphery and in *every* center.

Trade between both poles has been constrained of late, as much as in the past, by the U.S.A.'s dual role of primary goods producer and exporter. To this we must add the multiple and varied protectionist tariffs applied to Latin American exports of higher competitive power, which are only occasionally relaxed by that country.

These and other circumstances have determined a characteristic trade pattern between the U.S.A. and Latin America as a whole, the main feature of which is that our countries (in relative terms) export to the U.S.A. less than the volume they import from that country. This is caused, to a large extent, by both the influence of U.S.A. businesses in the area and because of financial commitments.[28] Latin America's usually unfavorable balance of trade with

[28] For instance, in the late sixties nearly 40 per cent of Latin American imports came from the U.S.A.; however, only a little more than 33 per cent of her exports went to this country.

the U.S.A. is, or has to be, compensated with positive balances with Europe and Japan. At the same time, this is a significant Latin American contribution to the U.S.A.'s balance of payments, along with those involving capital transactions. This structure also limits the Latin American ability to take advantage of opportunities in other Centers.

Finally, we shall recall the previous point concerning the nature and implications of the U.S.A.'s new type of investment in the area. These characterize the system's relationships with respect to both the traditional scheme as well as the (still) dominant one in the Europe–Africa relationship.

It is not necessary to recall that these general observations conceal sharp differences concerning the specific situations of various Latin American countries. In Mexico, Argentina, Uruguay, Venezuela, or Chile, the set of relationships and their implications appear with their own features, although we do not believe that the outline characterizing the whole may differ or disappear. However, a more detailed analysis would force us to describe some peculiarities.

Japan's position in the Center–Periphery general system differs considerably from that existing in the prewar period. In short, Japan has turned from an Asian power to a world power, due particularly to her trading relationship. Japan's trade extends both to other centers, such as the U.S.A. and Europe, and to various peripheral regions. This indicates a clear policy of diversification and balance with her export and import customers.[29] Japan has thus become an important factor in the trade expectations of areas such as Latin America. Her dominant position is likewise evident in the Asian area where the diffusion of the "consumption society" has a Japanese style. From this viewpoint, we may assume that sensitive adjustment problems will emerge in the future as China comes out of its relative isolation, or the Soviet Union puts more emphasis on the development of its Eastern area. The fact is that at present, and as far as Latin America is concerned, the dispersion and importance of Japanese activity represents a significant event in the area's "negotiating position."

2. Relationships with the Socialist Center

Given the modest purpose of this paper, it is difficult to detail considerations regarding the European socialist sphere and its relationship to the Periphery. Nevertheless, we shall attempt some tentative reflections.

On one side, in regard to the socialist area itself, it would seem logical to find a "microsystem" in it with a dominant center, the Soviet Union, and a

[29] For instance, in 1968, Japan sent to developed areas little more than half of its exports (and little more than 35 per cent to the U.S.A.) and 43 per cent to "developing" areas. About 5 per cent out of this total was assigned to Latin America and the largest part to the Asian area.

Periphery (the associated countries). Yet this identification would have a political rather than an economic significance, since even though there exists a hegemonic power at the first level, the essential characteristics of a Center–Periphery constellation are not reproduced in the second one. This is due to a fundamental reason which we have already mentioned: the trade relationship scheme is not settled in the "classic" division between primary producers and manufacturers. Owing to historical reasons and resource distribution and also to the heavy thrust given to industrialization processes in each country during the postwar period, trade patterns are considerably diversified and, in some cases, the industrialized component has a larger share in some affiliated or "dependent" countries (at the political level, as East Germany or Czekoslovakia) than in the "hegemonic power." In short, an analysis of the socialist area's internal relationships has to be guided by other approaches or categories different from those used in the usual Center–Periphery approach.

The other point to be considered is the nexus of the socialist group or the U.S.S.R. (as the system axis of the new center) with the Periphery. In this matter, very interesting ideas were pondered in the fifties, once the Soviet Union had recovered from its dreadful war wounds. A common assumption predicted increasing relations with and a high trade volume between the large socialist power and the underdeveloped market in the foreseeable future. This outlook was based upon very convincing ideas that might be outlined as follows: the most outstanding characteristic in Soviet development has been the great emphasis assigned to heavy industry and the modest growth of consumption-oriented activities. Under these assumptions, it would be feasible and profitable for her to expand her international commerce based on primary and consumption industrial goods imported from the Periphery, with machinery and equipment exported from the U.S.S.R. This would enable the Soviet economy to continue her "historic" specialization in those areas where she has more comparative advantages and, at the same time, she would open a dynamic stable market (at least, free from cycles), promoting industrialization for and in the Periphery.

Despite this consistent argument, the fact is that these and other alternative optimistic predictions were not fulfilled (nor did they seem to be on their way to fulfillment) in the late sixties. Indeed, in 1968, for instance, the export distribution of European socialist countries was approximately as follows: about 65 per cent to their own countries; 25 per cent to developed capitalist economies; 10 per cent to "developing" areas. Out of this latter percentage, 3 per cent corresponds to Latin America, including Cuba. We must furthermore mention that Cuba and the Middle East (especially Egypt) are exceptions to the rule due to political, not economic, causes.

It seems obvious that this penomenon so different from the logical forecasts already cited is not primarily generated, as it used to be argued, by constraints or impositions of rival capitalist powers. These might be a significant factor in specific situations with respect to given countries or products (the so called "strategic" goods), but the relative rigidity of the foreign trade structure of the socialist area in the last decade persuades us to seek other explanations.

The problem is of capital importance (at least potentially) for the Periphery's "negotiation capacity," making it worthwhile to review some related hypotheses. The central one is that political considerations as well as economic realities lead to a resource concentration in the socialist area itself. The initial hypotheses need no discussion—although there is some doubt as to whether the conditions leading to and/or forcing a "closed" socialist development or making it as self-sustaining as possible in the past, still hold. As for the economic considerations, it is useful to recall socialist Europe's great variety of resources (which diminishes its "physical" need for imported resources), and to keep in mind the enormous requirements and possibilities involved in pursuing, enlarging, and enhancing development in these countries.

Given these fundamental facts, it seems clear that trade with the "rest of the world" has a marginal significance in Soviet strategy. Paradoxically, the most vital markets from an economic viewpoint are those of the most developed capitalist countries, since they are (by means of trade or other arrangements) sources of technological progress which should be assimilated.

It is likely that in the mid 1950s the U.S.S.R. had also considered foreign trade strategies such as those which were foreseen, but it is obvious that they were not carried out. We might speculate in the sense that the socialist superpower had then to weigh several important claims on the use of its economic surplus, that is:

(a) The development of its own "hinterland" and, specifically, of its "agricultural periphery." We have to remember that more than half of the economically active population still works in rural sectors, which is an extremely obvious sign of its productivity relative backwardness;

(b) The pressure or need to increase the consumption standards at a faster rate, especially those of the urban centers, with a greater weight in the "social equilibrium";

(c) To accelerate progress in technological spheres of military significance in order to diminish or remove the U.S.A.'s advantages;

(d) To assist her associates and especially her sphere's "underdeveloped giant," that is, China;

(e) To assemble a trade-and-aid scheme like that previously described, with economic and general targets (especially the expansion and diversification of Soviet consumption and growth of her influence in the Periphery).

As we stated above, it is clear that point (e) was ignored (except for very special emergencies, like Cuba). It likewise occurred with point (d), and therein could lie the main reason of the breakdown in Chinese–Soviet cordiality. Instead, it is obvious that point (c) maintained its priority and also that the goals of point (b) were pursued as is suggested by the program to expand the production of consumer durables and automobiles. It is even more difficult to have a clear idea about the relative weight assigned to point (a) which might well be considered very important from the standpoint of necessary "homogenization" in both the productive and the social structure.[30]

Returning to the subject in which we are interested, a substantial reformulation of the U.S.S.R.'s (and socialist world's) global strategy would be necessary so that this new and *sui generis* center, could have a more tangible economic representation in the external problems of the Periphery.[31]

C. Changes in the Structure and in the Internal Relationships of the Periphery

Two points seem to be evident in examining this problem: The first is the increasing *differentiation* within the Periphery as compared with the generic situation of the model's "classical" stage. It has been encouraged by domestic changes in the countries and areas referred to and, to a lesser extent, by those which have occurred in their external relationships.

Generally speaking, we may identify a first group made up of economies that, apart from remaining specialized in a few primary product exports, have not succeeded in establishing alternative dynamic bases to foster their growth. They are, briefly, the typical primary-exporting countries with a dual structure of an active export–import sector, while "the rest" vegetates in a subsistence economy.

At the other extreme, it would be possible to identify economies which might be classified as "developed Periphery." They are mainly the old "branches" of the British center (Canada, Australia, New Zealand). Obviously, they are neither centers nor part of them, suffering various degrees of dependence that trouble them. However, from the viewpoint of their structure, they are simultaneously developed economies with relatively wide possibilities for domestic implementation of an inward-looking economic activity.

It is easy to see that Latin American countries are in an intermediate category—although particular countries may approach both extremes. According to their relative development structure or level, they have somewhat

[30] In this respect, see the analysis in the paper "Concentración de los frutos del progreso técnico en el desarrollo latinoamericano" [9].

[31] An additional and significant piece of evidence for what we are asserting is the rather reticent U.S.S.R. attitude toward the Periphery arguments in the UNCTAD conferences.

diversified production systems which have, consequently, different "endogenous" expansion opportunities and possibilities.

The significance of these differences should not be underestimated in a closer analysis of peripheral areas. Nevertheless, what we have previously pointed out is that the Latin American experience must be weighed with the fact that economies of relatively higher development are just the place where the dependent integration processes, through control and diffusion of the Center's direct private investment, appear with greater emphasis. This is, as we have said, the basic foundation of this new type of dependence.

The intra-Periphery relationships are the other elements to be considered. We intend to call the reader's attention to only two important matters.

The first is related to the advances and limitations of joint action by primary producers at the international level *vis-à-vis* the central economies. There is no space here to recall the intricacies of the world trade conferences, yet it is useful to note that the mere association of the "underdeveloped front" is an event of historical importance, which would be senseless to underestimate in light of the poor results obtained thus far. As we know, this is not only due to the main center resistance but also derives from the difficulty in adjusting the positions of a large and diversified constellation of countries—which the aforementioned "vertical arrangements" indeed support.

The other topic we have to consider is that of the measures for policy coordination and the integration of economies at a regional level. With regard to our region, the progress that has been made with the establishment and performance of a specifically Latin American mechanism (CECLA) for negotiations with the U.S.A. and other centers is fairly well known. Whatever the opinion might be about its efficiency and future possibilities, it would be unwise here (with a much better reason than in the Periphery as a whole) to disregard the tremendous present and potential significance of the process.

Progress in terms of subregional integration is no less significant. Apart from the criticisms (sometimes justified and to be discussed later on), it is not possible to ignore the changes that have occurred at the institutional level as well as in inter-Latin American trade flows. Between 1960 and 1968, this interchange expanded at a rate of more than 9 per cent per annum,[32] which doubles that of global exports, and also exceeds the exceptional *world* trade performance of this period (8.2 per cent). On the other hand, the trade among the five countries making up the Central American Common Market increased at an extraordinary rate between 1963 and 1967: 30 per cent annually.

Though the share of these internal flows is still small in the total of regional exports (7.7 per cent in 1961 as compared with 12.3 per cent in 1969), the shares of various countries being quite uneven (Argentina, Brazil, Mexico,

[32] The increase was 13 per cent in 1969.

and Venezuela represent two thirds of total exports), we have to insist again on the undoubted importance of these changes and trends.

It is not our goal here to review the controversial and well-known arguments about regional integration. Nevertheless, it is useful for our purposes to establish some ideas.

The first is that the clearly distrustful opponents of such integration projects inevitably start from an obvious yet seldom explained notion: every move forward in that direction would transfer to a wider and higher plane some problems presently noticed at national levels. For instance, the denationalization of the dynamic sector would imply at best our *integration* by foreign multinational corporations or investors.

It would be difficult to disagree with the argument in general, however, we think it disregards some obvious considerations. First, *in the worst case*, this evolution would mean nothing but projecting an already existing context onto another level. Secondly and foremost, this viewpoint disregards the essentially contradictory character of every social process, that puts in motion forces working in various directions; they are sometimes divergent and even opposite but, given some historical, cyclical, or social circumstances, open a richer and different variety of options.

From this standpoint, and though many and even all the reservations and objections about integration might be shared, it would always be valid to assume that it indeed transfers these problems to another level that might have greater chances of being settled and that positive approaches can be generated in an international context where there is apparently no solution in a national framework.

On the other hand, the point cannot be discussed, as it usually has been, either in terms of a Latin American parochialism or within narrow projections of political–ideological transplants (which overlook, for instance, the fact that this is also a delicate problem emerging in the socialist area). As a matter of fact, there is a fundamental concern which, at the same time, had priority in ECLA's first statements on the subject: we are living in an age in which the national framework is being superseded. Those intending to follow old models (except the superpowers which, because of their origin and structure, surpassed that framework) shall surely be anachronisms in tomorrow's world.

All these arguments may be judged "optimistic" in some cases or as "reformist" in others.[33] Needless to say, we do not consider them so. Nevertheless, our aim is neither to legitimize nor to promote them. Our goal is a very simple one: to show here as well as elsewhere, the existence of new facts, which must be identified, analyzed, and evaluated as such, without regard to or insistence upon old approaches or categories used in other specific histori-

[33] For instance, the argument "first revolution later integration" is ingenious, but history continues—even though some or many countries have not made the revolution.

cal frameworks. At any rate, even when differences in interpretation arise or are indeed very sharp, a discussion in the present should be contemporary and not "archaeological."[34]

IV. Some Conclusions about the New Center–Periphery Relationship Scheme

A tentative and preliminary attempt to state the substantive character of the new Center–Periphery relationship scheme should emphasize the following points:

(i) The relative marginalization of the Periphery at the different levels described has its basic roots in the factors emphasized by ECLA's original analysis, that is, the uneven distribution of technical progress and the Periphery's "old" way of participation in international trade through primary products specialization. This has meant that the "exaction mechanism," involving the worsening of the terms of trade, still operates.

(ii) In a sense, the above phenomenon has to some extent been counterbalanced by capital and credit flows. However, this means of integration into the Center—apart from not solving the widening gap between the system's poles—has reinforced the already complex dependence of the Periphery by stressing and expanding foreign productive activities, increasing its indebtedness and making technological subjection more decisive and extended.

(iii) Insofar as both processes are maintained and enlarged it seems reasonable to assume an increasing sharpness in the implicit contradiction. By way of speculation let us consider some alternatives, namely,

(a) The continuation of marginalization, thus weakening the relationships characterizing "dependent integration;"

(b) The reduction of marginalization through the addition of other forms of "insertion" into the central system, for example, an increasing volume of manufactured exports. This alternative might mean either a fall in or an enhancement of "dependent integration" according to the form taken by the process. In other words, and as a simple illustration, economic integration

[34] Though we are cautious with quotations, a pernicious rather than useful instrument, it seems appropriate to reproduce the thought of a spokesman for the revolutionary position in Latin America, Regis Debray: "We are never contemporary in our present. History moves forward in a disguised fashion: it enters the stage with the previous scene's mask, and nobody knows anything in the play. Each time the curtain is raised the plot must be started again. The fault is not indeed history's, but our ideas, too full of remembrances and images. We observe the past as overlapped with the present, even when this present is a revolution."

limited to light manufactures managed by international corporations, would surely aggravate the overall problem. However, it could also alleviate the cited contradiction and postpone its eventual "maturity." The emergence of other trading structures or "foreign colocation" of the Periphery (or parts of it), might lead to a different situation in terms of both integration and dependence;

(c) A progressively growing cohesion of the Periphery (or regions within it) and the full use of larger room of maneuver offered by the Center's differentiation and the presence of the socialist system, might lead to new realities in the areas considered.

In connection with these last points and also with the Periphery's search for new and different modes of relations with the Center, we cannot ignore the contributions made by ECLA (from 1949 to the present day), in the promotion of analysis of these problems.

REFERENCES

[1] Caputo, O., and Pizarro, R., Imperialismo, dependencia y relaciones internacionales. Univ. de Chile, CESO (1970).

[2] Cardozo, F. H., and Faletto, E., "Dependencia y desarrollo en America Latina," pp. 22–28. Editorial Siglo **XXI**, Mexico, 1969.

[3] ECLA, "Economic Survey of Latin America, 1949," pp. 15–45. United Nations, New York, 1951.

[4] ECLA, "Economic Survey of Latin America, 1969." United Nations, New York, 1970.

[5] ECLA, "Economic Survey of Latin America, 1970." United Nations, New York, 1971.

[6] ECLA, Trends and Structures of the Latin American Economy, Foreign Sector, "Economic Survey, 1970," April 1971.

[7] ECLA, The Expansion of International Enterprises and Their Influence on Latin American Development, "Economic Survey of Latin America, 1970," Vol. 2, Chap. 1. United Nations, New York, 1970.

[8] ECLA, "Development Problems in Latin America." Univer. of Texas Press, Austin, 1970.

[9] Ensayos de interpretacion economica; Concentración de los frutos progreso técnico. Universitaria and El Trimestre Economico No. 125.

[10] Fores, M., Britain's Economic Growth, Lloyd Band Rev. No. 99 (1971).

[11] Servan-Schreiber, J. J., "The American Challenge," Atheneum, New York, 1968.

[12] Statistical Abstract of the United States, pp. 738–784. U.S. Dept. of Commerce (1969).

[13] "Statistical Yearbook." United Nations, New York, 1969.

CONSEQUENCES OF THE EXISTENCE OF "IMMOBILE" INDUSTRIES

JAN TINBERGEN
Nederlandse Economische Hogeschool, Rotterdam, The Netherlands

I. Some Definitions

Among the many activities in which an economy is engaged, a number can be baptized "immobile or national." By this phrase we will indicate *two* types of activities, namely, *primary* production and the production of what Little [1] has called "*nontradables*." Primary production is immobile in the sense that it must be done on the spot where the natural resources needed for it are available: land, climate, geographic situation, and mineral deposits. Production of nontradables must be done in the country, since the products cannot at all or can hardly be moved. The clearest examples of nontradables are buildings and services. Among the services are not only the services rendered by buildings (the things we pay rent for), but a long series of other services: transportation between two given localities, personal services, such as the famous haircut, retail trade services, education, government services (or disservices), and so on. There are also categories which we will classify as nontradables rather than tradables, although strictly speaking they can be traded. This may be so since some products can be moved only at considerable expense. The so-called heavy goods are examples, or also electricity. The possibility of transporting them is not absent, but relatively slight. As a consequence, the borderline between tradables and nontradables is not sharp. Even so, the distinction is useful. While some authors—among whom Iversen and Leontief, have introduced the concept (under other names)—the distinction is only used in a small portion of economic literature. Its neglect has some consequences which have been dealt with elsewhere in recent years; it seems worthwhile to list these consequences, enabling us to pay a tribute to

Raúl Prebisch, who has dealt with some of them although in a different form [3].

After the definitions we present, a crude statistical indication of the *relative importance* of immobile activities is desirable in order to avoid the impression that we are speaking about something only of academic importance.

The important part primary production plays in developing countries is well known. Often almost half of these countries' income is earned in the primary sector. The reader should be reminded, however, of the fact that the immobile activities are the first phase of production only, that is, the production of raw primary products. Their processing, even the simplest, should not be classified as immobile or, in fact, primary.

The production of nontradables has been estimated to be close to 50 per cent of national income in developed countries and somewhat less (sometimes as much as 20 per cent of national income) in developing countries. As a consequence, the remaining activities, *mobile* or *international* activities, are a small part of total production in some developing countries.

Another piece of information will be useful, namely the *capital-output ratios* of immobile activities. On inspection of the—admittedly sometimes shaky—material available, we find that these capital-output ratios tend to be, in the scale of all such ratios, at the extremes. On one hand there are a number of very low capital-output ratios for immobile industries, such as those for some parts of agriculture, building, and personal services. On the other hand there are some of the highest capital-output ratios also applying to industries producing nontradables: energy, transportation and communication, and housing services, especially if we exclude the very primitive ways of transportation and communication, which are hardly applied anywhere anymore. Also the other type of mobile activities, primary production, shows some examples of very high capital ratios, mainly mining.

We will now discuss the consequences of the existence of immobile activities in the remaining sections of this chapter.

II. How to Cure Balance of Payments Difficulties

A number of countries, developing as well as developed (but the former rather more than the latter), are facing *balance of payments difficulties.* The problem is that their monetary reserves are diminishing, that is their imports, in the widest sense of that expression, are surpassing their exports by more than the planned capital inflow. A standard advice to countries in such difficulties has been often formulated, namely that they should *restrict their total national expenditure* to the value of their income. The advice may be based on the simplest conceivable definition of national income:

$$Y = X + E - M, \tag{2.1}$$

where

Y is national income,
X is national expenditure,
E is exports, and
M is imports.

If Y is taken gross, that is before deducting depreciation allowances, then X should also be taken gross; that is, investment, which is part of X, should include depreciation. From Eq. (2.1), it follows that:

$$M - E = X - Y, \qquad \text{and} \qquad M - E = 0, \qquad \text{if} \quad X = Y. \tag{2.2}$$

The existence of nontradables, however, creates complications during the execution of the standard advice. Since a considerable portion of expenditures is spent on nontradables, any reduction in expenditures automatically also reduces expenditures on nontradables. These can only be produced for the home market, however, and as a consequence their production falls. Thus, balance of payments equilibrium can only be attained at a considerably *lower level of national income.* I have tried to estimate the size of the fall in income [5], and a realistic estimate is that it is 5 times the original deficit on the balance of payments. This fall in income would not occur if there were no nontradables. Their existence implies that the execution of the standard device is much less easy or attractive than has often been thought.

The only acceptable way out is to produce and sell relatively more tradables. To sell them, the country's competitiveness must be enhanced. A general device here may be devaluation, and it has often been applied. If the elasticity of demand for the country's main products with regard to their price is low, devaluation will not, however, work out very favorably; that is, a considerable degree of devaluation will be needed. This is true, in particular, for developing countries, although not necessarily for all of them.

The perspective of devaluation not being promising, several countries have tried instead to raise production by raising investment. Under the circumstances, this leads to *inflationary pressures.* It is Raúl Prebisch, in particular, who has drawn the attention of economists and politicians to this "*structural theory of inflation*," in contradistinction to the monetary theory of inflation, which, in its simpler forms, neglects the existence of nontradables and hence belittles the difficulties involved in carrying out the "standard device" which was inspired by the monetary theory. Prebisch's theories may be said to represent the awareness of the existence of nontradables.

III. Macroplanning of Development

From the preceding statements, it follows that on the macrolevel there is a definite necessity, in planning a country's production structure, to keep some balance between the production of tradables and nontradables. A country, especially a poor one, cannot afford to invest in heavy infrastructural projects (which belong to the immobile sector) without at the same time investing in the production of tradables. This makes a joint planning for both types of projects, already often complementary at the microlevel, desirable.

With a given rate of growth of national income, *planning for the nontradables* is often simpler than for the tradables. Since nontradables can only serve the home market, their demand can be estimated more easily than the demand for tradables, which depends on the world market, on trade policies, and on future competitiveness, none of which is easy to estimate. This is true, in particular, if demand is of some importance, as will be the case whenever the country concerned has a large share in world supply. If it does not have a large share, and provided the quality it is able to supply is satisfactory, demand factors are not so important.

For macroplanning as a first stage in planning, the *average capital-output* ratio for a country at large will often be used. This ratio shows a relative stability in comparison with the huge differences between capital-output ratios for single activities. This stability is the reason why the concept has been used at all, contrary to what theorists would have suggested, theorists usually being aware of the possibilities of substitution between factors of production. The reason for this relative stability may again be seen as a consequence of the existence of nontradables: as already stated in Sect. I, not only must nontradables always be produced in each country and represent an important portion of any country's national product, but also the extreme values of capital-output ratios are to be found in that portion of the economy. Taken together, this makes for a rather stable average ratio, irrespective of the particular mobile industries the country has or plans. For macroplanning purposes, this is helpful, since in the absence of data for the country concerned we may take international figures as a first approximation.

IV. Choosing the Sectors to Develop

The next stage in planning consists of choosing the *sectors* to develop in the future. The choice should be centered around the choice of which *international* industries to develop. The immobile sectors will have to follow as a consequence. Generally speaking, those international sectors should be chosen which show the highest comparative advantages. One general principle which may be helpful in tracing such sectors is the well-known *Heckscher–Ohlin principle*, which says that the factors of production needed by the sectors to be developed should be as close as possible to the factor endowment of the country. The endowments with natural resources will be decisive in part. For another important part, relative endowment with capital, both physical and human, will be decisive. For developing countries, the quantity of physical capital available per capita is low and so is the quantity of human capital. The best development efforts notwithstanding, the relative positions on both counts, in comparison with the developed countries, will remain low for quite some time. The sectors contributing most to raising developing countries' income will therefore be the ones showing a modest capital–labor ratio, such as clothing and textile manufacturing, leather products, and the production of finished metal products. What matters, however, is not exactly the capital intensity of the international sectors considered by themselves, but rather the capital intensity of a complex—sometimes called "bunch"—of industries. The reason for it is again to be found in the existence of nontradables. Every sector producing tradable goods needs for its operation the inputs of a number of nontradables: energy, transportation, services, and buildings. Since these, as already observed, can only be produced in the country, no international sector can be established or expanded in isolation. Such establishment or expansion has to be accompanied by the expansion of immobile industries, and we will call the combination of a given piece of international industry and the complementary national industries, in their appropriate proportions, the *bunch* corresponding to that piece. The structure of the bunch will determine its capital-output ratio and any other parameters relevant to its attractiveness for the country concerned. It may deviate from the corresponding parameter for a single international industry.

One way to ascertain the *composition of the bunch* is the so-called *semi-input–output method*; the name indicates that it uses the method of input–output analysis, but only part of the information of the full input–output matrix of coefficients. Some attempts have been made to attain numerical results illustrating the point made [2, 4].

It seems interesting to explore the question of in which cases the capital-output ratio is likely to rise by the introduction of the bunch concept, and in which cases it will be lower for the bunch than for the international industry itself. Such a provisional exploration may be based on the assumption that most of the capital-output ratios of international industries are in the middle range, and that the capital-output ratios of many national industries are outside that range (see Sect. I).

It will be clear that international industries using relatively much energy or transportation will show a higher capital-ratio for their bunch. Examples of industries using much energy are the heavy chemical industries, metal smelting, and paper production. Examples of industries using relatively much transportation are industries producing heavy goods, such as fuels, fertilizer, ores, and building materials. In several of these cases, the capital ratio of the international industry itself is already high: this applies to heavy chemicals, fuels, and fertilizers, for instance. The bunch capital-output ratio will then be even higher.

Examples of international industries which show relatively higher inputs of labor-intensive nontradables are industries using relatively big buildings, either because they are themselves labor intensive or for other reasons, for instance tourism, handicrafts, and secretariats of international organizations.

Apart from the role played by nontradables the choice of international sectors is related in another way to the existence of immobile sectors, as defined in the beginning of this essay. In many developing countries *primary production* shows considerable comparative advantages in the sense that the comparative advantages of any other activities are decidedly less, at least during the first stages of development. This is another way of saying that it is difficult for the least-developed countries to get out of their state of underdevelopment.

V. Concluding Remarks

From the survey given of some recent research, it appears that the existence of immobile sectors, defined as sectors producing nontradables plus sectors of primary production, affects planning for development of developing countries in different ways and in various respects makes development more difficult than in the absence of these sectors. For this reason it seemed useful to bring together these various impacts of the existence of immobile sectors.

REFERENCES

[1] Little, I. D. M., unpublished mimeographed report.
[2] Netherlands Economic Inst., unpublished rep. for the Government of Ethiopia (1969).
[3] Prebisch, R., Economic Development or Monetary Stability: The False Dilemma, *Econ. Bull. Latin Amer.* **6**, No. 1, 1 (1961).
[4] Rasul, G., "Input-Output Relationships in Pakistan 1954." Rotterdam, 1964.
[5] Tinbergen, J., Spardefizit und Handelsdefizit, *Weltwirtschaft. Arch.* **95**, 89 (1965).

A LONG-RUN ECONOMIC GROWTH MODEL FOR DEVELOPING COUNTRIES *

PAUL ZAREMBKA

University of California, Berkeley, California

The theory of economic development of low-income countries is one of the more underdeveloped areas in the science of economics; development economists are usually able to make statements about the importance of increased savings or of the foreign exchange bottleneck but are rarely able to pin down the magnitude of the effects or the best policies to pursue to increase the rate of growth. As an attempt to strengthen development theory, this paper builds a testable model of economic growth around the basic principle of profit maximization. As a result, a general equilibrium framework for approaching the longer-run problems of economic development is obtained by emphasizing the supply rather than the demand for outputs.

Section I is the substantive contribution of the paper. It develops in detail the model of economic growth. Section II provides some estimates for Colombia and prewar Japan of those equations relating directly to the international sector and as such is only an introduction to full estimation of the model (which has been reported elsewhere). Section III concludes the paper by comparing the present model with two other development models.

* This paper represents a revision and condensation of the author's 1967 doctoral dissertation at the University of Wisconsin. Professors Robert E. Baldwin and Arthur S. Goldberger contributed importantly to the study through their continued suggestions for improvements. Professor Allen C. Kelley is thanked for helpful comments on an earlier draft, while Professor Charles C. Holt called attention to an omission that led to reestimation of the model. Comments by Professors Albert Fishlow, Lovell Jarvis, and Lawrence R. Klein on later drafts are also gratefully acknowledged. The University of Wisconsin Research Committee provided the computer time for the initial estimation. The final draft was completed under the Project for the Explanation and Optimization of Economic Growth, Institute of International Studies, University of California, Berkeley, California, as financed by the Ford Foundation and the National Science Foundation.

I. The Model of Economic Growth

The economy of developing countries is first disaggregated into three producing sectors: the primary or agricultural sector, the secondary or manufacturing sector, and the tertiary or service sector. This disaggregation is based upon the belief that the most useful breakdown of an economy is in terms of the sectors that are thought to have considerably different production functions and yet which are aggregate enough so that an understanding of the model is not subverted by detail.[1]

The basic structure of the model is then rather simple in conception: (i) Each sector has a production function which relates its inputs to its output; (ii) With one exception (agricultural labor) the utilization of factor inputs in the production process is determined by static profit maximization at the industry level (with appropriate microeconomic aggregating assumptions indicated), given the cost of labor and capital inputs and taking expected output price as a function of the output level; and (iii) Finally, the behavior of wage rates which clear the markets for labor services is derived, and the behavior of price levels is obtained. The international market plays a role in the behavior of prices.

While the approach is simple, the final structural model contains 28 equations—19 behavioral equations and 9 identities. The model is presented by first introducing the production functions, then the markets for capital and labor, the wage rate equations, the domestic price equations, and finally the international market. After the presentation of the model a list of endogenous and exogenous variables is provided.

A. Production Functions

The inputs of the production functions are specified to be capital, labor, and, in agriculture, land. However, there are many types of capital and many distinctions among laborers and among types of land. A sufficient condition for no aggregation bias is that proportionality among the inputs within each

[1] Green [3, pp. 119–120] has pointed out:

> The choice of the type and degree of aggregation of independent variables, however, is to be determined by the balancing of two types of cost—the cost of using variables which are numerous and/or difficult to estimate, and the costs associated with the unsatisfactory predictions which may result if the number of variables is small.

With the great lack of knowledge of the determinants of economic growth that exists at the present time and with the difficulty of obtaining accurate data in underdeveloped countries, the latter costs seem much smaller.

input class is always maintained. Such proportionality may be due to fixed coefficients among inputs of a variable input class or to proportional movement of the input prices within the class. In either case, this model assumes a proportional movement of factor inputs within the classes of capital stock in buildings, of capital stock in equipment, of labor, and of land. Thus the various types of capital stock in buildings and in equipment are aggregated, as are the various levels of labor skills and types of land.

The industry production function at a given point in time is a function of capital in buildings, capital in equipment, labor, and (for agriculture) land. However, these production functions assume a given technology and a given level of labor skills. At subsequent points in time, technology and labor skills are presumably advancing. Therefore, a time trend for technological change and skill improvement is also introduced into the production function.

The elasticity of substitution between any two inputs for a given level of output expresses the percentage change in the ratio of the utilization of two inputs given a unit percentage change in the price ratio for those inputs. For simplicity of analysis, we assume the elasticity of substitution equal to one in each industry between every factor. It then follows directly that no distinction can be made between neutral and nonneutral disembodied technological change, and that the functional form for the production function is Cobb–Douglas in the variable inputs. Assuming the factor input land for the production function in the primary sector ($i = 1$) fixed (any changes in land quality or in land acreage are assumed absorbed by the time trend), then

$$Y_i = e^{a_i + b_i t} K_i^{\mathrm{b}\alpha_i} K_i^{\mathrm{e}\beta_i} L_i^{\gamma_i} \qquad i = 1, 2, 3, \tag{1)–(3}$$

where Y_i is real output, K_i^{b} is real capital stock in buildings, and K_i^{e} is real capital stock in equipment, all valued at base-year prices, while L_i is labor.

The sum of the outputs of the three sectors gives total domestic output:

$$Y = Y_1 + Y_2 + Y_3. \tag{4}$$

B. Capital and Labor Markets

The underlying principle determining the behavior of producers is static profit maximization. Thus, given the production function, producers determine that level of utilization of each variable input which maximizes their profits (revenue less costs of production) in the current period. Although it may be expected that producers in less-developed countries do not as accurately succeed in maximizing profits as in developed countries, they are nevertheless likely to operate in the vicinity of the points of maximum profits.

In other words, a distinguishing characteristic of less-developed countries may be that, while producers do attempt to maximize profits, they are less accurate in achieving their goal than their counterparts in developed economies—the variance of actual profits around the point of profit maximization is greater in underdeveloped countries.

Since the model is an aggregate one, profit maximization is derived at the industry level with respect to the utilization of the variable factor inputs.[2] In the secondary and tertiary sectors, the maximization is with respect to capital stock in buildings, capital stock in equipment, and labor. In the primary sector, the family unit is considered predominant, so that the labor force is given and only buildings and equipment are freely variable inputs (land is taken to be fixed). Such a specification in agriculture allows for disguised unemployment in the sense that the marginal product of labor may be less than the wage rate.

The profit equation is specified in terms of relative prices, i.e., the price of output and the prices of inputs are taken relative to the domestic price level. Alternatively stated, profits are in real terms. Since at a point in time the domestic price level is given, such an approach does not change the point of profit maximization.

Also the industry maximizes, not real profits, but real *expected* profits: it does not know exactly how to price its output in order to sell all its produce (planned inventory accumulation is assumed zero), but rather has expectations as to this required pricing. Therefore, the profit equation is written

$$\Pi_i^* = \left(\frac{P_i}{P}\right)^* Y_i - \frac{q_i^{\mathrm{b}}}{P} K_i^{\mathrm{b}} - \frac{q_i^{\mathrm{e}}}{P} K_i^{\mathrm{e}} - \frac{w_i}{P} L_i, \qquad i = 1, 2, 3,$$

[2] Profit maximization at the industry level does not necessarily imply that our three sectors are controlled by monopolists (e.g., the government), although we speak below of *a* producer in a sector. One set of aggregating assumptions, and probably the most acceptable, is that all firms in an industrial sector (not necessarily constant in number since free entry is permitted) maximize profits, have the same production function of constant returns-to-scale, and face the same output and input prices uninfluenced by individual firm behavior (these assumptions are implicit in Zarembka [10]). The fact that individual firm output level is indeterminant, unless a factor such as land is fixed, does not affect the aggregate equations; also, external economies or diseconomies can lead to an *industry* production function of nonconstant returns-to-scale (see Zarembka [9]).

A second set of aggregating assumptions is that microeconomic firms maximize profits, are constant in number, have the same production function (not necessarily of constant returns-to-scale), and face the same declining marginal net-revenue curve. Then all firms are the same size. In both cases, the aggregate equations are the same as obtained here. Of course, we do not believe either set of aggregating assumptions holds exactly, but how far is one or the other in error in its predictive ability?

where for the ith industry, we define the variables as follows:

Π_i^*	expected real profits,
$(P_i/P)^*$	expected relative price of output,
q_i^{b}	rental price of buildings,
q_i^{e}	rental price of equipment,
w_i	nominal wage rate, and
P	general domestic price level.

These profit equations are the basic equations of the growth model around which other equations are obtained. The remaining behavioral equations are directed toward determining the prices relevant to these equations and then obtaining the utilization of the variable factor inputs through maximizing profits with respect to these inputs. Positing that the factor prices are taken by each industry as given, the behavioral equations for these prices are left to be developed in subsequent sections. The expected relative price of output, however, does depend upon industry output and is specified in this section, along with the solution equations for the factor inputs given factor prices.

The expected relative price $(P_i/P)^*$ that the producer receives for his output can be interpreted in terms of his expected average revenue or demand curve. The shape of the demand curve is determined by the response of relative price to the quantity of output sold—perfect competition in the product market is not assumed (thus theoretically permitting production functions of constant or even increasing returns to scale with still a determinate level of output for the producer). This curve is assumed to have a constant elasticity with respect to per capita output. Furthermore, the demand curve shifts upward as real per capita national income increases.[3] If the influence of income also has a constant elasticity, then the expected relative price $(P_i/P)^*$ of output is

$$(P_i/P)^* = c_i(Y_i/N)^{-\delta_i}(Z/N)^{\rho_i}, \qquad i = 1, 2, 3, \tag{5)–(7}$$

where N is total population of the country, Z is real national income, $-1/\delta_i$ is the price elasticity of demand for the industry output and ρ_i/δ_i is the income elasticity of demand. Real national income is defined by

$$Z = Y + R - D, \tag{8}$$

[3] Since important population changes occur, the effects of these changes are incorporated by introducing the reals in "per capita" terms. Note that the shift of the demand curve relative to national income is an acceptance of current income as the important influence on current consumption. For a long-run model such a specification is not particularly untenable.

where R is real net foreign income remittances to the economy in domestic currency and D is real depreciation of capital, so that

$$D = \sum_{i=1}^{3} (d_i^{\mathrm{b}} K_i^{\mathrm{b}} + d_i^{\mathrm{e}} K_i^{\mathrm{e}}), \tag{9}$$

with d_i^{b} and d_i^{e} fixed rates of depreciation.

The rental price of capital is the value of capital depreciated plus interest on capitalized value. Thus, the rental price is written

$$q_i^{\mathrm{b}} = (d_i^{\mathrm{b}} + r) P^{\mathrm{b}}, \qquad i = 1,2,3,$$

$$q_i^{\mathrm{e}} = (d_i^{\mathrm{e}} + r) P^{\mathrm{e}}, \qquad i = 1,2,3,$$

where r is the real rate of interest, P^{b} is the supply price of capital in buildings, and P^{e} is the supply price of capital in equipment.

The depreciation rate is often assumed invariant over time and is so assumed here, but the real rate of interest may, in fact, vary. This real rate of interest could be specified as the nominal rate of interest minus the rate of inflation; however, there is considerable difficulty in obtaining a *single* nominal interest rate series in a less-developed country which adequately reflects the nominal cost of borrowing. The vast majority of funds is obtained internally to the firm. Of those which are not, some are obtained abroad. Therefore, the assumption that seems to be the least violation of reality is that the real rate of interest is constant over time. Thus the cost of each capital good is simply taken as moving with its supply price—e.g., since buildings are constructed by domestic producers, P^{b} can be assumed to move with the domestic price level in the secondary sector P_2; and, since equipment may be largely imported in underdeveloped countries, P^{e} can be assumed to move with import prices in the secondary sector.

In sum, profit maximization for the industry requires the maximization of

$$\Pi_i^* = c_i (Y_i/N)^{-\delta_i} (Z/N)^{\rho_i} Y_i - \frac{P^{\mathrm{b}}}{P} K_i^{\mathrm{b}} - \frac{P^{\mathrm{e}}}{P} K_i^{\mathrm{e}} - \frac{w_i}{P} L_i, \qquad i = 1,2,3,$$

with respect to K_i^{b}, K_i^{e}, and L_i for $i = 2,3$, and with respect to K_i^{b} and K_i^{e} for $i = 1$. Using the production functions given by Eqs. (1)–(3), the partial derivatives of Π_i are obtained with respect to K_i^{b}, K_i^{e}, and L_i in the secondary and tertiary sectors, and with respect to K_1^{b} and K_1^{e} in the primary sector. These derivatives are set equal to zero, and the equilibrium condition that the relative factor shares are equal to the relative elasticities of output is obtained. Specifying that the wage rates in the secondary and tertiary sectors are equal, w_n, (or proportional), the behavioral equations are given in Table I for utilization of the factor inputs.

TABLE I

UTILIZATION OF FACTOR INPUTS

Primary Sector

(10) $$\ln K_1{}^{\mathrm{b}} = \text{constant} + \frac{\mathrm{b}_1}{\Delta_1} t + \frac{\delta_1}{\Delta_1} \ln N + \frac{\rho_1}{\Delta_1} \ln \frac{Z}{N} + \frac{\beta_1(1-\delta_1)}{\Delta_1} \ln \frac{P^{\mathrm{b}}}{P^{\mathrm{e}}} + \frac{\gamma_1(1-\delta_1)}{\Delta_1} \ln L_1 - \frac{1}{\Delta_1} \ln \frac{P^{\mathrm{b}}}{P}$$

(11) $$\ln K_1{}^{\mathrm{e}} = \text{constant} + \frac{\mathrm{b}_1}{\Delta_1} t + \frac{\delta_1}{\Delta_1} \ln N + \frac{\rho_1}{\Delta_1} \ln \frac{Z}{N} + \frac{\alpha_1(1-\delta_1)}{\Delta_1} \ln \frac{P^{\mathrm{e}}}{P^{\mathrm{b}}} + \frac{\gamma_1(1-\delta_1)}{\Delta_1} \ln L_1 - \frac{1}{\Delta_1} \ln \frac{P^{\mathrm{e}}}{P}$$

where $\Delta_1 = 1-(\alpha_1+\beta_1)(1-\delta_1)$.

Secondary and Tertiary Sectors ($i = 2, 3$)

(12), (15) $$\ln K_i{}^{\mathrm{b}} = \text{constant} + \frac{\mathrm{b}_i}{\Delta_i} t + \frac{\delta_i}{\Delta_i} \ln N + \frac{\rho_i}{\Delta_i} \ln \frac{Z}{N} + \frac{\beta_i(1-\delta_i)}{\Delta_i} \ln \frac{P^{\mathrm{b}}}{P^{\mathrm{e}}} + \frac{\gamma_i(1-\delta_i)}{\Delta_i} \ln \frac{P^{\mathrm{b}}}{w_n} - \frac{1}{\Delta_i} \ln \frac{P^{\mathrm{b}}}{P}$$

(13), (16) $$\ln K_i{}^{\mathrm{e}} = \text{constant} + \frac{\mathrm{b}_i}{\Delta_i} t + \frac{\delta_i}{\Delta_i} \ln N + \frac{\rho_i}{\Delta_i} \ln \frac{Z}{N} + \frac{\alpha_i(1-\delta_i)}{\Delta_i} \ln \frac{P^{\mathrm{e}}}{P^{\mathrm{b}}} + \frac{\gamma_i(1-\delta_i)}{\Delta_i} \ln \frac{P^{\mathrm{e}}}{w_n} - \frac{1}{\Delta_i} \ln \frac{P^{\mathrm{e}}}{P}$$

(14), (17) $$\ln L_i = \text{constant} + \frac{\mathrm{b}_i}{\Delta_i} t + \frac{\delta_i}{\Delta_i} \ln N + \frac{\rho_i}{\Delta_i} \ln \frac{Z}{N} + \frac{\alpha_i(1-\delta_i)}{\Delta_i} \ln \frac{w_n}{P^{\mathrm{b}}} + \frac{\beta_i(1-\delta_i)}{\Delta_i} \ln \frac{w_n}{P^{\mathrm{e}}} - \frac{1}{\Delta_i} \ln \frac{w_n}{P}$$

where $\Delta_i = 1-(\alpha_i+\beta_i+\gamma_i)(1-\delta_i)$.

Employment in the primary sector is simply labor supply. The U.N. Department of Economic and Social Affairs [7, pp. 12, 14, 22] world study of labor force participation suggests that labor supply in both urban and rural areas is approximately a constant fraction of population aged 15–65 in those areas. Since this model does not examine age distributional effects, the labor supply in the urban and rural areas is taken as a constant proportion of total population in the areas. Therefore, if s_n is the proportion of urban population in the urban labor force (L_n), then L_n/s_n is total urban population and $N - L_n/s_n$ is rural population. If s_1 is the proportion of rural population in the labor force, then rural employment equal to rural labor supply is

$$L_1 = s_1(N - L_n/s_n) = s_1 N - (s_1/s_n) L_n. \tag{18}$$

Summarizing the present status of the model, the production functions have been specified, the behavioral equations for factor input utilization have been obtained, and a few identities of the model have been provided. To complete the model, the cost of labor and the determination of domestic prices must be specified, and the international market must be introduced.

C. Determination of Wage Rates

As indicated in the previous section, competitive conditions in urban areas are specified to equate the wage rates in the secondary and tertiary sectors. Furthermore, the market for labor services in the urban areas is cleared—labor demand equals labor supply.[4] In this section the demand and supply equations for urban labor are set forth in order to determine the urban wage rate. At the end of the section, the rural wage rate is specified.

The demand for labor in the secondary and the tertiary sectors has already been given by Eqs. (14) and (17), respectively. Since employment equals labor demand:

$$L_n^{\mathrm{D}} = L_n = L_2 + L_3, \tag{19}$$

where L_n is employment in the secondary and tertiary sectors.

The supply of labor has three components. First, since there may be rigidities in moving from urban to rural areas, the supply of labor in the current period is a function of the supply in the preceding period.[5] Secondly, the incentive to move out of the rural areas depends in part upon the wage differential between the urban areas (w_n) and the rural areas (w_1)—the higher the urban wage relative to the rural wage, the greater the incentive for leaving the rural areas. Thirdly, as population increases, labor supply to the secondary and tertiary sectors increases (independently of shifts between the urban and rural areas). Thus, labor supply (L_n^{S}) in the current period relative to last period is given by

$$L_n^{\mathrm{S}}/L_{n-1}^{\mathrm{S}} = L_n^{\mathrm{S}}(w_n/w_1, N/N_{-1}),$$

where N = total population.

[4] However, the equations of this section would still obtain *mutatis mutandis* if there were a constant percentage level of urban unemployment.

[5] If there were complete mobility, supply in the preceding period would play no role in supply for the current period.

Positing the demand for urban labor equal to its supply, the constant elasticity equation can be obtained:

$$\ln(w_n/w_1) = j_0 + j_1 \ln(L_n/L_{n-1}) + j_2 \ln(N/N_{-1}), \tag{20}$$

where $j_1 \geqslant 0$ and $j_2 \leqslant 0$. It may be that urban wages are a constant ratio of rural wages; in this case, $j_1 = j_2 = 0$. A constant ratio could be the result of perfect mobility between the urban and rural sectors (with the differential in wages due to economic and psychological costs of moving).

For the primary sector, all income except rental on capital is treated as if it were wage income. In other words, farmers do not distinguish between their imputed wages and their profits (or losses). Therefore, the relevant wage rate for the primary sector is given by

$$w_1 = [P_1 Y_1 - (d_1{}^{\mathrm{b}} + r) P^{\mathrm{b}} K_1{}^{\mathrm{b}} - (d_1{}^{\mathrm{e}} + r) P^{\mathrm{e}} K_1{}^{\mathrm{e}}]/L_1. \tag{21}$$

D. Domestic Prices

The causes of the high inflation rates that have been observed in underdeveloped countries have been much debated. Among Latin American economists particularly, two schools seem to have developed (see Campos [1], reprinted in Meier [6, pp. 210–213]). One school, the monetarists, believes that rapid increases in the nominal supply of money by domestic monetary authorities have led to the rises in price levels. This school would argue that decreases in the rate of growth of money supply would contribute greatly to stabilization of the price levels.

The second school, the structuralists, holds the view that the bottlenecks created by a rapidly transforming economic structure are the principal causes of price level rises. Thus, for example, large increases in gross domestic product are accompanied *pari passu* by large increases in the price level, since underdeveloped societies have not developed the communication and transportation systems necessary for efficiently supplying producer raw materials or outputs. Furthermore, restrictions on the ability to import through tariff duties, exchange devaluation, or import licensing often make it difficult to obtain foreign raw materials or capital equipment for production purposes, or to obtain consumer goods. Therefore, inflation is a concomitant of economic growth that cannot be avoided.

This model does not take an a priori position on the accuracy of the arguments of either of these schools, but rather introduces elements of both schools in explaining the rate of change in the domestic price level. The monetarist position is represented simply by the changes in money supply relative to changes in real output. The structuralist position, however, is represented by three factors: the rate of change of real total output in order to incorporate effects of strains on infrastructure when output is increasing, the rate of change of import prices (in domestic currency after adjustment for import duties) to incorporate the direct effects of import prices on costs of production and consumption, and finally the ratio of total imports to total output in order to introduce the effects of import restrictions. Therefore, the change in price level is represented by the following behavioral equation, again using the constant elasticity functional form:

$$\ln(P/P_{-1}) = g_0 + g_1 \ln(\mathrm{Mo}/\mathrm{Mo}_{-1}) + g_2 \ln(Y/Y_{-1}) + g_3 \ln(P_{\mathrm{m}} E/P_{\mathrm{m}-1} E_{-1}) + g_4 \ln(M/Y), \tag{22}$$

where Mo is nominal money supply, P_{m} is the general level of import prices in dollars, E is the exchange rate with the dollar, M is total real imports, and $g_1 \geqslant 0$, $g_2 \geqslant -1$, $g_3 \geqslant 0$, $g_4 \leqslant 0$. If the monetarists are correct, $g_1 = -g_2 = 1$ (assuming money velocity constant) and $g_3 = g_4 = 0$; otherwise the structuralist argument should be at least partially accepted.

Since Eq. (22) gives an expression for the general price level, the equations for the sectoral price levels can now be obtained. Equations (5)–(7) specify the *expected* relative price for each sector. Of course, expectations may not be fulfilled. Assume the expectations are uniformly in error in all sectors (in percentage terms). Then the sectoral price level is obtained by scaling (up or down) the expected relative price after multiplication by the general price level.

The scaling factor is determined by calculating a weighted sum of the expected relative prices—which, if expectations are perfect, should add to one. The weights are the sectoral to total output ratios for the base year of the price indices. In other words, the sectoral price levels are given by the equations

$$P_i = \frac{P(P_i/P)^*}{\sum_{i=1}^{3} (P_i/P)^* (Y_{i0}/Y_0)}, \qquad i = 1, 2, 3, \tag{23)–(25}$$

where the subscript 0 refers to the base year output levels.

E. International Market

In the previous section on domestic prices, total imports play a role in the determination of the domestic price level. But imports of underdeveloped countries are often dominated by one sector, so that little is served by disaggregating imports when the rest of the model is concerned with only total imports. Now the total quantity of imports available to the country is determined primarily by the purchasing power of foreign exchange earnings: the greater the foreign exchange earnings, the greater the importation possible. Other factors such as foreign economic assistance, capital movements, changes in foreign currency reserve holdings, and international credit are ignored as of secondary importance in a long-run model. Therefore, total imports are simply given by the identity

$$M \doteq P_x X / P_m, \tag{26}$$

where P_x is an index of export prices and X is total real exports.

Total exports are determined by two factors. First, the greater is world real per-capita income, the greater are total exports. Secondly, the greater are export prices in domestic currency relative to domestic prices, the greater are total exports—alternatively, the greater the domestic rise in prices relative to export prices, the more exporters are squeezed out of the market. These two factors—world income and relative prices—are presumed to dominate the export market. Normalizing total exports for world population and using the constant elasticity functional form, the export equation is then written

$$\ln(X/N_w) = k_0 + k_1 \ln(W/N_w) + k_2 \ln(P_x E/P), \tag{27}$$

where W is world real income in dollars and N_w is world population. In some countries the supply of exports may be completely inelastic with respect to moderate changes in export prices relative to domestic prices. In this case, k_2 would be equal to zero.

The exchange rate with the dollar (E) has entered the model in Eqs. (22) and (27). Although the exchange rate could be assumed exogenous, greater interest may attach to any simulation of the model if an attempt is made to explain the behavior of this rate over time. The explanation is introduced now by considering the supply and demand for foreign exchange.

First, the supply of foreign exchange is earned by exporters who are usually required to turn this supply over to the central bank in return for domestic currency. This foreign exchange is demanded by investors and consumers who wish to buy foreign products (government purchases are not separately considered here). If the demand for foreign exchange exceeds supply, then (i) foreign exchange reserves may decrease; (ii) devaluation of the currency may take place; (iii) credit may be obtained from abroad; (iv) import duties or quotas may be instituted; or (v) import licensing may be introduced. Decreases in reserves or obtaining credit from abroad are generally considered to be in the nature of short-run mechanisms. Import duties or licenses are possible long-run controls, but are not as important in controlling long-run *changes* in excess demand as exchange rate adjustments. Thus, even though the underdeveloped country may not be under a flexible exchange system, greater and greater pressure is put upon the government to change the exchange rate when domestic price increases cause the real earnings of exporters to decrease and import prices to become relatively cheaper. Therefore, the long-run movement in the exchange rate should be determined by changes in the domestic price level relative to import prices (in dollars).[6]

Since there may be considerable lags between changes in the domestic price level relative to import prices and changes in the exchange rate, and since there is no a priori knowledge about the types of lags involved, the model assumes that the current exchange rate is a function of a distributed lag of domestic prices relative to import prices (after adjustment for import duties). Let the exchange rate be a function of $(P/P_m)^*$, a distributed lag of domestic prices relative to import prices, so that

$$\ln E = p_0' + p_1 \ln(P/P_m)^*.$$

Now let

$$(P/P_m)^* = [(P/P_m)(P_{-1}/P_{m_{-1}})^{\lambda}(P_{-2}/P_{m_{-2}})^{\lambda^2}\cdots]^{1-\lambda},$$

where λ is a parameter such that $0 \leqslant \lambda < 1$, and where P is the domestic price level in domestic currency and P_m is the import price level in dollars. When $P/P_m = P_{-1}/P_{m_{-1}} = P_{-2}/P_{m_{-2}} = \cdots$, then $(P/P_m)^* = P/P_m$. Also, if $\lambda = 0$, then there are no lags in adjustment.

Substituting the second equation into the first, carrying out the usual lagging of this equation by one time period and multiplying by λ, and then subtracting this lagged equation from the first equation, we have

$$\ln E = p_0 + \lambda \ln E_{-1} + p_1(1-\lambda)\ln(P/P_m). \tag{28}$$

Thus, Eq. (28) is an expression for the current exchange rate in terms of the exchange rate last year and the current ratio of domestic prices to import prices. If the exchange rate is solely determined in the long run by the domestic price level relative to the general level of import prices, p_1 would equal one.

F. Summary

All of the behavioral equations and identities have now been introduced so that the growth model is complete. There are 19 behavioral equations: 3 of them establish the production functions (Eqs. 1–3); 9 determine the

[6] Export prices (which face exporters) are not separately considered. Also the import prices relevant here are after adjustment for import duties; increases in duties can lower the pressure on the exchange rate. Thus, the model does not exclude the influence of import duties on rationing the supply of foreign exchange.

utilization of factor inputs (Eqs. 10–18); 4 establish price levels (Eqs. 5–7, 22); 2 represent the behavior of exports and the exchange rate (Eqs. 27, 28); and one determines urban wages (Eq. 20). Also, 9 identities (Eqs. 4, 8, 9, 19, 21, 23–26) have been introduced into the model. Table II lists all the variables of the model (P^b and P^e are not included, since they will generally be posited to move with other included variables).

TABLE II

LIST OF VARIABLES

Symbol	Description
	Endogenous Variables
Y_i	real output of the ith sector
Y	total real output
Z	real national income
K_i^b	real capital stock in buildings in the ith sector
K_i^e	real capital stock in equipment in the ith sector
L_i	employment in the ith sector
L_n	employment in the secondary and tertiary sectors together
w_n	nominal wage rate in the secondary and tertiary sectors
w_1	nominal wage rate in the primary sector
P	general domestic price level
$(P_i/P)^*$	expected relative price in the ith sector
P_i	price level in the ith sector
D	total real depreciation of capital stock
X	total real exports
M	total real imports
E	domestic currency to U.S. dollar exchange rate
	Exogenous Variables
1	number one
t	time trend
N	total population
W	world real income in dollars
N_w	world population
R	net real income remittances from abroad
Mo	nominal money supply
P_m	general level of import prices in dollars after adjustment for the rate of import duties
P_x	general level of export prices in dollars

II. Estimation of the International Sector with Colombian and Prewar Japanese Data: A Cursory Investigation

The model given in the preceding section has been estimated using two-stage least squares with some data for the Colombian economy (1925–1953) and the Japanese economy (1902–1938). Since this volume honors an economist strongly interested in the international influences on development, estimates for those equations directly relating to the international sector, namely, the equations for total exports, the exchange rate, and the general domestic price level, are mentioned here. Results from estimating the core of the model given by Table I are reported in Zarembka [10], while general comments on estimation and data procedures are given in Chap. 3 of Zarembka [8].

First, the estimates for the export equations are

Colombia:

$$\ln(X/N_{\mathrm{w}}) = \underset{(0.068)}{1.957} + \underset{(0.114)}{0.574} \ln(W/N_{\mathrm{w}}) + \underset{(0.134)}{0.022} \ln(P_{\mathrm{x}} E/P), \qquad R^2 = 0.511,$$

Japan:

$$\ln(X/N_{\mathrm{w}}) = \underset{(9.395)}{0.346} + \underset{(0.714)}{2.888} \ln(W/N_{\mathrm{w}}) + \underset{(1.593)}{0.163} \ln(P_{\mathrm{x}} E/P), \qquad R^2 = 0.443,$$

where world income and world population are given by the relevant observations for the United States. On the one hand, these estimates demonstrate the importance for exports of the income of the purchasers of exports and, interestingly, indicate the income elasticity of demand for exports to be less than one for Colombia, which exported primary goods, while greater than one for Japan, which exported secondary products. On the other hand, while the price coefficients have the expected sign, they are not significantly different from zero. The expectation is that increasing export prices relative to domestic prices would lead to an increasing supply of exports. In sum, only income of importers, not prices, strongly influences export volume.

The two endogenous variables of the model that affect total exports are the exchange rate E and the general domestic price level P. Reporting results for these equations in turn, the exchange rate equation estimates are

Colombia:

$$\ln E = \underset{(0.096)}{0.055} + \underset{(0.093)}{0.967} \ln E_{-1} + \underset{(0.093)}{0.014} \ln(P/P_{\mathrm{m}}), \qquad R^2 = 0.939,$$

Japan:

$$\ln E = \underset{(0.495)}{1.157} + \underset{(0.113)}{0.755} \ln E_{-1} + \underset{(0.083)}{0.184} \ln(P/P_{\mathrm{m}}), \qquad R^2 = 0.808.$$

In Colombia there is no indication that domestic prices relative to import prices affect the exchange rate, while for Japan there is evidence that this relative price does have an impact, but with a rather long average lag $(0.755/(1-0.755) = 3.08$ years). The Japanese estimate is the expected result, while the Colombian is left unexplained.

The Colombian and Japanese estimates of the domestic price level equation are:

Colombia:

$$\ln(P/P_{-1}) = \underset{(0.261)}{0.310} + \underset{(0.277)}{0.748} \ln(\mathrm{Mo}/\mathrm{Mo}_{-1}) - \underset{(1.366)}{1.221} \ln(Y/Y_{-1})$$

$$+ \underset{(0.209)}{0.222} \ln(P_M E/P_{M_{-1}} E_{-1}) + \underset{(0.123)}{0.159} \ln(M/Y), \qquad R^2 = 0.478,$$

Japan:

$$\ln(P/P_{-1}) = \underset{(0.133)}{-0.052} + \underset{(0.177)}{0.605} \ln(\mathrm{Mo}/\mathrm{Mo}_{-1}) - \underset{(0.361)}{0.883} \ln(Y/Y_{-1})$$

$$+ \underset{(0.184)}{0.094} \ln(P_M E/P_{M_{-1}} E_{-1}) - \underset{(0.082)}{0.042} \ln(M/Y), \qquad R^2 = 0.415.$$

These estimates are quite interesting, since they provide a test of the monetarist versus structuralist arguments about the causes of inflation in underdeveloped countries. If the monetarists are correct, the change in money supply should have a coefficient of 1.0 and the change in output a coefficient of -1.0, with the other two coefficients zero. If the structuralists are correct, the change in output should have a coefficient greater than -1.0, the change in import prices should have a positive sign, the ratio of imports to output should have a negative sign, and the change in money supply should have a positive coefficient (to the extent that money supply changes accommodate to the price change due to structural bottlenecks).

Clearly, the ability-to-import variables offer no important explanation of price changes. Thus, the hypothesis that $g_1 = -g_2 = 1$ remains to be tested. Obtaining the appropriate F-statistics for this joint hypothesis, the test results are $F_{23}^2 = 1.72$ for Colombia, and $F_{31}^2 = 2.57$ for Japan. At the 5% level of significance, the null hypothesis is accepted for both countries. Thus, the estimates lead to acceptance of the monetarist position. However, while the "monetarists" may be correct in saying that money supply is the important influence on price level, this result does not necessarily imply that the price level has much to do with the "reals" of growth.

III. Comparisons of the Model with Other Development Models

The development model of this paper can be best contrasted with two approaches to development theory: that of Lewis [5] and elaborated upon by Fei and Ranis [2], and that of Jorgenson [4]. The various fixed-coefficient production models, such as the Harrod–Domar model or the many input–output studies, do not lend themselves to ready comparison with this long-run model—fixed coefficients are generally an untenable assumption for anything but the short run.

The Lewis–Fei–Ranis, or surplus labor, approach posits agricultural real wages constant at a subsistence level with urban real wages higher by some constant amount. Assuming competition and profit maximization in the urban areas, labor is employed there until the marginal productivity of urban labor is equal to the urban wage rate. The rural labor force exists under surplus conditions: the marginal productivity of rural labor is zero or, if positive, less than the rural wage rate. Development proceeds when labor is drawn from the rural sector to the urban sector as either capital is accumulated in the urban sector, or as labor-using innovations are incorporated in the urban sector.

In the model of this paper the underdeveloped economy is divided into three sectors, so that services can be separately considered from manufacturing in the urban sector. The rural wage rate is not posited to be at the subsistence level but rather is revenue less costs of agricultural production per worker. Labor is not "surplus," since a Cobb–Douglas production function is assumed, which implies that a reduction of the agricultural labor force reduces agricultural output. Additionally, the urban sectors can only induce labor off the farms by raising urban wages relative to rural wages.

Thus the only way in which this model can be said to exhibit characteristics of the Lewis–Fei–Ranis approach is in the assumption that the rural labor force is determined by supply and that, therefore, the marginal productivity of rural labor may happen to be less than the rural wage rate. But the model does not depend upon a zero marginal productivity of rural labor and is not concerned with the relation of rural wages to rural marginal productivity of labor.

Jorgenson's "neoclassical" model is more in accord with the methodology behind this model, although he also has only one urban sector. As here,

Jorgenson assumes the marginal productivity of labor in agriculture always positive; in fact, he also employs a Cobb–Douglas production function with technological change. Secondly, as in this paper, Jorgenson assumes the real wage rates in the sectors to be variable, not fixed as in the surplus labor model of Lewis, Fei, and Ranis. However, in contrast to this model, Jorgenson assumes the urban–rural real wage ratio to be constant; this model assumes that the ratio is related to the change in demand for urban labor. Also, unlike here, Jorgenson assumes that population growth at low levels of income is related to per capita agricultural output. But he does not consider this specification fundamental to his approach.

Thus the model of this paper should be considered more as a generalization in several directions of Jorgenson's model rather than any sort of an agricultural labor surplus model. The model is more general than Jorgenson's in that:

(i) The urban–rural relative wage rate is specified to depend upon the demand for urban employment—it is not specified to be a constant;

(ii) The economy is disaggregated into three sectors, and capital is disaggregated into buildings and equipment;

(iii) The international market is introduced, though only through domestic price behavior; and

(iv) The specification of profit maximization is more explicitly formulated.

However, the model suffers relative to both the surplus labor approach and Jorgenson's neoclassical approach when the behavior of capital is considered. The other two models tied capital growth to savings (although in a simple way). In this paper no such link is developed, because the secondary sector is not disaggregated into consumer goods and capital goods. Thus an important improvement of this model would be to determine a method for allocating both domestic secondary sector output and secondary sector imports into capital and consumption goods so that capital stock could be more closely tied to production and to imports.

REFERENCES

[1] Campos, Roberto de Oliveira, Two Views on Inflation in Latin America, "Latin American Issues" (A. O. Hirschman, ed.), pp. 69–73. Twentieth Century Fund, New York, 1961.

[2] Fei, J. C. H., and Ranis, G., "Development of the Labor Surplus Economy, Theory and Policy," Irwin, Homewood, Illinois, 1964.

[3] Green, H. A. J., "Aggregation in Economic Analysis, An Introductory Survey." Princeton Univ. Press, Princeton, New Jersey, 1964.

[4] Jorgenson, D. W., The Development of a Dual Economy, *Econ. J.* **71**, 309–334 (1961).

[5] Lewis, W. A., Economic Development with Unlimited Supplies of Labour, *Manchester School* **22**, 139–191 (1954). Also, Unlimited Labour: Further Notes, *Manchester School* **26**, 1–32 (1958), and the contribution to this volume.
[6] Meier, G. M., "Leading Issues in Development Economics," Oxford Univ. Press, New York, 1964.
[7] United Nations Dept. of Econ. and Social Affairs, "Demographic Aspects of Manpower, Report I, Sex and Age Patterns of Participation in Economic Activities." United Nations, New York, 1962.
[8] Zarembka, P., A Long-run Economic Growth Model for Underdeveloped Countries, unpublished doctoral dissertation, Univ. of Wisconsin (1967).
[9] Zarembka, P., A Note on Consistent Aggregation of Production Functions, *Econometrica* **36**, 419–420 (1968).
[10] Zarembka, P., Notes on Testing Symmetry Conditions between Factor Demand Equations, *Economica* **38**, 52–60 (1971).

IV. ECONOMIC POLICY, FOREIGN TRADE, AND DEVELOPMENT

The fourth part of this book includes a series of essays which, whether from a theoretical or empirical point of view, refer to aspects of economic policy in the light of foreign trade and development.

The essays by Balassa, by Fishlow, and by Bhagwati and Cheh are empirical in character. Balassa indicates the beneficial effects of development policies based on exports in Taiwan and Korea while Fishlow examines the policies of import substitution followed in Brazil. Finally, Bhagwati and Cheh's essay is an important empirical contribution to elucidate the relationship between exports and the "size" of a country, and other interesting considerations.

Among the essays which are in themselves theoretical, we can mention Corden's and Chipman's. The former is especially concerned with the effects of protective policies on economic development. The latter analyzes stages related to the theory of exploitative trade and investment policies within the frame of Center–Periphery relationships.

Dagum's and Elías' works stand out as being the most clearly econometric. Dagum is concerned with a stochastic model of the functional distribution of income, and Elías tries to show us how to quantify the external sector's contribution to national income. Both papers include a good number of empirical results tending to support the explanatory power of their models.

Finally, de Bernis' paper is an essay of theoretical–institutional character. The author analyzes the historical conditions and possible trends in international economic relations by drawing a parallel between the neoclassical scheme of growth and the industrialization theory inspired by Prebisch's ideas.

The paper written by *Balassa* takes as its aim an analysis of the industrial policies followed by Taiwan and Korea after World War II. His essay begins with a rapid overview of development strategies in Latin American countries and Asia, which he finds basically conform to two very distinct approaches: (a) a substitution policy for imports of manufactures ("inward looking"); and (b) a policy built upon a system of export incentives ("outward looking"). The author points out the reasons adduced by Taiwan and by Korea in taking the second approach. Balassa then examines the results of the incentive system, that is, the beneficial effects such policies have had on exports and economic growth, and the interrelationship between the two.

As might be expected, the bulk of the attention is paid to the manufacturing sector—its export performance, growth, and structure. Finally, Balassa explores the present and future prospects for the national economies of Taiwan and Korea with reflections on the applicability of an "outward-looking" development strategy to other countries.

The paper written by *Bhagwati* and *Cheh* on the exports of developing countries deals with a cross-sectional analysis to examine two hypotheses for LDC exports: (a) Does the "size" of a country correlate with the share of exports in its national income; and (b) does the share of manufactured exports in its total exports tend to reflect that country's share of manufacturing value added to its national income, and the latter in turn to reflect the country's income per capita? The regression results bear out these hypotheses.

Corden's contribution to this volume is an attempt to systematize some points relating the level of protection to the growth rate of real income. There are two issues implied in this problem. The first is concerned with "protection to make the best of growth" (for instance, the initial theory of Dr. Prebisch); the second deals with the effects of protection upon the rate of growth (and this is the writer's concern). In fact, there are two aspects to this theme: one refers to positive economics, mentioned above; the other is analyzed in terms of welfare economics, whose main object is to determine whether an increase in the rate of growth through a given protective structure should be considered an argument strong enough to justify imposing or changing it. The argument subsequently turns to how protection affects savings (the real-income, income-distribution, and other effects), to the policy implications of these effects, to the "linkage" effects, and to the interdependence between learning and the growth rate. Relating these aspects, Corden points out that policy measures should be supported not only by a clear rationale based on economic theory, but be founded on the special circumstances of the country concerned.

The paper written by *Chipman* on the theory of exploitative trade and investment policies is devoted to the theoretical analysis of a model first formulated by Kemp, and further studied by Jones, of two countries, each capable of producing two commodities with labor and capital, when capital is internationally mobile. The problem is to ascertain the kinds of tariffs on traded commodities and taxes on income from foreign investment that would maximize a country's national advantage—whether this be an advanced industrial Center vis-à-vis the Periphery, or an underdeveloped country or region vis-à-vis the Center. Attention is focused on the latter, and especially on the case in which the lending country produces both commodities. It is found that in the absence of restrictive commercial policies, nothing is to be gained from interference with international capital movements, which is therefore justified only as an adjunct to commercial policy. Furthermore, a criterion is developed to determine whether foreign investment in the peripheral countries should be encouraged or penalized: if the Periphery exports goods whose production is labor intensive in the Center, then commercial policy, by improving the terms of trade of the Periphery, also lowers profit rates in the Center, making it possible and advantageous for the Periphery to tax income from foreign investments. On the other hand, if the Periphery exports goods whose production is capital intensive in the Center, measures to improve its terms of trade will also drive up profit rates in the Center, raising the cost of capital to the Periphery and making it necessary and advisable to subsidize income from foreign investments, in order to prevent foreign capital from being withdrawn. After an introduction, Chipman deals with these topics: (a) a production function for foreign exchange; (b) the offer curve when capital is mobile; (c) the problem described above; and (d) exploitative tax and tariff policies. Finally, the author uses some of the results to derive interesting implications for the theory of exploitative trade and investment policies.

Dagum's paper is a stochastic model of the functional distribution of income, which sketches the main lines of thought related to the theories of income distribution, and later describes two fundamental approaches: (a) the structural analysis, and (b) the dynamic analysis. The possibilities and scope of the former are elucidated by means of the theory of games, while the latter is presented through the specification of a set of postulates from which a logistic behavior pattern of the labor share in national income is derived. The model is found to have explanatory power both by countries (time-series analysis) and between countries (spatial analysis). In the first case, parameters have been estimated with time-series data for Canada, U.S.A., France, Sweden, and other countries, whereas in the cross-section analysis sample data for 37 countries (for 1967) have been used to investigate the stochastic properties of the estimators.

de Bernis' contribution to this volume is a study of the industrializing industries and the economic integration of less-developed countries and is a rather extensive analysis of the problems of underdevelopment. Taking as his starting point the comparison between neoclassic growth theory and the theory of industrialization inspired by Prebisch, the writer points out the two determinants of a general theory of industrialization: (a) structural conditions, and (b) the content of an industrial policy. Within this framework, de Bernis analyzes a second set of features: industrial process, cohesive industrial structure, accumulation process, sectoral allocation of investment, and selection of techniques. Using the concept of "industrializing industries," he reviews the historical situation and possible trends in advanced and underdeveloped countries in terms of agricultural and industrial productivities and from the point of view of the process of commodity exchange. He then proceeds to an examination of the "conditions" a policy of industrialization must meet: *internal* conditions (social structure, control of essential resources) and *external* ones (breaking of "vertical" dependence relations, the creation of "horizontal" linkages, such as regional economic integration). For this last, two types of coherence are treated, the spatial and temporal ones. de Bernis concludes by indicating that the increasing distance between developed and less-developed countries is not a product of chance or ignorance, but should be attributed to imperialism, under which any industrial policy such as the one proposed is impossible. However, as a way of getting rid of preanalytic "economism," the writer thinks that a politically based vision of development (by means of horizontal integration) will destroy imperialism through an attack on its weaknesses and contradictions.

The paper written by *Elías* on trade's contribution to the growth of national income is a methodological essay on the "accounting of growth," and deals with quantification of external factors. The essay contains a theoretical formulation as well as a brief empirical investigation. The model is designed to provide a formal introduction of the external sector in the explanation of income growth (basically through the behavior of the terms-of-trade). The analysis that follows develops the importance that changes in existing differences between domestic and world prices may have in the contribution of trade to income (which is worked out in a version of the familiar cost of protection approach). Employing his model, Elías concludes with some preliminary results which attempt to evaluate the significance of international trade in Argentine economic development.

Fishlow's paper examines the process of import substitution in Brazil from its first appearance on a large scale in the textile industry at the end of the 1890s to the final decade of significant substitution, in the 1950s. It shows how early industrialization was the result of exchange-rate variation in response to internal inflation, rather than related to an explicit state policy of protection through tariffs. It also demonstrates that, despite the continued expansion of industry during World War I, by 1920 Brazil was far from industrialized.

The great spurt of industrial growth occurred during the Depression. Not only was industrial growth significant, but it was also labor intensive, as the proportion of the labor force in industry increased between 1920 and 1940 from 3.5–10 per cent of the economically active population. The war once again gave a boost to industrial production on the side of demand. But more interesting, after the war the overvalued exchange rate, in combination with higher prices for coffee, permitted large imports of capital goods. Thus, although there was actually reverse import substitution between 1939 and 1949, it occurred in such a way that the process of industrialization as a whole was favored.

During the 1950s, there was for the first time active state policy to encourage import substitution in the consumer durables sector. This meant substantial foreign investment, and resulted in sensitivity to cyclical influences at the beginning of the 1960s. The slow-down in growth was less due to underconsumption than to overinvestment and creation of excess capacity. Finally, Fishlow shows that the concept of import substitution places too much emphasis on the demand side, and does not adequately recognize that subsidies on the supply side were essential to the process. For that reason, when the import coefficient was reduced, people mistakenly began to talk of the exhaustion of the process and failed to understnad that continued growth was feasible.

INDUSTRIAL POLICIES IN TAIWAN AND KOREA *

BELA BALASSA

Johns Hopkins University, Baltimore, Maryland
and International Bank for Reconstruction and Development, Washington, D.C.

I. "Inward-Looking" and "Outward-Looking" Development Strategies[1]

In the postwar period several Latin American and Asian countries adopted an "inward-looking" development strategy based on import substitution in manufacturing carried out behind high protective barriers. This strategy made it possible to attain high rates of economic growth during the period of "easy" import substitution when imports of nondurable consumer goods and the intermediate goods used in their manufacture were replaced by domestic production. The conditions prevailing in the countries in question suited the manufacturing of these commodities, as they can be produced efficiently on a relatively small scale, require mostly unskilled and semiskilled labor, and rarely necessitate the application of sophisticated technological methods.

However, once practically all such imports had been replaced, the expansion of the production of nondurable consumer goods and their inputs could not continue to exceed increases in domestic demand. In seeking new sources of industrial growth, most countries following inward-looking strategies then turned to import substitution in other intermediate products, machinery and durable consumer goods. In so doing, they have encountered limitations due

* Reprinted from *Weltwirtschaftliches Archiv*. **106** (1971).

[1] The first few paragraphs are based largely on my Growth Strategies in Semi-Industrial Countries [3].

to the narrowness of their domestic markets and the technological and capital requirements of the industries in question. These industries generally need high levels of output for efficient operation, and costs increase to a considerable extent at lower output levels—both in the manufacturing of the product itself and in the production of its parts, components, and accessories. They further require the availability of skilled workers and technicians, the use of sophisticated technological methods, and tend to be capital intensive, thereby raising the investment requirements of additional increments in national income.

Apart from permitting the establishment of high-cost firms, high levels of protection under an inward-looking strategy tend to discourage improvements in technology and in product quality and have detrimental effects on export performance. Exporters of primary goods are penalized by the high cost of industrial inputs and overvalued exchange rates associated with protection. There is also a bias against exporting manufactured goods, since producers can get a substantially higher price in protected domestic markets than abroad. In countries following an inward-looking strategy, the result has often been a slowdown in the expansion of exports with adverse effects for the growth of the national economy. In the second stage of import substitution, growth is also hampered by the high cost of domestic manufacturing and the large capital requirements of the new industries.

The Republic of China (Taiwan) and Korea, too, started out with import substitution in nondurable consumer goods and their inputs; by the late fifties, they had replaced virtually all such imports. Instead of concentrating on import substitution in intermediate products, machinery, and durable consumer goods, however, the two countries subsequently embarked on an export-oriented policy. This policy was adopted in Taiwan towards the end of the Second Four Year Plan period (1957–1960) and continued during the period of the subsequent Four Year Plans. In Korea certain changes in policies were made in 1961, but the major policy shift occurred at the time of the exchange rate reform of 1964.[2]

The "outward-looking" strategy adopted in Taiwan and Korea has entailed changes in the system of incentives in favor of exports. Also, the extent of protection in the manufacturing sector has been reduced, while primary activities have benefited from the adoption of more realistic exchange rates. Still, the major effect of this policy has been on the exportation of labor-intensive manufactured goods, and the expansion of these exports has importantly contributed to the acceleration of economic growth in the two countries.

[2] Several studies describe the policy changes carried out in the two countries. On Taiwan, see Ken C. Y. Lin [16], and Kuo-shu Liang [17]; on Korea, Kanesa-Thasan [15], and Brown [5].

After a short discussion of the policies applied during the fifties, we will consider the reasons for adopting an outward-looking strategy in Taiwan and Korea and the methods applied in carrying out this strategy. Subsequently, we will examine the effects of the policies followed on exports and on economic growth, and the interrelationship between the two. Special attention will be given to the manufacturing sector—its export performance, growth, and structure. Finally, we will analyze the present problems and future prospects for the national economies of Taiwan and Korea, with some considerations on the applicability of an outward-looking development strategy to other countries.

II. Industrial Policies during the Fifties

The industrialization of Taiwan and Korea began in the interwar period under Japanese occupation. While during the twenties industrial activities were, by and large, restricted to food processing, in the following decade the Japanese developed some heavy industries, among them aluminum (Taiwan), steel (Korea), cement, paper, and chemicals (in both countries) to assist their war effort. Industries producing nondurable consumer goods were, however, discouraged, as Japan wished to conserve for its own industry the market outlets for these commodities in the two territories. In exchange, they sold a variety of foodstuffs, fishery products, and some raw materials to Japan.

Neither country continued with the development of heavy industries in the period following the second world war. In Taiwan, war-damaged industrial plants were more or less restored, but the domestic market offered few possibilities for the expansion—or even the full utilization—of existing capacities. In Korea, most heavy industrial plants remained in the North after partition and, apart from fertilizers, the development of these industries in the South was hindered by the lack of sufficient home demand.

By contrast, industries producing nondurable consumer goods and their inputs provided opportunities for replacing imports by domestic production in the two countries. Independence from Japan not only made it possible to develop such industries but, because of the loss of assured markets for certain primary exports, it also necessitated savings in imports that could be realized in commodities such as textiles, shoes, and clothing.

In both countries, import substitution was carried out behind high tariff walls and was fostered by exchange controls. In Taiwan, it was also helped by the inflow of Chinese entrepreneurs and the increased needs of the population augmented by immigrants from the mainland. In Korea, the development of industries producing nondurable consumer goods and their inputs became part of the reconstruction effort after the end of hostilities with the North.

Import substitution in textiles, clothing, and shoes and other leather products contributed to the rapid growth of industrial production in Taiwan and Korea during the fifties. By the end of the decade, however, import substitution in these industries was virtually completed, with imports accounting for less than 10 per cent of domestic consumption, and both countries came to experience sluggish growth as well as balance-of-payments difficulties. Accordingly, new policies had to be devised to improve the balance of payments and to attain high rates of economic growth which had become a political as much as an economic objective.

III. Reasons for Adopting an "Outward-Looking" Strategy

As regards the policy choices available to Taiwan and Korea around 1960, the first consideration is the poor natural resource endowment of the two countries. They have few minerals and the ratio of the population to arable land is high. Reduced demand for sugar, rice, and some other primary products in Japan further limited the possibilities for relying chiefly on agricultural exports to attain rapid economic growth in Taiwan. Korea, too, encountered market limitations in some of its primary exports to Japan (e.g., laver and agar-agar).

With import substitution in nondurable consumer goods and in the intermediate products used in their manufacture virtually completed, production for domestic markets in these industries did not offer sufficient possibilities for rapid growth either. At the same time, the smallness of domestic markets in Taiwan and Korea restricted the scope—and raised the cost—of import substitution in intermediate products, machinery, and consumer durables. In 1960, the total market for manufactured goods, including food processing, was about $0.7 billion in the two countries as against $23 billion in India, $14 billion in Brazil, and $10 billion in Argentina.[3] Thus, the possibilities for import substitution were much smaller in Taiwan and in Korea than in the last mentioned countries, while the economic cost of import substitution was more apparent.[4]

The choice among development strategies is also affected by the opportunities for regional integration in the form of a customs union or common

[3] Data on the size of domestic markets for manufactured goods, defined as industrial output plus imports minus exports, have been taken from Balassa and Hughes [4]. Revised estimates for Taiwan and Korea are shown in Table I.

[4] It should be added, however, that, market size limitations notwithstanding, small countries such as Chile and Algeria passed to the second stage of import substitution.

market. Instead of adopting export-oriented policies, Central American countries with even smaller markets ($0.2–0.4 billion) have endeavored to expand their industries in the framework of a customs union, for example. For geographical and political reasons, this choice was not open to Taiwan and Korea around 1960, nor have recent efforts for industrial cooperation between the two countries met with much success.

The adoption of outward-oriented policies in Taiwan and Korea has further been influenced by the availability of a well-motivated labor force with a high educational level and relatively low wages that provides the two countries with a competitive advantage in exporting labor-intensive goods. The expansion of these industries also offered possibilities for absorbing unemployment while requiring less capital per unit of output than does the production of most intermediate goods, machinery, and durable consumer goods.

Mention should finally be made of the determination of the leadership in the two countries to attain high rates of economic growth, and the virtual lack of constraint on their ability to make decisions and to carry them out. In this connection, one should note that vested interests in import substitution were less important in Taiwan and Korea than in countries such as Argentina and Chile, where import substitution extends to intermediate products, machinery, and durable consumer goods.

IV. The System of Incentives

Prior to 1960, both Taiwan and Korea applied a system of incentives characteristic of countries following inward-looking policies. Tariffs and quantitative restrictions provided high levels of protection against imports and, in the absence of export subsidies, there was a bias against exporting manufactured goods. The protection of manufactured goods also penalized the primary sector through the high prices of manufactured inputs and low exchange rates that reduced the domestic currency equivalent of foreign exchange earnings.

In Taiwan, a drastic overhaul of the system of incentives took place in the years 1958–1961. The multiple exchange-rate structure was replaced by a dual rate in April, 1958, and by a single exchange rate of 40 Taiwanese dollars per U.S. dollar in August, 1959, that has been in effect ever since. In conjunction with the exchange reform, the import quota system was liberalized and the prior deposit requirement on import applications removed.

In addition to adopting a realistic exchange rate, a variety of tax and credit measures were introduced to promote exports. The transformation of

TABLE I

COMPARATIVE DATA FOR TAIWAN AND KOREA[a,b]

	Taiwan				Korea			
	1953	1960	1964	1969	1953	1960	1964	1969
Basic Data								
Gross domestic product ($ million)	972	1550	2285	4782	1673	2325	2971	6947
Population (thousands)	8261	10612	12070	14312	21440	24695	27631	31410
Per capita gross domestic product ($)	118	146	189	334	78	94	108	221
Manufacturing value added per head ($)	14	25	39	61	6	11	16	45
Share of manufacturing in gross domestic product (per cent)	11.6	17.3	20.8	23.5	7.6	12.1	14.8	20.3
Exports and Imports								
Total exports per head ($)	15	15	36	80	2	1	4	20
Exports of manufactures per head ($)	1	5	14	51	0[c]	0	2	15
Share of manufactured exports in total exports (per cent)	6	30	39	67	10	12	49	76
Total imports per head ($)	23	28	36	86	16	14	15	48
Imports of manufactures per head ($)	5	15	18	54	5[c]	7	7	34
Share of manufactured imports in total imports (per cent)	52	53	51	64	33	48	51	58

Manufacturing (excluding food, beverages, and tobacco)								
Manufacturing output ($ million)	217	561	1066	2045	264	573	899	2601
Domestic market for manufactured products ($ million)	309	669	1117	2079	374	736	1047	3186
Ratio of exports of manufactures to manufacturing output (per cent)	3.7	8.7	15.8	36.1	1.5	0.7	6.5	18.4
Ratio of imports of manufactures to domestic market for manufactured products (per cent)	32.4	23.5	19.6	37.1	30.5	22.7	19.7	33.3
Average wages in manufacturing ($/day)	0.74	0.92	1.10	1.61[d]	na	1.07	0.61	1.15[d]
Investment and Saving								
Share of domestic savings in gross product (per cent)	8.5	12.0	19.2	23.8	8.2	2.4	7.5	18.3
Share of investment in gross product (per cent)	13.9	20.0	19.2	26.3	16.2	10.9	14.6	29.5
Share of manufacturing investment in total investment (per cent)	25.0	30.2	32.1	33.03	20.0	20.0	23.9	19.3
Financing of Investment								
Domestic savings (per cent)	62.5	62.7	102.1	90.4	50.6	21.7	51.4	61.9
Foreign savings (per cent)	37.5	37.3	−2.1	9.6	49.4	78.3	48.6	38.1

[a] Sources: Korea, "Economic Statistics Yearbook" and "Major Economic Indicators"; Taiwan, "Statistical Data Book"; U.N., "Yearbook of National Accounts Statistics," "Statistical Yearbook," "Yearbook of International Trade Statistics," "Commodity Trade Statistics".

[b] Values in U.S. dollars at current prices and exchange rates.

[c] 1954.

[d] Wages for Taiwan are averages for the first five months of 1968, for Korea, all of 1968.

Taiwan's industrial structure has been further helped by the encouragement of foreign investment, the liberalization of policies regarding the establishment of new firms in existing industries, and the creation of the Industrial Development and Investment Center and of the China Development Corporation.

Similar policy changes are observed in Korea, except that in this country the changeover was made in two steps, in 1961 and in 1964, of which the second was of far greater importance. In early 1961, the dual exchange rate system applied in previous years was unified, with the official exchange rate devalued from 65 *won* to 130 *won* per dollar; import restrictions were also eased. In subsequent years, however, inflation ate away part of the incentives the devaluation had provided to exports; it necessitated imposing severe restrictions on imports and led to the reintroduction of multiple exchange rates.

Following the foreign exchange crisis of 1963, a unified exchange rate system was again adopted in May, 1964, when the official rate was raised from 130 *won* to 255 *won* to the dollar. At the same time, a comprehensive export promotion system was introduced and imports were liberalized. The number of import items not subject to import prohibitions was increased from 420 to 1630 by the end of 1965 and to 2490 by the end of 1966. These actions were accompanied by internal stabilization measures aimed at stemming inflationary pressures.

The described policy changes, together with the measures taken in subsequent years, have transformed the system of incentives in the two countries from emphasis on import substitution to emphasis on export promotion. In fact, compared to most other developing countries, the distinguishing characteristic of the incentive system applied in Taiwan and Korea is the advantageous treatment of both primary and manufactured exports. On balance, however, manufactured exports are favored over primary exports, since several of the export incentives reduce to a greater degree the cost of inputs of the former than of the latter.

Export incentives in Taiwan comprise rebates of customs duties (including harbor dues and defense surtaxes) and of indirect taxes on imported raw materials and components used in making export goods; retention of foreign exchange earnings for the purchase of raw materials and machinery subject to import permits, together with the possibility of selling such import rights to other firms; exemption from the business tax and the stamp tax; deduction of two per cent of annual export earnings from taxable income; low interest rate loans to finance the importation of raw materials and machinery used in exporting; and export insurance by a governmental organization. There are also direct subsidies to exports in a few industries, such as cotton spinning and rubber products, financed through manufacturers' associations. Finally, exports have been assisted by governmental institutes for market research and, since 1965, by the creation of a duty-free zone for processing of imported materials.

In Korea, the measures used to promote exports include exemptions from customs duties on imported materials and capital equipment used in the production of export commodities; exemptions from the business activities and commodity tax; reduction by 50 per cent of income taxes on profits earned from exports; export credit and loans for the purchase of raw materials and equipment at preferential rates; an export–import linkage system that permits exporters to import goods on the prohibited list for own use or for resale; high wastage allowance on raw materials imported for use in exports; and preferential electricity and transportation rates. Governmental assistance in export promotion abroad by KOTRA, an official trade organization, and by Korean embassies has also been of importance. Finally, mention should be made of informal pressures exerted by the president on business leaders to expand exports.

The incentive measures introduced in the two countries have improved the profitability of exports; in some instances exportation is more profitable than production for the domestic market. The resulting expansion of exports has "loosened" the balance-of-payments constraint and, apart from permitting high rates of economic growth, this has made possible the liberalization of import policy. The system of import restrictions is rather flexible in the two countries and tariffs are generally lower than in developing nations at similar levels of industrialization. Thus, while in Latin American countries average tariffs on imports are often in the 100–150 per cent range, the corresponding averages in Taiwan and Korea are about 20–30 per cent.

Relatively low levels of protection of manufacturing industries also mean that agriculture in the two countries is less penalized by high prices of inputs and overvalued exchange rates than is the case in most developing nations. Agriculture has further been assisted by direct policy measures, especially in Taiwan. These include, among other things, the provision of extension services, credits, improved seeds, as well as incentives for the use of machinery and for multiple cropping.

V. Export Performance and Economic Growth[5]

The policies followed during the sixties have led to the rapid expansion of exports in Taiwan and Korea. Between 1960 and 1969, the two countries

[5] Unless otherwise indicated, data on export performance and growth have been taken from Table II. In the case of developing countries, the figures shown in the table have been adjusted to exclude certain groups of countries.

increased their exports of manufactured goods at annual rates of 34 and 69 per cent, respectively, with higher rates in Korea in part explained by the lower initial base. In the same period, manufactured exports from developing countries other than those following export-oriented industrialization policies (apart from Taiwan and Korea, Hong Kong, Israel, Singapore, and, in recent years, Pakistan) rose at an annual rate not exceeding 8 per cent.

It should be emphasized that high rates of export growth were maintained throughout the period and that exports of manufactured goods assumed considerable importance in absolute terms. Thus, in 1969 the exports of manufactured goods from Taiwan and Korea, taken together, were approximately three times as large as from Latin America (excluding trade within LAFTA), which has an industrial output about eight times greater.[6]

The system of incentives applied has also encouraged the expansion of primary exports. The exports of primary products in Taiwan and Korea rose at average annual rates of 13 and 20 per cent between 1960 and 1969 as against 3 per cent a year in the nonoil-producing developing countries. As a result, total exports grew 23 per cent a year in Taiwan and 39 per cent in Korea during this period. By contrast, in the nonoil-producing developing countries, the average annual rate of increase of exports was about 5 per cent.

The rapid expansion of exports has importantly contributed to economic growth in the two countries. Taiwan experienced growth rates of GDP of 9.9 per cent and Korea 9.2 per cent in the period 1960–1969 as against approximately 4.5 per cent in the nonoil-producing developing countries. In Taiwan, economic growth proceeded at consistently high rates throughout this period, while in Korea growth accelerated to a considerable extent following the 1964 reforms (Table II).

Exports contribute to economic growth in various ways. To begin with, by permitting specialization according to comparative advantage, an export-oriented strategy permits a better use of a country's resources. As noted earlier, in Taiwan and Korea exports of nondurable consumer goods have utilized the educated manpower of the two countries, while import substitution in intermediate products, machinery, and consumer durables would have required substantial amounts of capital. In this connection, data on employment and on fixed investment are of interest.

In Taiwan, total employment increased at an average annual rate of 4.1 per cent between 1960 and 1969, while the rise of employment in manufacturing was considerably faster. In Korea, the increase in total employment was 2.8 per cent and in manufacturing employment 11.7 per cent a year during the period 1963–1969, for which data are available. In the same period, manufacturing absorbed three-fifths of the increases in the Korean labor force

[6] U.N. [7] and national statistics.

TABLE II

AVERAGE ANNUAL GROWTH RATES IN TAIWAN, IN KOREA, AND IN ALL DEVEOLPING COUNTRIES[a,b]

	Taiwan				Korea				Developing Countries			
	53–60	60–64	64–69	60–69	53–60	60–64	64–69	60–69	53–60	60–64	64–68	60–68
Gross Domestic Product[c]	6.9	9.6	10.2	9.9	5.0	6.3	11.4	9.2	4.9	4.8	4.8	4.8
Population	3.6	3.3	3.2	3.0	2.0	2.8	2.3	2.6	2.5	2.4	2.4	2.3
Per Capita Gross Domestic Product[c]	3.1	6.1	6.8	6.5	3.0	3.3	8.9	6.4	2.3	2.3	2.3	2.3
Agriculture[c]	3.9	5.6	4.7	5.0	2.3	6.5	3.1	4.6	2.9	3.1	2.5	2.8
Manufacturing[c]	10.1	23.0	16.1	18.0	13.6	9.7	22.0	16.0	7.2	6.8	5.8	6.3
Total Exports[d]	3.6	27.5	18.8	23.1	−2.8	38.0	39.0	38.9	6.6	5.7	6.2	5.9
Total Exports Excluding Petroleum[d]	3.6	27.5	18.8	23.1	−2.8	38.0	39.0	38.9	2.0	4.5	5.1	4.8
Exports of Manufactured Goods[d]	29.5	36.1	34.2	34.5	0.2[e]	89.7	55.0	69.0	6.4	9.6	13.3	11.4
Total Imports[d]	6.4	9.6	24.2	19.0	−0.0	4.2	36.0	21.0	4.8	4.0	7.0	5.5
Imports of Manufactured Goods[d]	6.7	8.7	28.5	19.2	6.6[e]	5.4	40.0	26.0	6.3	4.3	9.0	6.6

[a] Source: same as Table I, p. 165.
[b] All figures are in per cent.
[c] Constant prices.
[d] Current prices.
[e] 1954–1960.

[19, 21].[7] By contrast, increases in manufacturing employment were small in developing countries following inward-looking policies, several of which (e.g., Chile and Colombia) experienced very little increase during the sixties [23].

The rapid rise of employment in the two countries has brought about a decline in unemployment, both in absolute and in relative terms. Between 1963 and 1968, the number of unemployed declined from 200 to 72 thousand in Taiwan and from 705 to 496 thousand in Korea; expressed as a proportion of the labor force, the decrease was from 5.3 to 1.7 per cent in Taiwan and from 8.4 to 5.1 per cent in Korea. Here again, we find a contrast with developing countries following inward-looking policies; most countries for which there are published data experienced increases in the rate of unemployment during the sixties [24].

At the same time, the capital needs of rapidly rising output—as indicated by incremental capital-output ratios—have been relatively low in Taiwan and Korea. In the 1960–1969 period, these ratios averaged 1.7 in the two countries,[8] whereas among developing countries for which comparable data are available, capital-output ratios were around 3 in Guatemala, Ecuador, and Paraguay, and around 3.5 in Bolivia, Colombia, and Peru [27].

The growth of exports has also made it possible to apply large-scale production methods in consumer goods industries and has led to improvements in technological methods and in product quality. Moreover, exports have contributed to economic growth indirectly through increased demand for domestic materials, higher incomes, and an improved balance-of-payments position. In the Taiwanese food-processing industries, for example, the rise in exports has encouraged the further development of intensive agriculture. In both Taiwan and Korea, the higher incomes obtained in exports and in the export-related sectors have increased demand for consumer goods of domestic manufacture. Last but not least, the foreign exchange revenue provided by exports has augmented the availability of imports needed for economic growth.

The leading role of exports in the growth process is indicated by the rise in the share of exports in GDP. Export shares increased from 11 per cent in 1960 to 23 per cent in 1969 in Taiwan, and from 1 per cent in 1960 to 9 per cent in 1969 in Korea. From the point of view of the contribution of exports to the growth of the economy, however, the *incremental* ratio of exports to GNP is of greater interest. In 1960–1969, the ratio of the absolute increase in the value

[7] The figures for Taiwan have been derived by interpolation.

[8] Taiwan [22], and Korea [18]. Incremental capital-output ratios have been calculated by dividing the value of gross fixed investment for the years 1960–1968 by the increment in GDP between 1960 and 1969, both expressed in constant prices.

of exports to the absolute increase in GDP was 39 per cent in Taiwan and 29 per cent in Korea.[9] The differences between these ratios indicate that, with a larger initial export share, the contribution of exports to GDP can be greater despite a lower rate of growth of exports.

VI. Manufacturing Output and Exports

The application of an "even-handed" system of incentives has contributed to the rapid growth of both agriculture and manufacturing in Taiwan and Korea. Between 1960 and 1969, value added in agriculture grew at an average annual rate of about 5 per cent a year in both countries. Given its excellent export performance and the increased home demand for nondurable consumer goods at higher income levels, the growth of the manufacturing sector has been even faster. During the period under consideration, value added in manufacturing grew at an annual average rate of 16 per cent in both Taiwan and Korea. The growth of manufacturing has further accelerated after the overhaul of the incentive system in 1964 (Table II).

The expansion of the manufacturing sector in the two countries has been conditioned by the growth of manufactured exports. One way of quantifying this relationship is to calculate the incremental ratio of exports to output in manufacturing. For the 1960–1969 period, this ratio was approximately 35 per cent in Taiwan and 25 per cent in Korea.[10] It should be added that this ratio underestimates the contribution of exports to the growth of manufacturing, since there is a certain amount of double-counting in the output figures that include both the production of final goods and that of intermediate products used in their manufacturing. Moreover, the data do not indicate the indirect effects of exports on industrial output through higher incomes.

By comparison, in developing countries following inward-looking policies not more than 2–3 per cent of industrial output is exported and, apart from the increase of trade among the LAFTA countries in recent years, this ratio has been unchanged over the last decade. Nor do manufactured goods provide more than 4–5 per cent of the total exports of most developing countries, while they account for two-thirds of exports in Taiwan and three-fourths in Korea.[11]

[9] The calculation has been made in constant prices from data given in the sources referred to in Table I.

[10] Compare the previous footnote.

[11] Table I and Balassa and Hughes [4].

VII. Export Composition and Industrial Structure

In Taiwan, the leading manufactured exports are clothing, telecommunications equipment, plywood, cotton fabrics, and plastic articles. If manufacturing is defined to include food processing, canned mushrooms, canned pineapple, and canned asparagus would also come into this category, raising the share of manufactured goods in total exports to 74 per cent (Tables III and IV). Among primary exports, bananas and sugar are of importance. But while banana exports have increased to a considerable extent following trade liberalization in Japan, sugar exports have been adversely affected by rising domestic production costs and declining world market prices.

Korea's major manufactured exports include plywood, wigs, clothing, fish, cotton fabrics, and wool and synthetic fabrics, in this order. Among these, plywood and cotton fabrics were of greatest importance during the first half of the sixties while clothing and, especially, wigs have assumed importance

TABLE III

MAJOR EXPORT COMMODITIES: TAIWAN[a,b]

Commodity	1953	1960	1964	1969
Agricultural Products				
Rice	8.7	3.1	4.6	0.4
Bananas	2.6	4.1	6.8	5.3
Sugar	69.5	44.1	28.2	4.3
Tea	5.3	3.7	1.8	1.2
Processed Agricultural Products				
Canned pineapple	2.0	4.9	3.0	1.9
Canned mushrooms	—	0.1	4.4	2.9
Canned asparagus spears	—	—	0.1	2.8
Manufactured Products				
Plywood	—	1.5	6.0	5.9
Cotton fabrics	na	7.3	4.5	4.7
Cement	0.8	0.7	3.0	1.0
Telecommunications equipment	—	—	0.3	7.6
Clothing	na	na	3.8	12.6
Plastic articles	na	na	1.5	4.3
Major Exports	88.9	69.5	68.0	54.9
Minor Exports	11.1	30.5	32.0	45.1
Total Exports	100.0	100.0	100.0	100.0

[a] Sources: U.N. [7, 26].
[b] Figures are given in per cent.

TABLE IV

MAJOR EXPORT COMMODITIES: KOREA[a,b]

Commodity	1953	1960	1964	1969
Agricultural Products				
Fresh fish	4.7	4.9	4.0	2.8
Rice	—	11.8	2.0	—
Dried laver	na	4.0	4.6	1.8
Processed Agricultural Products				
Processed fish	0.9	3.5	3.4	0.4
Shrimp and shrimp products	2.2	0.4	3.8	0.0
Other Primary Commodities				
Raw silk	6.2	3.1	4.9	3.4
Iron ore and concentrates	na	7.7	5.0	0.9
Tungsten ore and concentrates	44.1	14.8	3.9	1.8
Agar-agar	4.9	3.0	1.7	0.2
Manufactured Products				
Plywood	—	0.1	9.6	11.3
Cotton fabrics, woven	na	7.7	9.3	2.4
Other fabrics, woven	—	—	0.9	2.3
Clothing	—	—	4.7	8.2
Human hair and wigs	—	—	3.0	8.6
Major Exports	60.8	61.0	60.8	44.1
Minor Exports	39.2	39.0	39.2	55.9
Total Exports	100.0	100.0	100.0	100.0

[a] Sources: U.N. [7, 26], and Korea [18].
[b] Figures are in per cent.

since. Korea does not export processed food in appreciable quantities but continues to sell raw silk and fresh fish abroad.

Until the mid-sixties, a high degree of commodity concentration characterized the exports of both Taiwan and Korea. The degree of concentration has diminished to a considerable extent in subsequent years, and the five principal export products now provide only about one-third of export earnings. By contrast, the concentration of exports by nation has changed little, with the United States and Japan accounting for some 70 per cent of Korean and 50 per cent of Taiwanese exports. The United States, the main purchaser of the manufactured exports of the two countries has, however, gained in importance at the expense of Japan, which continues to import mainly primary commodities from Taiwan and Korea.[12]

[12] For sources, see Tables III and IV.

While nondurable consumer goods and relatively simple intermediate products dominate the export pattern of the two countries, Taiwan is more advanced in the exportation of machinery and equipment. Telecommunications apparatus, including condensers, memory systems, semiconductors, vacuum tubes, and transformers accounted for 13 per cent of exports in 1969.[13] The share of machinery and transport equipment is lower in Korea, which has only recently started exporting radios and parts and components of computers for assembly abroad. Taiwan is also ahead of Korea in the exportation of chemicals, metals, and metal products, which it sells chiefly in the developing countries of Southeast Asia.

The export pattern of the two countries is characteristic of their industrial structure. In Taiwan, nondurable consumer goods and the intermediate products used in their manufacture accounted for about 21 per cent of value added in manufacturing in 1968, while in Korea the corresponding proportion was 36 per cent. Food processing, too, had a smaller share in Taiwan (21 per cent) than in Korea (24 per cent). By contrast, the share of metals and machinery was 22 per cent in the former and 17 per cent in the latter, and that of intermediate goods 36 and 23 per cent (Table V).

Differences in the shares of intermediate products and machinery in Taiwan and Korea in part reflect the higher proportion of intermediate products and machinery in the manufacturing output of Taiwan in the early postwar period: in 1953, the combined share of these products was 35 per cent in Taiwan as against 20 per cent in Korea. The structure of industries has further been affected by differences in the policies followed by the two countries over the last fifteen years.

In Taiwan, the government succeeded in containing inflation, thus avoiding a decline in the "real" exchange rate (the nominal exchange rate adjusted for increases in domestic prices). Realistic exchange rates have provided incentives for the domestic production of machinery and equipment, while relatively low levels of protection have assured the expansion of those branches where Taiwan has actual or potential comparative advantage.

By contrast, in the second half of the sixties, domestic price increases without commensurate adjustments in the exchange rate have led to an overvaluation of the currency in Korea. To offset the adverse effects of overvaluation on exports, the government has provided increasing export subsidies. But subsidies in the form of duty-free entry of machinery and materials used in export production, and preferential credit facilities for their importation, have also induced domestic producers to use imported inputs and have discouraged the domestic production of such inputs. In fact, the expansion

[13] At the end of 1968, altogether 125 electronics factories were in operation or being established, of which two-fifths represented foreign investment [11].

TABLE V THE STRUCTURE OF MANUFACTURING INDUSTRIES IN TAIWAN AND KOREA[a,b]

	Taiwan[c]			Korea[d]		
	1953	1960	1968	1953	1960	1968
Food, Beverages, and Tobacco	*33.1*	*31.7*	*20.8*	*39.1*	*31.7*	*24.0*
Food	23.6	28.2	16.6	17.6	15.0	10.9
Beverages	0.5	0.6	0.7	10.9	10.9	6.1
Tobacco	9.0	2.9	3.5	10.6	5.8	7.0
Nondurable Consumer Goods Industries	*31.5*	*23.2*	*21.4*	*40.9*	*43.1*	*36.3*
Textiles	20.5	12.8	12.5	28.1	29.6	25.9
Clothing and footwear	3.0	3.3	3.2	3.9	5.4	3.0
Furniture	1.0	1.0	1.1	2.3	1.5	0.8
Printing and publishing	3.9	4.6	2.6	5.3	4.9	4.4
Other manufactures	3.1	1.5	2.0	1.3	1.7	2.2
Intermediate Goods Industries	*28.3*	*29.7*	*35.7*	*12.2*	*15.0*	*22.9*
Wood products	5.1	4.2	3.8	2.9	3.0	3.2
Paper and paper products	3.3	3.9	3.0	1.1	1.6	2.1
Leather and leather products	0.4	0.3	0.1	1.3	0.9	0.5
Rubber products	1.4	1.3	1.1	1.8	2.4	1.4
Chemical industries	9.8	6.6	11.4	3.0	3.4	6.9
Petroleum and coal products	4.2	5.4	9.3	0.6	1.3	4.3
Nonmetallic mineral products	4.1	8.0	7.0	1.5	2.4	4.5
Metals and Machinery	*7.1*	*15.4*	*22.1*	*7.8*	*10.2*	*16.8*
Metal products	2.0	3.1	2.7	1.3	1.5	{5.2}
Basic metals	0.9	4.1	1.8	0.9	2.9	
Nonelectrical machinery	1.7	2.3	3.4	2.6	2.6	2.3
Electrical machinery	1.1	2.1	8.6	0.6	0.8	3.2
Transport equipment	1.4	3.8	5.6	2.4	2.4	6.1
Total	100.0	100.0	100.0	100.0	100.0	100.0

[a] Sources: U.N. [10], Taiwan [25], IBRD rep. [8].
[b] Figures are in per cent.
[c] Current factor costs.
[d] Constant market prices.

of the production of intermediate products in Korea has been largely confined to petroleum products and chemicals, which have received special benefits, and in the electrical machinery sector export subsidies have encouraged radio assembly but not the production of parts and components.

VIII. Some Adverse Effects of the Incentive System

Just as import substitution, exports may also be carried too far. This will be the case if subsidies induce producers to expand exports to the point where the domestic resource cost of an additional dollar in export earnings exceeds the resource cost of saving a dollar through import substitution. For exports taken as a whole, this is not likely to have happened in Taiwan and Korea since the average rate of export subsidy does not exceed that of import protection. However, as a result of differential subsidies, exports in certain industries have increased more, and in others less, than would have been desirable, and, especially in Korea, the domestic cost of some export products is rather high.

A study prepared by the Korean Trade Research Center [20] shows, for example, that in 1966 the direct plus indirect domestic cost of earning a dollar through exports of electrical machinery, mainly radios, exceeded 600 *won*, at a time when the exchange rate was 271 *won* to the dollar. This conclusion is confirmed by a study of the Korean Traders Association [1] according to which radios receive considerably larger export subsidies than the difference between domestic costs per dollar and the exchange rate. Similar results are shown for plywood and knitted fabric. Finally, one may question the desirability of providing export subsidies of 40–50 per cent to some textile products.

Differential export subsidies in Korea are in part the result of the proliferation of various forms of subsidies which have been imposed to offset the effects on exports of the increasing overvaluation of the exchange rate. Improvements in resource allocation and reductions in the domestic cost of earning and saving foreign exchange would require a simplification and unification of the system of subsidies, the exact amount of some of which is not even known. In order to encourage the domestic manufacturing of intermediate goods and machinery, it would further be desirable to equalize the incentives provided to the use of domestic and imported inputs in the production of exports. The equalization of incentives would also be served by reforming the tariff system and replacing import quotas by tariffs.

While the incentive system is generally more equitable in Taiwan, improvements would need to be made in this country also. Foremost among the changes that appear to be desirable is the replacement of the system of import controls by tariffs. The tariff schedule also needs to be revised and export incentives simplified with the aim of providing equal incentives to exports and to import substitution in the various branches of industry. In this connection, it may be added that Taiwan's tariff schedule is still based on the one applied in mainland China before 1949.

IX. Future Prospects

Korea and Taiwan continue to have a wage advantage over their major competitors in the labor-intensive branches of manufacturing. In 1968, average manufacturing wages per day were $1.15 in Korea, $1.61 in Taiwan, around $2.50–3.00 in Singapore, and $6.00 in Japan [9, 12].[14] But rapid increases in wages, especially in Korea, narrow this advantage and the two countries will eventually have to shift to more sophisticated exports. This would involve, on the one hand, upgrading exports which now often entail only relatively simple processing (e.g., grey cloth, veneer sheets) and, on the other, expanding the labor-intensive branches of the machinery and machine-tool industries that utilize workers with a higher educational level.

A shift towards more sophisticated exports would reduce the export share of standardized goods and increase that of differentiated products. But while the former do not require particular selling efforts, the latter require the creation of marketing facilities abroad or the establishment of business connections with foreign firms. A promising avenue is increased participation in the international division of the production process through subcontracting. Apart from ensuring foreign markets, subcontracting would provide additional advantages in the form of the utilization of the relatively cheap skilled labor in Taiwan and Korea and the importation of new technology. The potential for subcontracting is particularly great in producing parts, components, and accessories for assembly in Japan. Despite progress made in recent years in Taiwan, and to a lesser extent in Korea, these potentialities are now utilized only to a small degree.

Upgrading exports and expanding the labor-intensive branches of the machinery and machine-tool industries would tend to raise the share of domestic value added in exporting. It has also been proposed that Taiwan and Korea should increase this share, in general, and reduce their dependence on imports through "backward integration" that would involve replacing imports of intermediate goods, parts, components, and accessories by domestic production.

[14] Data for Taiwan refer to the first five months of 1968, those for Singapore are our estimates.

The objective of reducing dependence on imports has in some cases led to the establishment of small-scale plants with high operating costs, as in plastics and synthetic fibers. The planned increase in the production of automobile parts and components would also involve high costs. These considerations apply especially to Korea, where plants in these industries produce chiefly for domestic markets, while in Taiwan efforts are made at an early stage to assure that new plants be eventually able to export. The output of the proposed Korean steel mill is also destined for domestic consumption, yet costs could be lowered by specializing in a few varieties of steel products for domestic use and exports while importing other varieties.

The examples indicate that pursuing the objective of backward integration could easily lead to establishing high-cost industries which, in turn, would adversely affect the competitiveness of exports by increasing input costs and by raising claims on scarce factors. To avoid this danger and to increase the export potential of the two countries, it would be desirable instead to encourage projects that make the maximum *net* contribution to national income, irrespective of their import content. This could be accomplished by continuing with the policy of outward-looking industrialization and making it more consistent by doing away with discrimination against the domestic production of intermediate products and machinery. Such general measures could be supplemented by special measures in cases when the long payoff period of investment would call for government intervention.

X. Conclusions

We have examined in this paper the industrial policies applied in Taiwan and Korea during the sixties. It has been shown that, following the virtual completion of the process of import substitution in consumer nondurables and their inputs in the late fifties, both countries have adopted an outward-looking development strategy with emphasis on the exports of labor-intensive manufactured goods. This strategy has resulted in rapid increases in exports; the expansion of exports in turn has led to an acceleration of economic growth in the two countries.

Exports of labor-intensive manufactured goods have contributed to the growth of the national economies of Taiwan and Korea by utilizing the two countries' abundant resource, labor, and economizing on its capital; by permitting the use of large-scale production methods and encouraging technical improvements in export industries; as well as by creating demand for domestic materials, raising incomes, and augmenting the availability of imports.

The contrast with other developing countries is evident: during the sixties, per capita incomes rose at an annual rate of 6.5 per cent in Taiwan and Korea, compared to slightly over 2 per cent a year in the nonoil-producing developing countries.

The question arises if the outward-looking strategy adopted by Taiwan and Korea could be applied also in other developing countries. In this connection, some have suggested that the high rate of economic growth in the two countries has been made possible by the large amount of foreign aid they have received.[15] This explanation cannot, however, account for the fact that the rapid reduction of foreign aid in recent years has been accompanied by increases in growth rates, especially in Korea.[16] At the same time, both countries maintain a large military establishment which absorbed a large part of foreign aid in the early part of the period and cost more than the amount of foreign aid in recent years. Also, statistical studies indicate that in developing countries the contribution of exports to economic growth exceeds that of foreign aid by a considerable margin.[17]

This is not to deny that a massive inflow of aid would be helpful in supplementing domestic savings and export earnings in developing countries; but the proper use of this aid requires appropriate economic policies. Also, while the availability of relatively cheap labor is a boon to Taiwan and Korea, the adoption of an outward-looking strategy has made it possible to use this labor to advantage. Similarly, this strategy can be used to exploit the opportunities available in other countries.

More generally, an outward-looking strategy offers possibilities to utilize appropriately a country's resources for economic growth and to avoid the adverse effects of import substitution on production costs, technological change, and product quality in particular. Developing countries are therefore well advised to learn from the experience of Taiwan and Korea in applying export-oriented policies.

ACKNOWLEDGMENTS

The author is indebted for helpful discussion and comments to friends and colleagues at the World Bank, the International Monetary Fund, and in Taiwan and Korea.

[15] On Taiwan, see Jacoby [13].

[16] According to official statistics, in the two countries the ratio of foreign aid to GNP declined from 8–10 per cent in 1960 to 4–5 per cent in 1964 and below 2 per cent in 1969.

[17] See Balassa [2] and Cohen [6]. For a theoretical justification see Johnson [14].

REFERENCES

[1] "A Study on International Competitiveness of Korean Export Industries." Korean Traders' Association, Seoul, 1969.

[2] Balassa, B., Economic Growth, Trade and the Balance of Payments in the Developing Countries, p. 18. IBRD (March 15, 1968) (mimeo).

[3] Balassa, B., Growth Strategies in Semi-Industrial Countries, *Quart. J. Econ.* **LXXXIV**, (February 1970).

[4] Balassa, B., and Hughes, H., Statistical Indicators of Levels of Industrial Development. IBRD Econ. Dept. Working Paper No. 45, Table 12 (May 1969) (mimeo).

[5] Brown, G. T., Economic Policy and Development: A Case Study of Korea in the 1960s (May 1970) (mimeo).

[6] Cohen, B. I., Relative Effects of Foreign Capital and Larger Exports on Economic Development, *Rev. Econ. Stat.* L (May 1968).

[7] "Commodity Trade Statistics." United Nations, New York, 1969.

[8] Current Economic Position and Prospects of the Republic of Korea. IBRD Rep. (1970).

[9] "Economic Statistics Yearbook, 1970," p. 357. Bank of Korea, 1970.

[10] "Growth of World Industry." United Nations, New York, 1970.

[11] "Highlights of the Fifth Four-Year Development Plan of the Republic of China," p. 9. Council for Int. Econ. Cooperation and Develop., 1969.

[12] International Labor Office, *Bull. Labor Statist. 1970* 1st Quarter, p. 49, Korea (1970).

[13] Jacoby, N. H., "U. S. Aid to Taiwan: A Study of Foreign Aid, Self-Help and Development." Praeger, New York, 1968.

[14] Johnson, H. G., "Economic Policies Toward Less Developed Countries," Chap. 2. The Brookings Inst., Washington, D. C., 1967.

[15] Kanesa-Thasan, S., Stabilizing an Economy—A Study of the Republic of Korea, IMF Staff Papers, pp. 1–26 (March 1969).

[16] Ken C. Y. Lin, Industrial Development and Changes in the Structure of Foreign Trade. The Experience of the Republic of China in Taiwan, 1946–1966, IMF Staff Papers, pp. 290–321 (July 1968).

[17] Kuo-shu Liang, Foreign Trade and Economic Development in Taiwan: 1952–1967. Ph.D. dissertation submitted to Vanderbilt Univ. (1970).

[18] "Major Economic Indicators, 1958–1969," p. 17. Economic Planning Board, Seoul, 1970.

[19] "Major Economic Indicators, 1958–1969," p. 84. Economic Planning Board, Seoul, 1970.

[20] "Measures to Increase Net Foreign Exchange Earnings for Exports." Korean Trade Research Center, Seoul, 1969

[21] "Taiwan Statistical Data Book, 1970," pp. 7–8. Council for Int. Econ. Cooperation and Develop. (1970).

[22] "Taiwan Statistical Data Book, 1970," pp. 13, 20. Council for Int. Econ. Cooperation and Develop. (1970).

[23] "Statistical Yearbook, 1969," pp. 83–84. United Nations, New York, 1969.

[24] "Statistical Yearbook, 1969," pp. 85–87. United Nations, New York, 1969.

[25] Taiwan, "National Income of the Republic of China." Directorate General of Budgets, Accounts, and Statistics, 1971.

[26] "Yearbook of International Trade Statistics," United Nations, New York, 1970.

[27] "Yearbook of National Accounts Statistics, 1968," Vol. 1, United Nations, New York, 1968.

LDC EXPORTS: A CROSS-SECTIONAL ANALYSIS *

JAGDISH BHAGWATI and *JOHN CHEH*

Massachusetts Institute of Technology, Cambridge, Massachusetts

This paper examines two questions relating to LDC exports, using cross-sectional methods: (i) Does the "size" of a country correlate with the share of exports in its national income (Sect. I); and (ii) does the share of manufacturing exports of a country in its total exports tend to reflect that country's share of manufacturing value added in its national income, and the latter in turn to reflect the country's income per capita?

The strong relations which emerge from our cross-sectional regressions are, like similar work of other economists (e.g., Chenery), only broadly suggestive. Thus, for example, we find that the so-called South Korean "miracle" of a fantastically rapid expansion of exports during the 1960s is to be viewed against an "abnormally low" late-1950s export performance in terms of our size-regressions: South Korea starts well below the regression line in 1958, for all indicators of size, and even the "miraculous" rate of export growth leaves it below the line in each case by 1967.

I. LDC Country Size and Share of Exports in GDP

Does the "size" of a country correlate with the share of exports in its national income? It may be useful to know the answer to this question for the simple reason that often economists ask other economists questions such

* The research underlying this paper has been supported by the National Bureau of Economic Research in connection with a Project on Exchange Control and Liberalization in LDCs, being directed by Bhagwati and Krueger. Some of the data was collected by Ray Hartman; the calculations were carried out by John Cheh.

as the following: Is India "inward looking" in her trade policy, or is South Korea "outward looking"? The correct answer to these questions, of course, is to examine through structural analysis of each country itself whether its trade policy is import substituting or export promoting *vis-a-vis* what its optimal policy ought to be.[1] However, it may be quite suggestive to see also what a country's "position" looks like on a curve which may be fitted to cross-country data, as Chenery likes to do; and it may be equally suggestive to see what it looks like on its own "long-run trend," as Kuznets often does.

In this section, we have put together the available information for LDCs, on three proxies of size: population, GDP, and area. We reproduce the cross-sectional regressions for an "uncontrolled" and varying sample of LDCs, based purely on the principle that, in each case, as many LDCs should be included as the ones for which we have the needed data. As the share of exports in income, we have taken the share of exports in GDP.[2] We have chosen four years to conduct our analysis: 1958, 1963, 1965, and 1967—one-year analyses could be treacherous for LDCs, where bad harvests, drastic declines in exports, etc., could seriously affect export and GDP magnitudes.

Table I presents the linear and log-linear regression estimates when the export shares are regressed on population; Table II presents these regression estimates when the export shares are regressed on GDP; and Table III contains the results when the export shares are regressed on area.

The regressions establish a statistically significant relationship between export shares and both *population* and *GDP*. All the regression coefficients for the independent variables (in these two cases) are negative and significantly different from zero at the 5% level (for the 2-tail test).

The fits with *area* are somewhat inferior, although the coefficients are still negative and significant in the linear regression for 1958, and negative and significant in log-linear form for 1958 and 1963.

It would appear, therefore, that "size" in nearly all proxies we can think of correlates negatively and well with export shares. "Large" countries do tend to have lower export shares, whereas "small" countries tend to have higher export shares.[3]

[1] We deliberately emphasize in this connection the need to compare the trade policy *vis-a-vis* the "optimal policy," because much too often the words "import substitution" and "export promotion" are bandied about in the literature in a loose way or as pure statistical artifacts created by comparison with some balanced-growth norm which has no policy implication from a welfare point of view. In this connection, see Desai [2].

[2] GDP was chosen exclusively because it was available for the largest number of LDCs and for the largest number of years. It should really make no significant difference if we were to take other measures of income.

[3] We have not examined shares of imports in GDP, because imports would reflect factors such as foreign aid flows.

TABLE I[a]

ESTIMATES OF THE EQUATION: (Export/GDP) (%) = $a + b$ (Population) + u

Regression Form	Year	Coefficients: Constant	Coefficients: Population (in million)	R^2	F-Level	Number of Countries
Linear	1958	23.332	−0.071 (1.986)[f]	0.053	3.943	72[c]
	1963	23.479	−0.068 (2.047)[f]	0.053	4.193	77[d]
	1965	23.619	−0.065 (2.197)[f]	0.064	4.827	73[e]
	1967	21.357	−0.052 (2.086)[f]	0.069	4.351	61[b]
Log-linear	1958	3.124	−0.202 (3.397)[f]	0.142	11.544	72[c]
	1963	3.179	−0.216 (4.067)[f]	0.181	16.539	77[d]
	1965	3.259	−0.236 (4.769)[f]	0.243	22.742	73[e]
	1967	3.201	−0.224 (3.954)[f]	0.210	15.640	61[b]

[a] Variables and sources for Tables I–III. Exports: In millions of domestic currency, or millions of U.S. dollars when so given. From U.N. Yearbooks of International Trade Statistics; Export conversion factors: From U.N. Yearbooks of International Trade Statistics; GDP at factor cost: In millions of U.S. dollars. From U.N. Yearbooks of National Accounts. Area: In million square kilometers. From U.N. Demographic Yearbooks. Population: In millions, based on mid-year estimates. From U.N. Demographic Yearbooks.

[b] Argentina, Barbados, Bolivia, Brazil, Burma, Cameroon, Ceylon, Chile, Colombia, Congo, Costa Rica, Cyprus, Dominican Republic, Ecuador, El Salvador, Ethiopia, Fiji, Ghana, Greece, Guatemala, Guyana, Honduras, India, Iran, Iraq, Israel, Ivory Coast, Jamaica, Jordan, Kenya, Korea (South), Kuwait, Lebanon, Libya, Madagascar, Malawi, Mauritius, Mexico, Morocco, Nicaragua, Pakistan, Panama, Paraguay, Peru, Philippines, Senegal, Sierra Leone, Southern Rhodesia, Sudan, Syria, Taiwan, Tanzania, Thailand, Trinidad and Tobago, Tunisia, Turkey, Uganda, United Arab Republic, Uruguay, Venezuela, Zambia.

[c] Same as *b*, except Ghana, Malawi, Philippines, Turkey, Zambia; plus: Algeria, Cambodia, Central African Republic, Chad, Dahomey, Gabon, Gambia, Hong Kong, Liberia, Malaysia (West), Niger, Nigeria, Reunion, Surinam, Togo, Upper Volta.

[d] Same as *b*, except Ghana; plus: Algeria, Cambodia, Central African Republic, Chad, Dahomey, Gabon, Gambia, Hong Kong, Liberia, Malaysia (West), Mauritania, Niger, Nigeria, Reunion, Surinam, Togo, Upper Volta.

[e] Same as *b*, except Ghana; plus: Cambodia, Central African Republic, Chad, Gabon, Ghana, Liberia, Malaysia (West), Mauritania, Niger, Nigeria, Surinam, Togo, Upper Volta.

[f] Coefficients significantly different from zero at 5% level.

II. The Share of Manufacturing Exports in Total Exports of LDCs

In this section, we examine the hypothesis that the share of manufacturing exports by LDCs in their total exports will tend to reflect their share of manufacturing value added in GDP; and that the latter, in turn, will tend to reflect their GDP per capita.

This hypothesis suggests that countries tend to export what they produce—a conclusion which is compatible with either the theory of comparative advantage or the observed fact that several LDCs, having import-substituted in manufacturing tend to move quickly thereafter, under balance-of-payments difficulties, into subsidization to export the very manufactures whose produc-

TABLE II

ESTIMATES OF THE EQUATION: (Export/GDP) (%) = $a + b$ (GDP) $+ u$

Regression Form	Year	Coefficients: Constant	Coefficients: GDP (in million U.S.$)	R^2	F-Level	Number of Countries
Linear	1958	24.513	−0.001 (2.356)[a]	0.073	5.652	74[c]
	1963	24.519	−0.001 (2.529)[a]	0.081	6.652	77[d]
	1965	24.743	−0.001 (2.923)[a]	0.104	8.271	73[e]
	1967	23.005	−0.001 (3.0)[a]	0.134	9.100	61[b]
Log-linear	1958	4.262	−0.217 (3.487)[a]	0.144	12.160	74[c]
	1963	4.357	−0.222 (3.961)[a]	0.173	15.690	77[d]
	1965	4.662	−0.256 (5.028)[a]	0.263	25.282	73[e]
	1967	4.959	−0.294 (4.926)[a]	0.291	24.261	61[b]

[a] Coefficients significantly different from zero at 5% level.
[b] Same as *b* in Table I.
[c] Same as *c* in Table I, plus Malawi, and Zambia.
[d] Same as *d* in Table I.
[e] Same as *e* in Table I.

TABLE III

ESTIMATES OF THE EQUATION: (Export/GDP) (%) = $a + b$ (Area) + u

Regression Form	Year	Coefficients: Constant	Coefficients: Area (in million sq. kilometers)	R^2	F-Level	Number of Countries
Linear	1958	24.444	−3.061 (2.161)[a]	0.06	4.67	72[c]
	1963	24.249	−2.755 (1.772)	0.04	3.143	77[d]
	1965	24.072	−2.367 (1.568)	0.034	2.461	73[e]
	1967	21.359	−1.535 (1.127)	0.021	1.272	61[b]
Log-linear	1958	2.671	−0.111 (2.465)[a]	0.08	6.077	72[c]
	1963	2.688	−0.104 (2.473)[a]	0.075	6.116	77[d]
	1965	2.763	−0.080 (1.789)	0.043	3.201	73[e]
	1967	2.672	−0.007 (1.659)	0.045	2.753	61[b]

[a] Coefficients significantly different from zero at 5% level.
[b, c, d, e] Same as *b*, *c*, *d*, and *e* in Table I.

tion they have been encouraging in a sheltered market.[4] Since we confine our statistical analysis to regression techniques, the results are also compatible with the phenomenon of "export-led growth" under which manufacturing exports lead growth in manufacturing production and in GDP per capita.

Perhaps the most serious drawback of the hypothesis, which in consequence of its compatibility with several alternative theories of trade sounds eminently plausible, is that exports refer to *gross values*, whereas manufacturing production refers to *value added*. It is therefore perfectly in order to expect that a country which adds very little value added to domestic materials (e.g., diamonds) or imported materials (e.g., quasientrepot trade) and hence has a low ratio of manufacturing value added in GDP will have simultaneously a very high ratio of manufactured to total exports. Thus Zambia, almost at the bottom of the scale on share of manufacturing value added in GDP, has, for

[4] Bhagwati [1] describes this process somewhat cynically, though realistically, as tantamount to a new theory of comparative advantage which states that an LDC will produce whatever it imports and will export whatever it produces!

example, over 90% of its exports in SITC 6, which is traditionally classified as manufactures (along with SITC 5, 7, and 8), and closer scrutiny shows that this consists almost entirely of nonferrous metals and other minerals, with presumably the bulk of its value in the mineral ores and a very small percentage of value added in manufacturing. A reverse problem arises for some of the countries with a high share of manufacturing value added in GDP. The use of SITC categories 5–8 for defining manufacturing exports and the adoption of the UN classification of manufacturing activity to deduce the share of manufacturing value added in GDP leads to difficulties such as the following: Argentina ends up with less than 10% share of manufactured exports because "meat preparations," amounting to over 20% of total exports, are classified under SITC 1, whereas they are clearly included in manufacturing activity in the national accounts; Persia similarly gets her exports of manufactures seriously "understated" because "petroleum products" (SITC 3) are left out, but not from manufacturing value added. There is really no systematic *and* feasible way to get around this difficulty, although we hope later to rerun the regressions by converting the manufacturing value added data into gross production data if data on this relationship can be reliably put together for a sufficient number of LDCs.

Nonetheless, it is somewhat remarkable that the regressions which we have run, for the years 1958, 1963, 1965, and 1967 (to avoid reliance on single-year estimates in view of the serious fluctuations in GDP and exports which many LDCs experience), turn out to be significant in a fair number of cases, aside from the coefficients having the correct sign.

We have run the regressions in both linear and log-linear form for the largest possible set of LDCs for which the needed data is available.[5] Only the regressions which were statistically significant at 5% and 10% level and between have been included, although the regressions were run for each of the four years listed:

(1) For the uncontrolled sample of LDCs, ranging from 33–50 in number, all the regressions registered a positive relationship between GDP per capita and percentage of GDP in manufacturing, the coefficients uniformly being significantly different from zero at 5% level (Table IV).

(2) The relationship between the share of manufactured exports and GDP per capita was significant for the log-linear form for 1963, 1965, and 1967 and for linear form for 1967 (Table V). The sample ranged from 44–54 countries.

[5] We did try to run the analysis for a "controlled" sample but found that we could do this for only 13 LDCs, a sample which seemed too limited to be of any use, and the regression results were uneven.

(3) The regressions of share of manufactured exports on percentage share of GDP in manufacturing were the least satisfactory. The sample used here ranged from 18–33 countries. Nonetheless, the two regressions which turned up statistically significant fits in the log-linear form did have positive coefficients (Table VI).

TABLE IV[a]

REGRESSIONS FOR THE EQUATION:

% GDP in Manufacturing = $a + b$ (GDP/Population) + u

Regression Form	Year	Coefficients: Constant	Coefficients: % GDP in Mfg.	R^2	F-Level	Number of Countries
Linear	1958	8.279	0.023 (3.993)[f]	0.301	15.942	39[c]
	1963	9.367	0.019 (3.660)[f]	0.233	13.395	46[d]
	1965	10.014	0.013 (2.175)[f]	0.133	7.373	50[e]
	1967	11.004	0.513 (3.331)[f]	0.264	11.099	33[b]
Log-linear	1958	0.529	0.381 (4.583)[f]	0.362	20.996	39[c]
	1963	0.120	0.460 (5.508)[f]	0.408	30.341	46[d]
	1965	1.121	0.252 (2.451)[f]	0.111	6.007	50[e]
	1967	0.695	0.366 (4.497)[f]	0.395	20.219	33[b]

[a] Variables and sources for Tables IV–VI. Exports, manufactured exports: as with Tables I–III (manufactured exports: SITC groups 5–8). Export conversion factor: as with Tables I–III. GDP at factor cost: as with Tables I–III. Population: as with Tables I–III. % GDP (at factor cost) in manufacturing: From U.N. Yearbook of National Accounts.

[b] Argentina, Burma, Ceylon, Chile, Colombia, Cyprus, Dominican Republic, Ecuador, Greece, Guyana, Honduras, India, Iran, Jamaica, Jordan, Kenya, Korea, Mauritius, Mexico, Morocco, Pakistan, Panama, Paraguay, Philippines, Southern Rhodesia, Taiwan, Tanzania, Thailand, Trinidad and Tobago, Tunisia, Turkey, Uganda, Zambia.

[c] Same as *b*, except Iran, Jordan, Philippines, Tanzania, Tunisia, Turkey, Zambia; plus Algeria, Barbados, Bolivia, Congo, El Salvador, Guatemala, Iraq, Malawi, Nigeria, Peru, Sudan, Surinam, Togo.

[d] Same as *b*, except Jordan, Zambia; plus Bolivia, Cambodia, El Salvador, Ethiopia, Fiji, Iraq, Ivory Coast, Malawi, Malaysia (West), Nigeria, Peru, Sierra Leone, Sudan, Togo, Venezuela.

[e] Same as *b*, plus Bolivia, Cambodia, El Salvador, Ethiopia, Gabon, Guatemala, Iraq, Ivory Coast, Liberia, Libya, Malawi, Malaysia (West), Nicaragua, Nigeria, Peru, Sierra Leone, Surinam.

[f] Coefficients significantly different from zero at 5% level.

TABLE V

REGRESSIONS FOR THE EQUATION:

Manufactured Exports/Total Exports = $a + b$ (GDP/Population) + u

Regression Form	Year	Coefficients: Constant	Coefficients: GDP/Capita	R^2	F-Level	Number of Countries
Linear	1967	15.928	0.010 (2.12)[a]	0.097	4.505	44[c]
Log-linear	1963	−0.146	0.371 (1.192)[b]	0.030	1.421	48[d]
	1965	−0.110	0.409 (1.774)[b]	0.057	3.149	54[e]
	1967	−0.096	0.435 (1.775)[b]	0.070	3.149	44[c]

[a] Coefficient significantly different from zero at 5% level.

[b] Coefficient significantly different from zero between 5% and 10% level.

[c] Argentina, Brazil, Ceylon, Colombia, Costa Rica, Cyprus, Dominican Republic, Ecuador, El Salvador, Ethiopia, Fiji, Ghana, Greece, Guatemala, Guyana, Honduras, India, Iran, Israel, Ivory Coast, Jamaica, Jordan, Kenya, Korea, Kuwait, Madagascar, Malawi, Mexico, Morocco, Nicaragua, Pakistan, Panama, Philippines, Sierra Leone, Syria, Taiwan, Tanzania, Thailand, Trinidad and Tobago, Tunisia, Turkey, Uganda, United Arab Republic, Zambia.

[d] Same as *c*, except Brazil, Dominican Republic, Ghana, Jordan, Kuwait, Malawi, Morocco, Sierra Leone, Syria, Tanzania, Zambia; plus Burma, Cameroon, Chad, Dahomey, Gabon, Hong Kong, Liberia, Malaysia (West), Mauritania, Nigeria, Peru, Reunion, Sudan, Surinam, Togo.

[e] Same as *c*, except Ghana; plus Burma, Cambodia, Cameroon, Central African Republic, Chad, Gabon, Malaysia (West), Mauritania, Nigeria, Southern Rhodesia, Surinam.

TABLE VI

REGRESSIONS FOR THE EQUATION:

Manufactured Exports/Total Exports = $a + b$ (% GDP in Manufacturing) + u

Regression Form	Year	Coefficients		R^2	F-Level	Number of Countries
		Constant	% GDP in Mfg.			
Log-linear	1958	−1.733	1.203 (2.402)[a]	0.265	5.770	18[b]
	1963	−1.510	1.194 (2.238)[a]	0.139	5.011	33[c]

[a] Coefficient significantly different from zero at 5% level.

[b] Algeria, Argentina, Burma, Ceylon, Colombia, Cyprus, Ecuador, El Salvador, Greece, Honduras, India, Jamaica, Korea, Mexico, Nigeria, Surinam, Thailand, Trinidad and Tobago.

[c] Same as *b*, except Algeria, Surinam; plus Ethiopia, Fiji, Guyana, Iran, Ivory Coast, Kenya, Malaysia (West), Pakistan, Panama, Peru, Philippines, Sudan, Taiwan, Togo, Tunisia, Turkey, Uganda.

REFERENCES

[1] Bhagwati, J., *Theory and Practice of Commercial Policy*, Princeton Ser. No. 8 (1968).

[2] Desai, Padma, Alternative Measures of Import Substitution, *Oxford Econ. Papers* (November 1969).

PROTECTION AND GROWTH *

W. M. CORDEN

Nuffield College, Oxford, England

The formal body of international trade theory is in the main static and has often been criticized for this reason. Some of this criticism has been inspired by the stimulating writings of Dr. Prebisch. As a result of this weakness of orthodox theory, the relationship between protection and the rate of growth of real income has never been explored in a systematic manner, there being only fragments in the literature and much unrigorous speculation. While the infant industry argument for protection, which has such a long history, is essentially dynamic in nature, it has usually been treated in partial equilibrium terms, and, in any case, displays only one facet of the relationship between protection and growth.

This relationship can be regarded as having two aspects: The first aspect concerns "protection to make the best of growth." One assumes a growing and changing economy, perhaps one where the terms of trade are expected to change in particular ways because of particular patterns of domestic and world growth, and examines the effects of this growth on optimum protection policy. Thus one might develop an argument for protection on the basis of an expected deterioration of the terms of trade. The celebrated "Prebisch model" could be put under this heading. One could show how the optimum tariff structure would change over time as an economy's factor proportions change or as the expansion of the domestic market allows more and more economies of scale to be realized, and perhaps makes more and more import-competing industries viable with little or no protection. The tendency of some private

* This paper was written while the author was a visitor in the Faculty of Economics and Politics of Monash University, Australia, in 1969. I am indebted to helpful comments from Harold Lydall and Richard Snape.

decision-makers to plan on the basis of present, rather than future expected prices may also provide a case for social intervention, possibly in the form of protection.

The second aspect of the protection-and-growth relationship concerns the effects of protection on the rate of growth. This is the subject matter of the present paper. To be precise, we are here concerned with two questions: First, what is the effect of protection on the rate of growth? Second, if protection, or a particular protective structure, raises the rate of growth, is this an argument for imposing or altering the structure? The first question is thus a matter of positive economics and the second of welfare economics.

Protection could affect the rate of natural increase of the population. It might increase urbanization, and an urban population is usually more inclined to limit its birth-rate. Similarly, the death-rate may be dependent on consumption per head, and this will be affected by protection, but it will be assumed here that the rate of population growth is given. Furthermore, we assume that there is no migration and no capital inflow or outflow. The connections between protection and international movements of labor and capital are obviously important but can conveniently be analyzed separately. The relationship between protection and foreign investment has been discussed in another paper [2].

At various points in this paper there will be references to the community's aggregate or total real income. This concept begs certain questions and ignores income distribution considerations. It is perhaps best understood as *compensated* or *potential* real income. By "protection" is meant any trade intervention, such as tariffs, quantitative restrictions, multiple exchange rates, export taxes, subsidies, and so on. In general, we shall mean import tariffs.

The paper is not concerned with "foreign exchange gap" problems, and it is assumed that balance-of-payments equilibrium is continuously maintained by appropriate exchange rate or internal price adjustments combined with fiscal or monetary policies that keep domestic absorption of goods and services at the level set by the country's real output, terms of trade, and net international transfers. This is obviously not a realistic assumption for many less-developed countries, but is made here to isolate clearly other aspects of our problem. It needs to be remembered that, in addition to the effects discussed here, protection could affect the rate of growth via its effects on the balance of payments.

This paper is only a first attempt to introduce some systematic thinking on the relationship between protection and growth. It does not profess to deal with all important aspects of this subject and, like much of economic theory, is to a great extent merely classificatory. It is not concerned with the effects of protection on international knowledge diffusion—the focus is wholly on its effects on domestic capital accumulation.

No direct policy conclusions can or should be drawn from such simple theorizing. If we say that a certain policy is "second best," this does not mean that it is not an appropriate policy, given that constraints apply which do not make the first-best policy feasible. In any case, policy conclusions must rest not just on clear thinking aided by economic theory, but also—as is very evident in the work of Dr. Prebisch—on detailed knowledge and consideration of the circumstances of the country concerned.

I. How Protection Affects Savings: The Real Income Effect

Protection may affect savings, hence investment, hence the rate of capital accumulation, and hence the rate of growth of real income. These simple relationships will now be spelled out in more detail.[1]

Suppose for a moment that a country's aggregate savings depend only on its total real income, and not on income distribution or on relative prices, except insofar as the latter affect real income. We assume the marginal propensity to save to be positive. Hence a rise in real income causes savings to go up and a fall, to go down. It is well known that protection may raise or lower a country's static real income. The effects of protection on static real income have been analyzed in international trade theory. If there are no "domestic distortions" and the country cannot influence its terms of trade, protection is likely to lower real income. In that case it will cause savings to fall. On the other hand, protection may yield favorable effects on the terms of trade, and so real income may be raised and some part of the gains in real income will then be saved. Similarly, there may be a "domestic distortion," such as an excess of the wage-rate that has to be paid by the industrial sector over the social opportunity cost of labor, and tariffs at appropriate levels could then raise real income and hence savings.[2]

The next step is to assume that investment is determined by *ex-ante* (intended) savings. We could suppose that the rate of interest is so adjusted as to achieve this, or alternatively that public investment is varied so as to absorb the savings available. Hence investment will rise when real income rises and will fall when real income falls.[3] (Complications resulting from changes in

[1] For a more rigorous development of this argument, see Corden [3].

[2] If there is unemployment the wage-rate must exceed the opportunity cost of labor, which is then zero. Tariffs on labor-intensive industries may then increase employment, hence real incomes, and, insofar as any of the extra wage payments are saved, also savings. This case of "structural "unemployment is a special case of the more general situation of the wage-rate exceeding labor's opportunity cost.

[3] All this remains true if savings are positively related to the rate of interest. A rise in income, leading to a rise in saving at a given interest rate will lead to a fall in the rate of interest, and a positive relationship between savings and the interest rate then means that the final increase in savings and investment will not be as great as it would have been if savings had been interest inelastic.

the relative prices of investment-goods are ignored for the moment.) Thus a protective structure that imposes a cost of protection (a fall in real income) will reduce investment.

The change in investment, in turn, will alter the rate of capital accumulation. Suppose that it falls because protection has reduced real income. Assuming that the marginal product of capital is positive, the rate of growth of output will then fall below what it would have been otherwise. In terms of the simple Harrod–Domar growth equation, protection affects the rate of growth through altering the capital-output ratio, quite apart from any possible effects on the investment propensity.

It is not always understood that protection will affect the rate of growth even when the average propensity to save and invest is constant. Yet it is not an original point. Adam Smith wrote:

> The industry of the society can augment only in proportion as its capital augments, and its capital can augment only in proportion to what can be gradually saved out of its revenue. But the immediate effect of every such regulation is to diminish its revenue, and what diminishes its revenue is certainly not very likely to augment its capital faster than it would have augmented of its own accord had both capital and industry been left to find out their natural employments [13].

If for "revenue" we read "real income" and bear in mind that not "every such" regulation may reduce real income, we see that Adam Smith has anticipated the simple argument here.

The effect of protection on capital accumulation is not really additional to the static effects of protection. Rather, it is an implication of the static effects. When protection inflicts a static cost, and so reduces static real income, consumption and investment are reduced. The lower consumption inflicts a current welfare loss, while the lower investment reduces the rate of growth and so inflicts a future welfare loss. The cost of protection is the sum of these two losses.

II. How Protection Affects Savings: Income Distribution Effect

Protection can affect savings and investment through its effects on income distribution. If the marginal propensity to save differs between different sections of the community, the ratio of total savings to total incomes will alter. This effect of trade and protection on growth via its effects on income distribution has often appeared in the literature, first in the writings of the classical economists and then in the recent economic development literature, but modern formal trade theory, being static, has not found a home for it.

Various effects and relationships are conceivable. The marginal propensity to save out of profits may be higher than out of other incomes. Hence any redistribution towards profits will raise the overall savings propensity. In Ricardo's model it was assumed that all savings were out of profits and that a movement towards free trade (abolition of the Corn Laws) would shift income distribution away from rural rents towards profits. It followed naturally that free trade would raise the rate of growth.

In the case of those less-developed countries today which export land-intensive products, the effect is often claimed to be the other way: Protection of manufacturing industry is likely to raise profits and so increase savings. It is, of course, an empirical question whether the marginal propensity to save out of rural incomes is less than out of urban incomes derived from manufacturing. It cannot be assumed automatically. One may be misled by the difficulty of measuring saving and investment in agriculture, especially by peasant smallholders.

Protection may also reduce the profits of the commercial sector through reducing the volume of trade, and an interesting question then is whether the marginal propensity to save out of commercial profits is greater or less than out of manufacturing profits. On the other hand, if protection takes the form of quantitative import restrictions it may increase the profits of the commercial class, or at least of those elements in this or another class that are lucky enough to obtain the scarce import licence privileges. The propensity to save out of some types of profits may be higher than that out of other types, the issue then being how protection affects the composition of total profits.

The marginal propensity to save may depend not on the functional type of income but simply on the level of a person's income. The question is then simply how protection affects the degree of income inequality. The overall propensity to save would then be reduced by a protective structure which consists of high tariffs on "luxury" goods consumed by the well-off and low or zero tariffs on "essentials" consumed mainly by the poor. Quantitative import restrictions which yield monopoly profits to a limited number of traders and so increase income inequality would raise the overall savings propensity.

It cannot be assumed automatically that protection which redistributes incomes towards a high-savings sector must cause total savings, and hence investment and the rate of growth, to increase. The overall average propensity to save will rise only if the redistribution is towards the sector with the higher *marginal* propensity to save; conceivably, this might not be the sector with the higher average propensity. More important, total savings may fall if protection reduces total real income. It was stressed earlier that a fall in real income will reduce savings if the marginal propensity to save is positive; this must be combined with the income redistribution effect. For example, if protection reduces wages by $100 and raises profits by $70, and if the marginal propensity to save out of wages is 15% and out of profits is 20%, then total savings and the rate of growth will fall, even though there has been a redistribution in favor of profits and hence a rise in the overall propensity to save.

Protection can also affect savings and investment through its effect on government revenue. This is really a particular type of redistribution effect. The marginal propensity to save and invest of the government may be higher or lower than that of the sections of the community which pay taxes.

It is also possible that the marginal social productivity of public capital is higher than that of private capital, so that the shift from private investment to public investment which is likely to result when private savings are replaced at the margin by public savings would raise the overall productivity of capital and so the rate of growth. Alternatively, the government might use extra revenue to finance military expenditures which are unlikely to contribute to raising the rate of growth.

There are two types of revenue effect: First, tariffs raise revenue and output subsidies cost revenue. Secondly, protection may affect income tax collections. The best way to look at this is to suppose that for each sector there is a marginal propensity to pay income tax, depending on levels of income and institutional considerations, just as there is a marginal propensity to save. Thus total income tax collections may rise or fall, depending on whether protection shifts incomes towards those sectors prone to pay high marginal taxes (perhaps the corporate sector) or towards sectors paying low or no taxes (perhaps the unincorporated services sector in some less-developed countries), and also on whether it reduces or raises total real income.

III. How Protection Affects Savings: Other Effects

So far we have assumed that savings and investment vary only with real income and its distribution. We shall now assume away the income distribution effect by supposing the marginal propensity to save of different sectors of the community to be identical. We shall continue to assume that investment expenditures are brought to equality with *ex-ante* savings by changes in the rate of interest (or in public investment). But we shall now consider some other channels through which protection can cause investment, hence the rate of capital accumulation, and hence the rate of growth to vary.

First, the relative price of capital goods to consumption goods may be changed by protection. It may be that exportables are in general consumption goods and importables capital goods. Tariffs will then raise the domestic relative prices of capital goods. This is an effect which is conceivable in an economy which is an exporter of food and an importer of manufactures, and which imposes tariffs on a wide range of manufactured imports. Probably a more common situation is where a country deliberately discriminates in its tariff system *in favor of* imports of capital goods, with high tariffs on imports of manufactured consumer goods and low or zero tariffs on imports of capital goods. Even though the unprotected exportables may also be consumer goods, the net result is then to lower the relative prices of capital goods. A similar result follows from the typical regime of quantitative import restrictions where severe restrictions are imposed on imports of most consumer goods but capital goods are allowed in freely.

Sometimes countries start their industrialization process by protecting only manufactured consumer goods, hence lowering the relative price of capital goods. Then they move gradually to protection of intermediate manufactured goods that are inputs into capital goods and finally to finished capital goods, so that, if exportables are consumption goods, the prices of capital goods relative to consumption goods as a whole (including exportables) rise over time.

A change in this consumption goods–capital goods price relationship could affect the amount of investment in *real* terms.[4] The point can be made most simply if we assume that the propensity to save, expressed as a proportion of total money expenditure, is constant. Hence the proportion of expenditure on investment is constant. It follows immediately that if the relative *price* of capital goods falls, the relative *quantity* of capital goods to consumption goods absorbed by the economy must rise to the same extent. In *real* terms, the average propensity to invest has then risen, though in money terms it has stayed constant.

In fact it is not really necessary to assume that the propensity to save in money terms is constant. One need only assume that there is *some* substitution between consumption goods and investment goods in the community's "utility function" (as manifested by its propensity to save), in the sense that a change in their relative prices will lead to *some* change in their relative quantities in the opposite direction.

We now proceed to another conceivable effect of protection on savings. If quantitative restrictions or tariffs are imposed on imports of some consumption goods, we might expect consumers to substitute other consumption goods, whether unprotected importables or exportables. But it is also possible that they substitute savings instead, in the expectation that eventually the import restrictions or tariffs will be removed. In the present context, there would be

[4] A more rigorous exposition of the argument of this and the next paragraph, and its integration into a two-sector neoclassical growth model, is in Corden [3].

no sense in substituting savings if the restrictions were believed to be permanent. But if the restrictions are believed to be temporary, a consumer may optimize his utility over time not by substituting the purchase of other goods for the restricted goods but rather by saving with the intention of buying the same goods later.

This analysis is related to the well-known "demonstration effect" [11]. It has been argued that the availability of cheap and attractive imports produced in advanced countries causes consumers in less-developed countries to reduce their savings, or to be reluctant to increase them, since they wish to use their incomes to live as close as possible to the standards of living the advanced countries have "demonstrated" to them. If the imports were not available, it is suggested, there would be less pressure to consume, and hence more savings. This argument clearly requires that the opening of trade, the improvement of the terms of trade, or the restriction of imports is expected to be temporary. Even then, it must be remembered that the real income effect of restriction will cause savings to fall, so that on balance an increase in savings is by no means certain.

One might also take into account the effect of the availability of foreign goods on the incentive to work. The availability of cheap imports may lead to a substitution effect between leisure and goods, including future goods; one might expect people in less-developed countries to work harder to obtain these desirable goods, both to consume more now and to save more, and conversely for a restriction of imports to reduce savings for this reason.

IV. The Effects of Protection on Savings: Policy Implications

Do all the possible effects of protection on savings discussed in Sect. III yield new arguments for or against protection? It has already been pointed out that arguments for or against protection are not altered just because some part of an increase in real income induced by protection or by a reduction in protection will be saved. Given reasonable assumptions, a rise in real income is always desirable and a decrease undesirable irrespective of whether it is used for consumption or investment. Let us now consider the other effects on savings.

Is there an argument for a protective structure that lowers the relative prices of capital goods so as to increase the propensity to save and invest in real terms? There would be no argument for protection in this case if there were no divergence between the privately optimum and the socially optimum propensity to save. Let us suppose then that the socially optimum savings propensity is higher either because the social weighting of future relative to present consumption is higher or because the socially-perceived or expected productivity of investment is higher. Private decision-making will then lead to less expenditure on investment goods relative to consumption goods than is socially desirable. In terms of the analysis of "domestic distortions" familiar from the recent international trade literature, there is a domestic *expenditure distortion.* In the absence of deliberate intervention, the pattern of expenditure is "distorted"—that is, diverges from—the socially-desirable pattern.

It is a theme of the recent international trade theory literature that a domestic distortion should ideally be dealt with *directly*—by direct taxes or subsidies at the point of the distortion—rather than by the use of trade taxes, subsidies, or other trade interventions.[5] While there are some difficulties and complications in this approach (to which we shall refer below), it is generally useful and will be applied here. It follows that if the ratio of investment to national product is inadequate, first-best optimum policy is directly to subsidize or supplement saving or investment. This could be done by raising taxes in such a way as to minimize distorting effects, using the revenue to feed loanable funds on the capital market, so bringing the rate of interest down until investment is at the desired level, the revenue representing the desired extra savings. Alternatively, the revenue could be used to subsidize uniformly the purchase of investment goods, whether they are imported or produced at home. Another possibility is to use the revenue to finance public investment, so that the inadequate private investment would be supplemented by public investment.

The use of trade taxes—for example, tariffs on consumption goods while capital goods enter the country duty free—is second best, since these will not only alter the pattern of real expenditure in the desired direction but will also discourage domestic production of capital goods relative to the production of consumption goods, hence creating a distortion in the pattern of production away from the optimum, and so imposing a *production cost* of protection.[6] The analysis of the "theory of domestic distortions" is completely relevant: to deal with an *expenditure distortion*, first-best policy is to tax or subsidize the relevant category of expenditure; using trade taxes or subsidies is second best.

The same analysis applies to a protective structure which raises the prices of some or all consumption goods so as to induce the postponement of consumption. Given that it is socially desirable to increase savings, first-best policy would be to encourage savings directly and avoid inflicting a *production cost.*

[5] The clearest statement of this argument is in Johnson [8]. See also Bhagwati and Ramaswami [1].

[6] On the concept of "cost of protection," see Leamer and Stern [9] for a good exposition; and also Johnson [7].

The welfare analysis of protection designed to increase savings via income distribution effects is the same in principle. Again we assume that the savings generated by the free trade situation—this time, in particular, by the free trade pattern of real incomes—are below the social optimum.

First-best policy is to subsidize saving or investment directly, as described above, and to use taxes and subsidies to attain whatever income distribution is desired. There are two targets, optimum savings and optimum income distribution, and their achievement calls for the use of two direct tax-subsidy instruments.

Second-best policy would be to use direct taxes and subsidies to alter the income distribution in favor of the sections with relatively high marginal propensities to save. This is obviously second best, since it means that the income distribution will no longer be optimum (that is, the socially desirable distribution), except by chance. If the only instrument of policy is one that can alter income distribution, the second-best optimum will involve a "trade-off" between the two targets, income distribution being more unequal and savings lower than at the first-best optimum.

Third-best policy would be to impose subsidies on production of particular products so as to raise the incomes of those factors intensive in their production, these factors having the relatively high marginal propensity to save. Not only will income distribution be distorted from the optimum in order to raise savings, but in addition a production cost will be imposed, because the pattern of production will be distorted towards the subsidized industries.

Finally, tariffs to protect industries intensive in factors that have a high marginal propensity to save are fourth best, since they add a distortion in the consumption pattern to the production and the income distribution distortions.

Arguments which are sometimes advanced for encouraging capital-intensive manufacturing industries in less-developed countries because they are more likely to reinvest their profits than labor-intensive industries can be analyzed in these terms.[7] If it would not be optimum to establish these industries in the light of the usual cost criteria, allowing for distortions and so on, then a production cost of protection is incurred for the sake of increasing the overall propensity to save—and, as pointed out earlier—it is

[7] See Sen [12], who is concerned with the choice of a technique in a given enterprise, the main argument being that the technique should be more capital intensive than otherwise if savings are suboptimal. The optimality of income distribution *per se* is not an issue in his approach, since he assumes that the enterprise in question is publicly owned, so that "profits" imply surplus earned by the state itself, which it can reinvest. A similar approach—that savings be fostered by chosing investment projects on the basis of a shadow wage that is higher than it would be if savings were optimal (or if there were no limits to taxation)—can be found in Little and Mirrlees [10].

possible that total savings and investment fail to increase even though the propensity to save increases.

Protection to raise government revenue so as to finance public investment will also be second or third best, unless only trade taxes are administratively feasible or the collection costs of alternative taxes are very high. In some less-developed countries the latter is indeed true, and perhaps the revenue argument for tariffs is the strongest of all.

If one reason for a tariff is to raise the incomes of import-competing producers so that part of the increase in incomes will go to income tax, then we have a very indirect approach to raising revenue. Looking at this matter in partial equilibrium terms, the tariff is equivalent to a tax on consumers which finances customs revenue and a subsidy to import-competing producers. This subsidy equivalent raises the incomes of producers, and part of this then goes in income tax, part remaining with the producers. Consumers have paid for the customs revenue, for the extra income tax, for the after-tax increase in producers' incomes, and for the production and consumption costs of protection, the latter being distortion costs. A straightforward consumption tax—the rate of tax being the same for imported and for home-produced goods—could raise just as much revenue but would avoid both the increase in incomes to producers and the production cost.

Having said all this, we must note some important qualifications to the underlying approach in this section of the paper. It is always first best to subsidize that activity, factor of production, or item of expenditure which is closest to the point of the "distortion," *provided it is possible to finance the subsidy and to distribute it to the recipients without any costs.* The assumption that this is so has been implicit so far.

In fact, there are costs of financing as well as costs of distributing the subsidy. The same is true of the use of taxes as first-best devices for discouraging production or consumption of products which are being overproduced or overconsumed. We need not elaborate on the nature of these costs here, since they are well known. They may, indeed, be so high that they rule out what have been called "first-best" measures in this paper.

But the existence of such costs does not destroy the usefulness of this sort of analysis. It directs attention to the need to look at the costs of taxing and subsidizing as directly as possible and to weigh these costs against the distortion costs of using tariffs. For example, if a tariff is used to discourage consumption of luxury goods and leads to the byproduct of fostering domestic production of uneconomic industries that produce such goods, the resultant production cost of protection must be set against the alternative cost of imposing a tax on domestic producers at the same rate as the tariff (and in addition to it), and so ending up with a sales tax on the product. Similarly, if a tariff is used to foster an infant industry which produces an intermediate good, and so causes using industries to underutilize the product of the protected industry because of its higher price, the resultant consumption cost must be weighed against the alternative costs of financing a direct subsidy to the infant industry.

Once there are inevitable costs of correcting a "distortion," it will normally be undesirable to make a full correction, since this would simply mean replacing one cost—the cost of the original distortion—with another. Rather, the optimum is likely to require only a partial correction. Of course, since all these distortions and costs are not precisely measurable in any case, and sometimes one can only guess at them in the most general way, this is a rather formal point.

V. Protection and the Inducement to Invest

Protection may raise or lower the marginal efficiency of capital schedule for the economy as a whole, thus affecting the "inducement to invest." It will obviously affect the schedules of particular industries, and direct resources into some industries and out of others. But here we are concerned with the effect on total investment. The following discussion has been stimulated by Hirschman [4], who has emphasized the need to "maximize 'induced' investment decisions" in a less-developed country.

The first question is whether the "inducement to invest" matters. In our analysis so far, it has not mattered. Total investment was determined by savings, and an increase in the private inducement to invest would do no more than raise the equilibrium rate of interest or reduce the ratio of public to private investment. It was, of course, assumed that there is no capital inflow or outflow, an assumption we shall continue to make here. Let us then see through what channels a change in inducement to invest could affect total investment.

The familiar Keynesian problem is that there may be a floor to the rate of interest, or alternatively that investment may not be interest elastic, so that either the rate of interest could not fall sufficiently or, if it did fall, it might not succeed in bringing investment to the level of *ex-ante* savings generated at full employment. Hence the marginal efficiency of capital schedule would have to be shifted sufficiently to maintain full employment. But one wonders whether in most less-developed countries this is a problem. The problem is that demand is too great relative to available productive capacity, not too little: Investment is limited by the availability of savings, not the lack of desire to invest.

If lack of investment and demand were a problem, then, as Keynes pointed out, one way would be to increase public investment sufficiently, financed by credit from the central bank. Public and private investment combined can always be brought to equality with *ex-ante* full employment savings. But while this method could certainly deal with the employment problem, it would not necessarily lead to the most efficient pattern of investment and hence the highest rate of growth given the available savings: Private investment may be socially more productive at the margin than public investment, so that there may be a case for trying to raise the marginal private efficiency of private capital in order to raise the private content in total investment (though in some advanced countries, as Galbraith has pointed out, the case may well be for raising the share of public investment).

It is also possible that to some extent investment generates its own savings, which is probably what Hirschman had in mind. If investment becomes more profitable, extra resources may become available to finance it, either through reduced consumption or through reduced leisure, entrepreneurs and others working harder so as to finance the investment. If an incerase in the inducement to invest generates higher savings, then, in fact, savings are profit or interest elastic. Resources for investment will increase if incentives are sufficient. Hence raising the inducement to invest might indeed raise total private investment, and thus the rate of growth, even in the absence of capital inflow or outflow.[8] Whether this is so will vary between countries. In any case, assuming now that the inducement to invest is relevant for the rate of capital accumulation—as probably it is in some of the Latin American countries Hirschman had in mind—let us see how protection could affect it.

The question is simply how protection affects expected profits, which can be assumed to depend on current profits. Simple static analysis can be used here. If protection reduces aggregate real income, it may also reduce the rate of profit, at least if there is no great difference in factor-intensities between industries. In terms of the simple two-sector model familiar in trade theory, protection will raise the rate of profit if capital-intensive products are protected, and reduce it if the other products are protected.

If capital is sector specific, with a separate supply curve for different types of capital, each responding to its own profit rate, protection may raise some profit rates and reduce others, this being the usual income distribution effect. Increases in profits will induce investment, and decreases will discourage it. If protection raises profits in those industries where the elasticity of supply of new capital is high at the expense of profits in industries where the elasticity of supply is low, as well as at the expense of other factor incomes, then total investment will increase.

[8] In some countries savers hoard gold unless the expected profitability of productive investment is high enough. If we regard an addition to the stock of private gold holdings as a form of unproductive investment, then raising the inducement to invest productively brings about a switch in the pattern of investment which will raise the rate of growth.

There may be a *threshold effect*, this being an element in Hirschman's analysis. New investment into an industry will only be induced if the rate of profit increases above a certain threshold; small increases or decreases in profits would have no effect. If it is desired to induce an increase in total investment, protection must then concentrate profits, raising profits in some industries substantially, even though this is at the expense of other industries. Large profit increases in a few industries associated with modest profit decreases in many other industries will then raise total investment.

Finally, given that intervention through protection or other devices can raise the overall inducement to invest and that an increase in the inducement can actually raise investment and the rate of growth, the question still remains whether such intervention is justified. Should a static optimization policy be supplemented by a deliberate investment-inducing policy which will lead to some departure from the static optimum?

Essentially this depends on considerations previously discussed, namely whether private and social time preference diverge, and whether private expectations of the returns on investment fall short of the correct expectations —or, at least, fall short of expectations based on the (presumably) superior information of the policymakers. There may also be externalities associated with investment; these would not enter the private calculus but should enter the social calculus.

We can apply the "domestic distortions" analysis here (while bearing in mind its qualifications). If it is socially desirable to foster new investment, then first-best policy would be to subsidize new investment directly. A method which subsidizes an industry so as to induce new investment also draws existing capital and labor into the industry and hence causes some misallocation of existing resources, apart from possibly undesirable income redistribution effects. Hence subsidization of output of an industry into which new investment is expected to go is second best. A tariff to foster the industry adds a consumption cost, and so is third best.

VI. Backward Linkage

Hirschman has stressed the need to maximize "linkage effects" in order to induce investment and so foster the industrialization process [5]. This idea is worth examining with some care.

When a particular activity is protected, its own actual or potential profit rate will be increased. Now the question is how actual or potential profitability of investment in other activities will be affected. Hirschman focuses on backward linkage. Profits or potential profits in activities which produce inputs for the protected activity will increase. These must be nontraded inputs, or at least inputs which, because of economies of scale, would be wholly domestically produced and hence nontraded if the demand for them were sufficient.

If cloth were protected, so that the weaving industry expanded, the demand for yarn (which can be produced domestically if the scale of output is large enough) would also expand, and a backward linkage effect would be generated. This might be contrasted with protecting another product which does not require produced inputs that could be produced domestically, or where there may be some domestic production of the inputs, but any extra demand for them would be supplied from imports available at given world prices. The argument is that protection of cloth should be favored relative to the latter type of industry.

Hirschman is not specifically concerned with protection, this being just one device for "rearranging and concentrating the pattern of imports"[6] so as to induce sufficient demand for those inputs where there is a possibility of a backward linkage effect. Protection of cloth, in this example, raises profits in weaving and spinning and so induces investment in these two activities. Assuming that this is a net addition to the stock of capital, and is not just capital diverted from going somewhere else, there may then be some case for fostering the cloth industry.

Yet this is only half the story. Protecting cloth may reduce profits and hence investment in other industries. Labor may be drawn into weaving and spinning from other industries, and these two activities may use nontraded inputs, including the services of public utilities, which are also used by other industries. While spinning is complementary with weaving, there will be activities directly or indirectly competitive with weaving. The backward linkage effect is no doubt the main complementary effect, but it is by no means the only effect to take into account. Even if the supply of unskilled labor were perfectly elastic, other activities may be competitive in the use of skilled labor and some nontraded inputs. Investment in these industries will become *less* attractive.

If tariffs are the instruments of protection, one must bear in mind that the effective protection of the using industries will be reduced unless they are compensated by appropriate increases in their nominal tariff rates, while if the using industries are export industries they will suffer negative effective protection from tariffs on inputs unless they benefit from "export drawback" or similar arrangements, or obtain compensating export subsidies.

Finally, if a tariff is seen as a method of indirectly subsidizing a using industry so as to induce investment via the backward linkage effect into other industries which supply inputs to it, it is a very indirect approach and sets up a whole series of unnecessary distortions. If indeed there is any inducement-to-invest problem, it would obviously be more sensible to subsidize directly investment into the industries concerned.

VII. Learning and the Rate of Growth

To conclude, let us introduce "invisible" capital accumulation. When an industry's cost curve falls over time because it is learning by experience, we could say that the learning process represents the accumulation of "invisible" capital—we could call it knowledge or "human capital," if we liked. The fall in the cost curve is the fruit of this special form of capital accumulation.

An infant industry, as this term is often understood, is an industry that is undergoing such a learning process. If we make use of this simple concept of invisible capital accumulation, we can relate our previous analysis to the more familiar analysis of infant industry protection. This analysis usually takes a partial equilibrium form, but here we consider the implications of infant industry protection for the rate of growth in a simple general equilibrium model.

We consider an economy with only two industries, A and B, in both of which learning is related to the scale of current output. Thus production of A generates invisible capital K_a and production of B invisible capital K_b, which will yield fruits in later years. If the current "visible" outputs of A and B are X_a and X_b, respectively, then true current output is $X_a + X_b + dK_a + dK_b$. A part of current income will be saved and invested in the ordinary way. Hence total investment consists of "ordinary" investment plus "invisible" investment.

Now suppose that it is desired to increase the rate of growth by fostering industries with learning. Protection then shifts the output pattern from one industry to another, say from A to B. Learning in A will go down and in B up. Let us assume that, measured in terms of the productivity of learning—that is, in terms of the value of the increment to future output (measured at world prices)—this raises total learning. We might then say that invisible capital creation has increased, and so the rate of capital accumulation *on this account* has increased. But it must be borne in mind that if the shift in output imposes a current cost of protection, and hence lowers current real income, it is likely to reduce ordinary saving and investment out of current income for the reasons set out earlier. Thus against the increase in invisible capital creation must be set a decrease in ordinary investment.

It is perfectly possible that protection of genuine infant industries reduces the rate of growth, even though total learning or invisible capital creation has clearly increased. This could happen if a large cost of protection is required to bring about a shift to industries with relatively high learning rates and if the propensity to save out of current income is high.

Another way of looking at this matter is as follows. Protection which shifts the output pattern towards high-learning industries has the following effects. First, it reduces current income and hence current consumption. Secondly, because of the fall in current income, ordinary savings and investment also fall. And thirdly, it raises invisible investment. Thus the increase in invisible investment has been partly at the expense of consumption and partly at the expense of ordinary investment. The reduction in consumption represents an increase in the economy's savings (defined as consumption foregone), while the other effect represents a switch in the pattern of investment. It is possible that the switch in the investment pattern is uneconomic, hence causing output at later dates to be less than it would have been in the absence of protection (and in the absence of the extra total savings), and further, that it decreases output at later dates so much that it more than offsets the gain to future output which results when current consumption is foregone for the sake of invisible capital creation.

Finally, it should be noted—though no formal proof is attempted here—that if all learning were internal to firms and firms were able to finance current losses by borrowing on the capital market or out of their own resources, profit-maximizing firms would forego current profits or even incur losses for the sake of obtaining the benefits of learning only to an extent required to equate the expected marginal productivity of learning with that of ordinary investment. They would not invest in invisible capital to an extent that reduced expected future output and hence the rate of growth. Of course, their expectations may be mistaken, which may lead them to overinvest in learning, or alternatively and more likely, they may undervalue the rewards of learning and so may underinvest in activities which require relatively long loss-making periods while experience is being gained.

REFERENCES

[1] Bhagwati, J., and Ramaswami, V. K., Domestic Distortions, Tariffs and the Theory of Optimum Subsidy, *J. Political Econ.* **71**, 44–50 (1963).

[2] Corden, W. M., Protection and Foreign Investment, *Econ. Rec.* **43**, 209–232 (1967).

[3] Corden, W. M., The Effects of Trade on the Rate of Growth, *in* "Trade, Balance of Payments and Growth: Papers in Honor of Charles P. Kindleberger" (Bhagwati *et al.*, eds.). North-Holland Publ., Amsterdam, 1971.

[4] Hirschman, A. O., "The Strategy of Economic Development." Yale Univ. Press, New Haven, Connecticut, 1958.

[5] Hirschman, A. O., "The Strategy of Economic Development," Chap. 6. Yale Univ. Press, New Haven, Connecticut, 1958.

[6] Hirschman, A. O., "The Strategy of Economic Development," p. 116. Yale Univ. Press, New Haven, Connecticut, paperback edition, 1961.

[7] Johnson, H. G., The Cost of Protection and the Scientific Tariff, *J. Political Econ.* **68**, 327–345 (1960).

[8] Johnson, H. G., Optimal Trade Intervention in the Presence of Domestic Distortions, *in* "Trade, Growth, and the Balance of Payments" (Baldwin *et al.*, eds.). Rand-McNally, Chicago, Illinois, 1965.

[9] Leamer, E. E., and Stern, R. M., "Quantitative International Economics," Chap. 8. Allyn and Bacon, Boston, Massachusetts, 1970.
[10] Little, I. M. D., and Mirrlees, J. A., "Manual of Industrial Project Analysis in Developing Countries," Vol. 2, Chap. 13. Development Centre of the O.E.C.D., Paris, 1969.
[11] Nurkse, R., "Problems of Capital Formation in Underdeveloped Countries." Oxford Univ. Press, London and New York, 1953.
[12] Sen, A. K., "Choice of Techniques," 3rd ed. Oxford Univ. Press, London and New York, 1968, especially the introduction to 3rd ed.
[13] Smith, A., "The Wealth of Nations," (Everyman, ed.), Vol. 1, p. 402. J. M. Dent and Sons Ltd., London, 1910.

THE THEORY OF EXPLOITATIVE TRADE AND INVESTMENT POLICIES: A REFORMULATION AND SYNTHESIS *

JOHN S. CHIPMAN

University of Minnesota, Minneapolis, Minnesota

I. Introduction

Traditional doctrine has long held that free trade and free international mobility of capital are in some sense optimal. However, nations continue to pursue their own advantage, and at the same time it is recognized in the more sophisticated versions of classical doctrine that achievement of an international optimum would require not only a consensus as to the optimal distribution of output (say in the form of specification of an international social welfare function) but also a willingness to implement that consensus by undertaking lump-sum redistributions of income—itself a form of market interference. Even if such a utopian program were to be carried out, it would still be necessary at the negotiating stage for nations to know how much they stand to gain or lose from abandoning restrictionist policies.

In this paper, I shall examine a model first presented by Kemp [17], and subsequently further analyzed by Jones [14], of a two-country, two-commodity, two-factor (labor and capital) world, in which capital is (physically) perfectly mobile, and the "home" country pursues its national advantage and

* Research was made possible by a single-quarter leave granted by the University of Minnesota in the Spring of 1970, and carried out at the Institute for Advanced Studies in Vienna, Austria. The support of both these institutions is gratefully acknowledged.

the "foreign" country reacts passively.[1] I shall use the term "exploitative" to describe such policies, to convey the idea that the rest of the world is exploited in the same sense that natural resources are, as well as to avoid the somewhat insidious term "optimal." The term will therefore cover not only the types of policies that might be pursued by advanced industrial nations *vis-à-vis* the underdeveloped countries, but equally well to describe the kinds of policies that might be pursued by the Periphery (to use Dr. Prebisch's term [23]), to improve its relative position in the world, or to counteract adverse tendencies, real or alleged, emanating from the industrial Centers.

Elsewhere I have shown (Chipman [4]) that if world output can be efficiently produced by both countries producing both commodities, then under a very mild condition which can always be expected to be fulfilled whenever production functions are of a smooth neoclassical kind and are not identical as between countries, the world production possibility frontier will have a flat segment corresponding to such output combinations. Furthermore, sufficient conditions were obtained for the existence of efficient world output combinations when both countries diversify; simpler and very appealing conditions for this result have since been obtained by Uekawa [30].[2]

The above result has interesting implications for the theory of exploitative trade and investment policies. Consider first a situation in which, on the contrary, at least one of the countries specializes, and suppose that commodity trade is free but capital movements are subject to restriction. If the home country is a lender and the foreign country specializes, it will be to the home country's advantage to induce its citizens to withdraw some of their capital from abroad, since this will have the effect of raising its rate of return; by taxing income from capital invested abroad, the lending country can induce the withdrawal and capture the resulting increase in the return on foreign investment. Likewise, if the home country is a borrower and the foreign country specializes, it will be to the home country's advantage to encourage the foreign country to withdraw some of its capital, since the resulting excess of capital in the lending country will lower its rate of return there, thus lowering the opportunity cost of borrowing capital; this allows the home country to tax the income from foreign capital invested on its soil by the amount of the drop in the profits abroad, and the tax also serves to induce foreigners to withdraw their capital.

[1] Removal of the assumption of passive reaction would be a natural next step in the study of this model. For the case in which trade is unrestricted and only capital flows are subject to interference, a way has been shown by Hamada [10].

[2] Ethier and Ross [7] have considered this problem in a comparative dynamics setting in which capital is assumed to be produced and ownership patterns may change as a result of saving. They have characterized types of saving behavior that allow for the possibility of efficient production with diversification in the long run.

The above analysis, first set forth by Kemp [15, 16], no longer holds if the two countries both diversify. In such a case, and if commodity trade remains unrestricted, autonomous movements of capital into or out of the exploited country will not affect its rate of return there. An "optimal" policy for the exploiting country to pursue in such circumstances is one of noninterference with capital flows—always assuming absence of restrictions to commodity flows.

The rationale for taxing income from home capital invested abroad, or from foreign capital invested at home, is quite a different one when the foreign country diversifies. Its role is no longer to raise or lower the foreign rate of return (by driving capital out) and thus capture the differential, but rather to capture a differential in rates of return that results as a byproduct of commercial policy. If the home country imposes a tariff on its import good (Commodity 2), or a tax on its export good (Commodity 1) which improves its terms of trade (the relative price of Commodity 1), this will—by the Stolper–Samuelson theorem—either raise or lower the foreign rate of return on capital according as Industry 1 in the foreign country is capital or labor intensive. If the home country is a lender, then in the former case the tariff will have, in addition to the favorable terms-of-trade effect, the added advantage of raising foreign profit levels, which can be tapped if a tax is levied on investment income earned abroad; in the latter case, if the fall in foreign profits is not too great, it will be to the home country's advantage to subsidize foreign investment in order to capture the predominating commodity terms-of-trade effect; whereas if the decline in foreign profits is great enough to outweigh the terms-of-trade effect, the home country should subsidize imports and lower its terms of trade in order to capture the resulting increase in profits on its foreign investments. Likewise, if the home country is a borrower and Industry 1 (its export industry) is labor intensive abroad, then a tariff (or export tax) which improves its terms of trade will have the additional effect of driving down profit rates abroad, making it possible to tax foreign profits earned in the home country by the amount of the decrease; however, if Industry 1 is capital intensive abroad, foreign profit rates will be driven up and foreign capital withdrawn unless subsidized to stay; if the subsidy cost outweighs the direct terms-of-trade gain, it will be advantageous for the borrowing country to subsidize imports or exports and lower its terms of trade, so as to drive down foreign profits and make it possible to increase taxes on foreign income earned in the home country.[3] [The above discussion is all set out quantitatively in Table I (Sect. V).]

[3] An important difference should be noted between the model studied here and that of Mundell [22]. In Mundell's, production functions are assumed to be identical as between countries, and it follows from this that if a single instrument is introduced (a tariff or a tax on income from invested capital), and reversal of factor intensity is ruled out, equilibrium

The cases in which the tariff rate and tax rate on income from foreign investment have opposite sign have been termed "paradoxical" by Kemp [17]. However, casual observation suggests that they are by no means pathological. For instance, Chile and Venezuela have both traditionally been heavy borrowers of foreign capital, yet their export industries (copper and petroleum) are highly capital intensive not only in those countries themselves but in the United States as well. The possibility, therefore, cannot be excluded that commercial policy, by improving these countries' terms of trade, would also raise profit rates in the U.S.A. and thus raise the cost of borrowing, leading to withdrawal of foreign capital unless accompanied by remedial measures.

All the arguments of this paper apply equally well to a model in which labor, rather than capital, is the mobile factor (see Ramaswami [24]). However, in this case they carry the insidious implication that immigrants' income should be subject to a discriminatory tax (or subsidy), which would be unconstitutional in most countries if overtly pursued.

The remainder of the paper is organized as follows: Section II brings out into the open the important "reciprocity" relations of Samuelson [26] that underlie the theoretical analysis of the later sections, and develops a concept due to Samuelson which I describe as a "production function for foreign exchange." This is defined as the maximum obtainable value of output, at

---

with diversification is not possible. This is no longer the case if we allow (as we must—see Chipman [4]) production functions to be different as between countries, in both industries. This can be seen from the following simple argument: Let $g_i(w,r)$, $g_i^*(w^*,r^*)$ be the minimum-unit-cost functions for commodity i in the home and foreign countries, respectively, where w, r, and w^*, r^*, denote the wage rate and rental of capital in the home and foreign country. Let the home country be a borrower and suppose a tax of $100t'$ % is imposed on the income of foreign capital, so that $r^* = (1-t')r$ (see Eq. 5.14′, Sect. V); let Commodity 1 be exported by the home country and a tax of 100τ % be imposed on exports, so that $p_1^* = (1+\tau)p_1$, where p_i, p_i^* are the prices of commodity i at home and abroad, and $p_2 = p_2^* = 1$ (see Eq. 5.12, Sect. V). Then trade and capital mobility together with diversification of production in both countries imply the existence of a solution to the equations

$$g_1(w,r) = p_1, \qquad g_1^*(w^*,(1-t')r) = (1+\tau)p_1,$$
$$g_2(w,r) = 1, \qquad g_2^*(w^*,(1-t')r) = 1.$$

If $g_i = g_i^*$, for $i = 1,2$, and if $t' = 0$ and $\tau > 0$, the bottom two equations imply $w = w^*$, contradicting the top two; this is essentially Mundell's result. Likewise, if $g_i = g_i^*$, for $i = 1,2$, and if $t' > 0$ and $\tau = 0$, then the top pair of equations state that the points (w,r) and (w^*,r^*) both lie on the curve $g_1(w,r) = p_1$, and the bottom pair state that these same points both lie on the curve $g_2(w,r) = 1$. Then these curves must cross (or coincide) at two different points, implying factor intensity reversal.

If $g_i \neq g_i^*$, for $i = 1,2$, and an isolated solution to the above equations exists for $\tau = 0$ and $t' = 0$, then a slight increase in one or both of the parameters τ and t' is equivalent to a slight perturbation of the functions g_1^* and g_2^*, hence an isolated solution will continue to exist. Compare the argument in Inada and Kemp [12].

fixed world prices, expressed as a function of the country's endowments of labor and capital; the peculiar flat conic section of this production surface (depicted in Figs. 1 and 2) is what leads to the results of special interest. Section III deals with the hypothesized passive behavior of the foreign country, and Sect. IV formulates the optimum problem for the home (exploiting) country. This leads finally to the analysis of exploitative tariff and tax policies in Sect. V.

II. A Production Function for Foreign Exchange

Let a country be endowed with nonnegative amounts L and K (not both zero) of labor and capital, respectively, and produce amounts y_1 and y_2 of two commodities in accordance with production functions

$$y_i = f_i(L_i, K_i), \qquad i = 1,2, \tag{2.1}$$

which are assumed to be positively homogeneous of degree 1, twice continuously differentiable, with isoquants *strictly convex to the origin.*[4] Here, L_i and K_i represent the employment of labor and capital in industry i, assumed to satisfy

$$L_1 + L_2 \leqq L, \qquad K_1 + K_2 \leqq K, \qquad L_i \geqq 0, \quad K_i \geqq 0. \tag{2.2}$$

Thus, labor and capital are exogenously determined, inelastically supplied, and perfectly mobile as between industries. The *production possibility set* $\mathscr{Y}(L, K)$ is defined as the set of all nonnegative output combinations (y_1, y_2) for which there exist input combinations (L_i, K_i) satisfying (2.1) and (2.2.)

Suppose that world prices $p_1 \geqq 0, p_2 \geqq 0$ (not both zero), are given for the two commodities, and that any amounts can be imported or exported at these prices. Define the function[5]

$$\Pi(p_1, p_2, L, K) = \max\{p_1 y_1 + p_2 y_2 \colon (y_1, y_2) \in \mathscr{Y}(L, K)\}. \tag{2.3}$$

Since $\mathscr{Y}(L, K)$ is closed and bounded, this function is well defined. For each combination L, K of factors, it defines the maximum value of output obtainable at the given world prices p_1, p_2. Under competitive conditions, this

[4] That is, given any $(L_i^0, K_i^0) \geqslant (0,0)$, there exist $w^0 > 0$ and $r^0 > 0$, such that

$$w^0 L_i + r^0 K_i > w^0 L_i^0 + r^0 K_i^0$$

for all $(L_i, K_i) \geqslant (0,0)$, such that $f_i(L_i, K_i) = f_i(L_i^0, K_i^0)$ and $(L_i, K_i) \neq (L_i^0, K_i^0)$ (see Hurwicz and Uzawa [11, p. 131]). Here the symbol $\geqslant$ has the usual meaning that $(L_i, K_i) \geqslant (0,0)$ if and only if $L_i \geqq 0$, $K_i \geqq 0$, and not both $L_i = K_i = 0$.

[5] This function was first defined by Samuelson [26, p. 10]. Mathematically it is the support function of the set $\mathscr{Y}(L, K)$; see Fenchel [8].

corresponds to the gross domestic product (GDP), and by hypothesis it is available for purchase of goods from abroad at prices p_1, p_2. For fixed p_1, p_2, the function Π may therefore be regarded as a *production function for foreign exchange*. We shall see presently that it has the general properties of production functions, but with one peculiar special feature.

Consider Fig. 1. Isoquants are drawn corresponding to production of a dollar's worth of each commodity; if both prices are positive, these are the amounts of labor and capital satisfying $f_1(L, K) = 1/p_1$ and $f_2(L, K) = 1/p_2$, respectively. A dollar or more of foreign exchange can therefore be obtained from resources $V' = (L', K')$ if these are all allocated to Industry 1 and $f_1(L', K') \geqq 1/p_1$; or from resources $V'' = (L'', K'')$ if these are all allocated to Industry 2 and $f_2(L'', K'') \geqq 1/p_2$. Thus for any λ_1, λ_2 with $0 \leqq \lambda_i \leqq 1$ and $\lambda_1 + \lambda_2 = 1$, if resources

$$V = (L, K) = \lambda_1(L', K') + \lambda_2(L'', K'')$$

are available, and allocated to each industry according to

$$V_1 = (L_1, K_1) = \lambda_1(L', K'), \qquad V_2 = (L_2, K_2) = \lambda_2(L'', K''),$$

then outputs in the respective industries will be (by homogeneity)

$$f_1(L_1, K_1) = \lambda_1 f_1(L', K') \geqq \lambda_1/p_1,$$
$$f_2(L_2, K_2) = \lambda_2 f_2(L'', K'') \geqq \lambda_2/p_2,$$

yielding a value of

$$p_1 f_1(L_1, K_1) + p_2 f_2(L_2, K_2) \geqq \lambda_1 + \lambda_2 = 1.$$

Given that

$$L_1 + L_2 = \lambda_1 L' + \lambda_2 L'' \leqq L,$$
$$K_1 + K_2 = \lambda_1 K' + \lambda_2 K'' \leqq K,$$

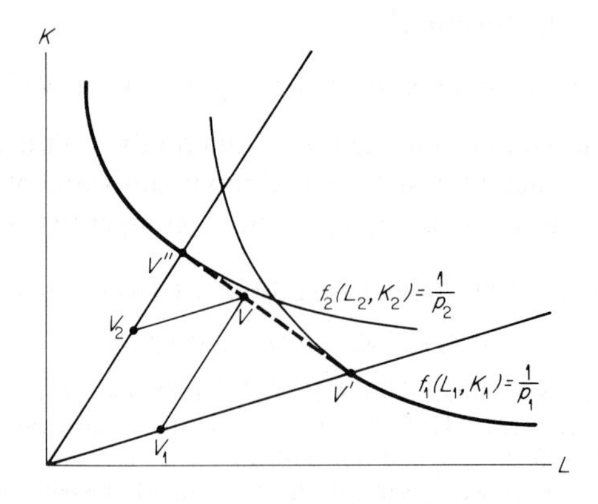

Fig. 1.

it follows from the definition of Π that

$$\Pi(p_1, p_2, L, K) \geqq p_1 f_1(L_1, K_1) + p_2 f_2(L_2, K_2) \geqq 1.$$

Therefore the point $V = (L, K)$ is on or above (in the diagram it is on) the isoquant for the production of one dollar's worth of foreign exchange.

The converse is also true; that is, given any $V = (L, K)$ such that

$$\Pi(p_1, p_2, L, K) \geqq 1,$$

we can find $V' = (L', K')$ and $V'' = (L'', K'')$ such that for some λ_i with $0 \leqq \lambda_i \leqq 1$ and $\lambda_1 + \lambda_2 = 1$, we have

$$V = \lambda_1 V' + \lambda_2 V'',$$

and

$$f_1(L', K') \geqq 1/p_1, \qquad f_2(L'', K'') \geqq 1/p_2.$$

(If $p_1 = 0$, say, we can take $\lambda_1 = 0$ and set $L' = K' = \infty$.) For, suppose

$$\Pi(p_1, p_2, L, K) = \pi \geqq 1.$$

Then by definition of Π, there are L_i and K_i satisfying

$$L_1 + L_2 = L, \qquad K_1 + K_2 = K,$$

(equality being justified by the argument following (2.6) below) such that

$$\Pi(p_1, p_2, L, K) = p_1 f_1(L_1, K_1) + p_2 f_2(L_2, K_2).$$

Defining

$$\lambda_i = p_i f_i(L_i, K_i)/\pi, \qquad i = 1, 2,$$

and

$$V' = (L', K') = (L_1, K_1)/\lambda_1, \qquad V'' = (L'', K'') = (L_2, K_2)/\lambda_2,$$

we see that $\lambda_1 + \lambda_2 = 1$ and that V' and V'' satisfy the required conditions.

Summarizing, we can state this result formally as follows.

THEOREM 1. The set $\{(L, K): \Pi(p_1, p_2, L, K) \geqq 1\}$ is the convex hull of the sets $\{(L, K): f_i(L, K) \geqq 1/p_i\}$, $i = 1, 2$.

In Fig. 1, the isoquant $\Pi(p_1, p_2, L, K) = 1$ (for fixed p_1, p_2) is shown by the thick curve. Its special feature is the flat segment (indicated by a broken line in the figure) within the cone corresponding to diversification of production. Within this cone, labor and capital are perfect substitutes in the production of foreign exchange, and the wage–rental ratio (the slope of the isoquant) is invariant with respect to factor endowments. This property of the isoquants is, in fact, the essence of the factor price equalization theorem. The characterization given by Theorem 1 is perfectly general, and readily extended to the case of m factors and n products.

Suppose in Fig. 1 that one imagines the quantity of labor to be fixed and the country's endowment of capital to be variable. Then as the endowment point moves upward from the horizontal axis along a vertical line, the output of Commodity 2 will be zero and that of Commodity 1 will increase until the diversification cone is reached; as the point continues upward inside the diversification cone, the output of Commodity 1 will fall and that of Commodity 2 will rise until, at the edge of the cone, the output of Commodity 1 has reached zero; from then on it stays equal to zero, and the output of Commodity 2 continues to increase. This is all depicted in Fig. 2. The dark solid lines depict $p_1 y_1$ and $p_2 y_2$ as functions of K (for fixed p_1, p_2, and L); these are the *Rybczynski functions* (cf. Rybczynski [25]), which are linear within the diversification zone. The function Π, regarded as a function of K with p_1, p_2, and L fixed, has the usual properties of production functions except for the flat segment (indicated by the broken line in Fig. 2) corresponding to diversification. The slope $\partial\Pi/\partial K$ of this segment will correspond to the rental of capital in this region, which will be independent of the capital stock.

The figures correspond to the special case of absence of factor intensity reversal. If, for instance, the isoquants for the two commodities intersected twice instead of once, there would be two diversification cones, and two flat segments instead of one on the isoquants of the function Π. In this case, there would exist some prices p_1 and p_2 for which the product isoquants would meet at a point of tangency, and the diversification cone would degenerate to a ray. If the country's factor endowment vector should happen to be on this ray, outputs would no longer be unique. In Fig. 2, this would show up in the linear segments of the Rybczynski functions becoming vertical; thus they would no longer be single-valued functions, but (multivalued) correspondences. The country's production possibility frontier will in this case be flat; we shall see below that this is the only case (when there are two products and factors) in which it is flat, i.e., in all other cases the production possibility frontier will be strictly concave to the origin.

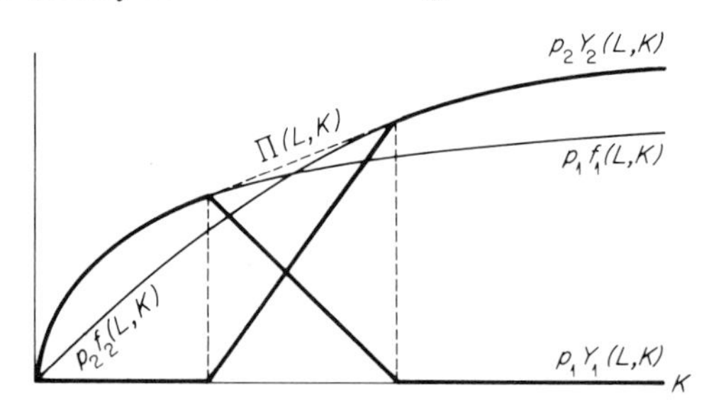

Fig. 2.

We now proceed to a more precise analysis of these questions.

The Lagrangean expression for problem (2.3) is

(2.4)
$$\mathscr{L}(L_1, K_1, L_2, K_2, w, r; p_1, p_2, L, K) = p_1 f_1(L_1, K_1) + p_2 f_2(L_2, K_2) + w(L-L_1-L_2) + r(K-K_1-K_2),$$

where w and r are Lagrangean multipliers. The Kuhn–Tucker necessary and sufficient[6] conditions are

(2.5)
$$\frac{\partial \mathscr{L}}{\partial L_i} = p_i \frac{\partial f_i}{\partial L_i} - w \leqq 0, \qquad L_i\left(p_i \frac{\partial f_i}{\partial L_i} - w\right) = 0, \qquad i = 1, 2,$$
$$\frac{\partial \mathscr{L}}{\partial K_i} = p_i \frac{\partial f_i}{\partial K_i} - r \leqq 0, \qquad K_i\left(p_i \frac{\partial f_i}{\partial K_i} - r\right) = 0, \qquad i = 1, 2,$$

together with

(2.6)
$$\frac{\partial \mathscr{L}}{\partial w} = L - L_1 - L_2 \geqq 0, \qquad w(L-L_1-L_2) = 0,$$
$$\frac{\partial \mathscr{L}}{\partial r} = K - K_1 - K_2 \geqq 0, \qquad r(K-K_1-K_2) = 0,$$

(see Kuhn and Tucker [18]). Now from the strict convexity to the origin of the production isoquants, we have $\partial f_i/\partial L_i > 0$ and $\partial f_i/\partial K_i > 0$, for $i = 1, 2$, and since by hypothesis either $p_1 > 0$ or $p_2 > 0$, it follows from (2.5) that we must have $w > 0$ and $r > 0$. Therefore equality must hold in (2.6), i.e., both factors must be fully employed.

Define the *production possibility frontier* $\hat{\mathscr{Y}}(L, K)$ as the set of all (y_1, y_2) satisfying (2.3) for some semipositive[7] prices p_1, p_2. This frontier is defined as *strictly concave to the origin*[8] whenever, for all (y_1^0, y_2^0) on the frontier, there exist prices $p_1^0 \geqq 0, p_2^0 \geqq 0$ (not both zero), such that

$$p_1^0 y_1^0 + p_2^0 y_2^0 > p_1^0 y_1 + p_2^0 y_2,$$

for all $(y_1, y_2) \in \hat{\mathscr{Y}}(L, K)$, such that $(y_1, y_2) \neq (y_1^0, y_2^0)$.

[6] The sufficiency follows from the fact that both the production functions and the constraints are concave; see Theorem 3 of Kuhn and Tucker [18].

[7] The vector (p_1, p_2) is said to be semipositive, written $(p_1, p_2) \geqslant (0, 0)$, if $p_1 \geqq 0$, $p_2 \geqq 0$ but not both $p_1 = p_2 = 0$.

[8] Compare the definition in footnote 4.

As is well known, the set $\mathscr{Y}(L, K)$ is convex.[9]. We shall now establish a necessary and sufficient condition for $\hat{\mathscr{Y}}(L, K)$ to be strictly concave to the origin, for all $(L, K) \geqslant 0$.[10]

THEOREM 2. In order that $\hat{\mathscr{Y}}(L, K)$ be strictly concave to the origin for all factor endowments $(L, K) \geqslant 0$, it is necessary and sufficient that

$$\begin{vmatrix} \partial g_1/\partial w & \partial g_1/\partial r \\ \partial g_2/\partial w & \partial g_2/\partial r \end{vmatrix} \neq 0, \qquad \text{for all} \quad w > 0, \quad r > 0, \tag{2.7}$$

where $g_i(w, r) = \min\{wL_i + rK_i : f_i(L_i, K_i) \geqq 1\}$.

Remark. By the envelope theorem of production theory,[11] $\partial g_i/\partial w$ and $\partial g_i/\partial r$ are the amounts of labor and capital used per unit of output of industry i, so at positive output and positive labor input levels, (2.7) can be written

$$\begin{vmatrix} L_1/y_1 & K_1/y_1 \\ L_2/y_2 & K_2/y_2 \end{vmatrix} = \frac{L_1 L_2}{y_1 y_2}\left(\frac{K_2}{L_2} - \frac{K_1}{L_1}\right) \neq 0, \tag{2.8}$$

yielding the familiar condition of nonreversal of factor intensity.

Proof. The sufficiency is shown as follows: Let a point $y^0 = (y_1{}^0, y_2{}^0)$ be on the production possibility frontier $\hat{\mathscr{Y}}(L, K)$; then there is a pair $p^0 = (p_1{}^0, p_2{}^0) \geqslant 0$ of prices such that $p_1{}^0 y_1{}^0 + p_2{}^0 y_2{}^0 \geqq p_1{}^0 y_1 + p_2{}^0 y_2$ for all $y = (y_1, y_2)$ in the production possibility set $\mathscr{Y}(L, K)$. Let $y^1 = (y_1{}^1, y_2{}^1)$ be on the production possibility frontier, and $y^1 \neq y^0$. We are to show that $p_1{}^0 y_1{}^0 + p_2{}^0 y_2{}^0 > p_1{}^0 y_1{}^1 + p_2{}^0 y_2{}^1$. Suppose not, i.e., let $p_1{}^0 y_1{}^0 + p_2{}^0 y_2{}^0 = p_1{}^0 y_1{}^1 + p_2{}^0 y_2{}^1$. Let L_i^j, K_i^j be such as to satisfy

$$y_i^j = f_i(L_i^j, K_i^j), \qquad \text{for} \quad i = 1, 2, \quad j = 0, 1,$$

and denote, for $0 < \theta < 1$,

$$L_i^\theta = (1-\theta) L_i{}^0 + \theta L_i{}^1, \qquad K_i^\theta = (1-\theta) K_i{}^0 + \theta K_i{}^1, \qquad i = 1, 2.$$

[9] A formal proof goes as follows: Let $y^0 = (y_1{}^0, y_2{}^0)$ and $y^1 = (y_1{}^1, y_2{}^1) \in \mathscr{Y}(L, K)$, and let $f_i(L_i{}^h, K_i{}^h) = y_i{}^h$ and $L_1{}^h + L_2{}^h \leqq L$, $K_1{}^h + K_2{}^h \leqq K$, for $h = 0, 1$. Denote $y^\theta = (1-\theta) y^0 + \theta y^1$, $L_i{}^\theta = (1-\theta) L_i{}^0 + \theta L_i{}^1$, $K_i{}^\theta = (1-\theta) K_i{}^0 + \theta K_i{}^1$, where $0 \leqslant \theta \leqslant 1$. We are to show that $y^\theta \in \mathscr{Y}(L, K)$. By the concavity of f_i, we have

$$f_i(L_i{}^\theta, K_i{}^\theta) \geqq (1-\theta) f_i(L_i{}^0, K_i{}^0) + \theta f_i(L_i{}^1, K_i{}^1) = y_i{}^\theta.$$

Define $\lambda_i = y_i{}^\theta / f_i(L_i{}^\theta, K_i{}^\theta)$ if $y_i{}^\theta > 0$ and $\lambda_i = 0$ if $y_i{}^\theta = 0$; then $f_i(\lambda_i L_i{}^\theta, \lambda_i K_i{}^\theta) = y_i{}^\theta$ by the homogeneity of f_i, and moreover $\lambda_1 L_1{}^\theta + \lambda_2 L_2{}^\theta \leqq L_1{}^\theta + L_2{}^\theta \leqq L$, and $\lambda_1 K_1{}^\theta + \lambda_2 K_2{}^\theta \leqq K_1{}^\theta + K_2{}^\theta \leqq K$. (Note that in this last argument, all that is actually used is the continuity and monotonicity of f_i, so the conclusion still follows even if homogeneity is not assumed.)

[10] This may be generalized to the case of n commodities and m factors, in which case the condition corresponding to (2.7) is that any set of k rows of the Jacobian matrix $\partial g/\partial w$ be linearly independent. In particular, this requires $n \leqq m$ (see footnote 12). [*Note added in proof:* Since this paper went to press I have learned that this result has been independently obtained by Chulsoon Khang in an article to be published in *Econometrica*.]

[11] See Shephard [28].

Then the point $(f_1(L_1^\theta, K_1^\theta), f_2(L_2^\theta, K_2^\theta))$ belongs to $\mathscr{Y}(L,K)$, hence

(2.9)

$$p_1^0[f_1(L_1^0,K_1^0)-f_1(L_1^\theta,K_1^\theta)]+p_2^0[f_2^0(L_2^0,K_2^0)-f_2(L_2^\theta,K_2^\theta)] \geqq 0.$$

On the other hand, by the strict convexity to the origin of the production isoquants we have, for $0<\theta<1$,

$$f_i(L_i^\theta, K_i^\theta) \geqq f_i(L_i^0, K_i^0), \qquad i=1,2, \tag{2.10}$$

with equality holding if and only if

$$(L_i^1, K_i^1) = \lambda_i(L_i^0, K_i^0), \qquad \text{for some} \quad \lambda_i > 0. \tag{2.11}$$

It follows from (2.9) and (2.10) that Eq. (2.11) holds whenever $p^0 > 0$.

Suppose one of the prices is zero, say $p_1^0 = 0$. Then since $w>0$ and $r>0$, it follows from (2.5) that $(L_1^0, K_1^0) = (L_1^1, K_1^1) = (0,0)$, hence $y_1^0 = y_1^1 = 0$. Since $p_2^0 > 0$, it follows that $y_2^0 = y_2^1$, contradicting the assumption that $y^1 \neq y^0$. Therefore, $p_1^0 > 0$, $p_2^0 > 0$, and from Eq. (2.11), we have

$$(L_1^1, K_1^1) = \lambda_1(L_1^0, K_1^0), \qquad (L_2^1, K_2^1) = \lambda_2(L_2^0, K_2^0).$$

Since both factors must be fully employed, we have

$$\begin{aligned} L_1^0 + L_2^0 &= L, & K_1^0 + K_2^0 &= K, \\ \lambda_1 L_1^0 + \lambda_2 L_2^0 &= L, & \lambda_1 K_1^0 + \lambda_2 K_2^0 &= K. \end{aligned} \tag{2.12}$$

Now $\lambda_i \neq 1$, otherwise $y_i^1 = y_i^0$ and hence (since $p^0>0$) $y^1 = y^0$, contrary to hypothesis. From Eqs. (2.12), we have

$$(1-\lambda_1, 1-\lambda_2)\begin{bmatrix} L_1^0 & K_1^0 \\ L_2^0 & K_2^0 \end{bmatrix} = (0,0). \tag{2.13}$$

If one of the outputs is zero, say $y_1^0 = 0$, then $(L_1^0, K_1^0) = (0,0)$ and Eq. (2.13) implies $(L_2^0, K_2^0) = (0,0)$, hence $y_2^0 = 0$; but the origin cannot belong to $\hat{\mathscr{Y}}(L,K)$, so $y_1^0 > 0$ and $y_2^0 > 0$. Then Eq. (2.13) contradicts (2.8) and thus (2.7). This proves that the condition (2.7) is sufficient.

To prove that (2.7) is necessary, suppose the determinant in (2.7) to vanish for some $w^0 > 0$, $r^0 > 0$. Then for some $L^0 \geqq 0$, $K^0 \geqq 0$ (not both zero), we have

$$\partial g_i/\partial w = \lambda_i L^0, \qquad \partial g_i/\partial r = \lambda_i K^0, \qquad i = 1,2,$$

hence from (2.8), it follows that

$$\hat{\mathscr{Y}}(L^0, K^0) = \{(y_1, y_2)\colon \lambda_1 y_1 + \lambda_2 y_2 = 1\}. \qquad \text{QED}$$

Henceforth condition (2.7) will be assumed to hold. It follows from

Theorem 1, therefore, that for each p_1, p_2, there will be unique y_1, y_2, maximizing (2.3) for given L, K. This defines the functions

$$(2.14) \qquad y_1 = Y_1(p_1, p_2, L, K), \qquad y_2 = Y_2(p_1, p_2, L, K),$$

and thus we have

$$(2.15) \qquad \Pi(p_1, p_2, L, K) = p_1 Y_1(p_1, p_2, L, K) + p_2 Y_2(p_1, p_2, L, K).$$

If $L > 0$, then, owing to the condition $L_1 + L_2 = L$, either $L_1 > 0$ or $L_2 > 0$; if, say, $L_1 > 0$, then $w = p_1 \, \partial f_1 / \partial L_1$, from (2.5), hence w is uniquely determined. Similarly for r, if $K > 0$. If $L > 0$ and $K > 0$, we therefore have the functions

$$(2.16) \qquad w = W(p_1, p_2, L, K), \qquad r = R(p_1, p_2, L, K).$$

Finally, for given y_i, w, and r, the factor demands L_i and K_i are determined in accordance with (2.1) and (2.5), giving rise to the functions which we shall denote

$$(2.17) \quad L_i = \tilde{L}_i(p_1, p_2, L, K), \qquad K_i = \tilde{K}_i(p_1, p_2, L, K), \qquad i = 1, 2.$$

Our aim in the rest of this section is to study the properties of the functions (2.14), (2.16), and (2.17).

The functions (2.14), (2.16), (2.17) are continuous, and must by definition satisfy the following relations identically in the variables p_1, p_2, L, and K:

$$(2.18a) \qquad \tilde{L}_1(p_1, p_2, L, K) + \tilde{L}_2(p_1, p_2, L, K) = L,$$

$$(2.18b) \qquad \tilde{K}_1(p_1, p_2, L, K) + \tilde{K}_2(p_1, p_2, L, K) = K,$$

(2.18c)

$$Y_i(p_1, p_2, L, K) = f_i[\tilde{L}_i(p_1, p_2, L, K), \tilde{K}_i(p_1, p_2, L, K)], \qquad i = 1, 2,$$

(2.18d)

$$W(p_1, p_2, L, K) \geqq p_i \frac{\partial}{\partial L_i} f_i[\tilde{L}_i(p_1, p_2, L, K), \tilde{K}_i(p_1, p_2, L, K)], \qquad i = 1, 2,$$

(2.18e)

$$R(p_1, p_2, L, K) \geqq p_i \frac{\partial}{\partial K_i} f_i[\tilde{L}_i(p_1, p_2, L, K), \tilde{K}_i(p_1, p_2, L, K)], \qquad i = 1, 2.$$

Moreover, in any neighborhood in which $\tilde{L}_i(p_1, p_2, L, K) > 0$ throughout the neighborhood, (2.18d) must hold with equality throughout the neighborhood; similarly in any neighborhood in which $\tilde{K}_i(p_1, p_2, L, K) > 0$, (2.18e) must hold with equality there. Conversely, if (2.18d) holds with strict inequality in any neighborhood of (p_1, p_2, L, K), then $\tilde{L}_i(p_1, p_2, L, K) = 0$

identically in that neighborhood; likewise if (2.18e) holds with strict inequality in a neighborhood, $\tilde{K}_i(p_1, p_2, L, K) = 0$ identically there. These considerations give us what we need to establish the following theorem, which is a rigorous statement of a result first stated by Samuelson[12]:

THEOREM 3. If (2.7) holds, then in any neighborhood of (p_1, p_2, L, K) in which each of the functions

$$\tilde{L}_i, \quad \tilde{K}_i, \quad W - p_i \frac{\partial f_i(\tilde{L}_i, \tilde{K}_i)}{\partial L_i}, \qquad R - p_i \frac{\partial f_i(\tilde{L}_i, \tilde{K}_i)}{\partial K_i}, \qquad i = 1, 2,$$

remains either positive or zero, the following properties hold:

$$\frac{\partial Y_i}{\partial p_j} = \frac{\partial Y_j}{\partial p_i}, \qquad \frac{\partial W}{\partial K} = \frac{\partial R}{\partial L}, \qquad \frac{\partial Y_i}{\partial L} = \frac{\partial W}{\partial p_i}, \qquad \frac{\partial Y_i}{\partial K} = \frac{\partial R}{\partial p_i}. \tag{2.19}$$

Proof. The proof consists in establishing: (i) that Π has continuous second-order partial derivatives in the prescribed neighborhoods, and (ii) that

$$\frac{\partial \Pi}{\partial p_i} = Y_i, \qquad \frac{\partial \Pi}{\partial L} = W, \qquad \frac{\partial \Pi}{\partial K} = R. \tag{2.20}$$

The conclusion (2.19) then follows immediately. Property (i) follows from a result of Alexandroff [1], and a detailed proof will not be indicated here. It remains to establish (2.20). We have from (2.15) and (2.18c),

(2.21)

$$\begin{aligned}
\frac{\partial \Pi}{\partial p_i} &= Y_i + p_1 \frac{\partial Y_1}{\partial p_i} + p_2 \frac{\partial Y_2}{\partial p_i} \\
&= Y_i + p_1 \left[\frac{\partial f_1}{\partial L_1} \frac{\partial \tilde{L}_1}{\partial p_i} + \frac{\partial f_1}{\partial K_1} \frac{\partial \tilde{K}_1}{\partial p_i} \right] + p_2 \left[\frac{\partial f_2}{\partial L_2} \frac{\partial \tilde{L}_2}{\partial p_i} + \frac{\partial f_2}{\partial K_2} \frac{\partial \tilde{K}_2}{\partial p_i} \right] \\
&= Y_i + \left[p_1 \frac{\partial f_1}{\partial L_1} - W \right] \frac{\partial \tilde{L}_1}{\partial p_i} + \left[p_1 \frac{\partial f_1}{\partial K_1} - R \right] \frac{\partial \tilde{K}_1}{\partial p_i} + \left[p_2 \frac{\partial f_2}{\partial L_2} - W \right] \frac{\partial \tilde{L}_2}{\partial p_i} \\
&\quad + \left[p_2 \frac{\partial f_2}{\partial K_2} - R \right] \frac{\partial \tilde{K}_2}{\partial p_i} + W \left[\frac{\partial \tilde{L}_1}{\partial p_i} + \frac{\partial \tilde{L}_2}{\partial p_i} \right] + R \left[\frac{\partial \tilde{K}_1}{\partial p_i} + \frac{\partial \tilde{K}_2}{\partial p_i} \right].
\end{aligned}$$

Now the last two terms on the right side of the third equality of (2.21) vanish upon differentiating both sides of the identities (2.18a) and (2.18b) with respect to p_i. The remaining four terms following Y_i are also seen to vanish: for instance, $(p_1 \partial f_1/\partial L_1 - W)\partial \tilde{L}_1/\partial p_i$ vanishes, since either

[12] Samuelson [26, p. 10] stated the proposition for n commodities and m factors, omitting mention of the requirement of nonswitching from specialization to diversification, as well as of the condition $n \leqq m$ needed to assure the single-valuedness of the functions Y_i.

$\tilde{L}_1 > 0$ and the term in parentheses vanishes by the equality of (2.5), or else $\tilde{L}_1 = 0$ identically, in which case $\partial \tilde{L}_1/\partial p_i = 0$ as well. Thus

$$p_1 \frac{\partial Y_1}{\partial p_i} + p_2 \frac{\partial Y_2}{\partial p_i} = 0. \tag{2.22}$$

This establishes the first equality of (2.20). (Note that when $(y_1, y_2) > (0,0)$, Eq. 2.22 simply states that the slope of the production possibility frontier $\mathscr{Y}(L,K)$ at (y_1, y_2) is the price ratio p_1/p_2.)

The second and third equalities of (2.20) are obtained in similar fashion, so it suffices to establish the second. We have, from (2.15) and (21.8c),

(2.23)

$$\begin{aligned}\frac{\partial \Pi}{\partial L} &= p_1\left[\frac{\partial f_1}{\partial L_1}\frac{\partial \tilde{L}_1}{\partial L} + \frac{\partial f_1}{\partial K_1}\frac{\partial \tilde{K}_1}{\partial L}\right] + p_2\left[\frac{\partial f_2}{\partial L_2}\frac{\partial \tilde{L}_2}{\partial L} + \frac{\partial f_2}{\partial K_2}\frac{\partial \tilde{K}_2}{\partial L}\right] \\ &= \left[p_1\frac{\partial f_1}{\partial L_1} - W\right]\frac{\partial \tilde{L}_1}{\partial L} + \left[p_1\frac{\partial f_1}{\partial K_1} - R\right]\frac{\partial \tilde{K}_1}{\partial L} + \left[p_2\frac{\partial f_2}{\partial L_2} - W\right]\frac{\partial \tilde{L}_2}{\partial L} \\ &\quad + \left[p_2\frac{\partial f_2}{\partial K_2} - R\right]\frac{\partial \tilde{K}_2}{\partial L} + W\left[\frac{\partial \tilde{L}_1}{\partial L} + \frac{\partial \tilde{L}_2}{\partial L}\right] + R\left[\frac{\partial \tilde{K}_1}{\partial L} + \frac{\partial \tilde{K}_2}{\partial L}\right].\end{aligned}$$

The first four terms on the right of the second equality of (2.23) vanish by the preceding reasoning. Differentiating both sides of the identities (2.18a) and (2.18b) with respect to L, we see that $\partial\tilde{L}_1/\partial L + \partial\tilde{L}_2/\partial L = 1$ and $\partial\tilde{K}_1/\partial L + \partial\tilde{K}_2/\partial L = 0$, establishing the second equality of (2.20). QED

The functions Y_i of Eq. (2.14) are the *Rybczynski functions* (see Rybczynski [25]); for fixed world prices p_1, p_2, they specify the form of output variations as functions of factor endowments. The functions W and R of Eq. (2.16) may be called the *Stolper–Samuelson functions* (see Stolper and Samuelson [29]), since they specify, for fixed factor endowments, the form of factor price variations as functions of variations in commodity prices. Denoting the labor-output and capital-output coefficients in industry i, as functions of the wage rate and rental of capital, by $a_i(w,r)$ and $b_i(w,r)$, respectively, we have

$$\begin{aligned} a_1(w,r)y_1 + a_2(w,r)y_2 &= L_1 + L_2 = L, \\ b_1(w,r)y_1 + b_2(w,r)y_2 &= K_1 + K_2 = K, \end{aligned} \tag{2.24}$$

and since

$$\begin{bmatrix} a_1 & a_2 \\ b_1 & b_2 \end{bmatrix} = \begin{bmatrix} \partial g_1/\partial w & \partial g_2/\partial w \\ \partial g_1/\partial r & \partial g_2/\partial r \end{bmatrix}, \tag{2.25}$$

and this matrix is nonsingular by (2.7), we can solve Eqs. (2.24) to obtain

$$
\begin{aligned}
Y_1(p_1,p_2,L,K) &= a^1(p_1,p_2,L,K)\cdot L + a^2(p_1,p_2,L,K)\cdot K,\\
Y_2(p_1,p_2,L,K) &= b^1(p_1,p_2,L,K)\cdot L + b^2(p_1,p_2,L,K)\cdot K,
\end{aligned} \tag{2.26}
$$

where

$$
\begin{bmatrix} a^1 & a^2 \\ b^1 & b^2 \end{bmatrix} = \begin{bmatrix} a_1(W,R) & a_2(W,R) \\ b_1(W,R) & b_2(W,R) \end{bmatrix}^{-1}. \tag{2.27}
$$

In accordance with Theorem 1, when $y_1 > 0$ and $y_2 > 0$, the functions a^i and b^i are independent of L and K. Moreover, since the functions $\partial g_i/\partial w$ and $\partial g_i/\partial r$ are homogeneous of degree zero in w and r, the functions a^i and b^i are homogeneous of degree zero in p_1 and p_2, i.e., they depend just on the ratio p_1/p_2. Thus, for given p_1/p_2, the functions Y_1 and Y_2 are linear within the cone of diversification. We therefore have the result that when the country diversifies,

$$
\frac{\partial W}{\partial L} = \frac{\partial^2 \Pi}{\partial L^2} = 0, \qquad \frac{\partial W}{\partial K} = \frac{\partial^2 \Pi}{\partial L\,\partial K} = \frac{\partial R}{\partial L} = 0, \qquad \frac{\partial R}{\partial K} = \frac{\partial^2 \Pi}{\partial K^2} = 0, \tag{2.28}
$$

and, by Eqs. (2.19) and (2.26),

$$
\frac{\partial R}{\partial p_1} = \frac{\partial Y_1}{\partial K} = a^2, \qquad \frac{\partial R}{\partial p_2} = \frac{\partial Y_2}{\partial K} = b^2, \tag{2.29}
$$

which depend on p_1/p_2 but are independent of L and K. Since Y_1 and Y_2 are positive within the diversification cone, the functions a_i and b_i are also positive there, hence the diagonal elements a^1 and b^2 of the inverse matrix have opposite sign to the off-diagonal elements a^2 and b^1; moreover, since W and R are homogeneous of degree 1 in p_1 and p_2, we have by Euler's theorem

$$
\begin{aligned}
p_1 a^1 + p_2 b^1 &= p_1 \frac{\partial W}{\partial p_1} + p_2 \frac{\partial W}{\partial p_2} = W,\\
p_1 a^2 + p_2 b^2 &= p_1 \frac{\partial R}{\partial p_1} + p_2 \frac{\partial R}{\partial p_2} = R.
\end{aligned} \tag{2.30}
$$

It follows that one of the elasticities $(p_i/R)\,\partial R/\partial p_i$ is negative and the other greater than unity—which is, in essence, simply the Stolper–Samuelson theorem (see Chipman [2]). Thus we have either

$$
\frac{\partial R}{\partial p_1} < 0, \qquad \text{and} \qquad \frac{\partial R}{\partial p_2} > \frac{R}{p_2}, \tag{2.31a}
$$

or

$$\frac{\partial R}{\partial p_1} > \frac{R}{p_1}, \qquad \text{and} \qquad \frac{\partial R}{\partial p_2} < 0. \tag{2.31b}$$

On the other hand, in a region in which a country specializes, say in Commodity 2, we have $Y_1 = 0$ identically in a neighborhood, whence by Eq. (2.19)

$$\frac{\partial R}{\partial p_1} = \frac{\partial Y_1}{\partial K} = 0, \qquad \frac{\partial R}{\partial p_2} = \frac{\partial Y_2}{\partial K} = \frac{\partial f_2}{\partial K} = \frac{R}{p_2}. \tag{2.32}$$

These relations are basic to the analysis that follows.

III. The Offer Function When Capital Is Mobile

Consider a country capable of producing two products with labor and capital, when the quantity L of labor is fixed but the quantity K of capital is variable, capital being internationally mobile. Assume that the inhabitants have titles of ownership to a fixed amount C of capital at home and abroad. Let prices p_1 and p_2 be determined on world markets. Then we wish to determine the country's excess demand for each commodity as a function of p_1, p_2, and K.

Let there be N consuming units, and let the νth unit have command of L^ν units of labor and title to C^ν units of the world capital stock, where

$$\sum_{\nu=1}^{N} L^\nu = L, \qquad \sum_{\nu=1}^{N} C^\nu = C. \tag{3.1}$$

The νth unit's income will be given by

$$I^\nu(p_1, p_2, L, K) = L^\nu W(p_1, p_2, L, K) + C^\nu R(p_1, p_2, L, K), \tag{3.2}$$

and its demand function for the ith product will be

$$x_i^\nu = h_i^\nu[p_1, p_2, I^\nu(p_1, p_2, L, K)] \equiv X_i^\nu(p_1, p_2, L, K). \tag{3.3}$$

It will be assumed that each commodity has positive marginal utility, hence demand is finite only if all prices are strictly positive; moreover, under this assumption all income will be spent, so the equation

$$p_1 X_1^\nu(p_1, p_2, L, K) + p_2 X_2^\nu(p_1, p_2, L, K) = I^\nu(p_1, p_2, L, K) \tag{3.4}$$

holds identically. Defining

$$X_i(p_1,p_2,L,K) = \sum_{\nu=1}^{N} X_i^{\nu}(p_1,p_2,L,K),$$

(3.5)

$$I(p_1,p_2,L,K) = \sum_{\nu=1}^{N} I^{\nu}(p_1,p_2,L,K),$$

we obtain by summing Eqs. (3.4) over the consuming units and using Eqs. (3.1), (3.2), and (3.5),

$$\begin{aligned} p_1 X_1(p_1,p_2,L,K) &+ p_2 X_2(p_1,p_2,L,K) \\ &= I(p_1,p_2,L,K) \\ &= LW(p_1,p_2,L,K) + CR(p_1,p_2,L,K). \end{aligned} \tag{3.6}$$

Now from (2.5) and Euler's theorem, we have

$$L_i W + K_i R = p_i\left(L_i \frac{\partial f_i}{\partial L_i} + K_i \frac{\partial f_i}{\partial K_i}\right) = p_i f_i, \tag{3.7}$$

hence

$$\begin{aligned} p_1 Y_1(p_1,p_2,L,K) &+ p_2 Y_2(p_1,p_2,L,K) \\ &= \Pi(p_1,p_2,L,K) \\ &= LW(p_1,p_2,L,K) + KR(p_1,p_2,L,K). \end{aligned} \tag{3.8}$$

Defining excess demand for the ith commodity (quantity imported if positive, exported if negative) by

$$z_i = Z_i(p_1,p_2,L,K) = X_i(p_1,p_2,L,K) - Y_i(p_1,p_2,L,K), \tag{3.9}$$

we have from Eqs. (3.6) and (3.8) the basic identity

(3.10)

$$p_1 Z_1(p_1,p_2,L,K) + p_2 Z_2(p_1,p_2,L,K) = (C-K)R(p_1,p_2,L,K).$$

From Eqs. (3.6) and (3.8), this yields

$$I(p_1,p_2,L,K) = \Pi(p_1,p_2,L,K) + (C-K)R(p_1,p_2,L,K), \tag{3.11}$$

i.e., the excess of gross national product over gross domestic product is equal to the deficit in the balance of payments on merchandise account.

In Sect. V it will turn out to simplify matters to consider the special case in which all consumers have identical homothetic utility functions. In that case, they have identical demand functions, and Eqs. (3.3) and (3.5) become

$$x_i = h_i[p_1,p_2,I(p_1,p_2,L,K)] = X_i(p_1,p_2,L,K). \tag{3.12}$$

Making use of Eqs. (3.11) and (2.20) we obtain

$$\frac{\partial X_i}{\partial K} = \frac{\partial h_i}{\partial I}\left[\frac{\partial \Pi}{\partial K} - R + (C-K)\frac{\partial R}{\partial K}\right] = \frac{\partial h_i}{\partial I}(C-K)\frac{\partial R}{\partial K}. \tag{3.13}$$

In particular, if $\partial R/\partial K = \partial^2 \Pi/\partial K^2 = 0$, i.e., if the country diversifies, then $\partial X_i/\partial K = 0$, that is, movements of capital have no effect on income, hence none on demand. This result is perfectly general, and does not depend on the assumption that consumers have identical homothetic utility functions; for from Eqs. (3.2), (2.20), and (2.28), we have, when the country diversifies,

$$\frac{\partial I^\nu}{\partial K} = L^\nu \frac{\partial^2 \Pi}{\partial L\, \partial K} + C^\nu \frac{\partial^2 \Pi}{\partial K^2} = 0, \tag{3.14}$$

hence from Eq. (3.3),

$$\frac{\partial X_i}{\partial K} = \sum_{\nu=1}^{N} \frac{\partial X_i^\nu}{\partial K} = \sum_{\nu=1}^{N} \frac{\partial h_i^\nu}{\partial I^\nu}\frac{\partial I^\nu}{\partial K} = 0. \tag{3.15}$$

IV. The Problem Formulated

Let there be two countries, a home (exploiting) country and a foreign (exploited) country. Following the notation of Kemp [17] and Jones [14], variables referring to the foreign country will have asterisks attached, and those without asterisks will refer to the home country.

It is given that the foreign excess demands are determined by the functions

$$z_i^* = Z_i^*(p_1^*, p_2^*, L^*, K^*), \qquad i = 1, 2, \tag{4.1}$$

which are assumed to satisfy the budget equation

$$\begin{aligned} p_1^* Z_1^*(p_1^*, p_2^*, L^*, K^*) + p_2^* Z_2^*(p_1^*, p_2^*, L^*, K^*) \\ = (C^* - K^*)\, R^*(p_1^*, p_2^*, L^*, K^*) \end{aligned} \tag{4.2}$$

identically in the variables p_1^*, p_2^*, and K^* (see Eq. 3.10). The quantity C^* of world capital owned by its inhabitants is assumed to remain constant throughout. The total world stock of capital will be denoted by $\mathbf{K}$; thus

$$K + K^* = C + C^* = \mathbf{K}. \tag{4.3}$$

It will further be assumed that the Z_i^*'s are continuously differentiable for positive prices, and unbounded if either p_1^* or p_2^* is zero.

The home country is assumed to have a Samuelsonian social utility function $U(x_1, x_2)$ which is determined by distributing domestic incomes in such a way as to maximize a social welfare function (see Samuelson [27]). If factor supplies are immobile, this could, in principle, be accomplished by means of a system of sliding income tax rates and subsidies, fine tuned so as to be adjusted to changes in domestic prices and incomes. It should be emphasized that the determination of such tax rates is likely to be a far more complicated matter than the determination of the tariff rates and tax rates on foreign capital (or on domestic capital invested abroad) needed to effect the exploitative trade and investment policies. The function U will be assumed to be continuously differentiable and strictly increasing in both arguments.

The problem we consider is therefore posed as follows:

$$\text{Maximize} \quad U(x_1, x_2)$$

subject to

$$(p_1) \qquad f_1(L_1, K_1) - x_1 - Z_1^*(p_1^*, p_2^*, L^*, K^*) \geqq 0,$$

$$(p_2) \qquad f_2(L_2, K_2) - x_2 - Z_2^*(p_1^*, p_2^*, L^*, K^*) \geqq 0,$$

$$(w) \qquad L - L_1 - L_2 \geqq 0,$$

$$(r) \qquad \mathbf{K} - K^* - K_1 - K_2 \geqq 0,$$

$$(s) \qquad \mathbf{K} - K^* \geqq 0.$$

We form the Lagrangean function

$$(4.4) \quad \mathscr{L}(x_1, x_2, L_1, L_2, K_1, K_2, p_1^*, p_2^*, K^*; p_1, p_2, w, r, s)$$
$$= U(x_1, x_2) + p_1[f_1(L_1, K_1) - x_1 - Z_1^*(p_1^*, p_2^*, L^*, K^*)]$$
$$+ p_2[f_2(L_2, K_2) - x_2 - Z_2^*(p_1^*, p_2^*, L^*, K^*)]$$
$$+ w(L - L_1 - L_2)$$
$$+ r(\mathbf{K} - K^* - K_1 - K_2)$$
$$+ s(\mathbf{K} - K^*).$$

Differentiating (4.4) partially with respect to the respective variables, we obtain the necessary conditions

$$(x_i) \qquad \frac{\partial U}{\partial x_i} - p_i \leqq 0,$$

$$(p_i^*) \qquad p_1 \frac{\partial Z_1^*}{\partial p_i^*} + p_2 \frac{\partial Z_2^*}{\partial p_i^*} \geqq 0,$$

$$(K^*) \qquad p_1 \frac{\partial Z_1^*}{\partial K^*} + p_2 \frac{\partial Z_2^*}{\partial K^*} + r + s \geqq 0,$$

$$(L_i) \qquad p_i \frac{\partial f_i}{\partial L_i} - w \leqq 0,$$

$$(K_i) \qquad p_i \frac{\partial f_i}{\partial K_i} - r \leqq 0.$$

Each of these fourteen inequalities becomes an equality if the variable indicated on the left is positive; this is to be understood whenever any of them is referred to as a "condition."

Conditions (L_i), (K_i), (w), and (r) are the necessary and sufficient conditions for the solution of the problem (2.3), hence may be eliminated and replaced by

$$(4.5)\quad \begin{aligned} w &= W(p_1, p_2, L, \mathbf{K} - K^*), & y_1 &= f_1(L_1, K_1) = Y_1(p_1, p_2, L, \mathbf{K} - K^*), \\ r &= R(p_1, p_2, L, \mathbf{K} - K^*), & y_2 &= f_2(L_2, K_2) = Y_2(p_1, p_2, L, \mathbf{K} - K^*). \end{aligned}$$

Since the foreign excess demand functions are assumed to be unbounded if either price is zero, no solution is possible with zero prices p_1^*, p_2^*, and similarly for home prices p_1, p_2. Thus, conditions (p_i) and (p_i^*) must be equalities. In order to simplify the problem at this stage, we shall put aside the cases in which $K^* = 0$ (i.e., all the world stock of capital is located in the home country) or $K^* = \mathbf{K}$ (all of it is located in the foreign country). These possibilities must, of course, be allowed for and included in a classification of all possible solutions, but this will not be considered in the present paper. We, therefore, will restrict attention at present to the case in which the solution has the property

$$(4.6)\qquad 0 < K^* < \mathbf{K}.$$

The first of these inequalities implies that equality holds in condition (K^*), and the second states that strict inequality holds in condition (s), hence $s = 0$.

We have eliminated conditions (L_i), (K_i), (w), (r), and (s), and replaced the inequality signs in (p_i^*) and (K^*) by equality signs (with $s = 0$). It remains to simplify conditions (p_i) and (x_i). Taking account of Eq. (4.2) and the fact that equalities hold in (p_1) and (p_2), we have, with the aid of Eqs. (4.5),

$$(4.7)\quad \begin{aligned} p_1 x_1 + p_2 x_2 &= \Pi(p_1, p_2, L, \mathbf{K} - K^*) - p_1 Z_1^*(p_1^*, p_2^*, L^*, K^*) \\ &\quad - p_2 Z_2^*(p_1^*, p_2^*, L^*, K^*) \\ &= \tilde{I}(p_1, p_2, p_1^*, p_2^*, K^*). \end{aligned}$$

The second equation of (4.7) defines the home country's GNP (in domestic prices) as a function $\tilde{I}$ of home and domestic prices and capital stock in the foreign country; it consists of GDP (the function Π), valued in domestic prices, plus the deficit in the home country's balance of trade. From (4.7) and conditions (x_i), we have

$$(4.8)\quad x_i = h_i[p_1, p_2, \tilde{I}(p_1, p_2, p_1^*, p_2^*, K^*)] \equiv \tilde{X}_i(p_1, p_2, p_1^*, p_2^*, K^*), \qquad i = 1, 2.$$

Our fourteen conditions have now been reduced to the two conditions (4.8), the two conditions (p_i^*), and the condition (K^*)—five in all. There are five unknowns: p_1, p_2, p_1^*, p_2^*, and K^*. Now it is immediately verified that the conditions remain invariant with respect to multiplication of either pair (p_1, p_2) or (p_1^*, p_2^*) by a positive constant. Therefore one price can be fixed arbitrarily in each country, or alternatively some other normalization can be adopted such as requiring their sum to be constant, for example. It is customary to suppose that the home country will impose a tariff on its imports but leave exports unrestricted; it turns out that there is a slight gain in cleanness of mathematical notation if instead we suppose the distortion to be introduced in the domestic price of the home country's export good,[13] which we may think of as Commodity 1.[14] We shall, therefore, adopt the convention that

$$p_2 = p_2^* = 1. \tag{4.9}$$

We are, therefore, left with the following three equations in the three unknowns p_1, p_1^*, and K^*:

$$p_1 \frac{\partial}{\partial p_1^*} Z_1^*(p_1^*, 1, L^*, K^*) + \frac{\partial}{\partial p_1^*} Z_2^*(p_1^*, 1, L^*, K^*) = 0, \tag{4.10a}$$

$$p_1 \frac{\partial}{\partial K^*} Z_1^*(p_1^*, 1, L^*, K^*) + \frac{\partial}{\partial K^*} Z_2^*(p_1^*, 1, L^*, K^*) + R(p_1, 1, L, \mathbf{K} - K^*) = 0, \tag{4.10b}$$

$$Y_1(p_1, 1, L, \mathbf{K} - K^*) - \tilde{X}_1(p_1, 1, p_1^*, 1, K^*) - Z_1^*(p_1^*, 1, L^*, K^*) = 0. \tag{4.10c}$$

They may be interpreted quite simply.[15] Equation (4.10a) states that the domestic relative price of Commodity 1 in the home country should be equal

[13] The fact that it is immaterial whether the distortion is introduced in the domestic price of the import or export good is, of course, the substance of Lerner's symmetry theorem; see [19].

[14] This is only to "fix ideas"; the subsequent analysis in no wise depends, and indeed should not depend, on this interpretation, since we cannot know in advance which commodities will be imported or exported.

[15] See the lucid discussion by Connolly and Ross [5], who emphasize that conditions (4.10a) and (4.10b) simply characterize efficiency, and do not depend on the particular choice of a social welfare function (which enters only via the function $\tilde{X}_1$ in Eq. 4.10c). It should also be stressed, however, that this possibility of splitting up the optimization problem into an efficiency problem and a distributive problem *does* depend on the hypothesis that there is *some* social welfare function which forms the basis for the subsequent redistribution (by a system of taxes and subsidies supplementary to those to be discussed in the following section).

to the negative of the slope of the foreign offer curve; Eq. (4.10b) can be interpreted as saying that the domestic rental of capital should be equal to the marginal productivity of foreign investment; finally Eq. (4.10c) expresses the equilibrium condition of demand and supply.

From here on, the analysis can proceed in either of two directions. First of all, we can classify the types of solutions to (4.10) according as the foreign country specializes or diversifies, and examine the tax and tariff structure that would be required in each case. This is the procedure followed by Kemp [17] and Jones [14]. By itself, such an analysis is not a sufficient guide for policy purposes, however—even in principle—since we do not know in advance which solution (if either—keeping in mind the possibilities excluded by (4.6)) will prevail. Secondly, therefore, we need to find some conditions that will determine the nature of the solution. Since conditions (4.10) are necessary, and not necessarily sufficient, this entails: (i) establishing the existence of a solution to the problem itself, and (ii) finding conditions that will guarantee (4.6) and exclude one of the remaining two possibilities (specialization and diversification). This program will form the subject of a future paper, and will not be taken up here; in the following section, therefore, we confine ourselves to describing the types of solutions that may be expected to occur.

V. Exploitative Tax and Tariff Policies

To gain insight into the nature of the problem, it is helpful to consider the home country's *indirect social utility function* V, defined by

$$(5.1)\qquad V(p_1,p_1{}^*,K^*) = U[Y_1(p_1,1,L,\mathbf{K}-K^*) - Z_1{}^*(p_1{}^*,1,L^*,K^*),$$
$$Y_2(p_1,1,L,\mathbf{K}-K^*) - Z_2{}^*(p_1{}^*,1,L^*,K^*)].$$

This definition incorporates the market clearing conditions (p_i) of the previous section, as well as the conditions (4.5) of efficient production. As is to be expected, therefore, we obtain from conditions (x_i) and Eq. (2.22)

$$(5.2)\qquad \frac{\partial V}{\partial p_1} = p_1\frac{\partial Y_1}{\partial p_1} + \frac{\partial Y_2}{\partial p_1} = 0.$$

Likewise, we have

$$(5.3)\qquad \frac{\partial V}{\partial p_1{}^*} = -p_1\frac{\partial Z_1{}^*}{\partial p_1{}^*} - \frac{\partial Z_2{}^*}{\partial p_1{}^*},$$

which when set $=0$ becomes Eq. (4.10a). Defining the function $\tilde{R}$ by

$$\tilde{R}(p_1, K^*) = R(p_1, 1, L, \mathbf{K} - K^*), \tag{5.4}$$

and making use of (2.20), we obtain

$$\frac{\partial V}{\partial K^*} = -p_1 \frac{\partial Z_1^*}{\partial K^*} - \frac{\partial Z_2^*}{\partial K^*} - \tilde{R}, \tag{5.5}$$

which when set $=0$ becomes Eq. (4.10b).

Differentiating the identity (4.2) with respect to p_1^*, we may express Eq. (5.3) in the form

$$\frac{\partial V}{\partial p_1^*} = (p_1^* - p_1)\frac{\partial Z_1^*}{\partial p_1^*} + Z_1^* + (K^* - C^*)\frac{\partial R^*}{\partial p_1^*}. \tag{5.6}$$

Likewise, differentiating (4.2) with respect to K^* and adopting the assumption that consumers in the foreign country have identical homothetic utility functions,[16] we may with the help of Eq. (3.13) put Eq. (5.5) into the form

(5.7)

$$\frac{\partial V}{\partial K^*} = (R^* - \tilde{R}) - (p_1^* - p_1)\frac{\partial Y_1^*}{\partial K^*} + \left[p_1 \frac{\partial h_1^*}{\partial I^*} + \frac{\partial h_2^*}{\partial I^*}\right](K^* - C^*)\frac{\partial R^*}{\partial K^*}.$$

Before proceeding to discuss optimal tax and tariff formulas, it is instructive to consider the optimal direction of change starting from a position of unrestricted free trade in which $p_1^* = p_1$ and $r^* = r$. Then the first term on the right in Eq. (5.6) vanishes, hence it will be in the interest of the home country to take measures to improve its terms of trade if $Z_1^* = Y_1 - X_1 > 0$ (i.e., if it is exporting Commodity 1) and if at the same time it is a lender, and Commodity 1 is produced and is capital intensive in the foreign country (i.e., $\partial R^*/\partial p_1^* = \partial Y_1^*/\partial K^* > 0$). Under these circumstances, in addition to the traditional terms-of-trade effect, the home country gains the increased profits from its investments abroad, which it can capture by imposing a tax to maintain the differential $r^* - r > 0$. However, if the home country is a lender and $\partial R^*/\partial p_1^* = \partial Y_1^*/\partial K^* < 0$, i.e., Commodity 1 is produced and is labor intensive abroad, then the fall in profits on foreign investment might offset the terms-of-trade effect and there is no *a priori* presumption as to which effect is stronger. On the other hand if the foreign country specializes in Commodity 2 (hence $\partial R^*/\partial p_1^* = \partial Y_1^*/\partial K^* = 0$), then the terms-of-trade effect is the only one to consider.

[16] This assumption is implicit in the treatments of both Kemp [17] and Jones [14], that is, they both tacitly assume that the foreign offer function is derived by maximization of an aggregate utility function.

If the home country is a borrower which exports Commodity 1, then an increase in its terms of trade $p_1{}^*$ will have an unambiguously favorable effect if the foreign country specializes in Commodity 2, or if it produces Commodity 1 and Commodity 1 is labor intensive in the lending country. The increase in $p_1{}^*$ will lead to a fall in profits in the foreign country, making it possible for the home country to tax foreign investment income by a corresponding amount. If production of a commodity is labor intensive (respectively, capital intensive) at home if and only if it is labor intensive (respectively, capital intensive) abroad, and if the lending country exports its capital-intensive product and the borrowing country exports its labor-intensive product, then the traditional rule will hold that either country stands to gain from an improvement in its commodity terms of trade. But the rule need not hold: if a borrowing country is exporting a capital-intensive product, a reduction in its terms of trade could have the additional effect of lowering foreign profit rates to such a degree that the resulting differential in marginal productivities of capital in the two countries—which it could collect by taxing income from foreign-owned capital—would more than make up for the direct effect of the worsened terms of trade.

Formula (5.7) may be analyzed in similar fashion. At an initial position of unrestricted free trade, the first two terms on the right vanish, and the bracketed term is equal to unity. Equation (5.7) then reduces to

$$\frac{\partial V}{\partial K^*} = (K^* - C^*)\frac{\partial^2 \Pi^*}{\partial K^{*2}}, \tag{5.8}$$

a formula which goes back to Kemp [16]. If the home country is a lender and the foreign country specializes in one of the commodities, then $\partial V/\partial K^* < 0$, i.e., the home country should withdraw some of its capital from the foreign country. This was suggested by MacDougall [20] and established by Kemp [15]. If the foreign country diversifies, however, then $\partial V/\partial K^* = 0$, and there are no first-order gains to be had from restriction of foreign investment. Differentiating (5.7) and evaluating the result at $p_1{}^* = p_1$, we find that when $\partial^2 \Pi^*/\partial K^{*2} = 0$,

$$\frac{\partial^2 V}{\partial K^{*2}} = -\frac{\partial \tilde{R}}{\partial K^*} = \frac{\partial R}{\partial K} = \frac{\partial^2 \Pi}{\partial K^2} \leqq 0. \tag{5.9}$$

This is negative if the home country specializes, and zero if the home country diversifies. Suppose now that free commodity trade is imposed, and Eq. (5.6) is replaced by the condition $p_1{}^* = p_1$; and suppose that the foreign country diversifies. Then if the home country specializes, the optimal policy with respect to capital movements is one of noninterference; on the other hand, if the home country diversifies, it is a matter of indifference whether capital movements are interfered with or not. Interference with capital flows in such circumstances (when free commodity trade is imposed) is justified only when the foreign country specializes, because only in that case can the home country affect profit rates in the foreign country.[17] On the other hand, changes in commodity terms of trade can affect foreign profit rates, so these conclusions concerning interference with capital flows no longer follow when interference with trade flows is also allowed.

Formula (5.8) may be explained in the following terms: If the home country is a lender and the foreign country specializes, then a withdrawal of capital from the foreign country raises its marginal product there, making it possible for the home country to tap this increase by taxing its citizens' foreign investment income. If the home country is a borrower and the foreign country specializes, by inducing a withdrawal of foreign capital it brings about a drop in the marginal productivity of capital abroad, allowing it to tax the profits on the remaining foreign capital by the amount of the discrepancy in the marginal productivity of capital in the two countries.

Thus, if the exploited country specializes, it will be in the interest of the country that adopts the exploitative investment policy to move in the direction of autarky on capital account. The outcome is qualitatively the same, regardless of which country adopts the policy (and collects the taxes), namely, that the total amount of foreign lending (or borrowing) should be reduced.

This appears to be in conflict with the analysis presented by MacDougall [20], who argued that Australia stood to gain from increased capital imports from Britain. The difference, however, is in MacDougall's premises, which are that the capital inflow is autonomous and that Australia reacts passively. The appropriate indirect social utility function for this case would then be

$$W(p_1, K) = U[Y_1(p_1, 1, L, K) + Z_1(p_1, 1, L, K), Y_2(p_1, 1, L, K) + Z_2(p_1, 1, L, K)], \tag{5.10}$$

[17] These propositions have been lucidly set forth by Corden [6, pp. 214–217] within the framework of traditional partial equilibrium analysis. One of the advantages of the concept of a production function for foreign exchange, combined with that of an indirect social welfare function, is that it provides a formal framework which justifies this type of analysis. Thus, the function $\tilde{R}$ of Eq. (5.4) may be regarded, for fixed p_1, as the supply function of foreign capital; on the other hand, the function V of Eq. (5.1) may be regarded, for fixed p_1 and p_1^*, as the home demand for and social marginal product of foreign capital. What is missing from Corden's analysis is an explanation of the conditions under which the foreign supply curve of capital will be infinitely elastic and those under which it will be upward sloping; what the Kemp–Jones analysis provides, combined with our substitution theorem [4], is the information that the first case corresponds to diversification, and the second to specialization, in the foreign country (assuming that the home country diversifies). The use of the consumers' surplus concept by writers such as Corden [6] and MacDougall [20], is another matter; however, it may be justified by means of the techniques introduced in Chipman [3] for the special case in which the social utility function U is of the log-linear type.

and from Eqs. (2.20), (3.10), and conditions (x_i) of Sect. IV, we obtain

$$\frac{\partial W}{\partial K} = -(K-C)\frac{\partial^2 \Pi}{\partial K^2}, \tag{5.11}$$

which is MacDougall's measure of Australia's gain per unit of capital inflow,[18] and is positive if Australia is a borrower and specializes. The conclusion is correct, but is based on the supposition that British investors would actually be willing to supply the additional capital, even though this would lower the return on their investments abroad. On the contrary, they would have to be induced by a subsidy which, if paid by Australia, would result in a loss to Australia as measured by (5.8).

Let us now consider the tax structure required to sustain an optimal solution, obtained by setting the expressions in Eqs. (5.6) and (5.7) equal to zero. Ruling out the case in which $z_1^* = z_2^* = 0$ at the optimum, which would entail $K^* - C^* = 0$ and $p_1^* = p_1, r^* = r$, we may assume $z_i^* \neq 0$ for some i, and hence for $i = 1$ without loss of generality. If Commodity 1 is exported by the home country and an export tax of $100\tau\,\%$ is imposed, it will satisfy

$$p_1^* = (1+\tau)p_1. \tag{5.12}$$

If, instead, Commodity 1 is imported and a tariff of $100\tau'\,\%$ is imposed, it will satisfy

$$p_1 = (1+\tau')p_1^*. \tag{5.12$'$}$$

We shall adopt the convention that

$$(1+\tau)(1+\tau') = 1, \tag{5.13}$$

so that if $\tau < 0$, this means either that exports of Commodity 1 are subsidized at a rate of $-100\tau\,\%$, or that there is a duty of $100\tau'\,\%$ on imports of Commodity 1, where $\tau' = -\tau/(1+\tau)$.[19]

[18] The amount $-(K-C)(\partial^2\Pi/\partial K^2)\,dK$ corresponds to the area of the rectangle $EDJI$ in MacDougall's Diagram I [20, p. 15]. (We remark that the W of (5.10) bears no relation to the W of (2.16).)

[19] Alternatively, keeping in mind the convention (4.9), and the fact that the essential relations corresponding to Eqs. (5.12) and (5.12′) are

$$\frac{p_1^*}{p_2^*} = (1+\tau)\frac{p_1}{p_2}, \qquad \frac{p_1}{p_2} = (1+\tau')\frac{p_1^*}{p_2^*}, \tag{5.12a}$$

if instead of (4.9) we adopt the normalization $p_1 = p_1^* = 1$, then we have

$$p_2 = (1+\tau)p_2^*, \qquad p_2^* = (1+\tau')p_2. \tag{5.12b}$$

Then if $\tau < 0$, this can be interpreted as meaning either that imports of Commodity 2 are subsidized at a rate of $-100\tau\,\%$, or that exports of Commodity 2 are taxed at a rate of $100\tau'\,\%$.

If the home country is a lender, and its government taxes its residents' income from foreign investment at a rate of $100t\%$, this tax rate will satisfy

$$r = (1-t)r^*. \tag{5.14}$$

If, instead, the home country is a borrower, and its government taxes the income on capital owned by nonresidents at a rate of $100t'\%$, this tax rate will satisfy

$$r^* = (1-t')r. \tag{5.14'}$$

As in the previous case, we adopt the convention that

$$(1-t)(1-t') = 1, \tag{5.15}$$

so that a negative tax rate of $100t\%$ imposed by a borrowing country should be interpreted as a positive tax rate of $100t'\%$ on income from foreign capital, where $t' = -t/(1-t)$.

An actual subsidy of $-100t\%$ (where $t < 0$) on home income from capital invested abroad would entail $r = (1-t)r^* > r^*$, which would encourage movement of foreign capital to the home country, unless it was accompanied by a tax of at least $100t'\%$, where $t' = -t/(1-t) > 0$, on foreign income from capital invested at home. With this proviso, a negative t could be interpreted as a subsidy to the home country's lending abroad. Likewise, a subsidy on foreign capital invested at home of $-100t'\%$ (where $t' < 0$) would entail $r^* = (1-t')r > r$, and this would encourage movement of domestic capital abroad unless accompanied by a tax of at least $100t\%$, where $t = -t'(1-t') > 0$, on income from home capital invested abroad.

Equating (5.6) and (5.7) to zero and substituting Eqs. (5.12) and (5.14), we obtain, upon factoring out $p_1^* z_1^* \neq 0$ and $r^* > 0$ and making use of the condition $\partial R^*/\partial p_1^* = \partial Y_1^*/\partial K^*$ from (2.19), the equations

$$-\frac{\tau}{1+\tau}\eta^* + 1 + \varepsilon^* = 0, \qquad t - \frac{\tau}{1+\tau}\gamma^* + \iota^*\delta^* = 0, \tag{5.16}$$

where η^* is the elasticity of the foreign country's excess demand for imports defined (following Marshall [21, pp. 337–8]) by

$$\eta^* = -\frac{p_1^*}{Z_1^*}\frac{\partial Z_1^*}{\partial p_1^*}, \tag{5.17}$$

where

$$\iota^* = p_1\frac{\partial h_1^*}{\partial I^*} + \frac{\partial h_2^*}{\partial I^*}, \tag{5.18}$$

and where, following Jones [14] and Kemp [17],[20]

(5.19)
$$\gamma^* = \frac{p_1^*}{R^*}\frac{\partial R^*}{\partial p_1^*}, \qquad \delta^* = \frac{K^*-C^*}{R^*}\frac{\partial R^*}{\partial K^*}, \qquad \varepsilon^* = \frac{K^*-C^*}{Z_1^*}\frac{\partial R_1^*}{\partial p_1^*}.$$

Now, from the assumption that consumers in the foreign country have identical homothetic utility functions, it follows that their demand functions have unitary income elasticity, i.e., $\partial h_i^*/\partial I^* = h_i^*/I^* > 0$, hence neither good is inferior, so $\partial Z_1^*/\partial p_1^* < 0$. Equating (5.6) to zero and using Eqs. (5.17) and (5.19) we see that *if the home country exports Commodity 1*, i.e., $z_1^* > 0$, then[21]

(5.20)
$$\eta^* > 0, \qquad \text{and} \qquad \eta^* - 1 - \varepsilon^* = -\frac{p_1}{Z_1^*}\frac{\partial Z_1^*}{\partial p_1} > 0,$$

whereas these two inequalities are reversed if the home country imports Commodity 1. In either case, $\eta^* \neq 0$ and $\eta^* - 1 - \varepsilon^* \neq 0$, and we can solve the equations (5.16) to obtain

(5.21a)
$$\tau = \frac{1+\varepsilon^*}{\eta^*-1-\varepsilon^*},$$

(5.21b)
$$t = \frac{1+\varepsilon^*}{\eta^*}\gamma^* - \iota^*\delta^*,$$

as well as

(5.21a′)
$$\tau' = -\frac{1+\varepsilon^*}{\eta^*},$$

(5.21b′)
$$t' = \frac{\eta^*\iota^*\delta^* - (1+\varepsilon^*)\gamma^*}{\eta^*(1+\iota^*\delta^*) - (1+\varepsilon^*)\gamma^*}.$$

These are the formulas developed by Kemp [17] and Jones [14], generalized to cover all cases. They are, of course, subject to the usual cautions concerning their proper interpretation, since the functions defined by Eqs. (5.17)–(5.19) depend on p_1, p_1^*, and K^*. Thus, the optimal τ and t cannot be computed in general without knowing the optimal values of these three variables.[22] Equivalently, formulas (5.21) are based on the first two equations of (4.10), whereas a complete solution requires taking account of all three.

[20] The notation adopted here for γ^*, δ^*, and ε^* is the same as that of Kemp [17] and Jones [14]; however, the sign of their η^* is the reverse of that of the Marshallian definition (5.17) adopted here.

[21] In terms of Eq. (5.21a) below, condition (5.20) is equivalent to the requirement that $\tau > -1$.

[22] For a discussion of the "paradoxes" which result from erroneous interpretation of formulas such as (5.21), see the excellent discussion by Graaff [9, p. 136].

If the optimal solution finds the home country exporting Commodity 1 and the foreign country specialized in the production of Commodity 2, then $\partial R^*/\partial p_1^* = \partial Y_1^*/\partial K^* = 0$ in accordance with Eq. (2.32), whence $\gamma^* = \varepsilon^* = 0$, and Eq. (5.21a) reduces to the well-known optimal tariff formula for the traditional case of factor immobility (see, e.g., Johnson [13]). It follows from (5.20) that when $z_1^* > 0$, an optimal solution requires $\eta^* > 1$, so $\tau > 0$. Since neither good is inferior, $\iota^* > 0$, so $t > 0$ if and only if the home country is a lender; if it is a borrower, we have $t' > 0$. Note that the result does not depend on whether Commodity 2 is imported or exported; the latter possibility holds when the home country is a borrower. This may also be seen by considering the case in which the home country exports both commodities and the foreign country is specialized in the production of Commodity 1. Then $\partial R^*/\partial p_1^* = R^*/p_1^*$ in accordance with Eq. (2.32), hence from Eqs. (5.19) and (4.2), we have

$$(5.22) \qquad 1 + \varepsilon^* = \frac{1}{Z_1^*}\left[Z_1^* + (K^* - C^*)\frac{R^*}{p_1^*}\right] = -\frac{Z_2^*}{p_1^* Z_1^*} < 0,$$

so that $\tau < 0$. In accordance with our convention (5.13) (see footnote 19), this means that a tax of $100\tau'\%$ should be levied on the export of Commodity 2, which is the same result as the above with the numbering of commodities interchanged.

If the home country imports both commodities, which is possible when it is a creditor, the foreign country must obviously diversify. If it imports one commodity and exports the other, and the foreign country specializes, we come back to the case just considered. It remains, therefore, only to consider the cases in which the foreign country diversifies.

When the optimal solution finds the foreign country diversifying, various "paradoxical" cases can, at least on the face of it, arise, as first noticed by Kemp [17]. In this case we have $\delta^* = 0$. Following Jones [14], denote

$$(5.23) \qquad \mu^* = \frac{(K^* - C^*)\, R^*}{p_1^* Z_1^*},$$

so that

$$(5.24) \qquad \varepsilon^* = \mu^* \gamma^*.$$

Since $\delta^* = 0$, Eqs. (5.21b) and (5.21a') yield

$$(5.25) \qquad t = -\tau'\gamma^* = \frac{\tau}{1+\tau}\gamma^*.$$

Thus, τ and t have the same sign if and only if $\gamma^* > 0$. If the home country exports Commodity 1, then it follows from (5.20) and (5.21a) that

TABLE I

EXPLOITATIVE TARIFF AND TAX PATTERNS WHEN HOME COUNTRY EXPORTS COMMODITY 1 AND FOREIGN COUNTRY DIVERSIFIES

	$K^* - C^* > 0$ $(\mu^* > 0)$	$K^* - C^* < 0$ $(\mu^* < 0)$
$(K^* - C^*)\dfrac{\partial R^*}{\partial p_1^*} > 0$ $(\varepsilon^* > 0)$	$\tau > 0,\ t > 0$	$\tau > 0,\ t' > 0$
$0 < Z_1^* + (K^* - C^*)\dfrac{\partial R^*}{\partial p_1^*} < Z_1^*$ $(-1 < \varepsilon^* < 0)$	$\tau > 0,\ t < 0$	$\tau > 0,\ t' < 0$
$Z_1^* + (K^* - C^*)\dfrac{\partial R^*}{\partial p_1^*} < 0$ $(\varepsilon^* < -1)$	$\tau < 0,\ t > 0$	$\tau < 0,\ t' > 0$

$\tau > 0$ if and only if $\varepsilon^* > -1$; moreover, the sign of μ^* is the same as that of $K^* - C^*$. This together with Eq. (5.24) gives us what we need to ascertain the possible[23] patterns of tariff and tax rates and the conditions that give rise to them; these were obtained by Jones [14, pp. 14–15], and are displayed in Table I. As Jones observed, it is not possible for τ and t both to be negative when the home country is a creditor, nor for τ and t' both to be negative if the home country is a debtor.

The conditions given in Table I can be interpreted very simply by referring back to Eqs. (5.6) and (5.7). From an initial situation of unrestricted free trade, we have

$$\left.\frac{\partial V}{\partial p_1^*}\right|_{p_1^* = p_1} = Z_1^* + (K^* - C^*)\frac{\partial R^*}{\partial p_1^*}, \tag{5.26}$$

giving the expression in the left margin of Table I. The first term, Z_1^*, measures the benefit to the home country through commodity trade of an improvement in its terms of trade; the second term, $(K^* - C^*)\,dR^*/dp_1^*$, measures the benefit through the increase in the return on home capital invested abroad (if $K^* - C^* > 0$) or through the decrease in the cost of borrowing from abroad

[23] The term "possible" is subject to the reservation that the existence of solutions with the sign patterns indicated in Table I must still be established; thus "not proved impossible" would be more accurate. Nevertheless, the discussion following Eq. (5.26) will provide a basis for an existence proof, though a formal proof will not be attempted here.

(if $K^* - C^* < 0$). As observed earlier, when the foreign country diversifies, we have

$$\left.\frac{\partial V}{\partial K^*}\right|_{p_1^* = p_1, r^* = r} = 0, \tag{5.27}$$

so the rationale for the home country taxing income from capital invested by one country in another is to capture the effect of changes in the terms of trade on profit rates in the foreign country. If the commodity and capital effects are both positive, so should be the tariff and tax rates. If the total effect is positive but outweighed by the commodity effect, the tariff should be positive and the tax negative. If the capital effect is negative and so strong that the total effect is negative, the tariff should be negative and the tax positive. What Table I tells us is that *the same criteria hold for optimal tariffs and taxes as for incipient ones.* In order to establish the existence of optimal tariff and tax patterns corresponding to each of the six cases of Table I, it is therefore sufficient to establish: (a) the existence of an initial free-trade equilibrium with the appropriate sign patterns for $\partial V/\partial p_1^*$ and with diversification of production; and (b) that the optimum is reached within the regime of diversification.[24]

Table I does not exclude the possibility that the home country exports both commodities; however, this is compatible only with two of the entries. Clearly, the possibility exists only when the home country is a debtor. Now consider the case $\tau > 0, t' < 0$; this requires $K^* - C^* < 0$ and $\partial R^*/\partial p_1^* > 0$, and from (2.31b) it then follows that $\partial R^*/\partial p_1^* > R^*/p_1^*$. Thus, from the budget equation (4.2), we have

$$0 < Z_1^* + (K^* - C^*)\frac{\partial R^*}{\partial p_1^*} < Z_1^* + (K^* - C^*)\frac{R^*}{p_1^*} = -\frac{Z_2^*}{p_1^*}, \tag{5.28}$$

from which it follows that at the optimum for which $\tau > 0$ and $t' < 0$, we must have $z_2^* < 0$, i.e., the home country must import Commodity 2. Therefore, if the home country exports both commodities, the optimal tax rate on foreign profits earned in the home country must be positive. In this case, a negative τ will be interpreted as a tax at the rate $\tau' = -\tau/(1+\tau)$ on the exports of Commodity 2 (see footnote 19).

The only cases excluded from Table I are those in which the home country imports both commodities. For the sake of symmetry, therefore, we shall

[24] Inada and Kemp [12] have shown that if an initial free-trade equilibrium with diversification exists, then a tariff-cum-tax equilibrium with diversification will exist if the tariff and tax are sufficiently small. A similar continuity argument could extend this to optimal tariff and tax rates, if conditions could be found under which the benefits from further extension of these rates come to an end before specialization has been reached.

display the configuration of tariff and tax rates corresponding to all cases in which Commodity 1 is imported; this is displayed in Table II. In accordance with the convention (5.13), a negative export tax rate τ on Commodity 1 will be interpreted as a tariff at the rate $\tau' = -\tau/(1+\tau)$ on imports of Commodity 1, and a positive τ (negative τ') will be interpreted as a tariff at the rate τ on Commodity 2 if it is imported.

If the home country imports both commodities, it must, of course, be a creditor. An argument similar to the above shows that the entry $\tau' > 0, t < 0$ of Table II must also be excluded. This case requires $K^* - C^* > 0$ and $\partial R^*/\partial p_1^* > 0$, hence $\partial R^*/\partial p_1^* > R^*/p_1^*$, so the budget equation (4.2) yields

$$(5.29) \quad 0 > Z_1^* + (K^* - C^*)\frac{\partial R^*}{\partial p_1^*} > Z_1^* + (K^* - C^*)\frac{R^*}{p_1^*} = -\frac{Z_2^*}{p_1^*},$$

whence at the optimum for which $\tau' > 0$ and $t < 0$, we must have $z_2^* > 0$, i.e., the home country must export Commodity 2. Consequently, if the home country imports both commodities, the optimal tax rate on the profits from its investments abroad must be positive; and there will be a positive tariff on the imports of one or the other of the commodities.

The preceding analysis has been based on the assumption that both instruments τ and t are used. However, it is well worthwhile investigating the consequences of not using the second. Space does not permit more than a

TABLE II

EXPLOITATIVE TARIFF AND TAX PATTERNS WHEN HOME COUNTRY IMPORTS COMMODITY 1 AND FOREIGN COUNTRY DIVERSIFIES

	$K^* - C^* > 0$ ($\mu^* < 0$)	$K^* - C^* < 0$ ($\mu^* > 0$)
$(K^* - C^*)\frac{\partial R^*}{\partial p_1^*} < 0$ ($\varepsilon^* > 0$)	$\tau' > 0,\ t > 0$	$\tau' > 0,\ t' > 0$
$Z_1^* < Z_1^* + (K^* - C^*)\frac{\partial R^*}{\partial p_1} < 0$ ($-1 < \varepsilon^* < 0$)	$\tau' > 0,\ t < 0$	$\tau' > 0,\ t' < 0$
$Z_1^* + (K^* - C^*)\frac{\partial R^*}{\partial p_1^*} > 0$ ($\varepsilon^* < -1$)	$\tau' < 0,\ t > 0$	$\tau' < 0,\ t' > 0$

brief outline of the principal problems. First we may observe that Eq. (4.10a) still holds, but Eq. (4.10b) is replaced by the condition

(5.30) $$R^*(p_1^*, 1, L^*, K^*) = R(p_1, 1, L, \mathbf{K} - K^*).$$

Consequently, formula (5.21a) still holds but Eq. (5.21b) is replaced by $t = 0$. Now assume that both countries diversify, and suppose for example that Industry 1 is relatively capital intensive in each of them; then if a tariff has the "normal" effect of increasing p_1^* ("improving the terms of trade") and reducing p_1 ("protecting" Industry 2), then it must raise r^* and lower r, in violation of Eq. (5.30). It follows that if Industry 1 is relatively capital intensive in both countries (or relatively labor intensive in both countries), p_1 and p_1^* must move in the same direction; thus, the terms of trade are "improved" if and only if the "wrong" industry is protected. The sign patterns are readily determined by applying the implicit function theorem to the set of four equations in footnote 3, and we find that

(5.31) $$\frac{dp_1}{d\tau} = \frac{a_2^*\Delta}{J(\tau)} p_1, \qquad \frac{dp_1^*}{d\tau} = \frac{a_2\Delta^*}{J(\tau)} p_1,$$

and

(5.32) $$\frac{dr}{d\tau} = -\frac{a_2 a_2^*}{J(\tau)} p_1, \qquad \frac{dw}{d\tau} = \frac{a_2^* b_2}{J(\tau)} p_1, \qquad \frac{dw^*}{d\tau} = \frac{a_2 b_2^*}{J(\tau)} p_1,$$

where (see Eq. 2.25)

(5.33) $$\Delta = \begin{vmatrix} a_1 & a_2 \\ b_1 & b_2 \end{vmatrix}, \qquad \Delta^* = \begin{vmatrix} a_1^* & a_2^* \\ b_1^* & b_2^* \end{vmatrix},$$

and

(5.34) $$J(\tau) = a_2\Delta^* - (1+\tau)a_2^*\Delta.$$

We find readily (see Chipman [4, p. 209]) that $J(\tau) = [a_2 a_1^* - (1+t)a_2^* a_1]/r$, hence starting at unrestricted free trade equilibrium, if Industry 1 is relatively capital intensive in both countries, a tariff will increase the terms of trade if and only if $a_1/a_2 < a_1^*/a_2^*$, i.e., if and only if the home country uses relatively less labor per unit of output in Industry 1 than in Industry 2, as compared with the foreign country. The opposite condition holds if Industry 1 is relatively labor intensive in both countries. Under the conditions corresponding to the first two rows of Table I, in which $Z_1^* + (K^* - C^*)\partial R^*/\partial p_1^* > 0$, hence $\tau > 0$, there is perhaps a weak *a priori* presumption that the tariff will "improve" the terms of trade.

Something definite can at least be said. At a second-best "optimum" when the foreign country diversifies, we have $\partial V/\partial K^* = (p_1{}^* - p_1)\,\partial Z_1{}^*/\partial K^* = -(p_1{}^* - p_1)\,\partial Y_1{}^*/\partial K^*$ from Eq. (5.7), so when $\tau > 0$, K^* should be increased or decreased according as Industry 1 is relatively labor intensive or capital intensive in the foreign country. Thus, a borrowing country exporting Commodity 1 which is relatively labor intensive in the foreign country, and importing Commodity 2 which is relatively capital intensive in the foreign country, will want to drive some of the foreign capital out so as to lower foreign output (hence increase foreign imports) of Commodity 1 and raise foreign output (hence increase foreign exports) of Commodity 2; in this way it can collect more revenue from its export tax or import duty, as the case may be.[25] The essence of the matter is that by *driving capital out*, the home country will be *more dependent upon trade, hence better able to exploit its monopoly position in trade*. If, on the other hand, its export good is relatively capital intensive abroad and its import good relatively labor intensive abroad, then it will be in the borrowing country's interest to attract still more foreign capital, because this will now lower foreign output of Commodity 1 and raise foreign output of Commodity 2, thus increasing foreign imports and exports of these commodities, and permitting more duties to be collected. This time, it is by *drawing capital in* that the borrowing country becomes more dependent upon trade, and better able to exploit its monopoly position in trade. In both cases the criterion, which furnishes the question for empirical research, is the same: whether, in a regime of protectionism with unimpeded capital movements, capital inflows or outflows make a country more dependent upon, and therefore better able to exploit, international trade.

REFERENCES

[1] Alexandroff, A. D., Almost Everywhere Existence of the Second Differential of a Convex Function and Some Properties of Convex Surfaces Connected with It (in Russian), *Uch. Zapiski Leningradu, Ser. Matemat. Nauk* **6**, No. 37, 3–35 (1939).

[2] Chipman, J. S., Factor Price Equalization and the Stolper-Samuelson Theorem, *Int. Econ. Rev.* **10**, 399–406 (October 1969).

[3] Chipman, J. S., External Economies of Scale and Competitive Equilibrium, *Quart. J. Econ.* **84**, 347–385 (August 1970).

[25] The general formula (when the foreign country diversifies) is

$$\frac{\partial V}{\partial K^*} = R^* - R - (p_1{}^* - p_1)\frac{\partial Y_1{}^*}{\partial K^*} - (p_2{}^* - p_2)\frac{\partial Y_2{}^*}{\partial K^*},$$

where $\partial Y_i{}^*/\partial K^* = -\partial Z_i{}^*/\partial K^*$ on account of Eq. (3.15). If instead of Eq. (4.9) we assume $p_1 = p_1{}^*$ and interpret τ as a tariff on imports (see footnote 19), then in a situation of unimpeded capital flows, we have $\partial V/\partial K^* = (p_2 - p_2{}^*)\,\partial Y_2{}^*/\partial K^* = \tau p_2{}^*\,\partial Y_2{}^*/\partial K^*$. Under Eq. (4.9) we have $\partial V/\partial K^* = -\tau p_1\,\partial Y_1{}^*/\partial K^*$ (see Eq. 5.12).

[4] Chipman, J. S., International Trade with Capital Mobility: A Substitution Theorem, *in* "Trade, Balance of Payments, and Growth: Papers in Intrenational Economics in Honor of Charles P. Kindleberger" (J. N. Bhagwati, R. W. Jones, R. A. Mundell, and J. Vanek, eds.), pp. 201–237. North-Holland Publ. Amsterdam, 1971.
[5] Connolly, M., and Ross, S., A Fisherian Approach to Trade, Capital Movements, and Tariffs, *Amer. Econ. Rev.* **60**, 478–484 (June 1970).
[6] Corden, W. M., Protection and Foreign Investment, *Econ. Rec.* **43**, 209–232 (June 1967).
[7] Ethier, W., and Ross, S. A., International Capital Movements and Long Run Diversification, *J. Int. Econ.* **1**, 301–314 (August 1971).
[8] Fenchel, W., Convex Cones, Sets, and Functions. Princeton Univ. Dept. of Mathematics, Logistics Res. Project (September 1953).
[9] Graaff, J. de V., "Theoretical Welfare Economics." Cambridge Univ. Press, London and New York, 1957.
[10] Hamada, K., Strategic Aspects of Taxation on Foreign Investment Income, *Quart. J. Econ.* **80**, 361–375 (August 1966).
[11] Hurwicz, L., and Uzawa, H., On the Integrability of Demand Functions, *in* "Preferences, Utility, and Demand" (J. S. Chipman, L. Hurwicz, M. K. Richter, and H. F. Sonnenschein, eds.), pp. 114–148. Harcourt Brace, New York, 1971.
[12] Inada, Ken-ichi, and Kemp, M. C., International Capital Movements and the Theory of Tariffs and Trade: Comment, *Quart. J. Econ.* **83**, 524–528 (August 1969).
[13] Johnson, H. G., Alternative Optimum Tariff Formulae, "International Trade and Economic Growth" pp. 56–61. Allen & Unwin, London, 1958.
[14] Jones, R. W., International Capital Movements and the Theory of Tariffs and Trade, *Quart. J. Econ.* **81**, 1–38 (February 1967).
[15] Kemp, M. C., Foreign Investment and the National Advantage, *Econ. Rec.* **38**, 56–62 (March 1962).
[16] Kemp, M. C., The Benefits and Costs of Private Investment Abroad: Comment, *Econ. Rec.* **38**, 108–110 (March 1962).
[17] Kemp, M. C., The Gain from International Trade and Investment: A Neo-Heckscher-Ohlin Approach, *Amer. Econ. Rev.* **56**, 788–809 (September 1966).
[18] Kuhn, H. W., and Tucker, A. W., Nonlinear Programming, *Proc. 2nd Berkeley Symp. Math. Statist. Probability*, pp. 481–492. University of California Press, Berkeley and Los Angeles, California, 1951.
[19] Lerner, A. P., The Symmetry between Import and Export Taxes, *Economica, N. S.* **3**, 306–313 (August 1936).
[20] MacDougall, G. D. A., The Benefits and Costs of Private Investment from Abroad: A Theoretical Approach, *Econ. Rec.* **36**, 13–35 (March 1960).
[21] Marshall, A., "Money, Credit, and Commerce." Macmillan, London, 1923.
[22] Mundell, R. A., International Trade and Factor Mobility, *Amer. Econ. Rev.* **47**, 321–335 (June 1957).
[23] Prebisch, R., Commercial Policy in the Underdeveloped Countries, *Amer. Econ. Rev., Papers Proc.* **49**, 251–273 (May 1959).
[24] Ramaswami, V. K., International Factor Movement and the National Advantage, *Economica, N. S.* **35**, 309–310 (August 1968).
[25] Rybczynski, T. M., Factor Endowment and Relative Commodity Prices, *Economica, N. S.* **22**, 336–341 (November 1955).
[26] Samuelson, P. A., Prices of Factors and Goods in General Equilibrium, *Rev. Econ. Stud.* **21**, 1–20 (1953).
[27] Samuelson, P. A., Social Indifference Curves, *Quart. J. Econ.* **70**, 1–22 (February 1956).

[28] Shephard, R. W., "Cost and Production Functions." Princeton Univ. Press, Princeton, New Jersey, 1953.

[29] Stolper, W. F., and Samuelson, P. A., Protection and Real Wages, *Rev. of Econ. Stud.* **9**, 58–73 (November 1951).

[30] Uekawa, Y., On the Existence of Incomplete Specialization in International Trade with Capital Mobility, *J. Int. Econ.* **2**, 1–23 (February 1972).

A STOCHASTIC MODEL OF THE FUNCTIONAL DISTRIBUTION OF INCOME

CAMILO DAGUM

The University of Ottawa, Ottawa, Canada

I. Introduction

The present paper is concerned with the time and space analysis of the functional distribution of income. For this purpose, we have introduced a set of postulates which specify a stochastic model and have analyzed the model's statistical properties. A structural analysis of the distributional problem (which belongs to the domain of the theory of games) is done in Sects. II and III.

The model specified was used to explain both the functional distribution *by countries* (time-series analysis), especially for developed economies such as the United States, Canada, France, Sweden, etc., and *between countries* (cross-section analysis), by means of a sample of 37 countries with data from the period 1966–1968.

II. Theories of Income Distribution

The economic theory approach to the analysis of income distribution is twofold: (i) personal distribution, and (ii) functional distribution. These categories are complementary, and they influence each other according to the degree of intersectoral efficiency and fluency of a national economy. If these characteristics operate, an equitable functional distribution condition an equitable personal distribution of income. On the other hand, the existence of structural dualisms and heterogeneities, which practically split a national economy into independent subsystems, allows the coexistence of a reasonable functional distribution of income in aggregate values, with a strong personal concentration of incomes, due to marginated brackets of the population, a characteristic which is observed in developing as well as underdeveloped economies.

The analysis of the personal distribution of income and wealth is a contribution of the Italian School of Economics, Statistics and Sociology, founded by Vilfredo Pareto [13] and Corrado Gini [8, 9]. These writers offered a theoretical and empirical analysis of the personal distribution of income and wealth, applying Paretian models and Gini's concentration index. Contemporary authors have been improving the early research carried on by Pareto and Gini.

The study of the functional distribution of income has been one of the economist's concerns since the end of the 18th century. We can distinguish main lines of thought according to the theoretical and methodological points of view of these authors, and with regard to the common principles applied by them, we can group these lines under three headings:

A. Principles of Automatic and Harmonic Distribution

These theories introduce, explicitly or implicitly, the principle of automatic and harmonic distribution, which means that economic agents considered as units of decision have no influence in modifying the structure of distribution (for which reason it is automatic); and the distribution achieved being optimal (for which reason it is harmonic), it can cause no conflicts. The following theories about the functional distribution of income belong to this category: (i) Ricardian or classical; (ii) neoclassical; (iii) empirical; (iv) post-keynesian (Kaldor–Pasinetti); and (v) linear programming.

B. Principles of Automatic Distribution and Domination (Nonharmonic): Marx, Kalecki, Perroux

These theories recognize the dominant power of strong groups with an economic strength capable of discretely modifying the structure of the functional distribution of income. Belonging to this category we have: (i) the Marxist theory that develops Ricardo's principle of the distribution of economic surplus; (ii) the institutional theory or "mark-up theories" of Kalecki

[10] and the theory of François Perroux [14], who introduces and develops the dominating power of the macro-organisms considered as macrodecision-makers.

C. Principle of Nonautomatic and Nonharmonic Distribution

This theory explicitly reveals the domination, negotiation, and coalition power of the macroeconomic agents on the distribution of the net national product and, especially, the economic surplus. The suitable mathematical method (i.e., the theory of games of von Neumann and Morgenstern [15]) is applied strictly and successfully to the structural analysis of the distribution of income. Nyblén [12] has attempted the systematic application of the theory of games to the study of the functional distribution of income.

III. Economic Surplus and Theory of Games

In developed countries we can observe a smooth functioning of research and development that allows the growth of the national product proportionally greater than the corresponding increase of inputs. This is the result of increased efficiency, particularly due to a highly qualified labor force, and a greater endowment of capital equipment which secures increasing economies of scale. A national economy operating at a relatively greater level of efficiency, produces an economic surplus whose imputation (distribution) is a consequence of an n-person game between the macroeconomic agents (macro-organisms), that is played in each successive production period. The n "players" are macroeconomic agents and their relationships of power, domination, bargaining capacity, organization of coalitions, and lateral payments determine their optimal strategies and the final outcome in the imputation of the economic surplus. Their most important features are: (i) lack of symmetry; (ii) the nonhomogeneity of their members; and (iii) the existence of a small and finite number of players (macroeconomic agents) with a discrete power (non-infinitesimal) to change the structure of the distribution, and their decisions (macrodecisions) can influence the level of economic activity.

Some of the most relevant macroeconomic agents that act in a national economic unit are: national associations of manufacturers and of landowners, national labor confederations, farm workers associations, etc. Their own domination power depends partly on the institutional order, social concepts and ideas, and the level of economic development. In short, the imputation of the economic surplus between the macroeconomic agents is the consequence of competition or struggle for its appropriation in an effort tending to increase or maintain their relative shares in the national product.

The specific case of a three-person game, for example, among industrial businessmen, rural entrepreneurs, and national labor confederations, can be shown geometrically by means of the fundamental triangle or the negotiation triangle [15]. Let S be the set of points that belongs to the simplex in three-dimensional space and e_i $(i = 1, 2, 3)$, their corresponding unit vectors; then we have:

$$S = \{(x_1, x_2, x_3) | (x_1, x_2, x_3) = \lambda_1 e_1 + \lambda_2 e_2 + \lambda_3 e_3;\ \lambda_i \geqslant 0, \lambda_1 + \lambda_2 + \lambda_3 = 1\}.$$

Thus, Simplex is an equilateral triangle contained in the secant plane to the axis at the points with coordinates e_i $(i = 1, 2, 3)$ (Fig. 1). The sum of the distances (from any point that belongs to the simplex) towards its three sides is equal to the height of the triangle. If we transform the simplex into an equilateral triangle with unit height, we obtain the fundamental triangle or negotiation triangle which is the geometrical figure appropriate to the normal form of a three-person constant-sum game. If the height of such a triangle indicates the economic surplus to be distributed, then for all nonnegative solutions there exists a unique point that belongs to the negotiation triangle, the distances from which to each side denote the percentage share of the macroeconomic agents in the economic surplus. Its sum, being equal to one, *exhausts* the imputation of the surplus.

Every point belonging to one of the triangle's sides represents the case of a player excluded from the surplus imputation. This indicates a player discriminated against by a coalition of the other two players. Every point outside the triangle implies a negative allocation for the player (the discriminated one), that is, he contributes a part of his share to the national income in order to increase the coalition share in the surplus. An example of such a case is one

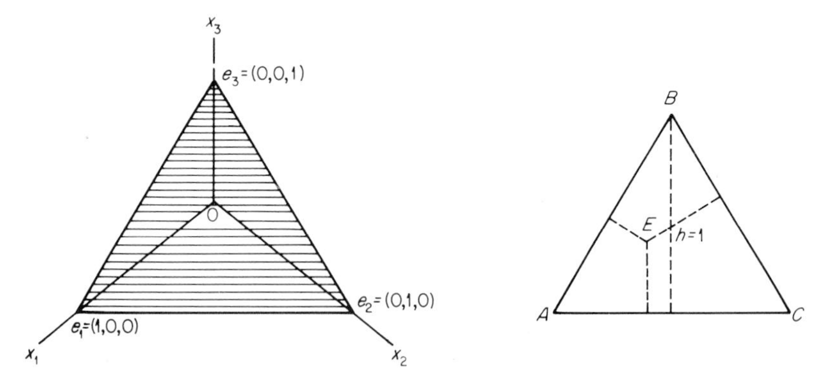

Fig. 1. Unit simplex and negotiation triangle in the case of three macroeconomic agents.

in which there is a coalition between businessmen and the workers' union, resulting in a wage increase for unionized workers and a price increase for business. If the third player is the nonunionized player, his relative share in the national income declines, and part of this deterioration is the contribution that increases the economic surplus which is to be distributed among the coalition's members.

IV. Structure and Dynamics of Income Distribution

In Sect. III the structural analysis of distribution was introduced applying the theory of games. The imputation of the economic surplus is the result of an n-person game between the macroeconomic agents, which takes place successively for each period of production. Their outcome condition the time path of the functional distribution of national income. As a consequence, we have two categories of analysis: (i) structural analysis, and (ii) dynamic analysis.

Structural analysis deals mainly with the degree of efficiency incorporated into the economic activity, the macro-organisms that participate in the productive process, their decision to fight or cooperate, their ability to negotiate and form coalitions, and the present institutional order. From these considerations, we get a *structure of production* and a *structure of distribution* that can be regarded as a consequence of two simultaneous and interdependent games: (i) *the production game*, and (ii) *the distribution game*. Much more specifically, the distribution game for each period is used to solve the imputation of the economic surplus, considering that there is a "part" already committed that belongs to the cumulative results of the preceding games, which determines the structure of income in the period $t-1$. These cumulative results, that is, the *committed distribution*[1] valued at the level of prices of inputs and final outputs in the period $t-1$, *plus* the resulting distribution for the economic surplus, determine the time path of functional distribution of income and define a stochastic process.

In the following sections the functional distribution of income is regarded as a stochastic process. Two alternative models are specified to explain the temporal behavior of the functional distribution of income by countries and its distribution intercountries. Finally, the parameters of these models for a sample of 37 countries are estimated and their econometric properties analyzed.

[1] This committed distribution coming from period $t-1$ can be marginally modified if the game of the distribution for the economic surplus contains a negative imputation, as was shown in Sect. III.

V. Specification of Model I

The national income is composed of wages and salaries earned and property income (profits, dividends, interest, etc.). In the applications, the data used were provided by national income accounts.

A. Notations

Let

$$\Omega = \{\omega | \omega = 1, \ldots, N\} \tag{1}$$

be the sampled space by countries (or national economic units);

$$I = \{t | t = 1, 2, \ldots\} \tag{2}$$

be the set of positive integers representing production and distribution periods;

$$R = \{t | -\infty < t < \infty\}, \tag{3}$$

be the set of real numbers, that is, the domain of the time variable in a continuous analysis;

$$Y = Y(\omega, t) \tag{4}$$

be the national income at constant prices of a country ω at time t;

$$P = P(\omega, t) \tag{5}$$

be the population of a country ω at time t;

$$y = y(\omega, t) = Y(\omega, t)/P(\omega, t) \tag{6}$$

be the national income per capita;

$$u = u(\omega, t) \tag{7}$$

be a stationary stochastic process;

$$\mu = \mu(\omega, t) \tag{8}$$

be the labor share in the national income of a country ω at time t;

$$\rho = \rho(\omega, t) = 1 - \mu(\omega, t) \tag{9}$$

be the property share in the national income of a country ω at time t.

The variable in Eq. (8) and its complement to one introduced in Eq. (9) define a stochastic process whose specification and analysis is the subject matter of this paper. For a fixed ω (in the realization of a stochastic experiment, for example, we observe the ωth country), the variable in Eq. (8) is a function of time, whose values for each t is a sample realization of the stochastic process Eq. (8), denoted as $\mu_\omega(t)$, and when it is evident from its context, as $\mu(t)$. When t remains constant and ω varies in Ω, we obtain the stochastic variable $\mu_t(\omega)$, or simply $\mu(\omega)$. The same symbolic simplification will be used for those functions set out in Eqs. (4)–(7), and (9).

In the specification of the model, t is assumed continuous, and its domain is given by Eq. (3). In the applications, t is a discrete variable, usually representing annual periods, and its domain is specified by Eq. (2).

B. Postulates

POSTULATE 1 (P.1). The function $\mu(y)$ is an unbiased predictor (*eo-ipso* predictor) [16] of $\mu(\omega)$ and $\mu(t)$, respectively. Namely[2]

$$\mu(t) = \mu(y(t)) + u(t) = \mu(y) + u(t), \tag{10}$$

$$\mu(\omega) = \mu(y(\omega)) + u(\omega) = \mu(y) + u(\omega). \tag{11}$$

POSTULATE 2 (P.2). The growth rate of the unbiased predictor $\mu(y)$ (with respect to $y(\omega)$ and to $y(t)$) from a real origin $\alpha < \mu(y)$ is a linear decreasing function of the unbiased predictor. Symbolically,

$$\frac{1}{\mu(y)-\alpha}\frac{d\mu(y)}{dy} = \delta\left(1-\frac{\mu(y)-\alpha}{\lambda}\right), \qquad \delta,\lambda > 0, \quad \mu(y) > \alpha, \quad y > 0. \tag{12}$$

POSTULATE 3 (P.3). $u(\omega,t)$ is a strictly normal and stationary stochastic process.

Postulates P.1–P.3 specify the primary form of a logistic model with respect to the functional distribution of income and its corresponding reduced form. P.2 rationalizes the empirical behavior of $\mu_\omega(t)$ and $\mu_t(\omega)$. In fact, the temporal behavior of $\mu(t)$ is an increasing function of the income per capita, with diminishing velocity of growth, converging to a finite and constant limit μ^* plus a purely stochastic term. A similar empirical behavior is observed among countries for constant t, that is, $\mu(\omega)$. To specify the primary form, to derive the reduced form, and to estimate the model's parameters by the least-squares method, the normality assumption set out in P.3 is not required. However, its introduction will be necessary in testing the hypotheses.

[2] For an analysis between *countries* (cross-sectional data of countries) $\mu(y) = \mu(y(\omega))$, $\omega \in \Omega$. For an *intertemporal* analysis (time-series) $\mu(y) = \mu(y(t)), t \in R$.

C. Derived Propositions

From Postulates P.1–P.3 jointly with Definitions (1)–(9), we deduce:

LEMMA 1. The expected value of the random variable $u(\omega)$ and that of the sample realization $u(t)$ of the stochastic process $u(\omega, t)$ is equal to zero.[3]

By definition of an unbiased predictor, we have:

$$E(\mu(\omega)|y) = \mu(y), \tag{13}$$

where

$$E(u(\omega)|y) = 0, \tag{14}$$

and taking the mathematical expectation in relation to income $y(t)$ on both sides of Eq. (14), we obtain

$$E(u) = E_y E(u(\omega)|y) = 0. \tag{15}$$

A similar result is achieved for $u(t)$, that is, the ensemble average and the time average of the stochastic process $u(\omega, t)$ are equal, according to the Birkhoff–Khintchine ergodic theorem.

LEMMA 2. $y(\omega, t)$ and $u(\omega, t)$ are independent stochastic processes.

From Eq. (14), we have

$$E(uy|y) = yE(u|y) = 0. \tag{16}$$

Therefore,

$$E_y E(uy|y) = E(uy) = E(u)E(y) = 0. \tag{17}$$

Then the disturbance term u has zero mean by Lemma 1, and by Lemma 2 it is independent from y.

LEMMA 3. The unbiased predictor $\mu(y)$ is a logistic function with four parameters.

Equation (12) may be equivalently written as

$$\frac{1}{\mu(y)-\alpha}\frac{d(\mu(y)-\alpha)}{dy} = \delta\left(1-\frac{\mu(y)-\alpha}{\lambda}\right), \tag{18}$$

and solving the differential equation, we have

$$\mu(y) = \alpha + \frac{\lambda}{1+\beta\exp(-\delta y)}, \tag{19}$$

[3] The formal structures of the proofs for $u(t)$ and $u(\omega)$ are similar; that is why we use $u(\omega)$ in this section.

where

$$\beta = \lambda e^{-k} > 0, \tag{20}$$

with k a constant of integration.

THEOREM 1. The labor share in the national income is a logistic function of the income per capita.

Substituting Eq. (19) into Eq. (10), we have

$$\mu(t) = \alpha + \frac{\lambda}{1+\beta \exp(-\delta y)} + u(t), \qquad \beta, \delta, \lambda > 0. \tag{21}$$

VI. Characteristics of the Unbiased Predictor

The unbiased predictor $\mu(y)$ has the following characteristics:

(a) It is a monotonic increasing function of y, that is,

$$\frac{d\mu(y)}{dy} = \beta\delta\lambda \exp(-\delta y)[1 + \beta \exp(-\delta y)]^{-2} > 0, \tag{22}$$

since $\beta, \delta, \lambda > 0$, according to Eqs. (12) and (20).

(b) It asymptotically converges to a unique and finite limit. In fact,

$$\lim_{y \to \infty} \mu(y) = \alpha + \lambda = \mu^*. \tag{23}$$

(c) For all $\varepsilon > 0$, there exists a finite income per capita y_n, such that

$$(\forall\, y(t) > y_n) \Rightarrow \mu^* - \mu(y) < \varepsilon. \tag{24}$$

This result is a consequence of Eqs. (22) and (23).

(d) There is a point of inflection whose coordinates are

$$\left(\frac{1}{\delta} \log \beta, \alpha + \frac{\lambda}{2}\right) = \left(\frac{1}{\delta}(-k + \log \lambda), \alpha + \frac{\lambda}{2}\right), \tag{25}$$

according to Eq. (20). To the left of the inflection point, the unbiased predictor $\mu(y)$ is convex to the origin, and is concave to the right of such a point. Hence,

$$\left.\frac{d^3 \mu(y)}{dy^3}\right|_{y = k/\delta} = -\frac{2\delta^3}{8} < 0, \tag{26}$$

according to Eq. (12).

(e) Using Eqs. (22), (23), (25), and (26), we obtain

$$\lim_{y\to\infty} \frac{d\mu(y)}{dy} = 0, \tag{27}$$

$$\frac{d^2\mu(y)}{dy^2} \begin{cases} > 0, & \forall y < \frac{1}{\delta}\log\beta, \\ = 0, & \text{for } y = \frac{1}{\delta}\log\beta, \\ < 0, & \forall y > \frac{1}{\delta}\log\beta. \end{cases} \tag{28}$$

(f) The unbiased predictor of Eq. (19) explains the time-behavior of the labor share in the national income, and its complement to one, under Eq. (9), explains the temporal share belonging to property income. For a fixed t and ω variable in Ω, we observe the *spatial* behavior of labor and property shares. The two curves intersect each other at the income point

$$y = -\frac{1}{\delta}\ln\frac{2\mu^* - 1}{\beta(1-2\alpha)}. \tag{29}$$

(g) The derivative of the unbiased predictor (Eq. 12) shows the growth of the labor share per unit in the national income as equal to the growth of property income but with opposite sign. Then for each t, the production factors' shares are divided into two components:

(i) The committed share, for the period $t-1$, as a result of the functional distribution of income in period t; that is,

$$\mu(y(t))\,Y(t+1) \qquad \text{committed share;} \tag{30}$$

(ii) The additional share resulting from the functional distribution of the economic surplus in period $t+1$, say,

$$\mu'(y(t))\,Y(t+1) \qquad \text{net increase over committed share,} \tag{31}$$

where

$$\mu'(y(t)) = \frac{d\mu(y(t))}{dy(t)}.$$

In accordance with Eqs. (22), (23), (27), and (28), *the labor share in the economic surplus* increases until it reaches its highest value at the inflection point of the unbiased predictor, from which it decreases converging to a zero value.

Letting $E(t+1)$ be the economic surplus in the period $t+1$, valued at prices of period t, we have,

$$E(t+1) = Y(t+1) - Y(t), \tag{32}$$

where

(33)

$$\begin{aligned}\mu(y(t+1))\,Y(t+1) &= \mu(y(t))\,Y(t+1) + \mu'(y(t))\,Y(t+1)\\ &= \mu(y(t))\,Y(t) + \mu(y(t))\,E(t+1) + \mu'(y(t))\,Y(t+1).\end{aligned}$$

On the right-hand side of Eq. (33) the first term is the labor share achieved in period t, and the two remaining terms define their shares in the economic surplus. The second term represents the committed share in accordance with the level reached in period t, and the third expresses its increase according to Eq. (31).[4]

VII. Parameter Estimation

In this and in the following sections, we will give a much more limited statement of P.3:

POSTULATE 3a (P.3a). The sample realization of $u(t)$ and the corresponding random variable $u(\omega)$ in the stochastic process $u(\omega, t)$, are, respectively, temporally and spatially independent random variables distributed with zero mean and a constant and finite variance. Namely,

$$u(t) \overset{d}{=} N(0,\sigma^2), \qquad u(\omega) \overset{d}{=} N(0,\sigma^2), \tag{34}$$

(35)

$$\begin{aligned}E(u(t)\,u(s)) &= 0, \qquad \forall t \neq s,\\ E(u(\omega_i)\,u(\omega_j)) &= 0, \qquad i \neq j.\end{aligned}$$

From P.1, P.2, and P.3a, we conclude that the least-squares estimators of parameters in Eq. (21) are identical to the maximum-likelihood estimators.

[4] In Argentina, since 1955—with the exception of 1958 and the period 1963–1966—the government-supported wage policy stated that all salary increases would take place in proportion to productivity increases. This statement implies that $\mu(y)$ is *held constant*. According to Eq. (33), we have

$$\mu(y(t+1))\,Y(t+1) = \mu(y(t))\,Y(t) + \mu(y(t))\,E(t+1),$$

where

$$\mu(y(t+1)) = \mu(y(t)),$$

by Eq. (32). When such a policy was established (at the end of 1955) the labor share in the national income declined from 0.52 to 0.45 (present level); then, in terms of the theory of games, we conclude that in Argentina there has existed, since 1956, a sole dominant coalition.

Given a random sample of size n (n periods of time for country or alternatively, n countries at the period t), we obtain, using Eqs. (21), (34), and (35), for the log of the likelihood function,

(36)
$$\log L = -\frac{n}{2}\log 2\pi - \frac{n}{2}\log\sigma^2 - \frac{1}{2\sigma^2}\sum\left(\mu - \alpha - \frac{\lambda}{1+\beta\exp(-\delta y)}\right)^2,$$

where

$$\max_{\theta}\log L = \min_{\theta}\sum_{t=1}^{n} u_t^{\,2} = \min_{\theta}\sum_{t=1}^{n}\left(\mu_t - \alpha - \frac{\lambda}{1+\beta\exp(-\delta y_t)}\right)^2, \tag{37}$$

where maxima and minima are computed over the parameter space

$$\theta = \{(\alpha,\lambda,\beta,\delta)|(\lambda,\beta,\delta) > 0, \alpha\,\text{real}\}. \tag{38}$$

Denoting by $\hat{\theta} = (\hat{\alpha},\hat{\lambda},\hat{\beta},\hat{\delta})$ the parameter vector belonging to the space of Eq. (38) which maximizes the likelihood function, and introducing the variable Z:

$$Z_t^{-1} = 1 + \hat{\beta}\exp(-\hat{\delta}y_t), \tag{39}$$

from Eq. (36) we deduce

$$n\hat{\alpha} + \hat{\lambda}\sum_1^n Z_t = \sum_1^n \mu_t, \tag{40}$$

$$\hat{\alpha}\sum_1^n Z_t + \hat{\lambda}\sum_1^n Z_t^{\,2} = \sum_1^n \mu_t Z_t, \tag{41}$$

$$\hat{\alpha}\sum_1^n Z_t^{\,2}\exp(-\delta y_t) + \hat{\lambda}\sum_1^n Z_t^{\,3}\exp(-\hat{\delta}y_t) = \sum_1^n \mu_t Z_t^{\,2}\exp(-\hat{\delta}y_t), \tag{42}$$

(43)
$$\hat{\alpha}\sum_1^n y_t Z_t^{\,2}\exp(-\hat{\delta}y_t) + \hat{\lambda}\sum_1^n y_t Z_t^{\,3}\exp(-\hat{\delta}y_t) = \sum_1^n \mu_t y_t Z_t^{\,2}\exp(-\hat{\delta}y_t).$$

The maximum likelihood estimator of the variance is then

$$\hat{\sigma}^2 = \hat{\sigma}_u^{\,2} = \frac{1}{n}\sum_{t=1}^{n}\left(\mu_t - \hat{\alpha} - \frac{\hat{\lambda}}{1+\hat{\beta}\exp(-\hat{\delta}y_t)}\right)^2. \tag{44}$$

There is no mathematical method to solve the system of Eqs. (40)–(43). However, their unknown parameters can be estimated by iteration to any degree of approximation desired, by means of a suitable program of electronic computation.[5]

[5] The author, with the valuable collaboration of Drs. L. Corona Treviño and A. Flores Victoria of the Instituto de Investigaciones de Ingeniería, Universidad Nacional Autónoma, México, has estimated those parameters for the cases analyzed in Sect. XI.

VIII. Asymptotic Covariance Matrix of the Estimators

The asymptotic covariance matrix is deduced from the Cramér–Rao inequality [1], which gives the lower bound for the estimators' variance.

Letting $v = \sigma^2$, the unknown parameters vector in Eq. (21) is

$$\xi = (v, \theta) = (v, \alpha, \lambda, \beta, \delta) \in V \times \theta, \tag{45}$$

where the parameter space $V \times \theta$ is the cartesian product of the space $V = \{v | v > 0\}$, with the space θ set out in Eq. (38). Denoting by $I(\xi)$ the information matrix, we obtain

$$I(\xi) = I(v, \alpha, \lambda, \beta, \delta) = \begin{bmatrix} I(v) & 0 \\ 0 & I(\theta) \end{bmatrix} = -E \begin{bmatrix} \dfrac{\partial^2 \log v}{\partial v^2} & 0 \\ 0 & \dfrac{\partial^2 \log L}{\partial \theta^2} \end{bmatrix} \tag{46}$$

where the partial derivatives are evaluated for $\xi = \hat{\xi}$.

The inverse of the information matrix Eq. (46) is equal to the asymptotic covariance matrix of the estimators. From Eqs. (36) and (46), we have

(46a)

$$I(\xi) = \begin{bmatrix} \dfrac{n}{2\sigma^4} & 0 \\ 0 & I(\theta) \end{bmatrix}$$

$$= \begin{bmatrix} \dfrac{n}{2\sigma^4} & & & & \\ 0 & \dfrac{n}{\sigma^2} & & & \\ 0 & \dfrac{1}{\sigma^2}\sum_1^n \dfrac{1}{(1+\beta\exp(-\delta y_\varepsilon))} & \dfrac{1}{\sigma^2}\sum_1^n \dfrac{1}{(1+\beta\exp(-\delta y_\varepsilon))^2} & & \\ 0 & -\dfrac{\lambda}{\sigma^2}\sum_1^n \dfrac{\exp(-\delta y_\varepsilon)}{(1+\beta\exp(-\delta y_\varepsilon))^2} & -\dfrac{\lambda}{\sigma^2}\sum_1^n \dfrac{\exp(-\delta y_\varepsilon)}{(1+\beta\exp(-\delta y_\varepsilon))^3} & \dfrac{\lambda^2}{\sigma^2}\sum_1^n \dfrac{\exp(-2\delta y_\varepsilon)}{(1+\beta\exp(-\delta y_\varepsilon))^4} & \\ 0 & \dfrac{\lambda\beta}{\sigma^2}\sum_1^n \dfrac{y_\varepsilon\exp(-\delta y_\varepsilon)}{(1+\beta\exp(-\delta y_\varepsilon))^2} & \dfrac{\lambda\beta}{\sigma^2}\sum_1^n \dfrac{y_\varepsilon\exp(-\delta y_\varepsilon)}{(1+\beta\exp(-\delta y_\varepsilon))^3} & -\dfrac{\lambda^2\beta}{\sigma^2}\sum_1^n \dfrac{y_\varepsilon\exp(-2\delta y_\varepsilon)}{(1+\beta\exp(-\delta y_\varepsilon))^4} & \dfrac{\lambda^2\beta^2}{\sigma^2}\sum_1^n \dfrac{y^2\exp(-2\delta y_\varepsilon)}{(1+\beta\exp(-\delta y_\varepsilon))^4} \end{bmatrix}$$

where

$$\mathrm{I}^{-1}(\zeta) = \begin{bmatrix} \dfrac{2\sigma^4}{n} & 0 \\ 0 & I^{-1}(\theta) \end{bmatrix} \tag{47}$$

Matrices (46 a) and (47) are symmetric. Zeros in the first row and column represent the stochastic independence between the variance estimator and the estimators of the other unknown parameters.

If $\tilde{\xi}$ is any other unbiased estimator of ξ with covariance matrix $\operatorname{var}(\tilde{\xi})$, it can be shown that $|I^{-1}(\hat{\xi})| \leqslant |\operatorname{var}(\tilde{\xi})|$, since $\operatorname{var}(\tilde{\xi}) - I^{-1}(\hat{\xi})$ is a symmetric and positive semidefinite matrix.

IX. Asymptotic Distribution of the Estimators

In accordance with the asymptotic properties of maximum-likelihood estimators, the estimate,

$$\hat{\theta} = (\hat{\alpha}, \hat{\lambda}, \hat{\beta}, \hat{\delta}) = \operatorname{est} \theta, \tag{48}$$

is, under general conditions of stochastic regularity, consistent, asymptotically unbiased and asymptotically efficient. Likewise, $\hat{\theta}$ converges stochastically to a multivariate normal distribution with mean θ and covariance matrix $I^{-1}(\theta)$, that is,

$$\hat{\theta} \xrightarrow{d} N(\theta, I^{-1}(\theta)). \tag{49}$$

X. Specification of an Alternative: Model II

In Sect. V, we introduced a set of postulates which completely specify a logistic model (Model 1) of the functional distribution of income, and which satisfy the empirical and logical characteristics [3, 7]. The following alternative specification (Model II) also yields satisfactory results with respect to the goodness of fit and the covariance matrix of the estimators. We start with the following set of postulates:

Postulate I (P.I). Similar to P.1 of Sect. V.

Postulate II (P.II). The income elasticity of the unbiased predictor $\mu(y)$, with respect to $y(\omega)$ and to $y(t)$ from a real origin $\alpha < \mu(y)$, is a linear decreasing function of the unbiased predictor. Therefore

(50)

$$\frac{d \log(\mu(y) - \alpha)}{d \log y} = \delta\left(1 - \frac{\mu(y) - \alpha}{\lambda}\right), \qquad \lambda, \delta > 0, \quad y > 0, \quad \mu(y) > \alpha.$$

POSTULATE III (P.III). Similar to P.3 of Sect. V.

POSTULATE IIIa (P.IIIa). Similar to P.3a of Sect. VII.

With these postulates we get the same results obtained in Lemmas 1 and 2. Solving the differential Eq. (50), we have

$$\mu(y) = \alpha + \frac{\lambda}{1+\beta y^{-\delta}} \tag{51}$$

$$= \alpha + \frac{\lambda}{1+\beta \exp(-\delta \log y)}, \qquad \lambda, \beta, \delta > 0,$$

a result corresponding to Lemma 3. Then,

$$\mu(t) = \alpha + \frac{\lambda}{1 + \beta \exp(-\delta \log y)} + u(t). \tag{52}$$

The characteristics of the unbiased predictor Eq. (51) are equivalent to those set out for Model I (Sect. VI). The coordinates of the inflection point are:

$$\left(\left(\frac{\beta(\delta-1)^{1/\delta}}{\delta+1}\right), \ \alpha + \frac{\lambda(\delta-1)}{2\delta}\right), \qquad \forall \delta > 1. \tag{53}$$

If $0 < \delta < 1$, the unbiased predictor does not have an inflection point, since $y > 0$.

If in Model I we replace the income per capita with its log, we obtain similar mathematical expressions for the likelihood Eqs. (40)–(43), the residual variance Eq. (44), the asymptotic covariance matrix of the estimators Eq. (47), and the asymptotic distribution Eq. (49).

XI. Applications

Models I and II were used as explanatory models of the *intercountry*, and *intertemporal* functional distribution of income.

In the parameter estimation for the intertemporal analysis, sample data of several developed countries (United States, Canada, France, Sweden, and others) were used. For the cross-sectional study, statistical information of the income per capita (in 1967 dollars) was available. Labor's share in the national income by country was obtained by averaging the period 1966–1968. A sample of 37 countries was available (data displayed in Table I).

TABLE I

PER CAPITA INCOME (IN 1967 DOLLARS) [$y(\omega)$] AND LABOR SHARE IN THE NATIONAL INCOME (IN PER CENT) [$\mu(\omega)$] BY COUNTRY

Country	$y(\omega)$	$\mu(\omega)$
Tanganyika	71.33	30.818
Korea	144.33	33.466
Ceylon	150.00	48.251
Bolivia	159.50	42.733
Paraguay	219.33	44.904
Ecuador	232.33	50.944
Honduras	233.00	50.161
Taiwan	246.67	47.870
Guatemala	285.00	49.723
Colombia	287.00	44.215
Malaysia	299.00	47.215
Peru	312.50	47.960
Costa Rica	410.67	52.559
Jamaica	528.00	61.348
Uruguay	562.33	47.977
South Africa	592.67	61.712
Spain	807.00	55.982
Venezuela	902.67	57.542
Japan	1044.33	56.103
Ireland	1060.00	61.057
Italy	1218.33	59.112
Austria	1413.33	66.141
Finland	1497.00	63.333
Netherlands	1750.67	65.422
Belgium	1987.33	62.437
United Kingdom	1993.00	74.903
Germany	2017.33	66.413
New Zealand	2073.00	61.975
Australia	2099.33	64.457
Luxembourg	2107.67	66.200
Norway	2117.33	67.146
France	2238.33	62.135
Denmark	2423.33	64.071
Switzerland	2613.00	63.641
Canada	2752.33	70.322
Sweden	2988.00	69.953
United States	3868.33	70.294

Next, we supply the results obtained:

Model I

$$\hat{\mu}(y) = -37.680 + \frac{108.966}{1 + 0.330 \exp(-0.0015\, y)},$$

$$R^2 = 0.71, \qquad \hat{\sigma}_u = 5.16, \tag{54}$$

$$\hat{\mu}^* = \lim_{y\to\infty} \mu(y) = 71.286.$$

TABLE II

SAMPLE ESTIMATE OF THE ASYMPTOTIC COVARIANCE MATRIX (MODEL I)

ξ \ ξ	σ^2	α	λ	β	δ
σ^2	39.4050				
α	0	591,286.03			
λ	0	−593,112.01	594,948.04		
β	0	2,277.37	−2,284.41	8.774	
δ	0	1.40	−1.41	0.005	0.0000036

TABLE III

SAMPLE ESTIMATE OF THE CORRELATION MATRIX (MODEL I)

ξ \ ξ	σ^2	α	λ	β	δ
σ^2	1.00				
α	0	1.00000			
λ	0	−0.99999	1.00000		
β	0	0.99986	−0.99986	1.00000	
δ	0	0.96214	−0.96271	0.96457	1.00

The sample estimate of the asymptotic covariance matrix of estimators is shown in Table II; Table III includes the sample estimate of the correlation matrix of estimators taken from the results of Table II.

Model II

$$\hat{\mu}(y) = -4.575 + \frac{83.282}{1+13.465\,y^{-0.560}},$$

$$(55) \qquad R^2 = 0.87, \qquad \hat{\mu}_u = 3.74,$$

$$\hat{\mu}^* = \lim_{y\to\infty} \mu(y) = 78.707.$$

Table IV presents the sample estimate of the asymptotic covariance matrix of estimators, and the sample estimate of the correlation matrix of estimators taken from the results of Table IV, is offered in Table V.

TABLE IV

Sample Estimate of the Asymptotic Covariance Matrix (Model II)

ξ \ ξ	σ^2	α	λ	β	δ
σ^2	10.53				
α	0	11,998.68			
λ	0	−13,909.94	16,466.89		
β	0	7,770.99	−9,224.54	5,187.31	
δ	0	74.66	−89.28	50.47	0.4972

TABLE V

Sample Estimate of the Correlation Matrix (Model II)

ξ \ ξ	σ^2	α	λ	β	δ
σ^2	1.00				
α	0	1.0000			
λ	0	−0.9979	1.0000		
β	0	0.9933	−0.9981	1.0000	
δ	0	0.9748	−0.9866	0.9937	1.00

A remarkable fact revealed in the estimates made for Model I as well as for Model II for the analysis *by country* (time-series data) and for the analysis *between countries* (cross-sectional data) is the significant correlation found between the estimators. This fact is perhaps not so striking if we consider that we are dealing with a logistic curve, that is, a *saturation curve*, with an exogenous variable and four parameters. In this case we should expect an interdependence between values given by the finite range of the function; particularly, in our case, the interval is (0,100).

With respect to the asymptotic characteristic of the logistic model, we can say, in accordance with Eq. (23), that variations of the parameters α and λ are conditioned by Eq. (23). As one increases, the other should decrease, so that their sum is held constant. That is why we obtain a negative correlation between the estimators. Moreover, as shown in Tables III and V, it is practically equal to minus one.

Likewise, the parameters β and δ are mutually conditioned, contributing simultaneously, to determine the velocity of convergency to the asymptotic value $\mu^* = \alpha + \lambda$. By observing the sign of δ, we can see that the correlation between the estimates is positive. In all the cases analyzed, the estimates were practically equal to 1, as evident from Tables III and V.

These observations illustrate the necessity of working with confidence regions rather than with confidence intervals for each particular parameter. Hypothesis testing should be done for linear combinations of the parameters. Among these linear combinations, the most important one from a theoretical and practical viewpoint is the following (once the goodness of fit has been proved):

$$\mu^* = \alpha + \lambda.$$

For Model I, we have

$$\hat{\mu}^* = 71.286,$$

where

$$\operatorname{var}\hat{\mu}^* = \operatorname{var}\hat{\alpha} + \operatorname{var}\hat{\lambda} + 2\operatorname{cov}(\hat{\alpha}, \hat{\lambda}). \tag{56}$$

For the sample estimate of μ^*, we get

$$\hat{\sigma}^2_{\hat{\mu}^*} = 10.05, \qquad \hat{\sigma}_{\hat{\mu}^*} = 3.17.$$

For Model II, the results are

$$\hat{\mu}^* = 78.707, \qquad \hat{\sigma}^2_{\hat{\mu}^*} = 445.6951, \qquad \hat{\sigma}_{\hat{\mu}^*} = 21.11.$$

Having in mind that maximum likelihood estimators [1] are, under general conditions of stochastic regularity, consistent, asymptotically normal, and asymptotically efficient with a covariance matrix given by the lower bound of the Cramér–Rao inequality, and considering that a linear combination of normal variables is normally distributed [2], then

$$\hat{\mu}^* \xrightarrow{d} N(\mu^*, \operatorname{var}\hat{\mu}^*). \tag{57}$$

Applying the conclusions of Eq. (57), we infer that in both Models I and II, the null hypothesis for the parameter μ^* must be rejected.

The difference between the two estimates of the parameter μ^* has been statistically tested and the null hypothesis accepted. The values of the multiple correlation coefficient R obtained for both Models I and II reject the null hypothesis, hence accepting the goodness of fit.

XII. Conclusion

The aim of this chapter has been to investigate the factors that explain labor's share in the national income. The results obtained are used for decision purposes in [6] to determine some target parameters and formulate a model for stability and development. A basic target parameter is μ^*. Given the goodness of fit of the two models proposed, to achieve the target objective for developing countries we suggest using the arithmetic mean of the two resulting estimates, that is,

$$\mu^* = 75.$$

REFERENCES

[1] Cramér, H., "Mathematical Methods of Statistics." Princeton Univ. Press, Princeton, New Jersey, 1946.
[2] Dagum, C., Transvariación en la hipótesis de variables aleatorias normales multidimensionales, *Proc. 32nd Session Int. Statistical Inst., Tokyo* **38**, Book 4, (1960).
[3] Dagum, C., On Method and Purposes in Econometric Model Building. *Z. Nationalokonom.* No. 4, 381–398 (1968).
[4] Dagum, C., A Logistic Decision Model for Stability and Development. *Proc. 37th Session Int. Statistical Inst., London* V.XLIII, Book 2, pp. 14–16 (1969).
[5] Dagum, C., Inflación estructural y modernización: Notas para una teoría sociónómica de la inflación. *Rome: Congr. Inst. Int. Sociolog.* (1969).
[6] Dagum, C., L'inflation structurelle: Un modele économétrique. *Economies et Sociétés, Cahiers de Economie Mathematique et Econometrie* IV, No. 3, pp. 497–517 (1970).
[7] Dagum, C., and Dagum, E. M. B., Introducción a la econometría. Mexico: Siglo XXI, 1971.
[8] Gini, C., Il diverso accrescimento delle classi sociali e la concentrazione della ricchezza. *Giornale degli Econ.* Ser. II, **37** (1909).
[9] Gini, C., "Ricchezza e Reddito" (Raccolta di scritti editi ed inediti con prefazione e note del Prof. A. De Vita). U.T.E.T., Torino, 1957.
[10] Kalecki, M., "Theory of Economic Dynamics." Holt, New York, 1954.
[11] Masse, P. and Barnard, P., "Les dividendes du progrès." Editions du Seuil, Paris, 1969.

[12] Nyblen, G., "The Problem of Summation in Economic Science." Gleerup, Lund, 1951.
[13] Pareto, V., "Cours d'economie politique." Lausanna, 1897.
[14] Perroux, F., "L'économie du XXe siècle." Presses Univ. de France, Paris, 1961.
[15] von Neumann, J., and Morgenstern, O., "Theory of Games and Economic Behavior." Princeton Univ. Press, Princeton, New Jersey, 1944; 3rd ed., 1953.
[16] Wold, H., On the Consistency of Least Squares Regression, *Sankhya*, *Ser. A* **25**, Part 2, 211–215 (1963).

INDUSTRIALIZING INDUSTRIES AND THE ECONOMIC INTEGRATION OF LESS-DEVELOPED COUNTRIES*

G. DESTANNE de BERNIS

Institut de Recherche Economique et de Planification
Université des Sciences de Grenoble, Grenoble, France

Raúl Prebisch's works have played a determining role in the reconsideration of the general theory of international economic relations. By questioning the neoclassic theory of transmitted growth, inherited from a Ricardian tradition rooted in its hypotheses and distorted in its targets,[1] Prebisch has paved the way for a consideration of the most concrete factors in a development policy. The succession of reports he has given us over the past twenty five years constitute a group of fundamental contributions which allow us to try to define the lines of force of a general theory of industrialization.

In light of the latest report we have seen [26], we can set forth the following preliminary findings:

* This article owes much to preliminary discussions with R. Borrelly, who has read the first draft and suggested the inclusion of many points.

[1] Ricardo was not merely an abstract theoretician. Also a banker, he looked after the interests of the English industrialist bourgeoisie and he told them what the conditions for a rapid industrialization of England were: that is to say, to mold international relations, as it was able to do thanks to its relative power, to create the conditions for an international division of labor which would be more fully explained later by Heckscher–Ohlin's famous theorem to which would be added some paradoxes (the famous Leontief) whose quasi-ideological function consists in reinforcing the optimistic nature of the theory.

It is indeed "paradoxical" to want to use the theory created for the industrialization of the most powerful country to industrialize those who happen to be the present victims of the division of labor imposed by it during its industrialization.

a. There are no grounds for limiting import substitution to industries providing consumption goods; industries making capital goods are equally affected;

b. The international division of labor is blocked by the refusal of the industrialized countries to open their frontiers to manufactured products from underdeveloped countries;

c. The transformation of the social and economic structures inherited from the past, and greatly influenced by the phenomena of foreign economic domination, constitutes a preface to any development policy;

d. The small size of most underdeveloped countries prevents them from going ahead if they do not implement a policy of regional coordination oriented toward common industrialization.

The general coherence and the mutal reinforcement of these elements need not be stressed. Moreover, they are observable not only in Latin America, but also in Asia and Africa, which afford us quite compelling illustrations, though each time on different levels. A commentary on them furnishes the elements of a theory of industrialization which can be expressed in two sets of propositions concerning, in succession, its *structural conditions* and its *content*.

It might seem logical to begin by studying the conditions which must be met before industrialization is possible. But, to be quite clear, we prefer to start with the necessary content of industrialization and then go back to its internal and external conditions, which will then appear more firmly grounded. On the level of action, these conditions must first be sought; otherwise any attempt at industrialization, even on the basis of structural content, which we will define herein, would lose all its effectiveness.

I. The Content of an Industrialization Policy

We must first settle a preliminary question: Have we the right to speak of *a* content, of *an* industrialization policy? The answer to this question cannot be merely empirical; it depends on the very nature of the process of industrialization. The latter may be defined as a process of permanent restructuring under the pressure of complexes of machinery (F. Perroux), as the filling in of the interindustry (input–output) matrix, or as the gradual substitution of mechanized work—being more productive—for less-mechanized work. Any one of these formulations gives the identical theoretical content to any industrialization process, above and beyond the differences which the historical level of the development of techniques may introduce into the list of the specific industries concerned. This identical theoretical content is founded upon driving effects, the notion of a "coherent industrial structure," and the nature of the process of accumulation.

By actually spotting the driving effects, we see that these do not arise in just any industries and act on just any other industries.[2] The restructuring of a given economic and social group under the pressure of complexes of machinery can only be carried out automatically if these *machines* are *available* in the economy under consideration, and they are available only if the balance of payments makes it possible to buy them from an outside manufacturer (who is willing to sell them) or if they are made domestically.

A "*coherent industrial structure*" can be defined from an interindustry matrix when the different sectors are not only connected with the outside world by their imports (machinery, raw materials) and by their exports (raw materials, finished products) but are also themselves interconnected by their inputs and outputs, which implies the existence of sectors engaged in equipment production and of processing sectors. The concrete content of these two sectors is obviously linked to the nature of other vertically associated sectors, but for all that, the principle is not changed.

As for the process of accumulation, it would not be possible to analyze the rate of money savings by starting with a single variable. The intertemporal allocation of resources, that is to say, the rate of accumulation cannot be studied independently of the intersectoral allocation, that is to say the structure of realized investment.

Even when Domar [8, Chap. 9] undertakes to reduce Feld'man's model[3] to an aggregate one by writing down the effective coefficient of investment in the two sectors (consumption goods, equipment), he is obliged to maintain the distinction between these two sectors in order to give the "real" conditions for the savings policy which is deemed desirable.[4] This statement may be extended

[2] The first half of the 19th century in Europe shows the preponderant influence of mechanical engineering (textiles play a part by imposing the manufacture of machines, later came the railways). The second half shows the influence of the pair, mechanical engineering–chemistry. The successive new sources of energy merely allowed the old system of steam engines to be altered to adapt itself to the development of new productive forces.

The history of the U.S.S.R. reveals the same connections. Each of the Latin American countries that has initiated a true development process has done so in its own way. Mexico is associated with steel making and the chemistry of hydrocarbons. Brazil links together a great steel center and a great chemical center and thus gives their full meaning to assembly plants which before that were merely appendages of foreign industries, etc. . . ..

[3] Since then, Feld'man's article has been published in English in its full text by Spulber [28]. We owe a lot to the first comments made on this pattern by Younes [33].

[4] The marginal propensity to save must be equal, in the balance, to the share of the total investment allocated to the sector making capital goods. Indeed, if we call λ the share of the investment allocated to the capital goods sector, β_1 the coefficient of effectiveness of investment (Domar's coefficient) in this sector, β_2 the same coefficient in the consumption goods sector, and σ' the marginal propensity to save, Feld'man's pattern leads us to write

$$\sigma' = \frac{\lambda\beta_1}{\beta_2 - \lambda(\beta_2 - \beta_1)},$$

and if $\beta_1 = \beta_2$, $\sigma' = \lambda$.

This conclusion can be found in the same way by using P. C. Mahalanobis's pattern [19, 20].

to all the models of the Harrod type, and since Domar's demonstration, we have been able to "read" the models stating—even globally—the conditions for balanced growth by adding to them a series of real conditions which spell out in a useful way the discussions about the necessary equality of warranteed and natural growth rates.[5]

The same holds true to an even greater degree for multisector models. Models with three sectors, like A. Lowe's[6] or patterns derived from Keynesian hypotheses like Pasinetti's (1965), demonstrate this directly. The same conclusion, provided that the specific conditions of the underdeveloped countries are taken into account, can be drawn from models deriving from that of von Neumann. Indeed, growth cannot be achieved in such countries merely by means of a proportional increase in the size of each sector: an effort must be made to try and build a capital structure as quickly as possible and, within the framework of the general hypotheses of turnpikes, accumulation in the producers' goods sector enjoys top priority, as we can easily understand.[7]

In all these models, the growth rate (insofar as it is linked to the process of accumulation) is determined by the share of investment allocated to the equipment sector. We can demonstrate that this process cannot be left to the fluctuations of foreign trade.[8] Above all, and contrary to what may have been

[5] Balance according to Harrod being regular only if $g_w = g_n$, the expression of g_w in which the propensity to save is itself formulated in real terms

$$\sigma = \frac{I_0 e^{\lambda\beta_1 t}}{Y_0 + I_0\{1 + [(1-\lambda)/\lambda]\cdot(\beta_2/\beta_1)\}(e^{\lambda\beta_1 t} - 1)}$$

with the same symbols as in footnote 4 and σ for the average propensity to save, (Y_0 and I_0 for the initial values of the national income and investment), restores to this equality ($g_w = g_n$) a homogeneous content in terms of: effectiveness of the investment; allocation of capital to the different sectors; technical progress ($g_n = l + p + lp$, with l for the rate of increase in the population and p for the growth rate of the productivity of labor). But the productivity of labor is itself dependent on the effectiveness of the investment and on its allocation to the different sectors (more highly-mechanized work replacing less-mechanized work). Finally, the allocation of the investment is the variable essential for a balanced growth policy.

[6] Here the growth rate of the overall economy is, as we know, directly determined by the growth rate of the machines destined to produce other machines.

[7] An application of this analysis has been made in the case of Algeria by Stoleru [29].

[8] The machines imported from abroad are not necessarily adapted to the technical problems to be solved; by systematically importing them the technological dependence and the general dependence are increased. The industrialized countries do not necessarily accept to ensure the industrial equipment of the new countries, as soon as a surplus of their balance does not give them the freedom of their purchases; the rate of technical progress becomes dependent on the production that ensures the equilibrium of the balance and therefore on world prices fixed by groups who have an interest in maintaining and reinforcing their dependence; the conditions of this "unequal exchange" (A. Emmanuel) raise the "cost" of this progress.

feared on the level of an argument that is too empirical or that leaves out agriculture, we can show that it is a necessary condition for a long-run rise in the standard of living of the population.[9]

Having touched on these three themes, the *metaphor* of the turnpike must now hold our attention. The effectiveness of an industrialization policy is linked to the speed with which we can locate ourselves on the logical "path" of industrialization, thanks to the *resorption* of the different types of imbalance at the outset.

We thus define *synthetically*, that is to say, without any possibility of noting discrepancies among them, several levels of abstractions, or more exactly, of successive ideas put in their concrete form. To speak like O. Lange, these are: the most abstract level, where the only question is to ensure the highest rate of capital foundation, making allowance for consumer requirements;[10] an intermediate level determined by the level of the development of productive forces on a planetary scale, and which will consist in defining at each moment of their evolution what content must be given to this building up of capital;

[9] Three remarks must be made here: First, in the long run, the growth rate of consumption is determined like that of investment by the λ, already seen in connection with the Feld'man–Mahalanobis pattern:

$$I_t = I_0 e^{\lambda\beta_1 t},$$

$$C_t = C_0 + I_0 \frac{1-\lambda}{\lambda} \cdot \frac{\beta_2}{\beta_1}(e^{\lambda\beta_1 t} - 1)$$

(with C for consumption). (In the long run, the λ of the exponential prevails over the coefficient $(1-\lambda)/\lambda$); Secondly, in short term, and until the curves of consumption with different λ (from 7 to 15 years) intersect, it is the increase in agricultural production (progress in organization or agricultural reform and progress in implements), which are not taken into account in the pattern, which ensures the increase in the standard of living. Finally, we must once again recall the fact that the radical opposition between consumption and investment ($R = C + I$, everything that is not invested is consumed) tends to leave out of the argument an essential category of consumer expenditure which raises labor productivity (improvement in nutrition, a rise in the level of health, development of education) and which, due to this, cannot be treated in terms of "human capital."

[10] During the first phases of development and subject to the "development consumption" mentioned in footnote 9, we are obliged to give top priority to the rapid development of productive investment with some restraint on the standard of living per capita, whence the term "requirements." But the most recent experience of the socialist countries shows that a reversal finally takes place in which one of the dynamic factors of development can be consumption. In capitalist countries it continues to be characterized by the contradictions between the value of the goods produced and the reinforcement of exploitation, the two contradictory aspects of the determination of profit rates. This comment reinforces those in footnote 5 concerning the role of technical progress, which initiates a new tendency, that of the fall in the profit rate, if it is not thwarted by an increase in the rate of exploitation. This can be done only within the limits tolerated by the necessity of recovering the value of the goods produced.

and a very concrete level, that of the economic policy of each country which, within the framework of its specific geography[11] and history, must determine empirically what structural distortions keep it outside the "path" of industrialization and how to eliminate them as quickly as possible.

Considering that the first level is established by the foregoing, and postponing the third one to the case studies below, except when we draw concrete sources of experience from it, it is to the second level that we must devote our attention: defining it for the moment[12] as the content of any industrial policy whatsoever, which consists in defining the types of industries essential for the implementation of a "coherent industrial structure" or of a rapid accumulation process. Having given a positive answer to our preliminary question, we are now able to proceed with an analysis of this content.

The connection we noted in Feld'man–Domar between the propensity to save and the *real* structure of capital is essential for our purpose.[13] Industrialization will take place all the more quickly—making allowances for our remarks made about foreign trade stresses—the more rapidly the volume of the production of equipment increases. This growth rate depends, of course, on two sets of variables, the quantity of monetary capital it is possible to assemble, or, to express it differently, the volume of surplus it is possible to accumulate, and the orientation given to this when used for investment.

[11] It is perfectly normal for the responsible authorities in underdeveloped countries to stress the "specific character" of their country's situation, often insisting on the fact that their development policy must not be dominated by any extraneous model.

In this we may see too great a concern for national problems, which prevents them from looking beyond their frontiers or a conception of development distorted by an ideological representation conveyed by the experts of the "developed countries" set on maintaining "vertical" relations. But it would be far too superficial to be content with that.

It is, indeed, common knowledge that during the first phases of humanity, the hold of the "geographic" over the history of man was considerable, man being obliged to adapt himself to a nature that he neither knew how to nor could yet dominate. The history of the development of mankind is in a sense the history of the reversal of this hold of the geographic over the historic. Indeed, we note that the "geographic" factors now exert only an anecdotal influence on industrial countries (nobody is amazed by the Italian steel industry). We should go much further and note that the developed countries have succeeded in despoiling the nonindustrialized ones of their geography: the oil market is currently an example. If we leave aside the North American third and the socialist third (roughly), the other third is characterized by nonconsuming but producing countries and nonproducing but consuming countries brought together by private corporations external to both. We know that all of them do not draw the same advantages from this!

[12] Without forgetting the lesson of history, of course (see footnote 2).

[13] It is moreover confirmed by all the sector patterns of optimal growth. Subject to the determination of the optimal rate of savings, the maximization of the preference function is dependent on the quickest possible realization of a capital structure which afterwards allows a regular development of the economy.

A.

The *volume of the surplus available for accumulation* depends on the surplus produced and the share of this surplus which is mobilized.

1.

The *volume of the surplus produced* will be greater as the difference between consumption and production is greater. Let us admit, to be brief, that we allow ourselves some minimal consumption level per capita and that we limit the development consumptions to those that facilitate the achievement of investment programs, so that in order to make things easier, we can integrate this cost into the very expenditure on investment. The problem then comes back to the maximization of existing production, and it is less commonplace than it would seem from this short statement.

All economies have an agricultural base, and occasionally—in the most pronounced cases of underdevelopment—have *only* an agricultural base, at the only possible source of an internal surplus. Therefore the first condition for industrialization lies in increasing the productivity of agricultural labor. The *latter* is in part linked to this basic agrarian reform, which must create the conditions for an evolution in technique, to which we shall return below. It also depends on placing at the disposal of agriculture, in sufficient quantities and at prices that are acceptable under the prevailing conditions of yield, a clearly determined variety of equipment of industrial origin, whose production cost is such that, if the equipment is not produced in the country itself, the transport costs from the industrialized regions will constitute an insuperable barrier to widespread diffusion.

These goods are essentially *equipment*,[14] from the tractor and motor, with everything that accompanies them, to the pump and the most ordinary implements, *cement* (buildings, silos, etc.) and chemicals (fertilizers, pesticides, plastics with their manifold uses in any modernizing agricultural sector, rubber, etc.).

So we come back from the maximization of agricultural output to the demand for well-defined products from industry. We have at least established the fact that *there can be no industrialization policy without an active agricultural development policy*. The all-too-well-known dilemma of choosing between

[14] One can never sufficiently stress the fact that having adequate and well-adapted equipment is the condition for an effective mastery of nature. F. List noted as early as the beginning of the 19th century that there is no agriculture that progresses unless it is in contact with industry; the ridiculously inadequate equipment of the African farmer, linked of course to the social and economic conditions of his tenure of the land, is an obstacle that impedes the slightest desire to progress.

development by agriculture or by industry is one of many dramatically false ideas which are nevertheless widespread and generally accepted.

But the economies of certain countries are also lucky enough to have an important mining sector. Never can the surplus it is possible to produce in this sector be considered a substitute for an agricultural surplus, because the whole of the available surplus must be maximized. But when one does exist, it nevertheless represents an appreciable contribution. We are naturally thinking of hydrocarbons, but the other mineral resources of the underdeveloped countries are also considerable.[15]

Their rational exploitation in the process of industrialization brings up two questions, the choice of the rate of extraction of the underground reserves (which determines the volume of the surplus), and the choice of the mobilization point of the surplus.

Subject to the necessity of this choice, but only insofar as the country concerned controls the exploitation of its own natural resources—and we shall come back to this point—it is not always in its best interest to speed up the rate. Indeed, on the one hand, it runs the risk of exhausting its reserves and of mortgaging its future: it must neither kill the goose that lays the golden eggs, nor eat its corn on the stalk. On the other hand, it is in the interest of the customer countries to exploit such resources rapidly and thus bring about a fall in the purchase price. In this we see another reason for never overlooking the importance of the agricultural surplus.

The choice of the mobilization point thus rejoins the question of the overall industrialization policy. The problem can perhaps be represented as follows: making allowance for the part that certain mineral resources (iron ore, hydrocarbons) may be called upon to play in the internal production processes, it is not always advisable to maximize the "revenue at the pit," because we must maximize the total economic surplus to be drawn from all the activities connected with this resource. On the proportion exported in the crude state to finance purchases of industrial equipment that must be procured abroad, the maximization of the surplus directly deducted is indispensable.[16] On the proportion of the resource which is to be processed domestically, it does not

[15] This supposes of course that the phase of bullionist mercantilism has been transcended intellectually and that the accumulation of wealth in the form of stocks of precious metals in the hands of the sovereign or of the ruling class is no longer the criterion of effectiveness or the target of economic policy. The first Congress of the Association of Arab Economists (Algiers, October, 1970) whose theme, as it happened, was "oil and development" explicitly wrote down in its conclusions that both as a source of wealth and as raw materials (see above), the whole policy concerning hydrocarbons must make of it an instrument for economic development.

[16] Subject to a calculation of the minimax type, maximization of the surplus with minimization of the quantities sold, which was perfectly understood—at long last—by the oil-producing countries during the recent negotiations in Teheran.

seem to be either useful or advisable to deduct an initial surplus.

Indeed, the industrial processing activities, in order to be feasible, must have a technical dimension which is often huge in relation to the domestic outlets of the country under consideration,[17] and this makes it necessary to envisage the export of the surplus to ensure their optimum level of activity. Considering the difficulties created by the industrialized countries when nonindustrialized countries try to enter the international market in manufactured goods, the question of price is important. Now, this free access to the international market is the condition for the smooth functioning of big production units and therefore for the attainment of all possible economies of scale inside the developing economy. By degrees, the mineral resources thus processed give rise to a series of development effects within the economy until the moment when, in its definitive form (fertilizers, machines), these can be used to increase the productivity of agriculture and to build up the industrial sector. The surplus it produces then blends into the surplus it generates.[18]

2.

In turn, the mobilized proportion of this new level of surplus must be maximized. If, in this case, the problem is very simple as far as the mineral resources are concerned, subject to a direct intervention of the political power in the field of prospecting for, producing, and transporting these resources, the question is much more ticklish as far as agriculture is concerned. With certain exceptions, the latter remains the essential source of a mobilizable surplus.

The surplus already produced in the agricultural sectors of nonindustrialized countries is relatively considerable. But this surplus is either withdrawn by the marketing sector in the form of profits, transferred abroad by the big trading companies (United Fruit, Unilever, Lesieur, etc.), or consumed on the spot by all the unemployed who are shown hospitality by those of their fellows who still have a patch of land and productive work. It is a question of making this surplus available for the economy concerned, and, also, of being able to mobilize the additional surplus generated by this improvement in production.

Within the framework of this study, we cannot tackle all the problems associated with this maximization of the proportion withdrawn from the surplus: reorganization of the internal marketing channels, applying a price policy consistent with these imperatives of development;[19] minimization of

[17] See R. Prebisch's report already quoted.

[18] Of course, this method of calculation can be considered (and therefore optimized) only in a socialist economy with full mastery over its production units so that the commercial categories draw aside and make way for the circulation solely of products which make the labor costs transparent [2].

[19] This form of deduction in advance closely resembles primitive accumulation. If the

transfers of surpluses abroad;[20] creation of labor structures in agriculture so that farmers without land and jobs can contribute productively, in return for the food they receive, to the work of developing the land and harnessing the water so as to raise the productivity of agricultural labor generally.[21]

It is the whole national policy of agrarian structure and the technical orientation of agriculture that is concerned. We are beginning to acquire and control instruments which will enable us to build up patterns for the choice of crops on the scale of a whole country by reference to the different targets that planners may assign to agriculture. This preference function may very well be the function of the produced and mobilized surplus and these patterns ought to take the multiple connections between industry and agriculture into account.

But it is not enough to withdraw a considerable proportion from the surplus. This proportion must also be used effectively.

B. Allocation of Investment by Sectors

What we have been led to say about the conditions for the maximization of the available surplus tends to show that this surplus ought to grow even larger as industry places at the disposal of agriculture the products the latter requires for its inputs, that is to say, as industry develops its metallurgical, mechanical engineering, cement, and chemicals sectors.

But it would be unthinkable to stop here. The whole analysis on which we are grounding our arguments is conducted in real terms as opposed to arche-global formulations, which are necessarily of a monetary nature. Of course,

State does not control these channels and does not recover the surplus thus deducted in advance, it is but a pure and simple exploitation of farm labor. Obviously, it is not this type of accumulation that is effective.

[20] It is certainly necessary to go on exporting in order to get the foreign exchange necessary to buy equipment and thus accumulate the surplus. The great world monopolies are very heedful about the maintenance of "unequal exchange" (A. Emmanuel), and it would not solve the problem, in our opinion, merely to tax exported products. However, the recent Teheran negotiations have just shown that the cartellization of producers can be effective even with relation to a very powerful "coordinated oligopole."

[21] We know that there is a correlation between overpopulation and the degradation of land (see Poncet).

Consequently, it is in the countries that are most marked by the tendency to be overpopulated that there are the greatest opportunities for conservation work in the fields of water and land. Besides, it is often possible to develop more productive techniques that are more labor intensive. It has recently been demonstrated, in connection with Algeria, that it was possible to bring about a considerable and lasting increase in the number of productive farm jobs without counting the temporary jobs (but of a nonnegligible duration, 10–20 years!) for the work of land development [12].

investment in each period can be defined by starting with savings. But without any doubt, owing to our reserves levels and the very few degrees of freedom that international trade leaves in open economies, one can never invest more than the total sum of capital goods made during the period. The putty–putty or putty–clay abstractions are merely academic hypotheses devoid of any possibility of application in the real world. Consequently, the decisions concerning the structure of production in a given period are also going to determine the structure of the product throughout the life of the types of equipment that are installed, and therefore the share of the product that will necessarily go into investment. If the amount of savings does not correspond to this, the result would be a twofold imbalance, overproduction of the means of production, and a shortage of consumer goods. After a period of such disturbances, it is indeed the monetary equilibrium that would have to readjust itself to the real structure. The only degree of freedom comes from the utilization of non-specific producers' goods, and here again it is the decision about initial types of production that determines the degrees of freedom in the structure.

The result is that decisions about industrial production cannot depend only on the requirements of agriculture:[22] they must also be based on the imperative of laying the foundations for the progressive building up of a structure for the production of capital goods, which meet the "actual requirements" of the industrialization process. Furthermore, the question of knowing just what is meant by that phrase crops up.

The difficulty comes from the point of knowing how to define the content of what we have so far called the capital goods sector. Must we understand by that only the "final industries" (in the sense used by Chenery and Watanabe, for instance), or must certain intermediary industries be added? We know that Hoffman included ferrous and nonferrous metals, machinery, the construction of vehicles, and chemical industries [11].

This attitude, tending to use definitions, is due to the fact that Hoffman's theoretical interest was in analyzing the growth process. The structure of production, from this perspective, consists of both fixed capital and a series of other intermediary products whose production exerts a determining influence on the technical structure of fixed capital. Paving the way for Perroux's analyses of growth industries, Hoffman came within the framework of a definition of capital which includes fixed capital and circulating capital. But he did not, however, isolate raw materials, because their production has never had any

[22] Except in very large countries, agriculture does not seem to be able to justify by itself big industrial complexes (except those directly concerning it, as, for instance, the overall direct production of agricultural implements or the last stage in the production process of fertilizers) but it constitutes a sideline outlet that can be a determinant for a series of "projects" (plastics, synthetic rubber, ammonia, motors, pumps, etc.) without which the construction of the industrial sector would not be able to work to full output.

driving effects anywhere, which is why most models describe integrated sectors. Nevertheless, he might have included the production of energy, but he was writing at a time when "industrial" consumption still had very little significance and before modern techniques for the construction of big power plants had given the plants their present capacity, which allows them to have powerful driving effects.[23]

We shall maintain his perspective in its the essential points. Nevertheless, the work done by Leontief's team [18] enables us to improve on Hoffmann's classifications. Thanks to them, we have tables of intersectoral capital coefficients for the United States. But, automatically, even these coefficients, whose nature is to be contrasted to the technical coefficients of the current flows of intermediary goods, concern only fixed capital goods in the strictest sense.

Such being the case, we see that, in the United States in 1939, 23 industries were selling capital goods. If we leave out agriculture (which supplies capital only to itself), construction, and the sectors with trifling contributions, we get a square table with 16 headings left. By triangulating this matrix, Younes has shown that there exists "a bloc of 4 sectors which provide capital goods to the other sectors." These sectors are:

34. Industrial and household equipments not specified elsewhere (including pumps and compressors);
35. Machine tools;[24]
30. Motors and turbines;
38. Iron and steel not specified elsewhere (including tool production).

Younes also stresses the fact that the connection between the machine-tools sector and that of motors and turbines is very close.

Thus, for the enumeration of ferrous and nonferrous metals, and construction of vehicles and machinery, we may substitute the list of four sectors taken from the Leontief tables. It is more restricted, for its range does not cover the whole range of the former, but it is more exact and consists of essential types of production.

Its composition does not enable us to isolate power production as a specific sector, but it has been demonstrated that it is not power production as such which has an industrializing effect because, in any country, this accompanies

[23] Martin analyzed these effects first in his report to the 1st International Economic Congress in Córdoba [21], then in a series of studies done under his direction at L'Institut Economique et Juridique de l'Energie of the University of Grenoble on induced innovations in the production of capital goods by the innovations realized in the sector of power production.

[24] On several occasions we have had the opportunity to examine the problem of the building up of a machine-tools industry in underdeveloped countries. We are not going back to this at length here.

industrial development. The industrializing effect comes from what is vertically linked to power, either the great technological innovations brought about by the construction of big power plants, or the industries which are large consumers of energy, and particularly the chemical industry.

To this enumeration derived from Leontief, we shall add (thus to an extent adopting Hoffman's position), the great sectors of the chemical industry: in mineral chemistry, the great mineral chemical industry (sulphur and its by-products, electrochemistry) and the manufacture of nitrate fertilizers; in organic chemistry, the basic products, the major intermediary products, plastics, and synthetic rubber. Indeed, these sectors meet the very criteria by which we have defined industrialization:

1. They are the source and the cause of powerful driving effects from one to another, and their driving effect is as great with respect to other industrial branches. They are the basis of the process of "chemicalization" which, according to many writers, characterizes contemporary industry;
2. They constitute an essential factor in the filling out of the interindustry matrix;
3. They deliver products which are bearers of technical progress and thereby raise labor productivity and consequently the surplus in many sectors and thus contribute to the general goal of capital accumulation.

This coupling of metals' processing and of chemistry corresponds at the same time to the requirements peculiar to both of these industries, to the needs of agriculture, to those of the building up of capital in agreement with the

---

We merely mention as a reminder that many machine tools are still made in small batch production in the industrialized countries. It is with them that the start must be made, using, for instance, the experience of the socialist countries who have passed from the simplest types of machines to more sophisticated types, building on experience that had been progressively acquired (see Judet and J. Perrin's report on Hungary, quoted in footnote 27).

Moreover, it is striking to note that very often underdeveloped countries have a certain stock of machine tools that are very seldom used (teaching, repair workshops, etc.), and that the system would become more effective by rationalizing their use.

We must never forget a specific character that machine tools share with computers: it is the machine tools of one generation that make it possible to produce the more sophisticated machine tools of the following generation. They form a sector that carries within itself not only an internal quantitative dynamism (it is the only sector producing machines that can be used indifferently in this sector or others; they are really nonspecific capital goods) but also a qualitative dynamism, for it is within it or by it that the technical progress which will be diffused to the other sectors is achieved.

Generally, the dimensions of the production units that make them are not very big, which makes their organization easier. The problems brought up by the size of their markets are not more difficult than for other industries, and we shall deal with them along with those of the other industries.

European experience of the 19th century, and some positive development experiences in Latin American countries. So the remarks we may make, concerning the importance of capital-production or capital-labor ratios, optimum project dimensions, the timelags for conception, construction, and breaking in, lose their capacity of objections, but become stresses which demand all the greater exactness of execution. What good would it do to draw on surplus to set up industries with low capital coefficients, small dimensions, and short timelags, if such industries have only ridiculously small industrialization effects?

However, such an enumeration does not solve all the problems: the essential question of the *choice of techniques* has not yet been touched. This is not only a question of the degree of capital intensity,[25] as it was thought for far too long a time, but it is a much more central question of the internal coherence of the industrialization process, the place where the concept of "coherent industrial structure" is going to have its greatest impact. Indeed, the techniques chosen can have the following effects:

1. They can be adapted to the conditions which already exist in the economy undergoing industrialization or be the pure and simple transfer of the techniques used in the most highly industrialized countries, because they are the most adapted to such countries;[26]
2. They can foster coherence among the different national industrial sectors by calling upon the same types of techniques, or types of production capable of being developed on the spot or, on the contrary, entail a permanent and total dependence for each of the sectors, with respect to imported supplies; or
3. They can reduce or reinforce preexisting technological dependence.

Now, with modern industrial growth (more and more complex techniques, the massive nature of investments arranged around continuous processes, particularly in the fields of steelmaking and chemistry, etc.), the function of conception and realization which implements the choice of techniques has become increasingly important. It has finally acquired, in the framework of an increasing social division of labor, a role of its own as it has passed from the research departments of large firms to real *engineering companies* which are autonomous with respect to their clients.[27]

[25] Although Granick's distinction between central processes and auxiliary processes is essential to reduce the capital coefficients, provided that one is able to work within the framework of the social structures that stimulate worker productivity.

[26] Not with reference to geography in this case, but to the historically realized economic conditions. The work done by Jorge Sabato on this subject is particularly rich in concrete experience and in the lessons to be drawn from it (see footnote 11).

[27] Here we use the work done at the IREP under the direction of P. Judet on industrial engineering and particularly a series of stenciled notes [3, 13, 14, 15, 16, 23, 27, 32].

In turn, this development in industrial engineering has effects on industry, particularly on the equipment industry.[28] We must particularly emphasize two of them:

(a) An exact definition of the basic function of industrial engineering is called for. Borrelly defines it as "the building up of fixed capital, and even its production, if we admit that capital is an *arranged* whole and not only the sum total of nonconsumable goods." Consequently, as a work of conception (even if this is not followed by implementation) industrial engineering has an indispensable part to play in the production of capital. It is the intervention of such work in the production of capital which leads Judet to consider that this arranged whole which constitutes capital "results from an onerous arrangement. . . ." From this angle, industrial engineering is situated in the very center of the process of the production and building up of capital and, in the first place, of "industrial capital." In this way, too, industrial engineering intervenes in the heart of the industrialization process, since "beyond the factories and infrastructures it is commissioned to conceived and realize, it plays a leading part in the restructuring of a given economic and social complex under the influence of coherent systems of machinery."

Borrelly does not merely draw theoretical consequences from this analysis, no matter how important they may be.[29] It does not seem possible to reserve a separate sector for industrial engineering in a discussion of growth patterns, for it intervenes in the production of many different types of equipment, whatever their purpose may be. It seems preferable—on the level of growth patterns—to treat it along with the capital-producing sector, subject of course to

[28] Judet writes [13, p. 2]:

> In turn, engineering has an effective action on industry, particularly on the equipment industry. By furnishing its experience and its general view of the problems, industrial engineering enables the supplier to situate his equipment in the plant; it helps him to solve the problems of scale and with him it examines the systems of readjustment, automation, and safety which will be best adapted to the equipment required.
>
> On the other hand, engineering has had to perfect the methods made necessary by the complexity and dimension of the industrial units to be conceived and achieved, methods of calculation for industrial projects, and methods for the orderly evolution of the work; it has thus helped to endow industry with effective methods for organization and decision making.
>
> Industrial engineering is the fruit of industrial development; once created, in turn, it becomes a promotional factor of industry and particularly of equipment industries and of industries using advanced techniques. The example of several countries (Spain, Brazil) brings out the dynamic role played by engineering in industrialization.

[29] Questioning the hypotheses of the malleability of capital and of the "substitutability" between labor and capital [3].

discussing elsewhere its institutional organization.[30] But, under these conditions, it becomes evident that countries which want to become industrialized cannot contemplate the idea of entrusting the long-run task of industrial engineering to countries that are already industrialized. An industrialized country must endow itself with all the elements necessary for the progressive building up of its own capital resources.

(b) This necessity is all the more imperative as the further development of engineering strengthens the domination of the most powerful developed countries. In a certain way the kind of international dependence shifts and "goes from lower to higher, from consumer goods to capital goods, organized by engineering into complex units around modern processes. . . . Today, whole complexes of machinery and equipment are bought, and advanced countries try to keep the exclusive rights to supply them, thanks to departments of research and development and licences linked to their implementation." But above all, the recent development in the electronics and automation of industrial processes reinforces even more this dependence in favor of the specialized engineering companies in this field and of the countries where such organizations are developing at the present time: foremost the U.S.A., then Europe and Japan. Moreover, we note that the dominant country, the U.S.A., "sells very few industrial complexes, it sells only patents and licences and advanced techniques which ensure it an ever increasing preponderance" [13, p. 4].

Thus we have defined what the central nucleus of industrialization may be, and, in our opinion, it must take place within the general conditions prevailing at the present time. But it is also obvious that a definition of what is essential remains absolutely useless if not matched by a statement of the conditions without which industrialization is impossible. Then the reminder of the content of the nexus of a rapid industrialization policy will convey its full meaning: it is obvious that the conditions for its creation are not the same as those prevailing in the creation of other industries. It is a fact that the developed countries do not want the underdeveloped countries to have these "industrializing industries"[31] and the former are using the considerable means they still have to prevent the latter from getting them.

[30] One may conceive of either specialized types of industrial engineering linked to each of the sectors (a big oil company—Pemex, Sonatrach—may have its own industrial engineering department for its own work, or a concern building metalwork structures may create an engineering department for the handling of the orders it receives) with the advantages of a probably far greater dynamism and the risks arising from the difficulty of making the decisions reached in each sector more coherent; or a national engineering board depending, for instance, on the central planning authority with the inverse advantages and risks.

[31] Perhaps it is not impossible to use industrializing for "the industry or group of industries whose fundamental economic function is to entail in its localized and dated

Consequently, another unavoidable question crops up. When we reflect on how vigourously the neoclassical theory of international specialization still reigns triumphant in a large number of universities, it is necessary to ask whether it is economically rational to believe that the underdeveloped countries can become industrialized by starting from the nucleus which has just been mentioned.

We would almost be tempted to suggest that at the level of abstract rationality where the neoclassical school is traditionally situated, we must go even farther than the following three sets of perfectly established statements:

1. The productivity of agricultural labor is much higher in industrialized countries than in nonindustrialized ones, because farmers possess much more highly perfected equipment, but also because their history has led them to adopt a highly productive behavior and a professional technique which can only be reached very slowly by farmers in underdeveloped countries, by means of an evolution which will take several decades;

2. On the other hand, history proves that, subject to necessary adjustments [22, 30], industrial workers in underdeveloped countries very quickly reach a level of productivity comparable to that of workers in industrialized countries. When Ferrer [10] compared labor productivity in branches of industry using similar equipment in the U.S.A. and in different Latin American countries, he did not note any significant differences;

3. Finally, the underdeveloped countries possess considerable mineral resources on their own territory, those of the traditional industries (iron, copper), as well as those of the essential industries of today and tomorrow (hydrocarbons, oil, and, above all, natural gas, uranium, bauxite, etc.), whereas their arable lands are worked out and at the very limits of exhaustion, while that of the developed countries has always been kept in good condition and is astonishingly fertile. Among the former many tend to suffer shortages of water, whereas the latter maintain a very balanced supply, especially if they do not waste too much in industry.

Ricardo's own logic gives the solution to this problem: the so-called underdeveloped countries must (according to the rationality of our reasoning) be the site of the great industrial achievements of tomorrow and the day after tomorrow, while their industrialization will help to absorb the agricultural surpluses

---

vicinity a systematic filling in or a structural alteration of the interindustry matrix and of the changes in the productive functions by placing at the disposal of the general economy new complexes of machines which increase the productivity of one of the factors or overall productivity. In turn, these changes induce economic and social restructuring and a change in the behavior functions in the whole complex under consideration" (see Destanne de Bernis, a report presented at the 1st International Economic Congress of Córdoba [7]. This report contained a number of demonstrations which we have considered here as established facts).

of the temperate countries whose agricultural vocation becomes evident. First the great basic industries, and then the new industries whose technique is still unknown, are going to repair progressively to places where they will dispose of the best overall factory supplies. The countries which experienced the wave of industrialization in the 19th and 20th centuries will quickly exhaust their own natural resources (subject to the discovery of substitutes obtainable within their own territory). But they will be able to buy consumption goods from those others who will buy their wheat, fruit, and vegetables, thanks to the revenues they will get from an agricultural sector that will recover its prosperity if the equilibrium of the balance enables it to procure the equipment and chemicals which are absolutely necessary.[32] With this reserve, this agriculture need not fear that artificial substitutes, such as proteins from petroleum, will compete with it too soon, because the new industrialists will not waste either their time or their money on producing them, as they will be well aware that the old industrial countries can furnish them "natural" products on excellent terms of trade. Then, moreover, Samuelson's paradox will cease being paradoxical, the rates of remuneration of the factors will be equalized (this time at both ends of the chain), but later on it will stop being exact, for one is permitted to think that the remunerations will move away from equilibrium in an . . . unwanted . . . direction.

Unfortunately, the world monopolies still control world markets, and many underdeveloped countries let them control their resources and domestic markets. The realization of the more rational system just outlined is linked to a condition which we are obliged to call political, even if it is but the condition for the implementation of the worldwide collective advantage of the most perfectly liberal type. It is not inconceivable, even if the political situation of the world today makes it unrealistic, that all the underdeveloped countries would merely have to stop trading with the developed countries. We understand why the dominant countries try so hard to control the diplomatic services of the others as well as their system of alliances.

In all events, this fable or this utopia—but utopias are never useless—has put its finger on the nature of the conditions for a successful industrialization policy.

II. The Conditions for an Effective Industrialization Policy

None of the foregoing is very original and yet, the past twenty five years have been characterized by the radical failure of all the industrialization policies

[32] But bearing in mind the advice they lavished on the then underdeveloped countries in the days of their short-lived prosperity, their own experts will advise them to add to their agricultural activity, a tourist activity on a large scale. Of course, as had been the case, this activity will make no change whatsoever in the basic structural problem!

in the LDCs. The second "Decade of Development" will not contribute any more than the first one[33] did if the reasons for this failure are not analyzed, that is to say, if we do not go beyond the statement of what should be done by spelling out how it would be possible to reach the goal.

The above analysis, if made in isolation, would make the irreparable mistake of economism, by which we mean the error of isolating economic phenomena from political phenomena. This does not mean that we believe in determining the economic aspect of things by means of the political, if we deny the unrestricted determination of the second by the first. A certain autonomy of the political sphere confers on it the power to promote economic structures for the benefit of the dominant powers, to impose and maintain relations of production which block the development of the productive forces, and, as it happens, to prevent contradictions from reversing these social relations.

And it so happens that the conditions we must examine are situated at the point of contact between the political and the economic. In turn, their realization presupposes a profound change in the alignment of forces at the national and the international level.

But experience also shows that this change in the relations of forces is generated from the dogged struggle for the conquest of power, and this struggle itself is traceable to the first stages of industrialization. True economic independence appears as the result of a series of successive decisions which reinforce each other, the progressive construction of real national economic power and the building up of the sections capable of industrializing.[34]

In this sense, if the conditions we will enumerate below are logically prior, they will only be brought about progressively, some of them only being possible thanks to the early decisions of industrialization. But we are obliged to keep the dichotomy in mind, because the concrete way in which these measures will have to be implemented depends at all times on the momentary form of the concrete alignment of forces.

While keeping this in mind and without specifying any order or hierarchy among them, we shall distinguish between internal and external conditions. The latter—as history shows—are not necessarily more difficult or easier to deal with than the former. Very often, the internal structures of a dominated country result from the imposition of economic and social structures prior to independence by the system of external domination which grew up during the

[33] Most certainly the Pearson report is more optimistic. But once we integrate the value of the big oil firms' production into the GNP of Saudi Arabia, we cannot see why this product would not increase even faster than that of the industrialized countries that import oil: oil is becoming more and more important in the power schedules and the production of power increases faster than the GNP in the industrialized countries!

[34] The example of Algeria since 1962 could serve as an illustration of this dialectic argument.

colonial period, and so they may be extremely rigid. However, we shall merely enumerate the internal conditions very rapidly, for we do not want to let ourselves be tempted to develop the analysis of all the aspects of setting up "industrializing" industries. We want to come as quickly as possible to one of the points on which Prebisch particularly emphasizes.

A. Internal Conditions

Here we must tackle three groups of problems.

1. Social Structures

The *agrarian* economic and social structures must be profoundly modified in order to maximize the agricultural surplus. The concerns of a policy of agrarian reform are:

a. The regimes of land tenure;
b. The distribution of the latifundia;
c. The reorganization of the minifundia into cooperative societies of production;
d. The creation of structures capable of furnishing productive employment to farmers without land and without work.

But the *industrial* structures must also be adapted to the requirements of development. We must particularly underscore two essential imperatives.

On the one hand, the industries which make up the nucleus of the industrialization policy cannot be left to the hazardous principles of private maximization of profit, the more so if the owner or owners are foreigners. In the literal meaning of the term, these are activities for the common weal and only the state is in a position to administer them correctly by placing them at the service of the national community.

On the other hand, by the fact that the underdeveloped countries are obliged to economize on their scarce resources (constituted by capital) one must distinguish between the central processes—necessarily highly mechanized, or even automated—and the auxiliary processes in which the more labor-intensive techniques are advisable. This implies that the workers must be effectively induced to render sufficiently intense efforts. The material incentives may have their part to play, but they are never sufficient, if they alone exist.

It is in this connection that we must bring up the question of adapting machines to men. We cannot possibly think that this problem will be solved overnight. In capitalist countries, the separation between the worker and his tools suffices to explain why man must above all adapt himself to machines. The heritage of capitalism and the economic conditions prevailing in the world explain, but do not justify, why this essential question has not yet even begun to be answered. Let us merely note that the building up of an independent economy should not entirely neglect this aspect of the industrial problem.

2. Control of Essential Resources

The necessity for exactness in the triad:

a. maximization of the surplus,
b. maximization of the mobilized share of the surplus,
c. maximization of the effective utilization of the mobilized share of this surplus,

must result in a threefold form of control by the public authority:

a. Over the *natural resources*, which implies, in one form or another, the nationalization of mineral deposits and the direct control of their exploitation;[35]
b. Over the *distribution channels*, so that they may meet the targets of the plan and fulfill the function of mobilizing the surplus;
c. Over the *financing channels*, which implies the nationalization of insurance companies and banks, and with their reserves being in the hands of nationals, a very strict control by the state. The importance of financial planning cannot be stressed too much.

3. Exact Planning

This means the existence of an *authority* capable of exercising *power* over the productive apparatus, the commercial apparatus, and the financial apparatus.

B. External Conditions

These consist in throwing off the bonds of "vertical" dependence with respect to the dominant international powers as well as in building up "horizontal" partnership links with neighboring countries with comparable levels of development. This is for the common attainment of the targets which are indispensable for each of them, but which none of them can reach alone, except when its size is exceptional for an underdeveloped country.

[35] At the first Congress of the Association of Arab Economists (Algiers, October, 1970) on "Oil and Development," the Algerian delegation kept insisting on the necessity of putting an end to the oil-concession contracts.

1. The Radical Severance of the Bonds of Imperialist Dependence

The imperialist countries have a genius for cloaking these bonds of dependence under the pretext of sentimental or ideological relations (defense against communism, maintenance of order). Our attempt to be clear must bring out the central points of this dependence, and it is certain that in terms of "market logic" this breaking off cannot help being costly. Nevertheless, it remains the condition for true economic liberation.

Besides what has already been said about the control of natural resources, this breaking off implies:

a. The systematic choice of multilateral financing methods matched by guarantees;

b. The obtaining of guarantees concerning access to world markets for manufactured products as an offset against any sale of raw materials or "strategic products." Indeed, besides transforming the internal surplus into foreign exchange—the condition for obtaining industrial equipment—exports fulfill two other functions: (i) the smooth operation of big industrial complexes, and (ii) the maintenance of the "quality" of the products;

c. The systematic search for customers and suppliers among the other underdeveloped countries so as to develop progressively the conditions for an "alternative" to dependent trade relations.

Indeed, it is important to note that all the countries described as "underdeveloped" or "developing" (and about which it is useless to recall once again the fact that their levels of development vary widely) are able to supply one another with a large part of the goods that they get separately from the developed countries.

Practically without exception, this is a matter of course for foodstuffs. It is also a matter of course for consumer goods of industrial origin, which are the object of mass consumption.

The difficulties begin to appear in certain consumer goods reserved for that minority of people with high incomes, for which no "national" market could justify the setting up of local production. Without discussing here the usefulness of maintaining this type of consumption, we may consider either that the persistence of the traditional import inflows affords no major drawbacks, or that the outlets thus open to such industries now being installed here and there in the Third World would very soon justify their creation. But this remains a minor point in the dynamic we are trying to analyze.

The real difficulty appears with reference to capital goods, since this is where dependence on dominant countries makes itself most distinctly felt. This difficulty arises from the fact that these goods are generally considered as belonging to the field of the almost "natural" production of the developed countries, from the fact that they demand technical experience and highly skilled manpower still in very short supply in the underdeveloped countries, and finally from the fact that the "national" outlets for these goods remain too restricted for national production.

However, we must at once add that some Latin American countries are already making capital goods and that they could easily increase their productive capacity if they found outlets. In the same way, the experience of the European socialist countries with the most backward industries, 20 years ago, shows that it is possible to accede very rapidly to industries of this type once a country is linked to a large market. Finally, it does not seem that so far all the possible or desirable advantages have been drawn from the existence of UNIDO, whose explicit task is to promote the industrial development of underdeveloped countries.

We cannot ignore the fact that the dominance of the great capitalist monopolies is based on pressure groups inside each country, and that they can thus block the development of "horizontal" exchanges (between countries at the same level of development), but we are not giving proof of a disparaging attitude when we wonder whether the governments of the underdeveloped countries themselves do not also have a certain responsibility, for instance, when they draw up their trade policy and sign their trade pacts.

The fact remains that such a policy on a worldwide scale is difficult to implement, considering the repeated interventions of the imperialist forces. That is why it is indispensable to envisage in a more immediately realistic way the types of cooperation needed among neighboring countries, making up one and the same "region" of nations.[36]

2. Regional Economic Integration

A kind of regional cooperation whose different dimensions must be set forth very exactly seems to us to be an absolutely essential condition for the setting up of these "industrializing industries." At the same time, the analysis of the content of such cooperation allows us to predict the effect of industrialization at a more concrete level. It is certainly not by chance that Prebisch has been led to insist more and more on the imperative of regional cooperation.

It has been said—and in our opinion without exaggerating—that most underdeveloped countries do not have the choice between industrialization by means of mutual cooperation or on their own. The only real choice open to them is between industrialization in common and nonindustrialization:

[36] Here we use the term "region" in its usual geographical meaning. In the language of the United Nations, one must speak of "subregions" or even only of regional complexes of countries. It is in the latter meaning only that we shall use the term of "region" so as to use a simpler language.

1. Cooperation is the condition for escaping from the network of "unequal" relations or for acquiring the power to negotiate less unequally;

2. Cooperation is the only solution for the contradiction, so often analyzed by Perroux, between the development of modern industries, which are technically large scale, and the market dimensions of the underdeveloped countries, which are often very small;[37]

3. Some operations indispensable for industrialization cannot be carried out in the spatial framework delimited by frontiers which, whatever their history may be, may have no significance with respect to these operations (stamping out certain diseases, agrarian and industrial development of river basins, etc.);

4. Regional "common markets" do not furnish a satisfactory answer to this problem, for they are often merely the organization, on behalf of the locally dominant power, of a large market for its own products. It is a very different case for regional organizations that implement "common policies" in "specific sectors."

Finally, such regional cooperation is imperative because it gives the industrialization policy both a "*spatial*" coherence and a *temporal* coherence, when what we have described as "coherent industrial structure" is set up.

The following analysis of this spatial and temporal coherence is not only a detailed statement of the conditions for an industrial policy, it is also a new way of approaching the effects of industrialization.

Spatial coherence. Regional cooperation cannot be promoted by installing in a single spot all the industries necessary for the industrialization of all the countries in the region. Indeed, three considerations are opposed to this, all somewhat different in nature but still complementary.

As long as the cooperating countries remain sovereign, each one of them must watch after its own balance of payments.

No country would accept complete dependence on another for all its industrial production. The fact that each would have effective control over key parts of the common edifice is a guarantee of stability of the mutual consensus.

Finally, and perhaps most importantly, in a plan of regional development embracing a vast area, no single industrial center would be able to induce

[37] Most certainly there are hopes of making a breakthrough in the field of the miniaturization of techniques, and the success of the "mini-ironworks" is a proof of this assertion. But these new techniques can be perfected only within the framework of centers for technical research which, in turn, will be effective only if they are built on the scale of several countries having identical problems to be solved.

This effort to find new techniques will not be limited to the question of miniaturization: it should include everything that conditions the full utilization of the local technical resources.

UNIDO should be able to furnish valuable help for the creation and the operating of such research centers.

industrialization effects that would diffuse in all directions to the limits of the said region. Experience proves that a given space with sufficiently large dimensions can only become truly industrialized (the overall political and social preconditions having been fulfilled in other respects), when it is enmeshed in a network of complementary exchanges among a small number of essential poles of development.[38]

So, from the outset, we must envisage the technical and economic coherence of our industrial structure as being reinforced by spatial coherence, that is to say, expanding as it were, in the multinational space, with regard to the three stresses that have just been enumerated. This spatial coherence must make itself felt by achieving a *specialization* of each of the industrial centers envisaged in the zone, it being understood that this *is* a specialization of the industrial centers and not of the countries.[39]

In the first stages of development—for instance, for some African regions—this specialization will have to be of the *inter*sectoral type. But very soon, and in any case when the first stages of industrialization have been passed (as is already the case in many Latin American regions), this specialization will have to have an *intra*sectoral character. Without even mentioning the metallurgical or mechanical engineering industries, the steel industry alone will have to provide widely different products (structural iron, sheets, tubes, and special steels, only to mention a few of the main categories). And above all, what can be said about

[38] So the pattern to be created implies that we take into account: (a) the minimal reduction of the technical operating costs of the complex and of each of its elements (losses of heat, for instance); (b) the transport costs whose total (between the elements of the complex then between these elements and the ultimate consumers) must be minimized, subject to solving the problem of the other stresses, and (c) industrialization effects which must be such that their diffusion entails progress in each of the points of the regional area under consideration.

Without any doubt, the traditional econometric patterns have difficulty in taking these different elements into account. The progress made in the method of graphs can help to shape concrete questions systematically and to seek solutions (see the pattern realized at the IREP, Grenoble, on the optimization of the system of power-producing equipment in E.E.C. by the year 2000 and Ponsard [25].

[39] One can indeed envisage the reconstitution of an international division of labor in which some will provide the agricultural produce, others the products of the mining industries, whereas others would have only a university, and finally one alone would have all the industry. We would then witness the return of the phenomena of unequal development and of the domination of the one or several countries, and this would very quickly become unbearable for the former. This risk would be particularly great in a vast region, which would be a victim at the outset of many dislocations.

This specialization will have to make allowance for a number of factors, for those that are taken into account in Ricardo's theory, but also for these activities that already exist and for the political stresses that cannot be eliminated. It is not a matter of saying that they are costly or that they are irrational elements. They exist, and the fact that they must be considered is the condition for effectiveness.

an endeavor like the chemical industry? If some technical considerations imply the regrouping of certain types of closely-linked production in the same locale, there are many, on the other hand, for which such a regrouping is not technically necessary.

So, several countries can each develop several lines of production among the industrializing industries, but inside each of these branches they will undertake (or further develop, for those that already have the beginnings of an industrial base) only the production of certain products or groups of specific products, and they will buy the others from the other centers of the region.

Agoston notes that this type of specialization "is particularly important for the development of mechanical, chemical, and metallurgical (ferrous and non-ferrous) industries.... The basic conditions for specialization in these branches are: standardization of products and specialization in standard types; and maximum development of all the raw materials and energy-producing materials existing in the countries" [1, p. 120].

It is neither necessary nor possible for us to dwell upon the procedures to be followed in this regard. We should like to limit ourselves to two main remarks:

(a) The first technical condition for this intrasectoral specialization in the field of mechanical engineering (and it is also one of its most obvious advantages) is the reduction in the number of types and models for everything concerning machines, tractors, transport vehicles, commercial vehicles, etc.

An excellent image of the "lists," which occur in the underdeveloped countries, where the major firms of the dominant powers tilt at one another in their competitive struggle is, indeed, that of the mosaic of machines of all sorts (tractors, trucks, and machinery, generally ill adapted rather than well adapted) and of all the makes to be found there. A sign of external domination, this situation is also the cause of other bottlenecks: there may be a shortage of component parts or no skilled repairmen (the existing ones may be accustomed to another make), and so the machine can no longer be used due to some minor detail. The dealer profits by this, and his agency more often than not carries new stock rather than spare parts, but here we have the source of very obvious wastefulness.

More and more countries are strictly limiting the number of makes of vehicles and machinery authorized for import. This measure is the first step on the way to making a policy of integration and intrasectoral specialization easier to achieve.

(b) In particular, such specialization constitutes an imperative condition for the production of essential industrial equipment in the region that is being industrialized. Here moreover, we must make a distinction between what we shall call the industries producing specific capital equipment (for other basic industries), and those producing machine tools, strictly speaking.

Martin, in his article from which we have already quoted, shows how regional economic integration can enable modern power stations to exert powerful upward effects, in so far as the total power-producing equipment to be set up within the whole area justifies the existence of a type of plant that would not be justified in individual installations of each country taken separately. This example can and must be generalized to all kinds of specific equipment (capital goods which are situated at the intermediate stages of capital production between nonspecific capital goods, such as the universal machine tool, and the production units of chemistry, power, mechanical engineering, etc.). The region as a whole will thus be in a position to produce its own equipment for mines, blast furnaces, smelting works, rolling mills, the chemical industry, etc. The fabrication of these different products demands operations that are sufficiently varied so as to justify their not all being made in the same place.

As for the machine-tool industry, it must complete this process of the regional production of equipment, to allow the region to master technical innovations as soon as they become available, enable it to adapt the production processes to regional conditions, and determine, by itself, the rate of acquisition of its real capital.

Such units can be set up only on the basis of intrasectoral specialization.

Of course, the fact that we have asserted that these industrial centers must be correctly situated in space does not deny the eventual existence of a hierarchy among the chief centers (for instance, a spatial concentration in the early stages of the production process) and the secondary centers. Otherwise, a coherent structure would no longer exist. But, in this way we see the concept of relays appears, since each of the centers created can serve as a relay to diffuse further the industrialization effects emitted by the overall industrial structure.[40] The concept of relays is useful not only to help us to establish the spatial coherence of the system, but in other ways as well.

Temporal coherence. Full industrialization, as well as the setting up of the first coherent network of industrializing industries, will take time. The timelags must be made as short as possible and be exploited with maximum effectiveness. It is also by starting with these timelags that we can determine the stages necessary for regional construction.

(a) *The temporal relays.* When timelags are inevitable—for instance, for really compelling material reasons—the relay mechanism must serve in preventing too serious imbalances from appearing or by then allowing the real industrializing pole to act that much faster. It will also have to play the same

[40] The industrialization relay would then be defined, in this spatial perspective alone, as a center of secondary importance capable of picking up an industrialization effect that is too diffuse to be effective, of giving it greater intensity, and then of propagating it more effectively in the immediate vicinity of the "relay."

role of preparation to begin the next step in an area which has gone beyond a given stage of modernization or industrialization.

(i) *The preinvestment relay.* We shall start from a concrete example: It may be thought that in West Africa, two steel-making units should be built, one on the coast, the other inland. The optimal site for the inland steel center is near the future hydroelectric dam of Gouina (Mali). But the completion of the preliminary surveys and the duration of the construction work on this dam are such that one cannot hope to see it become operational before a timelag of eight to ten years. Of course, this timelag can be cut down as far as possible by adapting the work so that the steel plant and the dam will become operational at about the same time. But it may happen that the coastal factory will take far less time to become operational.

Whatever the present decisions may be, it will be impossible to prevent the coastal factory (which will have begun delivering steel) from exerting industrialization effects on its zone of influence, and so from running the risk of creating cumulative imbalances which increase the retardation of the hinterland and, what is far more serious, the risk of compromising overall development possibilities.

Without there being any question of mere prestige, for sound economic reasons, it is therefore important to be able to set up a relay in the hinterland. Now, for reasons of distance and communications, on the one hand, and, on the other hand, because of the size of the coastal center in relation to its natural zone of influence the hinterland relay cannot be set up by starting from the coastal center. So even if techniques adapted to small-scale production are used, it may be necessary to set up a small steel works with a production, for instance, of 30,000 tons per year (based on medium quality iron ore and lignite or else on electricity by building at once one of the dams on the Félou, which will acquire fuller significance later on when the whole complex is developed).

Either of these relays or both of them—it will be necessary to determine which is the more effective—will have three functions to fulfill:

1. A direct and obvious function is that of furnishing at once a certain quantity of steel in the hinterland so as to avoid cumulative imbalances; we need not come back to this point;
2. There is also a preinvestment function with reference to the future dam (even if the solution of a temporary dam on the Félou is not chosen) since the structure can be built with steel produced within the zone itself; from then on a partial balance is established, even if the cost of the steel from the relay unit is higher than it would be from the larger works; the solution of an electric furnace with a dike on the Félou offers the additional advantage that it can be purely and simply integrated into the big works that are planned;
3. Another function of the preparation of the structures in the zone is to

receive a large quantity of steel; indeed, by putting 250–300,000 tons per year in one sweep at the disposal of an area which has never produced any steel before, there is a risk of making bottlenecks appear at certain stages of the processing, consequently, the first deliveries made by the relay unit can make it possible to work out the necessary technical details more smoothly.

We present this example only to illustrate these preinvestment functions. Such relay functions can be conceived in many ways. Thus, such and such a hydroelectric dam[41] could not possibly be justified under the present level of anticipated demand for electricity at the focus of the generating station. Successive additions of small nuclear energy plants, which can be quickly paid off, might very easily raise demand to a level that will progressively justify the existence of the dam. It may even be possible to set them up at the production facilities, which will help in the construction of the dam and thus cut its cost considerably. Different techniques may thus reinforce one another within the framework of the overall plan. But we already see that we are passing progressively from the preinvestment relay to the relay preparing for another stage of industrialization.

(ii) *The relay preparing for a further stage of industrialization.* It is not necessary to insist on this point, but we must note that, as usual, development problems must be envisaged within a dynamic framework. Once industrialization has begun, we cannot forget that our problem will still be to act in such a way that the process may continue as rapidly as possible.

If the development of industrialization is then achieved, the result will be a constant improvement in technique, productivity, and, consequently, in the consumption of industrial products. The relay first set up to fulfill the functions we have set forth will then be able to play a more and more important part and multiply its operations. In the area where it is situated, the effects of the conglomeration will soon be felt. Ultimately, its task will be to involve itself more deeply in the systems of *junctions* between the poles and to become a real industrial center, linked to the great poles, which will in turn see their own role advancing toward ever greater intrasectoral specialization, thanks to this promotion of relays.

On the other hand, we must now consider—though briefly—a definition of the stages necessary for this construction.

(b) *Stages in the attainment of regional cooperation.* Sometimes a certain radicalism may lead one at the outset to envisage a plan common to all the countries concerned, or at least a greater coordination of the plans. From a theoretical point of view and also from the most concrete experience, this position seems both unrealistic and abstract. Indeed, on the morrow of the

[41] That is to say, the Inga dam in Congo-Kinshasa.

independence of such countries, one might have thought such coordination and regrouping would take place very quickly. This overlooked, however, the fact that pre-occupation with national "construction" was going to prevail everywhere[42] and witnessed the breakup or the precarious state of the most carefully thought out attempts (Federation of Mali, The Ghana–Guinea–Mali Union, the U.A.R., etc.). It seems to be the most flexible types of co-operation that are viable.

Impatience is proof of a lack of realism. Social realities can only be transformed slowly in a progressive dialectic of structures and mentalities. But the structures proceed too far ahead of the mentalities, just as the latter cannot develop unless something in the former incites them to do so. There exists a pedagogy of multinational cooperation, just as there is an indispensable general pedagogy for development. By respecting the stages, one is sure to achieve effectiveness.[43]

We can, so it seems, distinguish three stages if we accept to make an approximate, or even rough analysis. Discussing the European experience, Bye distinguished the stages of harmonization, of common policies, and of "com-

[42] This is why we were compelled to think that, as a result of the conversations which had taken place in Tunis or Rabat during the Algerian war between the GPRA and the governments of these two capitals, the Great United Maghreb would come into being with the independence of Algeria.

[43] Everybody knows the precision of the stages during the realization of the E.E.C., and the principle of proceeding by stages has just been reasserted in connection with the passage to the monetary union.

On this subject, the experience of Comecon is also interesting. Even if we cannot make a more subtle analysis, let us be content with saying that until 1960–1962, it was a matter of "attempts to coordinate bilateral trade pacts and technical and scientific aid" at first, then of denouncing sources of wastefulness resulting from misappreciation of the criteria of economic rationality in the matter of prices, costs, orientation of exchanges, setting up of antagonistic equipments, as well as of the damage caused by economic nationalism." Since 1960–1962, a second stage has been undertaken: if, in the short term, priority is given to simple coordination, which is also a form of rationalizing what exists, even if it is a superior form, "it does seem that in the long run, community priority, adopting the form of specialization, should tend to have a more coercive aspect than is yet the case." And we know that the third stage, which was recently begun, has given rise to many reservations that could not possibly be dispelled at one sweep, at a time when the ideological community provides a much stronger basis for common orientations than what we can envisage in other regions of the world. Finally, we must add that considerable aid has been given by the U.S.S.R. particularly to the least industrialized countries or the smallest ones (for instance, Roumania and Bulgaria), a situation that cannot be experienced by regions whose member-countries are all at the same level of underdevelopment.

These quotations are taken from Caire's study [5]. On this subject we can also consult Kaiser [17], Agoston [1], [6], and Emmanuel [9].

munity planning".[44] We cannot transpose the experience of industrialized countries to a group of countries which are trying to lay the foundations of their industrialization, and the content of each of these phases could not possibly be the same. We are nevertheless very much aware of the formal similarity of the analysis we are proposing with Bye's analysis when we distinguish between: (a) a pure and simple rationalization of that which already exists, (b) a policy of common goals and regional specialization, and (c) the harmonization and then the general coordination of the plans.

These three stages are deeply dependent on one another and, in a way, are only abstract "names" to designate the short term, medium term, and long term or very long term targets. Each can be given some concrete content.

The rationalization of that which exists requires a true desire to cooperate, a desire to exploit existing equipment to its best advantage, the suppression of too disruptive discrepancies across national frontiers, etc. A rationalization of that which exists would at least put a stop to the process of balkanization within certain regions and would already help to bring about a considerable improvement in the balance of each country with reference to the dominant nation. This is not a question of just any policy of regional free trade and in particular it excludes the possibility that this may be the best way of organizing the regional market as an outlet for the dominant outside nation. We are very, very far from the harmonization of the coordination of the plans, even more so from a system of "regional" planning, and in the present state of the nonindustrialized economies that we know, the latter may seem to be very much lacking in realism.

The essential goal of the common realizations or of regional specialization will have to be the creation of industrializing industries,[45] prepared during the preceding stage. Actual harmonization and then the coordination of national plans can only follow later on.

But, if these stages must be distinguished in order to analyze the general process of industrialization, let us not conclude for all that, that this process can be linear or automatic. Each stage will condition the following one but will not necessarily give rise to it. Consequently, it is not the general process of integration that we should study now but its strategic phase. Of course, the

[44] We know that he defined *integration* as the action which consists in "making as compatible as possible the plans of the decision centers which make up (the whole that is being integrated)" [4].

[45] We can easily go back to the definition of international specialization given by Vajda, "The commitment made by a country—on the basis of bi- or multilateral international agreements—for the priority development of a branch of production or of products so as to satisfy, not only its own needs, but also those of the other countries participating in the agreement, in return for which the other contracting parties give up the production of the specialized products" [31, p. 29].

rationalization of what exists must come first, but it depends on the lucid good will of the participants and is only the beginning of a system of cooperation. (let us say a declaration of intentions put down in concrete form). True cooperation will only begin with the policy of common realizations and industrial specialization, and it is only this stage that will introduce a structural alteration capable of creating productive developments later on. It is this stage and this stage alone that we have considered here, in order to try and begin the study of its possible content. Indeed, if the industrializing industries are grounded on the industrialization process and if they cannot be set up within the framework of economically isolated states, they must be the first goal of the specialization envisaged.

Finally, we are faced with a twofold dynamic, whose elements are closely dependent on one another, the dynamic of industrialization which is based on, and gives a content to, the dynamic of integration itself. The meeting between the two takes place, above all, during this specific phase of the integration process, which is the beginning of specialization and during the specific phase of the industrialization process, which consists in setting up industrializing industries. Without denying the possibility of nonnecessity in passing from one stage to another, we have the right to think that their inception at the same time reinforces the chance of seeing them come to a successful conclusion.

So we are able to conclude by formulating another question and by trying to furnish an element of the answer.

The fact that the gap has progressively widened between the developed and underdeveloped countries is not due to chance or ignorance, but to imperialism.[46] So it is difficult to consider such an industrialization policy without wondering whether it is feasible within the framework of imperialism as it now exists. To this question, a negative answer seems to be in order. But if we were content with such an answer, we should remain at the pre-analytical stage.

Imperialism is not a homogeneous and coherent whole. Three remarks must be made about it:

1. First of all, it is the ground of conflicting interests. If it is in the interest of the overall imperialist structure to maintain underdevelopment, certain groups *within* the structure of imperialism are nonetheless under attack by other more powerful ones, and may discover a specific interest in a policy favoring the sale of equipment or making investments which can be clearly favorable to an industrialization policy of the underdeveloped countries.

2. Likewise, imperialism is made up of a complex of links, and some of them are weaker than others. Even apart from the contradictions between French imperialism and American imperialism, it is easier for Algeria to escape progressively from the domination of the French economy than might be the case with respect to a more powerful nation.

[46] On the nature of the latter, we must go back to Lenin's initial works and for their application to the present world to those of Palloix [24] and Frank.

3. Finally, imperialism has global weaknesses, that is to say its need for outlets[47] or its need for raw materials. Even if, in their isolation, the underdeveloped countries cannot exploit this weakness, their mutual understanding gives them real effectiveness. The recent Teheran negotiations are, of course, very interesting due to the obvious and immediate results obtained. We find them even more interesting because they are both the first manifestation of a real understanding among the producing countries and the first setback for the companies belonging to the Cartel. In this way, a new dynamic asserted itself, and if the producing countries maintain the unity which has already paid off, we have the right to consider that it is now possible to question the regime of the concessions. This example will be followed in other fields.

Of course, here again, no movement will be exactly linear, and imperialism will develop other means of defense and aggression. But, from stage to stage, without running the risk of erring by "economism" and, more specifically, provided that there is never any denial of the fundamentally political dimension of the industrialization policy, it will be up to political economy to analyze the weaknesses and contradictions of imperialism in order to devise the means of overthrowing it.

REFERENCES

[1] Agoston, I., "Le marché commun communiste, principes et pratique du Comecon," 2nd ed. Droz, Geneva, 1965.

[2] Bettelheim, Ch., "Calcul économique et formes de propriété," Maspéro, Paris, 1970.

[3] Borrelly, R., L'engineering, quelques éléments pour une analyse théorique, *I.R.E.P.*, Grenoble (September 1970), cyclostyled.

[4] Byé, M., "Relations économiques internationales," 3rd ed. Dalloz, Paris, 1971.

[5] Caire, G., Problèmes de planification supranationale au sein du bloc socialiste, Paris (1969), cyclostyled.

[6] Centre d'etudes de planification socialiste, Le commerce extérieur dans l'économie socialiste, *Problèmes de planification*, no. 8, Paris, EPHE, cyclostyled.

[7] de Bernis, G. Destanne, Industries industrialisantes et contenu d'une politique d'intégration régionale, *Economie Appliquée* (July–December 1966; January–March 1968).

[8] Domar, E. D., "Essays in the Theory of Economic Growth," Oxford Univ. Press, London and New York, 1957.

[9] Emmanuel, A., La division internationale du travail et le marché socialiste, *Problèmes de planification*, no. 7, Paris, cyclostyled.

[10] Ferrer, A., "La economia argentina." Fondo de Cultura Economica, Mexico, 1963.

[11] Hoffmann, E. G., "The Growth of Industrial Economies." Manchester Univ. Press, Manchester, New Hampshire, 1958.

[12] I.R.E.P., Développement industriel et production agricole en Algérie, Grenoble (December 1969), cyclostyled.

[47] We are not lapsing into Luxembourg and Steinberg's analysis if we consider that the imperialist countries need outside or preliminary markets' outlets. This does not imply that they have no other ways of maintaining their domination.

[13] Judet, P., Engineering et industrialisation, *I.R.E.P.*, Grenoble (October 1970), cyclostyled.
[14] Judet, P., Siderurgie, évolutions techniques et engineering, Report presented at the 1st Seminar for the Development of Steel Making in the Arab Countries (December 1970).
[15] Judet, P., and Perrin, J., Planification des industries mécaniques et situation de l'engineering en Hongrie, *I.R.E.P.*, Grenoble (December 1970), cyclostyled.
[16] Judet, P., Perrin, J., and Tiberghien, R., L'engineering, *I.R.E.P.*, Grenoble (May 1970), cyclostyled.
[17] Kaiser, M., "Comecon, Integration Problems of the Planned Economics." Oxford Univ. Press, London and New York, 1965.
[18] Leontief, W., *et al.*, "Studies in the Structure of the American Economy." Oxford Univ. Press, London and New York, 1953.
[19] Mahalanobis, P. C., The Approach of Operational Research to Planning in India, *Sankhya, Indian J. Stat.*, **16**, Parts 1 and 2 (December 1955).
[20] Mahalanobis, P. C., "Talks on Planning," Indian Statistical Series No. 14. Asia Publishing House, New York and Calcutta, 1961.
[21] Martin, J. M., Les centres d'énergie facteurs d'intégration economique, *Economie Appliquée* (July–December 1966).
[22] Morgault, M. E., "Pour un nouveau dialogue: l'Afrique et l'industrie," Fayard, Paris, 1959.
[23] Palloix, C., L'engineering, quelques orientations de travail, *I.R.E.P.*, Grenoble (September 1970), cyclostyled.
[24] Palloix, C., "L'économie mondiale capitaliste," Maspero, Paris, 1971.
[25] Ponsard, C., "Un modèle topologique d'équilibre économique interrégional." Dunod, Paris, 1969.
[26] Prebisch, R., Change and Development, Latin America's Great Task. Report submitted to the Interamerican Bank, Washington (1970).
[27] Roberts, J., L'engineering en Inde, *I.R.E.P.*, Grenoble (November 1970), cyclostyled.
[28] Spulber, N., ed. "Foundations of Soviet Strategy for Economic Growth, Selected Soviet Essays, 1924–1930," 2nd ed. Indiana Univ. Press, Bloomington, Indiana, 1965.
[29] Stoleru, L., An Optimal Policy for Economic Growth, *Econometrica* (May 1967).
[30] Trystram, J., L'ouvrier mineur marocain, Rabat, 1960.
[31] Vajda, I., "Le commerce extérieur socialiste. Le C.A.E.M. et la division internationale socialiste du travail." Budapest, 1963.
[32] de la Vega Navarro, A., La société nationale mexicaine Pemex et l'engineering, *I.R.E.P.* (December 1970), cyclostyled.
[33] Younès, Y., La théorie du capital, Paris (1963), typescript.

THE CONTRIBUTION OF FOREIGN TRADE TO NATIONAL INCOME

VICTOR JORGE ELIAS

Universidad Nacional de Tucumán, Tucumán, Argentina

I

How to measure the different elements which explain the growth in income has lately been a constant concern for a group of economists who have used tools such as production functions and productivity indexes for the purpose.

In their early essays, they found that the direct application of the production function, with inputs measured according to the traditional methods, could only account for 40–50% of this income growth. This resulted in the difficult problem of explaining the difference. Since that time several hypotheses have been developed in order to identify the so-called "residual," and to that end economists have appealed to different specifications of the production function, improved the measurement of capital and labor inputs (taking into account errors in measurement, changes in quality, etc.), and have considered the problem of specifying the best means for aggregating products, inputs, etc.

In some countries, the development of such a methodology led, after a time, to an almost complete identification of the elements which "explained" the residual mentioned above. This made us think about the problem posed at the beginning, that is, whether it was completely elucidated or not.

Many economists working in the field of international trade have tried to emphasize the role of foreign trade in the economic growth of a country. Some of them are particularly interested in stressing trade as one of the principal alternatives for developing countries; this is achieved by means of various models of an open economy and the application (from a static point of view) of the theory of comparative advantage.

These are the reasons which induced us to tackle the problem of how the foreign trade component of growth should be incorporated into the "growth accounting" methodology. From this we expect to provide an insight into how much this sector can contribute in the future to the economic growth of a given country.

In the first part of the paper, we attempt formally to incorporate the foreign sector in an explanation of the growth of income, which operates through the terms of trade effect, so that we get an implicit definition of it. In the second part, we will discuss an alternative model emerging from the protectionist policies followed by almost every country (we will try to relate this to the first analysis). Finally, we have made a limited empirical study for Argentina to see how our results operate.

II

The income of a given country for a certain period of time can be broken down into goods that remain within the country and commodities used as exports to get goods from abroad (both locally produced). For both products a production function is defined, from which we get the following definition of income:

$$Y = D(L, K) + T \cdot X(L, K), \tag{1}$$

where the variables are defined as follows:

- Y national income;
- D real value of the goods that remain in the domestic market (net of foreign inputs);
- X real value of the export goods (net of foreign inputs);
- T terms of trade;
- L labor input;
- K capital input.

Next, consider the relative rate of change of Y to identify its components and to evaluate the importance of the foreign sector. Lower case letters will be used to represent relative rate of changes. For example, if

$$y = \frac{1}{Y}\frac{dY}{dt},$$

then

$$y = w_D a_D l_D + w_D b_D k_D + w_X a_X l_X + w_X b_X k_X + w_X t, \tag{2}$$[1]

[1] t represents here the relative rate of change of T.

where the variables are defined as follows:

w share of D and TX in Y;
a share of labor input in D and X;
b share of capital input in D and X.

In the last two cases it is implicitly assumed that the factor markets are in equilibrium.

This formulation only makes clear the contribution of foreign trade and not that of the whole foreign sector, which is the reason we concentrate mainly on T. Other contributions of the foreign sector in general are reflected on capital movements (which are incorporated in K), or through knowledge of new technologies (which can be identified through qualitative changes in inputs). Our model can be adjusted for these cases.

Now let us discuss how to measure t, on which we are going to put our main empirical effort for the time being. It is implicitly defined from the balance of trade definition

$$\sum_i P_i M_i = B \sum_j Q_j X_j, \tag{3}$$

where the variables are defined as follows:

P_i, M_i prices and quantities of import goods;
Q_j, X_j prices and quantities of export goods;
B *relative* balance of trade ($B = 1$ when the balance of trade is settled or imports equal exports in value).

By taking the relative rate of change of Eq. (3), we have

$$\sum_i w_i(p_i + m_i) = \sum_j v_j(q_j + x_j) + b, \tag{4}$$

where w_i measures the relative weight of $P_i M_i$ in the total of imports, and v_j is the relative weight of $Q_j X_j$ in the total of exports.

From Eq. (4) we get the implicit definition of t

$$\sum_i w_i m_i - \sum_j v_j x_j - b = \sum_j v_j q_j - \sum_i w_i p_i, \tag{5}$$

where

$$t = \sum_j v_j q_j - \sum_i w_i p_i \tag{6}$$

or its dual,

$$t = \sum_i w_i m_i - \sum_j v_j x_j - b. \tag{7}$$

In using Eq. (6) to measure t we have to express P and Q in CIF and FOB terms, respectively. These expressions for t imply a definition of T by M/BX or Q/P, where its components represent a certain kind of aggregation, due to the fact that t is a *Divisia* index [2].

III

In measuring t we might have various problems due to the poor data quality for the foreign sector, and to government intervention in this sector through tariffs, exchange control, quotas, etc. All of these might cause important errors in the measurement of P and Q, so that we will obtain biased estimate of T. For example, suppose that instead of observing q and p, we observe q' and p', defined as

$$p_i' = p_i + c_i, \tag{8}$$

$$q_j' = q_j + d_j. \tag{9}$$

Therefore

$$t' = \sum_j v_j' q_j' - \sum_i w_i' p_i', \qquad t' = t + s, \tag{10}$$

where the bias s is given by:

$$s = \sum_j v_j' d_j - \sum_i w_i' c_i + \sum_j (v_j' - v_j) q_j + \sum_i (w_i - w_i') p_i. \tag{11}$$

The variables c and d involve different kinds of official intervention, such as tariffs, exchange controls, etc. What counts is the measurement of the price that the *country* pays for its imports (not the importers' prices) and the price that the *country* receives for her exports (not the exporters' prices).

It is interesting to observe that we also have the problem of quality changes in the import and export goods. In one respect, we can say that these changes are included in c and d. Having this in mind, we can predict the sign of s for certain countries due to the particular composition of their import and export goods and the kind of protectionist policy they have followed (for example, in the Argentine case we can predict a negative bias).

IV

The advantage which is offered by foreign trade could have been enjoyed totally or only in part, due to official interventions in the foreign sector through different kinds of controls. Since we have previously considered terms of trade variation, we disregard that question here.

We may obtain some idea of the degree of proficiency of the advantages of foreign trade through an index of the discrepancy which exists between the domestic and world prices for the different products. This discrepancy purports to represent the difference between internal and external costs, which represents resource misallocation (we leave out some dynamic aspects of the problem on which some arguments are based in favor of protectionist policies, even though part of it will be implicitly considered).

Due to the fact that foreign trade also includes intermediate goods and that there are some domestic distortions, the discrepancy between domestic and world prices does not reflect cost differences alone. To make this clear, we present three cases: (a) in Fig. 1, we present a case of trade in final import goods; (b) Fig. 2 presents a case of final export goods; (c) Fig. 3 presents a case in which the production of importables utilizes some foreign inputs which are also subject to tariffs. Here, P^D and P^W are the domestic and world prices for import goods, respectively; and Q^D and Q^W are the domestic and world prices for export goods, respectively.

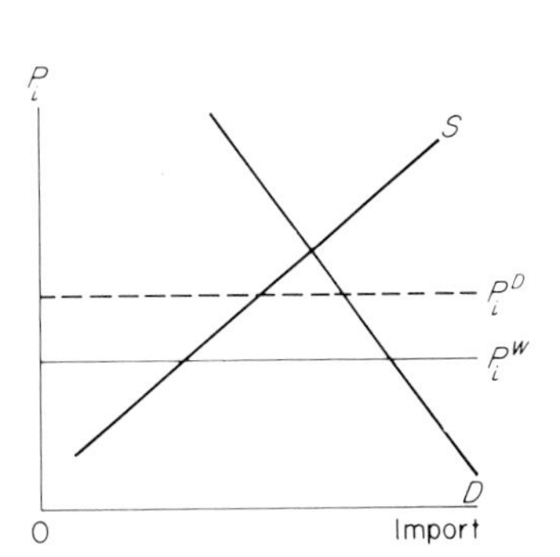

Fig. 1. Import of final goods.

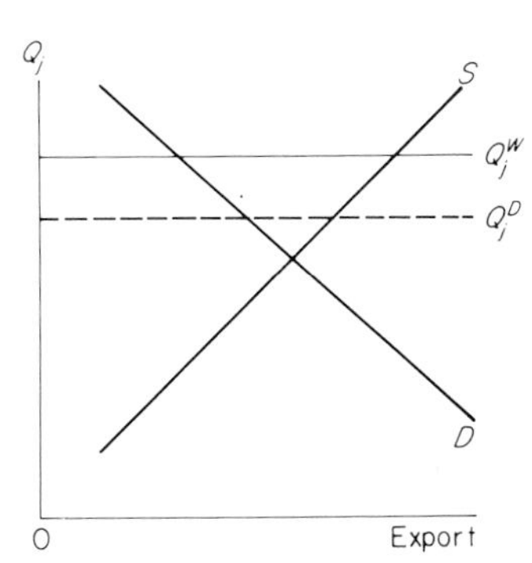

Fig. 2. Export of final goods.

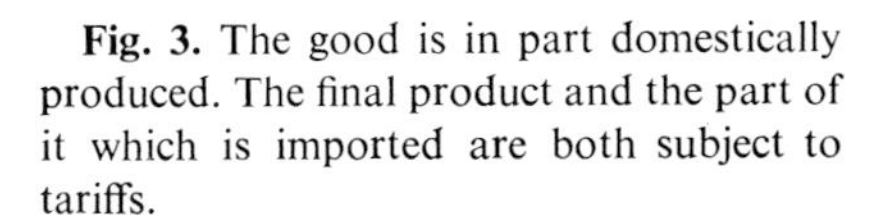
Fig. 3. The good is in part domestically produced. The final product and the part of it which is imported are both subject to tariffs.

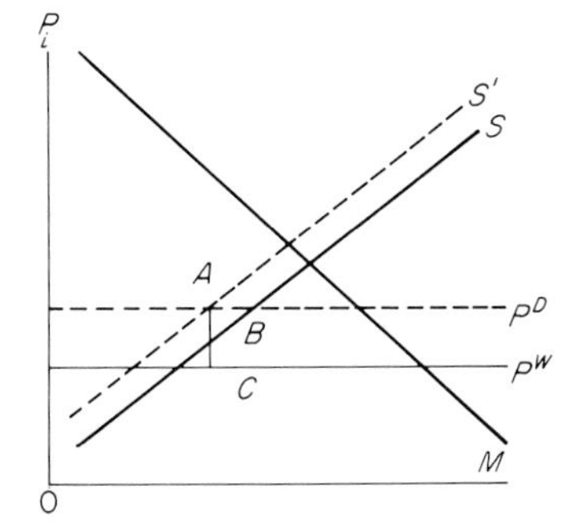

In the cases of final goods, we can see in Figs. 1 and 2 that the difference between domestic and world prices correctly estimates the excess of cost or benefit per unit of good between both markets. However, in the third case (Fig. 3) this difference (AC) overestimates the real difference (BC).

The construction of the index of discrepancy between domestic and world prices creates the problem of choosing a weighting scheme. A solution to this problem could be to evaluate the importance each product has in total imports and exports, considering just local production. Another alternative is to consider directly the implicit weight that is offered by the cost-of-protection formula. Let

$$P_i^D - P_i^W = E_i, \qquad Q_j^W - Q_j^D = F_j,$$

and define variables as follows:

- C cost of protection,
- ΔM_i^D domestic production increase plus decline of import consumption,
- ΔX_j^D production decrease of exportables plus the decrease in their domestic consumption.

According to the traditional formula of the cost of protection (final goods only), we have[2]

$$C = \tfrac{1}{2}\sum_i E_i \Delta M_i^D + \tfrac{1}{2}\sum_j F_j \Delta X_j^D, \tag{12}$$

and, taking relative rate of change of this expression,

$$c = \left[\sum_i \alpha_i e_i + \sum_i \alpha_i (\delta m)_i\right] + \left[\sum_j \beta_j f_j + \sum_j \beta_j (\delta x)_j\right], \tag{13}$$

where we use $(\delta m)_i$ and $(\delta x)_j$ for the relative rate of change of ΔM_i^D and ΔX_j^D, respectively, and

$$\alpha_i = \frac{E_i \Delta M_i^D}{C}, \qquad \beta_j = \frac{F_j \Delta X_j^D}{C}.$$

By the first alternative, the index could be approximated by

$$C' = \sum_i E_i M_i^D + \sum_j F_j X_j^D, \tag{14}$$

where the variables are defined as follows:

[2] The presence of tariffs on inputs presents the problem that we discussed in Fig. 3 [1].

M_i^D domestic production of importables,
X_j^D production of exportables.

Hence,

$$c' = \left[\sum_i \alpha_i' e_i + \sum_i \alpha_i' m_i\right] + \left[\sum_j \beta_j' f_j + \sum_j \beta_j' x_j\right], \tag{15}$$

where

$$\alpha_i' = \frac{E_i M_i^D}{C'}, \qquad \beta_j' = \frac{F_j X_j^D}{C'}.$$

Taking the difference between c and c', we have

$$\begin{aligned} c' - c &= \sum_i e_i(\alpha_i' - \alpha_i) + \sum_i [\alpha_i' m_i - \alpha_i(\delta m)_i] \\ &\quad + \sum_j f_i(\beta_j' - \beta_j) + \sum [\beta_j' x_j - \beta_j(\delta x)_j], \end{aligned} \tag{16}$$

which measures the bias using c' instead of c[3]. We have the additional bias due to the existence of intermediate goods in foreign trade.

[3] Some idea of the bias for a particular case can be given expressing C and C' in elasticity form. Consider just a case of an import good and define ε, supply elasticity; and η, demand elasticity. Let

$$H = \frac{P_i^D - P_i^W}{P_i^W}.$$

V_1 is domestic production of imports; V_2 is consumption of imports;

$$\pi_1 = \frac{V_1 \varepsilon}{V_1 \varepsilon - V_2 \eta}, \qquad \pi_2 = \frac{V_2 \eta}{V_1 \varepsilon - V_2 \eta}.$$

We have

$$C = \tfrac{1}{2} H^2 (V_1 \varepsilon - V_2 \eta), \qquad C' = H V_1.$$

Hence, in terms of relative rate of change,

$$c = 2h - \pi_1 \left(v_1 - \frac{1}{\varepsilon}\frac{d\varepsilon}{dt}\right) - \pi_2 \left(v_2 - \frac{1}{\eta}\frac{d\eta}{dt}\right),$$

$$c' = h - v_1.$$

If $\varepsilon = \eta$, and does not change over time, we have $v_1 = v_2$, and from this,

$$c - c' = h.$$

V

We can consider the behavior of c as part of the gains or losses which can be obtained through t, and as a result of this, we can consider the whole contribution of foreign trade as equal to

$$w_x(t+c), \tag{17}$$

having from this a final expression for y in the following form:

$$y = w_D a_D l_D + w_D b_D k_D + w_X a_X l_X + w_X b_X k_X + w_X(t+c). \tag{18}$$

With this formulation, we believe the door is open for the empirical study which we plan to undertake for the Argentine case for the period 1935–1968.

VI

In what follows, we present some efforts made in order to evaluate the importance of foreign trade in Argentine economic growth. Most of the empirical effort is still in progress, and here we would like to present some results that, although preliminary, give some idea of what can be done in the future.

We estimated t (terms of trade effect) using about 70 per cent of the exported goods and 40 per cent of the imported goods. The data came from publications of foreign trade series of value and quantity by products (or group of homogeneous products), where a ratio of value to quantity could be taken as a reasonable approximation to unit prices. Imports and exports are considered net of tariffs and are evaluated at the Argentine ports. (We have already started to collect data on individual prices from different Argentine and foreign sources which will give more reliable estimates of individual prices.)

We have used the value of the product at the beginning of the year to *weight* the rate of change of its price. As we were unable to obtain general price indices to deflate the export and import prices, we did not deflate them before computing the relative rates of change, since if we use the same index for both concepts they cancel out.

From the Argentine national income accounts we computed w_x, which varied around 12 per cent in the period 1950–1968.

In order to get some idea of the cost of protection, we used information collected directly from the Central Bank of Argentina regarding the prices of imports of durable goods net of tariffs and including them (with all the additional charges on import goods). From this source we made a tentative estimate of relative rate of change of the cost of protection, and the figures look very high indeed. This does not appear to be very reasonable.

In the Table I we present the index of the national product at factor cost (Y), which is taken from the Argentine Central Bank estimates; the index of total capital stock ($K_D + K_X$) and total labor input measured in homogeneous man-hours ($L_D + L_X$), which are taken from previous research done by the author ("The Capital-Product and Labor-Product Ratio in Argentina," mimeo); and the implicit indices of the terms of trade T and cost of protection C, which result after estimates of t and c are made respectively.[4]

TABLE I

PRELIMINARY RESULTS[a]

Year	Y	K	L	T	C
1955	85.4	61.9	77.4	[b]	[b]
1956	86.7	65.1	80.3	[b]	[b]
1957	91.6	68.9	88.0	[b]	[b]
1958	98.2	70.5	91.0	[b]	[b]
1959	92.6	82.0	99.7	[b]	[b]
1960	100.0	100.0	100.0	100.0	100.0
1961	107.0	93.9	96.5	101.8	361.0
1962	105.0	118.5	102.2	93.4	545.1
1963	101.2	133.3	95.4	104.0	1062.9
1964	109.4	138.8	[b]	106.6	1541.2
1965	117.9	147.7	[b]	100.6	2157.7
1966	119.3	153.8	[b]	95.7	[b]
1967	121.7	180.3	[b]	91.6	[b]
1968	127.7	[b]	[b]	93.4	[b]

[a] Year base 1960.
[b] An estimate was not attained.

[4] This paper was presented at the IInd World Congress of the Econometric Society in Cambridge, England. September 1970. The author wishes to acknowledge helpful comments made by members of the Institute of Economic Research, Univ. of Tucumán.

REFERENCES

[1] Johnson, H., The Theory of Effective Protection and Preferences, *Economica* (May 1969).

[2] Jorgenson, D., and Griliches, Z., The Sources of Productivity Changes, *Rev. Econ. Stud.* (July 1967).

ORIGINS AND CONSEQUENCES OF IMPORT SUBSTITUTION IN BRAZIL *

ALBERT FISHLOW

University of California, Berkeley, California

Import substitution as a strategy of industrialization has been much analyzed from the standpoint of its origins and its consequences. There is an extensive postwar literature, beginning with Raúl Prebisch's oft-cited 1949 ECLA report, justifying the strategy and, more recently, an accumulating series of writings which emphasize the inherent inefficiencies of such inward-turned development. Surprisingly, however, there has been much less empirical attention to the different phases of the process itself. Frequently, we find experiences of World Wars I and II, the Great Depression, and the conscious policy-directed efforts of the 1950s indiscriminately listed as examples of import substitution. Yet their characteristics are sufficiently different to merit more detailed examination.

In this paper the following propositions concerning the nature of the import substitution process as it historically evolved in Brazil will be established:

(1) Its first appearance was in the 1890s as a direct consequence of inflationary finances, and not influenced by tariff protection;

(2) War-related import substitution was most significant for its impulse to demand, and although unaccompanied by extensive capacity increases, did generate profits later utilized for investment;

(3) The impulse of the Great Depression was important both for the increased rate of growth and the wider variety of goods produced domestically, but represented technologically inferior substitution;

* I wish to acknowledge the valiant and invaluable research assistance of Peter Bloch, Astra Meesook, and John Wells in preparing this paper.

(4) The postwar sequence was relatively modest in terms of the reduction of the aggregate import coefficient, much of which had occurred previously, but was distinguished by the greater sophistication of the industrialization, its increased capital intensity, and the guiding hand of public policy.

One implication of these findings is that instruments of conscious policy such as tariffs were not very efficacious in evoking domestic import substitution and industrialization prior to the 1950s. The early surge of industrialization in Brazil was largely fortuitous and was reinforced at various intervals by exogenous forces. Another is that those external stimuli, while diverting demand to domestic industry, did not affect supply equally constructively. As a consequence, the high rates of growth were achieved without correspondingly high rates of productivity growth or technological transfer. Finally, the results suggest the need to reinterpret the industrialization experience of the 1950s as one directed less by the existence of a captive domestic market to which import substitutes could be directed, than by the responsiveness of new industries, and foreign investments, to the lucrative opportunities created by public policy.

I

The principal components of the manufacturing sector in Brazil in the late nineteenth century were textiles and foodstuffs, especially the latter. As was characteristic of nineteenth-century market-guided development, domestic manufactures first evolved from processing agricultural inputs. As late as 1919, the date of the first industrial census, a third of industrial value added emanated from manufacture of foodstuffs, the share in value of production being substantially greater.[1] Within this sector, encompassing such diverse activities as sugar refining for export and the local supply of bakery products, import substitution never played a significant role. To be sure, imports of such products as lard, butter, and others were ultimately replaced in the first decades of the twentieth century, but their impact upon industrial output as a whole can be dismissed.

Rather, it was cotton textiles that represented the first meaningful instance of Brazilian industrialization through import substitution. Despite the domestic availability of raw cotton supplies, entry into manufacture came relatively late. While there were a few mills dating back to the 1850s, as late as 1885 Brazilian cotton cloth manufacture was limited to some 50 mills with an output of only slightly more than 26 million meters, concentrated in the grossest grades. This production represented not much more

[1] See Table III, p. 323.

than 10 per cent of national consumption. Twenty years later, production had expanded tenfold, became more diversified, and represented 60 per cent of consumption. The transition can be traced to a brief interval concentrated at the end of the 1890s.

TABLE I

IMPLICIT DOMESTIC PRODUCTION OF COTTON CLOTH[a]

Period	(1) Consumption 1885 Level Per Capita[b]	(2) Consumption 1905 Level Per Capita[c]	(3) Imports[d]	(4) Production 1885 Level[e]	(5) Production 1905 Level[e]
1880–1884	226	261	242	−16	19
1885–1889	248	287	244	5	44
1890–1894	276	320	306	−30	13
1895–1899	310	359	219	91	140
1900–1901	336	389	116	220	273
1902–1906	362	419	184	178	235
1911–1913	429	496	211	218	285

[a] Millions of meters.

[b] (1) Consumption, 1885: Sum of 1885 estimated production and 1885 estimated imports. Estimated production from Branner [14]; production for firms reporting incompletely is estimated. Estimated imports are the sum of U.S., U.K., and German exports divided by share of market in early 1900s, 0.88. Extrapolated on basis of population series in IBGE [19].

[c] (2) Consumption, 1905: Sum of 1905 estimated production and 1905 estimated imports [48]. Imports, kilos of cotton goods as reported in Stein [79], multiplied by a conversion factor of 15 meters per kilo verified from comparison of British meter exports and kilo imports reported in Brazilian statistics. Extrapolation as above.

[d] (3) Imports: 1880–1900, as described in column (1) above; 1901–1906 as in column (2); 1911–1913, imports from Stein, multiplied by factor of 17.9 as indicated by comparison of U.S., U.K., and German exports and Brazilian imports.

[e] (4), (5) Production: column (4) = column (1) − column (3); column (5) = column (2) − column (3).

Table I presents the basic data from which this inference can be derived. Columns (4) and (5) contain alternative production estimates based upon subtraction of imports from two different estimated consumption levels, obtained from per capita absorption in 1885 and 1905. While in the earlier years the latter yield higher production estimates that may be regarded as upper limits, the time pattern of domestic responsiveness is clear. The interval 1895–1899 is demarcated as the first significant upward impulse in either instance. The explanation for the increase in activity is equally obvious

—the substantial reduction in imports. Over a five-year span these declined by virtually one-third.

Indeed, it is plausible that such import substitution represented almost the complete basis for growth of domestic manufacture. Production in 1885–1889 was more than likely closer to the 44 million meters of column 5 than the 5 million implied by the low 1885 consumption per capita levels. On the other hand, a decade later, under conditions of cyclical decline, 91 million meters seems the more appropriate estimate. If in the intermediate quinquennium, the level stood somewhere in the vicinity of 30 million meters (as was actually produced in 1885), the *entire* growth between 1890–1894 and 1895–1899 would be attributable to a reduction of the import coefficient. That there was such a substantial domestic response to the decline of imports does not depend solely upon indirect inference. We have the additional evidence of contemporary comment:

> It is sometimes said that the decline in imports is due to the decreased purchasing power of the Brazilian people, and this is undoubtedly a partial explanation in regard to some classes of goods. In the main, however, the true cause is to be found in the increase of home production, and the process is likely to continue except as regards the finer and higher priced grades of goods [59].

The course of domestic production through the period 1895–1899 was one of rapid acceleration. By 1901, corresponding to the nadir in imports, Brazilian textile output must have closely approached the observed 1905 level of 242 million meters. Again, there is more than the reconstruction of Table I to go by: First, there are the annual production statistics of the state of São Paulo, which record only a ten per cent increase between 1900 and 1905. Secondly, federal excise tax receipts on textiles, a specific levy per meter, rose but 9.9 per cent over the same interval.[2]

Despite the recovery of imports in the first years of the century, production more than held its own due to extension of the aggregate market. This was to be the central factor in the continued success of the industry. Had consumption remained at its 1905 level and imports continued their recuperation, the predicted domestic production in 1911–1913 according to Table I is 285 million meters. In fact, a much higher level of 388 million meters was realized. This discrepancy is due to the rapid rise of incomes that accompanied this first surge of industrialization. Neither import substitution nor responsiveness to price decline provides satisfactory alternative explanations. The former, as the import coefficient was reduced from 44 to 35 per

[2] For São Paulo production statistics, São Paulo Directoria de Industria e Comercio [26]. For consumption taxes, Ministério da Fazenda [23, 24].

cent, contributed only one-third of the growth; the latter, under plausible assumptions, explains only ten per cent.[3]

The outbreak of the war, and the consequent reduction of foreign supply, marked the second phase of import substitution directed growth. Between 1911–1913 and 1919 consumption grew only slightly more than one per cent a year, but production by six per cent.[4] By the war's end, a national market satisfied predominently by domestic production had been created.

The origins and subsequent course of this first experience with import substitution trace a pattern that was not only unplanned, but ran counter to policy in some instances. Furthermore, the rise of the textile industry in the 1890s and thereafter puts into new perspective the real consequences of the "Encilhamento," the period of intense inflation and exchange devaluation at the beginning of the Republic. These points require elaboration.

When in 1889, in an effort to meet shortages of liquidity, new and liberal banking legislation was passed, the immediate and predictable outcome was a sharp expansion in the quantity of credit available. The number, and capitalization, of industrial enterprises quickly responded: the nominal capital of *new* manufacturing establishments founded between November 15, 1889 and October, 1890 amounted to 47,540 *contos* compared to a previous *total* capitalization three-fourths as large [29]. The pace did not slow until mid-1891. After it had, cotton mills listed on the Rio stock exchange had increased their nominal share capital from 13,500 *contos* in May, 1889 to 84,210 in January, 1892 [76].

The obvious speculation inherent in such intense financial activity, and the inevitable depreciation of the *milreis* attendant upon rapid domestic inflation, has led commentators to conclude that the episode was "false and deceptive from beginning to end."[5] Yet this judgment ignores the permanent consequences of this temporary stimulus to national entrepreneurial initiative. The paid-in capital of cotton mills, while increasing only half as much as the nominal, did increase fourfold in less than 3 years. Moreover, of the 198 mills operating in 1912, no fewer than 33 date to the interval 1890–1894, and many of the 23 recorded as belonging to the period 1885–1889 undoubtedly were founded in 1889. These 33 firms exceed in number those surviving from the succeeding decade [20]. We are talking here about something much more substantial and enduring than a South Sea bubble.

[3] Prices declined about 5 per cent, which assuming a unitary price elasticity, leaves a growth of 4.0 per cent out of the original 4.6 per cent to be explained by income. At an income elasticity of 1.5, an annual growth in per capita income of more than 2.5 per cent is implied.

[4] Production based on data presented in Stein [78]; consumption estimated by summing production and imports as in Table I.

[5] A contemporary English-language newspaper in Rio cited in Stein [75].

The principal reason relates to the lagged and magnified relationships of the exchange rate to domestic inflation generated by the large increase in the money supply. Initially, the exchange rate did not completely deteriorate—until June, 1891 the descent had carried it to less than one third of its full decline—and made foreign goods attractive purchases. For consumers, this meant continued purchase of foreign textiles. For potential producers, this meant machinery could be ordered and paid for at favorable terms with their new found *contos*. In addition, in 1892 the government authorized an issue of 100,000 *contos* to finance credit to industry; even at the discount at which they circulated, they permitted many of the new firms to survive [77]. It is relevant to note that imports of capital goods from Britain, in sterling, increased some 70 per cent between 1885–1889 and 1890–1894. The absolute level in real terms was not exceeded in any quinquennium up to 1909 [49]. After 1893, as the exchange rate decline accelerated making imports progressively more expensive and increasing the reluctance of export houses to extend credit, the process of import substitution was facilitated.

In the absence of an independent indicator of domestic prices, one can only speculate on the magnitudes involved. It is relevant to note, however, that movements of the paper money supply and exchange rate diverged in the period 1895–1899, as shown in Table II. The average circulation in that

TABLE II

MONEY SUPPLY AND EXCHANGE RATE, 1889–1904[a]

	Paper Money in Circulation (millions of *réis*)	Average Value of £ in *réis*
1889	211	9.1
1890	298	10.6
1891	448	16.1
1892	524	19.9
1893	632	20.7
1894	712	23.8
1895	678	24.2
1896	712	26.5
1897	780	31.1
1898	780	33.4
1899	734	32.3
1900	700	25.3
1901	680	21.1
1902	676	20.1
1903	675	20.0
1904	674	19.6

[a] Source: "Anuário Estatístico do Brasil" [17].

interval increased 40 per cent over the previous quinquennium, while the *reis* per pound sterling rose 62 per cent. A more precise measure of the deviation in the period is obtained by considering the residuals from the equation

$$\log P = A + b \log M - ct,$$

where P is measured by the exchange rate, M by the currency in circulation, and t is time, introduced to remove the trend effect of increasing output. This regression yields significant coefficients and a comfortable margin of explanation:

$$\log P = -3.64 + \underset{(0.12)}{1.07} \log M - \underset{(0.009)}{0.018}t, \qquad R^2 = 0.90.$$

It also reflects a high degree of autocorrelation, i.e., cyclical movement, of the residuals, as measured by the Durbin–Watson statistic (0.71). Thus during the years 1895–1899, the average relationship that holds over the whole period systematically and continuously understates the level of exchange rate realized. On average, the deviation is -11 per cent over the interval, becoming as large as -24 per cent in 1899. Such a deviation is a measure of the degree to which expectations and speculation succeeded in causing an excessive depreciation of the *reis*.

While a real devaluation causes an obvious shift against imports, it also stimulates exports by increasing their profitability. Sterling and dollar earnings are translated into larger income in domestic currency. Simultaneously with the depreciation of the 1890s, however, the world price of coffee in dollars was undergoing a precipitous decline. In part owing to the cyclical decline of incomes in the developed countries, but more in response to the increasing world supply of coffee, the price halved between 1893 and 1898. As a consequence incomes of the coffee sector were barely maintained in domestic currency over this interval, despite the favorable movement of the exchange rate.

In such an environment, the prospects for investment in import-substituting activities had greater appeal. The source of such transfer is not yet established; no studies have been done of the entrepreneurs of the mills brought into production at this time. Yet one likely source of capital for the reallocation, as brought out clearly by the researches of Dean, are import merchants:

> Of the thirteen cotton mills built before the turn of the century in São Paulo, eleven by 1917 were controlled by importing firms or by entrepreneurs who had started out as importers [39].

Cognizant of the market, with working capital a large part of their total resources, and with declining import activity, they were a logical source of both entrepreneurship and investment. The process, indeed, would seem to bear close resemblance to the initial rapid growth of American textile production in the first decade of the 19th century, stimulated by the Embargo Act, and financed by commercial interests.

Still another aspect of the operation of the exchange-rate devaluation mechanism is worth pointing out. Occurring as it did during an inflationary expansion, import substitution may have benefited from declining real costs as well as increasing price. To the degree wage levels lagged behind the cost of living (as is not infrequent during a substantial inflationary surge), the real unit outlay for labor can decline. When, in addition, the price of the product increases more than other prices—the characteristic of a potential import substitute during a real devaluation—a much larger profit margin is created. In response, resources flowed for the first time significantly to domestic manufactures.

Tariffs, the direct policy instrument for influencing industrial activity, while ostensibly abetting import substitution, in fact did not. Although the official *ad-valorem* rates (*razoes*), ratios calculated on the basis of official values, increased, the true *ad-valorem* proportions declined. Official values were converted at the 1890 exchange rate and were well below those actually prevailing in the market. Despite the imposition of various compensating surcharges, actual customs receipts as a proportion of the value of imports declined irregularly from 39 per cent in 1890 to an average of less than 30 per cent during 1895–1899.[6] Thus collections moved inversely, rather than proportionally, with import substitution. Such lower receipts, paradoxically, may have reinforced the exchange-rate mechanism as it operated. Customs revenues at this time represented about two-thirds of governmental income. Reduced collections checked the capacity of the government effectively to implement a deflationary policy as severe as it might have chosen. Over the period 1894–1897, while expenditures in current *milreis* were held constant (and declined in real terms), a deficit was nonetheless experienced. Not until 1898 did notes in circulation cease to increase annually, despite the revocation in 1891 of the privileges of banks of issue [30]. Maintenance of internal credit, in a phase of initial establishment of the industry, was probably more significant than protection afforded by the tariffs.

This de-emphasis of the contribution of protection to early Brazilian import substitution carries over to the post-1900 period as well. It is common to attribute the early 20th century growth of textiles, the "Golden Age," to the Tariff of 1900. That those rates were protective in intent and application is indisputable. Contemporaries referred to the Brazilian tariff as among the highest in the world, with apparent justification. Rates as high as 314 per cent

[6] Calculated from Ministério da Fazenda [22], passim.

on certain grades of cotton and silk cloth contrast to duties of 12 per cent in Argentina and 28 per cent in Mexico [41]. Such extremes exaggerate, but do emphasize the consequences of the Act of 1900. Revaluation of official prices, accompanied by subsequent appreciation of the *milreis*, created *ad-valorem* rates on textiles of between 75 and 100 per cent. Collections rose from 30 per cent of value in 1900 to 49 per cent in 1906. Yet such measures did not prevent imports from continuing their recovery and retaining almost as large a share of a much increased Brazilian market in 1911–1913 as they had earlier at the very beginning of the century. The reason is symmetrical to the success of domestic import substitution in the face of declining tariffs: changing exchange rates. Their appreciation, by more than 50 per cent between 1900 and 1906, made foreign prices relatively cheaper. Tariff collections on the other hand increased, because they were based on official prices greater than true market values.[7] Again, they are a spurious index of the stimulus afforded to industrial development.

Despite the *de-facto* reduction in the protection enjoyed by domestic producers, textile output resisted foreign competition as well as it did because of the growing productivity of the industry. The relative decline of domestic to import prices is well chronicled prior to World War I. Prices in 1913 of Brazilian grey, bleached, and printed goods were about 10 per cent less expensive than comparable imports in 1907; for dyed fabric, the decline was almost 40 per cent. In absolute terms, a 1914 comparison of wholesale prices of bleached shirtings showed Brazilian prices substantially lower than the imported item. "This is due to the intense competition among the native mills, which prevents them from reaping the full benefit of the protection granted [42, 47]. Production statistics do not permit unequivocal inferences to corroborate these relative price tendencies. The reported national output and employment for 1905 and 1915 indicate declining output per worker despite a rising number of spindles per man. Yet similar data for São Paulo affirm an increase in productivity of 16 per cent per decade. In absolute terms, of course, it was lower wages that made the industry viable. Productivity per man was one-

[7] Since the *milreis* official price is fixed, the increased revenue to the government from converting its paper receipts into gold more favorably is completely independent of the protection afforded if the domestic price does not move directly with the import price. Over the short term, this is what appeared to occur [60]. If R is the ratio of import to domestic price, we have:

$$R = \frac{P_{£} \cdot X_r + tP_S}{P_S},$$

where $P_{£}$ is the foreign price, X_r the exchange rate, and P_S the domestic (and official price). $dR/dX_r = P_{£}/P_S$, which is always positive. As the exchange rate appreciates, X_r falls, as does R, while the tariff percentage, $tP_S/P_{£} X_r$, rises.

third to one-half contemporary United States levels, and even slightly below that attained by the American industry a half-century earlier.[8]

This relative price behavior explains the declining import coefficient between 1905 and the outbreak of World War I, but it is insufficient to account for the high rates of growth of production realized. For that, the most plausible explanation seems to be increased demand related to increased incomes. The recovery of coffee prices, and coffee incomes, after 1905 presumably paid a significant role. Demand for textiles, and industrial products more generally, was probably linked closely to the fate of the coffee sector, as well as the rate of industrial dissemination itself. Note, then, how the role of the foreign sector was reversed: Reduced import capacity and international trade had earlier been critical to the initial establishment of the industry; now it was their growth that was a positive factor.

A second surge of import substitution occurred during World War I. An earlier view, attributed largely to Roberto Simonsen, held that the extent of such war-based expansion was considerably greater than achieved before or subsequently. Such a conclusion depended upon estimates of nominal industrial production (based upon excise tax receipts) deflated by a cost-of-living index. Dean has correctly called attention to the exaggeration implicit in such a method. Textile prices, and those of other industrial products, clearly rose more rapidly than the prices included in the deficient cost-of-living deflator. He also has correctly emphasized the degree to which the war not only produced a captive market, but also an interruption of needed capital goods and intermediate goods imports.

Yet perhaps his reevaluation has caused the pendulum to swing too far in the other direction. In the first instance, there was an undeniable favorable influence on production. Cotton textile output in 1918 exceeded that in 1914 by 57 per cent; even calculated from the higher 1911–1913 base—1914 was a depressed year—the increment was more than one-fourth. There is no question as to the basis of the expansion. It is almost entirely due to import substitution that increased the proportion of consumption supplied domestically from less than two-thirds to 85 per cent at the war's end. Of more immediate concern to mill owners, profits benefited from the large increase in prices made possible by war-time inflation. Neither wages nor the price of cotton matched the steep ascent of textile prices. Very large dividends in 1916 and 1917 were one consequence; accumulation of reserves for later purchase of capital equipment was another [46].

[8] The productivity estimate is by Clark [32], and based on comparison with contemporary North Carolina practice. Other, more aggregative, evidence affirms this judgment. The U.S. 1849 output per man per year from the Census was 7800 yards; the corresponding 1905 value was 15,134 yards. Brazilian workers in 1915 produced on average 5723 meters, and therefore not much more than 6000 square yards [33, 38, 78].

This phenomenon of growth was not restricted to textiles. A quantity index calculated on the basis of outputs reported for excise tax purposes, and weighted by 1919 value added, shows a similar tendency.[9] From 1914 to 1918 this index grows at an annual rate of 8.5 per cent, and a lower, but still appreciable, 4.4 per cent when the terminal points are altered to less favorable bases—1911–1913 and 1919. Admittedly heavily weighted by cotton textiles, this index represents, even at its inception, probably more than 60 per cent of industrial value added. It does exclude frozen beef and sugar, two products which grew exceedingly rapidly for the export market. Their absence biases the index downward, but by not as much as Dean's emphasis upon the "new" exports as the only positive stimulus to manufactures provided by the war would lead one to believe. A comparison of the increase of value of exports of manufactures and the estimated growth of the value of industrial production gives it a weight of only 20 per cent. Since the ratio of value added to value of product in the exports of beef and sugar is relatively low compared to manufactures as a whole, the share in value added is possibly even smaller.[10]

Compared to the entire decade of the 1920s, and its growth rate of less than 4 per cent, the wartime expansion is clearly superior. To be sure, it is no landmark acceleration upon which Brazilian industrialization was founded, but then again neither is the demand created during the conflict to be casually dismissed. The inability of inputs to grow as rapidly, the principal consequence being a lower level of capital formation, did not represent a permanent disability. To a certain degree domestic supply increases compensated. In the case of pig iron, for example, production grew from 3500 tons in 1915 to 11,700 in 1918 [73]. More generally, despite the smaller average size of the new firms, industrial establishments founded between 1915 and 1919 account for one-fourth of the reported capital in manufactures in the 1920 census.

Moreover, critics, in focusing upon the reduced investment during the war, ignore the role of the increased profits in financing subsequent capital formation as well as the stimulus afforded by demand to the purchase of new equipment. The large imports of more modern machinery in the early 1920s, and the initiation in Brazil of local manufacture of cement and steel, date from this postwar period. Slow and smooth growth may not be a viable mechanism of import substitution, even with protection. To overcome the barrier of

[9] The sources and method of calculation of the industrial index are discussed in Appendix I.

[10] Manufactured exports of all kinds grew from 8748 *contos* in 1913 to 303,366 in 1918, as reported in "Dicionário Histórico, Geográphico e Ethnográphico do Brasil" [21]; the nominal value of manufactures increased from 956,957 *contos* in 1914 to 2,370,600 in 1918 according to Simonsen's estimates [74]. Since international prices, as well as domestic prices, rose substantially, the comparison in nominal terms gives a valid approximation.

domestic resistance on the sides of both demand and supply, a continuing and positive stimulus is necessary. The state was not mobilized to provide incentives to industrialization except through tariffs, and their force is not enough, because it is too indirect and insufficiently discontinuous. The exogenous shock of the war permitted the earlier excess capacity to be utilized, and carried the industrialization process a step further to the point of substantial replacement of previous imports that hitherto had continued to compete.

In summary, then, Brazilian industry had achieved by 1919 substantial autonomy in its production of consumer goods. Foodstuffs were protected by the tariff of distance that militated against transport of processed products and depended largely on primary inputs from domestic agriculture. Textiles had achieved national domination through a phased process of import substitution and income growth, and while requiring protection to compete, showed signs of possible vitality. Yet, as a whole, industrial production was limited and unsophisticated, as Table III shows. More than 80 per cent of value added emanated from consumer goods, and a third from food processing alone. The counterpart of such a profile was heavy reliance upon imports of intermediate and capital goods. Virtually the only product of this type for which imports did not constitute more than half of supply was wood, abundantly found in its natural state and requiring little processing.

Moreover, the ratio of total imports to supply understates the true dependence of the economy upon imports. Foreign and domestic supply are not equivalent. The former represents a net addition to available factor resources and is more comparable to an increment of value added, than to gross sectoral production, whose sum exceeds national income. A direct comparison of imports of manufactures to industrial value added does not resolve the problem because the factor resources implicit in imports of finished manufactures include some from the primary sector: the value of cotton cloth includes the value added in the cultivation of raw cotton.

Morley and Smith have suggested as a consequence a method of decompostion of imports by use of an input–output table of technical relationships [65]. This distributes the value added to imports back to their original sectoral sources. Since such an exercise is typically performed at high levels of aggregation, in which only the grossest type of interindustry transactions matter, an even simpler rule suggests itself to carry out the necessary transformation for total imports of manufactures. The value added in the domestic industrial sector replaced by imports consists of two parts: the direct value added of the imports, plus the indirect value added of intermediate industrial stages. Or to put it another way, it is possible, by subtracting the inputs from the primary sector to the secondary sector implicit in the value of industrial imports, to approximate a total which is comparable to domestic value added in manufactures. So calculated, we have the equivalent of the domestic resources in

TABLE III

DISTRIBUTION OF VALUE ADDED BY USE[a] AND IMPORTS AS A PERCENTAGE OF TOTAL SUPPLY,[b] 1919[c]

	Percentage Distribution	Imports as a Percentage of Supply
Consumer Goods	80.2	
Textiles	24.4	13.7
Clothing	7.3	6.2
Food	32.9	11.5
Beverages	5.4	23.8
Tobacco	3.4	0.3
Rubber	0.1	70.7
Printing and publishing	na	na
Chemicals	4.2	57.0
Leather	0.2	32.0
Nonmetallic minerals	1.2	40.5
Miscellaneous	1.2	53.4
Consumer Durables	1.8	
Electrical	—	100.0
Transport	—	53.5
Furniture	1.8	2.2
Intermediate Goods	16.5	
Metallurgy	3.8	64.2
Nonmetallic minerals	2.8	40.5
Leather	2.0	32.0
Chemicals	0.8	57.0
Wood	5.7	6.1
Paper	1.4	58.3
Rubber	—	70.7
Electrical	—	100.0
Capital Goods	1.5	
Mechanical	0.1	96.7
Electrical	—	100.0
Transport	1.4	53.5
Total	100.0	24.7[d]

[a] Classification and subdivision of industries by use was based on content of subgroups reported in the census; all transport was treated as investment. Federal excise tax has been subtracted, and foodstuffs adjusted for inclusion of sugar refining and bakery production for comparability with later censuses.

[b] No finer breakdown of imports than by sectoral level was available, hence the percentages refer to the entire sector, and not specific use. For that reason, where industries appear under multiple uses, their percentage is repeated.

[c] Source: Industrial Census, 1920; and [84].

[d] Total excludes printing and publishing.

industry which would be required to produce the imports from their initial stages onward.

If we take the ratio of value added in manufactures to be 0.4 of the value of production, and if we further presume that the remaining 0.6 of inputs is divided equally between manufactures and primary materials, we arrive at a correction factor equal to 0.7. These assumptions seem compatible with such diverse input–output tables as the U.S. in 1919 and Brazil in 1959, as well as with the many others which have been constructed. This new synthetic total of manufactures imports, equal to 0.7 of the original series, must then be compared to domestic value added in industry.[11] Since the latter is by assumption equal to 0.4 of the value of production, our rule simplifies to multiplication of the original ratio of manufactures imports to domestic production by the factor 0.7/0.4, or 1.75. Thus the true contribution of imported manufactures exceeds by 75 per cent the apparent importance measured by direct comparison.

In specific historical terms, this means that the 1919 proportion of imports to total supply of manufactures reported in Table III is a considerable understatement. The more accurate measure indicates that domestic value added would have to have been almost 60 per cent larger than it was to compensate for the imports. Hence as a proportion of total supply, imports were not 25 per cent, but closer to 37 per cent! Note as well that the imports as reported exclude tariffs, a legitimate procedure if they are not competitive with domestic output, since domestic indirect taxes have also been subtracted. To the degree that they are competitive, however, and the internal price diverges from the international by the extent of the tariff, a real comparison requires addition of the tariff surcharge. Since we want an actual import-weighted average, rather than a measure of protection weighted by domestic production, average collections relative to imports will do directly; it is assumed that tariffs were collected on industrialized products only. On this basis, the direct ratio of value of imports to supply increases to 28 per cent,

[11] The full matrix method to obtain gross supply equivalent of industrial imports requires computation of M^*:

$$[1-A]^{-1}M = \frac{1-a_{11}}{(1-a_{11})(1-a_{22})-a_{12}a_{21}}M_{\mathrm{m}} + \frac{a_{21}}{(1-a_{11})(1-a_{22})-a_{12}a_{21}}M_{\mathrm{p}},$$

where subscripts refer to the primary and manufacturing sectors as 1 and 2, respectively. The rule given in the text simply calculates $[(1-a_{12})/(1-a_{12}-a_{22})]\,M_{\mathrm{m}}$ instead. Both measures are then multiplied by the ratio of value added in industry, $1/(1-a_{12}-a_{22})$. If $a_{12}=a_{22}$, and a_{21} is small enough to be ignored, the approximation reduces to the near equality of $(1-a_{22})/(1-2a_{22})$ and the correct factor $1/(1-a_{22})$. Actual calculations using the input–output method and the simplification suggested here show the latter to be less than 10 per cent greater for four different dates, 1919, 1939, 1949, and 1959.

and the total contribution to value added, 40 per cent.[12] Finally, imports in 1919 were at low levels compared to their magnitude in the early 1920s. If we extrapolate forward nominal industrial output as reported by the census by a multiplication factor estimated from the real production index and the cost of living, and use 1920 imports for our comparison, much higher import ratios result. The simple ratio to supply, including tariff is one-third, and the adjusted, close to one-half. The Brazilian economy was far from having completed the process of import substitution.

One further indication of just how much farther it had to go along the path of industrialization is afforded by the size of the labor force engaged in production of manufactures. Ironically, the apparently large participation indicated by the demographic census—almost 10 per cent—has been used in the opposite vein: as evidence of the extensiveness of early industrialization. More careful examination raises serious doubts about the validity of such a reading. Specifically, there is a disparity in 1920 between the industrial and demographic censuses by a threefold factor: the industrial census reporting a total of approximately 350,000, the demographic, 980,000. The difference is also clearly associated with composition by sex: the industrial census reckoning a ratio of two men for every woman, the demographic suggesting 1:1. The explanation seems to be straightforward and simple. Large numbers of tailors and seamstresses are apparently included in the 1920 industrial occupational count. This had also occurred, but explicitly, in 1872. Since later censuses correctly classify such occupations in services, the 1920 demographic data give a very favorably biased view of the relative size of the manufacturing sector at that date. Indeed, correctly calculated on the basis of the industrial census, the labor force in manufactures in 1920 was only 3.9 per cent of the total, compared with 9.5 two decades later.

Some international comparisons may also help to put the Brazilian experience in perspective. Table III has already indicated the limited role of intermediate and capital goods industry in Brazil in 1919. Ratios of consumers to nonconsumers in different countries as calculated by Hoffman have notorious deficiencies, not the least of which is their sensitivity to sectoral classification of the original census data. It is informative, none the less, that Brazil in 1919 has the dubious distinction of having the highest ratio among all countries examined, including India in 1925; Argentina, 1908; Chile, 1912; and Belgium,

[12] Note that the relevant tariff criterion when calculating the participation in value added is effective rather than nominal protection, which takes into account the differential tariffs on inputs of raw materials relative to those on final goods. Since rates of effective protection are typically higher than the nominal tariff for industrial goods (because inputs are subject to lower surcharges), the calculation in the text, which makes no correction for the divergency, is an understatement. If we applied the 1967 ratio of effective to nominal protection for manufactures, the contribution to value added would be 42 per cent.

1846.[13] And almost a century earlier, the United States labor force had attained the 1920 Brazilian participation in manufactures.

It is perhaps useful to contrast the earlier description of the implantation of industrialization in Brazil, and this examination of its extent in 1919, with Leff's more simplistic and excessively revisionist conclusion:

> Brazil experienced substantial industrialization earlier than has sometimes been assumed. Far from being the creation of the import difficulties during World War II, the Depression, or World War I, Brazilian industrialization had proceeded extensively and at rapid rates before these events. On the whole, Brazilian industrialization seems to have taken place under conditions similar to those of other regimes of recent settlement: in conjunction with rapid expansion of foreign trade and with strong government support in the form of tariff protection [63].

II

The 1920s were not very propitious from the standpoint of further propagation of the limited industrialization Brazil had attained by 1919. Textile production continued to expand only until 1922–1923, with the remainder of the period marked by increasing foreign participation in local markets. In 1928, the year of peak imports, the share of imports had reverted to its pre-World War I level, and provoked agitation for increased tariff protection, obtained in the following year. Since the 1900 tariff had been fixed in nominal terms, the protection it afforded had been reduced by increasing domestic prices. The difficult situation of the industry was further complicated by the heavy investment undertaken to expand and modernize capacity after the war. Although costs were thereby presumably reduced, the low level of production prevented realization of the expected profits. Industry, in general, reflected this same deceleration. Between 1922 and 1926, the index grows hardly at all, measured in 1939 prices, and performs not much better in those of 1919.[14] By the end of the decade some recovery is apparent. The rise in 1927 can be ascribed to recuperation in textiles—not only cotton, but silk and woolens, as well; the lesser rise in 1928 suffers from stagnation in cotton, but is sustained by newer industries—cement, iron and steel, and paper—on the one hand, and the continuing rise of traditional goods like shoes, hats, and tobacco.

[13] Hoffmann calculated the ratio of value added in food, drink, textiles, clothing, leather goods, and furniture, and compared it to that in iron and metal goods, machinery, vehicle construction, and chemicals as a measure of stages of industrialization. The lack of homogeneity across countries and over time of such categories, as well as the imprecise justification of such a measure, limits its value to crude comparisons. Table III illustrates the limited economic content of his categories by its reclassification of the "chemical" sector, mainly candles, soap, and matches, into consumer goods [53].

[14] The annual rate in 1939 prices is 1.0 per cent; in 1919 prices, 1.7 per cent. In general, as to be expected with an industrialization attendant with structural change, as experienced in the 1930s, the 1919 rates are higher throughout, especially in the 1930s.

There seems little doubt that this disappointing aggregate performance, like that of textiles in particular, was influenced by sharply increased imports during the decade. Nondurable consumer goods imports grew at an annual rate of almost 15 per cent between 1921 and 1928; those of durables still more rapidly. By contrast, imports of capital goods for domestic industry, after an initial rise after the war, did not sustain the advance beyond mid-decade. Imports were favored by their falling relative prices during the decade. Beyond the erosion of the high specific rates of 1900, there was again the fluctuating exchange rate. Between 1923 and 1926 the *milreis* appreciated due to sharply augmented coffee exports and tight monetary policies, with direct effect on the cheapness of foreign commodities.[15] Had domestic manufactures attended to the increased demand proportionately, the annual rate of growth of industry between 1922 and 1926 would have been a highly satisfactory 8 per cent. There was no lack of demand in general. With a much larger increase of real GNP of more than 10 per cent in both 1927 and 1928, there was greater spillover into industry. Note that the valorization scheme as it operated during the decade, while it helped by maintaining the income and demand of the coffee sector, had its negative aspects as well. Financed by foreign capital, it provided foreign exchange that was converted into competitive imports; thus despite continuously shrinking commercial balances after 1924, the exchange rate remained firm. By the validation of domestic coffee production, moreover, it prevented the reallocation of resources out of the sector, and exaggerated the surplus problem of the Great Depression.

That crisis soon rescued domestic industry from the floundering of the 1920s. After brief and mild exposure to the cycle between 1929 and 1931, gross domestic product exceeded its 1928 peak in 1932, and thereafter proceeded to evolve at a rate of 5.6 per cent until 1939, more rapidly therefore than its pace of the 1920s. Manufactures led the surge, increasing at a rate of 8.6 per cent while agriculture expanded only half as rapidly. Real imports declined to half their 1929 peak by 1934 and then stagnated for the succeeding five years. The precipitous decline in exports, which in turn set in motion the inevitable sequence of exchange controls, increased protection, and even despite these, deteriorating rates of exchange, explain the source of the import substitution of the 1930s.

Since production grew in this fashion after 1932 while the recovery of the foreign sector was limited, it is clear that internal demand was the impulsive factor in the growth of the 1930s. It is important to stress this point at the outset since Palaez' revealing researches upon the Great Depression, and particularly his concern with correcting Furtado's discussion of coffee policy,

[15] Prices of total imports, relative to a general deflator, declined by 50 per cent between 1921 and 1926. With an estimated price elasticity of 0.7 (see Appendix II), two-thirds of the observed quantity change can be attributed to the price decline.

sometimes obscure this simple truth [69, 72]. The relevant question, then, is how such internal demand was generated, not whether it existed.

Palaez has here made important contributions to our understanding of the decade. In the first place, he had called attention to the self-financing aspect of the coffee support program through export taxes. From its origins in 1931 to the beginning of 1933, two-thirds of the total disbursements of the National Coffee Council originated from such levies [70]. Yet he fails to discuss several additional features of coffee policy that place it in a more favorable aspect. There is, for example, the earlier stimulative impulse in 1930 of the acquisition of coffee by the state of São Paulo financed by foreign capital. The immediate disbursement of *milreis* maintained income, while the sterling exchange financed not imports, but debt service. Again, there is the multiplier effect upon the money supply that is neglected. The Federal government contribution of 250 million *milreis* in high-powered money to the Coffee Fund permitted other bank deposits to increase, just as the credit from the Banco do Brasil, in which other bank reserves were kept, allowed that multiplier to increase. This means that the one-third deficit financing had a more than proportional impact upon total outlay. Nor was the export tax itself a simple domestic reshuffling within the coffee sector. To some extent it was borne by the foreign purchaser, and to this degree maintained the income of the coffee sector at levels higher than would otherwise have prevailed. Indeed, there is a presupposition that the largest part of the tax was shifted to the foreigner due to the inelastic demand resulting from the dominant position of Brazil in the world market.[16] The upshot of all this is that while coffee policy was probably not as central to the initial recovery from the depression as Furlado maintained, nor as simple as he described, it was not as insignificant as Palaez has implied.

[16] Consider the demand and supply of coffee in Fig. a. The supply curve S'_{cof} reflects the impact of the tax, with the quantity of exports correspondingly reduced. As can be seen, the shaded area constitutes the domestic payment, which is a fraction of the total collection shown by the rectangle of new quantity times the tax. The more inelastic is demand, the greater the

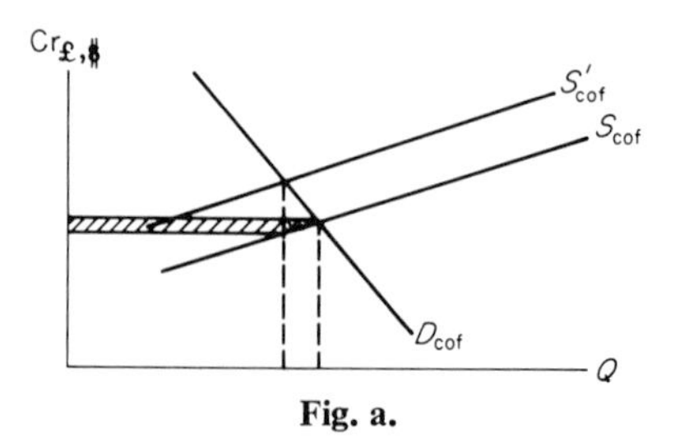

Fig. a.

incidence upon the foreigner; the more inelastic supply, the greater the burden upon coffee producers. Note that the small darker triangle represents the maximum net domestic real income loss. As the export tax improves the terms of trade, this loss becomes smaller, and changes sign as one approaches the optimum tariff.

His treatment of fiscal policy and the commercial balance, while again revealing, must be similarly qualified. Palaez is on secure ground when he argues the classical character of governmental fiscal policy in 1931, and only its chance conversion to a larger deficit in 1932 because of the insurrection in São Paulo. The Vargas government was no more advanced in Keynesian logic when it assumed power than the early New Deal and is not to be credited with conscious reflation. Nor can one dispute the important contribution to demand made by the greatly increased positive commercial balance in 1931 and 1932. To assert that this was an "external factor," as he does, is more questionable. The surplus was due to the much more rapid reduction of imports than exports, provoked by exchange controls and devaluation, deliberate instruments of policy. Reduced import capacity, not expanded international demand, was the operative force. Unlike the 1932 deficit, the objective was deliberate and unavoidable, given the large accumulated foreign debt on which payment was due.

TABLE IV

ESTIMATED AND REALIZED FEDERAL BUDGETS, 1931–1939[a,b]

Year	Estimated Receipts	Realized Receipts	Estimated Expenditure	Realized Expenditure	Estimated Deficit	Realized Deficit
1931	2,670.0	1,752.7	2,451.6	2,046.6	−218.4[c]	294.0
1932	2,242.4	1,682.4	2,217.3	2,859.7	−25.1[c]	1164.1
1933	2,125.4	2,095.8	2,100.9	2,391.8	−24.5[c]	296.0
1934	2,086.2	2,518.6	2,355.0	3,050.2	268.7	128.2
1935	2,169.6	2,722.7	2,691.7	2,872.0	522.1	149.3
1936	2,537.6	3,127.5	2,893.7	3,226.1	356.1	98.6
1937	3,218.5	3,462.5	3,726.0	4,144.0	507.5	681.5
1938	3,823.6	3,879.8	3,875.2	4,735.4	51.6	855.6
1939	4,071.0	4,297.6	4,065.5	4,850.3	−5.5[c]	552.8

[a] Source: Report on Economic and Commercial Conditions in Brazil [51] and [85].
[b] Thousands of *contos*.
[c] Minus sign indicates surplus.

After this period of early crisis, moreover, the federal government increasingly behaved in proper Keynesian fashion. Table IV presents a series of planned and realized federal receipts and expenditures from 1931 to 1939. Not only did planned deficits become more frequent policy, but also the realized shortfalls emanated from conscious additional expenditure rather than overestimated revenues. The large 1933 deficit was of this form. In 1935 and 1936, when the deficit was underattained, the excess of revenues would have generated a surplus in the absence of unplanned expenditures. The consequence of such policies was a regularly increasing issue of paper money that served as the basis for commercial bank expansion. Even in 1936, when the deficit was at its lowest level of the decade, a positive monetary policy was followed. It did not escape notice by the British Commercial Secretary: "Although the deficit of the 1936 budget outturn only amounted to 98,261 *contos*, this result was not achieved without inflation. Extra-budgetary expenditure resulted in an increase of 685,010 *contos* in paper money and in internal debt bonds [50]." Of this total two-thirds were circulating notes.

Added to the stimulus of deficit finance and federally inspired monetary expansion was the net monetary income of the coffee sector. Export receipts in *milreis* recovered by some 25 per cent from their 1932 low point until 1936. At the same time the receipts of the program of Readjustmento Economico—designed to reduce agricultural debt to banks—must have increased the income of coffee producers by as much as 20 per cent. Since export taxes declined from 1933 on as well, the combined effect may have been a substantial increase in real purchasing power. While irrelevant to the controversy over the source of internal demand in the initial recuperation after 1929, such rising income is clearly germane to the really central issue: the rapid continuing real growth during the 1930s.

That result depended very much upon the joint isolation of the domestic market—reinforced by the Tariff of 1934—and its reflation. Domestic production and consumption of cotton textiles both increased. The average 1925–1929 level of the former was 546 million meters, while ten years later it reached 887; the symmetrical values for consumption are 651 and 888. The divergence between the rates of growth of 5.0 and 3.2 per cent is a measure of the role played by import substitution in the process; put another way, even at this late date, elimination of the foreign source of supply accounted for a third of domestic growth. For cement and rolled steel products, substitution was a much more decisive factor than for textiles, which had begun their development long before. Both sectors initiated production in any significant fashion during the 1920s and, having small shares of the market, derived large and immediate advantage from the barrier against imports. The primary products, pig iron and steel ingots, although of recent vintage, had attained much larger shares of domestic supply in the 1920s. As a result, their growth in the 1930s depended much more upon the growth of the market. Table V presents pre- and postdepression average production and consumption for these key products.

These results can be generalized: The industries which grew most rapidly during the Great Depression were the intermediate and capital goods sectors. Metallurgy, nonmetalic minerals, and paper all grew considerably more rapidly than industry as a whole. Consumer goods, with the exception of durables, had

TABLE V

BRAZILIAN PIG IRON, STEEL, ROLLED STEEL, AND CEMENT PRODUCTION AND CONSUMPTION[a,b]

Annual Average	Pig Iron		Steel Ingots		Rolled Steel		Cement	
	Production	Consumption	Production	Consumption	Production	Consumption	Production	Consumption
1925–1929	25.2	32.7	14.8	21.8	16.7	441.2	50.4	483.6
1935–1939	104.6	105.4	84.2	91.6	74.7	404.6	547.6	612.0
Annual rate of growth	15.3	12.4	19.0	15.4	16.2	−0.9	27.0	2.4

[a] Source: Baer [6] and Palaez [71].
[b] Thousands of tons.

virtually completed the substitution process. Among the consequences was an increasing concentration of industrial production in São Paulo, which even earlier in 1919 had shown an industrial profile more oriented to newer, more technologically advanced sectors. By 1939 its dominance as the manufacturing center of the country was assured.

We can extend these conclusions by still another means. The demand for imports, because it is a residual difference between total demand and domestic supply, can yield information about the structure of both. We can thus separate out how much of the import substitution was due to price effects, and how much to displacement of the supply curve itself. Figure 1 illustrates how

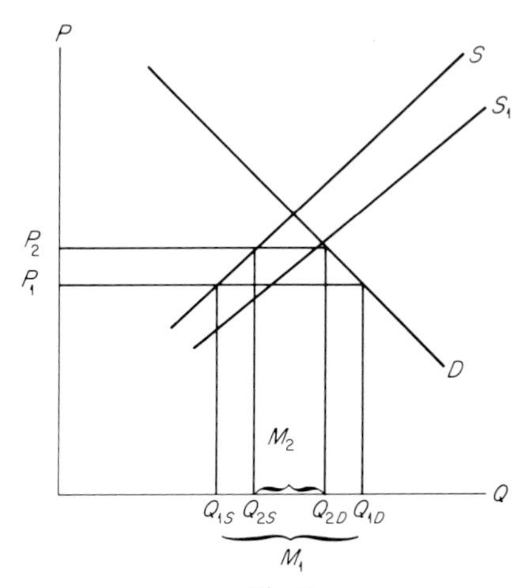

Fig. 1.

such sources contribute differentially. At price P_1 and with the indicated demand and supply curves S and D, the quantity $M_1 = Q_{1D} - Q_{1S}$ is imported. Suppose a higher tariff is levied, raising the price to P_2. Imports are reduced as indicated, even though the supply curve has not shifted out due to productivity change or capital accumulation. With both occurring, the curve shifts to S_1, establishing still a new equilibrium point. Knowing the response of imports to their price, income, and time enables us to estimate the slopes and positions of the original demand and supply curves.

In particular, as shown in Appendix II, by appropriate specification of the ratio of domestic supply of competitive imports, we can estimate the characteristics of the supply response by fitting regressions of the form,

$$\log M + xt = \log A + b \log Y + c \log P + edt,$$

where M is imports, either total, or sectoral; x is the rate of shift of the supply curve in the base period (here the 1920s); t varies from 0 in 1920 to 19 in 1939; Y is either domestic product, or in the case of capital and intermediate goods, industrial production; P is a price index for imports; d is a dummy variable taking values of 0 in the decade of the 1920s and 1 thereafter; and e therefore becomes a measure of the differential shift in supply in the depression compared with the 1920s.

In addition to estimation for total imports, such an excercise was undertaken for four groups of imports: consumer nondurables; intermediate inputs (excluding nonindustrialized products, principally wheat); total capital goods; and industrial capital goods. For consumer durables, with almost nonexistent domestic production, the demand for imports yields the total demand parameters directly, and there is no supply response to estimate. The regression results are reported in detail in Appendix II. Suffice it to say that despite some evidence of autocorrelation, the estimation is almost uniformly quite significant. Table VI reports the results implied for the demand and supply parameters. Two demand elasticities are reported for consumer durables, the first corresponding to the 1920s, the other to the 1930s. Although the latter is somewhat smaller, reflecting perhaps a downward revision in response to the political and economic uncertainties of the decade, it remains absolutely high. Yet the realized purchases in the 1930s fell far short of those in the previous period. The reason is to be found in the sharp increase in price of such imports, and the sensitivity of consumer demand to cost. In the instance of the other products for which domestic substitution was relevant, the results confirm a hierarchy of supply shifts comparable to that of the production series themselves. Investment goods lead, followed by intermediate products, and ultimately by consumer goods. Shifts in the supply curves, as opposed to movements along them, dominate in the production increase due to the modest estimated price elasticities of supply.

TABLE VI

IMPLIED RATES OF SHIFT OF DOMESTIC SUPPLY CURVES DURING THE GREAT DEPRESSION[a]

	Domestic Competitive Supply Relative to Imports	Price Elasticity of Demand	Income Elasticity of Demand	Price Elasticity of Supply	Shift in Supply Curve (% per year)
Consumer Nondurables	1.0	−0.4	0.6	0.2	3
Consumer Durables	0	−1.1	2.3 2.1	—	—
Intermediate Goods	0.6	−0.2	0.7	0.2	5
Investment Goods	0.4	−0.4	1.6	0.4	14
Capital Goods for Industry	0.4	−0.4	1.7	0.4	14
Total Imports	0.6	−0.4	1.2	0.3	6

[a] Source: See text and Appendix II.

Although they are somewhat sensitive to the assumptions made about the magnitude of the demand price elasticities, it is important to note that they are constrained in any event to values less than unity by the uniformly low level of the regression coefficients; hence the results are not an arbitrary conclusion. It is not only the case, therefore, that industrial production increased rapidly during the 1930s, but that the expansion was accomplished by more than greater employment of variable factors. Significant capital accumulation and/or technological change is implied in the new import substitution sectors, and for the industrial sector as a whole. For the first time, domestic inputs figure importantly in such investment.

This diversification of domestic production during the Great Depression is further revealed in Table VII. The structure of value added by use in 1939 has perceptibly altered in favor of intermediate and capital goods. Consumer goods have declined from 80 per cent of value added to a little more than two-thirds. Even within this rubric important changes have occurred. Food and beverages have declined from 50 to 40 per cent of the total. Textiles, chemicals, and printing and publishing have increased. Correspondingly, the sectoral distribution of imports indicates for the first time perceptible domestic participation

TABLE VII

DISTRIBUTION OF VALUE ADDED BY USE[a] AND IMPORTS AS PERCENTAGE OF TOTAL SUPPLY,[b] 1939[c]

	Percentage Distribution	Imports as Percentage of Supply
Consumer Goods	69.7	
Textiles	22.0	5.7
Clothing	4.8	3.5
Food	23.6	2.8
Beverages	4.3	8.5
Tobacco	2.3	0.0
Rubber	0.2	40.7
Printing and publishing	3.6	4.2
Chemicals	6.5	37.5
Leather	0.2	7.7
Nonmetallic minerals	1.0	13.6
Miscellaneous	1.2	40.5
Consumer Durables	2.5	
Electrical	0.4	65.8
Transport	—	56.2
Furniture	2.1	0.8
Intermediate Goods	22.9	
Metallurgy	7.6	41.4
Nonmetallic minerals	4.3	13.6
Leather	1.5	7.7
Chemical	4.2	38.7
Wood	3.2	4.3
Paper	1.5	37.5
Rubber	0.4	40.7
Electrical	0.1	65.8
Capital Goods	4.9	
Mechanical	1.3	79.5
Electrical	0.3	65.8
Transport	3.3	56.2
Total	100.0	20.4

[a] Division by use of certain industries followed titles of subgroups. For 1939, division of the electrical industry was based on the 1949 ratio between intermediate and capital goods for those groups; all of transport before 1959 was treated as investment, following Candal [31].

[b] Percentages in total supply refer to entire sector rather than particular use; for that reason, where industries appear under multiple uses, the percentage is repeated.

[c] Source: Industrial Census, 1940 [43].

in certain industries. Such intermediate sectors like metallurgy and chemicals produced domestically more than half the supply. Note particularly that the chemical sector, which in 1919 was directing more than 80 per cent of its output to consumer goods, in 1939 has proceeded to the point of almost equal division. Capital goods have increased their participation in value added by a factor of more than three, while the previously almost complete dependence upon imports has simultaneously receded.

We may therefore conclude that import substitution during the Great Depression, unlike during World War I or the prewar period, gave an impulse to the evolution of a more sophisticated productive structure. Corresponding to such an alteration was a shift in the distribution of imports in favor of more specialized products incapable of ready substitution. Partly guided by policy, but also by the price mechanism itself, essential and complementary imports could be obtained to reinforce the growth process.

The modest degree to which the import coefficient apparently had been reduced between 1919 and 1939 does not contradict this conclusion about the importance of import substitution. The simple ratio of imports of industrial products to total supply declines from 25 to 21 per cent excluding tariffs; inclusive of tariffs, from 28 to 25 per cent. From the 1920 relative import participation of 0.34, the reduction is more substantial still. But these current ratios distort the change over time because they fail to take into account the very substantial price increase of imports relative to domestic manufactures between 1920 and 1939; this change is estimated to have been more than 60 per cent. While the 1939 value ratio is as large as it is, real imports actually were smaller in 1939 than in 1920. To make an accurate comparison, therefore, relative prices of imports must be held constant. When this is done, the results are strikingly different. In 1920 relative prices, the decline in the import component of total supply is from 34 to 15 per cent; in 1939 prices, from 50 to 25 per cent. In value-added terms, the absolutes alter, but the relative decline is the same. Indeed, in no period subsequent to 1920 did the reduction in the import coefficient play so large a role as that between 1920 and 1939. This is all the more remarkable since the 1920s actually saw a reversal of the decline in import participation.

The final question of interest that remains is the productivity consequences of the externally enforced import substitution that occurred. That it was the latter, rather than inadequate interest in exports and an artificially high price of foreign exchange, must again be emphasized to appreciate the consequences. Real exports, i.e., in quantity terms, more than doubled between 1932 and 1939, and were characterized by an increasing substitution of cotton to offset the reduced demand for coffee. Between 1929 and 1939, while internal prices rose by less than one-third, the exchange rate declined by 132 per cent, representing a substantial real devaluation. The largest depreciation occurred before 1932, after which the internal price level and the exchange rate moved roughly together. The real devaluation, as had happened so frequently in the past, was indeed more decisive than tariffs in altering the relative prices in favor of import substitution.

The rapidity and unplanned nature of the industrialization process during the depression undoubtedly led to capital scarcities. The data upon cement and rolled steel consumption presented in Table V, as well as the quantity index of imported capital goods, seem to leave little doubt about that. Combining these series into a weighted index leads to an average value in 1925–1929 that exceeds the level of 1935–1939 by 20 per cent. Yet such a measure possibly exaggerates the true course of investment. There is no doubt that the industrialization was labor intensive. The São Paulo industrial censuses report employment growth of production workers between 1932 and 1937 at a rate of 10.4 per cent per annum, leaving a margin for productivity gain of less than 2 per cent per annum. But over the same interval, the ratio of horsepower per worker remained stationary, implying a horsepower–output ratio that declined but slightly. More significantly still, the same constant horsepower–labor ratio can be traced back to 1928.[17] Thus despite the severe limitations of access to imports of capital goods—which were as much as 50 per cent smaller during the beginning of the 1930s than during the preceding decade—the horsepower–output ratio underwent a deterioration of no more than 10 per cent.

Horsepower is, of course, an imperfect measure of capital emplacement. During a period of initial installation in which sources of energy to activate machines are crucial, its rate of growth may exceed that of investment as a whole. The contrary may occur subsequently. To seek to remedy the situation a capital stock in manufactures series has been constructed based upon reported census values in 1919 and 1939. To make such information usable, it is necessary to convert the historical cost totals into constant prices. This has been done two ways: direct deflation of the reported capital in the census by a method taking into account the variation in historical prices in the different years of investment; and by allocating the reported intercensal nominal flows on an annual basis by means of a quantity index of investment and price index. There is a surprising agreement in the results of the two methods.[18] On the basis of direct deflation of the census capital stock, the rate of growth between 1919 and 1939 is 2.9 per cent. From the annual allocation of investment we have 3.3 per cent. Both are considerably below the 5.1 per cent annual change in output.

[17] For employment, horsepower, and production data in São Paulo, see Suzigan [80].

[18] The deflator for the capital stock is derived by assuming that flows of net investment are directly proportional to output. This affords a means of distributing the gross capital stock into its historical flows, and thereby permits deflation for different price levels as

The principal deficiency is undoubtedly to be found during the depression itself. Supposing that the capital–value-added ratio remained constant during the 1920s, its implied decline in the following decade was substantial: from 2.1 to 1.4. Note again the need to distinguish constant and current price magnitudes. The latter actually show an increase in the capital–value-added ratio between the two censuses because of the relative rise of prices of investment goods during the 1930s. It was precisely such an increase that reflected the scarcity of imports, on the one hand, and attracted domestic resources, on the other. Even the pattern of development described above implies greater investment in the 1930s than the selective data upon cement and steel consumption and imports of capital goods indicate. It suggests that by the end of the depression gross investment had fully regained the levels of the late 1920s, in part owing to the recuperation and greater selectivity of imports,

---

well as depreciation for time. The formula to accomplish both operations simultaneously—under the additional assumption of constant decadal growth rates for simplification—is:

$$\frac{\Delta O_o \sum_o^{-j} (1+r)^{-i} + O_{-j-1}}{\Delta O_o \sum_o^{-j} (1+r)^{-i} (P_i/P_o) + dO_o \sum_{-1}^{-j-i} (1+r)^{-i} (P_i/P_o)},$$

where O_o and ΔO_o are the initial values for the output and increment in output, respectively; r is the rate of growth; d is the depreciation rate; O_{-j-1} is the level of output at the start of the period; and (P_i/P_o) is the price index. The period of summation is equal to $1/d$ to incorporate all relevant gross flows.

The price index until 1939 was constructed by weighting an import price index of investment goods, the price of cement, the price of rolled iron, and the cost of living index to reflect the approximate importance of construction domestic production of equipment and imports of capital goods. The implicit investment goods deflator employed in Economic Commission for Latin America [82], was used from 1939 to 1949 and, thereafter, the fixed capital deflator of the national accounts. The depreciation rate, d, was set equal to 0.033.

The alternative method constructed a nominal investment index, consisting of a quantity index inclusive of consumption of cement and rolled steel products, and imports of capital goods and the aforementioned price index. The nominal investment obtained by differencing the census capital stocks was then distributed in accord with the nominal index, and deflated back to real terms. An initial starting point for the capital stock at the end of 1919 was necessary and was assumed to be equal to twice the value of transformation in that census year.

The results of the two methods, both in millions of 1959 new *cruzeiros*, are:

End of	Direct Deflation	Interpolation of Flows
1919	90.9	84.6
1939	161.4	160.9
1949	328.9	319.9
1959	791.1	820.8

but even more to the increasing capacity for domestic production of cement, steel, and simpler types of machinery and equipment.[19]

Despite the adverse circumstances under which industrialization occurred labor productivity increased by 1.1 per cent over the two decades. Only 0.1 per cent can be explained by improved quality of the labor force, leaving the rest to utilization of capital and technological change.[20] Since the rate of use of machines was more intense during the depression—there is evidence of two and even three shifts daily—the flow of capital services presumably occurred at a rate corresponding more closely to output than the capital stock estimates cited above. Under the best circumstances, capital services might have kept pace with output. This still implies a rate of technological change of 0.4 per cent annually over the period.[21] To be sure, in the traditional industries the situation was less satisfactory, as the evidence on the age of distribution of machinery in the textile industry in São Paulo indicates.[22] But to focus on this alone is to miss the essential character of the depression industrialization—a diversification and extension into new fields, which inherently brought with it some technological advance.

Over the depression decade, then, Brazil significantly extended its earlier entry into industrialization. Largely in response to international conditions and previous oversupply of coffee, prices of imports rose, making domestic

[19] This conclusion is derived as follows: In the first instance, the net capital stock at the end of 1929 is estimated by applying the growth rate of output from 1919 to 1929 (4.2 per cent) to the initial 1919 capital stock in 1959 of $90.9 million. This value is 137.3, implying a net investment flow of 46.4 in the 1920s and a much smaller 24.1 in the 1930s. These net flows are distributed to quinquennia in proportion to the volume of output. Estimated depreciation is then calculated to reach gross investment magnitudes. The results indicate industrial investment in 1959 of $46 million in the period 1925–1929, and 40 in 1935–1939. This comparison probably still credits the 1920s with too much investment, since the level relative to a crude estimate of GDP in 1959 *cruzeiros* exceeds 11 per cent for the industrial sector alone in 1925–1929, and is less than 7 per cent in 1935–1939.

[20] The weights applied to labor and capital in this calculation are each 0.5. If the actual growth of the capital stock is used, the total factor productivity growth is 1.7 per cent annually, strengthening the conclusions.

[21] This is based upon the changed educational distribution of the male population aged 10–69 between 1920 and 1940, and adjusted by using the approximate income differentials reported in the urban budget studies of the Fundação Getúlio Vargas in the early 1960s. On the basis of more recent studies, the weights can be improved, but sensitivity tests have shown that this result is not likely to alter significantly.

[22] Suzigan [81]. But he may be exaggerating the situation by assuming that all machines reported as of unknown vintage were "much more than 10 years old." Since this group makes up half of the total, its correct average age is of some importance. Even if distributed in proportion to the ages reported, less than 10 per cent of the equipment would have been produced during the decade.

substitution an attractive field for development. Necessarily, because of limited imports, it was a capital-scarce industrialization absorptive of large inputs of labor, supplied at a virtually constant real wage. Over the short term such a growth was both feasible and profitable. Indeed, it represented an impressive response to the crisis conditions under which Brazil labored. Over the longer term, despite the horizontal diversification, such a pattern of development may have had more serious consequences. By perpetuating an antiquated technology in the consumer goods industries, whose productivity growth had already been minimal in the decade of the 1920s, the depression may have lain the basis for later contradictions. In the 1950s, under the pressure of rising wages in the expanding industrial sector, the same labor-intensive mode of production in these traditional sectors could not be employed efficiently, leading not to successful modernization, but to slow rates of growth and actual reduction of the initial labor force. These problems are partially the consequence of the unenviable circumstances of depression industrialization.

III

World War II prolonged the diminished role of imports in total supply, but with a difference: Circumstances during the conflict favored Brazilian exports to other Latin American countries, and brought United States support of the coffee market. Moreover, favorable prices were encountered. Thus, although imports stagnated, import capacity actually increased. This fact clearly differentiates the wartime experience from that of the depression and explains the much more liberal import policies made possible at the end of the conflict.

Another difference during the war was the increased ability of the economy to adapt to import shortages. Capital formation was less prejudiced than during the 1930s by virtue of the domestic capacity that had been created. Consumption of cement and steel show continuing increases during the conflict [1, 7]. Had it not been for such prior industrial development ,the consequences would have been far more severe. Imports of capital goods of all kinds averaged 20 per cent below their level in 1935–1939, despite the inclusion of large shipments of machinery for the Volta Redonda steel mill in 1943 and 1944 [43]. Lack of fuel was another handicap. Even so, industrial production managed to proceed at the creditable rate of 5.1 per cent. The only sectors fully prejudiced were those more dependent upon assembly than production. A good example is the assembly of motor vehicles, which presents one of the few cases of absolute decline during the war.

The impetus for industrial growth clearly came from expansive monetary and fiscal policies and the absence of foreign supply. Unlike the 1930s, when internal demand also had been the principal stimulus, much of the wartime expansion diluted itself in rapid inflation. Whereas prices rose perhaps 40 per cent between 1934 and 1939, in the quinquennium 1940–1945 they doubled.[23] This circumstance was to have profound implications for exchange rate policy, and with it, import substitution, in the postwar period.

Although the Brazilian inflation substantially exceeded that of the United States during the war, the same 1939 exchange rate was to remain in force in 1945, and indeed until 1953. Already in 1946, however, on a parity comparison with 1939, the exchange rate was overvalued by 70 per cent.[24] Such a disequilibrium inevitably immediately provoked large imports in 1946 and 1947, until reserves were sharply drawn down. It also led to another predictable consequence—the decline of noncoffee exports. Although in 1946 the government intervened to prevent exports of textiles in order to reduce internal price pressures, such action soon proved unnecessary. The market itself operated to produce the same result as costs rose while the *cruzeiro* equivalent of external sales remained constant.

Such a policy of overvaluation was defended for its anti-inflationary consequences, and the necessity to compensate for import deficiencies accruing from the war. It could only be maintained after 1947 by going to a system of direct controls, and also by the appreciable increase in coffee earnings over the period, which more than doubled between 1947 and 1950, providing the explanation for the 20 per cent gain in total export receipts. The crucial factor was the increase in coffee prices in the world market; what had been a steady price appreciation in the postwar period turned into a bonanza with the Korean War. As a result, despite the disincentive to other exports, total dollar proceeds increased by almost 15 per cent between 1947/48 and 1951/52.

Industrial imports were substantially cheaper because of the exchange-rate overvaluation than they otherwise would have been. As a consequence, the participation of imports of manufactures in the domestic market actually increased in real terms between 1939 and 1949, providing in the aggregate import substitution in reverse. Furtado has nevertheless maintained that the policy was favorable to industrialization.

[23] The industrial price index for the 1930s is estimated from sources reported in Appendix I. For the 1940s the industrial component of the wholesale price index was used; it is conveniently available in Baer [3].

[24] As calculated in Huddle [54].

> ...The industrial sector was doubly favored: on the one hand, because the possibility of competition from abroad was reduced to a minimum owing to import controls; and on the other, because raw materials and equipment could be acquired at relatively low prices. A situation extremely favorable to investments in industries connected with the domestic market was thus created. It was this situation which was responsible for the rise in the investment rate and the intensification in the process of growth in the postwar period [45].

Huddle has more recently argued against such a position for a variety of reasons [56]. Without entering fully into all the issues involved, it does seem clear that much of his criticism and revisionism is misplaced. Two different questions are involved, which Huddle confounds. The first is whether the mechanism described by Furtado actually operated, and whether incentives to industrialization would have been reduced by devalutation; the second is whether such a growth strategy divorced from market signals in this fashion was efficient.

TABLE VIII

PERCENTAGE DISTRIBUTION OF INPUTS BY USE[a]

	1935–1939	1946–1947	1948–1952
Consumer Goods	17.0	20.5	15.0
Nondurables	6.7	9.7	6.3
Durables	10.3	10.8	8.7
Fuel	12.2	9.4	12.9
Raw Materials	51.1	41.7	39.2
Capital Goods	19.8	28.4	32.9
Industry	6.5	9.1	11.6

[a] Source: [43].

On the first of these, which is his main interest, Furtado emerges with the sounder case. Although the allocation of import licenses was far from perfect, it did produce the desired results. The structure of imports evolved as indicated in Table VIII.[25] Three aspects stand out: First, the participation of consumers goods increased during the period of free importation in 1946 and 1947, only to be significantly compressed during the period of import controls. Secondly, the participation of nondurables shows even greater conformity to such a pattern, yet it was precisely such imports that represented the threat to domestic industry already in place. Durables mattered less from this standpoint, whatever the judgment about their necessity. Finally, there was the increased participation of capital goods, particularly marked in 1951 and 1952 as the system of priorities exerted itself progressively more effectively. This was even more characteristic of investment goods for industry, whose participation increased by 26 per cent between 1946–1947 and 1948–1952, while that of total capital goods advanced by 16 per cent.

[25] Huddle argues that levels must also be examined. This depends upon whether the quantity of imports would have been substantially different under an alternative exchange regime. Since noncoffee export earnings and foreign investment would have been larger with devaluation, as he himself maintains, it is not likely that substantial adjustments in the magnitude of imports would have been necessary. Hence what is more pertinent is the structure of imports under alternative regimes.

The consequence was a marked increase in the investment ratio measured in *real* terms: a given amount of savings could purchase a much larger amount of equipment due to its lower relative price. Measured in 1953 prices, the ratio of gross capital formation to gross national income averaged 18.7 per cent in 1951 and 1952; the 1952 level of gross investment was not surpassed until 1957.[26]

There is similarly little doubt that the implicit subsidy to industry inherent in the policy of overvaluation was substantial enough to influence industrial cost structures. A calculation of the gains bestowed on industry by the importation of inputs and capital goods at the fixed rate rather than the parity rate shows that it equals more than 5 per cent of the value of production of manufactures in 1949. Presumably part of this gain was passed along to final consumers, while at the same time permitting satisfactory profits, for the terms of trade turned *against* industry between 1947 and 1952. Huddle finds such an explanation unconvincing because the annual subsidies are so large compared to the *increment* in value added. Why he uses the increment in value added as the appropriate yardstick is not clear; not only were the subsidies not actual receipts, but their significance lies in the reduction in the *level* of costs they made possible. In any event, he considers it more probable that much of the subsidy was captured by exchange officials in illegal payments for licenses. There is, in fact, evidence for existence of such a market, not the least of which is the sudden closing by the government of the Carteira de Exportação e Importação in 1953 and the discovery that $100 million in import licenses was unaccountable for. Yet Huddle's corrections cannot be accepted at face value. They imply, for example, that in the years 1948–1952 exchange officials received in bribes almost the equivalent of total central government expenditures for wages and salaries of all personnel![27]

What undoubtedly occurred, in addition to corruption of unknown magnitude, was some reduction of the subsidy to industry through higher profits of importers. As long as importers charged only the import price to purchasers, the gain accrued to industry; but if internal prices were higher, as they could be because of the divergence between supply and demand, then the exchange-rate subsidy served only to enrich importers. Because there are no available

[26] Huddle reaches a contrary conclusion because he considers only private investment, and more important, he calculates the investment ratio in current terms. But this is a measure of savings sacrifice, not the investment goods put in place. Note further his erroneous subtraction of the terms of trade effect from product growth that permits him to assert that Furtado has overestimated economic expansion during the period [57]. Only if the original data were measured on an income basis, which they are not, would subtraction be correct. Addition is necessary to reach an income concept. (For estimates of product, income, and investment in real terms see IBGE [18].)

[27] Huddle's calculations are reported in [55]. For public sector expenditures see [35].

comparative data on import and domestic prices, it is difficult to judge how operative such a factor was. That it did not annihilate the subsidy we can infer from the behavior of relative industrial prices and the investment deflator during the period.

It is doubtful that devaluation in 1946 would have served equally well to stimulate industrial growth that measured 9.3 per cent as an annual average over the internal 1947–1952. In the first place, simple alteration of the exchange rate would have increased the profits of the coffee sector substantially, without altering real exchange receipts in any significant fashion. There is no indication that this would have represented an important source of accumulation for industrial investment. Secondly, while imports would have been more expensive, the additional protection afforded domestic manufactures was less significant at that juncture than the access to inputs and capital goods at lower prices. Due to the intervention of the depression and the war, as we have seen, Brazilian producers were forced back upon their own devices more than was desirable from the standpoint of efficiency. Moreover the licensing system did operate successfully, by and large, in limiting competitive imports while encouraging complementary.

Most important, overvaluation was a viable policy instrument in accomplishing these objectives. An explicit subsidy system for industry coupled with taxes on exports would have provoked far greater opposition, despite its more desirable technical properties. Efficacy of policies is frequently as significant as their pure efficiency. The exchange policy thus became a counterbalancing distortion to that of the 1930s, during which import prices had risen substantially relative to prices of domestic substitutes. Now the situation was reversed. Because controls were imperfect, however, resources were directed within the industrial sector not entirely without market guidance and potential competitiveness. It is relevant to note that over the interval 1948–1953 the structure of industrial growth was subject to smaller variance than in the decade subsequent or preceding; and that the domestic capital goods sector, in which comparative disadvantage was probably greatest, was not artifically succored. What was occurring was reinforcement of industrialization through a policy of *non*import substitution.

Yet such control of the price system necessarily had compensating costs. Overvaluation had a permanent effect on noncoffee exports and fostered Brazilian attitudes of pessimism and disbelief in the external market that characterized subsequent policy during the decade. In a similar fashion, the implicit subsidy and tax combination it created was a manifestation and reinforcement of what was to be continuing belief in the virtues of capital-intensive industrialization and neglect of agriculture. Finally, the system, for all its real allocative internal effects, did not adequately deal with one of the major problems for which it had been designed—equilibrium in the balance of

TABLE IX

PERCENTAGE DISTRIBUTION OF INDUSTRIAL VALUE ADDED BY USE[a,b]

	1949	1959
Consumer Nondurables	61.9	46.6
Textiles	19.7	12.0
Clothing	4.3	3.6
Food products	20.6	16.4
Beverages	4.5	2.9
Tobacco	1.4	1.3
Rubber	0.2	0.1
Printing and publishing	4.0	3.0
Chemicals	4.7	5.0
Leather	0.2	0.1
Nonmetallic minerals	0.7	0.5
Miscellaneous	1.6	1.8
Consumer Durables	2.5	5.0
Electrical equipment	0.3	1.9
Transport equipment	—	0.9
Furniture	2.2	2.2
Intermediate Goods	30.4	37.3
Metallurgy	9.4	11.8
Nonmetallic minerals	6.5	6.1
Leather	1.1	1.0
Chemical	4.7	8.3
Wood	4.2	3.2
Paper	2.3	3.0
Rubber	1.7	2.9
Electrical equipment	0.5	1.1
Capital Goods	5.2	11.1
Mechanical	2.1	3.4
Electrical equipment	0.8	1.0
Transportation equipment	2.2	6.7
Total	100.0	100.0

[a] Division by use followed titles of subgroups; all transport equipment production before 1959 was treated as investment following Candal [31].

[b] Source: Industrial Census, 1950 and 1960.

payments. Private capital inflow was discouraged by overvaluation and did nothing to offset the continuing pressure of demand for foreign exchange at such artificially low prices. Short-term compensatory credits and debt accumulated on such a scale in 1951 and 1952 that the system was no longer viable.

In the latter years, official compensatory finance alone was $615 million, more than one-third the value of imports (FOB).

The policy of fixed exchange rates thus gave way in 1953 to a more flexible system of multiple exchange rates, which nonetheless retained many previous features. The principal differences were two—variation in the exchange rate over time to accompany domestic rates of inflation, and reliance on rationing of exchange through an auction system rather than bureaucratic allocation of licenses. What remained was the subsidy of imports considered essential to the growth process, and the continuing implicit tax levied on exports to finance the former. Indeed, calculation of the absolute value of the subsidy conceded to importers of industrial equipment during 1955–1960 compares in magnitude to those conceded to *all* industrial imports between 1948 and 1952 [52].

However, for the remainder of the decade and into the beginning of the 1960s the strategy was to revert to a process of import substitution, for the first time more consciously guided by government direction. Through exchange-rate policy, exemptions from duty on intermediate inputs and capital goods after 1957 when an *ad-valorem* tariff was instituted, attraction of foreign capital, and internal channeling of credit, production was initiated in automobiles and other consumers durables, and substantially extended in chemicals, electrical machinery, and metallurgy. Of the efficacy of the incentives there can be no doubt. Table IX presents the percentage distribution of industrial value added by use in 1949 and 1959. In no other intercensal period, including that of 1919–1939, had such extensive structural change occurred. The share of consumer goods decreased by one-fourth, while the relative position of consumer durables and investment goods each doubled in current terms. In constant prices, the modification is more striking still, particularly for consumer durables. Their participation, measured in 1955 prices, rises from 2.4 per cent in 1949 to 8.3 per cent in 1959. Correspondingly, consumer nondurables decline still more precipitately from 66 per cent to less than 50 [13]. The sectoral composition conforms to expectation. The industries which grew most rapidly were plastics, transport equipment, electrical equipment, chemicals, and metallurgy.

Of the total growth in manufactures between 1949 and 1962, more than 31 per cent is associated with a decline in the import coefficient.[28] A similar calculation between 1949 and 1959, also measured in 1959 prices, shows a smaller, but still large, 26 per cent. At the relative prices of 1949, because imports were less expensive and therefore a smaller share of supply, the import substitution component is reduced to 21 per cent. All indications, therefore, point not only to renewal of import substitution in certain new sectors—transport equipment, electrical machinery, and chemicals exhibit declining imports that represent more than three-fourths of their increased production—but also its global significance.[29]

([28, 29] *see page 346*)

An important component of the new import substitution was the large role played by foreign investment in the process. Its participation was indispensable for two reasons: the necessary transfer of technology in the modern sectors and the self-financing in foreign exchange of the needed capital equipment. The importance of the latter is indisputable. What is striking about the evolution of imports in the decade of the 1950s is not so much their relative decline, but their absolute growth while export receipts in dollars were diminishing. With the exception of the wartime limitations, the constraint upon import capacity was more severe in this period than any other. It was precisely the role of policy to mitigate its effect. Foreign capital was actively sought. SUMOC Instruction 113 permitted direct import of equipment and its evaluation at the most favored exchange rate. This incentive to foreigners was compensated by extension to Brazilian firms of similar advantages on suppliers' credits advanced abroad to import capital goods [11].

[28] Based upon data presented in Morley and Smith [66]. The contribution of import substitution is measured in value-added terms as described in the text. The calculation of the share of production due to import substitution is:

$$\frac{IS}{\Delta VA} = \frac{\Delta VA - [VA_o/(VA+M)_o]\,\Delta(VA+M)}{\Delta VA}.$$

It is derived from the equation

$$\Delta VA = \frac{VA_o}{(VA+M)_o}\cdot\Delta(VA+M) + \Delta\left(\frac{VA}{VA+M}\right)\cdot(VA+M)_o + \Delta\left(\frac{VA}{VA+M}\right)\Delta(VA+M).$$

The second term represents the contribution of a changing import coefficient. The method of calculation therefore is an upper limit of the contribution of import substitution since it credits to it the interaction term. In Table X, we indicate the range of variation resulting from the inclusion of the interaction term in the contribution of domestic demand.

Note that Morley and Smith themselves report a larger proportion due to import substitution—42 per cent. The difference lies in their use of sectoral percentages subsequently weighted by changes in value added. This is equivalent to weighting initial imports by the sectoral rates of growth of supply and leads to exaggeration of the degree of import substitution. Morley and Smith also do not treat the problem of the sensitivity of the measure to the relative price structure selected, or the disposition of the interaction term.

[29] This is at considerable variance with the findings of Huddle [58], who attributes to import substitution a participation of less than 5 per cent between 1949 and 1963. The reason for the different results are twofold: Huddle uses the standard measure of import participation relative to gross production, and more important, has distorted absolute levels and rates of change in his import coefficient. His ratio of imports in total supply in 1938 is 0.15; using the value of imports of manufactures reported in [43] and the census value of production in 1939, the ratio is 0.27. Since this 0.15 is the subsequent base for his parity price calculations, it is not surprising that the role of imports is so small. Note finally that his implicit rate of growth of real imports between 1949 and 1958, obtained by parity price deflation, is of the order of 8 per cent *annually*. The real index value in [43] increases 2 per cent *in total* over the interval.

Despite these inflows, the balance-of-payments problem became increasingly onerous. Once more, while exchange-rate and commercial policy were used successfully as instruments to stimulate internal industrialization, they could not maintain external equilibrium inevitably. The inability and unwillingness to define a serious noncoffee export strategy was the reason. Brazilian export performance, taking fully into account the demand for its nontraditional products, was one of the worst for the developing countries in the postwar period [40]. So long as it was possible, whether by using coffee prices or capital inflows, to guarantee sufficient foreign exchange to allow for imports of capital goods and intermediate inputs, the poor Brazilian export performance could be ignored. Whereas earlier import substitution experiences such as those of the two world wars or of the Great Depression had derived from largely exogenous developments in international markets, that of the 1950s did not. Rather, it was the assumption that substitution was necessary, and the ingenuity to devise measures to compensate for falling exports, that distinguishes this period as one of conscious design.

Even after the establishment of the multiple exchange-rate system, and the greater flexibility to offer higher rates for noncoffee exports, the quantum response was limited. Nor was this simply because the exchange rate lagged behind inflation. In fact, through the 1950s there was continuing real devaluation, which in itself was insufficient to generate interest in the external market. The divergence between import and export rates widened through the latter 1950s and 1960s, equivalent to the imposition of an increasing implicit tax on exports [9]. Instead of the larger real devaluations that should have occurred to equilibrate the external market and to increase exports, higher protective barriers were used instead. Hence the actual trajectory of the real exchange rate is misleading.

Moreover, the discontinuities in the real exchange rate were considerable, particularly as inflation accelerated. Over the 1953–1959 period, the average monthly variation in the real rate was almost 4 per cent, while rates for individual products varied even more due to the differential bonuses conceded [8]. The potential significance of such variance is partially indicated by Brazilian export response after the policy of periodic devaluation was introduced. Other incentives such as drawbacks, tax credits, etc., have obviously been significant in this accomplishment as well. The combination has made it possible for exports to grow rapidly, although real export exchange rates are actually no more favorable now than they were in the early 1960s. Needed and lacking was a more positive and active policy rather than exclusive dependence on the weak market signals emitted by the exchange rate. Indeed, instead, there were administrative barriers, such as licences and bonuses, which discouraged participation in the external market.

The final and related dimension of the import substitution strategy was the reduction in the participation of consumer durables in total imports, and their replacement by domestic manufacture. The estimated participation of imports in total supply to consumer durables was equal to that of capital goods in 1949, approximately 60 per cent. Ten years later, only 6 per cent of consumer durables were imported, a third of capital goods. As a consequence, the average annual rate of growth of domestic production of consumer durables was in excess of 24 per cent over the decade [12]. One alternative to satisfying consumer demand in this fashion would have been by limiting supply of such goods. The other dimensions of such an option—still import substitutive—would have been greater incentives to the domestic capital goods industry, and, in particular, attention to production of equipment simultaneously advanced, yet modified to Brazilian needs. It does not seem obvious that such possibilities were foreclosed by the insufficient scale of the Brazilian economy to sustain efficient production of investment goods, or by the differential technological transfer implied. Such a policy would have inevitably led to more attention to the traditional sectors, and quite possibly to a development less inward oriented and more socially efficient.

Commitment to the sectoral profile actually chosen reinforced the strategy of capital attraction and foreign investment. Approximately half the equipment imported under Instruction 113 was destined for the automobile industry. Of the total growth between 1949 and 1962, foreign firms account for nearly one-third; yet their participation in import substitution, as a minumim estimate, was 42 per cent [10, 68]. Under the alternative strategy suggested above, foreign investment inevitably would have had an important role to play; whether it would have been as great is open to question. In such basic sectors as metallurgy, machinery, and electrical equipment, which also experienced import substitution, foreign participation was smaller in 1965 than in transportation equipment [67]. Leff, in his study of the capital goods industry, finds that domestic firms were more than competitive:

> ...in 1964, the foreign rather than the domestic firms were bearing a disproportionate share of its excess capacity and low profit margins.... In papermaking equipment, local firms had a better profit performance than a foreign firm with worldwide reputation. A similar situation generally prevailed in the sector's other product lines [61].

In the early 1960s the industrialization process began perceptibly to falter. It was common among contemporaries to view it as a stagnation following from exhaustion of the import substitution process. The latter, by divorcing the rate of increase of production from the rate of growth of internal demand, gave an initial stimulus. The difference between the two rates is precisely the consequence of the decline in the import coefficient. Now that the latter had attained low levels, "the internal market expansion... is not sufficient... to ensure the maintenance of the recent acceleration of the rate of industrial growth, which had been achieved largely by virtue of a reserved market for import substitution industries" [83]. Such a narrow market was the consequence of sectoral, regional, and social imbalance, themselves exacerbated by the process of import substitution, whose principal manifestation was the unequal income distribution. Subsequently, partially influenced by renewed growth, others have rejected this view in favor of short-term exogenous factors: political uncertainty and accelerating inflation followed by the inevitable output consequences of stabilization.

The stagnationists seem to be right in their search for an explanation directly rooted in the type of import substitutive industrialization that had occurred, but they err in attributing secular properties to what was essentially a cyclical phenomenon. Inherent in the import-substitution process is a tendency for production to grow rapidly at the outset, at rates clearly superior to those which can be sustained over the longer term. In the case of actual substitutes, such rates are due to displacement. In the case of new goods, which had neither been imported not produced, the reason is the response to lowered price. Effectively, due to prohibition or licensing, the price of the imported equivalent was extraordinarily high, while the domestic substitute was available at a cost within the relevant range. After this initial reduction in price and the response to it have occurred, growth is governed subsequently by income elasticity. Since an important part of the substitutive process in Brazil was in consumer durables, moreover, one had an added fillip to early demand response: the demonstration effect of consumption patterns elsewhere. This description accurately characterizes, for example, the introduction of automobile manufacture in Brazil where early production exceeded previous limited imports, and growth was initially quite rapid.

The deceleration in product output implied by the substitution process is inherently destabilizing. To counter it requires that expectations exactly move opposite to production statistics to restrain early euphoria, and to sustain optimism as the rate of growth diminishes. In view of the confidence in undiminished growth that abounded in Brazil in the late 1950s and the subsequent pessimism to which it soon gave way, it is doubtful that such compensation fully operated. Under these circumstances, after the early boom, there was some tendency for import-substitution producers, and their suppliers, to cut back on investment and expansion plans that had been made earlier. The reduction was further aggravated by another characteristic of the substitution process—large initial and indivisable capital expenditures.[30]

[30] Compare Leff's description of the investment boom in capital goods:

> Rather, the sector's excess capacity seems to be a case of sectoral over-building which occurred because of the way firms made their investment plans. Reacting to the favorable market conditions and expectations generated in the earlier period, the older firms and new entrants installed more capacity than the market could absorb over the short or medium term [62].

The upshot was that soon after establishment many of the new industries had substantial idle capacity that foreclosed their own continuing investment, and altered the plans of others. At the same time in the early 1960s the balance-of-payments crisis was looming larger. Between 1959 and 1962 the outflow of interest and profits on past investment almost doubled; in the latter year, amortizations plus service charges amounted to one-third of exports. Attempts to curtail profit remissions gained increasing support and were finally successful in 1962. In this context, and further fed by the unstable political climate after Jânio Quadros' resignation in 1961, foreign investment was sharply curtailed, foreclosing continued expansion into newer sectors yet. From an annual rate in excess of $100 million in 1959–1961, direct investment averaged but one-half in 1962–1963. On the assumption that all had been destined for the industrial sector, and assuming industrial investment on the order of one-third of the total, the implied direct decline in total investment from this source alone is 5 per cent; when one takes into account the complementary national investment directly linked to the foreign, the effects are further magnified.[31]

Thus, there were inherent real forces at work to restrain industrial growth in the early 1960s, quite apart from the additional perturbing element of the sporadic attempts to contain the accelerating inflation. What makes the process inherently cyclical, rather than stagnationist, is precisely the sharper decline in investment than in income that ultimately leads demand to grow up to previous capacity and motivates new capital formation once more. The high rates of growth from 1968 thus partake of a cyclical recovery, as well as a response to altered policy incentives. Even with an unequal and possibly worsening income distribution, the underconsumption argument must assume declining income elasticities in a large segment of the population in order to conclude that there is a continuing lack of demand stimulus. The aggregate income elasticity is an income distribution weighted average of class elasticities: $\eta_y = \sum w_i \eta_i$. Either the η_i must decline, or the w_i must shift in such a way as to shift income to classes with lower elasticities. There is no evidence that demand in the upper classes had been saturated, $\eta_u = 0$, or that its weight in income had increased drastically. The observed decline in demand for automobiles, for example, is traceable to the price phenomenon noted earlier. Moreover, even admitting reduced demand for certain key products and lags in relative prices and sectoral adjustments, this can explain a *decline* in income. Whether it can explain *stagnation* in an economy with high rates of

[31] Such assumptions are not unreasonable, implying a higher capital output ratio for manufacturers than for the economy as a whole, and a total allocation of net foreign investment to the sector. This further means that foreign investment was accounting for about 30 per cent of capital formation in manufactures, which if anything, is probably somewhat on the low side. Hence the calculation may be an understatement.

population growth and low rates of savings is another matter. Hansen's thesis would seem of even more doubtful value for contemporary Brazil than it proved to be for the United States in the 1930s.

If this last wave of import substitution of the 1950s had crucial limitations, it also had its impressive features. In particular, between 1949 and 1959 productivity per man in manufactures grew by 5.8 per cent. Much of the increase was due to the capital-intensive character of the process, another property predictable from its product orientation and the deliberate overvaluation of the exchange rate. While output increased at the considerable rate of 8.8 per cent annually, the estimated net capital stock accumulated still more rapidly at 9.2 per cent. Total factor productivity advance was of a much more limited magnitude. Depending upon the weights attributed to capital and labor, it ranged between 1.6 and 2.7 per cent.[32] Even at its lower limit it exceeds comparable magnitudes for the other periods. Subtracting the contribution of changing labor quality, which accounts for no more than one-fifth of the observed increase in total factor productivity, does not alter this conclusion; indeed, a striking aspect of industrial productivity growth in the 1950s is the extent to which the educational component is unaltered from the previous decade. Thus, in a conscious fashion, a modern industrial structure embodying new technology and catering to market tastes was introduced into Brazil.

The converse of this proposition is most obviously the limited employment absorption of the process. As has been convincingly shown, the growth of the industrial labor force in Brazil relative to the expansion of output in the decade of the 1950s was smaller than in other developing countries [12]. In spite of a rising share in total income, the industrial sector gave rise to employment of equal shares of the labor force in 1949 and 1964. In part the phenomenon is the result of the modernization of the traditional sector under the regime of favored capital importation; the most labor-intensive sector, textiles, shows a smaller absolute work force in 1959 than in 1949. The relative factor price structure that emerged from the import-substitution strategy was highly unfavorable to expanded employment because of the subsidy granted to import of capital goods. Moreover, while received industrial wages rose less than productivity over the decade, the sum of wages *plus* supplementary costs for social security, etc., did more or less maintain pace. Since the latter represents the cost of employing labor, it is the more relevant magnitude in discussing demand for labor. In addition, since the implicit industrial deflator rose substantially less than the cost of living index, we have the situation of

[32] The capital weight for the lower rate is 0.33, derived from the share of gross capital income to gross value added in both the 1950 and 1960 industrial censuses; the higher is based on a weight of 0.5 which may reflect more accurately the net productivity contribution. All data in this paragraph have been calculated on the basis of adjusted census data.

actual real wage payments as perceived by the worker rising by 3.5 per cent annually while costs to the employer increased by 5.7 per cent.[33]

Such a gain was partially purchased by reduced incomes of potential entrants to the industrial sector for whom no demand was generated at the average prevailing wage. Technological choice was not completely rigid, although much influenced by the product composition of the substitution process. In turn, this perpetuated and reinforced an income distribution favorable to disproportionate growth in consumer durables. The contrast with the circumstances of the 1930s is striking when real wages and labor productivity jointly increased at low rates, as large quantities of new workers entered industry.

By its very nature, in relying upon an internal market exclusively and neglecting agricultural productivity, the import-substitution strategy of the 1950s made it impossible to achieve significant technological advance and substantial labor absorption simultaneously. Only at very high and continuing rates of growth is such an equilibrium possible, virtually necessitating either high rates of income (and hence productivity) growth within agriculture, or exports of manufactures. Yet both were foreclosed by the policy emphasis of the period.

IV

The history of Brazilian industrialization from its origins through its great surge in the 1950s is thus no simple and uniform process of import substitution. Both in its initiation in the 1890s, and its concluding phase in the 1950s, domestic policies were decisive in altering relative profitabilities in favor of industry. In large measure, however, in the early period it was the fortuitous influence of inflation, rather than the tariff, that accomplished the result, just as in the early 1950s the policy of maintaining the exchange rate gave an important and unplanned subsidy to industrial capital formation. During the long intermediate period from World War I through the Korean War, exogenous influences loomed much larger. During such periods the rate of capacity creation was artificially compressed, and while feasible in the short run, brought with it, in the Great Depression, serious problems of technological inferiority.

Table X summarizes the influence of the declining import coefficient as a factor in the growth process in the intercensal periods since 1919. Ranges of the contribution of import substitution are presented, reflecting complete

[33] These calculations are based on census data. The implicit industrial price deflator is derived from the real industrial rate of growth in the *Conjuntura Econômica* and the census nominal increases.

TABLE X

CONTRIBUTION OF IMPORT SUBSTITUTION TO GROWTH

A. Imports as a Proportion of Domestic Value Added[a,b]

Year	Relative Prices 1920	1939	1949	1959
1920	0.90	1.75	0.70	1.00
1939	0.30	0.57	0.23	0.33
1949	0.39	0.73	0.30	0.43
1959	0.18	0.34	0.14	0.20

B. Import Substitution as a Proportion of Changes in Domestic Value Added[c]

Years	Relative Prices 1920	1939	1949	1959
1920–1939	0.52–0.28	0.68–0.40		
1939–1949		−0.21–−0.10	−0.11–−0.06	
1949–1959			0.21–0.10	0.27–0.14

C. Rates of Growth of Output and Inputs[d]

Years	Output	Capital	Labor	Labor Quality	Technological Change
1919–1939	5.1	2.9	4.0	0.0	1.7 (0.4)[e]
1939–1949	7.3	7.0	4.9	0.6	1.0
1949–1959	8.8	9.2	3.0	0.6	2.4

[a] Source: Imports of manufactures from "Estrutura do Comércio Exterior" [43] multiplied by 0.7, divided by value added from census; 1919 census adjusted to include sugar and bakery products, and extrapolated to 1920 by production and cost of living indexes.

[b] Imports include tariffs.

[c] Sources: first estimate, $\{\Delta VA - [VA_0/(VA_0+M_0)]\,\Delta(VA+M)\}/\Delta VA$; second estimate: $\Delta[VA/(VA+M)](VA_0+M_0)/\Delta VA$.

[d] Sources. Output: 1919–1949—Industrial Index, Appendix 1; 1949–1959—adjusted real index of transformation industry, *Conjuntura Econômica*; capital: deflated and depreciated census nominal gross capital applied as described in footnote 18; labor: total end of year personnel reported in census, 1919 adjusted for inclusion of sugar and bakery products; labor quality: income weighted index of educational attainment of male labor force 10–69, income differentials multiplied by 0.6 reflect other than educational inputs; technological change: $Q-0.5$ capital -0.5 (labor + labor quality).

[e] Calculated on the assumption that capital services increased as rapidly as output due to increased utilization.

inclusion and exclusion of the interaction term, respectively. On the whole, the conclusions are not much affected by the uncertainty. As is seen, the contribution is unequivocally greatest during the first period, concentrated in the less than ten years of the Depression. Note, moreover, that despite the war, expansion of imports in real terms thereafter was sufficient to increase the import coefficient above its 1939 level. Yet as we have seen, while this was occurring in the aggregate, its sectoral distribution was highly concentrated in capital and intermediate goods, thereby preserving the market for domestic consumer nondurables. Last, there is the final surge of the import substitution process, this time consciously, in the 1950s. Perhaps as much as one-fourth of the rapid growth of the decade is explained by displacement of the former import market.

Equally impressive is the lack of association between the rate of growth of output and the degree to which industrialization was import substitutive. The same is true of the rate of total factor productivity change, adjusted or unadjusted for labor quality change. Import substitution discussed merely in terms of the reduction of the import coefficient is a descriptive rather than analytic concept. Precisely for this reason, there has been a tendency to exaggerate the adverse implications of the exhaustion of the process as the role of imports has become progressively smaller. By definition, the former import demand will not serve as a guaranteed market any longer, but this demand focus is much too narrow. What made import substitution an effective source of growth were the differential incentives given to producers for the home market—whether by the enforced increased price of imports in the 1930s or the more deliberate subsidies of the 1950s. It may be easier to rely on such a process initially because the previous imports define the extent of the market with certainty. Such a virtue is overstated. Investors can project as well by the consumption structure of other countries. Automobiles, television sets, and other consumer durables did not so much replace existing imports in the 1950s as cater to repressed demand not served by foreign supply.

To speak of the easy phase of industrialization through import substitution and its subsequent exhaustion is therefore to miss the central point. Production will follow profits in a market system, and those profits are subject to policy influence. If exports had been subsidized to the extent of permitting producers to earn foreign exchange at any price, there would have also been a growing market that *ex post* would appear to explain a large part of industrial development. In similar fashion, domestic demand will be credited as new goods, potentially tradable but never imported, are produced by a more diversified and technologically responsive industrial structure. In misreading the cyclical tendencies of the import-substitution process as an indication of insufficient secular market demand, the pessimism of the early 1960s obscured the extent to which it was supply incentives rather than demand that was driving the system. It has contributed to an overconcern with sources of future growth and insufficient attention to the better application of policy incentives.

In the final analysis, the evaluation of the success of Brazilian industrialization reduces to the efficiency of the resource allocation it produced—this last in its broadest sense, by no means exclusive of the possibility that without the stimulus of industrial expansion resources would have been idle. This seems clearly to have been true during the Depression, for example. Nor are errors of excess to be judged by the same standards in circumstances where the limitations and barriers to economic activity are pervasive and occasionally unyielding. By any criterion, it is difficult to argue from the present vantage point that Brazilian industrialization was a mistake. It is equally strained to argue that its early import-substitutive character was misdirected by state policy. Tariffs, while they reached levels as high as 50 per cent and more in the 19th and early 20th centuries, tended toward uniformity. Exemptions on imports of machinery and equipment only reinforced the tendency to move into production of consumer goods with the least comparative disadvantage.

Yet for all its apparent efficiency, this layered development of consumer goods first, followed by selected intermediate goods in the 1920s, and finally, limited capital good production made necessary during the Depression, may have suffered from its excessive reliance upon the market. Instead of an articulated development bloc, in which investment in interdependent sectors is guided and directed by policy, there was more dispersed and less concentrated impact. Moreover, due to the overriding importance of the variable exchange rate in determining the effective tariff wall, private investment was subject to significant short-run as well as long-run forces. One cannot help but contrast the Brazilian pattern of early industrial development with that of the European latecomers, in which state action played a much more central role in creating new institutions and mechanisms of industrial response; or even with that of the United States, where simultaneous production of textiles and textile machinery occurred, and where the introduction of railways also immediately stimulated local producers of equipment.

Layered development may limit the economy not only by causing profitable social investments to be bypassed because interdependences are ignored, but also by impeding the development of an indigenous technology. Increasingly, it has become apparent that a much smaller part of increased income per capita is explained by capital accumulation pure and simple. Both technological change and improved quality of the labor force play large roles. Not until relatively late did such factors begin to receive attention in Brazil, masked by the apparently satisfactory process of industrial growth.

The guided import substitution of the 1950s, despite the backward linkages of the automobile industry, did not fully alter this pattern. Its emphasis upon consumer durables, as we have seen, continued the previous lack of vertical integration back to investment goods production. The reliance upon foreign investment, and particularly the favorable terms for importation of foreign equipment, was in the same vein. State policy altered the basic contours of the historical substitution process less than it might appear.

These generalizations require and merit further study. An understanding of the historical characteristics of the Brazilian industrialization process is no idle exercise. In few countries has the interpretation of the past so defined and discriminated among policy options in the present.

Appendix I

This appendix briefly describes the methodology utilized to derive the GDP and sectoral indices presented in Table A-1. GDP is a weighted average of the latter based on 1939 share in income originating as presented in the *Conjuntura Economica* [34]. The relative weights are: agriculture, 33.2; industry, 21.7; government, 9.0; transport, 8.4; electric energy, 1.5; and commerce 26.2.

The agricultural index is a 1939 Laspayres quantity index consisting of crops representing about 90 per cent of output in that year. No adjustments for differential value added by crop were made, however, nor is there any allowance for net investment in livestock. The available line stock series are linearly interpolated, the weight of changes is small, and the slaughter ratio, while increasing, does not grossly misrepresent movements in the sector as a whole. Meat products were not available from 1925. The basic source for all series except meat was the Getúlio Vargas Foundation [44]. The meat series reported there as cattle until 1939 is, in fact, total slaughter; the entries for 1940 and thereafter are inconsistent with the earlier ones, referring only to fresh, and not total, production. Correct data may be found in Serviço de Estatística Econômica e Financeira [27] and thereafter in Instituto Brasileiro de Geografia e Estatística [19]. For pork, the hog slaughter series was used consistently due to changes in coverage of the production series.

The decision to construct a separate index here, rather than rely upon the one presented in the 1968 Vargas Foundation study, was based upon three factors. One was the variable weight base of that index which makes comparisons with the other indexes difficult, as well as its own interpretation. The second was the aforementioned inconsistency in the series for meat production. The third is an even more serious error in 1940, when an entirely new series on wood production was linked to one previously based upon internal commerce in pinewood. The consequence is a substantial exaggeration in reported primary sector growth during the war: an increase of 60 per cent is reported between 1939 and 1941!

TABLE A-1

Year	GDP	Agriculture	Industry	Government	Transport	Electrical Energy	Commerce
1920	48	59	41	46	37	24	47
1921	48	61	40	45	35	24	47
1922	53	63	48	49	38	25	53
1923	54	64	48	52	45	26	53
1924	55	64	48	47	52	30	53
1925	55	62	49	50	59	33	53
1926	56	62	50	53	56	38	54
1927	61	68	55	58	63	42	59
1928	67	76	58	65	67	46	64
1929	67	77	56	72	71	48	63
1930	66	79	52	79	59	47	60
1931	65	75	55	73	61	47	62
1932	68	79	56	85	57	48	63
1933	74	89	61	76	61	53	70
1934	80	93	68	87	64	60	76
1935	83	92	77	82	71	67	82
1936	92	100	91	80	78	74	94
1937	95	100	93	90	85	80	96
1938	98	102	96	96	92	87	98
1939	100	100	100	100	100	100	100
1940	99	91	105	106	100	106	100
1941	107	98	117	104	106	116	110
1942	105	96	112	110	107	127	106
1943	113	103	124	110	112	139	116
1944	118	104	130	127	121	154	120
1945	121	103	135	144	123	166	123
1946	136	112	157	160	128	182	139
1947	135	110	162	142	131	201	141
1948	150	115	184	167	145	233	155
1949	162	122	201	192	150	254	168

The industrial index is a 1939 value-added composite of production series based upon excise tax collections.[34] Subsectoral, specific output, series were weighted by 1937 prices to form groups to which the 1939 census value-added weights could be applied. This procedure was necessitated by lack of full 1939 price information and failure to have value-added weights at such levels of disaggregation. In addition to value-added weights based on included groups, thereby implicitly attributing the same rate of growth to excluded production, the indices were aggregated to two-digit industrial levels and those

[34] An index based on 1919 weights was also constructed and used for calculating the rates of growth during World War I, and the comparisons in the 1920s.

weights applied. This assumes that excluded observations in each industry grow at the rate of the series available. The results are comparable, yielding slightly higher rates of growth. The individual group weighting was preferred due to the questionable homogeneity of the industry aggregation. As additional data became available, the final index was appropriately chained to avoid the bias inherent in previous attempts to use the same information. The basic series are to be found in three sources [16, 25, 27].

From 1939 to 1949 there already existed an index using 1939 value-added weights and hence fully comparable to our own. The series after 1939 is that of Loeb [64].

One important judgment relating to the cotton textile series should be mentioned. The most frequently cited series, as in Stein [78], for example, shows a 50 per cent increase in production in 1923, followed by a larger decline in the next, and subsequent continuation at the lower level. The 1923 level according to this series was not attained again until 1937. In view of the implausibility of such a pattern, and lack of qualitative evidence in its favor, we prefer the much more even development set out in "Quadros Estatísticos" [28].

Government activity is measured by estimated wages and salaries paid to employees deflated by the cost of living index to 1939 *cruzeiros*. Wages and salaries until 1939 are in turn derived from government outlays, found in Baer [4], and the 1939 factor payment ratio reported in *Conjuntura Econômica* [36]. This ratio is then interpolated linearly between its 1939 value and its subsequent 1947 level, again reported in the *Conjuntura Econômia*. For 1947–1949 the direct personnel expenditures are utilized. The cost of living index is reproduced in Baer [5].

Transport is a combination of railroad and coastal shipping quantity indices based upon reported revenue of the former, and estimated income of the latter. The estimate is derived from multiplying known tonnage by average length of haul and rate, obtained from Consultec [37]. (The 1950 shipping rate was obtained as a relative of the railroad ton-kilometer charge and then applied to 1939 railroad rates.) The railroad series is a Laspayres combination of passenger and ton-kilometers using 1939 relative prices. All underlying quantity series may be found in "Anuário Estatístico" [15] and "O Brasil em Números" [19].

Electric energy is consumption of electricity in Rio and São Paulo from 1928 to 1941, extrapolated back upon a series of installed capacity. From 1941 to 1949 a series on production of 10 enterprises responsible for about 80 per cent of total output is used. This is available in Loeb, "Números Índices." The capacity series has the deficiency of nonconstant utilization, but while erring in annual movements, correctly orients the trend. These data may be found in "Quadros Estatísticos" [27] and APEC, "A Economia Brasileria e Suas Perspectivas" [2].

Commerce is a synthetic geometric weighted average of the agricultural and industrial indices. These are weighted 0.36 and 0.64, respectively, based on a 1939 cross-sectional relationship among the states, of the form $(C/I) = a + b\log(A/I)$, where b is equal to the agricultural weight and $1-b$ the industrial.[35] Although seeming to depreciate the significance of agriculture, the weights make intuitive sense in associating increasing commercial activity with the more rapidly growing, urban-oriented industrial sector.

Appendix II

This appendix indicates the derivation of the parameters of the underlying demand and supply functions from statistical estimation of import demand equations. If the supply of imports is perfectly elastic, all variation in observed imports will reflect different points along the demand function. That demand function, in turn, is dependent upon demand for the product and its domestic supply: by definition, $M = D - S$. Since in reality there are two types of imports within a given category, those for which substitutes exist, and those without, we can further write

$$M = D_1(Y, P) + D_2(Y, P) - S_2(t, p) \tag{1}$$

where Good 2 has a domestic source of supply and Good 1 does not. Demand for each type of good is a function of income and price; the domestic supply is dependent upon price, and time. The latter is a proxy for such factors as capital accumulation, capacity utilization, and productivity change, all of which influence its position in the price plane.

Aggregating over demand for both goods, which are similar in use, we have the income elasticity of demand for imports equal to the income elasticity of the composite category times the inverse of the ratio of imports to total supply:

$$\eta_M = \eta_D\left(1 + \frac{S_2}{M}\right). \tag{2}$$

This result, as the others below, follows directly by derivation of Eq. (1) as indicated:

$$\eta_M = \frac{dM}{dY}\cdot\frac{Y}{M} = \left(\frac{dD}{dY}\cdot\frac{Y}{D}\right)\frac{D}{M} = \eta_D\cdot\left(1 + \frac{S_2}{M}\right). \tag{2a}$$

[35] $R^2 = 0.75$ and $t = 4.55$, both significant at the 1 per cent level for the 21 observations.

Similarly, the import price elasticity is equal to a weighted difference of the demand and supply price elasticities:

$$\varepsilon_M = \varepsilon_D + (\varepsilon_D - \varepsilon_S)\frac{S_2}{M}. \tag{3}$$

This again follows from manipulation of the underlying Eq. (1):

$$\varepsilon_M \equiv \frac{dM}{dP}\cdot\frac{P}{M} = \left(\frac{dD}{dP}\cdot\frac{P}{D}\right)\cdot\frac{D}{P} - \frac{dS_2}{dP}\cdot\frac{P}{S_2}\cdot\frac{S_2}{M} = \varepsilon_D\left(1+\frac{S_2}{M}\right) - \varepsilon_S\frac{S_2}{M}. \tag{3a}$$

Finally, the percentage rate of change of imports over time is equal to the shift in the supply curve times the ratio of domestic supply to imports:

$$\theta_M = \sigma\frac{S_2}{M}. \tag{4}$$

This last formulation is equally direct:

$$\theta_M \equiv \frac{dM}{dt}\cdot\frac{1}{M} = -\frac{dS_2}{dt}\cdot\frac{1}{S}\cdot\frac{S_2}{M} = -\sigma\frac{S_2}{M}. \tag{4a}$$

These parameters N_M, ε_M, and θ_M correspond exactly to the coefficients of a logarithmic import demand equation:

$$\log M = \log A + b\log Y + c\log P + et, \tag{5}$$

where $\eta_M = b$, $\varepsilon_M = c$, and $\theta_M = 1$. Hence, by specification of S_2/M, and some notion of ε_D, we can determine the income elasticity of demand, the supply price elasticity, and its shift over time. Unfortunately, S_2/M is not a directly observed magnitude. Although related to the share of domestic production in total supply, it is not identical to it. Goods which enter into supply without an import counterpart are excluded. Many consumer goods industries with small import shares are, therefore, irrelevant to the calculation. Coarse cotton textile production, for instance, falls into this category, since imports of such commodities had ceased by the 1920s. Only at the limit, where *all* domestic output is competitive with imports (as was probably true in the capital goods industries) does S_2/M become equal to the ratio of domestic output to imports. The effect of continuing import substitution therefore is to increase the ratio S_2/M, but not without limit. As S_2/M rises, some imports are totally eliminated, and both denominator and numerator are simultaneously affected.

In addition to the difficulty of its measurement, the use of S_2/M to calculate the underlying parameters presents a further problem. The logarithmic form Eq. (5) implies a constant import demand elasticity η_M. Since, in fact, S_2/M changes as the substitution process proceeds, this means a variable demand elasticity for the product. While some variation is admissible, substantial changes in the underlying elasticities are presumably not. For our purposes, we have used a constant S_2/M factor, with the recognition that it represents an indication of average behavior rather than an accurate reproduction of the changes over time. Ultimately, therefore, it must be the reasonableness of the results and their internal consistency that determine the validity of the arithmetic values for S_2/M and their assumed constancy.

A variant of Eq. (5) was actually estimated:

$$\log M + xt = \log A + b \log Y + c \log P + edt. \tag{6}$$

The dummy variable d assumes the value 0 from 1920 to 1929, and 1 thereafter. As a consequence, the coefficient e measures the differential rate of growth during the depression, relative to the base rate x of the 1920s. The latter is specified rather than estimated because of the problems of multicollinearity that arise. In fact, alternative values of x were chosen, and the corresponding e coefficients correctly compensated. On the basis of our knowledge of the 1920s, these can be reasonably chosen.

The regression equations used are reported below, with t values in parentheses. CG are consumer nondurables; DCG, durables; RM, intermediate inputs (excluding nonindustrialized products, principally wheat); KG, total capital goods; IK, capital goods for industry; and M, aggregate imports. All import indexes are derived from [43]. GDP and IP are the indexes for gross domestic product and industrial output respectively; the derivation of both is described in Appendix I. The price indexes for each group, $P\ldots/P$ include estimated tariffs and are relative to a general price index. The basic import price indexes are calculated from the value and quantity indexes contained in [43], to which adjustments are made for estimated duties:

$$\begin{aligned} \mathrm{CG} + 0.02t &= 0.38 + \underset{(2.91)}{1.23\,\mathrm{GNP}} - \underset{(3.70)}{0.96\,P_{\mathrm{CG}/P}} - \underset{(2.12)}{0.031\,dt}, \\ R^2 &= 0.71, \quad \mathrm{DW} = 1.18, \end{aligned}$$

$$\begin{aligned} \mathrm{DCG}^{36} &= -6.43 + \underset{(2.77)}{2.29\,\mathrm{GNP}} - \underset{(2.34)}{1.12\,P_{\mathrm{DCG}/P}} - \underset{(1.38)}{0.18\,d\mathrm{GNP}}, \\ R^2 &= 0.89, \quad \mathrm{DW} = \mathrm{x.xx}, \end{aligned}$$

$$\begin{aligned} \mathrm{RM} + 0.02t &= 0.16 + \underset{(4.27)}{1.19\,\mathrm{IP}} - \underset{(2.81)}{0.45\,P_{\mathrm{RM}/P}} - \underset{(2.96)}{0.031\,dt}, \\ R^2 &= 0.69, \quad \mathrm{DW} = 1.27, \end{aligned}$$

[36] Note that for consumer durables, for which no supply response is hypothesized, the form of the equation permits instead a readjustment of income elasticities in the 1930s.

$$\text{KG} + 0.01t = -4.52 + 2.29\,\text{IP} - 0.73\,P_{\text{KG}/P} - 0.057\,dt,$$
$$(5.70) \qquad (2.23) \qquad (2.60)$$
$$R^2 = 0.76, \quad \text{DW} = 1.71,$$

$$\text{IK} + 0.01t = -5.25 + 2.42\,\text{IP} - 0.70\,P_{\text{IK}/P} - 0.058\,dt,$$
$$(4.39) \qquad (1.47) \qquad (1.85)$$
$$R^2 = 0.61, \quad \text{DW} = 1.60,$$

$$\text{M} + 0.02t = 0.76 + 1.97\,\text{GNP} - 0.80\,P_{\text{M}/P} - 0.039\,dt,$$
$$(6.22) \qquad (4.55) \qquad (3.17)$$
$$R^2 = 0.84, \quad \text{DW} = 1.67.$$

On the basis of these coefficients, and the given values of S_2/M and ε_D in Table VII, the other parameters η_D, ε_S, and σ are calculated from Eqs. (2)–(4).

REFERENCES

[1] Análise e Perspectiva Econômica, "A Economia Brazileira e Suas Perspectivas," Vol. 9, p. 1–5. Rio de Janeiro, 1970.
[2] Análise e Perspectiva Econômica, "A Economia Brasileira e Suas Perspectivas," Vol. 7, p. 1–6. Rio de Janeiro, 1968.
[3] Baer, W., "Industrialization and Economic Development in Brazil," pp. 300–301. Irwin, Homewood, Illinois, 1965.
[4] Baer, W., "Industrialization and Economic Development in Brazil," Appendix F. Irwin, Homewood, Illinois, 1965.
[5] Baer, W., "Industrialization and Economic Development in Brazil," Appendix G. Irwin, Homewood, Illinois, 1965.
[6] Baer, W., "The Development of the Brazilian Steel Industry," p. 61. Vanderbilt Univ. Press, Nashville, Tennessee, 1969.
[7] Baer, W., "The Development of the Brazilian Steel Industry," p. 85. Vanderbilt Univ. Press, Nashville, Tennessee, 1969.
[8] Bergsman, J., "Brazil: Industrialization and Trade Policies," p. 35. Oxford Univ. Press, London and New York, 1970.
[9] Bergsman, J., "Brazil: Industrialization and Trade Policies," p. 38. Oxford Univ. Press, London and New York, 1970.
[10] Bergsman, J., "Brazil: Industrialization and Trade Policies," p. 77. Oxford Univ. Press, London and New York, 1970.
[11] Bergsman, J., "Brazil: Industrialization and Trade Policies," p. 73. Oxford Univ. Press, London and New York, 1970.
[12] Bergsman, J. and Candal, A., Industrialization; Past Success and Future Problems, *in* "The Economy of Brazil" (H. S. Ellis, ed.), p. 37. Univ. of California Press, Berkeley, California, 1969.
[13] Bergsman, J. and Candal, A., Industrialization; Past Success and Future Problems, *in* "The Economy of Brazil" (H. S. Ellis, ed.), p. 45. Univ. of California Press, Berkeley, California, 1969.
[14] Branner, J., "Cotton in the Empire of Brazil," pp. 42–43. Department of Agriculture Misc. Spec. Dept. No. 8 (1885).

[15] Brasil. Instituto Brasileiro de Geografia e Estatística, "Anuário Estatístico," Vol. 5, Apendice, 1939–1940.
[16] Brasil. IBGE, "Anuário Estatístico," Vol. 5, Apendice, pp. 1318–1335, 1939–1940.
[17] Brasil. IBGE, "Anuário Estatístico," Vol .5, Apendice, pp. 1353–1354, 1939–1940.
[18] Brasil. IBGE, "Brasil: Séries Estatísticas Retrospectivas," p. 216. Rio de Janeiro, 1970.
[19] Brasil. IBGE, "O Brasil em Números," Rio de Janeiro, 1960.
[20] Brasil. IBGE, "IV Recenseamento Geral do Brasil, Censo Industrial, 1920," p. xlv, 1927.
[21] Brasil. Instituto Histórico e Geográfico Brasileiro," Dicionário Histórico, Geográphico, e Ethnográphico do Brasil," Vol. 1, p. 530. Rio de Janeiro, 1922.
[22] Brasil. Ministério da Fazenda, "Proposta e Relatório," 1890–1900.
[23] Brasil. Ministério da Fazenda, "Proposta e Relatório," p. 51, 1901.
[24] Brasil. Ministério da Fazenda, "Proposta e Relatório," p. 769, 1906.
[25] Brasil. Ministério das Relaçoes Exteriores, "Brasil: Relação das Condiçoẽs Geográficas, Econômicas, e Socias," 1940–1941, 1942.
[26] Brasil. Saõ Paulo Directoria de Indústria e Comércio, *Boletim* No. 4 (1926).
[27] Brasil. Serviço de Estatística Econômica e Financeira," Quadros Estatísticos," 1935–1946.
[28] Brasil. SEEF. "Quadros Estatísticos," pp. 10–11, 1939.
[29] Calógeras, J. Pandia, "A Política Monetária do Brasil," p. 229. São Paulo, 1960.
[30] Calógeras, J. Pandia, "A Política Monetária do Brasil," pp. 280–281, 307, 309, 325, 329, 337, 338. São Paulo, 1960.
[31] Candal, A., "A Industrialização Brasileira." IPEA, Rio de Janeiro, 1968.
[32] Clark, W., "Cotton Goods in Latin America, Part II," p. 46. Department of Commerce Special Agents Ser. No. 36 (1910).
[33] Copeland, M. T., "The Cotton Manufacturing Industry of the United States," p. 21. Harvard Univ. Press, Cambridge, Massachusetts, 1912.
[34] *Conjuntura Econômica* **22**, No. 10 (October 1969).
[35] *Conjuntura Econômica* **22**, No. 12 (December 1969).
[36] *Conjuntura Econômica* **22**, No. 12 (December 1970).
[37] Consultec, "O Transporte Rodoviário No Brasil," Vol. 2, Tables I-1, V-36. Rio de Janeiro, 1962.
[38] Davis, L. and Stettler, H., The New England Textile Industry, 1825–1860, *in* National Bureau of Economic Research, Studies in Income and Wealth, Vol, 30, "Output, Employment and Productivity," p. 231. Columbia Univ. Press, New York, 1966.
[39] Dean, W., "The Industrialization of São Paulo, 1880–1945," pp. 28–29. Univ. of Texas Press, Austin, Texas, 1969.
[40] de Vries, B., "Expert Experience of Developing Countries." Johns Hopkins Univ. Press, Baltimore, Maryland, 1967.
[41] Downs, W. C., "Wearing Apparel in Brazil," p. 10. Department of Commerce Misc. Ser. No. 36 (1910).
[42] Downs, W. C., "Wearing Apparel in Brazil," pp. 11–12. Department of Commerce Misc. Ser. No. 36 (1910).
[43] Fundação Getúlio Vargas, "Estrutura do Comércio Exterior do Brasil, 1920–1964," Vol. 2. Rio de Janeiro, 1969.
[44] Fundação Getúlio Vargas, "Projections of Supply and Demand for Agricultural Products of Brazil," Rio de Janeiro, 1968.
[45] Furtado, C., "The Economic Growth of Brazil," p. 241. Univ. of California Press, Berkeley, California, 1963.
[46] Garry, L. S., "Textile Markets of Brazil," p. 23. Department of Commerce Special Agents Ser. No. 203 (1920).

[47] Garry, L. S., "Textile Markets of Brazil," p. 35. Department of Commerce Special Agents Ser. No. 203 (1920)

[48] Garry, L. S., "Textile Markets of Brazil," pp. 22–24. Department of Commerce Special Agents Ser. No. 203 (1920).

[49] Graham, R., "Britain and the Onset of Modernization in Brazil, 1850–1914," Appendix C. Cambridge Univ. Press, London and New York, 1968.

[50] Great Britain. Department of Overseas Trade," Report on Economic and Commercial Conditions in Brazil," p. 19, 1937.

[51] Great Britain. Department of Overseas Trade, "Report on Economic and Commercial Conditions in Brazil," Appendixes 1, 2, and 4, 1938.

[52] Gudin, E., "The Chief Characteristics of the Postwar Economic Development of Brazil," *in* "The Economy of Brazil" (H. S. Ellis, ed.), p. 11. Univ. of California Press, Berkeley, California, 1969.

[53] Hoffmann, W., "The Growth of Industrial Economies." Manchester, 1958.

[54] Huddle, D., Balanço de Pagamentos e Controle de Câmbio no Brasil, *Rev. Brasileira Econ.* **18** (June 1964).

[55] Huddle, D., Balanço de Pagamentos e Controle de Cambio no Brasil, *Rev. Brasileira Econ.* **18**, 281 (June 1964)

[56] Huddle, D., Furtado on Exchange Control and Economic Development: An Evaluation and Reinterpretation of the Brazilian Case, *Econ. Develop. Cultural Change* **15**, 269–285 (April 1967).

[57] Huddle, D., Furtado on Exchange Control and Economic Development: An Evaluation and Reinterpretation of the Brazilian Case, *Econ. Develop. Cultural Change* **15**, 277 (April 1967).

[58] Huddle, D., Postwar Brazilian Industrialization: Growth Patterns, Inflation and Sources of Stagnation, *in* "The Shaping of Modern Brazil" (E. Baklanoff, ed.). Lousiana State Univ. Press, Baton Rouge, Lousiana, 1969.

[59] Hutchinson, L., "Report on Trade Conditions in Brazil," p. 67. Department of Commerce Report (1906).

[60] Hutchinson, L., "Report on Trade Conditions in Brazil," p. 32. Department of Commerce Report (1906).

[61] Leff, N., "The Brazilian Capital Goods Industry, 1929–1964," p. 37. Harvard Univ. Press, Cambridge, Massachusetts, 1968.

[62] Leff, N., "The Brazilian Capital Good Industry, 1929–1964," p. 32. Harvard Univ. Press, Cambridge, Massachusetts, 1968.

[63] Leff, N., Long-Term Brazilian Economic Development, *J. Econ. Hist.* **29**, 490 (1969).

[64] Loeb, G. F., Números Índices do Desenvolvemento Físico de Produção Industrial, 1939–1940, *Rev. Brasileira Econ.* **7**, (March 1953).

[65] Morley, S., and Smith, G., On the Measurement of Import Substitution, *Amer. Econ. Rev.* **60**, No. 3 (1970).

[66] Morley, S., and Smith, G., Import Substitution and Foreign Investment in Brazil, *Oxford Econ. Papers* (*n. s.*) **23**, 125 (March 1971).

[67] Morley, S., and Smith, G., Import Substitution and Foreign Investment in Brazil, *Oxford Econ. Papers* (*n. s.*) **23**, 128 (March 1971).

[68] Morley, S., and Smith, G., Import Substitution and Foreign Investment in Brazil, *Oxford Econ. Papers* (*n. s.*) **23**, 126 ff. (March 1971).

[69] Palaez, C., A Balança Comercial, A Grande Depressão e A Industrialização Brasileira, *Rev. Brasileira Econ.* **22** (January/March 1968).

[70] Palaez, C., A Balança Comercial, A Grande Depressao e A Industrializaçao Brasileira, *Rev. Brasileira Econ.* **22**, 24 (January/March 1968).

[71] Palaez, C., A Balança Comercial, A Grande Depressao e A Industrializaçao Brasileira, *Rev. Brasileira Econ.* **22**, 40 (January/March 1968).
[72] Palaez, C., Acerca da Política Governamental, da Grande Depressao, e Industrialização no Brasil, *Rev. Brasileira Econ.* **23** (July/September 1969).
[73] Palaez, C., O Desenvolvimento da Industria do Aço no Brasil, *Rev. Brasileira Econ.* **24**, 194 (April/June 1970).
[74] Simonsen, R., "The Industrial Evolution of Brazil." São Paulo, 1939.
[75] Stein, S., "The Brazilian Cotton Manufacture," p. 87. Harvard Univ. Press, Cambridge, Massachusetts, 1957.
[76] Stein, S., "The Brazilian Cotton Manufacture," p. 88. Harvard Univ. Press, Cambridge, Massachusetts, 1957.
[77] Stein, S., "The Brazilian Cotton Manufacture," pp. 91–96. Harvard Univ. Press, Cambridge, Massachusetts, 1957.
[78] Stein, S., "The Brazilian Cotton Manufacture," p. 191. Harvard Univ. Press, Cambridge, Massachusetts, 1957.
[79] Stein, S., "The Brazilian Cotton Manufacture," p. 193. Harvard Univ. Press, Cambridge, Massachusetts, 1957.
[80] Suzigan, W., A Industrializacão de São Paulo: 1930–1945, *Rev. Brasileira Econ.* **25** (April/June 1971).
[81] Suzigan, W., A Industrializacão de São Paulo: 1930–1945, *Rev. Brasileira Econ.* **25**, 106.
[82] United Nations. Economic Commission for Latin America, "Analysis and Projections of Economic Development: The Economic Development of Brazil." New York, 1956.
[83] United Nations. Economic Commission for Latin America, The Growth and Decline of Import Substitution in Brazil, *Econ. Bull. Latin Amer.* **9**, 55 (March 1964).
[84] Villela, A., *et. al.*, "Aspectos do Crescimento da Economia Brasileira, 1889–1969," Table 5-VIII. Rio de Janeiro, 1971.
[85] Villela, A., *et. al.*, "Aspectos do Crescimento da Economia Brasileira, 1889–1969," Table 7.71. Rio de Janeiro, 1971.

V. FOREIGN INVESTMENT AND ECONOMIC DEVELOPMENT

A couple of essays have been collected under the above heading and deal with the behavior of foreign capital in its relation to economic development. It should be noted that these two papers reflect, to some extent, points of view of countries in the process of growth and those of advanced ones, respectively.

Although the approach of Ffrench-Davis and Arancibia makes use of analysis in a strong operational sense, Kindleberger's work puts more emphasis on analytical tools as such. In other words, although both papers may have policy implications, the essay by the Latin American economists is much more explicit (the political process is so strongly linked to the economic one, that decision-makers have only a few degrees of freedom in the new countries).

Finally, an observation on methodology seems to be appropriate to the papers included here. Kindleberger makes his analysis from a bilateral point of view (that is, the foreign firm facing a given country), a typically microeconomic scheme. On the other hand, Ffrench-Davis and Arancibia are more concerned with the global problem of planning; there is an essentially macroeconomic cast to their approach.

The paper presented by *Ffrench-Davis* and *Arancibia*, consists of an introduction and analysis of some fundamental aspects of the role played by foreign capital in Latin America. After the brief introduction, there is a section devoted to outlining the part that foreign capital plays in the process of development: its relation to domestic efforts, the difference between balance-of-payments loans and those for development, and an analysis of direct investment (technological knowledge, management capacity, and foreign markets). Next the writers consider some of the policy problems arising with foreign capital re-investment of profits and a related tax policy, the access to domestic credit, mixed corporations, foreign capital and economic integration, all of them illustrated in the Latin American context. To conclude, Ffrench-Davis and Arancibia present the results of their investigations, the most outstanding of which are: (a) the country whose leaders think and act as if they believed that development depends on what others may do for it has no destiny as an economically independent country; and (b) the policy devices for dealing with foreign capital are seriously inefficient (especially in the part referring to the distribution of costs and benefits).

Kindleberger's contribution is a study of direct investments in less-developed countries and tries to distinguish what have been their historical wrongs and their present values. At the outset, the author gives a detailed account of the scope of the analysis which is limited to relationships between host countries and foreign firms specializing in exportable primary products. Secondly, historical wrongs are taken for granted, so that no discussion is offered on this point. The writer points out that the analysis is not mathematical, although it makes use of three simple equations in order to organize the treatment of the "cost and profits to differing players in a nonzero-sum game" of direct investment in less-developed countries, and that of the costs and profits for the same players using different strategies. The work comprises an introduction of variables and three identities, and proceeds to look at intervening markets, labor and capital costs, technological and management aspects, taxes and government expenditures, external economies and diseconomies caused by investment, amortization methods and investment risks, nationalism involved in the problems, and the applied discount rates. Kindleberger's paper concludes by elaborating on some aspects related to the matter of the division of benefits between the investing country and the recipient one.

NOTES ON FOREIGN CAPITAL AND LATIN AMERICA*

RICARDO M. FFRENCH-DAVIS
Universidad Catolica de Chile, Santiago, Chile

SAMUEL ARANCIBIA
Banco Central de Chile, Santiago, Chile

I. Introduction

In the following notes, we intend only to introduce and analyze schematically some of the fundamentals related to foreign capital's contribution to the development of the Latin American countries. It is neither a question of treating every problem posed by foreign capital in developing countries, nor of dealing with features of the empirical type. On the contrary, it is our purpose to discuss some issues related to foreign capital, with special emphasis on countries like those of Latin America, stressing some aspects which seem to be relevant today.

It is most evident that any study about foreign capital will always be surrounded by strong prejudices in favor of or against it. We believe that an attitude towards foreign capital should never be of the "all or nothing" type. At the same time, we think that, although there seems to be a tendency for the second alternative in intellectual circles, the former is usually predominant in government spheres: an excessive dependence on eventual foreign capital inflows.

As in the economic life of countries it is government thought that has, in fact, a greater expression, our notes will mainly focus on the analysis of development strategies which give a predominant role to foreign capital.

* The authors wish to make acknowledgment for comments made at the seminar on "The Structure and Development of the Latin American Economy," headed by Prof. Osvaldo Sunkel, and at the seminar of CEPLAN, headed by Prof. Alejandro Foxley.

The two main conclusions of this paper are:

(a) The country whose leaders think or act as if they believed that development depends on what others may do for it will have no destiny as an economically independent country; and

(b) Present policy design towards foreign capital is seriously deficient. The empirical consequence is that the distribution of profits is remarkably favorable for foreign capital and embodies important forms of external dependence. The discussion that follows intends to tackle both problems.

II. Foreign Capital Role in the Process of Development

A. Foreign Capital and Domestic Effort

There still exists an old controversy over the question of whether or not it is possible to consider foreign capital as a substitute or a complement of domestic saving. Moreover, empirical work has shown contradictory results. The great variety of these results cannot be attributed to any reason other than the various forms of the treatment of foreign capital in underdeveloped countries, and the other public policies adopted by these countries.

A primary assumption states that the income level characterizing developing countries does not allow an investment margin large enough to warrant sustained and rapid development. As a natural conclusion it appears that foreign capital, in its various forms, is the alternative which may solve this inadequacy. On the other hand, it is not difficult to find orthodox economic models which may serve to "show" how foreign capital inflows can raise an economy's rate of growth.[1]

A simple quantitative example will help determine the role of foreign capital in the development process of economically weaker regions, specifically, in the process of Latin American development.[2] Data available on this point suggest that in 1967 Geographic Gross Product for Latin America reached approximately U.S. $136 billion. Considering, among other things, that the region intended to raise its rate of growth per annun by one per cent, relying for this purpose on foreign capital exclusively, it would require additional external resources in one year of about U.S. $4500 million. In other words, in the event that Latin America insisted on basing its main prospects for development on foreign capital, it would be necessary to obtain

[1] For an analysis of these models and their restrictions, as well as the adequate indicators to measure foreign capital's contribution to development, see Griffin, and Ffrench-Davis [5].

[2] For a complete development of this case, see the Appendix.

a yearly volume of resources two and one-half times greater than the external financing of the region in the year 1967.[3]

What has been said before demonstrates clearly that not only political reasons—such as the search for an independent Latin American development with its own features—but also reasons of feasibility, prescribe a shift in the attitude towards foreign capital and its assigned role in Latin American growth.

There is still another feature, often neglected, which reinforces the previous statement. The above estimations refer to the gross contribution of foreign *capital* to the *geographic* product. Nevertheless, foreign capital obtains a return consisting of profits or interests, which are shares of *geographic* product, but not so of *national* product. In short, the government authorities of a country should concentrate their efforts at the national product level, since this is the variable which reflects the volume of goods and services that increases personal income or the patrimony of the national community. It is rather easy to visualize that the gap between the geographic and national products could rapidly expand in the course of time. If we assume that the average return on foreign capital is 10 per cent, the gap would increase by $450 million in the first year, reaching about $2300 million by the fifth year. This means that in only five years, foreign factors of production would double their returns.

In summary, there are certain circles among whom the prevailing impression is that the only way to break the "poverty circle" is by means of assistance from abroad. But if we look at the magnitude of foreign aid that the underdeveloped world as a whole would require, we recognize that such an alternative is not possible.

In fact, the above argument constitutes a definitive demonstration that it is impossible to rely on foreign capital as the sole realistic alternative to overcome the condition of underdevelopment. The argument suggests that, within the context of an aggregate development plan, it should not occupy a predominant place at all.

Thus we must face the other single alternative—a substantial increase of the rate of national savings. Among the means to attain a greater rate of national savings, we can distinguish two different categories of change: marginal and structural. Among the former, there is always margin for policies to increase the level of domestic savings and to improve its allocation, from a social viewpoint, in any underdeveloped economy. In some of these, it will be necessary to create new savings instruments and/or to modify the existing ones, as well as to reinforce the present financial institutions. In others, it will be necessary to reformulate the tax system, and in many it will be essential to start an educational program designed to modify the consumption

[3] For a detailed analysis on the "foreign trade and savings gaps" of Latin America, see Marshall (6). On this point, and particularly on the case of Chile, see Foxley [4].

patterns of the population and to create patterns consistent with social and economic development. In all of them it will be convenient to reexamine the priorities of national investment. Yet, all these measures, despite their positive effects upon savings and its allocation, will probably produce only marginal increases in the level of savings.[4] It is through the introduction of social and economic reforms of a structural character that an increase of domestic savings to levels consistent with the eradication of unemployment and a vigorous, sustained, and *independent* development can come about. The introduction of structural reforms, which means the effective shift of power from oligarchic structures to national majorities, is the basic element for the creation of a "national conciousness of development," making it possible to implement a program for development.[5]

It can be easily foreseen that the introduction of reforms which involve changes in the economic system will often discourage the inflow of foreign, particularly private, capital. This situation reflects the true nature of man's social activity, wherein the choice of any alternative means resignation to something in return. The point, in this respect, is man's consciousness of the implications of every action or choice. Finally, the authors personally feel that

> foreign investment does not precisely belong to the type of activity which generates and maintains an ideological fervor propitious to social and economic development; this situation can only be the product of a truly domestic effort. In other words, it is not a question of substituting capital for ideological fervor, but of attracting domestic savings with the aid of that ideological fervor—national consciousness of development or whatever it might be—in such a way that domestic capital may completely replace the inflow of foreign capital. Thus, it would be undesirable to rely on financial capital imports as the key stimulus for development. They should rather be considered a complementary device, particularly where new national investment may have a foreign component putting pressure on the balance of payments [5, p. 26].

Once again, we must observe and emphasize that foreign capital yields revenue that opens a gap between the geographic and national product (i.e., between the social productivity of capital and that part remaining in the host

[4] Data relating to the Chilean economy, seem to reinforce this statement. In the last five years, there has been a substantial improvement in the financial market. However, the shortage of savings is the Achilles' heel of the Chilean economy.

[5] In certain political and financial circles, it is often stated that structural changes diminish the level of savings. This statement is made on the grounds of the historical experience of countries where drastic reforms have been announced, although they were never applied with the proclaimed intensity. On the other hand, there are cases where reforms have been made, without placing them within the clear context of planned development, which permit the use of every new situation favoring development. Lastly, those who support the above statement make no distinction between different sectors of savers. This statement might be valid for the case of *traditional private savings*, centered in big capitalist businesses. However, it is certain that the opposite prevails in the case of public savings and the rest of the private sector.

country). The substitution of external savings for national savings will eliminate that gap. Thus, a similar volume of national savings will have an impact upon national product substantially greater than a similar volume of foreign capital. The exception to this rule is in those foreign investments which contribute with technologies and external markets which otherwise *would not have been available*, and provide them at a cost below their social productivity.

In short, the above statements should not be thought of as an utter refusal to recognize the importance of foreign capital in the development process. We have just stated that there are at least some feasibility reasons which prevent us from considering it as a panacea for the problem of underdevelopment. We have also pointed out that the only realistic attitude will be to exhaust every possibility of increasing domestic savings. In this context, foreign capital should be considered a complement to the internal effort—a complement which takes into account the development of every potentiality, and which never moderates or substitutes for those structural reforms which, with the corresponding popular participation, are, at the present, prerequisites for overcoming underdevelopment. We estimate that these considerations should be taken into good account in determining the position of Latin American countries facing foreign capital.

B. Balance-of-Payments Borrowings and Development Loans

Foreign capital may assume different forms, among which we can distinguish loans and direct investment. Each form foreign capital inflows may adopt serves a different purpose. On this point, it would be desirable to know what are the conditions or the specific goals to be attained by these loans or direct investment, as a complement to the domestic effort of development.

Let us first examine loans, starting with short-term or balance-of-payments loans. Latin American economies, or at least a number of them, often face serious problems in their balance of payments. The adoption of adequate monetary, fiscal, and foreign trade policies, even though they may considerably reduce the possibility of facing these problems and their intensity, cannot, unfortunately, eliminate them altogether, although they do help strengthen the international reserves position of the countries concerned. Their causes often appear associated to conditions in the international market (faced by exports from developing countries), over which the exporting country has no control.

Under such conditions, a country hindered by worsening terms of trade should first turn to its own reserves. However, because of its traditional deficiency, the country should appeal to external loans in order to finance an acceptable import level. These loans should be short term, refundable at a time when external prices are recovered.

The international finance organization has recently experienced a significant improvement for Latin American countries. First, Latin American reserves have increased by about $3 billion between 1962 and 1970, having more than doubled during this period. Secondly, there are two encouraging innovations to be observed at the level of the International Monetary Fund: the creation of Special Drawing Rights (SDR)—meaning the availability of new resources, not limited by tied economic policies—at the disposal of any country which has a critical position in its balance of payments. In addition to this, the redesign of the Compensatory Financing Scheme in 1966, permitting countries undergoing a worsening in their terms of trade, to obtain a *nonconditioned* credit from the IMF, to an amount equal to 50 per cent of their share in that institution. Regarding this system, two valuable characteristics should be mentioned: (a) It made it possible to draw up to the amount of 50 per cent (representing a maximum of $982 million for Latin America) *whether or not* they are using stand-by loans, and (b) their automaticity, not subject to the condition of signing "bills of intention," given the worsening of the terms of trade. It is obvious that these innovations mark a positive, though insufficient, change for the IMF and contribute to a greater independence in developing countries. Finally, it is possible to obtain short-term lines of credit from banking institutions abroad. The use of these lines is closely related to an adequate investment of international reserves in time of improved terms of trade. On the other hand, we must remember that a reserve level of about $5 billion would permit the negotiation of short-term credits at an adequate level to cover the needs of countries undergoing foreign exchange difficulties. However, it would be necessary to create and strengthen the mechanisms of financial cooperation among Latin American countries in order to realize this situation. The signing of the Santo Domingo Agreement, setting up a mechanism to support the balance of payments in Latin American countries, meant a moderate but promising advance [2]. A steady advance in that direction, until reaching a Common Reserve Fund, will contribute to the support of the external sectors in these countries. Finally, Latin America should persist in its endeavor towards the regionalization of the International Monetary Fund [7]. This means essentially that standby loans at each economic region of the world will be governed by the regional authorities, according to consistent criteria and models, considering the specific characteristics of the region. Thus, a single criterion—worked out by developed countries—should be avoided for regions showing disparities like those in Latin America, Western Europe, and the Middle East.

There is another category of external loans represented by the so-called long-term or development loans. Remarks should be made on this point in order to show that, also in this case, foreign capital must only be considered a complement to the domestic effort. In short, we wish to call attention to the probable effects of public investment projects financed with foreign capital. Let us examine, as an illustration, the case requiring external financing for building schools, hospitals, or generally speaking, to develop projects containing a small proportion of foreign or imported inputs. For an economy enjoying a somewhat acceptable situation in its balance of payments and international reserves, the use of foreign loans entails the conversion of foreign currency into the domestic, to pay the wages and salaries of engineers, technicians, and workers engaged in the project, and to solve simultaneously the problem of domestic raw materials purchases for the purpose. This conversion, accomplished by selling foreign currency proceeds of the loan by the government to the central bank, determines the relative abundance of foreign currency in the hands of the latter. In order to make foreign capital useful, it must be employed in the financing of imports. Except for the case of a balance-of-payments deficit, this means that the authorities of the recipient country would temporarily give a greater flexibility to the importers, either by reducing real exchange rates or other restrictions, in their purchases abroad. In other words, the country accepting foreign capital under these conditions should also be willing to accept imports which, because of their temporary character, might compete with items domestically produced, and thus discourage many domestic industries already established to substitute for imports. In this case, we can say that appealing to long-term external loans for public investment financing, far from promoting import substitution, tends to delay development in the national industrial capacity. Consequently, although no one will question the necessity of having a greater number of houses, schools, or hospitals, there are sound reasons for opposing their financing via external credits, unless the country requires external aid on account of its negative balance of payments. In fact, the latter is particularly true when pressures upon the balance of payments are intensified as a result of the process of development itself, as the new domestic investment of productive character will contain a rather significant imported component. If this is the case, foreign capital will be contributing to the solution of a balance-of-payments problem.

In short, so-called "development loans" will also have the character of "balance-of-payments" loans, in order to be used effectively by the recipient country. That is, they should only be sought when balance-of-payments projections contained in a development plan indicate a shortage in foreign exchange needed to finance the additional importing of capital goods. External credit, otherwise devoted to the financing of expenditures in local currency, often creates difficulties for domestic activities, instead of contributing to a sound and rapid development.

C. Direct Investment: Technological Knowledge, Management Capacity, and Foreign Markets

We have already examined two possible forms which foreign capital inflows can take: loans applied to the solution of temporary problems in the balance of payments and those used as a complement in a planned effort of domestic savings. In both cases, such capital has a definite financing role. Yet, capital flows entering a country in the form of direct foreign investment, may have quite a different character, as a channel for attaining technological knowledge, management capacity, and foreign markets. Investment, at the political level, is not equivalent to credit, since it means granting direct decision power to a foreign center (the home office), whereas at the financial level, it means variable returns (profits) instead of fixed ones (interest rates).

In considering foreign capital in the form of direct investment, technological knowledge, management capacity, and foreign markets stand out as positive characteristics accompanying it. Direct foreign investment, however, on account of its own nature or because of circumstancial factors, poses a set of problems from the point of view of the independence or sovereignty of the host countries, which forces us to recognize a diversity or conflict of interests between the foreign investor and the national community in which he works. As stated before, foreign investment means granting decision power to a foreign center (from the political point of view). This is closely related to the phenomena of foreign dependence. This intrinsic characteristic of foreign investment, to a country trying to be free from dependence, poses the need of closing the entrance to the strategic development sectors and, in the remaining sectors, to prevent any excess over a level of "critical significance."

In pointing out the existence of "circumstantial" factors, we are trying to call attention to variables, such as the economic sector in which the investment is carried out, the characteristics of the productive process adopted, or the position needed to sell output on the international market. The existence of these, as well as other, problems is clearly reflected in the literature on the subject. Thus, whereas some authors justify a strict tax treatment for the case of foreign corporations as the only way to secure the permanence in the host country of a substantial portion of their profits, others think that such systems are responsible for braking the reinvestment of profits, thus preventing output expansion and discouraging other potential investors. Although there are some who claim that foreign investment prevents the development of a dynamic management class, others emphasize its contribution to its formation; whereas one group considers foreign labor and input use as exaggerated, another group takes it as the condition necessary to derive the highest returns from more advanced technologies. These are not the only elements or points for discussion: exchange rate policies, access to domestic credit sources, depreciation practices, price policies, and the monopolistic character of many foreign enterprises, are also significant parts of it.

The key to the problem lies in the role attached to foreign investment, whether it is primary or secondary: If it is the mechanism chosen to finance development, or if it consists of a device by which we try to obtain technologies and markets which otherwise would be beyond our reach.

When foreign capital is considered only as a complement in domestic development, it is generally believed that external credit may itself play such a role. Thus, direct investment is relegated to a nonfinancial role consisting of making development possible in economic activities which the host country is not capable of developing on its own. In these cases, the country should consciously choose whether to develop such an activity through foreign intervention or to reject it, and concentrate its efforts on other activities where it is possible to develop a particular technology or obtain it abroad, and where domestic market is sufficient or where there is the possibility of reaching markets abroad by means of integration agreements, direct commercial negotiations, or competitive international markets.

We will later refer to these problems. In the meantime, we would like to ask if it is possible to obtain mechanisms or agreements which, without presenting the difficulties of direct foreign investment, may lead to elements such as technological knowledge, management capacity, and foreign markets. The following quotation taken from one of the United Nations publications [8] may be useful in formulating an answer:

> Basic technology is naturally available, without the intervention of foreign firms, by means of access to the information published, training abroad, the activities of centers and research institutions and technological information, the hiring of foreign technicians, and the direct obtaining of technical knowledge abroad (permissions for license use, etc.). . . . However, the advanced knowledge required by modern industry, cannot usually be attained that way. . . .The transfer of operational experience (that of groups of managers, investigators, and technicians) incorporated in a developing country usually requires an active participation in the new work of such foreign firms as well as that of their personnel.

These considerations suggest an entire spectrum of knowledge from the technological to management capacity whose transfer possibilities, aside from the foreign firm in the abstract, would gradually decrease as we advance from the former to the latter. Although they are illustrative, these considerations do not explicitly incorporate elements which may be significant in relation to the problem. Technical knowledge may lend itself to a certain form of classification. Thus we can say that there are given technologies which might be classified as "static" in the sense that they are acquired "once for all," and that may be successfully used for a long while. In this case (technologies are available in the form of royalties, for instance), it would be wise to complement them with an adequate quota of foreign capital in the form of long-term loans and to give them over to the initiative of national firms, whether public or private. There exists a second category among these technologies, which is tied to progressive improvements and is hence characterized as dynamic. This category, in continuous evolution, is often not available, unless it is accepted with foreign capital in the form of direct investment. In this case, as an alternative to the firm with foreign management, it is desirable to consider the association of national and foreign production factors via the formation of mixed corporations. We shall return to this point later.

The significance of a rapid advance in developing a technology adequate to the economic characteristics of Latin American countries must be emphasized. This should be a selective effort, particularly in the case of areas of greater strategic importance for the process of independent development. In order to acquire this kind of selectivity, both in the development of a domestic technology and in the achievement of a foreign one, it would be necessary to have a centralized programming board of technological policy.

In short, there are well-defined areas where it is possible to complement the internal effort with foreign capital. There also exist clearly identified cases in which it is not desirable to resort to foreign capital. Among the former are loans to meet a temporary disequilibrium in the balance of payment, as well as those nonconditioned long-term loans to complement domestic savings, and direct investment as a means of obtaining certain technologies and markets. The acceptance of foreign capital inflows through any of these categories cannot efficiently be adopted in a decentralized form by productive units or firms. In economic terms, these are cases in which market or price systems will not correctly operate under any regime, whether socialist or capitalist. These are decisions which belong in the macroeconomic field and which should be adopted in a centralized form.

Among those cases in which the attitude should be of rejection, should be included the granting of privileges to foreign private capital aiming at a mass inflow as the means that will make an economic take-off possible for the country: the outcome, in a few successful cases in the economic field, would be a return to colonialism, and to a cultural, political, and economic denationalization. In most cases there will be frustrated expectations of development. As stated before, only an enormous internal effort will generate the conditions required to attain the elimination of underdevelopment and dependence.

III. Some Problems of Foreign Capital

A. Profits Reinvestment and Taxation

In the previous section, we mentioned some of the characteristic problems of direct foreign investment. Most of these problems are not mutually independent, a fact which should be taken into account in posing solutions.

One of these problems is that of profit remittances by foreign firms operating in Latin America. Taxation treatment given to these firms constitutes an important point of discussion about foreign capital. In this connection we have mentioned these aspects, as they illustrate what we have stated above. In order to give an adequate solution, it is not desirable to ask for the necessary conditions to maximize reinvestment of profits and then independently design a policy to follow in taxation matters. On the contrary, the point is to find a combination of both which might be considered optimal from the nation's point of view.

TABLE I

LATIN AMERICA'S EVOLUTION OF EXPORTS AND NET PAYMENT TO PRODUCTIVE FACTORS ABROAD (IN MILLIONS OF DOLLARS)[a]

Year	Commodity Exports (1)	Foreign Investment Profits (2)	External Loan Interest (3)	Total Payments (2)+(3) (4)	(2)/(1) × 100 (5)	(4)/(1) × 100 (6)
1960	7923.4	949.2	288.8	1238.0	11.9	15.6
1961	8163.9	1094.0	340.4	1434.4	13.4	17.6
1962	8590.0	1120.6	361.2	1481.8	13.0	17.3
1963	9034.3	1096.6	357.1	1453.7	12.1	16.1
1964	9729.2	1252.7	447.4	1700.1	12.8	17.5
1965	10,216.2	1303.4	545.2	1848.6	12.7	18.1
1966	10,772.9	1518.1	605.5	2123.6	14.1	19.7
1960–1966	9199.9	1190.6	420.8	1611.4	12.9	17.5

[a] Source: ECLA [3].

The usual concern about the level of profits and interests remittances has a solid base in reality. In fact, data referring to Latin America show significant and ever increasing amounts of payments (see Table I). In order to tackle the problem, it is often proposed to impose on foreign capital a high rate of compulsory reinvestment of profits. Thus we intend to avoid a significant part of foreign capital returns flowing to the original country. Moreover, the main goal will be to keep such resources and devote them to increasing the productive capacity of that economic sector where the initial investment took place or in associated industries. On the one hand, these plans do not always appear conditioned to the outcome of an analysis about the potentiality of the sector mentioned. In fact, no one can affirm that a sector, which at a given time justifies a certain rate of investment, will always have a social profitability high enough to deserve additional capital. (The mining sector, through the natural process of draining deposits of the highest quality, illustrates this.) On the other hand, there are reasons of even greater importance which suggest that the general solution best fitted for the case will not be the establishment of policies of compulsory profits reinvestment of foreign capital. To base our action on this alone means looking at the eventual problem of the balance of payments, presupposing that foreign investment is desirable *per se*. This neglects the greater significance represented by an increasing gap between geographic and national products, and the appropriation and control of the patrimony located within the country by foreign capitalists. On the other hand, in negotiating a foreign investment, there is a "price" to be paid for compulsory reinvestment. This price may assume the form of lower taxation, accelerated depreciation, domestically subsidized credits, tariff exemptions, etc. All of these definitely mean giving a higher rate of profitability to foreign capital in return for a part of their gains not being remitted abroad.

In short, a scheme should be worked out which, not being compulsory with regard to profit reinvestment, may assure that a significant share of them will remain in the country by fixing adequately high tax rates on such profits. Thus, the government, which is ultimately responsible for the task of determining priorities in the field of national investment, would obtain a volume of resources which might allow domestic capital stock and productive capacity to increase. In general, compulsory reinvestment constitutes the most burdensome foreign means for a developing country and suggests an excessive concern for balance-of-payments short-term problems, regardless of who controls the patrimony within a country's frontiers. The general advice should then be the highest dependence upon taxation, and the least upon compulsory reinvestment.

B. Access to Domestic Credit

A significant aspect in the definition of a general policy towards foreign capital may be the determination of the conditions under which foreign firms may or may not have access to internal short-term credit. To pose this problem may sound rather strange: what could the reason be for forbidding foreign capital from entering the financial mechanism to provide for short-term needs in times when internal credit is considered "another domestic input" (such as labor services and raw materials), and it is generally agreed that it would be desirable to maximize the use of domestic inputs by foreign firms? Let us begin by stating that in the real world we are most interested in optimizing the use of domestic inputs and, whereas domestic credit is effectively taken as "another domestic input," it demonstrates very peculiar characteristics. The main one is that it is a means which is particularly scarce in underdeveloped countries; credit means a form of using savings, and we started this chapter by emphasizing that one of the characteristics of underdevelopment is a shortage of savings.

There are two important features which should be pointed out here, which have a close relationship to each other. The first is the usual credit rationing observed in many Latin American countries; the other is the cost or interest of banking credit.

The existence of credit rationing is another way of suggesting that the financial banking market generally experiences an excess demand. Under these conditions, those who obtain a greater access to credit are not usually the ones who use it in the most efficient and useful way for the country, but rather those with better social connections, as well as financial ones with bank institutions. This explains the scarcity of credit available to farmers, artisans, and small and middle industries, which in many cases may better contribute to general welfare than some of the larger credit users. In limiting our concern to foreign firms, we find a characteristic similar to that of the domestic consumer who prefers, on the same basis, certain imported commodities to domestic ones. In banking administration there is also a bias in favor of credit to foreign firms, because of the notion that they have greater economic support and "responsibility" in discharging their obligations. This bias is even sharper, in its turn, when the bank is a branch of a foreign institution.[6]

Regarding the second feature—credit costs—we can say that it assumes a special significance in economies suffering from inflation. Traditional credit policy has always tried to keep the nominal interest rate constant. Thus, the real credit cost (the effective cost resulting after discounting inflation affecting the economy) turns out to be artificially low or *negative*. The lack of planning based on the real cost of credit results in a subsidy which favors the one who receives it. This kind of subsidy is generally financed by the saver himself. On

[6] Quantitative data, although fragmentary, will support this statement. At the end of 1968 just 48 foreign firms were having 31 per cent of the credits granted by foreign banks located in Chile. This percentage can be compared with the fact that 17 per cent of the stock shares of Chilean industrial corporations was held by foreigners.

account of the low real cost of credit, giving foreign firms access to internal credit under the terms described *means accepting a transfer of assets from the national community to foreigners.* In fact, foreign firms using such credit may derive a real profit from these borrowings, and nothing will prevent that profit from being eventually remitted to the original country; or in case of not being sent abroad, from increasing its share in the control and ownership of the patrimony within the national frontiers. In other words, a part of the profit obtained by foreign firms will not be assigned to its capacity, efficiency, or technological knowledge, but simply to the subsidy that the host country grants them in offering cheap credit. These remarks might lead us to modify what we said about profit reinvestment policy. Yet, if we analyze the problem in detail, we observe that the best way to avoid the dangers described here consists of being firm in determining the conditions under which access to internal credit is offered to foreign firms, and of determining precisely the cost of credit in such a way as to reflect its real cost to the national economy. In short, the use of credit in a country with a low savings level should not be subsidized, undervaluing nationals who save, and favoring foreign firms who use it.

Thus, in negotiating the terms for foreign capital inflows, the treatment given to credit should be taken into account. The use of internal credit, in turn, means granting *control* over a share of the national patrimony. Making that credit available at a low cost (lower than the one in external financial markets) constitutes a direct subsidy which represents an *ownership* transfer of national property.

C. Mixed Corporations

Some of problems of independence or sovereignty facing developing countries as a result of direct investment may be softened through the merging of foreign entrepreneurs and capital with the corresponding production factors of the host country. The advantages of such a merger will be effective, provided that they mean an actual *participation* of national entrepreneurs in the decision-making process. Thus, greater experience and knowledge in the management and technological fields on the part of the foreign entrepreneur will gradually be transferred to national firms through coexistence in the same business. The important aspect of this system, more than the sharing of profits, is active participation in the production process, management, technology, and the marketing of output. This will be an essential for the mixed corporation in order to soften or eliminate the negative features of foreign investment. Above all, the national institution associated with foreign capital should prevent itself from becoming a mere representative or lobbyist for the enterprise, seeking privileges and grants for the mixed corporation. Unfortunately, this is frequently the case.

D. Foreign Capital and Economic Integration

Integration by a group of developing countries may provide a way to defeat external dependence or to consolidate it. The existence of a greater market free from tariff barriers offers a temptation to foreign investment, especially for more dynamic industries of a regional character. Evidently, it may be an effective or positive contribution to regional development with the technologies introduced. However, a regional policy to face it should be selective and consistent among the member countries.

The difficulties this task implies are not neglected when recommending the ways to reach this harmony: this harmony is difficult to reach (even in the case of sharing the conclusions arrived at in Sec. II). There are many factors that justify a different evaluation by each country of the relative weight given to foreign capital in the process of development. We are rather trying to emphasize the priority that these countries, particularly those connected by links of regional economic integration, may give to their efforts in order to reach an agreement upon the basic concepts related to the treatment of foreign capital. Such an agreement or agreements should be basically aimed at avoiding: (a) competition among Latin American countries in attempting to attract foreign capital, a competition which will lead a single country to seek advantage at the expense of the welfare of Latin America's people; and (b) the establishment of hegemony by non-Latin American capital in the most crucial and dynamic industries of the future common market.

In the case of member countries of a process of economic integration, the agreements mentioned above are necessary to guarantee that the initiatives adopted by each country towards foreign capital will follow limitations common to every member. This means that the coordination required by the integration process (with respect to the different phases in the economic policies of participating countries) should cover all areas which directly or indirectly determine the treatment given to foreign capital.

With respect to this point, it should be noted that in Latin American subregions, the importance of the problem has been well recognized. Thus in posing the necessity of coordination of the various branches of economic policy, the Agreement for Subregional Integration recently signed by Bolivia, Colombia, Chile, Ecuador, and Perú emphasizes the harmonic treatment of foreign capital among all countries belonging to the subregion [1].

The efforts made in this direction by the commission of this agreement are quite promising. In case of attaining its goals, it will maximize the foreign capital contribution to the development of the subregion, but with a sovereign and independent scheme.

What has been just said, with special reference to the case of Latin American countries engaged in an integration process, will also hold for the situation of the region as a whole. Coordination with regard to a foreign capital policy will surely reduce or eliminate some of the costs which are at present incurred in relation to foreign capital. In fact, it would likely be difficult for a Latin American country by itself to be successful in trying to avoid an external credit acceptance which might imply a commitment, such as the purchase of certain capital goods and raw materials, or the use of some special means of transportion under given price conditions. The country in question will surely expect a substantial reduction in capital contribution compared with that which it would have received under different circumstances. The outcome will certainly be different if every Latin American country reaches a basic agreement regarding the conditions or terms under which it is willing to accept foreign capital.

IV. Conclusions

It would be desirable to point out once again—as a concluding remark—some of the problems posed in the above paragraphs:

(a) The amount of foreign capital that Latin America requires to begin its path towards development inevitably leads to recognition of the impossibility of relying on this alternative. A substantial increase of the domestic savings rate—through the introduction of social and economic reforms and the creation of a "national consciousness of development"—seems to be the main task for any underdeveloped country willing to make a serious effort to overcome its condition of poverty and dependence.

(b) Foreign capital should only be considered as a complement to the domestic effort. In this sense, we must think that balance-of-payments loans and long-term credits on the one hand, and direct investment on the other—the latter taken as the means of access to technological and management knowledge and to external markets—constitute definite ways through which foreign capital may contribute to the process of development of economically weaker countries.

(c) The questions posed by foreign capital in general are not mutually independent, and this fact should be taken into consideration in stating possible solutions. The establishment of a taxation treatment and criteria regarding the reinvestment of profits constitutes only an example of what has been said before. The greatest realiance upon taxes and the least upon compulsory reinvestment is recommended to solve this specific feature of the problem.

(d) Underdeveloped countries should be particularly cautious in determining the conditions under which access to internal credit is given to foreign firms, without leaving the task to the risk of "market forces." Not doing this may imply accepting a transfer of resources from the host country to the foreign sector.

(e) In developing countries facing problems of independence or sovereignty because of direct foreign investment, the establishment of mixed corporations emerges as a mechanism potentially acceptable not only to make foreign technology and managerial capacity available, but also to obtain effective participation in the firm's marketing policy. The design adopted by mixed corporations is crucial. In case it is faulty, the result might be an increase of the external dependence: foreign control of these firms, with domestic capital and labor serving the foreign capital. The objectives of mixed enterprise will only be met if the host country is allowed effective and progressive access to technological knowledge and development and to marketing channels.

(f) Progress in regional processes of economic integration raises the urgent question of harmonizing the policy of the member countries *vis-á-vis* foreign investment. Otherwise, the competition among countries to attract such a capital would result in an excess profit for foreign investment and in a process of development which would show an increasing picture of external dependence. Only adequate harmonization will permit the coexistence of foreign investment parallel with the pace towards a true independent development free from pressure and influence from abroad.

Appendix

The Gross Geographic Product (GGP) of Latin America amounted to $136 billion in 1967.[7] The GGP per capita has increased by 1.9 per cent per year in the period 1950–1967 [9]. Its increase to 2.9 per cent means an annual increase of $1360 million over 1967. Assuming that the marginal capital-product coefficient is 3.3, an additional annual investment of $4500 million would be required. The capital-product coefficient was obtained by weighting the coefficients of each of 18 Latin American countries according to their GGP level in 1967.[8]

[7] U.N. La Economía de América Latina en 1969, May 1970. Figures given in 1969 dollars have been corrected by the U.S. consumer price index to obtain data in 1967 values.

[8] For data about coefficients by country see [6, p. 185].

The net capital contribution (principal less refunding and depreciation) amounted to $1863 million in 1967. Thus, the additional contribution represents an increase of about 250 per cent over the 1967 level.

Estimations have been made in the simplest way possible, in order to show the probable ordering of magnitudes of the capital required and the interest and profits to be earned.

REFERENCES

[1] Acuerdo de Cartagena, Arts. 27 and 28.
[7] Boletin Mensual, Centro de Estudios Monetarios Latinoamericanos (November 1969).
[3] ECLA, Economic Survey of Latin America (1967, 1968).
[4] Foxley, A., Experiencia en la Utilizacion de Modelos Economicos para la Planificacion de Mediano Plazo en Chile, ODEPLAN (1968).
[5] Griffin, K., and Ffrench-Davis, R., El Capital Extranjero y el Desarrollo, *Rev. Econ.* No. 83–84, 86–87, Univ. de Chile (1964, 1965).
[6] Marshall, J., El Modelo de las Dos Brechas como medio de cuantificar los requerimientos de recursos externos de A. L. *in* "Estudios Monetarios II." Banco Central de Chile, 1970.
[7] Massad, C., and Carrasco C., Problemas Financieros y Monetarios de la Integracion Latinomericana: Algunos comentarios, *in* "Estudios Monetarios II." Banco Central de Chile, 1970.
[8] United Nations, Las Inversiones Extranjeras en los Paises en Desarrollo (January 1968).
[9] United Nations, Economic Survey for Latin America, Fig. 7, p. 10 (1968).

DIRECT INVESTMENT IN LESS-DEVELOPED COUNTRIES: HISTORICAL WRONGS AND PRESENT VALUES

CHARLES P. KINDLEBERGER

Massachusetts Institute of Technology, Cambridge, Massachusetts

I. Introduction

In an effort to narrow and simplify the scope of this paper, we shall deal only with the relations between host countries and foreign firms specializing in primary products for export. This leaves out consideration of the home country and the problems of investment in import-competing manufactures. The former could readily be added by extension of the technique; the latter by its modification, some suggestions toward which are indicated along the way at particular points.

The paper offers no real discussion of historical wrongs. For the most part they are assumed to exist, most probably objectively, but certainly in the perception of the officials and public of the host country. The facts in many cases will be cloudy or difficult to interpret. In the International Petroleum case in Peru, for example, the country and the company differ about the title to land which Peru deeded in 1826, after independence, to one of its citizens, and whether this title legitimately included mineral rights; about the lease which IPC obtained from the British owner in 1914; and about the legitimacy of the international arbitration to which Peru agreed, after some British arm-twisting, in 1922. The facts are complex and debatable; the emotions to which they give rise are not. And there are numerous cases of outright "exploitation." Diaz Alejandro contrasts the carpetbaggers who invaded Cuba (and especially the Isle of Pines) after 1898 to buy up sugar land, with the moratorium on new foreign investment in Germany after World War II, imposed until after monetary reform and the beginnings of reconstruction [4].

Where an original bargain is lopsided owing to ignorance on the side of the citizens or government of the host country, the moral history is even more debatable. Is it wrong to take advantage of advanced technology or wider access to information so long as there is no misrepresentation, no wrongful obtaining of insider information, no bribery, corruption, gunboats, or strong-arm tactics? Is the advanced foreigner under any obligation to share his knowledge and technology with owners of natural resources prior to fixing the terms of a concession? In many instances, of course, there is not knowledge of oil or ore deposits, but only a suspicion of their existence; such investment is risky. But suppose the foreigner had a monopoly of the technology, so that there was no other way to obtain it other than by making a deal with him, and suppose the proposition was risky *ex ante*, but paid off big *ex post*. Is that exploitation? Is it possible to have situations which were not exploitative *ex ante* but are properly regarded so *ex post*?

In economics, bygones are bygones. The past is forgotten when it produces no income. Historical wrongs, however, may well have payoffs. They produce streams of income for political figures or political parties and may easily produce a payoff for a country in xenophobic cohesion. Social and political cohesion which is tolerant of similar units on the same or higher and lower levels is likely to be considered superior to that based on antipathy. But the latter may be better than none. Social and political cohesion based on isolationism or xenophobia may be a consumption good which can substitute for real income in the welfare function of a country [2], or it may even be a producer's good, which spurs a people on to greater productive efforts or more saving, and incentive for the effort needed for development. It may keep the masses quiet while unequal income distribution stimulates capital formation and growth. Compare the Mexican formula for development as expressed by a cynic: "Revolutionary slogans and high profits."

The present values of the title are, of course, present discounted values. A foreign firm will undertake investment when the present discounted value (PDV) of the stream of income envisaged exceeds that of costs, which are largely but by no means solely current, both calculated at some appropriate discount rate. But a given foreign investment has a present discounted value for the host country, as well as for the firm undertaking it. It would be possible to calculate PDVs for various political and social elements in the host country on a disaggregated basis. Moreover, there will be alternative present discounted values of a given investment for a host country, depending upon different regulations or different rates of tax. In particular, there will be a different value for the investment depending upon whether it is operated by the foreign firm under nondiscriminatory national treatment, or if it is nationalized, which under international law, presumably, calls for compensation. The question in all these cases is what to include in the stream of income and what in the stream of costs—this is the subject of the present paper.

The discussion is not mathematical, although it makes use of three simple equations merely to organize the discussion of the costs and benefits to different players in the nonzero-sum game of direct investment in less-developed countries, and to the same player with different strategies. The models are extremely simple and would probably have to be modified for different primary products, such as tin in Bolivia or Malaysia, oil in Venezuela or Indonesia, bananas in Central America, or tea in India or Ceylon. Changes would be especially required, as already noted, if the models were to be applied to import-competing manufactures.

II. The Variables

New investment is undertaken or not undertaken on the basis of a simple formula for capitalizing a stream of income. In perpetuity, where the income is constant, it is expressed as

$$C = I/r, \tag{1}$$

where C is the capitalized value of the investment, I is the annual income on it in perpetuity, and r is the normal rate of profit expressed in per cent per year.[1] If C, the value of the asset, exceeds C', the value of the stream of costs, by some normal proportion the investment will be undertaken; if not, then it will not be. In what follows, I is disaggregated into various elements which are viewed from three vantage points: that of the foreign investor, f; that of the home country, h, but under two different circumstances, one when the investment is operated by a foreign investor, h_f, and one when it is nationalized, h_{nat}.

The three formulations permit three comparisons: first, the value of a given investment to the foreign investor and to the home country; second, the value of the investment to the host country in foreign ownership and after nationalization; and third, the value of the investment to the foreign investor and to the host country when the latter operates it itself. These three comparisons address the resulting issues in the literature: the distribution of the gains from foreign investment[2]; the appeal of confiscation of foreign investment by a developing country [3]; and the theory of direct investment.

[1] We disregard the complications introduced by an irregular time profile of earnings, which, of course, is the normal expectation.

[2] For the Prebisch contribution, see Economic Commission for Latin America [5, 6]. See also Singer [16].

III. Three Identities

The present discounted values may be approximated by three identities, as follows:

$$C_{\mathrm{f}} = \frac{(S_{\mathrm{f}} - w_{\mathrm{f}} L - r_{\mathrm{f}} K - T_{\mathrm{h}} - G_{\mathrm{f}}) z}{D_{\mathrm{f}}}, \tag{2}$$

$$C_{\mathrm{h_f}} = \frac{T_{\mathrm{h}} + (w_{\mathrm{f}} - w_{\mathrm{h}}) L - G_{\mathrm{h}} + \mathrm{EE}_{G_{\mathrm{f}}} + \mathrm{EE}_{\mathrm{f}} + N_{\mathrm{f}}}{D_{\mathrm{h}}}, \tag{3}$$

$$C_{\mathrm{h_{nat}}} = \frac{S_{\mathrm{h}} - w_{\mathrm{h}} - r_{\mathrm{h}} K - p\mathrm{RDM} - G_{\mathrm{h}} - A + \mathrm{EE}_{\mathrm{h}} + N_{\mathrm{h}}}{D_{\mathrm{h}}}, \tag{4}$$

where

C is the present discounted value of an investment;
S is annual sales;
L is labor required by the project;
T is annual taxes paid by the project over time;
K is capital stock;
G is the annual cost of services provided by government or government investments;
RDM is foreign technology and management;
EE is external economies;
A is annual compensation payments over a long period;
N is satisfaction from national ownership (n) or dissatisfaction because of foreign ownership (f), normalized as an annual return on a public good or evil;
D is the discount rate in per cent per annum;
p is the price of foreign technology and management per year;
w is the annual wage rate;
r is the rate of return on capital in per cent per annum;
z is an element of political risk, where $1 > z > 0$, and 1 represents no risk and 0 represents a certainty of loss owing to political factors.

IV. Marketing

First compare S_{f} and S_{h}, the sales of output of a particular investment in foreign hands, and after nationalization. Under well-functioning international markets and perfect competition, $S_{\mathrm{f}} = S_{\mathrm{h}}$. The nature of the ownership would be a matter of indifference to sales. But this is by no means the only outcome. Many observers in less-developed countries, such as Prebisch, and most marxist and strongly left observers, believe that S_h under nationalization would exceed S_f, because of the overcoming of monopsony. Julien, for example, or Magdoff claim that United States firms pay low prices but get large amounts of needed raw materials at high profits [9, 12]. Presumably when S is decomposed into PQ, Q may be high, but P is unduly low. With different ownership Q might remain the same or decline slightly, while P would rise by more than Q declined to raise total S. Or the typical Canadian fear is that an American company which owned a high-cost mine in the United States and a low-cost one in Canada, might cut back in depression according, not to economic, but to political considerations—how much more unpleasant it would find unemployment in Montana than in British Columbia, for example. Under these circumstances, $S_h > S_f$ and, other things equal, a shift to Canadian ownership would improve Canadian and world welfare.

This is by no means the only possibility, however. The theory of direct investment postulates that the foreign investor must have an advantage over the domestic investor in order to overcome the disadvantages of operating in a foreign culture and at a distance from its decision center. One of the possible advantages, especially relevant in bulky primary products like oil and iron ore that are costly to ship and store, is that a vertically-integrated company can sometimes coordinate different stages of production more efficiently than a system of disaggregated markets. Production, shipment, processing, and distribution must be articulated with some precision, if it is expensive to have excess supplies or gaps in supply at separate stages. This may require an overall directing brain which the disaggregated market, with separate decision-making at each stage, does not provide. Long-term contracts are a partial substitute for this vertical integration, but raise awkward questions of dependence at times of renegotiation and renewal.

There is an element of monopsony here, to be sure. Highly efficient units at a given stage may be unwilling to operate independently for fear of being cut off from sources of supply or potential marketing outlets by an oligopolistic industrial structure. Once vertical integration enters an industry with only a small advantage, it tends to spread with little or no economic justification. But the economic efficiency of coordinated operations in different stages of production, where there are economies to be gained from such coordination, must mean that there are many cases where $S_f > S_h$. This seems to be the explanation of why Japanese ownership in Australian iron mines is appropriate, why Hirschman may be wrong in recommending blanket divestment of foreign investment in Latin America, and which support Adelman's position that the large international oil companies will still find a place when and if they have been pushed out of producing areas, and when the consuming and producing countries have failed any longer to hold up the price of world oil [8, 1].

The foreign company's advantage over local enterprise may lie in marketing even without the economies of coordination just outlined. These economies are probably not important in copper, but both in Zambia and Chile arrangements for government acquisition of 51 per cent ownership of producing mines provide for management and sales by the foreign firm. In the case of Sociedad Minera El Teniente, SA, the Chilean Government owns 51 per cent and the Kennecott Copper Corporation (through the Braden Copper Company) 49 per cent, but Kennecott has a contract with the Board of Directors—a majority appointed by the Chilean government—to manage the operations of the mine and "an Advisory Sales Contract that calls for our advising the board on market conditions, pricing and related matters."[3] Where the marketing company has a special advantage, it must be presumed that the marketing fee includes a rent on its scarcity. But in complex bargaining situations of this sort, where there is no competitive standard, it would be difficult to measure such rent.

There is no clear indication whether S_f is equal to, exceeds, or falls short of S_h. Anything can happen—circumstances alter cases. There is every reason to examine the circumstances of a particular case and arrive at a judgment as to the extent of real economies of marketing and of monopsony power, both that which can be evaded, and that which cannot.

V. Labor Costs

In the enclave case, where the foreign company brings in workers from the home country (or even one hundred years ago in the guano industry in Peru from China), L must be subdivided into L_h and L_f, and possibly L_f into L_{home} and $L_{contract}$ [11]. Disregarding these cases, however, we may focus on the rent which local labor, L, may earn under foreign investment. This is $(w_f - w_l)L$ in Eq. (3) and is positive though not always sizeable. This increases domestic purchasing power, and thus has local benefits. It may also have the costs of creating a dual economy and disincentives for ordinary labor to work at occupations outside the foreign investment sector, as opposed to waiting for a job in that sector.

If the shadow price of domestic labor is zero, the total $w_f L$ is a gain for the less-developed country in Eq. (3), but the dual-economy complications are more serious. If labor unions organize and push up the discriminatory wage paid by foreign investors, the external economies in training from the foreign

[3] See Michaelson [14]. See also the similar arrangements between Zambia and the Roan Selection Trust, set out in the Statement by the Chairman, Sir Ronald L. Prain, accompanying the Roan Selection Trust Ltd. Annual Report for 1969.

investment may be reduced as more home-country labor is brought in, or more foreign capital to substitute for domestic labor.

VI. Capital Costs

Typically, one can expect $r_f < r_h$. This is another element of monopoly. One theory of direct investment asserts that plowed-back profits are the cheapest form of savings, and need to earn only slightly more than the government bond rate in the home country to make it worthwhile for the corporation to expand rather than to pay out earnings to its stockholders. Where continued expansion in its home market is likely to cut prices and profits, a company may go abroad and expand in a noncompeting area. Under this theory, a firm need not earn more abroad than at home to undertake foreign investments, or more abroad than its local competitors, so long as it earns more than the long-term government bond rate at home and is able to avoid depressing home profits. To the extent the theory applied at all, it is more relevant to direct investment in manufacturing than to primary production.

Even if we reject the cost-of-capital theory of direct investment, however, it is likely that $r_f < r_h$. This is the original basis for thinking that direct investment belongs to the theory of capital movements, rather than to—in the present view—oligopoly theory. With separated capital markets (and no other distinct advantage in technology, management, and the like) direct investment would flow, like portfolio capital, from capital-rich to capital-poor countries. Only with capital markets perfectly jointed and perfectly competitive, with $r_h = r_f$ for all kinds of borrowers, does the cost of capital become irrelevant to direct investment. The basis for thinking $r_f < r_h$ is either that capital markets are imperfectly joined or that they are not perfectly competitive, so that larger and better known firms have an advantage over smaller and less well-known borrowers. In this latter circumstance, the foreign firm may have an advantage in borrowing at a cheaper rate than host-country enterprise, even in the host-country capital market. It seems that McKinnon and Shaw are exploring the infant-industry aspects of capital markets in less-developed countries, to test the hypothesis that learning by doing is strong in them, and that there is merit in discriminating against the borrowing by foreign firms on the ground that this inhibits the step-by-step development of a flourishing capital market, vital to development.

A fortiori, the foreign firm has an advantage over the enterprise of the less-developed country when it comes to borrowing in the capital market of the developed country, especially when the borrowing record of the less-developed country is complicated by past defaults or rolling over of debts.

VII. Technology and Management

There is no counterpart for pRDM in Eq. (2), which expresses the present value of the investment to the foreign firm. This is because it is assumed that the costs of research and development and management, including market management, are sunk, and that incremental costs of extending these services to a particular foreign investment are negligible. This will not always be true, of course, particularly in instances where it is necessary to modify the technology appropriate to developed countries before it can be used in less-developed situations. In addition, in the long run, the company may feel it necessary to spread its overhead evenly over all operations. R & D could be regarded as an investment on which the company had to earn a return in every use. In this case it could be included with K on which the company wanted a return of r_f or with equity on which it required D_f. The question whether foreign subsidiaries are charged management fees, or whether these are lumped with profits and taxed may turn on such questions as whether a given subsidiary is a joint venture or 100 per cent owned. It may be necessary in some cases, therefore, to allow for a $p\text{RDM}_f$ which is distinct from $p\text{RDM}_h$.

Whether $p\text{RDM}_f$ is zero or positive, however, it is likely to be lower than $p\text{RDM}_h$. Local enterpreneurs in less-developed countries, who need technology or management services, including marketing, may be expected to pay for them at competitive and not monopoly prices, that is, when they can get the RDM services at all. Many firms in developed countries choose to invest abroad rather than to license, because they keep their proprietary interest in the technology inviolate by not renting it out, and because the market for technology does not squeeze out the last bit of rent available, as direct investment may do. Much technology is available on license, of course, and there is a borderline where the decision to license or not is a close one. Moreover, new technology can be produced to order by specialized research firms, though results cannot be guaranteed and the services are said to be expensive. A local firm in a less-developed country may find it sufficient to hire management consulting services rather than employ foreign enterprise full time. Nonetheless, there is likely to be a higher cost, or less service, in research, development and management when a firm is owned locally than when it is foreign.

VIII. Government Expenditure

G_h is provided by the host country; G_f is the annual cost of economic overhead capital of the sort usually provided by government which the foreign investor may be required to contribute, in a few cases of large companies investing in fairly primitive economies. Aramco's construction of ports and railroads in Saudi Arabia would be one example; or the United Fruit Company's initial investment in the Central American railroad. For the host country, this G_f may pay external economies (EE), but in most cases G_f serves primarily the interests of the foreign investor. Where it is a railroad such as that from Ras Tanura to Mecca, built by Aramco for the Saudi Arabian Government with little or no benefit to the company, it is evidently in lieu of taxes, and could be consolidated with T_h.

G_h is government expenditure which the host government must undertake to make the foreign investment viable. It is assumed to have no external economies or to be net of external economies. It is unlikely to be a net benefit, rather than a cost, although it might be that unanticipated external economies made the *ex-post* result positive, rather than negative. In any case it is assumed to be no different before or after nationalization.

IX. Taxes

Taxes raise a particular problem of the time profile because of the shift of bargaining power from a time before a foreign investment is installed until after it is fully developed. Before a concession is granted, the weight of bargaining power is largely on the side of the company. Countries grant tax concessions to compete for potential investments, although they are urged by such economists as Bhagwati, Diaz Alejandro, and Rosenstein-Rodan to form cartels and limit the erosion of contract terms. Once the investment has been made, however, the balance shifts. The increase in levels of taxation is most clearly seen in petroleum, where small royalties per barrel gave way to income-tax schemes, taxing corporate profits at levels which mounted from 25–50 and finally as high as 75 per cent, followed by calculating income on the basis of posted rather than actual prices and of hypothetical rather than realized income. The Organization of Petroleum Exporting Countries (OPEC) insists on the legitimacy of contract renegotiation, not unknown in Anglo-Saxon practice when the circumstances prevailing at the time of the original contract have drastically changed. Such renegotiation, when no objective circumstance has changed other than bargaining power, raises subtle questions of legality to which an economist has nothing to contribute.

Taxes on oil companies in the Middle East have risen from \$1 billion in 1960 to \$6 billion in 1969. We do not have data available on other primary products, such as tin in Malaysia and Indonesia, iron ore in Africa, Latin America, and most recently Australia, or copper in Africa and Chile. It is evident, however, that the variability of profits with export prices is an important qualification to Raúl Prebisch's controversial view that the long-run terms of trade tend to turn against primary producers. Such terms of trade on merchandise account fail adequately to measure the distribution of welfare between the industrial-investing country and the primary-producing host. For this purpose, we need what have been called variously the terms of trade on returned value [13] or the terms of trade on current account with the rate of profit earned by investor, which had been declining, shown as an offset to the decline of export commodity prices [10].

Note that the capacity of less-developed countries to tax is fairly well developed when they confront a few large raw-material producers but less so in import-competing lines. In the former case, they are not inhibited by the requirement of national treatment, and can tax directly, and indirectly, through other means such as multiple exchange rates, up to the limits of the companies' reserve price, at which they will pull out. It is important not to go too far. The rate of tax and the definition of what is income are both largely in the control of the host country. In import-competing industry, however, it is not so clear. There is growing evidence that some (a few? many?) foreign investors require their subsidiaries to buy equipment, components, and raw materials from an international subsidiary and charge higher than competitive prices. The purpose is to transfer profits from one jurisdiction to another, often a Panamanian- or Bahamas-based tax haven, in order to minimize taxes. The opportunities for this sort of manipulation are evidently less in raw-material production, where the bulk of the value added, apart from profit, is locally produced, than in import-competing manufacture. The remedy lies not in forbidding foreign investment, so much as reducing tariffs on the final product and increasing the sophistication of tax officials so that they will be in a better position to define the income on which the taxes are levied.

Taxes are the main benefit to the less-developed country from foreign investment in primary production. The rent to domestic labor and external economies, while interesting in particular cases, is typically less significant than the level of taxation. Here the host country wants high taxes on old investments where its bargaining power is strong, and low taxes on the new investments it hopes to entice. Case-by-case tax determination or a discriminating monopoly is the optimum strategy for such a less-developed country but is generally excluded by the nature of competition and the legal principle of nondiscrimination. Cartels to prevent competitive tax concessions, already referred to, are hardly proof against the real divergence of interests of rival countries seeking a single investment. But the national payoff to better training in tax law and fiscal economics is probably high.

X. External Economies and Diseconomies

EE are external economies and diseconomies. They fall into three categories: EE_{G_f}, the benefits to the local economy from economic and social overhead investment undertaken by the foreign investment firm, which may be taken to be positive; EE_f, and EE_h, which are the external economies, positive and negative, from the foreign investment itself, and from its nationalization. The external economies may include Hirschmann-type linkages which stimulate the growth process, and training effects, including those in technology and management which reduce dependence on foreign investment, change the bargaining position, and enable the host country over time to command an increasing share of the rent. It is assumed that all external economies accrue to the host country and none to the foreign firm, although this may not be true where the investor's advantage lies in his capacity to achieve economies of scale by articulating production in several markets. This last is more likely to be the case in import-competing manufacture—as for example, the articulation of Ford production in Britain, Belgium, and Germany—than in raw-material production. The enhanced benefit to the producer from vertical integration over competitive markets at separate stages of raw-material production has already been treated in the difference between S_f and S_h.

EE_h may well be negative if the country's credit standing is affected by its action in nationalizing particular foreign-owned property. The Peruvian government, for example, has taken two full page advertisements in the *New York Times* in an attempt to persuade investors that the trouble with the International Petroleum Company and the nationalization of certain Grace agricultural properties did not alter its policy of welcoming foreign investment [15]. These advertisements emphasize the continued investment programs of IT & T and the South Andean Copper Company, although the first involves some disinvestment, and there is evidence elsewhere in the press that the second represents a reluctant decision to keep on investing for fear of losing the substantial assets already accumulated. Any loss owing to the invoking of the Hickenlooper amendment or similar retaliation would be included under EE_h. EE_h differs from EE_f in two respects, therefore. While certain economies such as linkages are identical whether the investment is foreign or domestic operated, some training and management economies may be smaller with domestic operation, and some diseconomies may ensue from nationalization.

EE_h has a somewhat asymmetrical quality. A reputation attractive to foreign investors is difficult to build and easy to lose. An individual investor may be exasperating in the way he transgresses local law, extracts exorbitant profits, and the like, but he enjoys the protection against penalty that the local government wants to maintain a "good climate for foreign investment." With growing sophistication in the investment process on the side of investors and governments, however, it will ultimately be possible to deal with separate cases on their merits without concern for these externalities.

XI. Amortization

Where foreign investments are bought up locally, as in Chile, Ecuador, Bolivia, Peru in Latin America, and Tanzania and Zambia in Africa, there may or may not be compensation. The doctrine asserted by the United States in the Mexican Eagle case is that compensation should be "prompt, adequate, and effective," which means the capital value of the assets, payable immediately in convertible foreign exchange. In any event, this doctrine which requires a payment to the owners equal to D_{f}, has been watered down. Payment is usually made on an annual basis, often in kind in the product of the investment.

The formula for discounting a perpetual stream of incomes does not properly apply to a flow of compensation payments for a stipulated period. Where the period is a long one, and the discount rate is high, however, the difference is negligible. Yet in many cases host country and firm abandon all pretense of using present discounted values for estimating payments due, but rather adopt the fiction that a dollar tomorrow is the same as a dollar today. The practice is widespread in international debt negotiations of moving this year's debt service, which, say, Ghana or Indonesia cannot pay, forward to follow the last scheduled payment without regarding the debtor as in default. The present value of the payment may decline by as much as 90 or 95 per cent in these cases, depending upon the rate of discount applied. Creditors' consortia adopt this fiction, in defiance of the economic doctrine that bygones are bygones, because they are fearful that default and readjustment of principal may be infectious. By the same token, firms which are bought out by eminent domain and paid the nominal value of asset ceded, but over time and without interest, and their governments, accede in the arrangement from an inability to do better. But the economist should recognize that in these cases, while

$$\sum A = \mathrm{PDV}(S_{\mathrm{f}} - w_{\mathrm{f}} L - r_{\mathrm{f}} K - T_{\mathrm{h}} - G_{\mathrm{f}}),$$

that

$$\mathrm{PDV}(A) < \sum A.$$

XII. Risk

Ex post, of course,

$$\mathrm{PDV}(A) = \mathrm{PDV}[(S_{\mathrm{f}} - w_{\mathrm{f}} L - r_{\mathrm{f}} K - T_{\mathrm{h}} - G_{\mathrm{h}}) z],$$

where z is the risk of nationalization. But z must be calculated *ex ante* before a company can judge whether to undertake a given investment. Operationally, the *ex-post* value is of limited importance.

Note that it would be possible to include z with D_{f}, the foreign rate of discount. It is better to separate it out, however, so as to indicate that a given firm has one rate of discount for all investments, but different risks attaching to those in separate countries.

XIII. Nationalism

N, the satisfaction which a country gets from national ownership (N_{h}) or the dissatisfaction that it feels from foreign control over its resources (N_{f}), takes us again to the contribution of Breton in "The Economics of Nationalism." Presumably N_{f} is negative and N_{h} positive, that is, there is shame or unease from having domestic real assets owned and controlled from abroad, for reasons of group solidarity and xenophobia; and pride and satisfaction from domestic control. The values of N_{f} and N_{h}, expressed as negative or positive flows of income per year, depend upon (i) the extent of foreign ownership, with N_{f} being larger the larger the proportion of total enterprise controlled from abroad; (ii) the degree of development, with both N_{f} and N_{h} being larger for less-developed and smaller for developed countries per unit of foreign or domestic control, however measured; and (iii) the history of past investment, with N_{h} being larger the longer and more lurid the record of historic wrongdoing by foreign investors.

N_{h} may be positive for a country as a whole but negative for certain local groups of politicians and business men who work with foreign investors. Thus Frantz Fanon in "The Wretched of the Earth" believes it insufficient to nationalize foreign investment—it must be socialized as well [7]. On the other hand, the positive value of N_{h} may be small for the country as a whole and do little to reduce the situation of inequality, in which $C_{\mathrm{h_f}} > C_{\mathrm{h_{nat}}} - N_{\mathrm{h}}$, but N_{h} is of great importance to particular politicians and even business competitors. Thus N_{f} and N_{h}, aggregated and disaggregated, are important political variables in many less-developed countries and developed countries as well. The economist is perhaps in no position to measure them numerically, enabling them to be used to calculate $C_{\mathrm{h_f}}$ and $C_{\mathrm{h_{nat}}}$, in Eqs. (3) and (4), except by revealed preference.

XIV. Discount Rates

D, the rate at which streams of income are discounted to capitalize them, differs from r, the rate of interest on bonds, by virtue of business risks. z applies to political risks. Whether risks of foreign exchange control belong in D or z is a matter of indifference. As noted, z could be included in D but is not. The borderline is hazy.

In a riskless world, $z = 1$ and $r = D$. But in a classic world with a given state of the arts, economic men, modest government, no externalities, and competition, so that $S_f = S_h$, $w_f = w_h$, $r_f = r_h$, if there was still risk, D_f would probably be lower than D_h because of better capacity of some businessmen in some countries to manage business risk. This bears on the theory that direct investment arises from differences in the capacity of businessmen in different countries rather than any other advantage. In this classic world, $C_{f_{nat}}$ would be less than C_f, and foreign investment would be desirable from the standpoint of world welfare.

D_h does not enter into the comparison between Eqs. (3) and (4), since it is the same in both cases and so should play no part in any decision to nationalize a foreign investment. The difficulty is likely to arise when the host country is disaggregated and certain groups apply a high rate of discount to the negative items in Eq. (4), that is, to the need to pay for foreign capital, research, and management, and to the losses from discouraging future investments. In these cases political and business leaders presumably apply one rate of discount to the positive items S_h and N_h, and a different and higher discount to the offsets. Under these conditions, nationalization of foreign investment is irresistible.

XV. Conclusion

A comparison between C_f and C_{h_f} of Eqs. (2) and (3) addresses the question of the division of benefits between the investing and the host country. This was the issue raised by Prebisch and Singer more than 20 years ago. The distributional question has a number of asymmetries where a gain or loss for one is not necessarily a loss or a gain for the other, for several reasons: z, perceived risk, which is less than 1 for the investing country but does not raise the return to the host; external economies for the host country, with no cost to the investor; N_f, which poses a political cost for the host but with no evident benefit for the home country;[4] and even an equally divided stream of benefits would be discounted at different rates.

[4] This presumes that there is no offsetting pride in foreign direct investments in the home country akin to the pride which countries derived from colonies. Some critics who believe in neocolonialism and imperialism may dispute this.

It has already been suggested that C_f and C_h have both been growing, but C_{h_f} at a faster rate than C_f in oil, and probably other areas such as iron ore, bauxite, and copper, as well. More data are needed.

A comparison between C_{h_f} and $C_{h_{nat}}$ of Eqs. (3) and (4) poses Bronfenbrenner's problem of the appeal of nationalization. It is assumed that in most cases, the difference between all items but the last in the numerator on the right-hand side will be larger in Eq. (3) than in Eq. (4), and positive, so that apart from N_f and N_h, C_{h_f} would be larger than $C_{h_{nat}}$. This is especially the case if the external diseconomy from confiscation ($EE_h < 0$) is substantial, but is almost certainly the case otherwise. The critical issue is a political one. As noted, N_f is negative and N_h positive. They are not necessarily equal; they doubtless differ from country to country in absolute value, and they may have different time profiles. It is likely that in a country which feels strongly politically about foreign investment—perhaps by reason of historic wrongs—the pain of foreigner ownership ($N_f < 0$) is likely to remain high over a long time, albeit rising to periodic heights from time to time when the foreign corporations come into the news; whereas after nationalization, N_h, which is positive, will have a high value for only a short time and will thereafter decline. This may account for the willingness of some countries, such as Ghana, with a new government, to restore foreign ownership and management after nationalization.

A comparison between the value of a given project in foreign and in domestic ownership of Eqs. (2) and (4) can be used without any hint of nationalization to illustrate the theory of foreign direct investment. Leave A, EE_h, and N_h out of Eq. (4)—A because it is zero, EE_h and N_h since they may be presumed small. Normally S_f will exceed S_h, and $r_f K$ will be less than $r_h K$. pRDM, moreover, is a negative item in Eq. (4) not found in Eq. (2). The only advantage for C_h is cheaper labor.

With development, to be sure, S_h will approach S_f and even surpass it, as it contains substantial monopsony elements; $r_h K$ will approach $r_f K$ as the country's credit standing improves; and pRDM will decline towards zero as doing leads to learning. The equations leave out the disadvantage at which the foreign investor works by virtue of the strangeness of the culture and the distance from the decision center. But if the time profile of returns in Eq. (4) changes through time, the discounting formula must be altered. The weight that future higher returns contribute to the present discounted value of the investment in national ownership then depends heavily on D_h. When it matures, the infant industry must pay for its care in childhood.

REFERENCES

[1] Adelman, M. A., "The Multinational Corporation in World Petroleum" (C. P. Kindleberger, ed.), pp. 227–241, especially p. 241. M. I. T. Press, Cambridge, Massachusetts, 1970.
[2] Breton, A., The Economics of Nationalism, *J. Political Econ.* **72**, No. 4, 376–386 (1964).
[3] Bronfenbrenner, M., The Appeal of Confiscation in Economic Development, *Econ. Develop. Cultural Change* **3**, No. 3, 201–218 (1955).
[4] Diaz Alejandro, C. F., Direct Foreign Investment in Latin America, "The International Corporation" (C. P. Kindleberger, ed.), p. 321. M. I. T. Press, Cambridge, Massachusetts, 1970.
[5] Economic Commission for Latin America, "The Economic Development of Latin America and Its Principal Problems." United Nations, New York.
[6] Economic Commission for Latin America, "Economic Survey of Latin America, 1949," United Nations, New York, 1951.
[7] Fanon, F., "The Wretched of the Earth," Grove Press, New York, 1965.
[8] Hirschman, A. O., How to Divest in Latin America, and Why, "Essays in International Finance," No. 76. Princeton Univ. Press, Princeton, New Jersey (November 1969).
[9] Julien, C., "L'Empire americain." Grasset, Paris, 1968.
[10] Kindleberger, C. P., "The Terms of Trade: A European Case Study," p. 18ff. The Technology Press and Wiley, New York, 1956.
[11] Levin, J., "The Export Economy." Harvard Univ. Press, Cambridge, Massachusetts, 1960.
[12] Magdoff, H., "The Age of Imperialism: The Economics of U. S. Foreign Policy," p. 207. Modern Reader Paperbacks, New York, 1969.
[13] Mamalakis, M., and Reynolds, C. W., "Essays on the Chilean Economy." Irwin, Homewood, Illinois, 1965.
[14] Michaelson, C. D., Joint Mining Ventures Abroad: New Concepts for a New Era, the 1969 D. C. Jackling Award Lecture, American Institute of Mining, Metallurgical and Petroleum Engineers, Washington, D. C. (February 19, 1969).
[15] *New York Times*, September 28, 1969 and November 16, 1969.
[16] Singer, H. W., The Distribution of Gains Between Investing and Borrowing Countries, *Amer. Econ. Rev.* **40**, No. 2, 473–485 (1950). Reprinted in American Economics Association, "Readings in International Economics." Irwin, Homewood, Illinois, 1967.

VI. PROBLEMS OF REGIONAL DEVELOPMENT

This section includes two articles on regional aspects of development. Once again it is interesting to note the difference between the topics dealt with by these papers. Whereas Letiche deals with the characteristics of the African economy, Powelson is concerned with aspects of international politics and what he calls the Latin American economic theory.

In Letiche's work there are some hints on regional differences between development in Latin America and the African continent. Through the work of Raúl Prebisch and the ECLA, for Latin America, at least, it has been possible to elaborate a body of doctrines as an agglutinating element in the cause of Latin American economic development. We can observe here some common ground with Powelson's work, although the latter has taken a different approach.

Powelson's analysis is a critical study of the operation of certain American institutions and the strategy that Latin America should employ to obtain their political goals.

In brief, both economists examine the peculiarities which are characteristics of two important regions in the world now called on to play important roles in the delicate mechanism of international policy.

Letiche's paper about conditions and objectives in African economic development represents a comprehensive introduction to the socio-economic and institutional situation of the continent. The writer considers that in describing the framework explicitly, it will be possible to get a better understanding of African problems as such. After a deep and careful scrutiny, policy recommendations may be given. After a brief introduction, Letiche develops several themes for the reader: national construction (its achievements and problems), development conditions and opportunity costs (with the emphasis on African peculiarities), population growth, migration and unemployment, economic relations with metropolitan powers, the planning of economic development, and the potential role of monetary as well as financial institutions in the African economy. Letiche finally points out that, building on these conditions and objectives, he will carry on a program of research and evaluation of monetary systems used by the new African nations (those south of the Sahara), with special reference to their impact on the problems of economic development of the continent and trade among African countries.

Powelson's essay is an examination of the political impact of Latin American economics upon the United States. His work begins with a brief analysis of the arguments used at different levels, by both North Americans and Latin Americans, about problems of development and international policy. The writer points out the connection between political positions and economic theories, and draws on concrete situations (especially political strategies of Latin America over time). The considerations that follow are divided into three parts: (a) the policy of weakness of the 50s and the beginning of the 60s (analyzing the awakening of Latin American scholars and particularly the work done by ECLA); (b) the United States foreign policy machine (examining the actions of the president, the State Department, and the Congress); (c) some suggestions for Latin American strategy (in which the peculiarities of North American institutions and the characteristics of a "strong" policy for Latin America are emphasized). Powelson concludes his work by expressing the hope that his views can, in fact, serve the cause of all the countries of the western hemisphere.

CONDITIONS AND OBJECTIVES OF AFRICAN ECONOMIC DEVELOPMENT

JOHN M. LETICHE

University of California, Berkeley, California

I. Introduction

Africa, unlike Latin America, has not had an economic spokesman. Since World War II, Raúl Prebisch has not only raised the key issues facing Latin America, and proffered solutions for settling them, but he has perceptively and courageously altered some of his fundamental approaches and recommendations in the light of new evidence and superior analysis.[1] He has had a greater influence on Latin American international development policy than any other economist, and his influence on African government and academic economists has also been marked. For the fundamental issues facing Latin America—the struggle for orderly development of mankind in an epoch of revolutionary change, characterized by massive migrations from rural to urban areas often aggravating the spread of urban decay and the mounting unemployment in the major cities—have plagued most sub-Sahara African countries no less than those of Latin America.

[1] Three developments in Prebisch's writings can readily be distinguished: (i) the emphasis in the late 1950s on strengthening the Latin American industrialization process through differential tariff protection, import substitution, and the creation of a common market for trade and investment integration [28]; (ii) the recognition by the mid-1960s that the stage of "easy substitution" of domestic manufacturing production for imports had passed, and that Latin American exports should be promoted by industrial countries removing their trade barriers to imports of manufactures from Latin America [29, 30]; (iii) the stress in the late 1960s on tariff preferences for Latin American manufactures in the United States and other industrial nations, as well as upon more effective integration of the major Latin American economies through the use of Special Drawing Rights (SDRs) and the removal of their overvalued exchange rates [see 38, 39]. Raúl Prebisch expressed the latter views at a conference [31].

Understandably, therefore, the writings of Prebisch have served as important antecedents in preparing this paper. It is based on Chap. I of a study being prepared in response to an invitation by the Executive Secretary of the Economic Commission for Africa to examine and appraise the monetary systems of Africa. Any attempt to deal successfully with the particular problems facing African countries must begin with an appreciation of their objectives and an agreement about the basic underlying conditions. The clarification of these starting points owes much to consultations with African political leaders and monetary experts during personal visits in 1962, 1964, and 1969 to almost every African country. Since these understandings form the framework for the entire study's analysis and recommendations, it is preferable to state them explicitly in order that the reader may be in a better position to make whatever adjustments in his own reasoning he may deem fit. An endeavor has also been made to present the case of the African countries.

II. National Construction

A fundamental objective of the new African nations, often referred to as Africanization or "indigenization," has been the achievement of appreciable rates of economic growth with the transfer—as soon as possible—of political, economic, and financial control to Africans. This transfer applies particularly to those controls which are regarded as necessary for the avoidance of outside interference with the sovereignty of independent nation states. It is in this sense that, particularly in the early 1960s, a feeling of unity existed in Africa, a unity against alien control.

A basic expectation in the 1960s was that there would be much foreign assistance and rapid economic development. This unity of expectation and hope has been displaced by disunity and disappointment. The disunity within each nation even exceeds the conflicts between the new nations. Many African countries have suffered *coups d'état* or civil war, and current politico-economic trends provide no evidence that these will decrease.

The reasons for this phenomenon are neither simple nor singular. They are complex, deep rooted, and stem from common causes. In nearly all the new African countries obstacles to achieving the key condition for progress—political legitimacy and stability—have posed themselves in their most acute form. All of these countries have suffered from postindependence malaise. Contrary to expectations, the task of national construction has turned out to be much less glamorous and much more complex than the struggle for independence. As complex positive goals slowly had to replace the relatively simple and almost unanimous resentment of the former colonial power, the lack of a single-minded social purpose became manifest:

(a) There has been insufficient national unity; accordingly, the cohesive unifying role was thrust upon the state, which was rarely strong enough to achieve this task. In fact, the brittle crust of national unity frequently tended to break down as the state itself became the subject of divisive struggles for control. Political obligation often followed tribal, racial, or religious lines, in addition to economic interests. As these schisms in many of the new African nations turned the control of political authority into a matter of life and death, opposition understandably came to be considered sinister. Under such conditions, it is not surprising that the conflicts led to war or civil war. The first problem facing every new African nation is to develop minimum standards of political-national behavior based on ethical-legal norms rather than on coercive power or personal loyalty. Practically nowhere have the requirements for the formation of a modern nation state been met.

(b) The "development decade" of the 1960s failed, particularly in Africa. The most direct manifestation of this failure has been the dangerously growing masses of unemployed in the major cities as populations grew, and as young people drifted from the rural to the urban areas.[2] The ambitious economic development plans proved to be empty blueprints. While governments and their ministers expressed support for rapid economic development, the glaring disparity between showplaces and shanties widened.

(c) There has often been a misdirected stress on government responsibility for development. It is true that from 1960 to 1967 the GNP growth rate in several new countries south of the Sahara (e.g., Ivory Coast, Mauretania, Guinea, and Mali) has been above 5 per cent. But government investment and initiative, on which the "development decade' had based its hopes, has accounted for little of this growth. In most instances, when government undertook industrial projects, they turned out to be of doubtful viability. The evidence is overwhelming that where rapid progress occurred it centered in the private industrial and/or agricultural sector. A basic condition for more successful economic development must therefore be the recognition of the importance of confining the governments of Africa to those activities in industrial and agricultural development for whose execution they possess the required resources or can draw upon and train them.

[2] African officials of the leading capitals in East and West Africa estimated the percentage of working men unemployed in 1969 at a minimum of 20 per cent in several cities, rising to a maximum of 40 per cent in others. The Report of the Commission on International Development concludes: "The failure to create meaningful employment is the most tragic failure of development. All indications are that unemployment and underutilization of human resources have increased in the 1960s, and that the problem will grow even more serious" [11–13, 27].

The sub-Sahara developing countries are struggling with the often conflicting goals of concentrating their limited resources for the promotion of rapid economic development or for the establishment of institutions to support the building of new nation states. The forces of tribalism have made this particularly acute. Nationalism, primarily in the form of anticolonialism, was a more powerful force in commanding support for independence; but since independence, nationalism has been weakened by tribalism and has proved to be less powerful than anticipated in the process of modernization. The sub-Sahara countries have, therefore, been faced with the need to create and strengthen institutions expressly directed at nation building, which should concentrate, however, in efficiently adapting these institutions to African conditions. They are often, as in the case of large military and higher educational establishments, inappropriate transplants from abroad, extremely costly, and, in their present form, ultimately to be rejected by the body politic.[3]

III. Development Conditions and Opportunity Costs

To be effective, nation-building institutions must correspond to their historical environments. Under prevailing African conditions, this means setting up a government apparatus responsible for the framework and the underpinning of economic advance, thereby maximizing the flexibility for alternative occupational pursuits. Viable institutions must contribute to the political economy in a degree commensurate with the cost. In virtually all the new African countries, if the military establishment (whose function is twofold: strengthening the economy and reinforcing the identity of the state) is to justify its cost, a large proportion of the army recruits would have to be used in economically productive activities such as irrigation, reforestation, the building of roads, harbors, railways, wharfs, and schools. These are all part of a country's infrastructure. Most developed countries have used their so-called "army engineers" in similar ways when there was no other national

[3] Before independence, the United Kingdom and France often recruited a small number of officers, as well as enlisted men, from the better-educated tribal groups situated remote from the capital. This aggravated tribal and geographical imbalance and increased, rather than reduced, internal differentiation. After independence, political instability and weak institutions intensified military distrust of civilian political parties. This has tended to strengthen military controls and, with the grave shortage of civilian personnel to manage large-scale organizations, the assumption by the military of an increasingly large part in guiding economic and social development. Unfortunately, the experience of many developing countries has shown that their armies may also lack organizational and engineering skills. This has usually meant that the wider their sphere of economic involvement the less effectively have they been able to perform. Considerable research has been done on these issues, although not greater than the need. [6, 7, 15, 18, 35].

need for their services, a procedure which is taking hold in several African countries. Nevertheless, it does not eliminate the urgent necessity of postponing many of the alleged satisfactions afforded by large military establishments—and other symbolic institutions associated with nationalism—in order to secure more productive benefits for the country at large.

The national boundaries of the new African countries are, for the most part, residues of late 19th and early 20th century European balance-of-power diplomacy and of the post-World War II dissolution of the British and French empires. They certainly do not represent the realities of present, or even potential, economic viability. In most instances, absurdly small-scale national markets hinder economic specialization, check economies of scale, and militate against economic development. This has been aggravated by an emphasis on subregional equalization of economic development in an attempt to reduce political divisiveness.

Currently, the majority of African countries are not in danger of following orthodox economic policies of either the "left" or the "right"—although the number of exceptions is growing, particularly because of frustrations resulting from insufficient success in economic development and neglect by major Western powers. They are severely pragmatic. Those that are very much dependent economically on a single metropolitan power would like to reduce this dependency, to develop more extensive multinational relationships, and to benefit from the experience and aid of all countries willing to assist them. But they clearly recognize that, during the last decade, their political and economic importance to former metropolitan centers, as well as to the United States and the Soviet Union, has generally diminished. This, *inter alia*, has resulted in a decline in foreign aid supplied to them. Although subject to political and economic pressures of competing ideologies, most African countries south of the Sahara probably will be spared direct military involvements of foreign powers, and foreign aid will remain at approximately current proportional levels. Hence, with few exceptions, their economic development will have to depend primarily on their own efforts.

The similarities in the factors responsible for the economic backwardness of most African countries are greater than the differences. As a consequence, it is possible to analyze their economic problems with a considerable degree of generalization, in the sense that the conclusions are relevant and applicable to many nations south of the Sahara. However, in the procedures which have been used in dealing with their developmental problems, the differences are greater than the similarities.

Although strengthened central banking, commercial banking, and fiscal institutions are indispensable for African economic progress, the greatest constraints to African economic development are not of a domestic monetary nature. They are to be found in such fundamental factors as the degree of the people's readiness for modern agricultural and industrial advance—of their social and political "forwardness," of the will and skill of its leaders, of the inability to establish and manage the relevant institutional and business apparatuses which guide economic life. Essentially, it is the advance in productivity that is the determining factor. Specifically, therefore, the greatest constraints to African economic development are such real factors as the lack of qualified directors, trained manpower, and capital equipment.

In all African countries there is a critical, pervasive need for an expanded and more effective educational and training process—particularly in the primary and secondary schools—to overcome the overwhelming prejudices against manual work. This is indispensable for the entire course of economic development, especially because of the widespread but irrational preference for investment in capital equipment over investment in technical training, and for white-collar over blue-collar work. There is a great lack, in *combination*, of equipment and training, as well as adquate incentives and information for the pursuit of required skills. In the early stages of development, both equipment and training have to be imported; their importation is often inextricably linked; government direction and supervision of the interwoven indigenous training is essential.

The record of foreign companies in training Africans and appointing them to positions of responsibility is poor. Major emphasis must therefore be placed on the relationship between this problem and increased African training. In every new African nation, technical organizational ability is the resource in scarcest supply. This scarcity has been intensified by policies which have hindered rather than helped the expansion of this resource. It cannot be overemphasized that anything done to increase the availability of that resource would increase the rate of African industrial development. Just as with respect to capital formation, the economic choice is unavoidable: the new African nations must substantially increase their domestic rate of saving and investment, in training as in the acquisition of physical productive equipment, or, without the transfer of resources from abroad through foreign aid and investment, they will suffer from a lower rate of economic growth. But, in any case, at present more important than ownership is the effective participation of Africans in the management of local enterprise. This is a necessary, though not sufficient, condition whereby Africans can—and should—increase their share of ownership.[4]

[4] To the extent that there has been discrimination against nationals in employment, even though they could perform the work as efficiently, the elimination of the foreigners' monopoly gain would bring about a transfer of income from foreigners to nationals. But if the foreigners were receiving a price commensurate with their skilled qualifications, and nationalization involved replacing them with nationals of inferior skills at the same salary,

African economic development must be regarded in terms of generations rather than decades. There exists an understandable impatience on the part of many African leaders, frequently western trained, with the slow advance of their economies. They are disturbed over extreme regionalism, ultraconservatism matched by ultraradicalism, as well as occasional nepotism, graft, and inefficiency. This frustration tempts them to resort to autarchic comprehensive controls, which, however, cannot but lead to disappointment in the rate of progress, to still greater frustrations, to political and tribal turbulence, and, in many instances, to military rule.[5] Although the modern history of developing countries records that military establishments have often served as political arbiters and promoters of economic modernization, disaster usually follows when they become standby political authorities, injecting violence into politics and sapping the economic strength of the nation. If the military is to be successfully integrated into the politico-economic organization of African states, it must evolve into a respected but subsidiary, nonpolitical instrument of government.[6]

the effect would primarily be to transfer income not *towards*, but only *within* the national group, individuals favored with promotions, at the expense of the general community, which would bear the costs of poorer administration, inferior economic efficiency, or deterioration in the quality of service. For a discussion of the effects of nationalizing property as compared with nationalizing the civil service, or the administrative and executive jobs in a particular enterprise see [19, 20]. This is a controversial issue among African economists, particularly since it relates to the often small proportion of "retained value added" by expatriate manufacturing firms.

[5] In appraising the political role of the military in East Africa, Francophone Africa, Nigeria, and Ghana, Gutteridge with only minor excessive generality writes:

> It is less likely that the military will actually seize power than simply seek, in conjunction with other forces in the community, to transfer it from one set of hands to another. They are more likely to be the agents of current dissidence than the upholders of a consistent political philosophy [14].

[6] Practically all new nations have encountered these problems [10].

> By using the army as its political instrument *par excellence*," T. Halperin-Donghi illustrates from the experience of Buenos Aires, "the revolutionary government slipped into the habit of relying on force for the solution of its internal problems and it thus perpetuated precisely those political contradictions which it was trying to abolish. At the same time the indiscriminate use of the army added greatly to the financial burdens imposed on the population in the revolutionary areas [9].

What makes these issues more explosive today is the pressure of time and instantaneous communication. The developed nations cannot remain entirely unconcerned about them because historically the system of government which has brought about economic development—whether popular or authoritarian—has tended to be confirmed rather than radically changed by this achievement [24].

In practically all instances, the sub-Sahara countries that have experienced mounting government expenditures exceeding revenues have encountered a deterioration in the balance of payments, a loss in foreign reserves, even an exhaustion of expanded foreign credits, and an external crisis bordering on the breakdown of foreign and domestic confidence in the future of the economies. These crises are accentuated by the glaring perquisites of highly placed officials as contrasted with the modest earnings of the lower civil servants. Military coups have often occurred in an attempt to rectify these inequalities, but military regimes have also assumed power when responsible governments have tried to reduce expenditures and increase revenues. Such "budgetary revolutions" are a new, ominous phenomenon in Africa. They are related, in part, to the underdevelopment of alternative occupational opportunities in civilian life for government and military personnel—alternatives which are both scarce and less remunerative, i.e., their opportunity cost is usually very low. But regardless of the immediate events that brought these governments to power, experience has shown that the popularity of a military regime gradually begins to wane. It does not possess the required political, administrative, and bargaining expertise for long-term rule. As the fundamental restraints on rapid economic development again emerge, covert criticism of the government begins to mount, countered by increased government oppression. The longer a military regime remains in power, the more it usually endangers its own position, as well as its possible contribution to economic development.[7] Comprehensive administrative controls tend to stifle economic progress and create dissension. They militate against long-run economic adaptation, adversely affecting the process of development and usually causing the downfall of even the best-intentioned military regime.

IV. Population Growth, Migration, and Unemployment

The African continent on the whole is not bedeviled by the problem of population pressure.[8] Given reasonable availability of capital for the develop-

[7] Even the experience of early civilizations in nation building suggests the overriding importance of combining a framework of nonauthoritarian legality with progressive adaptiveness to the environment. Verifiable progress, wrote Walter Bagehot, was contingent upon "the change from the age of status to the age of choice . . . where the government was to a great and a growing extent a government by discussion and where the subjects of that discussion were . . . matters of principle" [3]. For a favorable modern interpretation of "Bagehot as Historian," see Jacques Barzun [4].

[8] Egypt, the Republic of Rwanda, and the Kingdom of Burundi do suffer from population pressure. Nigeria has encountered much concentration and high rates of population growth in the southwestern area; the Central Province of Kenya, the Upper Volta, and the

ment of agriculture and substantial mobility of persons from tribal area to tribal area, the ratio of population to cultivable land is not a serious problem for the African continent as a whole. However, recent estimates for most countries south of the Sahara indicate extremely high rates of population growth which could seriously impede their economic advance, particularly since the higher the population growth rates the larger the investment in capital, training and schooling that is absorbed in providing for the increase of population so that little—if any at all—is left over for raising the level of living. The key issue in this regard is not currently excessive population but the rates of growth, and their perverse effects on development and employment.

Compared with other developing areas, the amount of unutilized labor *and* unused but cultivable land in Africa south of the Sahara is considerable, making it more feasible to achieve a steady growth or even an acceleration of domestic production and consumption without inflationary pressures on the domestic price level. Imports of capital equipment and consumer goods, however, rise markedly with economic expansion. Unless the value of exports increases sufficiently, or larger foreign loans and grants are obtained, economic expansion may be expected rapidly to reduce foreign reserves and to undermine the value of the currency. These considerations are relevant for the foreseeable future even if in the longer run the problem would be solved by successful industrial development. Although, in general, inflation in the traditional sense of a rapid rise in domestic prices is not a present danger in Africa, foreign trade and investment, with their related effects on the stability or instability of currencies, will continue to play an important role in the success or failure of African economic development plans.

V. Economic Relations with Metropolitan Powers

For many African countries, trade with the sterling area and the franc zone constitutes a large fraction of their total foreign trade. From 1948 to 1970

Cameroons have experienced similar difficulties. But these latter problems are local and can be relieved by contiguous domestic expansion. Data on population growth rates for selected African countries, and projections for the period 1960–1975 are to be found in Keyfitz and Flieger [22, 23]. In most of the African countries, the population is rising at a 2.4–3 per cent annual rate, with extremely high crude birth rates (e.g., above 45 per thousand per year) and extremely high crude death rates (e.g., above 25 per thousand per year). This represents a demographic phase of development which has become obsolete even in other underdeveloped parts of the world. It resembles European conditions at about 1800; but African birth rates are generally higher than those of 18th century Europe. A sharp relative fall in crude death rates, which has already occurred in Mauritius, would result in record population growth rates in many African countries. For the best available studies to date, albeit demonstrating how little reliable information exists, see Brass *et al.* [5].

their share of world exports drastically declined. Although there are outstanding exceptions, particularly where petroleum, manganese, cobalt, copper, chrome, and phosphate rock dominated the figures, the exports of many key agricultural products increased at a slower rate than the production and incomes of the developed countries. At current prices their supply has usually been in excess of demand. But a substantial geographical diversification of this trade with the sterling area and the franc zone can occur only gradually.

Mutuality of interests among countries in the sterling area and in the franc zone is not merely economic. It also encompasses historical, political, and linguistic ties. All these associations, coupled with the fact that every country must keep a part of its real capital in the form of liquid reserves, make it practicable for the African countries in these zones to maintain close monetary, foreign-exchange reserve, and exchange-rate connections with their former metropolitan territories.

The extent to which many African countries obtain foreign aid from France, the European Economic Community (EEC), or the United Kingdom, via preferential marketing arrangements and investment grants, is sufficiently large that if this aid were to be reduced rapidly political stability would be endangered.

A peculiar characteristic of the so-called "dual economies" of Africa has been that a large part of the income earned in Africa was not spent in Africa but siphoned off to foreign countries.[9] In many cases, the indigenous tribal population is occupied principally in subsistence agriculture, whereas the nonindigenous population is engaged in the industrial, commercial, and monetary agriculture or export sectors. In these sectors the proportion of net domestic product exported is unusually high, while the proportion of income accruing to the indigenous population is often extremely low. Furthermore, the corporate profits and wages received by the nonindigenous population—sums frequently amounting to over 50 per cent of the net national domestic money income—are to a large extent transferred to the metropolitan territory through capital transfers, savings, and payment for imports of consumer goods.

In effect, most African countries as "dual economies" have long suffered from the overwhelming dependence of their production, incomes and demand on foreign, rather than domestic, markets. There were no domestic monetary and fiscal institutions for maintaining or expanding domestic effective demand to stabilize or raise the level of output. The struggle for independence strengthened the political pressures for economic "localization": African leaders have insisted that African countries should spend a larger proportion of their

[9] Ghana and Nigeria have been outstanding exceptions to this rule. See United Nations [37]. For a critical appraisal of the "dual-economy" concept under different conditions, see Aboyade [1], Itagaki [17], Dixit [8], and Jorgenson [21].

income on their own output. It is inevitable that this pressure will become greater and the structure of production, incomes, and consumption be altered by more extensive use of either monetary and fiscal measures operating through the market mechanism or by direct administrative controls.

The process of national self-determination has become interwoven with theories of macrodevelopment analysis, protectionist planning, and depression economics stemming from the West, and with theories of centralized comprehensive planning, nationalization, and government control over foreign trade stemming from the East. These influences have contributed powerfully to establishing the notion in many African nations that they are economic entities endowed with consistent objectives and a consensus in favor of realizing them by fundamentally nationalistic rather than cosmopolitan economic policies. But these theories and their policy implications are inapplicable to African condtions—they are based on the assumption of conditions which simply do not exist in the new African nations.

Current macrodevelopment analysis stems primarily from the Keynesian body of thought which takes for granted an advanced economy that has already accumulated a great stock of modern equipment and the skilled labor force needed to operate it. Both were idled by a deficiency of aggregate demand, and the policy prescription was to raise demand sufficiently to draw the existing labor force back into employment in manning the existing abundance of machines. Furthermore, land as an economic agent was considered unimportant and was completely disregarded, so that no attention was paid to such problems as the training of modern agricultural and industrial skills. In these conditions, the reemployment of resources could be accomplished by simply using expansionary fiscal and monetary policy to stimulate monetary expenditure. Part of the increase in expenditure would consist of investment expenditure, but it was not regarded as a prescription meant to deal with the long-run problems of the growth of productive capacity. There was no point in adding to the unemployed capital goods and skilled manpower. But these are just the essential requirements for self-sustaining economic development in African countries. It is true that even a poor country might suffer from a general insufficiency of demand, so that even its limited productive capacity was not fully utilized, in which case, the Keynesian prescription would be applicable, but that does not serve in any way to alleviate the basic African problem of insufficient productive *capacity*.

Two further elements in macrodevelopment theories were often applied to African economies:

(a) The rate of economic growth was seen as depending on the proportion of income saved and invested in additional physical productive capacity, and on a technologically given ratio of capital stock to total annual output of goods and services. Thus, if this ratio of capital to output is five to one, a growth rate of 5 per cent per year requires a rate of investment out of saving, or out of foreign aid, of 25 per cent of income;

(b) the underdeveloped countries were assumed to be characterized by massive disguised unemployment concealed in the subsistence agricultural sector of the economy. Hence, the transfer of these (disguised) unemployed to industry would not reduce agricultural output but leave an agricultural surplus which could be drawn on for economic development.

There has been no empirical support for these views; empirical studies have, in fact, drawn contrary conclusions. The prescriptions based upon them are dangerously misleading, especially for countries which are critically dependent upon foreign trade and investment. In all probability, they contributed to the belief, widespread even among African government officials, that there exists some mysterious source of untapped economic energy which, if only liberated, could provide both for development and for other national goals, so that self-sustaining growth—"take-off"—could be achieved within a "development decade." Not surprisingly, fiscal and monetary policies are often regarded as the effective instrument—the Aladdin's lamp—for releasing this economic potential.

VI. African Development Planning

In most of the new African countries, the economic views on domestic planning and on international trade planning are of a kind. Although there are divergent positions regarding the merits of a competitive market mechanism, a viable mixed economy, or a planned socialistic state, a consensus prevails on the advisability of comparatively high tariff protection and, somewhat less generally, of direct controls on trade and capital movements. Import substitution, in particular, is given too high a priority. Although judicious and selective import substitution can play an important role in the development process, practically without exception the experience of other continents has revealed a tendency to push this instrument beyond its effective limits. If exports are subsidized, a corresponding protection of domestic industries from imports is appropriate. But if tariff rates are higher than the subsidies given to exports, industrial development is hindered rather than helped. In practice, many intermediate goods are required for the production of advanced consumer and capital goods. Developing countries must import them in substantial amounts. The increased costs of import substitution generate, or strengthen, inflationary pressures; the high prices of tariff-protected and monopoly-ridden goods exaggerate the contribution of the protected industries to the growth in GNP; and the entire protective structure hardens disincentives to the learning and adjusting process of an emerging modern economy.[10]

Coordination of the planning, financial, and foreign trade ministries of each new African country is essential. The record of the last decade in virtually all African countries demonstrates that economic development plans built only on macroeconomic considerations are simply inadequate. The macroeconomic projections of investment and consumption can only be estimates of the expected results of microeconomic decisions by the managers of government and private individual plants, and the heads of agencies and individual households. In the new African countries there do not as yet exist either the effective institutions or a sufficient body of men with the required skills and executive responsibilities by which macrodecisions can be translated into the innumerable microdecisions that can bring them into actual being. In consequence, it is primarily the micromarket signals—profitable cost–price relationships—which for the foreseeable future will continue to be decisive for African economic development and growth.[11]

With limited exceptions, this applies to agricultural production and processing as well as to industrial output. But since 70 to 80 per cent of the population in the new African countries south of the Sahara is engaged in agriculture, attention must be devoted primarily to this sector. Unless demand for agricultural commodities is increased together with gains in productivity, and small-scale industry in the countryside is also increased, the exodus to the cities in excess of their absorptive capacity in terms of regular employment will become a disintegrating force. It will radicalize the urban population, exacerbate the urbanization problem, and render it a key obstacle both to development and to nation building. Overwhelming evidence has been piling up that African farmers are not hidebound by tradition but are effective "maximizers": their decisions are based on rational economic and,

[10] The experiences of Ghana, Guinea, and Mali clearly show that, in the new African countries, industrialization is contingent upon more fundamental factors than socialist or private-enterprise ideology or form of economic organization. See Amin [2] and Zolberg [40].

[11] Many African countries have prepared "economic guidelines" for their development, but strictly speaking these have not been "economic plans" even of a purely macro kind. They have not even constituted satisfactory projections. To formulate such plans, certain minimum basic data are required—data on investment, employment, the quantity of money, consumption, the labor force, taxes, etc. But the new African countries simply do not possess much of this data. Their economic planning would be greatly improved by increased knowledge of the underlying microrelationships which, in turn, would strengthen the interpretation of basic macrorelationships. For this, however, more and better facts—especially improved national accounts—are a prerequisite. On these points, see the convincing argument and evidence, based on lessons from Nigeria's development [36].

occasionally, noneconomic criteria within the context of prevailing institutions. Normally, agricultural output per acre or per man is closely related to the investment that has been made in agricultural extension, and in the education and training of young men in agricultural and engineering schools. The important question is whether the incentives they face, the relationships between costs and prices, are conducive to the attainment of national goals.[12] It is particularly in the *more-rapidly developing* African countries, where objective and impersonal criteria such as competitive costs and prices are lacking, that a satisfactory market mechanism would provide an essential ingredient for guiding economic development

In the *least-developed* countries and regions of Africa, the root causes of backwardness are associated with even more elemental factors than the supply of skills, resources, and incentive-setting institutions. Education, transportation, and communication are so undeveloped that the building of an infrastructure is essential before much increased income can be expected from any increased effort. The result is an arrested stage of nondevelopment. Because agricultural productivity has been extremely low, the required storage and transport facilities are often unavailable, so that market incentives alone could not have much effect. There is, in essence, a premarket level of economic organization. Increased productivity waits for the developed trading facilities which wait for the increased productivity that would justify them. This interdependence between increased productivity and creation of warranted—rather than inoperable or empty—economic institutions is a cardinal aspect of the beginning of nation building.

There is need for new better-trained and strengthened government, cooperative, and private institutions to accelerate the rationalization of agriculture to provide the basis for industrial development and to prepare for the establishment of integrated monetary, fiscal, and production-development targets. At present there often exist monetary stabilization measures side by side with practically unrelated production-development plans. Based particularly on what African economists have termed agro-allied industries—oil plant and rubber plantations, oil crushing, meat producing, processing, and canning complexes, sugar estates, fully integrated textile industries—African producers have shown that, given the opportunity, they have an excellent record for enterprise. This also would apply to basic industries such as

[12] For a general analysis of these issues, see the excellent discussion by Schultz [33, 34]. It has been shown that under a propitious environment agrarian reform and modernization could be phased right [26]. The Mexican government, making agricultural investment in the commercial sectors of large-scale agriculture and doing almost nothing with traditional agriculture, helped expand industries and cities while the *landed* peasants—satisfied with their immediate needs—slowly moved off their farms when alternatives were open to them, rendering feasible the disbanding of unnecessary armies.

chemical fertilizers and food processing, as well as to certain selected semi-manufactured and manufactured products for which the domestic demand is rapidly growing.

Emphasis on the gradual expansion from simple to more advanced manufactures, with more attention devoted to selective interregional investment in key projects—assisted by the freer entry of these products to the developed countries—holds greater promise for African industrial development than comprehensive domestic planning and extensive import substitution of intermediate products and capital goods.[13]

VII. Potential Role of Monetary Institutions

In the new African countries, government officials must be cognizant of the economic problem of the efficient allocation of extremely scarce resources. Such allocation among competing uses, including provision for future needs, is of prime importance. Effective financial institutions are indispensable for this task. Responsibly and independently managed, monetary and banking institutions can help create a formidable set of nation-building instruments. Regardless of whether they are primarily "single-dependency" nations (the franc-zone nations in Africa), more "multiple-dependency" nations (the sterling-area countries in Africa), more or less command moblization systems (Guinea, Zambia), reconciliation systems (Ivory Coast, Kenya), or traditional modernizing autocracies (Ethiopia), these financial institutions not only provide the framework for integrating government and business decisions, but they make available the required information for minimum standards of public accountability.

Modern monetary and banking institutions can play an important role in diversifying the structure of production and accelerating the rate of African economic development, as well as in stabilizing fluctuations in demand and utilizing more fully the limited productive capacity of the new African nations. Hitherto, financial institutions have not been able to deal effectively with African problems of development and stabilization because of the absence

[13] See Lary [25]. Although in 1965 less than 10 per cent of total imports by developed from less-developed countries constituted labor-intensive manufactures, this trade has been growing rapidly in recent years (see pp. 96–97). If the structure of wages in less-developed countries does not nullify their comparative advantage in labor-intensive products, the developed countries have it within their power, by reducing their barriers to importation of finished manufactures, "to influence greatly the export earnings of less developed countries and therewith their possibilities of economic growth" (pp. 109, 127). Further, the experience of Brazil in the latter 1960s has not only confirmed this Prebisch thesis, but it has also demonstrated the serious damage done to developing countries by their own high tariff protection and over-valued exchange rates.

of the basic political and economic institutions to formulate and to implement African objectives. Furthermore, the economic fluctuations in African countries were almost entirely dependent on foreign trade and investment. The essential role of modern financial institutions must, therefore, be to help develop and diversify the African economies—to promote industrial and agricultural projects for the expansion of *internal* production and consumption—as well as to offset general insufficiency or excess of demand resulting from external or internal deflationary or inflationary pressures.

The central banks of African countries have to perform functions which are neither required nor appropriate for central banks of the developed countries. As the main monetary authority, every central bank must have the responsibility of conscious and discretionary control over the money supply to assist in maintaining a steady and high level of activity, to build up the mechanisms through which local savings are promoted and made available for local investment, and to protect the value of the currency. However, the power of a central bank in Africa to stimulate or restrain effective demand through strictly monetary operations is limited. Not only do African countries generally have a large subsistence sector and a high degree of dependence on external trade, but they also have local money-using sectors such as manufacturing, service, and peasant enterprises which are only to a moderate extent susceptible to centralized monetary influence. In addition, they suffer from comparatively underdeveloped money and capital markets and fiscal institutions. It is precisely for these reasons that African central banks should take a more active role in stimulating economic development and in pursuing monetary policies for a more balanced economy. If they do not, they will become divorced from the fundamental economic problems facing Africa. Other government agencies which are more sensitive to political pressures will be compelled to undertake projects which, manifestly, could be better considered, formulated, and partially financed in conjunction with the supervisory and regulatory powers of the central banks.

The central banks of African countries should, therefore, directly furnish the useful services mentioned above and, in addition, give assistance to their governments by financing a legally limited proportion of short- and long-term government expenditures. Indirectly, they could furnish an important service by promoting the establishment of commercial banks as well as specialized investment and savings institutions for the launching of industrial and agricultural projects in both the private and the public sector. In most countries where a private body of well-informed critical opinion is in the earliest stages of formation, central banks could well play the role of catalysts in economic development, by supporting investment in manifold ways from both public and private sources.

The development of African monetary institutions must be regarded as a long-run process, with central banking operations becoming more effective and more efficient with the growth in the number and size of private and government financial, commercial, and industrial firms. At present, these conditions do not prevail in the new African countries. This limits the effective use of *general* monetary policy. Similarly, the governments of these countries cannot effectively use *general* fiscal policies. Their tax administration over both foreign and domestic firms is weak, and the general use of monopolistic licensing procedures to encourage investment invites corruption. Under such conditions, a central bank in collaboration with the ministry of finance and other government agencies is particularly suited to help establish and administer an "investment-funds" policy:

(a) By providing powerful financial incentives for firms to deposit their funds with the central bank in time of excessive demand and to withdraw them in time of insufficiency of demand, the central bank can both check inflationary pressures and fill deflationary lows while inducing investment in prearranged projects for the express purpose of steady economic development. This central bank function is particularly important in the new African countries.

(b) The cooperation between the central bank and a small number of large firms can be channeled into mutually productive efforts. The research staff of the central bank, in conjunction with the ministry of planning, can assist the private firms in setting up projects which they would be prepared to launch at short notice. Further, the central bank, in cooperation with the ministries of agriculture and labor, can participate in an investment-funds policy of expanding small-scale industries in the countryside.

(c) Another role that the central bank might play is to advise and assist in establishing and selecting managers of new public and private financial, commercial, and industrial firms. The growth and multiplication of such firms would gradually render more effective the utilization of more general monetary and fiscal policies.

It is practicable for a new African state to grant the central bank sufficient independence to insulate the management of its operations from the primarily political decisions of government, thereby ensuring that it can act as an effective obstacle to the misuse of the monetary instrument. This practice has the great advantage of providing the government, and especially the Minister of Finance, with a buffer against the ceaseless and inordinate demands for financing which are made upon them by innumerable powerful forces.

Conflicts of policy between the government and the central bank are inevitable at all stages of economic development, but are especially serious in newly-developing countries. Economic development plans of new African states invariably include both primary objectives—e.g., target growth rates of GNP, high levels of employment, rising levels of per capita income for all sections of the population—and subordinate objectives—e.g., price stabilization, external balance, improved distribution of income. An entire set of interdependent policies would be required for the achievement of these goals. Monetary policy constitutes only one instrument within that set. It is inappropriate for dealing with some of them—e.g., distribution of income—and ineffective, unless coordinated with budgetary and fiscal policies, for dealing with others—e.g., high levels of employment. These facts notwithstanding, the central bank in a newly-developing country often confronts situations which impel experimentation.

It must play a key role in economic development as government banker, adviser, assistant in the flotation of bonds and treasury bills, and so forth. However, when the central bank becomes too closely associated with the development process, it is in danger of becoming submerged to the interests of the Minister of Finance. The chief responsibility for the financing of economic development must rest with the Minister of Finance. It is he who should be Chairman of the Development Board. The Minister of Economic Development (or of Economic Planning) should be a member of the Development Board, as should also be the governor of the central bank. But the role of the governor of the central bank in the context of economic development must be that of an adviser.

Monetary history suggests that the primary responsibilities of the central bank should be:

(a) To maintain a reasonably stable price level—the overriding importance of this objective stems from the fact that loss of confidence in the currency is one of the great dangers facing a newly-developing open economy;

(b) To expand monetary demand in line with the economy's real capacity to grow;

(c) To promote balance-of-payments equilibrium.

Since monetary policy is part of total economic policy, African governments increasingly insist that the broad objectives of the central bank should be consistent with the general economic policy. However, many noncentral-bank measures affect price stability, aggregate monetary demand, and external balance. Thus, while the chief responsibilities of the central bank should be the endeavor to achieve these objectives, it cannot be held responsible for failure to achieve them if they are being thwarted by other government policies. In most African countries, government budgetary policy has recently been inconsistent with the attainment of these objectives. To achieve them, the central bank would have had to refuse finance to government boards and agencies.

It is important that the governor of the central bank be substantially independent of the Minister of Finance, but he cannot remain independent of the government as a whole without becoming a rival government. When fundamental differences in policy arise, the Governor should be free to formulate and to submit his views to parliament. It should not be possible for the central bank to block or thwart the economic program of the government if the latter is prepared to take complete responsibility for the required monetary (or balance-of-payments) policy. The government should, however, be responsible for placing the issues before parliament. Such announcements have the great advantage of putting both the government and the central bank in a position where there is no way in which either can avoid assuming responsibility for the monetary policy to be followed. Once the policies of the government are determined and announced, the governor of the central bank must either submit to them or resign. Accordingly, even in times of conflicts of policy between the government and the central bank, in this limited but important sense the governor of the central bank must ultimately remain independent.[14]

The crucial impact of a central bank on economic policy has never been determined by formal arrangements. Detailed and precise prescriptions in this field are inappropriate; they cannot effectively be applied to modern, ungeneralizable, unpredictable, and conflicting objectives and conditions. It is the authority and respect that the governor of a central bank can command that usually matters. This authority varies strikingly in the new sub-Sahara nations. Personal characteristics aside, it depends heavily on the governor's competence as an economist, on his possessing essential information, on his experience in the operation of financial markets and, above all, on the objectivity and cogency of his views as judged by experience. These attributes must to a considerable extent rely on a competent research staff, on a steady flow of relevant reports, and on widespread business and government contacts.

The specialized knowledge of the governor in the functioning of financial markets and key institutions is indispensable. These are the organs through which the bank implements its policies. Portfolio and debt-management, monetary and fiscal coordination—these are not merely technical operations. If the bank is to conduct its work in a manner that smooths the fluctuations of money markets, the governor must possess economic competence as well as

[14] Compare the discussion of these issues by two distinguished central bankers: Rasminsky [32], and in the same series, Holtrop [16]. I am pleased to note that where we are dealing with the same, or similar, topics, there is no substantial difference in views. The recommendation to submit fundamental differences in policy between the Governor of the Central Bank and the Minister of Finance to Parliament is based primarily on Canadian experience [See Statutes of Canada (4–16 E. II Chap. 88), 1967], which, of course, applies to African countries only in a normative sense. Its purpose is to emphasize that, particularly under African conditions, the power of the governor of the central bank should be increased.

financial sensitivity. When much capital is of foreign origin, skillful daily operations furnish a source of increased confidence, as well as of loanable funds. Such operations form the means of checking perverse market reactions when the bank takes monetary initiatives.

The most compelling task of central-bank management in Africa lies in limiting the potential damage of financial shocks and, wherever possible, preventing financial crises from arising. The success of these efforts depends not only upon the level of a country's monetary and financial development but also upon minimum standards of trust and confidence between the governor, senior members of the bank, and the financial community. These are prerequisites for the successful implementation of open-market operations. The bank's power, moreover, is critically limited by the technical competence of its personnel and by the institutions and instruments which are genuinely under its control. The intrinsic financial position of a central bank as expressed by its balance sheet—or in the franc-zone countries by the *compte d'operations*—is of fundamental importance in its operations. Consequently, for an appraisal of the contribution that central banking and monetary institutions can make to African stabilization and development, an analysis of their role within the relevant institutional setting is indispensable.

The contemporary African environment is no less subject to divisive and disruptive forces than the rest of the world. If monetary, banking, and other development institutions are to make an important, albeit limited, contribution to dealing with this situation, they will have to become more effective both in implementing their own specialized functions and in playing a more significant role within the council of government. They are better suited for providing assistance to African economic development than is usually realized. Although much of African economic planning requires government direction —and in certain cases government ownership and management of basic industries—for the most part, African conditions call for decentralized, market-oriented processes coupled with cooperative tribal arrangements.[15]

The central banks, as guardians of the currency and overseers of economic growth, have a special obligation to undertake the responsibility of explaining in understandable terms the complex forces operating at different times on

[15] This form of planning needs to be institutionalized by way of selective medium-term targets, appraised annually, thereby providing a sense of national urgency, timely adjustment, and credible accomplishment. In rural areas, where the demand for land is smaller than the supply at the going "contractual price," the problem is to increase the demand for it by raising the real returns in agricultural employment (e.g., through improved schools, running water, electricity, and storage and transport facilities). In urban areas, where the demand for labor is smaller than the supply at the going wage rate, the problem is to increase the demand for it by raising the real returns in manufacturing and service employment (e.g., through increased labor productivity, enlarged investment, and road and highway construction).

their economies, and in elaborating the basic rationale for the policies being followed. To the extent that monetary policy is effective, the political and administrative simplicity of changes in monetary policy—as compared with fiscal policy—lend support to their potentially greater usefulness in African economic development than has so far been accorded to them. The needs, however, are beyond current African resources. In the foreseeable future, the African continent is likely to witness a greater demand than supply for both real and financial capital. African countries will, therefore, have to accelerate the development of their new banking institutions and use the expertise of cooperating foreign banks in order to satisfy several growing needs: for short-term capital to finance foreign trade; for medium- and long-term capital to finance the transformation and investment of agriculture and industry; and for the importation of long-term capital from all parts of the world.

The African monetary systems, which developed during the colonial and neocolonial period, have progressed considerably since independence. Understandably, they are still far from effective in meeting national needs. They have been, and some of them are still, closely connected with restrictive trade and overvalued exchange-rate practices that have not been in the long-term economic interest of either the African countries or the metropolitan powers. It would be difficult to exaggerate the importance of devising means whereby these new nations, while retaining their friendly ties with the metropolitan territory, could gradually eliminate these restrictive practices. For the long term, they retard rather than speed economic development and economic independence.

In the context of the above conditions and objectives, the author is carrying out an analysis and appraisal of the various monetary systems used in the new African nations south of the Sahara, with reference to their impact on problems of African economic development and intra-African trade. This in turn calls for an analysis of the relations between the metropolitan and the new African financial and commercial institutions, their effects on the structure of African economic development, as well as on the directions and pace of African foreign trade. These conditions are more than a century behind those of most Latin American countries. Nevertheless, the new African nations often suffer from similar causes as those which have plagued Latin America—but in greater historical, political, and economic depth. Understandably, their objectives are closer to those of the leading Latin American countries than to the major industrial powers. The monetary and trade experience of Latin America, therefore, both in regard to its successes and failures, as well as the counsel of scholars in these fields, should be welcome knowledge to the writer, not only for improvement of the examination and appraisal of the emerging African monetary systems, but also for recommendations on possible courses of future action.

REFERENCES

[1] Aboyade, O., The Development Process, *in* "National Reconstruction and Development in Nigeria" (A. A. Ayida and H. M. A. Onitiri, eds.). Oxford Univ. Press, London and New York (in press).

[2] Amin, S., "Trois Experiences Africaines de Developpement: Le Mali, Le Guinee et Le Ghana." Presses Univ. de France, Paris, 1965.

[3] Bagehot, W., "Physics and Politics" (1872) *in* Baron de Montesquieu, "The Spirit of Laws," Vol. 2, p. 97, and the relevant discussion in Chap. 2, entitled The Use of Conflict, Chaps. 3 and 4. Nation Making, Colonial Press, New York, 1900.

[4] Barzun, J., *in* "The Collected Works of Walter Bagehot" (N. St. John–Stevas, ed.), Vol. 3, pp. 23–40. The Economist, Hazell Watson and Viney, London, 1968.

[5] Brass, W., Coale, A. J., Demeny, P., Heisel, D. F., Lorimer, F., Romaniuk, A., and Van de Walle, E., "The Demography of Tropical Africa." Princeton Univ. Press, Princeton, New Jersey, 1968.

[6] Coleman, J. S., and Price, B., Jr., "The Role of the Military in Underdeveloped Countries" (J. J. Johnson, ed.), pp. 360–378, 394–402. Princeton Univ. Press, Princeton, New Jersey, 1962.

[7] Coleman, J. S., and Rosberg, C. G., Jr., "Political Parties and National Integration in Tropical Africa." Univ. of California Press, Berkeley and Los Angeles, California, 1964.

[8] Dixit, A., Theories of the Dual Economy: A Survey. Inst. of Int. Stud., Univ. of California, Berkeley, Tech. Rep. 30, pp. 1–60. (October 1969), and sources cited therein.

[9] Donghi, T. Halperin-, Revolutionary Militarization in Buenos Aires, 1806–1815, "Past and Present, A Journal of Historical Studies," p. 105. July 1968.

[10] Donghi, T. Halperin-, "Storia dell America Latina." Piccola Biblioteca Einaudi, Torino, 1968.

[11] Eriksson, J. R., Wage Change and Employment Growth in Latin America Industry, in Manpower and Unemployment Research in Africa, A Newsletter, Centre for Developing Area Studies, No. 2, pp. 58–63. McGill Univ. Montreal, Canada (November 1970), and sources cited therein.

[12] Gutkind, P. C. W., Bibliography on Unemployment, in Manpower and Unemployment Research in Africa, A Newsletter, Centre for Developing Area Studies, No. 2 pp. 43–45. McGill Univ., Montreal, Canada (November 1969).

[13] Gutkind, P.C.W., Manpower and Unemployment Research in Africa, A Newsletter, Centre for Developing Area Studies, No. 2, pp. 1–9, 44–47. McGill Univ., Montreal, Canada (November 1970).

[14] Gutteridge, W., "The Military in African Politics," p. 135. Methuen, London, 1969.

[15] Gutteridge, W., "The Military in African Politics," pp. 141–159. Methuen, London, 1969.

[16] Holtrop, M. W., "Central Banking and Economic Integration," pp. 5–8. Konserthuset, Stockholm, 1968.

[17] Itagaki, Y., A Review of the Concept of the Duel Economy, "Developing Economies," Vol. 6, pp. 143–157.

[18] Janowitz, M., "The Military in the Political Development of New Nations," pp. 23–30, 75–89. Univ. of Chicago Press, Chicago, Illinois, 1962.

[19] Johnson, H. G., A Theoretical Model of Economic Nationalism in New and Developing States, *in* "Economic Nationalism in Old and New States" (H. G. Johnson, ed.), pp. 10–16. Univ. of Chicago Press, Chicago, Illinois, 1967.

[20] Johnson, H. G., The Ideology of Economic Policy in the New States, *in* "Economic Nationalism in Old and New States" (H. G. Johnson, ed.), pp. 126–130. Univ. of Chicago Press, Chicago, Illinois, 1967.

[21] Jorgenson, D. W., The Development of a Dual Economy, *Econ. J.* **71**, 309–334 (1961).
[22] Keyfitz, N., and Flieger, W., "World Population," p. 24. Univ. of Chicago Press, Chicago, Illinois, 1968.
[23] Keyfitz, N., and Flieger, W., "Population in the 1960s, Demographic Data and Techniques." Freeman, San Francisco, California, 1970.
[24] Kissinger, H. A., Central Issues of American Foreign Policy, *in* "Agenda for the Nation" (K. Gordon, ed.), p. 604. Brookings Inst., Washington, D. C., 1968.
[25] Lary, H. B., "Imports of Manufactures from Less Developed Countries," pp. 10–17, 97–137. Nat. Bur. of Econ. Res., New York, 1968.
[26] Nash, M., Economic Nationalism in Mexico, *in* "Economic Nationalism in Old and New States" (H. G. Johnson, ed.), pp. 79–84. Univ. of Chicago, Chicago, Illinois, 1967.
[27] Pearson, L. B., "Partners in Development" p. 58, Annex 1, p. 270. Praeger, New York, 1969.
[28] Prebisch, R., Commercial Policy in the Underdeveloped Countries, *Papers Proc., Amer. Econ. Rev.* **69**, 251–273 (May 1959).
[29] Prebisch, R., "Towards a Dynamic Development Policy for Latin America." United Nations, New York, 1963.
[30] Prebisch, R., "Towards a New Trade Policy for Development," pp. 20–25. United Nations, New York, 1964.
[31] Prebisch, R., 25th Anniversary of Bretton Woods, Queen's University Kingston, Ontario, June 2–3 (1967).
[32] Rasminsky, L., The Role of the Central Banker Today, "The Per Jacabsson Foundation," pp. 27–28. Int. Monetary Fund, Washington, D. C., 1966.
[33] Schultz, T. W., "Transforming Traditional Agriculture," Chaps. 5–7. Yale Univ. Press, New Haven, Connecticut, 1964.
[34] Schultz, T. W., "Economic Growth and Agriculture," Chaps. 1, 2, 4. McGraw-Hill New York, 1968.
[35] Shils, E., "Political Development in the New States," pp. 41–43, 66–75. Mouton, The Hague, 1962.
[36] Stolper, W. F., "Planning Without Facts," pp. 67, 92, 109. Harvard Univ. Press, Cambridge, Massachusetts, 1966.
[37] United Nations, "Scope and Structure of Money Economies in Tropical Africa," II.C.4.E/2739 ST/ECA/34, Tables 5–8, 15, 20–24. United Nations, New York, 1955.
[38] United Nations, Economic Bulletin for Latin America, Vol. 12, No. 1, pp. 35–55 (1967).
[39] United Nations, Economic Bulletin for Latin America, Vol. 12, No. 2, pp. 146–147 (1967).
[40] Zolberg, A. R., Economic Planning in Mali, *in* "Economic Nationalism in Old and New States," (H. G. Johnson, ed.), pp. 108–121. Univ. of Chicago, Chicago, Illinois. 1967.

THE INTERNATIONAL POLITICS OF LATIN AMERICAN ECONOMICS

JOHN P. POWELSON

University of Colorado, Boulder, Colorado

I. Introduction

In a volume dedicated to Raúl Prebisch, who has been both masterful economist and political force in Latin America, it is not inappropriate to devote a paper to the political impact of Latin American economics upon the United States. It should be understood from the beginning that the author is strongly in favor of most of the objectives of Latin American policy, such as unilateral trade preferences for developing countries, ample compensatory financing for fluctuations in primary-product prices, effective commodity agreements, or other arrangements to improve the terms of trade, and increased flow of capital through international lending agencies, principally the Inter-American Development Bank. Criticism of the strategy of Latin American diplomats is intended in spirit to be constructive, in the hope of finding more effective ways by which these goals can be achieved.

The Latin American strategy of the 50s and early 60s, it seems, has been grounded on weakness. Buttressed by theories emanating from the Economic Commission for Latin America, diplomats have preached the powerlessness of their countries, a powerlessness which underlies the theory of structural inflation: inflation is "there" and cannot be stopped without destroying growth. Declarations that the terms of trade are moving against producers of primary products emphasizes that Latin America is buffeted by international currents against which it can do nothing. Whenever Latin American economists state that foreign demand for their products is inelastic, they emphasize the inability of their countries to alter the export structure in favor of goods whose demand is more elastic. When Latin Americans argue for unilateral concessions in North American markets, they are also saying they are incapable of developing the vast interiors of Argentina and Brazil (for example), to open up mass consumption possibilities of their own.

The truth or falsehood of these assertions and theories is not the question here—in a political sense, it is irrelevant whether they are true or not. What is more important is to predict the reaction of North American diplomats and legislators to them, to determine how effective such arguments will be in confrontations with the United States.

Much of the Latin American rhetoric has been aimed at persuading North Americans how small the sacrifices need be on their part to produce great benefits for Latin America. How minor would be the impact of free access for Latin manufactures in the U.S. market, since U.S. producers are large, efficient, and monopolistic, while Latin competitors would be small, high cost, and subject to heavy transport expenses. How little the North Americans would give up if they recognized the 200-mile limit and bought fishing licenses, or if they paid another cent per cup of coffee, or if they allocated one per cent of their national income to international lending. What trivial sacrifices these would be for the *powerful* United States, and how great would be the benefit to a *weaker* Latin America.

That these arguments have had but little effect upon North American delegates to UNCTAD, OAS, commodity study groups, and other conferences has been a source of frustration and no small wonderment for the Latin Americans. The more sanguine among them may attribute the meager results to political affairs within the United States, stemming in part from provincialism, ignorance, and apathy of the people, and in part from politicians' unwillingness (more so in some Administrations than in others) to interpret international urgencies to their constituents. In large part, this interpretation is correct, but there is another subtlety about the North American way of thought to which Latin American economists and diplomats appear to have been oblivious.

North Americans—particularly those of the generation now in political power—have been taught to admire strength and to *despise* weakness. There is no need to explain Weber's "protestant ethic" or the sayings of Benjamin Franklin, for most Latin American intellectuals are already familiar with them. It seems, however, that Latin strategists have not grasped how strongly held these tenets are. Despite such Christian precepts as the parable of the Good Samaritan, North Americans learn early in their lives to brook no quarter for those who lose in competition. The weak are to be mercilessly destroyed.

This is a powerful indictment of North American society, and some explanation is required as to how this situation came about. But first it should be commented that there is considerable disaffection with this state of affairs, particularly among North American youth, to the extent that some argue that a revolution is currently under way which will drastically change the most revered national values. For whatever impact this revolution may have upon relations with Latin America, however, it has not succeeded yet. Latin American political strategists must count on dealing with the old values for at least another decade or two.

The legitimate destruction of the weak has become sanctified in political and economic theory. Even the weak are presumed to benefit from being destroyed, for they "gain" more by hanging on to the coattails of the strong than they could by preserving their own personalities. This principle stems from Adam Smith's invisible hand; it is found in Ricardo's law of comparative advantage; and it is a tenet of democracy and majority rule. The economic theory does not presume that all have equal bargaining power; rather, the richer the rich are, the better off will be the poor. The political theory does not presume that the minority have special "rights." There is no way by which a minority group can defeat a majority. Rather, a minority finds political force by allying itself in common cause with some elements of the majority, becoming a new majority sliced in a different way. North American liberals believe civil rights will come to Blacks when White-inspired institutions are made accessible to them. They may live in the suburbs and sit wherever they wish in a transport system that accords with an urban–work/suburban–dormitory pattern evolved out of White cultural values. In the same way, North American diplomats and strategists are convinced that the western hemisphere as a whole will gain by the universal promotion of economic and political institutions, such as private enterprise and competition, that emerged from Anglo-Saxon culture. In these institutions, weakness is despised and destroyed.

During the fifties and early sixties ECLA poured forth volumes of theories proclaiming the weakness of Latin America, and the moral or ethical obligation of the strong to make concessions to it. True to its own values, the United States has turned a totally deaf ear to these pleadings. Any concessions on the part of the United States, such as participation in the Inter-American Development Bank and the coffee agreement, despite initial misgivings, were not generated by a feeling of moral obligation but by temporary strong bargaining positions that the Latin Americans were able to achieve.

In the latter sixties, however, there surged a new strength in Latin America. The Mexican Government, which has been learning to operate from strength *vis-á-vis* the United States ever since 1917, instituted a variety of new laws controlling foreign investment and otherwise limiting the activities of North Americans in Mexico; it also refused to yield to U.S. insistence on isolating

Cuba diplomatically. The governments of Venezuela and Chile began to tax U.S. direct investment far more heavily than before. In 1968, a new military government in Peru expropriated the International Petroleum Corporation and set stringent rules for other foreign investment. In 1970, a left-wing government in Chile proclaimed its intentions to nationalize foreign investments sweepingly. Furthermore, Latin American governments have been learning how to form a united front before the United States, as in the Council for Latin American Economic Coordination (CECLA). However much the U.S. Government may have disliked this chain of events, nevertheless it has instilled into North American strategists a respect for Latin America that had been almost totally lost a decade before.

The remainder of this paper is divided into three parts: In the first Latin America's policy for weakness will be analyzed, which dates roughly from 1950 to 1965. In the next, some characteristics of the U.S. machine for foreign policy are explored, which it would be useful for Latin American diplomats to bear in mind. In the final part, certain suggestions to Latin Americans on how to prepare an effective foreign policy *vis-á-vis* the United States are proffered.

II. The Policy of Weakness: 50s and Early 60s

It is with some misgivings this is labeled the "policy of weakness"—perhaps it would be better to call it the "policy of declaring Latin America weak." For this policy did, in fact, play a significant role in making Latin America strong. It inspired in Latin American intellectuals a new spirit of indignation over the injustices inflicted upon them by foreigners, as well as an awareness of the archaic social structures of their own continent, and it united them in seeking ways to overcome both these indignities.

Nevertheless, the substance of the policy was to declare that underdevelopment in Latin America was due to forces beyond the control of Latin Americans: the terms of trade, high cost of foreign capital, political intervention, economic control from abroad, and the like. Even where feudal structures had been erected by Latin Americans, it has been supposed that these were supported and defended by the foreigner. To North Americans, whose political myth compels them to believe that man's duty is to overcome his environment, this declaration appeared as surrender. According to the North American myth, the greater the obstacle and the more it seems beyond the control of the individual, then the greater the challenge and the greater the glory in overcoming it.

The heart of the Latin American policy lies in the stream of economic theories emanating from the pens of ECLA economists. These theories relate principally to the terms of trade and to development process and strategy, including inflation, balance of payments, import substitution, and export promotion.[1] In one way or another, all these theories relate to the balance of payments, and they center on the point that over time, gross output and exports of Latin America must increase in proportion. The author agrees with this statement and there will be no attempt to analyze it. Rather, we turn our attention to those aspects of the theory which propose that exports are at the mercy of structural forces about which the Latin Americans can do nothing, at least in the short run.

To gain credence, any scholarly precept must have both theoretical and empirical validation. The two need not occur simultaneously. Often theories are proposed the validation of which comes later, and sometimes the theories do not lend themselves readily to empirical study. At other times, the empirical study comes first, and theories are spun from the results. Over time, however, the scientific method requires both.

ECLA's theory of the terms of trade—that over time they deteriorate for producers of primary products—rests on both empirical and theoretical arguments.[2] Readers are no doubt familiar with them, so they will be summarized only briefly.

The empirical case rests on a study of British trade data from 1876–1880 to 1936–1938, in which imports were valued CIF the United Kingdom, for want of adequate data from Latin American sources. This study has been widely criticized, principally by Ellsworth, who pointed out that international transportation costs had been going down during that period at a sufficient rate to make it likely that British importers were paying a lower price (CIF), while Latin American exporters were receiving a higher price (FOB) for the same goods [5]. Furthermore, ECLA took no account of changes in the quality and composition of British exports, its study suffering from the familiar problems of index-number use over long periods.

The theoretical case rests on three propositions. First, because of internal policies in the MDCs (especially the United States), innovations in manufacturing are not translated into lower prices (for exports and internal consumption); rather they go into higher wages and profits. Secondly, because of a rigidity in the price structure in MDCs, prices rise more during prosperity than they fall in depression; consequently, there is a long-term upward bias. Finally, because of Engel's law (that in high-income countries the income elasticity of demand for foodstuffs is not as great as that for manufactures)

[1] Representative writings of ECLA economists during the period under review have recently been reprinted [2].

[2] Both the theoretical and empirical cases were first made in Prebisch [10]. They have been further elaborated in other Latin American writings, such as Prebisch [11], and ECLA [1], reprinted in Theberge [12]. See also ECLA [3].

and because of the development of synthetics, the worldwide demand for primary products expands, over time, only in lesser proportion than that for manufactured goods. For all these reasons, the terms of trade have presumably been turning against the producers of primary products.

Though the facts may be correct, in each case there is a fallacy in the reasoning. The internal wage–price policies in the United States (expressed in dollars) should have no effect on the *real* prices at which exports and imports trade. Meier has shown that these depend on reciprocal offer relationships. If North Americans, with higher incomes stemming from innovations, do not *want* to consume 100 per cent of their increment but prefer to trade *some* of it (even the smallest part) for foreign goods, the terms of trade are bound to move against them, regardless of internal wage–price policy [7]. In two earlier articles the author has used examples to demonstrate how internal policies would be offset by opposite movements in the exchange rate [8, 9]. The same reasoning would apply to asymmetries in the business cycle, which are but one manifestation of the internal wage–price policy. Finally, neither Engel's law nor the substitution of synthetic for natural primary products would turn the terms of trade against Latin America *unless* the substitution of synthetics was great enough to reduce Latin American exports *in absolute terms*, not merely in proportion to manufactured goods. If increased manufacture in MDCs leads to *any* increase in demand for Latin American exports—and it obviously has—then the terms of trade would theoretically move in favor of Latin America.

Despite the intellectual demolition of both the empirical and the theoretical arguments, the proposition crops up again and again. In many of their speeches, Latin American officials state categorically that the terms of trade are moving against primary-producing countries, and often they base their data on such good years as 1950 (because of the Korean War) and 1954 (because of the coffee freeze), pointing out that prices have been lower in other years. It seems safe to say that by and large, Latin American officials *believe* the terms of trade are turning against their countries, while North American officials *believe* the case is far from proved. When an economic theory cannot be proved one way or another (because of loopholes in both the empirical and theoretical validations), it is interesting that the opinions about it should divide along national lines. It is here that one's cultural values play their role, such as whether weakness is to be sympathized with or despised, and that the "politics of economics" makes sense.

"ECLA economics" with respect to the balance of payments has faced an even more hostile reception in the United States. ECLA's principal thrust is that, unlike a century and a half ago when Europe and the United States were less developed, today's LDCs cannot achieve a reasonable rate of growth without incurring balance of payments deficits. Development, they say, requires capital goods which must in large part be imported. Unless financed by lending, these imports must be paid for by exports. But Latin American exports, both primary products and manufacturing, face inelastic demand in the MDCs. It is therefore to no avail for Latin America to adopt such exchange-rate, monetary, or fiscal policies as might, according to classical economic thought, increase her foreign exchange income, for what Latin America would gain through increased sales would be more than offset by decreased income through lower prices.[3] Even classical economic thought recognizes this possibility, in the Marshall–Lerner conditions, that devaluation will improve a country's foreign earnings only if the sum of the elasticity of demand for its exports and of its own demand for imports exceeds one.[4] The problem is not only to demonstrate that demand for traditional exports is inelastic, but that there is nothing Latin America can do—in introducing new exports—to make it more elastic.

Deficit in the balance of payments as an inevitable accompaniment of development has not found a very credent audience in the MDCs. In the first place, it has been inadequately documented. Most of the ECLA writings that refer to inelastic demand for their exports take for granted that this is the case, as if inelasticity is so obvious that no evidence of it need be offered. If there are studies to back up the proposition, they have not been given widespread circulation. Yet it is not altogether clear that the demand even for traditional exports is as inelastic as Latin American writers think. U.S. imports of coffee have been severely cut back in those years where the price was increased due to a freeze. Aluminium is substituting for tin, and copper producers (in the United States) have argued the price of copper must not be allowed to rise too high for fear other metals will be substituted. The very prospect that their primary outputs will be replaced by synthetics is an argument that demand is somewhat elastic. All the above is evidence that demand may be elastic when prices are raised. Unless there is a convincing argument for a kink in the schedule (and there does not seem to be such an argument), one might suppose that some products would find a degree of elasticity in case prices were lowered as well.

In the second place, ECLA's occasional statements that even the foreign demand for Latin American manufactures is inelastic meet considerable doubt. Instead, North Americans are more likely to conclude that Latin American exports of manufactured goods tend to be high priced because of inefficiencies in their production and failure to take advantage of economies of scale. Heavy protection of domestic manufactures has insulated them from foreign competition, and Latin American exporters, by postponing rather

[3] This argument is elaborated in ECLA [4].

[4] See Kindleberger [6].

than jumping to accelerate the date of completing the Latin American Free Trade Area, have shown themselves inclined to relax within that insulation. There is widespread belief in the United States that if these exporters would make themselves more efficient in production and would pursue modern marketing techniques, they could force their way into the MDCs despite import restrictions imposed by the latter. Given lower wages in Latin America, a judicious choice of goods accompanied by appropriate advertising, might well find favorable entrance. Latin American exports of manufactures are in fact increasing, both in absolute terms and in proportion to total exports, as is demonstrated by Figs. 1 and 2.

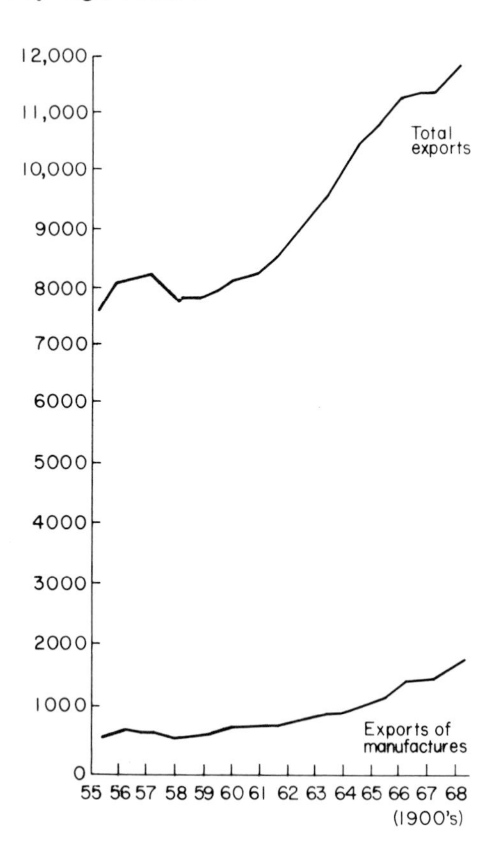

Fig. 1. Latin American exports, 1955–1968 (millions of U.S. dollars). Source: Statistical Bulletin for Latin America.

In sum, the ECLA economic thought that evolved during the 50s and early 60s appears to have been a source of unity among Latin American technicians

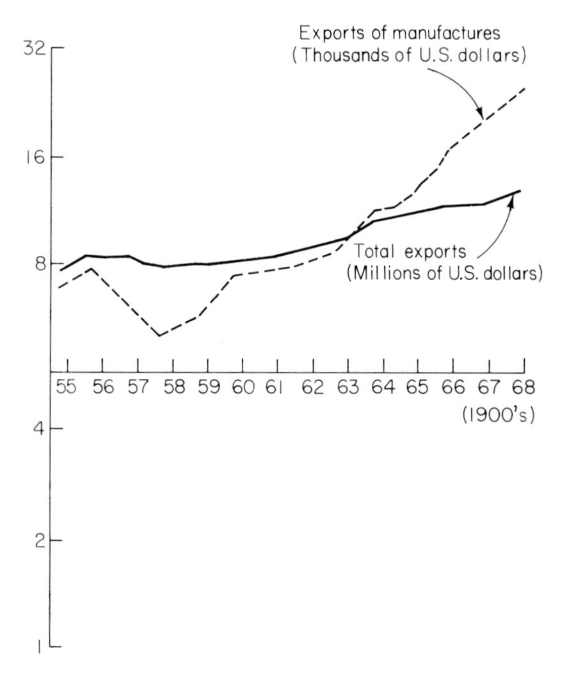

Fig. 2. Latin American exports, 1955–1968, in logarithmic scale designed to show percentage increments. Source: Statistical Bulletin for Latin America.

and the intellectual public, for it provided an ethnocentric basis by which disparate groups (e.g., industry, labor, military, students) might find goals in common (release from indignities imposed by the foreigner) and learn how to express common cause. This accomplishment should not be denigrated. On the other side of the coin, however, these same factors probably made it harder for North American diplomats to accede to Latin American wishes in international conferences. They painted Latin America as a picture of weakness, and unwittingly they set off, among North Americans, both a latent feeling of hostility and a belief that Latin America was not strong enough to enforce its demands.

III. The United States Foreign Policy Machine

Latin Americans often believe that foreign policy in the United States is composed in the State Department, and that this department represents the interests of a domestic constituency. While Latin officials very close to the diplomatic process have probably been disabused of this naiveté, nevertheless it is commonly held by the technicians who advise these same officials, and it is certainly held by the intellectual public at large. It is therefore appropriate at this time to deal with some of the subtleties of the U.S. diplomatic process.

The principal agencies that compose U.S. policy toward Latin America are the President, the State Department (including the Agency for International Development and its proposed successors), and the Congress. Each of these has separate functions, and there is considerable friction among them. A knowledge of how this friction operates might help Latin negotiators play one agency off against the other, where this is possible.

It would seem—at first blush—that the State Department and the Presidency are the same thing, since the President appoints the Secretary of State and the Assistant Secretary for Latin American Affairs, and they both serve at his pleasure. But the matter is not so simple. The State Department is a large apparatus, consisting mostly of career men who do not change jobs as the presidency changes hands. Most technicians, even of relatively high level, fall into this category. Only the very top positions, such as the Secretary and a few officials whose offices have been labeled political, do, in fact, change. Furthermore, the career technicians do not alter their views from presidency to presidency. Consequently, they act as stabilizers in the promotion of a long-run policy toward Latin America (and toward other parts of the world).

Their effectiveness, however, differs with different presidents. Some presidents rely on the Secretary of State implicitly, while other (such as Kennedy and Nixon) bypass him by creating White House advisors whose appointments do not outlast the term of the President and who may influence his thinking more than the officials of the State Department. Some Presidents will ignore the State Department if its officials do not agree with him on policy. Nevertheless, the president must rely on department officials to carry out everyday negotiations and to man international conferences, such as meetings to discuss jurisdiction over territorial waters, commodity study groups, and the like. The relationship between the president and his White House advisors, on the one hand, and the State Department officials on the other, is not always without tension.

The third arm in this policy triad is the Congress. Congress is directly responsible to its constituency, and its constituency—unfortunately—does not include Latin Americans. It is difficult to persuade a Congressman to favor a law that would promote Latin American exports into the United States when that law would run counter to the interests of the people who would vote for (or against) him. Fortunately, however, not all foreign policy issues need be settled by Congress. The extent to which the government will assist a company whose property is being expropriated in Latin America depends largely on the decision of the president, assisted by his White House advisors and technicians in the State Department. However, questions of preference for Latin American imports or participation in the coffee agreement cannot be decided without a favorable vote of Congress.

Now, the State Department—particularly career officials—consider themselves *mediators* between the foreigner (e.g., Latin American) on the one hand and the U.S. Congress and the president on the other. Their principal object is to find a satisfactory solution to an international problem, no matter who wins. The smoother the relationship between Latin America and the United States, the more successful they consider themselves to be. They do have a bias toward solutions favoring the United States, but it is not nearly so strong as many believe. Rather, if they can persuade the president to give *less* support to a U.S. company demanding compensation for expropriation, thereby bringing about agreement, they believe they have done their duty well. In conferences (e.g., Buenos Aires, 1967) on territorial limits over the sea, State Department negotiators were accompanied by representatives of the U.S. fishing industry. Though these latter had come to protect their own interests, nevertheless from the State Department's vantage point, they were there to learn about the Latin American position and about how complex such international issues are, in the hope that they would become more tolerant in their demands on Congress and the presidency.

Of the foreign policy triad, therefore, the State Department (including the U.S. ambassador) is the most flexible, the most willing to listen to Latin arguments. Often an ambassador behaves as if the country to which he is accredited were his constituency, arguing its case before the president. Though much admittedly depends on the personality of the incumbent, from the point of view of his office alone the U.S. official most likely to argue the case *for* joining the coffee agreement would be the U.S. ambassador to Brazil. The opponents would be the Congressmen representing General Mills, Chase and Sanborn, and other coffee roasters.

If there are any general principles that State Department negotiators would like to establish, they would *not* be simply "whatever is best for U.S. industry." In such disputes as fisheries and petroleum with Peru, petroleum with Argentina, and the like, the Department's objective would be to promote the sanctity of contract, especially where government is a party; the legitimacy of government continuity, so that each government assumes the obligations of its predecessors; and the acceptance of international law. Latin Americans may well argue that these principles would favor the U.S. contestant in a dispute, since agreements in favor of foreign enterprise were common in the case of dictators like Leguía, who laid down the terms on which the International Petroleum Corporation made its bed in Peru. Be that as it may. If clear rules of order are promoted by which U.S. investment is accepted or not in Latin

America, the State Department's object of promoting peaceful relations is vastly facilitated.

State Department officials (including the ambassador and AID officers) are the ones Latin American technicians are most likely to meet in international conferences. The question therefore is: What kinds of arguments are most likely to affect them? The answer is: *Not* arguments that stress how weak Latin America is. For these persuade department officials that Latin America will be compliant, that it can do nothing, and therefore peace will be more easily assured if they concede to the wishes of more powerful interests at home. To tell State Department officials that the United States ought to make trade concessions to Latin America because of inequities the North Americans have inflicted in the past, or because the cost to the United States will be so small and the benefit to Latin America so great, will—alas!—fall on deaf ears.

It is, perhaps, a good idea at this point briefly to review some of the opinions of Latin American development problems that have widespread currency in the United States. Just as ECLA theory and Latin American diplomats have been attributing lack of development to forces beyond the control of Latin Americans (e.g., terms of trade, foreign monopolies, political power of foreign investors, trade barriers of MDCs), so also the North Americans have been attributing it to factors internal to Latin America. Principal among these is the philosophy, believed to be widely held by Latin American businessmen, that profits are to be earned by monopoly and privilege in small markets highly protected from foreign competition; that administrative decisions should be made by a small business elite on the basis of inadequate information (e.g., inadequate cost controls and market research); that strict delineations by class should preclude decisionmakers from consulting their "inferiors" or laborers from contributing to productivity increase; and that proposals to develop mass markets through income redistributions (e.g., progressive taxes and agrarian reform) or through *effective* Latin American integration ought to be postponed. Under these circumstances, it is widely felt in the United States, Latin American businesses are necessarily inefficient and are unable to compete in international markets. This fact, rather than trade barriers in MDCs, is widely believed in the United States to be the principal obstacle to diversification of Latin American exports.

The extent to which these North American opinions are accurate is a matter that Latin Americans might well ponder. But it is irrelevant to the present discussion. We are here concerned with the reaction of U.S. policymakers to the ECLA thrust and are offering some opinions as to why international meetings, such as the two UNCTAD conferences, have made slow headway. The author believes it is because of widely divergent philosophies, on the part of Latin American and North American negotiators, on the causes of underdevelopment, and the peculiar way in which these philosophies have clashed. North American negotiators will yield only in the face of Latin American *strength.* The Latin Americans have done their utmost to persuade the North Americans of how *weak* Latin America really is.

IV. Some Suggestions for Latin American Strategy

It will seem the height of audacity for a North American now to suggest what Latin American strategy ought to be. Or it will seem like some sort of trick, in that North Americans have the reputation of trying to persuade Latin Americans that certain policy moves are in their own advantage, when in reality they are in ours. This author confesses to being one of the North Americans who believes that ultimately there is a wide area of mutual advantage, but also that U.S. policies (not only Latin American) have not been well designed to discover that area. Finally, however, the author is not proposing a new strategy. In the latter part of the 60s, the "policy of declaring Latin America strong" was already adopted by a few countries and is in the course of adoption by others. It can only be suggested that it advance as rapidly as possible.

The strategy depends on recognition of the following facts:

1. Certain elements of U.S. foreign policy are made primarily in the State Department, others primarily by the president, and others primarily in Congress. Latin Americans would do well to understand which elements are which, as well as to know that these three branches have differing degrees of independence and are frequently in conflict with each other.
2. The State Department's major objective is to "keep the peace" by finding solutions that yield the least friction. Often a solution will involve concessions by the United States.
3. Latin American negotiators have no access to the U.S. Congress, very limited access to the U.S. President, but ample access to the State Department.
4. In those policy areas for which it does not bear direct responsibility, the State Department is nevertheless the most powerful negotiating agent the Latin Americans have in confronting the U.S. President and Congress.
5. In their mission to "keep the peace," the State Department will pay far greater attention to Latin Americans who argue from a position of strength than to those who argue that Latin America is weak.

In recent years, policy makers in some countries have begun to take a much stronger stance *vis-á-vis* the United States. True, they use the doctrine of Latin American weakness in an effort to unify their own countries in policies of strength, for such unification depends on the existence of a "common enemy." It is not necessary to mention which countries they are, and what the policies of strength they have followed are, for these points are well known. The official attitude in the United States has been one of alarm, and the parent corporations of direct investment companies have shown considerable concern. At the same time, a new respect is being developed, which will doubtless be turned to Latin American advantage in the future.

This new policy of strength, it seems to me, ought to include further promotion of the following points:

1. Commercial advantage in international markets should be gained by bringing primary products under effective national control. This may be done under various arrangements, including private or government enterprise, foreign or national ownership. The important point is not the legal form of ownership but that essential economic decisions must be made at home.
2. Clear rules of order should be set for foreign investment: what kinds will be permitted, what kinds prohibited, and the manner in which business shall be conducted. Foreign businesses should be under effective national control and subject only to national laws.
3. Strength in international bargaining also depends on economic strength. This in turn depends on efficiency of production. The extent to which North American impressions of Latin American business philosophy may be true should be deeply pondered. Latin Americans should *not* depend on unilateral concessions of MDCs as their *principal* means of access to European and North American markets, for such concessions are bound to be slow and disappointing. They should depend far more on their own efficiency through competition and advantages of scale, gained by redistributing income through appropriate taxes and agrarian reform, and by economic integration. From this strength, they should bargain their way into the markets of the MDCs.
4. Latin American negotiators should inform their counterparts from the United States that once a specific list of grievances is satisfied—including unfair agreements with foreign companies that were made by dictators without popular support—that from that point on the Latin American governments will be willing to honor promises made by prior governments, and that disputes with foreign owners will be decided, not by administrative decision, but by open trial in *national* courts.
5. Latin America can negotiate with the United States much more effectively from the basis of economic integration. Not only would integration improve productive efficiency, as mentioned above, but it would prevent some countries from competing with others in trade negotiations and in the terms on which foreign investment may be acceptable.

The above suggestions are broad, for it would seem improper for a foreigner to spell out details. They are not designed to make the author popular either in Latin America or in his own country. The U.S. Government would not be happy with these suggestions, although the author believes himself to be a patriot in proposing them, for independent strength in Latin America is to the long-run advantage of his own country. The Latin Americans may not like the suggestion either that they have been declaring themselves weak or that to do so has been an unfruitful policy. This chapter has been written because the author was given the opportunity to participate in a book that might have some readership in Latin America, and there were a few points important enough to warrant its inclusion.

REFERENCES

[1] ECLA, "Towards a Dynamic Development Policy for Latin America," Chap. 1, E/CN. 12/680/Rev 1. United Nations, New York, 1963.
[2] ECLA, "Development Problems in Latin America," Univ. of Texas Press, Austin, Texas, 1970.
[3] ECLA, "Development Problems in Latin America," Chap. 1. Univ. of Texas Press, Austin, Texas, 1970.
[4] ECLA, "Development Problems in Latin America," Chap. 2. Univ. of Texas Press, Austin, Texas, 1970.
[5] Ellsworth, P. T., The Terms of Trade between Primary Producing and Industrial Countries, *Inter-Amer. Econ. Affairs* **10**, No. 1, 47–65 (1956).
[6] Kindleberger, C. P., "International Economics," pp. 166–168. Irwin, Homewood, Illinois, 1963.
[7] Meier, G., "The International Economics of Development," pp. 10–65. Harper and Row, New York, 1968.
[8] Powelson, J. P., Toward an Integrated Growth Model: The Case of Latin America, "Constructive Change in Latin America" (C. Blasier, ed.), pp. 57–85. Pittsburgh Univ. Press, Pittsburgh, Pennsylvania, 1968.
[9] Powelson, J. P., The Terms of Trade Again, *Inter-Amer. Econ. Affairs* **23**, No. 4, 3–11 (1970).
[10] Prebisch, R., The Economic Development of Latin America and Its Principal Problems. Published by ECLA in United Nations document E/CN.12/Rev. 1 (April 27, 1950).
[11] Prebisch, R., Commercial Policies in the Underdeveloped Countries, *Amer. Econ. Rev. Papers Proc. 71st Ann. Meeting Amer. Econ. Ass.* pp. 251–273 (May 1959).
[12] Theberge, J., "Economics of Trade and Development," pp. 292 ff. Wiley, New York, 1968.

VII. INTERNATIONAL COOPERATION

The paper written by *Johnson* on the "crisis of aid" is an evaluation of the programs of international cooperation and takes up the so-called "Pearson Report." After giving the problem an adequate place in the recent past, the author turns to the First Conference on Trade and Development of the United Nations (Geneva, 1964), born under Dr. Prebisch's inspiration. Next, a rapid review of research done at other levels—Johnson, Pincus, Geiger—about which the writer makes certain remarks and clarifies the distinction between official and academic approaches to the problem of development aid. A detailed analysis of the Pearson Report follows after an account of the formation of the Commission of Experts, and there is a careful examination of the reasons for the Report's failure to resolve the issues. Particular emphasis is given to the point that the Pearson Report does not supply any new motives for the advanced countries to offer more aid for development. In addition, there is also an analysis of the consequences that the Report may produce and especially the reaction in North America. Johnson concludes by remarking that the Pearson Report marks the end of an era in the promotion of economic development, and that the peripheral countries will now have to learn how to succeed by their own efforts—all of which is preshadowed in Prebisch's ideas on the alternatives facing the developing countries.

THE "CRISIS OF AID" AND THE PEARSON REPORT

HARRY G. JOHNSON

London School of Economics and Political Science, London, England and University of Chicago, Chicago, Illinois

I

One of the historically distinguishing characteristics of the period since the end of World War II has been the growth of concern in the advanced industrial countries over the widening gap in living standards between the rich and the poor countries, and the assumption of an obligation on their part to help promote the economic development of the poor countries through the contribution of substantial resources to development assistance. For some countries, such as France and the United Kingdom, development aid has been envisaged largely as an obligation to former colonial territories; for other European countries, the motivation has varied between a sense of moral obligation and a sense of ultimate commercial advantage. The big impulse to development assistance, however, came from the leadership example and pressure of the United States, which initially approached development assistance in the spirit of the Marshall Plan for European Economic Recovery, and after successful completion of that plan, under the visionary inspiration of President John F. Kennedy, turned its attention to the solution of the development problem of the poor two-thirds of the world's population. Development aid has become a major world endeavor, involving some $6.5 billion in official aid disbursements and some $4.5 billion in private investment and lending in recent years, and employing hundreds of thousands (perhaps even millions) of people as economists and administrators in national governments and international agencies, as technical advisers in all sorts of fields, and as trainees of various kinds.

The problem of European economic recovery, for which the Marshall Plan was developed, was however a quite different problem than the problem of promoting economic development in the poor countries. The war-ravaged European countries were established nation-states, culturally mature and economically advanced, lacking only an intensive but brief marginal injection of capital to restore their economies and set them on the path of "self-sustaining growth." The poor countries were in many cases newly-created states, lacking the political stability and cultural homogeneity of established nations; and their poverty reflected general backwardness in the industrial and agricultural arts and a general paucity of productive resources, including social and human capital as well as the material means of production. Their development would necessarily be a relatively slow, painful, and wasteful process of "learning by doing" and of accumulating a complementary equipment of infrastructure, labor skills, material capital, and industrial knowledge, often while coping with the problems of achieving political stability and modernizing the society. In these circumstances, the Marshall Plan approach —the "crash programme" approach to setting nations on their economic feet and equipping them quickly for "self-sustaining" growth—was doomed to disappointment, with respect both to the degree of success achievable and the foreseeability of an early end to the need for the effort.

By the early 1960s, it was apparent that a "crisis of aid" was approaching. On the one hand, the need for development assistance, or at least the demand for it, was rising rapidly as the numbers of the developing countries, and the rate of economic growth to which they aspired, steadily increased. At the same time, the political stability and capacity to use aid of many of them was also increasing, as the early excesses of national "liberation" were recognized to be counterproductive. On the other hand, two of the three major aid donors, the United Kingdom and the United States, were in balance-of-payments difficulties that put pressure on their governments to limit their aid programs, and public opinion in the United States was becoming both increasingly disillusioned with the apparent failures of United States development assistance and increasingly concerned about the domestic problems of race relations and poverty.

The emerging crisis of aid was symbolized by the First United Nations Conference on Trade and Development, held in Geneva in 1964 and largely inspired by the thinking of Dr Raúl Prebisch. The main theme of the conference was a demand by the developing countries for a "new trade policy for development"—largely the intellectual creation of Dr. Prebisch—involving international commodity agreements to raise and stabilize the prices of the primary products on which these countries depended for the bulk of their export income, and preferences in the markets of the developed countries for the manufactures on which they planned to base their industrialization. This demand reflected the recognition that the halcyon days of competition in aid-giving between the West and the Soviet bloc had ended, that aid-givers were becoming decreasingly generous and increasingly choosy, and that any hope for important new sources of external resources for development lay in the field of trade rather than aid. Recognition of the increasing stringency of official aid-giving was also reflected in the concern of the developing countries to obtain redefinition of the target for developed country aid of one per cent of national income so as to increase the actual amount of aid it represented, and to obtain changes in the techniques of development lending—softening of financial terms, and untying of the aid—that would have the effect of increasing the real resource transfers actually involved.

As a consequence of the interest stirred up by the 1964 U.N. Conference on Trade and Development, and particularly of the shock to informed American opinion of the confrontation there of United States trade and aid policies with the demands of the developing countries, the author was commissioned in 1965 by the Brookings Institution to make a study of the issues; similar studies by John Pincus and Theodore Geiger were commissioned by other sponsors. What emerged from these studies—reformulated in the light of hindsight, and stated very briefly—was, first, that none of the arguments from the self-interest of the advanced countries—political, military, and economic—that had been used from time to time in support of official aid-giving was at all persuasive; the prime case for aid had to be made in terms of the moral obligation of the rich to the poor, and was only as strong as that sense of moral obligation. Secondly, for a variety of economic reasons, the official measurements of aid transfers grossly overstated the amount of real resources both transferred by the aid-donors to the aid-recipients, and received by the aid-recipients from the aid-donors—two magnitudes which are not necessarily even approximately the same, Thirdly, while the developing countries could justifiably complain bitterly about the discrimination against their exports and thus their development implicit in the tariff and agricultural support policies of the developed countries and the rules governing commercial policy changes institutionalized in the General Agreement on Tariffs and Trade (GATT), the tariff preferences they were demanding would, if implemented, yield them negligible additional resources for development investment in the reasonably near term, while both experience and theoretical analysis showed that international commodity agreements of a substantially resource-transferring kind were very unlikely to be implementable—so that trade offered no real alternative as a substitute for additional aid. Finally, many of the exporting difficulties experienced by the developing countries were of their own making, the consequence on the one hand of heavy taxation of primary-producing export sectors and on the other of high-cost import-substitution policies, both of which impeded the growth of exports—so that even if expanded export opportunities were offered, they were likely to have little effect failing major changes in the developing countries' approach to development promotion.

II

It is relevant at this point to expand on the difference between the established official approach to development assistance and the approach of the economist, which underlies the last three of these points. The official approach, in this as in other areas of policy, is dominated by balance-of-payments considerations and works in terms of flows of foreign exchange, i.e., financial flows. This approach suggests, quite wrongly, that additional export earnings are equivalent in benefit to additional loans or grants. It also lumps together in the aid total a heterogeneous collection of tied and untied official grants and loans on varying concessional terms, the domestic money value of food aid, and various kinds of private capital flows. Further, it deducts the flow of servicing payments on past loans. This last practice, in turn, fosters the notion that debt service constitutes a "burden" on the economy, requiring "relief," which it should not be if the loans have been applied to good economic purpose. From the economic point of view, what matters is not the foreign exchange flows but the implicit transfer of real resources involved in any particular transaction. This involves, for official capital transfers, making deductions for any excess of the prices of the goods purchased with the aid over world market prices resulting from the tying of aid or the giving of aid in the form of surplus foodstuffs; and, for loans as contrasted with outright grants, reckoning the economic value at the value of the gift element involved in concessionary interest rates, grace periods, etc., and not at the much higher face value of the loan. On the same approach, the value of trade concessions to the recipient is not the resulting increase in the value of the trade concerned, unless that increase consists purely of an increase in prices, as with some forms of the proposed international commodity agreements. Otherwise, the value of a trade concession has to be reckoned in terms of the effect of additional export earnings in enabling a country to acquire importable goods more cheaply, in terms of resource cost, by exporting than it could obtain them by producing them domestically. As regards private capital transfers, which are included in the assistance totals, these being commercially profitable transactions presumably involve no cost to the citizens of the country from which they come, except to the extent that like other private capital exports they pay taxes to the country invested in, which are lost to the home country under double taxation agreements, and these taxes exceed the costs of the social overhead expenditure the government of the home country would have had to incur if the capital had been invested at home.

These differences between the official and the economically scientific measurements of development assistance have undoubtedly played a significant part in the growing disillusionment with the effectiveness of development assistance, as has the fact that much so-called aid has been given for political and military purposes, rather than the promotion of economic development, and may well indeed have been counterproductive in terms of promoting development. They have also helped to divert attention from recognition of the urgent importance of a larger volume of official aid in real terms, to schemes for extracting more real aid by subterfuge through the softening of aid terms, and to schemes for benefitting the developing countries by new trade arrangements and by linking aid to international monetary reform that hold either little promise of substantial benefit or little promise of acceptance by the developed countries. As a result, the "crisis of aid" had been steadily deepening.

The United States administration, Congress, and the public, in particular, have become increasingly unwilling to go on providing development assistance at recent levels, let alone at the rising levels required to meet calculated needs for such assistance by the developing world. This reluctance has acted as a brake on the generosity of other advanced countries—a generosity otherwise stimulated in some cases by the moral shock of the Geneva UNCTAD Conference—since for balance-of-payments reasons, other countries prefer not to get too far out of line with the scale of United States aid-giving. The growing relative scarcity of funds for development assistance has impinged most sharply on the International Bank for Reconstruction and Development (the "World Bank"), which is the U.N. institution most directly concerned with development finance and which, under its past president, George Woods, and its current president, Robert McNamara, has been aggressively converting itself from a conservative semi-commercial bank into a development assistance agency.

III

In October 1967, Mr. Woods suggested that a "grand assize" should be conducted by an international group of "stature and experience," to study the consequences and results of twenty years of development assistance and make recommendations for the future. In August 1968, Mr. McNamara followed up this suggestion by appointing the Right Honourable Lester B.

Pearson, a Nobel Peace Prize winner for his part in settling the Suez crisis, and former Prime Minister of Canada, a rich but small North American country which has long played the role of intermediary between developed and developing countries but has only recently become converted to belief in the importance of development assistance. Mister Pearson chose an appropriately distinguished group of colleagues: Sir Edward Boyle, a British politician and specialist in education; Roberto de Oliveira Campos, a distinguished Brazilian economist, public servant, and banker; C. Douglas Dillon, American banker and recently distinguished Secretary of the U.S. Treasury; Wilfred Guth, a German banker with experience at the International Monetary Fund; Sir Arthur Lewis, a pioneer in the academic field of economic development and in development advising; Robert Marjolin, French economic civil servant active in European economic integration; and Dr. Saburo Okita, eminent Japanese public-service economist recently active in promoting Japanese involvement with the development of the poor countries of the Pacific.

When the appointment of Mr. Pearson was first announced, many academic economists, concerned about the promotion of development but not involved in the official aid business, hoped that his commission would initiate some of the fundamental scientific research into aid and its effects that the field so obviously needed. The announcement of the names of the other commission members, however, made it clear that the Commission's work was to be a public relations exercise on behalf of increased aid, and especially of official and multilateral aid. And so it has proved to be. Mister Pearson set for his commission, and achieved, the target of producing its report within a year. This target of quick reporting necessarily meant dependence on a staff of experts in the official economics of aid, whose function would be to assemble and organize material rather than to undertake fresh research. (Mister Pearson, incidentally, adopted the American practice of entrusting his staff with the preparation of the report, rather than the British practice according to which the commission itself writes the report, a decision which, rumor has it, almost led to Sir Arthur Lewis' refusing to sign the report.) The need for speed also meant that the commissioners themselves consulted exclusively with the officials of governments and international institutions engaged in the aid business, and not at all with academic and political opponents of development assistance as currently practiced. Consequently the *Report* of the commission is a look at the aid business from the inside, so to speak: it raises no fundamental economic questions, but instead contents itself with the established concepts used in aid analysis; it combines an excessively aggregative overall approach with an excessively *ad hoc* treatment of the myriad details; and its ultimate emphasis in its recommendations is on economic administration rather than economic analysis.

IV

Given the public relations character of the Commission's assignment and the circumstances in which it was appointed, one might have expected its *Report* to serve two functions. The first, and more important, would be to provide some fresh and appealing reasons for the giving of aid by the advanced countries, appealing especially to the aid-fatigued American public. The second, complementary to the first, would be to provide a rather optimistic but still plausibly sober review of past experience with development assistance, combined with a set of well-reasoned and sensible suggestions for the improvement of the efficiency of current methods of rendering and administering development assistance, both designed to give fresh hope to underpin the fresh motivation for aid-giving.

In any event, the *Report* has succeeded reasonably well in the fulfillment of the second objective; its analysis and recommendations express the common-sense conclusions that would have been reached by most people asked to think about the contemporary aid-giving and aid-receiving process on the assumption that it was going to continue. But the second objective is subordinate to the first, and with respect to the first objective, the *Report* can only be described as a dismal failure. It has provided no new and appealing reasons for the expansion of development assistance by the advanced countries, and has instead produced a series of pseudoconsiderations whose hollowness and inconsistency with one another can only reinforce the arguments of the opponents of aid. The result is that both the ideological adherents and the ideological opponents of development assistance will be able to criticize the *Report* for the pusillanimous concessions it makes to the other side of the debate, while the open-minded average man will find the *Report* at once flabby and smug—if he bothers to read such a fat compendium of establishment wisdom at all.

The failure of the *Pearson Report* to provide a persuasive new reason for aid-giving is the inevitable result of the conflict between moral conception and the facts of reality that arises with any charitable operation such as development aid or the relief of poverty: the moral conception stresses the inherent dignity and worth of man as man, and hence leads to resentment on the one side and uneasiness on the other about the reality of economic difference, which is the occasion of the charity itself. This conflict is exacerbated when the participants in the charitable transfer are not individuals but nation-states jealous of their sovereignty. It can only be resolved by resort to the fiction on both sides of the charity transaction that the need for charity is temporary. Hence any effort to resolve the conflict within a general and consistent philosophy of sustained charity must prove self-defeating: charity can only be a continuing process if new reasons are continually being discovered as to why it will be temporary, and this precludes a general philosophy.

The failure of the *Pearson Report* with respect to its major function of remotivating aid-giving is epitomized in its title: *Partners in Development*. This title attempts to assert for nation-states the equivalent of the oft-asserted equality of man. It is propaganda on behalf of the sovereignty of the developing nation-states, or a polite fiction to paper over the vast inequalities in resources between rich and poor nations. In either case, it is certain to evoke attitudes on both sides inimical to enlargement of the flow of development assistance. If nations are really equals, as the fiction asserts, what is the necessity or the purpose of aid? If they are not equals, as is the reality, why should rich nations transfer resources to poor nations that pretend to be equal but are not? On the other hand, if nations should be equals but are visibly and indisputably not equals, why should aid transfers be regarded as charity rather than reparations for the injustice of the world? And why should the amount of charity be determined by the rich man's beneficence rather than the poor man's need? An alleged partnership formed out of the rich man's uneasy conscience and the poor man's resentful need is likely to disintegrate in mutual recrimination—as the aid relationship has indeed been doing.

The *Report* itself devotes a scant five pages to the crucial question, "Why Aid?" These five pages attempt to skate delicately over the major issues and to reconcile the irreconcilable with wise-sounding but empty platitudes. The argument begins negatively with the acknowledgment that aid will not buy a western ideology, political stability, or peaceful and internationally responsible behavior from the recipients. In other words, aid serves no political self-interest of the aid-givers. Its objective instead is "to reduce disparities and remove inequalities . . . so that the world will not become more and more starkly divided between the haves and the have-nots." But if avoidance of such division has no implications for ideology, political stability, or peace, the argument for it must be moral. But the moral argument immediately raises, at least for an American audience, the conflict between the relief of domestic and the relief of foreign poverty. The *Report* asserts that "Both wars must be won." Why should rich nations help poor ones when they have pressing poverty problems of their own? The *Report* asserts that "the simplest answer to the question is the moral one: that it is only right for those who have to share with those who have not. "But why should this moral obligation extend beyond the bounds of sovereign states? The Commission appeals to "a new and fundamental aspect of the modern age—the awareness that we live in a village world, that we belong to a world community." But awareness of the existence of others has only rarely and marginally been a reason powerful enough to motivate large-scale charity towards them; and in any case the question is one of charity extended by the national government of a rich country to the national government of a poor one, not from a rich individual to a poor individual. Instead of arguing a moral case for intergovernmental aid transfers, the *Report* abandons the subject by contradicting itself: "the moral incentive for cooperation in international development . . . is not the basis on which support for international development mainly rests."

"There is also the appeal of enlightened and constructive self-interest." Economically, there is "the fullest possible utilization of the world's resources, human and physical, which can be brought about only by international cooperation" and which benefits the rich countries through "direct benefits from a bilateral aid relationship" and through "the general increase in international trade which would follow international development." But the *Report* does not explain why aid, rather than other policies, presents the best way of promoting fuller utilization of world resources; nor does it examine whether the asserted economic benefits of aid-giving are worth their resource cost; and it is careful to state that donor countries should not expect development to create economic windfalls for them. It is also concerned to assert that nothing tangible in the way of political benefits should be expected.

Having in effect again disposed of self-interest as a motivation for aid-giving, the *Report* then appeals to "the acceleration of history" and the alleged consequential necessity to expand the concept of the national interest to embrace the common problems of the world, and asserts that the emerging awareness of the world community is "itself a major reason for international cooperation in development." But that emerging awareness of the world community is described as "an act of faith"; it does not by itself imply any commitment to help poor nations to develop; and even if it is so construed, it does not necessarily imply an expansion of development aid on present lines.

At this point, the *Report* refers to the fact that the developed countries have accepted a commitment to help the poor nations (the *Report* actually uses the question-begging phrase "impoverished nations") to develop. The argument thus returns full circle to the moral commitment which was earlier denied to be the main basis for support of development assistance. But it then asserts that "whatever is or is not done internationally, the poorer countries of the world have made their choice for development . . . . The only questions are: how fast, and by what means, and at what cost to themselves and to the world can development be achieved; and whether it has a clear and tangible goal." In other words, the *Report* abandons all pretense of discussing the justification for aid, and turns to the question—which assumes that such justification has been provided, though it clearly has not—of setting a target for aid.

"Our answer is that the goal of the international development effort is to put the less-developed countries as soon as possible in a position where they can realize their aspirations with regard to economic progress without relying on foreign aid." The *Report* then asks, and answers affirmatively, the question "But can the majority of the developing countries achieve self-sustaining growth by the end of the century? For us the answer is clearly yes. In our view, the record of the past twenty years justifies that answer." And it adds: "The thing to remember is that the process, global in scope, and international in nature, must succeed if there is finally to be peace, security, and stability in the world."

V

It may be remarked that the developing countries could achieve self-sustaining growth at any moment, by abandoning their dependence on aid, though this might involve growing at a slower rate (not necessarily slower, because the commission is unable to demonstrate that aid in the past has actually promoted growth). The question hinges on the rate of growth aspired to by the developing countries, a matter on which the *Report* is remarkably vague, presumably because of its acceptance of the principle of national sovereignty. It should also be noted that the thing the commission wants us to remember is precisely what it has earlier been at pains to deny, that aid for development will buy peace, security, and stability in the developing world.

The chain of observations presented by the Report on the justification for development assistance is a set of pious but selfcontradictory platitudes, designed to skate over the real issues while enabling the Commission to arrive at an ostensibly feasible compromise between the interests of the developed countries and the demands of the developing countries. That compromise consists, on the one hand, in adopting the view that if the average annual rate of growth of gross national product in the developing countries could be raised from the recent five per cent per annum to six per cent per annum by the end of the 1970s, these countries could, by the year 2000, finance their own growth and import requirements without concessional loans. It consists, on the other hand, in asserting that this change can be affected consistently with the already-accepted commitment of the developed countries to channel one per cent of their gross national products into development assistance, provided that they implement that commitment and accept the Commission's recommendations for increasing the element of real as distinct from nominal aid involved, notably by increasing the percentage of official aid from the 1968 percentage of 0.39 to 0.70 by 1975 or at latest 1980, and doubling the proportion in it of multilateral aid to 20 per cent.

In effect, the Pearson Commission *Report* says that the political demands of the developing countries for development assistance can be satisfied if the developed countries will only live up to their past moral commitments, while recommending various apparently sensible changes in aid policies that will, in fact, increase the real burden of those commitments substantially. At the same time it holds out to the aid-givers the promise that, though the initial crash-program of development aid has not solved the development problem, it can still be solved within the time-span of a generation, i.e., by the year 2000. Both the implication that no further great effort is required, and the promise of a foreseeable end to the need for charity, display a certain amount of political sagacity. But the compromise is very unlikely to succeed in practical political reality, and the offer of it is likely to provoke dissatisfaction on both sides of the development assistance transaction. For the developed countries, the *Report* fails to provide any cogent reason, other than the doubtfully relevant aspirations of the developing countries, why the developed countries should make the long jump from present levels of official aid to the levels required to fulfill its target for such aid: a past moral commitment to a target that has not only not been fulfilled but whose fulfillment has steadily been receding, proves neither that fulfillment of the target is desirable, nor that it will be relatively painless. For the developing countries and their sympathizers, an increase in the target minimum rate of growth from five per cent to six per cent for the rest of the century is a trivial *quid pro quo* indeed for the liquidation of the assumed moral obligation on the rich countries to improve the lot of the poor.

In my judgment, the failure of the *Pearson Report* to provide a new motivation for more generous aid-giving is attributable fundamentally to the fact that the commission has taken the sovereignty of the nation-state as given, and has concerned itself with relations between sovereign states that happen to be alternatively poor and rich, instead of concerning itself with the fundamental units involved in the poverty problem, which are people and not nations. In relations among sovereign nations, morality is an emotion without a cutting edge. In relations among people, however, the nation-state is an instrument of discrimination whose injustice and immorality can be clearly demonstrated. The nation-state discriminates economically in favor of its own citizens through its control of immigration; it discriminates further in their favor through its tariffs and other protective policies; and recently the richest nations have come to discriminate still further in favor of their own citizens (in their role as workers) through the imposition of restrictions on the outflow of capital. In this perspective, development assistance appears very much as conscience money paid by the rich to the poor to ease the conscience of the one and buy off the indignation of the other; and the problem of promoting development appears more as one of reducing the discriminations between people associated with the nation-state than as one of increasing the international flow of conscience money—though more conscience money would undoubtedly help. The *Pearson Report* might have been far more effective if it had attacked the discriminatory features of the nation-state directly, and insisted on the need either to reduce the discrimination or to increase the flow of conscience money, rather than attempting to wheedle more development assistance in the name of faith in the brotherhood of man.

VI

As already mentioned, the *Pearson Report* is far more successful in achieving its second (and secondary) objective—a reasonably optimistic review of past experience with development assistance, leading to a sensible set of suggestions for future improvement—than in achieving its first and crucial objective. A full review of its analysis of the development problem and of past achievements with respect to it, and of its recommendations for changes in development policies and practices, would be inappropriate to the present purpose. Four general themes of the *Report*, however, deserve some comment.

The first theme is that, despite the widely-felt disillusionment about the process of promoting the economic development of the poor countries, much more development has occurred than has generally been realized; that more is to come as infrastructure investment finally bears its fruits; that various past errors in approach are in the process of being corrected; and that much has been learned about how to promote development. All of this is true. But one would expect development to occur when people have at last decided that they want it, when they have the successful examples of the already developed countries before their eyes, and when the maintenance of high activity and the progressive liberalization of international trade by the developed countries is providing an unprecedented opportunity for growth by osmosis. One would also expect people to learn, albeit slowly, from their own errors. The real questions are whether development aid has promoted or retarded development, and if it has promoted it, how significant its influence has been. Many of the critics of aid believe that it has encouraged national governments in the developing countries to pursue counterdevelopmental policies and permitted them to preserve archaic social and political structures, and so has retarded rather than promoted the modernization process. The *Report* is, in fact, unable to adduce any clear evidence that aid has promoted growth; this may be largely because it lacked the time, staff resources, and economic competence to investigate the question in a properly scientific manner. Instead, it falls back on the undisputed fact that much aid was given for other purposes than development (how much was intended to promote development, and did it actually do so?), emphasizes the importance of the transfer of technology and ideas associated with aid (was the transfer always appropriate, and could it have been effected in some cheaper way?), and stresses the contribution of aid in supporting a psychological climate favorable to experimentation (good experiments, or bad?). The usefulness of aid in promoting development remains an act of faith; yet the rest of the *Report* depends on the assumption of its usefulness.

The second theme is the seriousness of the population problem in the developing countries, and the need for priority for population control. The Commission is right to view this subject with the gravest of alarm, but it fails to consider its full implications. The responsiveness of population to economic opportunity in the developing countries is one of the major reasons why developed countries are both reluctant to allow immigration from such countries and doubtful about the beneficial effects of assistance for economic development to these countries. Freer immigration into the advanced countries—which should be, but is not, currently considered a possible remedy for poverty in the developing countries—more aid, and freer trade, all run the risk of aggravating the problem of inequality by stimulating the breeding of more poor people at the expense of the less philoprogenitive rich. Family planning may well be not only more important than additional development assistance, but a prerequisite to the provision of increased assistance.

The third theme is an emphasis on education and on technical development as a major means to economic development, together—though this is implicit in the detail of the *Report*—with emphasis on more efficient selection of investment projects aimed at giving priority to those with high yields. The latter emphasis is important for the future, given the likelihood of increasing stringency in the availability of aid funds; but there is some danger that the emerging popularity of "cost-benefit analysis" will lead to more and more scarce resources being devoted to the allocation of funds among projects and less and less being available for the projects themselves. It is a well-known characteristic of bureaucracies that, the less money they have to spend, the more time and effort they devote to deciding exactly how to spend it.

The fourth theme is the desirability of increasing both the proportion of official aid in the total financial flows of development assistance, and the proportion of multilateral—as contrasted with bilateral—aid in the total of official flows. From the economic point of view, both changes would significantly augment the real flow of resources from rich to poor countries. But it is important to recognize the direction in which these recommendations lead. Essentially, they point in the direction of world government, not explicitly in the form of political federalism but implicitly in the form of a redistribution of income between nations through the instrumentality of international institutions and specifically of the World Bank. This may be a desirable direction of evolution, and indeed the only feasible path of human progress.

But it should be recognized and discussed for what it is, and not disguised as an obvious and sensible step towards increased efficiency in the administration of development assistance. Presentation in that guise—which is essentially a proposal to increase the taxation of the rich countries for the benefit of the poor while depriving them of control over the spending of their own money—is likely to prove unacceptable to the citizens of the rich countries. Again, in this connection, the failure of the Pearson Commission to consider the consequences of the organization of mankind into nations is a crucial weakness in its argument.

VII

The *Pearson Report* has, in my judgment, failed in its main purpose, a purpose crucial to its many sensible suggestions for reform, that of providing a new motivation for the giving of development assistance. Especially, it has failed to provide any arguments likely to appeal to the aid-weary and domestically-preoccupied American public. What are likely to be the consequences?

One major unfortunate consequence is likely to be that those who favor increased development aid will become increasingly shrill in their demands for increased aid, and increasingly intellectually dishonest in the arguments they present. This tendency is, in fact, already apparent. As one example, there is strong support in pro-development-assistance circles for the proposal to link international monetary reform to development finance by monetizing the new Special Drawing Rights at the International Monetary Fund, and distributing a large part or all of them to the developing countries to be earned back by unrequited exports by the developed countries. This is essentially a proposal to provide development assistance by inflationary world monetary expansion, based on the naive assumption that the governments of the advanced countries can be tricked by exploitation of the mysteries of money—which they can understand at least as well as the proponents of the scheme—into accepting a larger volume of aid commitments than they would be willing to provide by democratic budgetary vote. Another instance is the campaign currently being mounted in the United Kingdom to persuade the public to sanction additional aid allocations on the grounds that "trade follows aid," i.e., that the present sacrifice of aid resources will be economically justified by the gain of markets. If this proposition were true, which it is not, it would scarcely be necessary to advertise it. A third instance, evident at the recent Columbia University Conference on International Development, is the propensity of those who favor more aid for whatever reason to sign any document that recommends more aid, regardless of how silly or impracticable the specific proposals for giving more aid contained in it may be.

Another consequence is that the process of disillusionment of the American public with aid, and of American disengagement in the aid process, will continue. This is in spite of the fact that a presidential task force, reporting in March 1970, and clearly influenced by the *Pearson Report*, has recommended that the level of American assistance for economic development should be increased. Without powerful support from public opinion, such a recommendation is likely to perish in the Congress. And failing a powerful lead from the United States, other countries are unlikely to increase their development assistance contributions substantially.

The prospective decline of official aid obviously bodes ill for those who have made a career in the aid business, either as administrators or as advisors, or as outside, presumably independent, missionaries on behalf of aid to their fellow men. The world of official aid is, in fact, already showing many of the signs of a declining industry or community, and in particular showing a belated urgent concern about its own administrative efficiency. But will the decline in official aid actually seriously impair the process of economic development, to the detriment of the poor countries of the world?

The author is inclined, perhaps optimistically, to return a negative answer to this question. The decline of official development aid that can be foreseen will mean an increased dependence on the private market mechanisms of economic development, as contrasted with governmental planning and control of the development process. These mechanisms are, internally, the forces of competition and the desire to improve one's individual welfare by increasing one's earning power. Externally, the most important are competition in international trade, on the one hand, and the international operations of the multinational corporation, on the other. The author has considerable faith in the long-run powers of international competition to transform societies that have a latent urge to be transformed, though these powers may long be held in check by the use of political power to resist change and to attempt to capture the benefits of development for the politically powerful from the economically productive. The author also believes that the liberalization of world trade that has already been accomplished through GATT provides ample opportunities for the poor countries to develop through trade, though there is considerable scope for further widening of those opportunities. It is true, as already mentioned, that trade provides far fewer resources per dollar for development than does aid; but we are considering a process of development extending to the end of the century, and in that time trade opportunities should have full scope to do their work.

As regards the international corporation, this is a powerful agency for the transmission of technological progress, and the reallocation of capital resources, from the rich to the poor countries, which has already in the past two decades done much in its own way to diffuse the process of economic development around the globe. Too much should not be expected of the international corporation. It is a profit-seeking enterprise, which will diffuse development only to the extent that such diffusion is in its own interests. It is not a government, able to levy taxes on some people in order to invest in what it thinks will contribute to the economic development of others. But there is a considerable overlap of interests between the two. In particular, the corporation often finds it in its own interests, when operating in developing countries, both to invest in the training of local labor—both operative and managerial—and to invest in teaching modern efficient methods of production both to its supplier enterprises and to its customers. Where the interests of corporation and government conflict, it is not always obvious that government rather than the corporation has the better judgment of what is in the social interest.

To conclude, the *Pearson Report* may well represent the end, rather than the beginning, of a novel phase in world economic development—the end of a phase in which the powers of government to promote development by the use of its legal powers of control and planning and its economic powers of taxation of its citizens were grossly exaggerated, and the powers of free competition to promote growth were unduly discounted, rather than the beginning of a concerted move towards nations becoming "partners in development" and moving towards world government. The *Pearson Report*, in short, may be a tombstone rather than a milestone in the evolution of a developing world economy.

VIII. THE SOCIO-ECONOMIC APPROACH

As an epilogue to the present volume, we have included a paper by *Cornejo.* The introductory chapter consists of a brief synthesis of the economic ideas of Dr. Prebisch, and the scheme offered in this section tries to show the social content of Prebisch's theories on Latin American development. The underlying assumption is that development implies the promotion of greater distributive justice.

Underdevelopment is characterized, in fact, among other features, by profound distributive inequalities, a problem which Prebisch made his concern from his early writings. One of the roots of Latin American underdevelopment is the dynamic inadequacy of the activities in the agricultural sector of the economy which continually produces surplus labor which the emerging industry of the cities is unable to absorb. All this serves to give rise to phenomena such as underemployment and even outright unemployment, apart from other characteristics of underdevelopment (among them, the low level of national income and the increase in inequality which are at the same time both the cause and effect of underdevelopment itself).

This state of affairs is also characterized by a lack of social mobility, because of special privileges and the basic inbalance between the rural and urban areas, all of which produce serious social rigidities that endanger values which are worth preserving. Therefore, a solution must be found for the social question; if one is not, there may result a breakdown of the system, with very high political, human, and social costs.

According to Cornejo, Prebisch does not support any known system of social organization, although he esteems those values and principles among which are found personal freedom and democracy. Prebisch argues in favor of planning, without which no discipline of development could be established, but he opposes every system which would subordinate the will of some individuals to the arbitrary decisions of others. To oppose necessary reforms will not prevent them from coming. Besides, they might take place violently with the costs mentioned above, bringing with them an authoritarian state.

THE SOCIAL DOCTRINE IN PREBISCH'S THOUGHT

BENJAMIN CORNEJO

Universidad Nacional de Córdoba, Córdoba, Argentina

> *It would be disastrous if, in order to free man from necessity, we would have to dispense with other values, subordinating him to the demands of an arbitrary power. Nothing, in its essence, is consistent with the peculiarities of Latin American countries, with their hidden desire of being free from necessity to dignify man's personality to attain the full enforcement—by means of economic development—of democracy and human rights, particularly among members of that depressed half of the Latin American population. And in order that social mobility may push the best upwards in their search for economic development and democracy, it has to be so not only there, but also in every stratum of society. A social order without economic privileges, without the tremendous privileges that make a few rule over the ideas of all the others, over the creative forces of the spirit and over the deepest feelings of their hearts.*
>
> Raúl Prebisch

I

This paper is in response to several stimuli. Perhaps the most important is a sort of reaction of the writer toward erroneous insights so widely spread in the past and still, in the present, about what might be called Prebisch's "ideology" or about his ideas on economic development, in general, and that of Latin America, in particular.

There are many people who consider Prebisch's theory and his work—particularly, the work carried out as head of ECLA—as eminently technical in character. For instance, his arguments about the terms of trade, about import-substitution, the inadequate endowment of capital per capita, etc., contain a technical and objective explanation of the low level of development in our countries, upon which solutions could be based, although the attempt to build a social doctrine upon them as well has proven useless.

As we all know, economists do not consider development an exclusively technical or economic phenomenon, but also as something with very strong political and social implications. Although there is a kind of general agreement that the idea of economic development is associated with a sustained increase in per capita national income, and although the word "economic" would seem to give the concept a material content, economists—and in this particular case, those from ECLA—have not neglected any characteristic of underdevelopment of the noneconomic scope of an acceleration of development. In other words, it is easily observed that behind technical problems related to economic characteristics of underdevelopment, there are certain others which make it possible to classify some countries as poor or less developed, and others as developed or wealthy. At the same time, these characteristics may demonstrate a regrettable internal reality in the sharp contrasts between the greatest wealth and the greatest poverty of individuals and families, or as a phenomenon whose best illustrations are found in poor countries, where there is not only a great material inequality, but also inequalities associated with significant aspects of social, political, and cultural life.

It is this reality that gives inspirations to doctrines of the economists who are particularly interested in searching out the causes of economic backwardness and formulating policies which help to overcome them. From the very beginning, Prebisch showed himself to be a strong partisan of the doctrine that asserts that economic development as manifested in the increased wealth of nations, is only *a means*. In his first report for ECLA in 1949, Prebisch clearly states at the beginning, that "industrialization is not an end in itself but the principal means available by which those countries (the young ones) can obtain their share in the benefits of technical progress and gradually increase the living standard of the masses" [6].

In his earliest documents, Prebisch established bases for what in the long-run became a body of doctrines in which his ideas about Latin American development were established. These ideas were reformulated and enriched in the course of years to the extent that references to the living standard of the masses were stressed in a way that gives the expression its real significance. Economic development should not be considered in terms of wealth and power in their relationship to nations, as was formerly the case with the idea of progress. Development, landed today as the most desirable goal, has deeper roots and tends to increase the population's welfare by spreading to "the densest and deepest strata of a people's life" [5, p. 2].

Even a brief examination of the expressions and doctrines offered by Prebisch in a number of later documents will suffice to show us that the economic development ideal, which he conceived and fostered like anyone else in Latin America, implied from the very beginning an ideal redistribution of income in order to favor lower-income groups and establish a more equitable social and economic order.

Thus, the "social question" enters firmly into the economist's theories about Latin American development. In a passage in Prebisch's last book, written as Director of ECLA, we come across something which in our opinion can be taken as the Latin American version of the social question: "...it could be estimated that about a half of the present population has the very small average income of only 120 dollars a year. This large social group, with the highest undernourishment coefficient, the poorest clothing and worst housing facilities, as well as the highest levels of disease and illiteracy, only represents about one fifth of the whole personal consumption in Latin America" [3].

Now, we must realize that economic development considered only as an increase of per capita national income, just *an average*, does not necessarily mean a better distribution, as is often believed. "Although it is true that it is usually recognized that income distribution is not so skewed in advanced countries as in the underdeveloped ones, what has historically improved income distribution in more advanced countries has not been any phenomenon inherent in the growth process but rather social and tax legislation based upon ethical and moral considerations" [7]. That is, those who advocate development should not think that distributive justice will be wrought "in addition." Prebisch himself clearly stated this in various passages of his numerous papers in which he points out that the spontaneous play of economic forces in advanced countries has not resulted in an equitable distribution of income. Therefore, an increase in average wealth attained through technological progress, capital accumulation, industrialization, etc., will not have any positive effect if it serves only to increase the welfare of a few.

Prebisch, his followers, and economists concerned with development in general, have agreed to include the greatest distributive disparity as one of the elements characterizing an underdeveloped country. A developmental process unable to remedy or lessen that disparity would be incomplete, mutilated. The character of *means* given to the idea of development would be lost. If, however, the notion of development (with or without adding the word "economic") includes, besides political, cultural, and social features, some structural changes which may yield a more equitable distribution of a greater amount of goods of every sort, then we can say it becomes an *end* in itself.

This argument implies something more than a mere question of semantics. A development policy, in order to be successful, requires the population's general agreement, particularly the agreement of medium and low income groups, especially if it means a sacrifice for them (more savings, less consumption, more work, etc.), which they will not be willing to make unless they are promised increased distributive justice.

On the other hand, the existing inequalities in a developing country constitute a very significant fact to be taken into account in development strategy. Present relationships between income and saving levels are well known today, as well as the vicious circle of poverty based upon them: We are poor because we do not save, and we do not save because we are poor.

These, and other questions to be examined below, show us that the "social question" permeates the problem of development. Even in a brief examination of this point, we will soon discover other expressions of distributive inequalities which development should correct. The relations between rural and urban areas is a good example or more precisely, one in which Prebisch's theory assumes a particular relevance: The countryside (agriculture) generates surplus labor, while the city (industry) is unable to absorb it, thus creating a lack of equilibrium that illustrates the dynamic inadequacy of the underdeveloped country. Another, and perhaps more remarkable, example in analyzing these problems, is the inequality which is found between advanced or wealthy countries and the underdeveloped or poor ones. The former enjoy the advantages of technical progress, high productivity, a greater social and economic leveling of classes, and, finally, an abundance of gifts and the advantages of a political and commercial supremacy. The latter, at least in the extreme cases, are overwhelmed by backwardness, poverty, and the sharpest disparities and subordination at the international level.

Consequently, the main task of development should be to correct imbalances of this kind, which are closely related to one another, to the extent that they are taken as expressions of basically the same phenomenon in different fields and contexts.

The social approach we intend to take relates to the problem of justice, and this places us on the normative field. It can be carried out without sacrificing scientific objectivity. Prebisch himself, who often referred to distributive justice and frequently used a social reformer's tone, especially in his recent work, wisely posed the social problem in Latin America's less-developed countries, with a rigorous and objective scientific criterion. In one of his early essays (already quoted in this paper) he depicts the population's living standard as a phenomenon *not* associated with the wickedness or selfishness of the wealthy class, but with the productive structure of those countries, low capital endowment per worker, a high percentage of the working class employed in low productivity jobs, a lack of technological advances, etc. [5, *passim*].

Thus, we may conclude that everything related to social questions in Latin America and what may be called "social change," implies the analysis of economic development as well. But if we can effect a division of these concepts—putting economic development on one side and distributive justice on the other—we will clearly observe the close relationship between them, as well as the necessity of including *data* on the social question in a strategy for development. A short quotation from Prebisch's work summarizes everything that is implied in the statements above: "What is economic does not necessarily oppose what is social, but when growth is slow the distribution is nearly always very poor. The practising of social justice requires a strong rate of development, as well as a political distributive wisdom, which is in itself very difficult" [4, p. 3].

Social inequality involving the existence of large sectors of the population with very low consumption levels suggests one of the main factors working against an increase of industrial productivity: the narrowness of the domestic market and consequently the lack of stimulus of high effective demand. This is one of the basic elements of the dynamic inadequacy of the Latin American economy.

Prebisch's approach to this economy, with reference to the great forces that impede its progress, poses a *contradiction* between a deficient accumulation of capital and the increase in the labor force, which, despite the great differences, recalls the style of traditional socialist approaches. It is evident that the socio-economic reality of Latin America, as well as that of other underdeveloped countries in other regions, has peculiar characteristics quite different from those prevailing in industrialized countries. Here we are not dealing with a process of capital accumulation which may lead to speculation about the crisis of the system, but rather with the slowness of the rate of accumulation which prevents the attainment of technological and productivity levels which, besides increasing income, would help with the absorption of the increase in the labor force.

These considerations lead us to the study of what might be called Prebisch's social doctrine. It is not an easy task to distinguish this doctrine from the whole of his writings about Latin American development. As already observed, these social aspects, particularly those concerning distributive inequalities, are included in Prebisch's theory. We will try to focus our attention on the points related to the matter under consideration, without disregarding features and arguments which are, to a certain extent, essential for the economic analysis of development. For that purpose, we will rely almost exclusively on two books from Prebisch's most recent writings. The first, "Towards a Dynamic Development Policy for Latin America," contains a survey carried out at ECLA's Secretariat for the tenth period of the Commission sessions (Mar del Plata, May 1963), which was Prebisch's last report as director of such an organism; and the second, "Transformation and Development: Latin America's Great Task," is a report for IDB (Interamerican Development Bank, May 1970), on special request of the institution. The choice of these books is based on the fact that they are Prebisch's latest work, expressing his personal opinions, and in which the writer dwells more extensively on the subject than in any other document related to the social features of development.

The order in which the cases chosen will be dealt with may appear arbitrary to the reader, and it may be so. But it has been difficult for us to establish a logical ordering of subjects and features closely related to one another. We have diligently attempted to give a summary or synthesis because of the nature and object of this work. A number of omissions—although we hope none of importance—and more than one repetition have resulted.

II

The great inequalities in income distribution constitute a restraining factor in the industrialization process of developing countries. As Prebisch points out,

> Now we can easily understand the meaning of social integration of lower-income groups in the process of development in order to gradually attain its advantages. As we said before, about 60 per cent of the Latin American population belongs to these lower-income groups. This lower-income population, whose consumption may be considered negligible in relation to their rapidly increasing number, are the real victims of the social inequality of their economic system. A rough estimate of the problem indicates that less than 20 per cent of the total manufactured goods falls into their hands [4, p. 5].

As Prebisch affirms in his book: The social contrast, is simply astonishing. In fact, 50 per cent of the people accounts for only two tenths of the population's total consumption, and on the other end of the distributive scale, we find 5 per cent of the individuals enjoying approximately three tenths of the total quantity... [3, p. 5].

Any policy for development through foreign aid, investment incentives, etc., could be extended or, at the same time, designed to remedy such disparities, at least in a partial or limited way. But the initial effects would disappear and industrial expansion would not find a market wide enough to sustain its expansion. Still, we must recognize that the mere start of a process of industrialization helps to absorb the labor force, even though social justice is not attained, at least to the extent necessary to justify a system, and leads to a partial absorption of surplus labor.

In case these distributive disparities prevail along with the privileges which, according to Prebisch, have been prevailing for centuries in Latin America and have "deep historical roots," if social mobility is not promoted, and consumption among higher income groups is not compulsorily restrained in order to extend consumption among lower income groups as well as to promote capital accumulation, there would remain only the most harmful symptoms of underdevelopment. These are manifested mainly in the uneven distribution of income, inequality of job opportunities, and the feelings of frustration prevailing among popular sectors, particulary at the present time, when the "demonstration effect" can be easily observed:

> Higher income groups in Latin American societies tend to imitate the living standards of the people from advanced countries; and thanks to powerful elements provided by an ever-improving technique in mass communication, a desire for those living standards tends to penetrate to the lowest income groups, which are attracted by the appeal of a consumer society difficult to attain due to the meagerness of their income [4, p. 6].

We wish to put stress on these and many other expressions contained in Prebisch's writings, with special emphasis on his point about social inequalities. We have already seen that they were Prebisch's main concern in his early essay and, in the present, they are viewed as part of the analysis of Latin American development and the formulation of an economic policy to promote it. Yet, it should be noted that the interest Prebisch has shown in promoting social change has been increasing to the extent of becoming the central point of the whole argument.[1]

Thus, the problem of development is at the same time the social problem of an equal distribution of income. Posed in other terms, and insisting on what we have already said on this point, it is impossible to attain social justice without economic development, nor can this latter aim be completely achieved without the former. This is the only way for Latin American countries to transform the structures that prevent them from overcoming the low level of dynamism in their economies. Thus, we can ask, what will be the results of incorporating technological advances and creating new industries if they are unable to absorb the surplus labor which is gradually leaving the rural areas on account of demographic increases or technological advances that economize on labor in agriculture and rural industry? This question suggests to us, among other things, that a good development policy should form a set of different but consistent measures, that the various economic and social features should be integrated, that social reforms will be carried out,

[1] In one of the recent documents published by ECLA we read: since 1961, Latin American governments have committed themselves in a series of statements, to accelerate development and promote social justice.... It is to be implied that there is certainty in the sense that development should be interpreted as a mere process of growth.... Other important orientations have been stressed, particularly in (i) the reform and modernization of key institutions, such as public administration, fiscal systems and land tenure...; and (ii) the expansion and more equitable distribution of public action to raise living standards, increase productivity of the labor force and attain a social stability, putting emphasis on the problem of education, health, and housing [1].

and that, in the end, income redistribution does not consist merely in a division among those who now receive less of the surplus of the people who get more. What counts is to distribute the increase in income resulting from higher productivity and from every other factor representing a higher level of development.

After mentioning some points regarded as promising signs of growth, such as the tremendous increase of cities, evolution and diversification of industries, etc., Prebisch points out the "evident lack of ability shown by urban activities in the task of absorbing and making productive use of surplus labor, as well as the ever stronger social tension" [4, p. 12].

"In order to correct all this," Prebisch states, "it is most necessary to accelerate development and this means a substantial effort, a real discipline of development" [4, pp. 13–14]. This discipline entails sound political decisions and a definite plan; in their absence

> one or another compulsory form of development will dominate in the end. Because simple frustration is not an alternative: leaving things as they are is the same as popular frustration. Thanks to this insight, it has been possible to discover great social evils and promote a genuine desire for social integration in popular classes. However, as they have no strong convictions, or a well-congealed system of ideas, the population appeals to an inexhaustible source of emotions to acclaim charismatic personalities [4].

Therefore, we have two options: the one of "populism," which is frustrating by definition because of its emotional content is inclined to "immediatism"—a point to be later discussed—and that of an ordered and systematic development policy, that is, a discipline of development which, without neglecting reasonable immediate claims (in order to ameliorate stresses) aims at a real transformation of social, political, and economic structures, for the attainment of a steady pace in the increase in national product.

As is evident, what has been said up to this point clearly reveals the option Prebisch prefers. Let us now examine the fundamental features of the social problem, and what the obstacles are to be overcome in order to find a solution, where the dangers are which these solutions may entail, and which, in a word, are the values that economists, politicians, and social reformers want to preserve in this transformation process. In short, which are the values Prebisch wants to maintain? The task will give us some insight into the ideal society as conceived by this brilliant Latin American writer, unparalleled by any other in his concern about the development of the Latin American countries, nor in his influence upon their economic policies in the last two decades.[2]

[2] Prebisch's influence may be observed in documents prepared or made under his direction, particularly the ones for ECLA, and through the action of a number of his followers throughout the continent.

III

We have talked about obstacles, dangers, and values. Again, we must emphasize the necessary limits imposed on this essay—the "social question" in Prebisch's work—and the difficulty of separating features which are in reality inseparable. At any rate, we will now try to isolate some fundamental aspects, omitting features and points which are inessential in the context of Prebisch's theory as a whole.

In our opinion, Prebisch thinks that the first obstacle to development lies in the socio-economic structure of the great majority of the countries in the region. It should be observed, at this point, that generalizations made about socio-economic realities in Latin America overlook the peculiarities and differences which distinguish many of the countries belonging to the continent. Some of these have already reached a notable level of development, leaving the conventional image of an underdeveloped or developing country far behind.

"The social structure prevailing in Latin America represents a serious hindrance for technical progress and therefore, for economic and social development." The two main characteristics of this situation are the following: (a) social mobility is prevented; and (b) the structure is characterized by special privilege in distribution. This distributive privilege is not accompanied by a sound accumulation of capital but is shown in the extraordinary consumption patterns of higher-income groups in contrast to the poverty of the popular masses [3, p. 4]. In order to elaborate on this social structure, we should also distinguish two large economic sectors: the countryside and the city, representing agriculture and industry, respectively. In the light of the points under consideration, we must examine the relationships which connect them, and besides, take into account their demographic problems.

The greater part of the poor population lives in the countryside, and it is here that we can find the main factors accounting for internal "bottlenecks." As stated before, the dynamic inadequacy of Latin American development to date reveals itself in abundant surplus labor. This same inadequacy is also evidenced by "the meager rate of about one per cent a year by which income per capita has been increasing since the middle of the last decade [written in 1963] in Latin America as a whole." Parallel to this, there is

> another fact, which is perhaps the strongest source of social tensions, that is, a substantial part of the increase of the working-age population is not satisfactorily absorbed in the productive process.... This phenomenon holds particularly for the case of the population migrating from rural to urban areas.... And it is necessarily so in the course of economic development. But these people's fate *need not be so* [emphasis added]. Far from being integrated in the city life, from finding access to better living standards, they erect their miserable dwellings and earn their living by offering every kind of personal services for meager wages, with periods of outright unemployment.... The countryside, therefore, brings poverty, frustration and resentment to the cities [3].

Surplus labor does not wholly migrate to cities, but part of it also remains in the countryside. But the phenomenon of migration helps to explain the fact that while the share of the total labor force employed in Latin American agriculture before 1931 was about 63 per cent, this had declined to 41 per cent in 1969 [4, p. 192]. It is upon this half of the poor population—living mainly in the countryside—that the cost of import substitution falls, and of an exaggerated protection, of injurious marketing, and of social privileges they do not enjoy.

There are several reasons accounting for this situation. Among them, we can mention land tenure systems which make technical assimilation difficult, the inadequate action of the government in adapting and spreading new techniques, and the low level of investments.

In addition to the weak increase of income, which itself acts negatively upon the demand for agricultural products, we also have to add a meager food diet and the effects of the well-known economic law (Engel's law) according to which the higher the income, the lower will be the proportion to spend on foodstuffs. On the other hand, technical improvements that economize on labor and increase productivity per capita, may also intensify the migration process of people moving from agriculture to industry. But industry so far lacks the dynamics needed to absorb such an excess. So it happens that with the excess people in the countryside, they migrate to cities where urban industry generates a surplus of its own.

In order to understand the problem, it should be remembered that a slow improvement in production technique may also cause the labor force to move, unless a high rate of new investment is registered [3, pp. 29 ff.]. The employers' interests—easily understandable—tend to favor the use of cheaper techniques, which are usually labor saving. And we must not forget that the consumption of wealthy classes will tend to be biased toward industrial products containing little labor and much capital, which is a demonstration of the nonabsorbing effects of distributive differences.

The phenomenon of surplus labor extends to other sectors as well, and thus it is observed in services and public administration. Sometimes this is not considered as outright unemployment, but only as underemployment, or irregular, sporadic jobs with very low remuneration, performed by people whose work is nearly unnecessary [4, p. 30].

The above picture is not the same for all the countries of the region, and there are a variety of cases, but given the differences per capita product of people working in the industrial or agricultural sector, the fact that the surplus labor from the latter sector is not successfully absorbed in the former is one of the factors preventing a significant increase in production per man [4, pp. 32 ff.]

Industrial import-substitution has concentrated in markets for traditional imports, although, according to Prebisch, these are evident signs that this policy is losing its effectiveness. Industrialization is becoming "deficient and expensive because of market limitations and a very weak competence" as well as the exaggerated protection, and has not succeeded in transforming the traditional structure of foreign trade [4, pp. 181–182].

The demographic situation is a factor which partly determines the socio-economic structure and occupational pattern.

> The tremendous increase in demographic growth rates is a relatively new phenomenon in Latin America, which—excepting the long period of migration of the population to the U.S.A.—did not show a comparable intensity in the evolution of the present advanced countries. That tremendous increase started in the late 1930s and assumed special significance as scientific and technological advances reduced the mortality rate with no parallel reduction in the birth rate. During the last five years of the 1930s, the net demographic growth rate was 1.9 per cent with the population tending to double every 37 years. Now, at the beginning of the 1970s, that rate has reached 2.9 per cent, a rate which reduces the doubling time to every 25 years [4, p. 21].

Incidentally, we can observe that this is the same growth rate (doubling every 25 years) adopted by Malthus in his famous geometric progression, with the peculiar difference that where the well-known clergyman and economist postulated such a trend in a community without obstacles (such as lack of livelihood) where a population could breed freely, the trend observed in Latin America takes place in poor communities, which aggravate their poverty by means of the so-called "demographic explosion."[3]

According to Prebisch, the problem of capital accumulation and that of the external "bottleneck" reflect the extraordinary increase in population. He rejects or questions the efficiency of simple solutions such as family limitation, but urges that the problem be faced in a realistic way, on the grounds that "there would likely be an optimal population growth rate according to conditions prevailing in each country, to be found between absolute demographic stagnation and the biological upper limit which some Latin American countries are approaching, as they have already gone beyond an average annual rate of 3.5 per cent" [4, p. 192].

> It is necessary to overcome the increasing lack of equilibrium between population growth and capital accumulation. But God forbid that we fall into the simplemindedness of considering birth limitation as the alternative for a vigorous strategy of economic and social development. Of course, such a strategy should be the expression of inevitable national decisions, in which demographic policy appears as a clearly defined element in the light of long-run considerations, which by their nature are not strictly economic ones [4, p. 236].

There are also other considerations to be taken into account in examining this difficult issue, because "birth limitation arouses some deep and very

[3] The process is not consistent with Malthus' theory in its relation to human tendencies, although it confirms it in substance, i.e., that the main obstacle to progress of humanity lies in the tendency of human beings to reproduce far beyond the limits of subsistence.

respectable feelings" [4, p. 191]. In the economic field, Prebisch puts special emphasis on the following points. (i) the outcome of a policy based on restrictive measures can only be observed after 15–18 years; (ii) the results may be offset by other phenomena, such as the increasing incorporation of women into the labor force; (iii) birth limitation would make it easier to handle the problem of the government's social investments in health, housing, and education, which are very expensive and as a rule, have large accumulated shortages; (iv) at any rate, this is a problem of foreseeing the future. There is a need for a deep sense of collective responsibility which, whatever the limitations and obstacles to the solutions, should not be neglected or postponed [4, p. 192].

There are two additional observations made by Prebisch which are worth mentioning. The first suggests that we have reached a point at which family limitation is suggested as an alternative to international financial cooperation, to the extent that it has been stated that "1000 dollars spent on birth control would allow a substitution of many thousands of dollars in capital investments." For the writer under consideration, this is "self-defeatingly simplistic" and a strange comparison [4, p. 191]. The second observation entails a more obscure line of reasoning: "If demographic phenomena keep drifting on the present course, the crisis of the system will go deeper and deeper. Consequently, if we really mean to change the system—and to change it completely and even violently—it is quite reasonable to act against birth control" [4, p. 194].

Such is the position of those who are partisans of chaos, to oppose everything which might be considered as promoting progress and improvement of a social order, which will thus collapse with all the greater celerity. Manifestly, this is not Prebisch's position, as he was the creator and the strongest supporter of a discipline of economic development, having among its main elements a demographic policy seeking to find a solution, although one in the long run, for the problems affecting a deficient occupational structure and a chronic abundance of surplus labor.

IV

As can easily be observed, the idea of greater social justice and of a redistributive policy which does not consist of "confiscating the earnings of the upper-income minority in order to distribute them among popular masses," is always present in Prebisch's thoughts [3, p. 5]. Such a policy should be based upon development promotion, and this, in turn, upon capital accumulation, while this last, in its turn, depends upon savings made possible by a clear reduction in consumption outlays among higher-income groups. (External aid is not taken into account here.) And all this may be attained through the contributions of technology.

According to these premises, it is possible to elaborate a plan for development and work to have it carried out. But social pressures resulting from present inequalities call for immediate solutions. Prebisch is quite aware of the urgent claims by groups now marginated in the distribution of benefits of scientific and technical advances, as well as of goods enjoyed by higher-income classes. The poor must also suffer the major effects of inflation, nearly always present in the majority of the weak Latin American economies. Thus, we must beware of so-called "immediatism," according to Prebisch's terminology:

> We must warn," he says, "against the permanent harm which may arise from this point. The social tensions of our time will often induce us to use an exaggerated proportion of (social) resources in order to improve present consumption levels, or to make social investments for immediate welfare, at the expense of economic investments for future welfare. To give way to this pressure would defeat the social objective of secularly increasing the standard of living of the masses [3, pp. 17–18].

Such is the dilemma between urgent palliatives and substantive solutions. Will it be necessary to start the redistribution by running the risk of resorting to transient and superficial measures, overlooking the prospect of a permanent transformation of the social structure, attained by a fairer long-run distribution? Or, on the contrary, will it be unavoidable to impose on the masses the sacrifice of long unsatisfied expectations in order to assure the viability of the second alternative?

Prebisch is definitely forced to make his choice in favor of one of the solutions, in which both views are conciliated:

> The fundamental questions of capital accumulation and of income redistribution are posed [here] in very different terms compared with the capitalist development of advanced countries.... Capital accumulation took place there first, and then a gradual income redistribution was brought about. While, the two processes posed in our case must take place simultaneously—and this is inevitable—under the increasing pressures of the masses [3, p. 16].

Distributive disequilibrium, Prebisch would state later on, is the source of frequent tension and "it is politically and socially understandable that such rigidities must be remedied through redistributive measures, whether by means of adjustments in salaries or public expenditures." Thus, we create a "complex system of commitments which will lead, among other things, to the immediate redistribution of income. No matter that these measures were inspired by social justice, for even if there appears to be a temporary abatement of such rigidities, this so called redistributive immediatism will leave basic problems unsolved. And repressive attitudes will not solve them either" [4, p. 185].

In any event, it is necessary to preserve the real income levels of popular sectors suffering the effects of inflation. Given the case of masses facing necessary real sacrifices, these should be greater the higher the income classes; therefore, every measure should be guided by an established development policy.

> As we can easily observe, this is an eminently political problem, since its solution—besides involving rigorous decisions—requires popular support and the comprehension of lower-income groups, taking care that this support should not be jeopardized by pressures, premature or exaggerated demands, which will surely cause a disruption in the whole program of improvement and expansion [3, p. 62].

The mere fact that these questions have political implications lead to solutions which show immediate results apparently advantageous to the masses. Such is the case of inflation, which has not proven to be an efficient instrument for redistribution. On the contrary, inflation has historically been the "instrument of regressive redistribution favoring high-income groups." But, "we must well understand that pressure for social improvement has become a dominant factor in inflation in some of our countries. The inflationary spiral may actually bring a psychological relief when the slow growth of income, or even income contraction, or distributive maladjustments, combine themselves against the steady rise of the people's living standard."[4]

All these arguments illustrate the significance of the factor we are analyzing in order to consider the problems of development. The tendency towards immediatism may be found in the most diverse political or ideological situations, but perhaps for quite different reasons. Those who expect to receive the benefits of measures of an immediate rise in effective demand accept such measures in order to mitigate their difficulties, and the ones who take them—in this case, the government—hope to calm political agitation. As Prebisch points out, the former consider "immediate" measures an easy substitute for basic transformations; others, may have "a clear and long-run vision," but in case they do not have anything to show in the near future, "it will be difficult or even impossible for them to accept a persistent development discipline, beyond the period of excitement that the gift may arouse" [4, p. 186].

V

Prebisch does not characterize the new society in which distributive inequalities will have disappeared or softened, and at the same time, a high level of development closer to that of industrialized countries will have been attained. But the paths by which it is possible to attain a more equitable

[4] The False Dilemma Between Economic Development and Monetary Stability [3, p. 202].

economic order and a developed economy have, in Prebisch's work, a very strong social content and a clear ideological orientation. This does not mean he has a clear preference for a given political party or an implicit adherence to any school of social thought. It does mean that Prebisch takes a clear stand on certain points related to the process that Latin American countries should follow, on the requirements to be met, and the characteristics that the new society should present. The extent of the problem and the way in which Prebisch has dealt with it, especially in his latest work, prevent us from considering it as thoroughly as we should, in the framework of the present essay. Thus we can only reemphasize that we may be guilty of omissions and have tried to cut the risk of betraying Prebisch's thought.

As we have already seen, one of the essential requirements for development is capital accumulation. This is basically a continuing process: as productivity increases, more investment will be necessary; otherwise, surplus labor will make its appearance in the industry. A very slight rise in income will at least mean the possibility of small increases in savings, although capital requirements are much greater. Where should we look for savings in order to satisfy these needs? There are two main sources: the constriction of consumption in the higher-income groups, and international cooperation. The first is only a limited possibility, since an increase in incomes will cause a general rise in consumption (even by lowering the share of higher-income groups); the second is necessary because we will have to import capital and consumer goods as well [3, pp. 32, 37–39, Sect. C, pp. 81, ff; 4, Chap. 4, Sect. C, Chap. 5]. Moreover, it will also be necessary to obtain international financial resources in order to generate a process of domestic savings and to break another of the vicious circles in the Latin American economy, which does not save what it should, because it is wasting potential elements of production, and wasting these because it no longer saves [4, p. 127].

With regard to domestic savings, we can say there is a considerable savings *potential.* "In case upper-class consumption were restrained in such a way that it exceed 11 times that of the lower classes, it would be easy to move from an annual rate of income growth of 1 per cent per capita to a 3 per cent rate; and in case this consumption were reduced to 9 times the lower-class level, the rate would increase to a 4 per cent per capita yearly" [3, p. 127]. But domestic savings should not only come from wealthy groups. Medium- and small-income groups should also participate, either through measures to stimulate savings and investment or through others discouraging some forms of consumption.

Agrarian reform has a prominent place in the program of structural changes suggested by Prebisch and rests upon the premises of an anachronistic system of land tenure, a poor technology, and thus a very low productivity. We have already examined the conditions which prevail in agricultural activities with population growth causing redundant (surplus) labor in the countryside and thus a very low income level among rural groups of workers.

> This reform," he says, "is the most urgent for three main reasons: (a) to attain a structural change which will allow the greatest use of potential savings and promote social mobility, with its important econonmic, social, and political implications; (b) to meet the demands of a rapidly growing population eager to improve its diet, and (c) to raise the living standards of the rural masses [3, p. 47].

This is a problem of eliminating

> certain forms of privilege which substantially weaken incentives for technical progress in its different aspects and, consequently, the best utilization of the men of action and capacity that present technology requires.... The great inequalities observed in agricultural land ownership make the application of modern techniques to large farms almost impossible: the very large estate because it yields a plentiful produce without using sophisticated techniques, and the small property because of its poorness and inefficiency [3, p. 56].

For Prebisch, agrarian reform seems to have two fundamental advantages: the abolition of privilege and the increase in productivity with the introduction of technology. Many paragraphs of Prebisch's writings make us think that technology will have the dominant role. As we have just seen, most of the importance of distributive disparities lies in the fact that they constitute an obstacle for technology assimilation. Besides, such disparities are taken as secondary in considering "the peculiar cases of some countries in which natural factors or agrarian policy have achieved the desired results without land redistribution" [4, pp. 38–39] or when the form of income distribution is questioned. "If a considerable part of the income of the upper classes derives from the privilege of belonging to a dominant position in the system, the incentive to technical progress is weakened" [4, p. 183].

However, a thorough examination of Prebisch's work in its whole context, and particularly the part represented by his recent writings, reveals that the reasoning could be inverted: we aim to improve technology and increase productivity, for it would not be possible to attain greater social justice without them: "We must not think, as we often do, that an increase in agricultural productivity is always necessary to lower commodity prices in the cities. It is a requirement for the social integration of rural masses" [4, p. 201]. This is the background of urban social tension and the permanent struggle to distribute insufficient levels of output. Despite their low living standards, rural masses only seldom participate in this redistributive struggle: "the social integration of the excluded masses is a fundamental problem in Latin America" [4, p. 225].

The promotion of social mobility which, as was noted, constitutes one of the three reasons for agrarian reform, assumes a very particular significance in the doctrine under consideration. It will cause the appearance and increase of dynamic elements in every social stratum and any distributive disparities which may emerge will no longer be the outcome of privilege. The present stratification of society constitutes an obstacle for "men of decision, capable of taking risks and responsibilities," and the process of development requires more and more technicians at every level. "The starting point to reach this goal, social mobility, lies in education.... The first real expression of a policy of income redistribution should start here, that is, from social investment in human resources, in the finding and training of men, in the access to opportunities to reach every level of education" [3, pp. 54–55].

Prebisch puts special emphasis on this point of view and extends his argument as follows: "From the mobility viewpoint, development requires to the greatest extent, that the most skillful occupy the highest positions, thus avoiding a waste of potential abilities. The socio-economic structure, whose peculiarities we have already analyzed, works against the possibilities of social promotion" [3, pp. 11, 184, 210].

In this passage Prebisch clearly uses the language of the social reformers. Perhaps we could discover touches of Saint Simon's influence (from each according to his capacity, etc.), or detect some reminiscences of Pareto's doctrine, to which Prebisch devoted one of his earliest essays [2]. At any rate, a similar terminology is often found in many of his works, and particularly in the last chapters of his latest work [4], where he expresses his deep concern about a more equitable social order in terms traditionally employed to pose the social problem: a more equitable distribution of wealth.

But this new social order could be described by some of the many varieties conceived by philosophers, economists, politicians, and, in general, the numerous reforming schools, beginning with the utopians' candid conceptions down to the most rigorous models of present-day collectivism. None of the well-known labels can be considered as strictly consistent with Prebisch's schema. However, by means of some of the peculiarities attributed to the hierarchy of desirable things, it is possible to define his ideology. As a means of synthesis, the reader could refer to the passage quoted as epigraph for this essay, although we would rather try to clear up the point with a few final considerations.

Prebisch states that in order to accelerate development, attain technical progress, and introduce social mobility, structures and attitudes should undergo significant changes. Today we often observe a greater willingness to undergo changes than ever before, although we are most cognizant of the risks that changes may entail, especially stemming from those who resist them.

One of the first problems posed in this essay was the one referring to the possibility of restricting consumption and raising capital accumulation without using compulsory means or socialization, by imposing facts instead of ideologies. According to the socialist experience in some countries, this would lead to the cessation of political traditions, among these, the normal role of political parties. That is why, Prebisch says,

> in an objective study of these points it is necessary to give a clear explanation of the underlying political assumptions, even more so in those cases where paramount importance is attached to the progressive or gradual support for certain values and goals that—despite the obstacles to political evolution—keep on projecting an ideal image during the long struggle to reach them in Latin America [4, pp. 15–17].

The process of change will evidently bring with it new ways of living, yet, there is nothing in it,

> tending to subordinate human values to its requirements. On the contrary, contemporary technology opens an infinite number of possibilities for the individual's way of living and self-determination, which until recently were limited to a very small portion of humanity.... The concentration of economic power," he adds, "in one form or another means an ever-present danger to a true democracy. The State is not an abstract entity. Those who handle its affairs are moved by interests and emotions and not only by collective desires [3, p. 23].

Now, according to what we have already said, we come to the conclusion that there are values, such as liberty and democracy, which sould be preserved during the process of change as well as in the new system to be established. On the other hand, it is possible to believe that development will only be attained through the maintenance of social discipline, and this means interfering in the free play of economic forces. We all know that such free play is unable to promote development and secure an equitable distribution of income. Therefore, no objections are made to the necessity of state intervention, and "it is here that we come across the principal problem...: how to do this without having the state interfere in the individual's decisions by arbitrarily submitting them to its increasing authority" [4, pp. 187–188].

In order to control development, the state has used planning as a device. Prebisch's detractors have severely criticized planning, despite the clarity with which Prebisch has expressed his opposition to arbitrary state actions, and from the explanations given on what he himself considers to be "planning" and about its benefits from the standpoint of efficiency, competition, and the market mechanism. Thus, he says, "the intention of working upon those forces [the spontaneous forces of the economy] is often confused with overt state interference in the market mechanism," which "is still of great value since it is absolutely impersonal." Too, "socialist economies are now tending to perceive the case this way," and, in particular, there are countries "which are increasingly turning to competition." On the other side of the coin we note that great liberal countries such as the U.S.A., are not against the adoption of deliberate measures in order to correct or remedy poverty or lack of equilibrium.[5]

No doubt development could be accelerated by means of compulsory measures "but it is most important to make the high social and political cost explicit, as well as the human cost it represents" [3; 4, p. 235]. We all know what this social, political, and human cost is: it represents a loss of freedom, with power concentrated in the hands of a few or only one, and the people subordinated to arbitrary decisions of the central power, in a word, the elimination of democracy. From an economic point of view, it means competition's surrender.

According to our interpretations of Prebisch's thesis, Latin America is presently undergoing a process of evident change, in which there is a conflict between those who are the strong supporters of and those opposed to any change. One of Prebisch's books is devoted to both groups [3, p. 15]. The attitudes of both of these are full of pitfalls for the values and principles he would like to see preserved.

On one side, "Latin America is accumulating a great emotional power, that of great collective movements" [3], and "nonconformity and intransigence have become the dominant features of youthful unrest, which is steadily advancing.... As they do not find themselves heeded by the economic and social system, they strongly reject it" [4, p. 209]. He also writes, "Social inequality offends young people's imaginations and they begin to oppose the existing order, the type of society in which they live and even the fundamental values inherent in it" [4, p. 210]. This lack of conformity and the criticism of large industrial societies might have very sound implications, although they may also lead to the hazard of "an unconditional adoption of methods employed abroad" and, at the same time, that "the powerful appeal of extraneous conflicts may disturb the comprehension of what is ours" [4, p. 211].

Confronting this current of feeling favorable to change, which is fed more by emotional forces than by ideologies, and because of these liable to lead to undesirable ends, there is another current strongly opposed to structural changes. Its hope is to keep the traditional structure, but at the same time promising an efficient productive system and the preservation of values which, like personal freedom, are considered to be the very essence of Western

[5] See Prebisch [4, pp. 188, 206–207, 214, 219, particularly Sect. 5 in Chap. 6, pp. 203 ff.]. See also Prebisch [3, Chap. 4, Sect. B, p. 75] where we find the following phrase: "This task of guiding private initiative through government intervention is very important and may be achieved without compulsion by the mere use of inducements and discouragements."

society. These groups disregard the fact that "in case democracy's future course may concern them... there will be nothing to strengthen it except social mobility... and that an obstinate opposition to its attainment may force other people... to ignore the democratic rules" [3]. "It will not be possible," Prebisch remarks, "to halt changes in the system forcibly.... It may be possible to restrain subversion temporarily... but changes cannot be avoided," and "it is not possible to foretell how this force will be used; it might perhaps, be used to achieve such changes. But the sign and inspiration which guide them are also unpredictable, although the political and social cost are easily predictable" [4, p. 227].

In this way we arrive at a dilemma of two unpromising alternatives: either compulsory and violent change, which may lead to the concentration of power with a small group ruling over the others; or opposition, not less violent than the other, threatening to lead us to an authoritarian state. The first may lead us to a greater justice in the distribution of income but with a political and social cost and the sacrifice of the highest values inherent in human dignity. The second implies the establishment of a system of social injustice, with ever-present seeds of destructive violence and the risk of also losing such values under the power of force.

Prebisch does not forecast the outcome of the process, leaving us to "imagine which will be Latin America's goals and which course we would have preferred them to follow" [4, p. 20]. And after some urging on the need to act in a reasonable way, Prebisch concludes by emphasizing the task Latin America must fulfill in order to persuade others as well as herself:

> She has very little time left to find her own way, darkened by the obstinate interplay of interests and ideological confusions. It is not a question of finding a magic formula and waiting for the rest to be given us in addition. It is not a formula that is required. It is a process guided by significant purposes. We must find the way and follow it with audacity and the emotion that spurred great actions, with intelligence and care, without which it is not possible to transform today's unreality into tomorrow's truth [4, p. 221].

If we close this imperfect synthesis of Prebisch's social doctrine at this point, the reader will probably think that he does not agree with the terms of the problem as posed. He will think that neither of the two options may seem acceptable to Prebisch, an idea which may be strengthened if one considers his apparent coldness toward certain practical achievements, which have resulted in visible processes of change in the last decades. It should be noted that his way of examining things is more akin to philosophical quietness and scientific objectivity than to coldness. It is true that Prebisch does not explicitly adhere to any known system, and does not outline his own model for economic and social development with justice. Yet, in his writings we do find an explicit preference, resulting from his adherence to the principles of freedom, human dignity, social mobility with equal opportunities, an equitable income distribution, access to civilization's benefits for poor classes, as well as access to technological progress, and the attainment of higher levels by means of domestic efforts and loyal external cooperation. All the rest are only details which will probably be given "in addition." Even those things which in the present belong to a world of dreams and which is Prebisch's ideal for a united Latin America:

> Unity in that sense has always been a dream. People having very sound political ways of thinking have conceived of it with particular conviction. Although some time it may happen that a hundred and fifty years of sentimental and volatile eloquence, of an anguished divorce between a moving rhetoric and an obstinate reality, may appear unexpectedly and spontaneously [4, p. 217].

REFERENCES

[1] El cambio social y la politica de desarrollo social en América Latina. United Nations, New York, E/CN. 12/826/Rev. 1 (1969).

[2] La Sociologia de Vilfredo Pareto, *Rev. Ciencias Econ.* **9**, Ser. 2, No. 27, 154 (1923).

[3] Prebisch, R., "Towards a Dynamic Development Policy for Latin America." United Nations, New York, 1963.

[4] Prebisch, R., "Transformation and Development." Survey presented to the Inter-american Development Bank, Washington, D.C. (1970).

[5] "Problemas Teóricos y Prácticos del Crecimiento Económico." United Nations Document E/CN. 12/221, Mexico (1952).

[6] "The Economic Development of Latin America and its Principal Problems." Economic Commission for Latin America, United Nations E/CN. 12/89/Rev. 1 (1950).

[7] Urquidi, V. L., La Perspectiva del Crecimiento Económico y la Repartición del Ingreso Nacional, Re-impression of *Rev. Bancaria* 7, No. 1, 12 (1959).

APPENDIX
THE WORK OF DR. RAÚL PREBISCH

The chronological ordering of Dr. Raúl Prebisch's work has been made possible thanks to the invaluable cooperation of the United Nations' Latin American Institute for Economic and Social Planning, Argentina's Central Bank Library, and the Library of the School of Economics at the University of Buenos Aires. Some other references have been taken from the School of Economics Library at the University of Córdoba.

It is important to point out that not all the papers listed are Mr. Prebisch's personal undertaking. In some cases, it has been possible to mention the other contributors; in others—especially in the case of United Nations' work—it is obvious that the research has been done under his leadership. There are, of course, many articles which are his own products. Finally, the list we offer, however complete, is not exhaustive: there may exist aditional work which belongs to the distinguished Argentine economist which have not been recorded owing to lack of information.

1918

"Industrialización del Maíz" /s.l., s.e./, unpublished, 1918. 30 pp.

1919

"Teoría del interés," Buenos Aires, unpublished, 1919. 55 pp.

1920

El Ajuste de los Salarios al Costo de la Vida, *Rev. Econ. Argentina* (*Buenos Aires*), November–December, 333–341 (1920).

1921

Anotaciones sobre nuestro medio Circulante, *Rev. Cienc. Econ.* (*Buenos Aires*), (1921).

La conferencia financiera Internacional de 1920, *Rev. Econ. Argentina* (*Buenos Aires*) 119–135 (1921).

"Planes para estabilizar el poder adquisitivo de la moneda," pp. 1459–1514. Research Work at the School of Economics, Univ. of Buenos Aires, 1921.

1922

Anotaciones sobre la Crisis Ganadera, *Rev. Cienc. Econ.* (*Buenos Aires*) 383–440 (1922).

"Carácter y finalidad de los Cursos de Seminario," La Plata, Olivieri y Dominguez, 1922. 32 pp.

"Información Estadística sobre el Comercio de Carnes," Imp. Gadola, Buenos Aires, 1922. 75 pp.

1924

Aclaraciones al Proyecto de Colonización del Poder Ejecutivo, *Rev. Econ. Argentina* (*Buenos Aires*) September–October, 1924.

Determinación de la capacidad imponible, método australiano de promedios, *Rev. Econ. Argentina* (*Buenos Aires*) August, 121–134 (1924).

Establecimiento de nuestra administración financiera sobre bases comerciales, *Rev. Econ. Argentina* (*Buenos Aires*) March, 201–212 (1924).

1925

Anotaciones a la Estadística Nacional, *Rev. Econ. Argentina* (*Buenos Aires*) August, 85–104 (1925).

1927

El régimen de pool en el Comercio de Carnes; informe técnico, "Sociedad Rural Argentina," Buenos Aires; "El Pool de Frigoríficos," pp. 25–63. Buenos Aires, 1927.

Anotaciones demográficas, *Rev. Econ. Argentina* (*Buenos Aires*) March, 199–216 (1927); April, 287–304 (1927); May, 403–408 (1927); July, 19–29 (1927).

1944

Conversaciones en el Banco de México, S.A., "Antecedentes y Proyectos de Creación de un Banco Central en Argentina." México, 1944.

La Moneda y los ciclos económicos en la Argentina. Class Notes taken from Dr. R. Prebisch, Professor of Econ., School of Econ., Univ. of Buenos Aires, (by J. González del Solar, P. M. Martínez, and J. C. Menescaldi), 1944. 323 pp.

Observaciones sobre los planes monetarios internacionales, *El Trimestre Econ.* (*México*) July–September, 185–208 (1944).

1945

Introducción al Curso de Economía Política, *Rev. Cienc. Econ.* (*Buenos Aires*), July, 525–537 (1945).

El Patrón Oro y la Vulnerabilidad Económica de Nuestros Países, Jornadas II (1ª Sesión del Seminario sobre América Latina), El Colegio de México, Centro de Estudios Sociales, *Rev. Cienc. Econ.* (*Buenos Aires*) March, 211–213 (1944).

Se señalan en nuestra historia injusticias que impidieron un mayor progreso del país, *Finanzas* (*Buenos Aires*) September, 27–31 (1945).

1946

"Introducción al Curso de Economía Política; concepto preliminar a la Circulación de Ingresos," Buenos Aires, Imp. Córdoba, 1946. 15 pp.

1947

El capital y la tasa de interés en la teoría keynesiana, *Bol. Banco Central Venezuela* (*Caracas*) March, 12–17 (1947).

La Conjuncíon del ahorro y las inversiones en la teoría keynesiana, *Bol. Banco Central Venezuela* (*Caracas*) April–May, 14–20 (1947).

El sistema teórico keynesiano y sus proyecciones económicas y sociales, *Bol. Banco Central Venezuela* (*Caracas*) April–May, 21–28 (1947).

Las Teorías Económicas de Lord Keynes y las doctrinas de los Clásicos, *Bol. Banco Central Venezuela* (*Caracas*) January 18–23, (1947); February, 11–14 (1947).

"Introducción a Keynes," 1st ed. Fondo de Cultura Económica, México–Buenos Aires, 1947. 145 pp.

1948

Apuntes de Economía Política, (dinámica económica). Lectures by Prof. R. Prebisch. (Corrected version by Dr. J. Broide, Associate Professor, Buenos Aires.) /s.e./, 1948. 103 pp.

Introducción al Curso de Dinámica Económica, *Rev. Fac. Cienc. Econ.* (*Buenos Aires*) June, 448–463 (1948).

Dictamen acerca de los anteproyectos sobre Banco Central y Bancos, *Rev. Hacienda* (*Caracas*) September, 146–178 (1948).

1950

Estudio Económico de América Latina, *Rev. Econ.* (*Montevideo*) April–May, 577–582 (1950).

Economic Survey of Latin America 1949: The Economic Development of Argentina, *Rev. Econ. Argentina* (*Buenos Aires*) August–September, 171–187 (1950).

El estudio de las ciencias económicas en la Facultad de Buenos Aires, *Rev. Centro Estudiantes Cienc. Econ.* (*Asunción*) September, 25–28 (1950).

The Economic Development of Latin America and Its Principal Problems, *Amer. Econ. Rev.* (1949–1950).

1951

Economic Survey of Latin America 1949: Growth, Disequilibrium and Disparities Interpretation of the Process of Economic Development, UN Sales 51, II. G.1 (1951).

Theoretical and Practical Problems of Economic Growth, E/CN. 12/221, (May 18, 1951). (Introduction signed by Dr. Raúl Prebisch).

Interpretaçao do Processo do Desenvolvimento Económico *Rev. Brasil. Econ.* (*Brasil*) March, 7–117 (1951).

La Cepal y el Desarrollo Económico, *Rev. Econ.* (*México*) June, 156–164 (1951).

Discurso pronunciado el 29 de Mayo de 1951 en el IV período de sesiones de la Comisión Económica para América Latina, *El Trimestre Econ.* (*México*) July–September, 557–570 (1951).

1952

Cuáles son las Razones Económicas del Retraso Agropecuario? *Panorama Econ.* (*Chile*) September, 580–584 (1952).

El Desarrollo Económico de América Latina, *Comercio Exterior* (*México*) October, 365–368 (1952).

"Introducción a Keynes," 2nd ed. Fondo de Cultura Económica, México–Buenos Aires, 1952.

Notas sobre el desarrollo económico, la inflación y la política monetaria y fiscal, *Rev. Econ.* (*Santiago, Chile*) October, 34–45 (1952).

1953

Exposición del Dr. Raúl Prebisch en el V período de sesiones de la Comisión Económica para América Latina, Río de Janeiro, April 10, 1953, *El Trimestre Econ.* (*México*) April–June, 351–365 (1953).

1954

Perspectivas del Desarrollo Económico de América Latina, *Selección Contable* (*Buenos Aires*) July, 403–413 (1954).

Exposición del Dr. Raúl Prebisch, Director Principal a cargo de la Secretaría Ejecutiva de la Comisión Económica para América Latina (February 8, 1954); *Econ. Finanzas* (*Santiago, Chile*) February, 9–15, 20 (1954).

Premisas fundamentales de la Conferencia Interamericana de Río de Janeiro, *Probl. Agr. Ind. Méx.* October–December, 115–122 (1954).

Comentarios sobre el Informe Preliminar, *Clarín* (*Buenos Aires*) (December 7 and 14, 1954). Six articles.

The Stimulus of Demand, Investment and Acceleration of the Rate of Growth, *Econ. Survey Latin Amer.* (1954).

International Cooperation in a Latin American Development Policy, UN Sales II. G. 2 (November 1954).

Exposición ante la Sesión Plenaria del Consejo Interamericano de Comercio y Producción, *Temas Econ.* (*Venezuela*) October–November, 35–49 (1954).

1955

The Prebisch Report Text, *Rev. River Plate* (*Buenos Aires*) (October 31, 1955).

Outline of an Interpretation of Latin America's Economic Development, *Econ. Columbiana* (*Bogotá*) (November 1955).

Dr. Prebisch's Economic Policy Address to the Army, *Rev. River Plate* (*Buenos Aires*) (December 30, 1955).

Moneda Sana o Inflación Incontenible, Secretaría de Prensa de la Presidencia de la Nación, 1955, *Rev. River Plate* (*Buenos Aires*) (June 20, 1956).

Report on the Economic Situation in Argentina, *Rev. Econ.* (*Montevideo*) September–November (1955); December–February (1956).

Informe Preliminar Acerca de la Situación Económica Argentina, Buenos Aires. Presidencia de la Nación, Secretaría de Prensa y Actividades Culturales (1955). 95 pp.

A Report on Argentine Economic and Financial Conditions with Recomendations for a New Policy, Buenos Aires, Secretaría de Prensa de la Presidencia de la Nación (1955).

Teoría y Práctica del Desarrollo Económico: El Caso Argentino, Argentina (1955) (mimeo); *Panorama Econ.* (*Santiago*) (June 22, 1956).

The Prebisch Report Argentina's New Manual of Economics, *Comments Argentine Trade* (*Argentina*) November, 18–23 (1955).

Problemas del Desarrollo Económico Latinoamericano, *Bol. Mensual* (*Uruguay*) June–February (1955); 5–12 (April 19, 1955).

CEPAL—La Institución y sus Actividades, *Hispanoamericano* (*México*) January, 34–36 (1955).

Comentario del Informe Económico Financiero del Dr. Raúl Prebisch, *Bol. Bolsa Comercio Bs. As.*, December, 1961–1968 (1965).

The Country Must Understand That a Crucial Stage in Its History Has Been Reached, *Rev. of the River Plate* (*Argentina*) 21–26 (1955).

Informe Económico Presentado al Excmo. Sr. Presidente Provisional de la Nación, *Bol. Bolsa Comercio* (*Buenos Aires, Argentina*) October, 1316–1338 (1955).

Some General Projections Arising from Latin American Experience during the Last Quarter of a Century, "Analyses and Projections of Economic Development: An Introduction to the Technique of Programming," UN Sales II. G. 2. (November 1955).

La libre Empresa y el progreso económico, Buenos Aires, *Cámara Argentina Comercio* (1955). 87 pp.

La situación económica del país, Buenos Aires, Secretaría de la Presidencia de la Nación (1955). 29 pp.

Introducción al Informe sobre el Desarrollo Económico de Colombia (ECLA), *Rev. Banco Repúbl.* (*Bogotá*) 1226–1234 (October 20, 1955).

Discurso del Director Principal de la Comisión Económica para América Latina en la Conferencia de Ministros de Hacienda o Economía de Río de Janeiro, November 24, 1954, *El Trimestre Econ.* (*México*) April–June, 241–248 (1955).

1956

Desarrollo Económico y Política Social, Round Table at the University of Córdoba, Argentina, 1956.

Economic Recovery Programme and Final Report, *Rev. River Plate* (*Buenos Aires*) (June 20, 1956).

Principal Tendencies of Economic Development in Latin America, *Panorama Econ.* (*Santiago*) (June 22, 1956).

Economic Development Plan, *Rev. River Plate* (*Buenos Aires*) (October 19, 1956).

El papel de la Industria en el Crecimiento Argentino, *Bol. Bolsa Comercio* (*Buenos Aires, Argentina*) October, 1791–1798 (1956).

How the Dynamic Forces of the Argentine Economy Were Dissipated, *Rev. River Plate* (*Buenos Aires*) June, 21–27 (1956).

La Iniciativa Privada, la Industria y la Programación del Desarrollo Económico, *Bol. Bolsa Comercio* (*Buenos Aires*) October, 1559–1563 (1956).

La Economía del país, *Bol. Bolsa Comercio* (*Buenos Aires*) January, 1–10 (1956).

"Introducción a Keynes," 3rd ed. Fondo de Cultura Económica, México–Buenos Aires, 1956.

Moneda sana o inflación incontenible: plan de restablecimiento económico, Buenos Aires, Secretaría de Prensa de la Presidencia de la Nación (1956).

Moneda sana o inflación y plan de restablecimiento económico, *Bol. Bolsa Comercio* (*Buenos Aires*) January, 653–672 (1956).

Teoría y Práctica del Desarrollo económico: el Caso Argentino, *Bol. Bolsa Comercio* (*Buenos Aires*) 1249–1258 (July 30, 1956).

1957

La Política Económica de los Países menos Desarrollados, *Activ. Econ.* (*Perú*) March, 8–12 (1957); *Econ. Colombiana* (*Bogotá*) (1957).

Soviet Challenge to American Leadership: America's Role in Helping Underdeveloped Countries, *Com. Econ. Dev.*, New York (1957).

Problemas de Comercio Interlatinoamericano, *Rev. Conselho Nacional Econ.* (*Brasil*) January–February, 44–51 (1957).

Conclusiones de la Mesa Redonda de Economistas sobre las medidas de estabilización monetaria (by Raúl Prebisch, Roberto de Oliveira Campos, Ricardo Torres Gaitán, Isidoro Martínez, Julio Melnik, and José Antonio Mayobre), *Rev. Econ.* (*Oruro*) January–August, 151–155 (1957).

Teoría e Practica do desenvolvimento, *Rev. Cienc. Econ.* (*Sao Paulo*) January–March, 11–26 (1957).

1958

Multilateral Payments in a Policy for a Latin American Common Market, *Banco Central Ecuador* (*Quito*) November–December (1958).

1959

Commercial Policy in the Underdeveloped Countries, *Amer. Econ. Rev. Papers Proceedings* (*Evanston, Illinois*) May, 251–274 (1959).

Ten-Year Plan for South American Free Trade Zone, *Rev. River Plate* (*Buenos Aires*) (May 9, 1959).

The Steel Industry and Regional Economic Integration, *Econ. Finanzas* (*Santiago*) November (1959).

Latin America Common Market, *Bol. Informativo* (Inter-American Council of Commerce and Production, Montevideo), September–October (1959); *Econ. Grancolombiana*, UN Sales II, G. 4, August, 43–51 (1959).

Significance of the Common Market for the Economic Development of Latin America, Statement by Dr. Raúl Prebisch at the Second Session of the Special Committee to Study the Formulation of New Measures for Economic Cooperation of the OAS, Buenos Aires (April 29, 1959).

La Crisis Estructural de la Economía Argentina y la Orientación de sus soluciones, *Análisis Proyecciones Desarrollo Econ.: Desarrollo Econ. Argentina*, UN Sales II. G. 3, Vol. I (1959).

La CEPAL y el Mercado Común Latinoamericano, *Argo* (*Colombia*) July–August (1959).

Las tareas de América Latina, *Panorama Econ.* (*Chile*) September, 315–318 (1959).

Mercado Común Latinoamericano, *Bol. Informat. Ser. A* (Crónica Orientaciones) (*Montevideo*) September–October, 31–36 (1959).

Los Pagos multilaterales en una política de mercado común Latinoamericano, *Rev. Banco República Oriental Uruguay* (*Montevideo*) January, 32–43 (1959).

El Mercado Común Latinoamericano, *Bol. Banco Central Ecuador* (*Quito*) July–August, 19–28 (1959).

1960

Pagos y la Zona de Libre Comercio en América Latina, *Comercio Exterior* (*México*) January, 9–12 (1960).

Panoramas y Perspectives de la Industria Siderúrgica en América Latina, *Comercio Exterior* (*México*) January, 20–30 (1960).

Latin América: The Challenge and the Task Ahead, *Statist.* (*London*) Economic Survey of Latin America, March 26 (1960).

Transformación Estructural de la Economía Latinoamericana, *Política* (*Caracas*) July, 137–141 (1960).

The Structural Crisis in Argentina and its Prospects of Solution, *Conf. Econ. Develop.* Univ. of Texas, Austin, Texas (1958).

"Economic Growth: Rationale, Problems and Cases." Univ. of Texas Press, Austin, Texas, 1960.

"The Reciprocal Credits System for the Free Area," Montevideo, January 1960.

Vamos a tener más Recursos Exteriores en América Latina, pero estamos preparados para aprovecharlos al máximo?, *Rev. Naciones Unidas* October, 66–70 (1960).

Inflación y desarrollo económico, *Bol. Banco Central Ecuador* (*Quito*) September–October, 15–33 (1960).

"Introducción a Keynes," 4th ed. Fondo de Cultura Económica, México–Buenos Aires, 1960. 133 pp.

Los pagos multilaterales en una política de mercado común Latinoamericano, *Rev. Cienc. Econ.* (*Sao Paulo*) March, 45–62 (1960).

La Política Comercial en los países insuficientemente desarrollados (desde el punto de vista Latinoamericano), *Economía* (*Santiago, Chile*) 4° quarter, 25–45 (1960).

El Principio de la Reciprocidad, *Rev. Cienc. Econ.* (*Sao Paulo*) June, 79–82 (1960).

La oportunidad y la tarea de la América Latina, *Inform. Comercial Española* (*Madrid*) July, 65–71 (1960).

El Problema fundamental; elevar la tasa de capitalización, *Com. Exterior* (*México*) September, 487–489 (1960).

1961

Economic Development or Monetary Stability: The False Dilemma, *Econ. Bull. Latin America* (*Santiago*) March, 1–25 (1961).

Joint Responsibilities for Latin American Progress, *Foreign Affairs* (*New York*) July, 622–633 (1961).

Reflections on the Latin American Economic Integration, *Com. Exterior* (*México*) November (1961).

La Respuesta de América Latina a una Política de Cooperación Económica Internacional, *Com. Exterior* (*México*) July, 674–685 (1961); *El Trimestre Econ.* (*México*); *Bol. Mensual Banco República Oriental Uruguay* (*Montevideo*) July–August, 22–31 (1961).

Agrarian Reform and Other Problems of Latin America, *Rev. River Plate* (*Buenos Aires*) (July 11 and 31, 1961).

Los Obstáculos Estructurales y la Necesaria Revisión de la Política de Desarrollo y de Cooperación Internacional, *Com. Exterior* May, 276–278 (1961).

Economic Development, Planning and International Cooperation, E/CN. 12/582/ rev. 1, Un Sales II. G. 6, November (1961).

Producir vivir depende de Latinoamérica, *Combate* (*Costa Rica*) January–February, 23–29 (1961).

Commercial Policy in the Underdeveloped Countries, *Int. Bank Reconstruction Develop. World Trade Trends Patterns*, Washington, 251–273 (1961).

El falso dilema entre desarrollo económico y estabilidad monetaria, *Bol. Econ. América Latina* (*Santiago*) March 1–26 (1961); *Rev. Cienc. Econ.* (*Sao Paulo*) March, 3–61 (1961).

1962

El Desafío que Afronta América Latina, *Com. Exterior* (*México*) February, 74–75 (1962).

Exposición Pronunciada durante la Reunión Extraordinaria del CIES, *Punta del Este* August (1961); *El Trimestre Econ.* (*México*) January–March (1962).

Europe and the Structural Crisis of the Latin American Economy, *Rev. River Plate* (*Buenos Aires*) (November 30, 1962).

Confrontará Europa la Crisis Estructural de América Latina, Text of Dr. Raúl Prebisch's speech at the meeting of the International Union of Executives of Christian Enterprises, Brussels, November 21, 1962, *Notic. Cepal* (*Santiago, Chile*) (1962). 17 pp.

Economic Hanning, *Panorama Econ.* (*Santiago*) June (1962).

The Latin American Answer to the New Policy of International Economic Cooperation, *Rev. Univ. República* (Facultad Cienc. Econ. Administ.) (*Montevideo*) July (1962).

Economic Aspects of the Alliance, "The Alliance for Progress." Johns Hopkins Press, Baltimore, Maryland, 1962.

The Economic Development of Latin America and Its Principal Problems, *Econ. Bull. Latin America* **7**, No. 1 (1962).

Exposición del Dr. Raúl Prebisch en la 2da sesión plenaria del 2do período de sesiones de la conferencia de las partes contratantes de la Asociación Latinoamericana de Libre Comercio (ALALC/C.II/ di 8) (August 27, 1962).

Declaraciones sobre la ALALC, *Hacienda Públ.* (*Paraguay*) September, 19–21 (1962).

El mercado Común requiere Grandes Decisiones Políticas, *Rev. Naciones Unidas* (*México*) September, 31–36, 41–48 (1962).

El Rol de Europa en los Programas de Desarrollo Económico de América Latina, *Hacienda Públ.* (*Paraguay*) July 674–685 (1962).

Es Inaplazable tomar vigorosas decisiones políticas, *Suple. Com. Exterior* (*México*) September–October, 45–47 (1962).

Cuartro propuestas concretas para vigorizar y dinamizar la marcha de la Asociación Latinoamericana de Libre Comercio, *Zona* (*Buenos Aires*) August–September, 10–15 (1962).

El Director principal de la Comisión Económica para América Latina urge se tomen grandes decisiones políticas para impulsar decisivamente la integración económica latinoamericana; presenta 4 propuestas concretas encaminadas a vigorizar la lenta marcha de la Asociación Latinoamericana de Libre Comercio, *Notic. Cepal* (*Santiago, Chile*) August (1962). 14 pp.

La Planificación, el desarrollo y la democracia. Text of Dr. Prebisch's speech at the Inter-American Social and Economic Council held in Mexico, October 23, 1962, *Selección Contable* (*Buenos Aires*) December, 425–436 (1962).

Reflexiones sobre la Integración Económica Latinoamericana, *Rev. Econ. Estadística* (*Córdoba*) No. 1, 175–188 (1962).

La Integración Económica Latinoamericana, *Selección Contable* (*Buenos Aires*) September, 182–194 (1962).

El mercado común constituye una de las grandes reformas estructurales de América Latina, *Rev. Cienc. Econ.* (*Sao Paulo*) June, 36–52 (1962).

La Planificación económica, *Panorama Econ.* (*Santiago, Chile*) June 154–158, 178 (1962).

Texto del discurso pronunciado el 23 de Octubre de 1962 por el Dr. Raúl Prebisch subsecretario de la N.U. a cargo de la Comisión Económica para América Latina (CEPAL) ante el Consejo Interamericano Económico y Social (CIES), reunido en México a nivel ministerial, *Noticias CEPAL* (*Santiago, Chile*) November 2, 1–10 (1962).

1963

Planning of Economic Growth in Latin America, *Rev. River Plate*, (*Buenos Aires*) 21–22, 42–44 (June 11, 1963).

Memorandum indicating his ideas and recommendations of the lines on which he considers Argentina's financial and economic policy should be conducted if the country is to surmount the present crisis, *Rev. River Plate* (*Buenos Aires*) (May 31, 1963) (Submitted to the President of Argentina).

Hacia una Dinámica del Desarrollo Latinoamericano, UN Sales 64, II. G. 4 (1963); *Análisis* (*Buenos Aires*) May, 28–34 (1963).

Planificación y Controlismo, Lima, Perú, Univ. of San Marcos, Instituto de Investigaciones Económicas, *Estudios Modernos* No. 4 (1963).

Memorandum sobre la planificación económica y social, *Selección Contable* (*Buenos Aires*) June, 513–515 (1963).

Exposición del Dr. Raúl Prebisch, Director Principal a cargo de la Secretaría Ejecutiva de la Comisión Económica para América Latina, en la primera reunión plenaria del décimo período de sesiones, realizada en Mar del Plata, el 6 de Mayo de 1963, *Desarrollo Econ.* (*Buenos Aires*) January–March, 151–166 (1963).

1964

Hacia una Nueva Política Commercial en Pro del Desarrollo, E/ CN. 46/3. UN Sales No. 64 II. B. 4 (1964).

Proposiciones para la Creación del Mercado Común Latinoamericano (1964).

Las Aportaciones de recursos internacionales a los países en desarrollo, *Técn. Financ.* (*México*) March–April, 415–433 (1964).

Business, Undevelopment, the Geneva Marathon Starts, *The Economist* (*London*) 1123–1127 (March 21, 1964).

La Carta de Alta Gracia; los países latinoamericanos coordinan sus puntos de vista ante la Conferencia Económica Mundial de Comercio y Desarrollo, *Inform. Com. Española* (*Madrid*) No. 885, 1673–1678 (March 19, 1964).

Comisión especial coordinadora latinoamericana (CECIA), discurso del Dr. Raúl Prebisch en la Asamblea de Alta Gracia, Córdoba, *Selección Contable* (*Buenos Aires*) April–May, 281–285 (1964).

El espíritu de conciliación, *ONU* (Crónica Mensual) (*New York*) July, 79–85 (1964).

El Falso dilema entre desarrollo económico y estabilidad monetaria, International Bank of Reconstruction and Development, *Inst. Desarrollo Econ.* (Teoría crecimiento estud. generales sobre probl. desarrollo econ.) 1–70 (1964).

Informe de Raúl Prebisch, Secretario General de la Conferencia de la N.U. sobre Comercio y Desarrollo, *Rev. Econ. Política* (*Madrid*) January–April, 205–354 (1964).

La moneda y los ciclos económicos en la Argentina (Notes based on the lectures by Dr. R. Prebisch in 1944), Univ. of Buenos Aires, School of Econ. Inst. de Investigaciones Económicas y Sociales, 1964. 106 pp.

Nueva política comercial para el desarrollo; Report by R. Prebisch to the UNCTAD Conference at Geneva, Switzerland, May 23, 1964, Fondo de Cultura Económica, México–Buenos Aires, 1964. 148 pp.

La política comercial en los países insuficientemente desarrollados (desde el punto de vista Latinoamericano), International Bank of Reconstruction and Development, *Com. Int.* (*México, D. F.*) 192–211 (1964).

1965

A Conversation—American Business and Raúl Prebisch, U.S. Council of the International Chamber of Commerce (1965).

"Introducción a Keynes," 5th ed. Fondo de Cultura Económica, México–Buenos Aires, 1965. 131 pp.

Proposiciones para la creación del mercado común Latinoamericano, by Raúl Prebisch, José Antonio Mayobre, Felipe Herrera, and Carlos Sanz de Santamaría), *Documentos* (*Madrid*) No. 255, June, 33–63 (1965); *El Trimestre Econ.* (*México*) July–September 533–557 (1965).

"Hacia la integración acelerada de América Latina; proposals presented to the Latin America Presidents" (by José Antonio Mayobre, Felipe Herrera, Carlos Sanz de Santamaría, and Raúl Prebisch). Fondo de Cultura Económica, México, 1965. 197 pp.

1966

Algunos Problemas fundamentales sobre el Comercio Mundial, *ONU* (Crónica Mensual) (*New York*) February, 47–55 (1966).

Comisión Especial de Coordinación latinoamericana; intervención del Dr. Raúl Prebisch, *Com. Exterior* (*México*) July, 469–476 (1966).

Una política económica internacional para el desarrollo, *Com. Exterior* (*México*) February, 77–80 (1966).

Hechos y tendencias del Comercio y desarrollo en la Actualidad, *Rev. Econ.* (*México*) August, 226–238 (1966).

Problemas comunes de América Latina y las demás regiones en desarrollo, *Centro Estudios Monetarios Latinoamer.* (Boletín Mensual) (*México*) July, 309–317 (1966).

1967

"El Reto de Comercio y el Desarrollo para América Latina," Cámara Nacional de Comercio de la Ciudad de México, 1967.

Declaraciones del Secretario de la UNCTAD, Dr. Raúl Prebisch, en la sesión plenaria de la Comisión especial de coordinación latinoamericana, *El Trimestre Econ.* (*México*) January–March, 165–180 (1967).

La reunión de presidentes de América y la UNCTAD, *Com. Exterior* (*México*) May, 377–378 (1967).

Fragmento de sus declaraciones en la Reunión Ministerial del Grupo de los 77, celebrada en Argel entre el 10 y el 25 de octubre de 1967, *Comercio Exterior Suppl.* (*México*) November, 3–7 (1967).

Interview with The Banker, *The Banker* (London) September, 748–754 (1967).

1968

Hacia una estrategia global del Desarrollo, TD/3/Rev. 1. UN Sales 68 II. D. 6 (1968).

Significación del segundo período de sesiones de la Conferencia de las Naciones Unidas sobre Comercio y Desarrollo, TD/96/Rev. UN Sales 69 II. D. 3 (1968).

Statement by Dr. Raúl Prebisch, Secretary-General of the UNCTAD, during the 39th Session of the Conf., February 2, 1968, New Delhi (India), United Nations (1968). 13 pp.

1969

La Inversión privada extranjera en el Desarrollo Latinoamericano, OEA/Ser. H/X. 14 CIES/1371 (April 28, 1969).

Reflexiones sobre la Cooperación Internacional en el Desarrollo Latinoamericano, *Com. Exterior* (*México*) October, No. 10, 757–766 (1969).

La Marcha hacia el Mercado Común Latinoamericano, *La Nación* (*Buenos Aires*) June 13–14 (1969).

Problemas teóricos y prácticos del crecimiento económico, "América Latina: Ensayos de Interpretación Económica" (A. Bianchi, ed.), pp. 41-78. Santiago, Chile, 1969.

1970

Transformación y Desarrollo: La Gran Tarea de América Latina, Report by Dr. Prebisch, Interamerican Development Bank, Washington D.C. (April 17, 1970).

AUTHOR INDEX

Numbers in brackets are reference numbers and indicate that an author's work is referred to, although his name is not cited in the text. Numbers in italics show the page on which the complete reference is listed

SUBJECT INDEX